# *Readings and Cases in* INTERNATIONAL MANAGEMENT

## *A Cross-Cultural Perspective*

DAVID C. THOMAS
*Simon Fraser University*

SAGE Publications
*International Educational and Professional Publisher*
Thousand Oaks ▪ London ▪ New Delhi

*For information:*

Sage Publications, Inc.
2455 Teller Road
Thousand Oaks, California 91320
E-mail: order@sagepub.com

Sage Publications Ltd.
6 Bonhill Street
London EC2A 4PU
United Kingdom

Sage Publications India Pvt. Ltd.
B-42, Panchsheel Enclave
New Delhi 110 017 India

Printed in the United States of America

**Library of Congress Cataloging-in-Publication Data**

Thomas, David C., (David Clinton), 1947-
Readings and cases in international management: A cross-cultural perspective / David C. Thomas.
p. cm.
Includes bibliographical references and index.
ISBN 0-7619-2637-2 (pbk. : alk. paper)
1. International business enterprises—Management. 2. International business enterprises—Management—Cross-cultural studies. 3. Intercultural communication. I. Title.
HD62.4.T489 2003
658′.049—dc21 2003008544

This book is printed on acid-free paper.

03 04 05 06 10 9 8 7 6 5 4 3 2 1

*Acquisitions Editor:* Al Bruckner
*Editorial Assistant:* MaryAnn Vail
*Copy Editor:* Judy Selhorst
*Production Editor:* Diane S. Foster
*Typesetter:* C&M Digitals (P) Ltd.
*Proofreader:* Andrea Martin
*Indexer:* Jeanne R. Busemeyer
*Cover Designer:* Michelle Lee

# CONTENTS

# PREFACE

Globalization is shaping the role of managers as never before, and international management responsibilities and contact with other cultures are now commonplace. Therefore, understanding the influence of culture on management is now a fundamental aspect of business education. I hope that this book will help managers gain the understanding of cross-cultural interactions that is so important to managerial effectiveness in today's world.

## Coverage

This book is a compilation of readings and cases that have to do with managing in organizations that transcend national borders and in which organization members come from different cultural backgrounds. The bias of the book is that managing people in organizations is the key to organizational effectiveness. Therefore, the readings and cases have to do with the human aspects of management.

The rapid changes in management worldwide have clearly challenged the ability of academics to make courses in international management relevant. One of the best ways to enrich courses of this type is to supplement textbook material with recent articles and case studies. The readings and cases in this book are organized around three major themes in international management. These are a) the basis for understanding the influence of culture on international management, b) the key roles that international managers play, and c) important challenges that these managers face. In this regard it parallels the organization of my advanced text *Essentials of International Management: A Cross-Cultural Perspective,* also from Sage Publications. However, *Readings and Cases in International Management: A Cross-Cultural Perspective* is not limited to use as a supplement to that text. It is designed to be used on its own or as a companion to other international management texts or as a supplement for courses in organizational behavior, management, or international business.

## Selection of Materials

The readings and cases have been selected to be appropriate for both undergraduate and graduate students. Care has been taken to select readings that do not duplicate, but supplement, material typically contained in texts on this topic. Also, in as far as was possible, both readings and cases represent a broad geographic scope. While the cases are organized around the three themes identified above, most cases are integrative. That is, they address a number of topics and can be used at a variety of points in a typical course.

## Teaching Notes

Complete teaching notes for the readings and cases are available on a CD Instructor's Manual. Also in the website is a quick reference guide to the cases that identifies the topics most prominently addressed in each of the cases and also the countries involved. Additionally, users of the book are encouraged to contact me at dcthomas@sfu.ca with their comments and suggestions for using the readings and cases. These comments will be posted on the website so that we can all benefit from each other's experience.

## Acknowledgments

I am grateful to the authors who submitted cases to this volume and to the institutions that supported use of other material. Many of the cases are new, but there are also some old favorites that I just couldn't leave out. My thanks go to Marquita Flemming for encouraging me to produce this book and to Al Bruckner and MaryAnn Vail for shepherding it to completion. The staff at Sage Publications has done their usual professional job. My research assistant Alexandra Lebedeva provided invaluable assistance with the many details of the production of this volume. Thank you Sasha! Finally, I am, as always, grateful for the cross-cultural relationship that is the foundation for all that I do. Yes, Tilley, I know I'm the one who is different!

—David C. Thomas

# PART I

## Management and Culture

This section presents readings and cases that are helpful in understanding both the cultural context of international management and how culture influences the behavior of individual managers. International management is defined by the structure and content of managerial roles, but the very concept of management itself may be culture bound. Our ability to make sense of organizational and management behavior in an international context requires an understanding of what culture is and where it comes from. And, in order for culture to be valuable in explaining and predicting behavior, we must be able to systematically describe cultural differences and also understand the fundamental principles that influence the interactions among individuals who are culturally different. It is this kind of knowledge that forms the basis for the global mindset required of today's managers.

# Reading 1.1

## GLOBAL MANAGERS

### *Developing a Mindset for Global Competitiveness*

BEN L. KEDIA

ANANDA MUKHERJI

As the focus of business shifts from the domestic environment to the global, business leaders and managers will have to increasingly look for ways to redefine their strategies and realign their organizations to the new and more complex global realities. This, essentially, is the challenge for global managers—to articulate a viable global strategy, facilitate and develop supportive processes by which globalizations can be managed, and create appropriate conditions by which the overall strategy, process, culture, and structure can be meaningfully aligned to achieve organizational effectiveness. The challenges of global competition, corporate downsizing, industrial renaissance, and economic dislocation are the new watchwords of American business (Jusela, 1994). The challenges, however, are not restricted to meeting changes in the global competitive environment, but also to look at ways to improving organizational performance and increasing individual development simultaneously (Porras & Silvers, 1991).

In a world where communication and transportation technology have reduced barriers considerably, an additional challenge is to develop a mindset that is global to increase organizational effectiveness, and yet maintain efficient business operations. The question really is, what are firms to do to enhance their competitive abilities in the face of increased pressures of global competition, and yet maintain their long term viability as effective business entities? There is considerable evidence that large scale changes are taking place in the global arena. Although economic growth rates for developed countries have slowed down and stabilized between 2 and 4%, the growth rates of newly industrialized countries are burgeoning between 5 and 11% (*Fortune,* 1995). In an earlier report, the World Bank has forecasted that by the year 2020, the five largest economies, based on purchasing power parity, would be China, the US, Japan, India, and Indonesia (World Bank, 1992), displacing Germany and France from the ranks of the top five. The emerging economic reality with its new players implies that existing concepts may have to be seriously reviewed and reconsidered. For any business, the conventional model will no longer have the same validity, and the greatest opportunities and challenges would be from the global market and its attendant challenges to operate differently (Rhinesmith, 1993).

According to Yip (1992), the globalization phenomenon is taking place on account of four globalization drivers, and managers need to be

SOURCE: Reprinted from *Journal of World Business, Vol 34*, Kedia et al., "Global Managers," pp. 230–251. 

cognizant of these drivers. These are market drivers, cost drivers, competitive drivers, and government drivers. (1) *Market Drivers*—Although more salient in industrialized nations, per capita income has been increasing worldwide. This has resulted in greater purchasing power and an increased demand for goods worldwide. There has also been a convergence in lifestyles, tastes, aspirations, and expectations of consumers. Increased global travel has also created a new class of global consumers. (2) *Cost Drivers*—Another set of factors impacting globalization is lowered manufacturing and production costs. Consequently, economies of scale, availability of low labor costs, accelerated technological innovation, and improved transportation have been a part of cost drivers. (3) *Competitive Drivers*—Competitive drivers affecting globalization are new global competitors, increased formation of global strategic alliances, and more countries becoming competitive battlegrounds. (4) *Government Drivers*—Globalization is also impacted by government drivers. These include factors like the emergence of trading blocks, large scale privatization, and reduction in trade barriers.

Companies are now confronted by the rapid globalization of markets and competition, the increasing importance of speed and flexibility as key sources of competitive advantage, and the growing proliferation of partnership relations with suppliers, customers, and competitors (Ghoshal, Arnzen, & Brownfield, 1992). The prevailing conditions in the global environment make it necessary for companies to respond with radically different management approaches to succeed. Over the last few years there have been a number of writers who have helped define, develop, and better understand the mindset for global managers (see Jusela, 1994; Kefalas & Neuland, 1997; Rhinesmith, 1993; and Tichy, 1992). Similarly, there have been a number of articles on the strategic demands and challenges today's managers face in the global environment (Bartlett & Ghoshal, 1992; Murtha, Lenway & Bagozzi, 1998; and Prahalad & Lieberthal, 1998). Based on an extensive review of the literature, we propose to do two things. One, is to develop the essentials of the global mindset based on available literature and suggestions made by various scholars in the field. In this process, we propose to examine those mindsets that we feel are less useful in today's highly competitive and turbulent global environment. Two, is to briefly outline the forces facing managers in today's highly competitive global environment, and how our proposed global mindset may be useful in balancing and integrating the various forces and multiple challenges emanating from global business, regional/country pressures, and world-wide functions. The issues we specifically address in this paper are:

- Changing orientation of managers
- Developing a global perspective
- Role, qualities, and requirements of global leadership
- Evolution of managerial mindsets
- Strategizing and integrating globally

Globalization can be conceptualized as a situation where political borders become increasingly more irrelevant, economic interdependencies are heightened, and national differences due to dissimilarities in societal cultures are central issues of business. The world, on account of these complex and dynamic forces, becomes a "global marketplace" (Lane, DiStefano & Maznevski, 1997). This requires global managers to possess a global perspective. A global manager is one who has reorganized his or her way of thinking and has an altered mindset. Lane et al. (1997) suggest that thinking globally means extending concepts and models from one-to-one relationships to holding multiple realities and relationships in mind simultaneously, and then acting skillfully on this more complex reality. Thus, to be globally competitive, global managers need to have openness that allows a global mindset to form, evolve, and develop.

## Changing Orientation of Managers

Over the last decade or so, with notable changes taking place in the global competitive environment, the orientation of managers has changed considerably. This change has taken place both in terms of levels, and in terms of priorities. From a level perspective, most traditional training focused on the individual executive with the objective of broadening the perspective of managers with the hope that individuals will somehow find ways to influence choices and actions within their corporations (Ghoshal et al., 1992). The focus has shifted from the level of the individual manager to that of teams and groups, and indeed the target now is the entire organization that needs to be trained and reoriented to face the emerging global challenges (Tichy, 1992).

Other than level of training, managers were traditionally trained in what may be defined as "hard" as opposed to "soft" issues (Tichy, 1992: p. 210). The focus in "hard" issues training was to become the low cost producer. Consequently, the "hard" issues were oriented toward drivers of the bottom line, and the emphasis was on budgets,

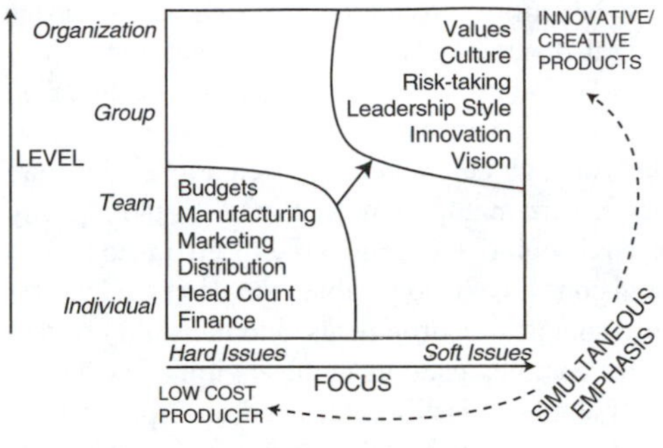


**Figure 1**

manufacturing, marketing, distribution, head count, and finances. However, in the face of reduced market power and increased global competition, the focus is now shared with "soft" issues that emphasize the need to be creative and to deliver innovative products simultaneously. The orientation, consequently, has shifted toward drivers of the top line and the emphasis is on values, culture, vision, leadership style, innovative behavior, and risk-taking. The framework given in Figure 1, adapted from Tichy (1992), illustrates this changed orientation of levels and of priorities. The challenge for global managers is the ability to focus on hard and soft issues simultaneously.

Earlier theoretical contributions suggested that the fundamental international problem facing managers was to reconcile the conflicting pressures of adapting to a standardized technology and product, or to respond to local market needs and requirements (Murtha et al., 1998). These conflicting pressures were considered to be mutually exclusive and existed linearly in terms of zero-sum trade-offs, that Fayerweather (1982: p. 211) termed as "unification" or "fragmentation" strategies.

However, technological and theoretical developments have indicated that international business strategy can be conceptualized along multiple dimensions. Rather than conceive strategy along one dimension, researchers (Doz & Prahalad, 1991; Prahalad & Doz, 1981, 1987) have suggested that strategy consists of balancing the twin pressures of global integration and local responsiveness concurrently. Consequently, paying simultaneous attention to various dimensions of strategy (Murtha et al., 1998) is considered to be an appropriate way to balance these forces. Organizational capabilities to exploit the full strategic potential of these complex pressures of integration, responsiveness, and coordination (Murtha et al., 1998) require global mindsets that equilibrate these forces rather than predispose decisions in favor of one dimension at the expense of the others (Prahalad & Doz, 1987). Bartlett and Ghoshal's (1989) definition of a transnational mentality implies the ability to balance these complex forces in pursuit of a unique strategy that blends them. It is worth mentioning that the organizational context, in terms of culture, corporate policies, and motivation, must be geared towards forming and sustaining a holistic global outlook. In other words, a transnational mentality or a global mindset is a completely different way of looking at the world and synthesizing the many complex forces.

Like much of strategy research on cognitive issues (Prahalad & Bettis, 1986; Grant, 1988), we focus on the mindset of the global manager whose impact is felt at the organizational level. We take the liberty of shifting our level of analysis from the manager to the organization in the belief that organizational actions, in terms of strategies and postures, are an aggregation of the mindset of the key and dominant decision makers. Like Prahalad & Bettis (1986), who used the manager's dominant logic to establish a linkage between the pattern of diversification and performance, we propose to use the mindset of global managers to explain actions and strategies of organizations taken in international business.

## Framework to Develop a Global Perspective

For managers to orient themselves and their priorities to the changed international realities, we suggest that a triad consisting of a global mindset, knowledge, and skills, is needed by managers to be globally competitive. Although a global mindset is a state of being essentially characterized by openness, and an ability to recognize complex interconnections, global managers need a certain set of supportive knowledge and skills to sustain the mindset. Knowledge and skills are needed to meet the changing, emerging, and increasingly complex conditions associated with globalization (Rhinesmith, 1993). Figure 2 provides an illustration of how global mindset, knowledge, and skills are interrelated.

### Global Mindset

A global mindset, according to Rhinesmith (1993: p. 24), "is a way of being rather than a set of skills. It is an orientation of the world that allows one to see certain things that others do not. A global mindset means the ability to scan the world from a

**Figure 2** Developing a Global Perspective

broad perspective, always looking for unexpected trends and opportunities that may constitute a threat or an opportunity to achieve personal, professional or organizational objectives." A global mindset is for each manager to realize his or her firm's interdependence on the global economy even when the firm's activities are seemingly confined to the domestic environment. However, to sustain and develop a global mindset, a manager also needs knowledge and skills.

We conceptualize a global mindset for global managers to be a necessary condition to effectively handle global competition, however, it is not a sufficient condition. The sufficient conditions that enhance and sustain a global mindset are knowledge and skills. A manager needs to have knowledge of different aspects of the interdependent world. Skills, on the other hand, are certain human and behavioral abilities that managers have that help them to do their work more effectively in the global context. It is this unique combination of global mindset, knowledge, and skills that is necessary and sufficient for the making of global managers.

Given the changed level of training and the new priorities for global managers, coupled with knowledge and skills required for a global mindset, global managers have to play a leadership role. To do this, global managers have to define their role, and develop certain qualities that make them true global managers (Kets de Vries & Mead, 1992). The primary role of the global manager, according to Kets de Vries and Mead, is to act as a catalyst within the organization. Here the global manager has to be sensitive to cultural diversity, and to manage cultural diversity. An effective global manager is one who values diversity and is able to leverage differences in a meaningful way. Apart from a catalytic role, global managers need to develop and possess certain important traits. One, is the capacity for envisioning and being able to give meaning to the vision. Two, is to be able to understand increasingly complex environments, and the ability to recognize complex patterns in the environment. Three, is to be able to instill values and to inspire others. Finally, an effective global manager should be able to build and maintain organizational networks at the global level.

In a general way, many requirements of global management may not differ from those of the non-global management mindset. At an abstract level, effective management, whether in the global or domestic environment, requires traits like creating vision and instilling values. However, apart from a common set of traits, global management requires a set of specialized skills, capabilities, and competencies that are not part of the traditional education system and managerial experience. Our focus is on this emerging set of capabilities that is increasingly assuming salience. A global mindset, to distinguish it from a non-global mindset, is one that is characterized by unique time and space perspectives, and a general predisposition (Kefalas & Neuland, 1997). A unique time perspective is one of taking a long-term view when dealing with international business activities. Similarly, a unique space perspective is one where managers with a global mindset will extend their personal space well beyond their immediate surroundings, both in terms of geography as well as in real and potential relationships with other people. Also, managers with a global mindset will exhibit a general predisposition by being more tolerant of other peoples and cultures, consider cultural diversity an asset, thrive on ambiguity, balance contradictory forces, and rethink boundaries (Kefalas & Neuland, 1997; Rhinesmith, 1993).

In addition, other characteristics of a global mindset include emotional connection, capacity for managing uncertainty, ability to balance tensions, and savvy (Gregerson, Morrison, & Black, 1998). The first of these is a genuine emotional connection with people throughout the organization's worldwide operations. The second is to have the capacity to manage under conditions that are constantly changing and inherently complex. The third is to confront and balance the various tensions of global a integration and local responsiveness (Prahalad & Doz, 1987). Finally, to exhibit business savvy and organizational savvy (Gregerson et al., 1998), where business savvy enables a manager to recognize worldwide market opportunities, and organization savvy implies intimate knowledge of the firm's capabilities, and the ability to mobilize worldwide resources to capture market opportunities.

### Knowledge for a Global Mindset

Knowledge is more attuned toward factual information rather than cognitive and behavioral skills. Knowledge is appreciation of the existence of differences, and it is the appropriate use of knowledge that requires skills. In this particular case, knowledge is to do with a number of factors that make a global manager's work more effective. One critical area of knowledge is mastery over technology, and the ability to the technology, information systems, and telecommunications effectively in an organization's global activities. Another important knowledge-based issue is to know about socio-political factors of different countries, and how these socio-political factors impact business operations. A third area of knowledge is that of culture and cross-cultural issues that impact management.

Thus, apart from the socio-political, economic, and cultural dimensions of the global environment and other countries, global managers need to be aware of the technical dimensions of knowledge. This does not only include the technologies associated with communication, information, and computers, but also the impact of technology on the global operations of the firm. The fact that technology drives business in subtle and powerful ways is something a global manager has to be aware of. Technology impacts the firm's production processes such as new and improved computer numeric control machines that drastically improve quality, to flexible manufacturing systems that make scale economies and long deliveries irrelevant. However, it is the power of technology to make certain products, processes, or services obsolete much faster today than it was a few years ago that is of critical importance. Moreover, with decreased product life cycle and increased and more expensive product development cycles, global managers are faced with a challenge of understanding technology, and assessing its impact on the global operations of the firm.

Increased global competition has impacted a number of areas, most notably manufacturing and communications. The role and function of manufacturing in the global environment have increasingly become a competitive weapon. Some of the more prevalent practices include total quality management (TQM), just-in-time (JIT), factory automation, employee involvement, and outsourcing (Fatehi, 1996). Communication and information technology are critical factors in the operations and successful performance of MNCs. Crossing national borders, MNCs are particularly vulnerable to multiple political, cultural, and economic systems within which they operate, and an effective management information system is crucial for the success of MNCs (Fatehi, 1996).

Knowledge requirements for global managers are the basic building blocks toward a global perspective, and a global mindset. Constantly striving for a bigger, better picture will expand one's knowledge (Rhinesmith, 1993), and that a global manager's technical, business, and industry knowledge is the most fundamental quality that allows him or her to successfully manage the competitive process, both domestic and foreign. This knowledge must be broad as well as deep, and must include a well developed international dimension that includes constant scanning of information, and competitive and market conditions on a global basis. Another important area is country-specific knowledge that implies some understanding of social, political, and economic development and policies of the concerned countries (Lane et al., 1997). This suggests that the relationship between trade, export, industrial, and agricultural development policies are important, as is information on taxation, banking, exchange rules, currency repatriation, and so forth.

As mentioned earlier, country-related information has to be complemented by cross-cultural knowledge as well. This is a true challenge for global managers in that they not only learn about the world and application of business principles, technology, and competitiveness to the international arena, but ultimately a challenge that becomes deeply personal in accepting and adjusting to other values, experiences, and lifestyles (Rhinesmith, 1993). One key to being a successful manager in a global organization is to understand cultural differences that exist among different nations and societies. Only an awareness of the complex phenomenon of culture will allow managers to become open-minded enough to move to the next level that allows an understanding of the different dimensions of culture, and how behaviors are affected.

### Skills for a Global Mindset

Skills are the ability to put knowledge into action. Managers may be knowledgeable, say for example about culture, but may not possess the complex skills to use that knowledge effectively. The skill in this case is to know how behavior is affected, and what the dimensions of culture are. Knowledge and understanding should be the basis to take action (Lane et al., 1997), as intellectual action may not transfer directly and automatically into a high degree of skill unless considerable practice is involved. Putting knowledge into practice is the essential way to develop skills. One important skill for the global manager is the need for acculturation of other cultures. Another important skill is the ability to lead and indeed leverage diversity to the advantage of the company.

The human factor may ultimately come to represent the new competitive edge for the global corporation, more than physical and other resources (Baird, Briscoe, Tuden, & Rosansky, 1994). The presumed strength of US firms in the quality of their management and their leadership training may in fact be their disguised weakness (Rhinesmith, 1993). A major shift affecting corporate America is from vertical values, such as individualism and autonomy, to horizontal values, such as interdependence and networking. It is a transformation from a predominantly masculine value system to an androgynous one. The new value set calls for each person to have both masculine and feminine characteristics. The nurturing style of expressing power, along with the sharing perspective of empowerment, seems to encourage productivity in high-performing organizations. In reinforcing the process perspective, Ribbens (1996) found in an empirical study that the most effective managers were those who changed their behavior or explained their actions. Managers who tried to influence the expectation of others or who avoided conflicting expectations were regarded as less effective.

The challenge for global managers is one of acculturation, followed by developing skills to lead and motivate a diverse workforce. In today's dynamic international environment, there is great need to be flexible and responsive. The world that managers face is one that is filled with complexity and contradictions. The earlier model of efficiency, hierarchy, control, and centralization is being replaced by a model of responsiveness, decentralization, partnership, and teamwork. To be globally competitive, organizations have to become increasingly more organic in structure, and more fluid in their responses. Structures in organizations have become more and more fuzzy, with ill-defined boundaries. To be globally competitive and responsive in this organic manner, strong process mechanisms need to be developed to support these needs along with a well developed global mindset.

The challenge for global managers is to understand what culture means, and look for creative ways to leverage diversity at the workplace towards greater organizational effectiveness, and higher levels of performance. American attributes of individualism, and goal- and achievement-orientation, along with being competitive and aggressive have to be accommodated with priorities of other cultures that stress shared goals and a communitarian outlook. Culture is a deep-rooted characteristic of persons and groups, and rather than think of changing other people's cultures, global managers should consider how best to use the different cultures of others to meet organizational objectives. Because culture and language are so closely connected, global managers could improve their skills by learning one or more languages. This is likely to increase their effectiveness when using a language that is understood by the people the global manager is managing.

Globalization will obviously require strategic thinking that involves identifying different ways for people to meet their goals and determine which actions will get them where they want to be (Stumpf, 1989). Given the increased complexity that a highly competitive global environment creates, Stumpf suggests that strategic thinking involves a number of key process-oriented factors. These involve a manager's ability, given the changed global circumstances, to know the business and markets, manage subunit rivalry, find and overcome threats, stay on strategy, be an entrepreneurial force, and to accommodate diversity. Awareness and understanding of culture and being able to use diversity of people effectively is essentially a form of strategic thinking.

For global managers to be acculturated requires that they develop greater sensitivity to foster greater levels of understanding. There are considerable benefits that are likely to accrue when managers are sensitive to culture, and have the skills to use this knowledge to benefit both the organization as well as the individual. In short, a combination of knowledge and skills will go a long way in increasing managerial effectiveness in international operations, developing cosmopolitan organizational representatives, improving cross-cultural skills of employees in general, and enhancing job effectiveness. Given the dynamics of today's complex world, a global manager has to have a global mindset based on knowledge and skills so that organizations can survive and grow.

## Developing a Global Mindset

"Constantly crossing cultural, language, political, social, and economic borders makes global business complex and uncertain, . . . and constant learning is required for success" (Gregerson et al.,

**Table 1** The Changing Managerial Perspectives

| *Mindset* | *Outlook* | *Strategy* |
|---|---|---|
| Ethnocentrism: Home-country perspective | Centralized/Controlled | International |
| Polycentrism/Regiocentrism: Host-country Perspective | Decentralized/Autonomous | Multinational |
| Geocentrism: Global perspective | Networked/Interdependent | Transnational |

1998, p. 23). Other than constant learning, these authors suggest global managers require adventuresomeness, curiosity, and open-mindedness, among other characteristics. However, the key question is how to develop and sustain the characteristics required for successful global managers? There are a number of strategies for developing successful global leaders (Gregerson et al., 1998), and include:

- *Foreign travel* to put potential leaders in the middle of a country so as to absorb its culture, economy, political system, market, and other crucial details.
- Establish *teams* in which individuals with diverse backgrounds and perspectives work closely together.
- Purposeful *training* developed around an effective and structured learning environment.
- *Transfers* to foreign locations to live, work, and learn from the experience of overseas assignments.

## The Changing Mindset of Managers

The terms globalization and global outlook have been increasingly used in business literature. As Rhinesmith (1993: p. 2) observes, "Globalization has arrived in the world but not in most of the world's organizations." He goes on to state that there is little doubt that to be viable during the next century, all organizations, whether international or domestic, will need to be more global in their outlook if not in their operations. There is increasing appreciation of the fact that more emphasis has to be placed in developing the human mind and, consequently, business organizations to remain competitive in the face of globalization.

The important question is, in what ways has managerial outlook evolved in the context of thinking globally? Among managers in western nations, there is one fundamental characteristic in the evolution of the global mindset. European managers, for historical, cultural, and political reasons, are generally exposed to a multitude of cultures, regions, languages, and customs. In short, they have far greater environmental heterogeneity to contend with. American managers, on the other hand, are usually exposed to a relatively more homogeneous environment. American managers, generally, are faced with lesser variety in terms of language and culture. One may use Chakravarthy and Perlmutter's (1985) framework of *ethnocentrism, polycentrism, regiocentrism,* and *geocentrism* to explain managerial mindsets (see Table 1).

The initial mindset of managers, especially those from a more homogeneous environment, when thinking globally is one of *ethnocentrism.* In this mindset, managers use a home-country standard as a reference point in managing international activities. The outlook is one of centralized decision-making and high control over operations. Managers with such a mindset may follow an international strategy of maintaining control from the home-country, and replicating home-country systems and procedures abroad. The next level of evolution is one of *polycentrism* or *regiocentrism,* and here, as international investment and involvement increase, the host-country culture and practices assume salience. This may be extended to include a number of similar countries in the region, and host-country, standards are used as a reference point in managing company operations. The strategies typically followed are likely to be multinational strategies that emphasize decentralized and autonomous global operations. For the evolutionary process to reach the level of a global mindset, a *geocentric* mindset has to be reached. Here the managerial outlook is one of creating a global network and a preference for following a transnational strategy that is integrative and interdependent.

## Managerial Mindsets

There has been a great deal of evolution and change in the perspectives of business managers. Here we will outline some typical mindsets that managers have and can be used to explain how these unique mindsets impact analysis of the environment and drive business decisions. The mindsets that have been conceptualized and developed here, and explained in the sections that follow have been adapted and modified from Baird (1994). The intent is not so much to chart a historical path but to provide an insight into different kinds of mindsets that currently exist, and how much work is involved in moving from one mindset to another. As competition, culture, and nation-states are closely bounded together, this exposition of four mindsets we provide will make clear that some mindsets are less effective in today's world of heightened global competition and increased economic interdependencies. The four mindsets are also closely associated with a firm's strategy that may range from the least global to the most global mindset, and are also indicative of the level of development of a global perspective consisting of a global mindset, knowledge, and skills. The four mindsets we classify and explain in some detail are: (1) Defender; (2) Explorer; (3) Controller; and (4) Integrator.

### The Defender

The *defender* is a traditional mindset that is internally focused, and is essentially oriented to the domestic market and its needs (Baird, 1994). The *defender* is basically uninterested in other markets and cultures, and assumes any foreign element in the domestic market to be an unwanted and a temporary aberration. If the activities of foreigners become significant or threatening to any degree, the *defender* looks to the government and other collective representations to protect itself and its markets. It is not uncommon for the *defender* to ask for trade barriers, quotas, duties, laws, and special agreements to obtain protection, and all this is done with the hope of discouraging foreigners from sharing the domestic market. The *defender* is satisfied with its domestic operations, and is generally uninterested in making foreign forays.

The attitudes and beliefs of the *defender* follow the theme that what is different, in terms of culture and people, is dangerous. The *defender* acknowledges that others exist, but is uninterested in their existence. Faced with limited foreign advertising, production, or distribution, the *defender* makes no conscious effort to cultivate or understand foreign clients, competitors, or markets. The *defender* is unaware that there exists a connection, in many cases a strong one, between the activities of foreign competitors and the future of the domestic market. When faced with increased competition, the *defender* prefers to retreat within the protective custody of the domestic legal and political system rather than aggressively confront the foreign competition. There is almost no international element in the business strategies that the *defender* formulates and implements.

A classic example of the *defender* mindset is the reaction of the American steel industry that was faced with a steep decline between the 1960s and the 1980s. Mueller (1985: p. 214) states that "The mid-1960s also marked the start of a political response by the large American steel producers to the increasing presence of foreign competition in their home markets. For this purpose, US producers arranged a truce with their traditional adversary, the United Steel Workers union (USW), and enlisted its support in vigorous publicity and lobbying campaigns against imported steel. These and subsequent efforts had considerable success in obtaining government intervention in the quantities and prices of steel brought into the United States. . . ." Another example of a *defender* reaction is the attempt by the US footwear industry to obtain import protection (that was denied by President Reagan) in the mid-1980s to combat severe competition from foreign producers. The attempts by the U.S. textile and machine tools industries to seek government relief and intervention in the mid-1970s when faced with stiff foreign competition indicates the working of a *defender* mindset.

### The Explorer

The *explorer,* although largely inward-looking like the *defender,* is aware that business opportunities may exist in foreign markets. The *explorer* is aware that there are differences across nationalities and cultures around the world, but does not necessarily consider foreign cultures to be dangerous or to be avoided. To the *explorer,* foreign markets, notwithstanding the different cultures, present opportunities for increasing sales and expanding distribution of products (Baird, 1994). The *explorer,* however, treats its international forays with a lot of caution while moving into foreign markets to find new customers for its products and services. The *explorer* also focuses on closely studying the foreign environment to help increase its own business. However, the international forays of the *explorer* are relatively small when compared to the size of its domestic business.

As long as the mindset is that of the *explorer,* the domestic market will always predominate. The foreign or international business of the *explorer,* whether it be manufacturing, distributing, or selling, is controlled from the head office located in the home country. The foreign forays the *explorer* undertake serve to provide intelligence to the head office to estimate foreign competitive threats, assess political changes, and monitor competitors. The foreign operations of the *explorer* are centrally managed from head office usually with highly centralized decision-making and operational control to oversee the communication and distribution lines established abroad. The *explorer* prefers to follow strategies like exporting and franchising, and has limited investment commitments overseas.

Attempts made some years ago by Lotus Corporation to go international indicate an *explorer* mindset. Although Lotus officials assumed from the start that business productivity software had a natural global market (Yoffe, 1990), nothing substantial materialized until the hiring of Digate as CEO. Although Lotus had considered international issues, its initial international ventures were basically a gigantic mess. Lotus took some lighthearted forays into international markets and its first attempt at an international plan "was bizarre, and needless to say it went nowhere" (Yoffe, 1990: p. 39). Similarly Seiko, the Japanese electronics giant, exhibited an *explorer* mindset in its initial international forays. Seiko's management made a number of trips to the United States and Europe to study production methods used in these locations (Yoffe, 1990). Seiko, however, was quick to learn and developed a more aggressive mindset from that of an *explorer* to one that was interested in developing long-range global plans and a dominant market share.

### The Controller

The *controller* is more externally oriented than the *explorer*. The *controller* wishes to dominate the overseas markets through well developed systems and procedures that have worked very well at home. Unlike the *explorer*, the *controller* is willing to make a larger investment commitment internationally, and the proportion of foreign sales to domestic sales is considerable. The *controller*, however, follows an ethnocentric mindset (Chakravarthy & Perlmutter, 1985). Ethnocentrism implies that strategic decisions are guided by the values and interests of the parent company in its international activities. The *controller* establishes full-scale development, production, and distribution facilities abroad (Baird, 1994). Because of a multitude of interactions in different foreign markets on account of the need to produce and sell abroad, the *controller* is forced to understand the nature of culture, and how it impacts business. The *controller* would, however, like to impose the home culture and practices on its foreign operations wherever possible. The foreign cultures and markets must be used to the extent that it furthers the interests of the parent company.

The *controller* may follow some variations of its unique mindset to further its own ends. One such variation is a polycentric mindset which implies that strategic decisions are tailored to suit the cultures of the various countries in which the *controller* operates, or a regiocentric mindset where decisions are blended between the interests of the *controller* and its subsidiaries on a limited regional (Chakravarthy & Perlmutter, 1985). The culture of the *controller*, however, is the dominant one in business operations and strategic decision making. The *controller*, while allowing for a certain degree of independence in the activities of its many dispersed units, maintains financial and strategic control. Most often it is in the form of payment to the parent company, or in the parent company making important transfer pricing decisions, distribution of corporate overhead charges, and allocation of resources. Most importantly, the *controller's* head office spends much time and resources on mechanisms for controlling, and to lesser extent coordinating, diverse units and geographic distribution. The approach is that the parent company is supreme, and all important decisions must have the approval and sanction of the head office.

Some industries, dictated by the nature of their products and unique business operations, take on a *controller* like mindset. Typically industries that have a high proportion of franchising in the food industry are likely to exhibit a *controller* mindset. For example, Coke, McDonald's, and Pizza Hut are firms from the fast food industry that, perhaps, exemplify managing and strategizing with a *controller* mindset. A *controller* mindset could also be associated with the traditional multinational corporations where foreign offices and investments were made to replicate home country cultures, systems, and procedures. For instance, McDonald's closing down of its India operations, and Pizza Hut shutting down its Moscow property may indicate shortcomings associated with a *controller* mindset. Recently, Coke overestimated the strength of its brand name among India's consumers as it based its advertising strategy on its worldwide image, only to find the advantage slip to Pepsi that had customized its campaign and specifically tailored it for the Indian market (Prahalad & Lieberthal, 1998). To cite a Coke executive, "We're so successful in international business that we applied a tried and true formula . . . and it was the wrong formula to apply in India" (quoted from Prahalad & Lieberthal, p. 72).

### The Integrator

The *integrator,* we argue, is the manager with a global perspective with a real global mindset based on heightened awareness (knowledge), and enhanced abilities (skills). The *integrator* holds a multiple cultural perspective and creates a worldwide web of relationships with suppliers, developers, designers, distributors, competitors, and customers (Baird, 1994). The *integrator* also weaves together a complex web of partnerships, alliances, and relationships that shift and reconfigure over time as new threats and opportunities appear. The *integrator* is able to use his or her knowledge skillfully in actions leading toward organizational effectiveness. The *integrator* is typified as one who is aware, who understands, and who is competent. The *integrator* creates a global perspective or global mindset by obtaining information about the world, using the information experientially, and develops abilities and skills by being totally immersed in the dynamics of the complex environment. The *integrator* has the ability to first understand the external world with its unique differences and opportunities. The *integrator* is also able to bridge differences in a meaningful way, and finally is able to manage the differences between people, values, and cultures.

The *integrator* is able to leverage differences and synergistically integrate the many disparate elements in his or her complex world. The *integrator* knows not only how to deal with a second party, but is also aware how the second party deals with the third, and how the third party deals with the second (Baird, 1994). *Integrators* coordinate more than they control, and spend a lot of their time and resources improving coordination and cooperation among the different elements of the worldwide system. The *integrator* sees his or her role as that of creating effective and embedded networks, which in turn allows appropriate linking and leveraging. The key to network building is active management of cross-company and cross-cultural issues (Hagel, 1996). A critical function for managers is to develop and sustain mechanisms for knowledge flow and transfer from one part of the global system to another. *Integrators,* in a sense, create information networks to manage mutual interdependencies and to increase the payoff from diversity. *Integrators* understand that competitive success comes from a win-win strategy (Brandenburger & Nalebuff, 1993), and not from the old win-lose (zero sum game) that may be a part of the mindset of *defenders, explorers,* and *controllers.* The *integrator* is more interested in leveraging than restraining, integrating than empire building, coordinating than controlling, and managing change than creating stability.

Attempts by Toyota of Japan may be examples of an *integrator* mindset. Toyota is not merely a company but a confederation of firms more properly called the Toyota Group (Yoffe, 1990). It is part of a *keirestu* whose distinguishing trait is the link among member firms that may be described as a thick and complex web of relationships not matched elsewhere. As Yoffe (1990) mentions, Toyota is at the apex of a hierarchy of firms worldwide that consist of primary, secondary, and tertiary suppliers and subcontractors. Toyota, along with Nissan, Hitachi, Mitsubishi, and other large Japanese firms, represents an *integrator* mindset in its outlook and strategy which is one of leveraging, sharing, and developing complementarities. However, Toyota, while following more of an *integrator's* mindset in some of its domestic operations, still retains a *controller's* mindset when operating overseas[2] in attempting to impose its culture and practices on its foreign operations.

Some of the illustrations provided here have been discussed in articles by Prahalad and Lieberthal (1998) when they suggest that organizations need to discard their imperial mindset regarding international business. The actions of Fiat of Italy is a classic attempt at evolving into and practicing with an integrator's mindset. Ford recently introduced its Escort model in India and priced it around $21,000, putting it straightway into the luxury car market, and far away from the real market and competition offered by the dominant and popular Maruti–Suzuki priced at $10,000. Fiat, with its experience in Brazil, another big emerging market like India, had already designed a car, the Palio, for the demanding Brazilian market. Fiat is now on the verge of transferring its knowledge and experience to India to compete with Maruti–Suzuki rather than Ford. Similarly, Philips Electronics introduced a two-in-one video-CD player in China that has sold over 15 million units. This product and its marketing is likely to be successful in other emerging Asian economies. Yet the same product has no market in the developed world. In contrast, both Revlon and Kellogg have found it difficult to succeed in China and India because these companies did not approach their markets in a holistic manner. As Prahalad and Lieberthal (1998, p. 72) state, "Tailoring products to the big emerging markets is not a trivial task. Minor cultural adaptations or marginal cost reductions will not do the job. Instead, to overcome an implicit imperialism, companies must undergo a fundamental rethinking of every element of their business model."

**Table 2** The Four Mindsets and Global Perspectives

| *Mindsets* | *Defender* | *Explorer* | *Controller* | *Integrator* |
|---|---|---|---|---|
| Level of global perspective | None | Surface level | Intermediate level | Deep level |
| Global identify self | Maintain self sufficiency | Define differences | Redefine self | Integrate |
| Others | Acknowledge | Explore | Control | Leverage diversity |

SOURCE: Adapted from Baird, 1994.

From an evolutionary or developmental perspective, the *defender* has little or no global orientation, and also has limited skills and knowledge to effectively operate in a globally competitive environment. The *explorer* has knowledge about the international environment, and a restricted set of skills to operate in the global environment in a limited manner. Because of its many limitations, and inadequacies, the *explorer* is able to pursue only a very limited range of international business activities on account of its surface level global perspective. The *controller* has more knowledge of the global environment as well as considerably more skills about the international marketplace. The *controller,* however, has a limited global mindset, and consequently it has an ethnocentric-efficiency orientation in its international operations. The *controller* has an intermediate level global perspective. The *integrator,* we suggest, has a well developed and a deep level global perspective. The *integrator* has a true global mindset with the appropriate level of knowledge and skills.

In facing global competitiveness, the *explorer* is the least effective, the *controller* is somewhat more effective, and the *integrator* is the most effective. We suggest that a given mindset is associated with a particular world view and perspective, and with a specific type of strategy. For mindsets and strategies to change, appropriate training efforts have to be made to move it from one mindset to another. Table 2 provides an overview of the four mindsets within a global perspective.

Readers may be concerned over our advocacy of the *integrator* mindset as being appropriate and relevant in today's complex global reality. With competition likely to take place in the big emerging markets of Brazil, China, and India, MNCs will no longer be able to consider these as new markets for existing products. In short, MNCs will have to discard their "imperialist mindset" (Prahalad & Lieberthal, 1998, p. 69), so as to adapt, design, manufacture, and market products that suit the unique requirements of these markets. The mindsets of *defenders, explorers,* and *controllers* will simply not be able to assess, understand, and react to the new global realities. It is only the *integrators* who have developed the mindset, skills, and knowledge to be dynamic and effective players in the global arena. Our argument is that the global mindset is an evolutionary process. Some managers and organizations remain at an early stage of the evolution, and progress to the level of a *defender, explorer,* or *controller.* Other managers and organizations evolve quickly through the various stages, or move effortlessly to mindset of *integrators.* We contend that *integrators* have the required mindset, capability, and flexibility to adapt and manage in today's complex global environment. Having any of the other three mindsets implies both limitations and a lack of capabilities in effectively managing today's complexities.

## Strategizing and Integrating Globally

The important issue in having a true global mindset is not to be able to do all things, rather it is to be able to understand the complexities of managing an interdependent and complex global network, and in playing the required part within the network to ensure high degrees of coordinating, leveraging, and integrating. Bartlett and Ghoshal (1992) have suggested that the key functions in a global environment are a combination of specialization and integration. The ability of a manager to integrate comes from having a global mindset that is based on requisite knowledge and skills needed to operate effectively in the global context. Researchers argue that key aspects of international strategic capabilities derive from managers' cognitive processes that balance competing business, country, and functional concerns (Perlmutter, 1969: Prahalad & Doz, 1987; Kogut, 1985; Bartlett & Ghoshal, 1989, and Hedlund, 1993).

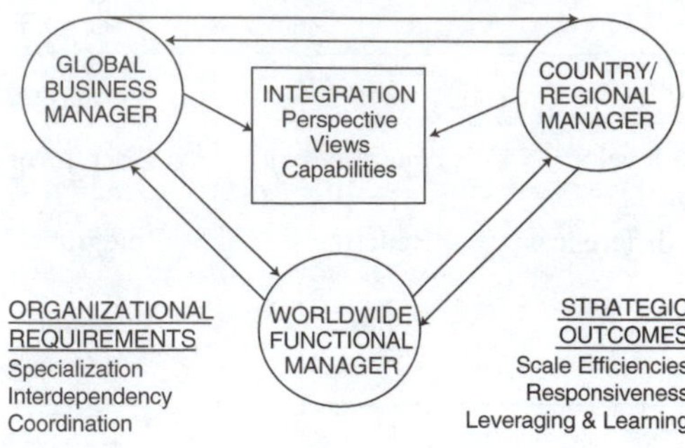


**Figure 3** Integrating and Strategizing Globally

SOURCE: Adapted from Bartlett & Ghoshal, 1992.

This view is supported by Bartlett & Ghoshal (1992) who suggest that there are three fundamental dynamics of global operations (see Figure 3). One, is global scale efficiency and competitiveness, and this is the responsibility of the global business manager. The global business manager's role is to be a strategist, architect, and coordinator. Two, is national level responsiveness and flexibility, and this is the responsibility of the country or regional manager. The country or regional manager's role is one of being a sensor, builder and contributor. Three, is worldwide leveraging and learning capability, and this is the responsibility of the worldwide functional manager. The worldwide functional manager's role is that of scanner, cross-pollinator and champion.

These three dynamics correspond to the business, country, and functional concerns mentioned earlier, and are, according to Bartlett & Ghoshal (1992), the triad on which global strategies can be built. The critical part is the meshing of these forces which entails integrating different perspectives, view balancing, resource leveraging and sharing, and capabilities building (Bartlett & Ghoshal, 1992). The higher the degree of integration, the more global and effective the strategy. Traditionally, there would be a high degree of coordination between two of these three forces, resulting in less than optimal global strategies. With managers developing a global mindset, we suggest that all three forces of strategizing globally can be meaningfully integrated resulting in true and effective global strategies. All three roles require a global mindset, but there is also the need to integrate the multiple pressures and challenges of business, function, and region, and here the manager with a global mindset, irrespective of the level or position within the company, plays a crucial role. In short, a global mindset is required not only at the business, regional, and functional levels, but also at the crucial corporate requirement to integrate all three forces. In addition, managers with a global mindset will need to balance and integrate the forces consisting of scale economies, responsiveness and flexibility, and resource leveraging and capability building.

## Conclusion and Discussion

Based on the dynamic changes taking place, there is a need to have global managers with a global perspective. This global perspective consists of a mindset, knowledge, and skills. A global mindset, in its simplest form will allow a manager from one part of the world to be comfortable in another on account of knowledge and skills that are based on understanding and awareness. A global mindset, in other words, will make a manager more competent and effective. A global manager must be able to lead and motivate diverse work teams, and this skill comes from knowing and using knowledge of cultural differences. Global managers have to coach teams as well as to lead. Global managers must seek out and acquire knowledge. Not only must he or she know how to use high technology in managerial activities, but also to understand and assess the impact of technology on the global activities of the firm.

We suggest that globalization has preceded, in many cases, the abilities of managers to grasp with the new and complex realities. As we have stated, there are still many managerial mindsets that are completely out of tune with the requirements of today's global business requirements. The challenges is to identify which mindsets managers belong to, and to understand how their mindsets are inhibiting them from being effective. The next challenge is to create an appropriate environment to move managers from a relatively dysfunctional mindset to one that creates a global perspective.

## Notes

1. A version of this paper was presented at the NIBS International Seminar, Rennes International School of Business, France in March, 1997.

2. We are grateful to one of our anonymous reviewers for pointing out why corporations like Toyota may simultaneously pursue different mindsets.

C 12
C 1.7



## References

Baird, L. (1994). *Meeting global challenges: The executive perspective.* Unpublished working paper. University of Boston, Boston, MA.

Baird, L., Briscoe, J., Tuden, L., & Rosansky, L. M. H. (1994). World class executive development. *Human Resource Planning, 17*(1): 1–10.

Bartlett, C. K. & Ghoshal, S. (1989). *Managing across borders: The transnational solution,* Boston, MA, The Harvard Business School Press.

Bartlett, C. K. & Ghoshal, S. (1992). What is a global manager. *Harvard Business Review,* Sep-Oct, *70*(5): 124–132.

Berry, J. K. (1990). Linking management development to business strategies. *Journal of Training & Development Journal, 44*(8): 20–22.

Brandenburger, A. M. & Nalebuff, B. J. (1993). The right game: Use game theory to shape strategy. *Harvard Business Review,* Jul-Aug: 57–71.

Chakravarthy, B. & Perlmutter, H. V. (1985). Strategic planning for a global economy. *Columbia Journal of World Business,* Summer: 3–10.

Doz, Y. L. & Prahalad, C. K. (1991). Managing DMNCs: A search for a new paradigm. *Strategic Management Journal,* Special Issue, *12:* 145–164.

Fatehi, K. (1996). *International management: A cross-cultural and functional perspective.* Upper River Saddle, NJ: Prentice-Hall.

Fayerweather, J. (1982). *International business strategy and administration.* New York, NY: Ballinger.

Fortune. (1995). *March, 20:* 109.

Ghoshal, S., Arnzen, B., & Brownfield, S. (1992). A learning alliance between business and business schools: Executive education as a platform for partnership. *California Management Review, 35*(1): 50–67.

*Global Economic Prospects.* (1992). Washington, DC: The World Bank.

Gregerson, H. B., Morrison, A. J., & J. S. Black (1998). Developing leaders for the global frontier. *Sloan Management Review, 1*(40): 21–39.

Hagel, J. (1996). Spider versus spider. *McKinsey Quarterly, 1:* 4–18.

Hedlund, G. (1993). Assumptions of hierarchy and heterarchy with application to the management of the multinational corporation. In S. Ghoshal and D. E. Westney (Eds.), *Organization theory and the multinational corporation* (pp. 211–236). New York, NY: St. Martin's Press.

Jusela, G. E. (1994). Meeting the global competitive challenge: Building systems that learn on a large scale. In W. L. French, C. H. Bell, & R. A. Zawacki (Eds.) *Organization development and transformation: Managing effective change* (pp. 369–397). Boston, MA: Irwin.

Kefalas, A. G. S. & Neuland, E. W. (1997). Global mindsets: An exploratory study. A paper presented at the Academy of International Business Conference in Monterey, Mexico.

Kets de Vries, M. F. R., & Mead, C. (1992). The development of the global leader within the multinational corporation. In V. Pucik, N. M. Tichy, & C. K. Bartlett (Eds.), *Globalizing management: Creating and leading the competitive organization* (pp. 187–205). New York, NY: John Wiley & Sons., Inc.

Kogut, B. (1985). Designing global strategies: Profiting from operational flexibility. *Sloan Management Review, 26*(4): 27–38.

Lane, H. W., DiStefano, J. J. & Maznevski, M. L. (1997). *International management behavior,* 3rd Edition. Cambridge, MA, Blackwell Publishers, Inc.

Mueller, H. (1985). The changing U.S. position in the international market: Output, trade and performance. In M. Hochmuth and W. Davidson (Eds.), *Revitalizing American industry: Lessons from our competitors* (pp. 213–262). Cambridge, MA: Ballinger Publishing Company.

Murtha, T. P., Lenway, S. A. & Bagozzi, R. P. (1998). Global mind-sets and cognitive shift in a complex multinational corporation. *Strategic Management Journal, 19*(2): 97–114.

Perlmutter, H. V. (1969). The tortuous evolution of the multinational corporation. *Columbia Journal of World Business.* Jan-Feb: 9–18.

Porras, J. I. & Silvers, R. C. (1991). Organization development and transformation. *Annual Review of Psychology,* 42: 51–78.

Prahalad, C. K. & Doz, Y. L. (1981). An approach to strategic control in MNCs. *Sloan Management Review,* 22: 5–13.

Prahalad, C. K. & Doz, Y. L. (1987). *The multinational mission: Balancing local demands and global vision.* New York, The Free Press.

Prahalad, C. K. & Lieberthal, K. (1998). The end of corporate imperialism. *Harvard Business Review,* July-August: 69–79.

Ribbens, B. A. (1996). Torn between expectations? *Academy of Management Executive, 10*(2): 65–66.

Rhinesmith, S. H. (1993). *A manager's guide to globalization: Six keys to success in a changing world.* New York, Irwin.

Stumpf, S. A. (1989). Work experiences that stretch the managers' capacity for strategic thinking. *Journal of Management Development, 8*(5): 31–39.

Tichy, N. M. (1992). Global development. In V. Pucik, N. M. Tichy, & C. K. Bartlett (Eds.), *Globalizing management: Creating and leading the competitive organization*, (pp. 206–224). New York: John Wiley & Sons, Inc.

Yip, G. S. (1992). *Total global strategy: Managing for worldwide competitive advantage.* Englewood Cliffs, NJ, Prentice Hall.

Yoffe, D. B. (1990). *International trade and competition: Cases and notes in strategy and management.* New York, NY, McGraw Hill.

# Reading 1.2

## CULTURAL CONSTRAINTS IN MANAGEMENT THEORIES

GEERT HOFSTEDE


### Executive Overview

Management as the word is presently used is an American invention. In other parts of the world not only the practices but the entire concept of management may differ, and the theories needed to understand it, may deviate considerably from what is considered normal and desirable in the USA. The reader is invited on a trip around the world, and both local management practices and theories are explained from the different contexts and histories of the places visited: Germany, Japan, France, Holland, the countries of the overseas Chinese, South-East Asia, Africa, Russia, and finally mainland China.

A model in which worldwide differences in national cultures are categorized according to five independent dimensions helps in explaining the differences in management found; although the situation in each country or region has unique characteristics that no model can account for. One practical application of the model is in demonstrating the relative position of the U.S. versus other parts of the world. In a global perspective, U.S. management theories contain a number of idiosyncracies not necessarily shared by management elsewhere. Three such idiosyncracies are mentioned: a stress on market processes, a stress on the individual, and a focus on managers rather than on workers. A plea is made for an internationalization not only of business, but also of management theories, as a way of enriching theories at the national level.


### In My View

Lewis Carroll's *Alice in Wonderland* contains the famous story of Alice's croquet game with the Queen of Hearts.

> Alice thought she had never seen such a curious croquet-ground in all her life; it was all ridges and furrows; the balls were live hedgehogs, the mallets live flamingoes, and the soldiers had to double themselves up and to stand on their hands and feet, to make the arches.

You probably know how the story goes: Alice's flamingo mallet turns its head whenever she wants to strike with it; her hedgehog ball runs away; and the doubled-up soldier arches walk around all the time. The only rule seems to be that the Queen of Hearts always wins.

Alice's croquet playing problems are good analogies to attempts to build culture-free theories of management. Concepts available for this purpose are themselves alive with culture, having been developed within a particular cultural context. They have a tendency to guide our thinking toward our desired conclusion.

As the same reasoning may also be applied to the arguments in this article, I better tell you my conclusion before I continue—so that the rules of my game are understood. In this article we take a trip around the world to demonstrate that there are no such things as universal management theories.

Diversity in *management practices* as we go around the world has been recognized in U.S. management literature for more than thirty years. The term "comparative management" has been used since the 1960s. However, it has taken much longer for the U.S. academic community to accept that not only practices but also the validity of theories may stop at national borders, and I wonder whether even today everybody would agree with this statement.

An article I published in *Organizational Dynamics* in 1980 entitled "Do American Theories Apply Abroad?" created more controversy than I expected. The article argued, with empirical support, that generally accepted U.S. theories like those of Maslow, Herzberg, McClelland, Vroom, McGregor, Likert, Blake and Mouton may not or only very partly apply outside the borders of their country of origin—assuming they do apply within those borders. Among the requests for reprints, a larger number were from Canada than from the United States.

## Management Theorists Are Human

Employees and managers are human. Employees as humans was "discovered" in the 1930s, with the Human Relations school. Managers as humans, was introduced in the late 40s by Herbert Simon's "bounded rationality" and elaborated in Richard Cyert and James March's *Behavioral Theory of the Firm* (1963, and recently re-published in a second edition). My argument is that management scientists, theorists, and writers are human too: they grew up in a particular society in a particular period, and their ideas cannot help but reflect the constraints of their environment.

The idea that the validity of a theory is constrained by national borders is more obvious in Europe, with all its borders, than in a huge borderless country like the U.S. Already in the sixteenth century Michel de Montaigne, a Frenchman, wrote a statement which was made famous by Blaise Pascal about a century later: "*Vérite en-deça des Pyrenées, erreur au-delà*"–There are truths on this side of the Pyrenees which are falsehoods on the other.

## From Don Armado's Love to Taylor's Science

According to the comprehensive ten-volume Oxford English Dictionary (1971), the words "manage," "management," and "manager" appeared in the English language in the 16th century. The oldest recorded use of the word "manager" is in Shakespeare's "Love's Labour's Lost," dating from 1588, in which Don Adriano de Armado, "a fantastical Spaniard," exclaims (Act I, scene ii, 188):

"Adieu, valour! rust, rapier! be still, drum! for your manager is in love; yea, he loveth."

The linguistic origin of the word is from Latin *manus,* hand, via the Italian *maneggiare,* which is the training of horses in the *manege;* subsequently its meaning was extended to skillful handling in general, like of arms and musical instruments, as Don Armado illustrates. However, the word also became associated with the French *menage,* household, as an equivalent of "husbandry" in its sense of the art of running a household. The theatre of present-day management contains elements of both *manege* and *menage* and different managers and cultures may use different accents.

The founder of the science of economics, the Scot Adam Smith, in his 1776 book *The Wealth of Nations,* used "manage," "management" (even "bad management") and "manager" when dealing with the process and the persons involved in operating joint stock companies (Smith, V.i.e.). British economist John Stuart Mill (1806–1873) followed Smith in this use and clearly expressed his distrust of such hired people who were not driven by ownership. Since the 1880s the word "management" appeared occasionally in writings by American engineers, until it was canonized as a modern science by Frederick W. Taylor in *Shop Management* in 1903 and in *The Principles of Scientific Management* in 1911.

While Smith and Mill used "management" to describe a process and "managers for the persons involved, "management" in the American sense—which has since been taken back by the British—refers not only to the process but also to the managers as a class of people. This class (1) does not own a business but sells its skills to act on behalf of the owners and (2) does not produce personally but is indispensable for making others produce, through motivation. Members of this class carry a high status and many American boys and girls aspire to the role. In the U.S., the manager is a cultural hero.

Let us now turn to other parts of the world. We will look at management in its context in other successful modern economies: Germany, Japan,

France, Holland, and among the Overseas Chinese. Then we will examine management in the much larger part of the world that is still poor, especially South-East Asia and Africa, and in the new political configurations of Eastern Europe, and Russia in particular. We will then return to the U.S. via Mainland China.

## Germany

The manager is not a cultural hero in Germany. If anybody, it is the engineer who fills the hero role. Frederick Taylor's *Scientific Management* was conceived in a society of immigrants—where large number of workers with diverse backgrounds and skills had to work together. In Germany this heterogeneity never existed.

Elements of the mediaeval guild system have survived in historical continuity in Germany until the present day. In particular, a very effective apprenticeship system exists both on the shop floor and in the office, which alternates practical work and classroom courses. At the end of the apprenticeship the worker receives a certificate, the *Facharbeiterbrief,* which is recognized throughout the country. About two thirds of the German worker population holds such a certificate and a corresponding occupational pride. In fact, quite a few German company presidents have worked their way up from the ranks through an apprenticeship. In comparison, two thirds of the worker population in Britain have no occupational qualification at all.

The highly skilled and responsible German workers do not necessarily need a manager, American-style, to "motivate" them. They expect their boss or *Meister* to assign their tasks and to be the expert in resolving technical problems. Comparisons of similar German, British, and French organizations show the Germans as having the highest rate of personnel in productive roles and the lowest both in leadership and staff roles.

Business schools are virtually unknown in Germany. Native German management theories concentrate on formal systems. The inapplicability of American concepts of management was quite apparent in 1973 when the U.S. consulting firm of Booz, Allen and Hamilton, commissioned by the German Ministry of Economic Affairs, wrote a study of German management from an American view point. The report is highly critical and writes among other things that "Germans simply do not have a very strong concept of management." Since 1973, from my personal experience, the situation has not changed much. However, during this period the German economy has performed in a superior fashion to the U.S. in virtually all respects, so a strong concept of management might have been a liability rather than an asset.

## Japan

The American type of manager is also missing in Japan. In the United States, the core of the enterprise is the managerial class. The core of the Japanese enterprise is the permanent worker group; workers who for all practical purposes are tenured and who aspire at life-long employment. They are distinct from the non-permanent employees—most women and subcontracted teams led by gang bosses, to be laid off in slack periods. University graduates in Japan first join the permanent worker group and subsequently fill various positions, moving from line to staff as the need occurs while paid according to seniority rather than position. They take part in Japanese-style group consultation sessions for important decisions, which extend the decision-making period but guarantee fast implementation afterwards. Japanese are to a large extent controlled by their peer group rather than by their manager.

Three researchers from the East-West Center of the University of Hawaii, Joseph Tobin, David Wu, and Dana Danielson, did an observation study of typical preschools in three countries: China, Japan, and the United States. Their results have been published both as a book and as a video. In the Japanese preschool, one teacher handled twenty-eight four-year olds. The video shows one particularly obnoxious boy, Hiroki, who fights with other children and throws teaching materials down from the balcony. When a little girl tries to alarm the teacher, the latter answers, "what are you calling me for? Do something about it!" In the U.S. preschool, there is one adult for every nine children. This class has its problem child too, Glen, who refuses to clear away his toys. One of the teachers has a long talk with him and isolates him in a corner, until he changes his mind. It doesn't take much imagination to realize that managing Hiroki thirty years later will be a different process from managing Glen.

American theories of leadership are ill-suited for the Japanese group-controlled situation. During the past two decades, the Japanese have developed their own "PM" theory of leadership, in which P stands for performance and M for maintenance. The latter is less a concern for individual employees than for maintaining social stability. In view of the amazing success of the Japanese economy in the past thirty years, many Americans have sought for the secrets of Japanese management hoping to copy them.

There are no secrets of Japanese management, however; it is even doubtful whether there is such a thing as management, in the American sense, in Japan at all. The secret is in Japanese society; and if any group in society should be singled out as carriers of the secret, it is the workers, not the managers.

## France

The manager, U.S. style, does not exist in France either. In a very enlightening book, unfortunately not yet translated into English, the French researcher Philippe d'Iribarne (1989) describes the results of in-depth observation and interview studies of management methods in three subsidiary plants of the same French multinational: in France, the United States, and Holland. He relates what he finds to information about the three societies in general. Where necessary, he goes back in history to trace the roots of the strikingly different behaviors in the completion of the same tasks. He identifies three kinds of basic principles (*logiques*) of management. In the USA, the principle is the *fair contract* between employer and employee, which gives the manager considerable prerogatives, but within its limits. This is really a *labor market* in which the worker sells his or her labor for a price. In France, the principle is the *honor* of each class in a society which has always been and remains extremely stratified, in which superiors behave as superior beings and subordinates accept and expect this, conscious of their own lower level in the national hierarchy but also of the honor of their own class. The French do not think in terms of managers versus nonmanagers but in terms of *cadres* versus *non-cadres;* one becomes cadre by attending the proper schools and one remains it forever; regardless of their actual task, cadres have the privileges of a higher social class, and it is very rare for a non-cadre to cross the ranks.

The conflict between French and American theories of management became apparent in the beginning of the twentieth century, in a criticism by the great French management pioneer Henri Fayol (1841–1925) on his U.S. colleague and contemporary Frederick W. Taylor (1856–1915). The difference in career paths of the two men is striking. Fayol was a French engineer whose career as a *cadre supérieur* culminated in the position of Président-Directeur-Général of a mining company. After his retirement he formulated his experiences in a path-breaking text on organization: *Administration industrielle et générale,* in which he focussed on the sources of authority. Taylor was an American engineer who started his career in industry as a worker and attained his academic qualifications through evening studies. From chief engineer in a steel company he became one of the first management consultants. Taylor was not really concerned with the issue of authority at all; his focus was on efficiency. He proposed to split the task of the first-line boss into eight specialisms, each exercised by a different person; an idea which eventually led to the idea of a matrix organization.

Taylor's work appeared in a French translation in 1913, and Fayol read it and showed himself generally impressed but shocked by Taylor's "denial of the principle of the Unity of Command" in the case of the eight-boss-system.

Seventy years later Andre Laurent, another of Fayol's compatriots, found that French managers in a survey reacted very strongly against a suggestion that one employee could report to two different bosses, while U.S. managers in the same survey showed fewer misgivings. Matrix organization has never become popular in France as it has in the United States.

## Holland

In my own country, Holland or as it is officially called, the Netherlands, the study by Philippe d'Iribarne found the management principle to be a need for *consensus* among all parties, neither predetermined by a contractual relationship nor by class distinctions, but based on an open-ended exchange of views and a balancing of interests. In terms of the different origins of the word "manager, the organization in Holland is more *menage* (household) while in the United States it is more *manege* (horse drill).

At my university, the University of Limburg at Maastricht, every semester we receive a class of American business students who take a program in European Studies. We asked both the Americans and a matched group of Dutch students to describe their ideal job after graduation, using a list of twenty-two job characteristics. The Americans attached significantly more importance than the Dutch to earnings, advancement, benefits, a good working relationship with their boss, and security of employment. The Dutch attached more importance to freedom to adopt their own approach to the job, being consulted by their boss in his or her decisions, training opportunities, contributing to the success of their organization, fully using their skills and abilities, and helping others. This list confirms d'Iribarne's findings of a contractual employment relationship in the United States, based on earnings and career opportunities, against a consensual relationship in Holland. The latter has centuries-old roots; the Netherlands were the first republic in Western Europe (1609–1810), and a model for the American republic. The country has been and still is governed by a careful balancing of interests in a multi-party system.

In terms of management theories, both motivation and leadership in Holland are different from what they are in the United States. Leadership in Holland presupposes modesty, as opposed to assertiveness in the United States. No U.S. leadership theory has room for that. Working in Holland is not a constant feast, however. There is a built-in premium on mediocrity and jealousy, as well as time-consuming ritual consultations to maintain the appearance of consensus and the pretense of modesty. There is unfortunately another side to every coin.

## The Overseas Chinese

Among the champions of economic development in the past thirty years we find three countries mainly populated by Chinese living outside the Chinese mainland: Taiwan, Hong Kong and Singapore. Moreover, overseas Chinese play a very important role in the economies of Indonesia, Malaysia, the Philippines and Thailand, where they form an ethnic minority. If anything, the little dragons—Taiwan, Hong Kong and Singapore—have been more economically successful than Japan, moving from rags to riches and now counted among the world's wealthy industrial countries. Yet very little attention has been paid to the way in which their enterprises have been managed. *The Spirit of Chinese Capitalism* by Gordon Redding (1990), the British dean of the Hong Kong Business School, is an excellent book about Chinese business. He bases his insights on personal acquaintance and in-depth discussions with a large number of overseas Chinese businesspeople.

Overseas Chinese American enterprises lack almost all characteristics of modern management. They tend to be small, cooperating for essential functions with other small organizations through networks based on personal relations. They are family-owned, without the separation between ownership and management typical in the West, or even in Japan and Korea. They normally focus on one product or market, with growth by opportunistic diversification; in this, they are extremely flexible. Decision making is centralized in the hands of one dominant family member, but other family members may be given new ventures to try their skills on. They are low-profile and extremely cost-conscious, applying Confucian virtues of thrift and persistence. Their size is kept small by the assumed lack of loyalty of nonfamily employees, who, if they are any good, will just wait and save until they can start their own family business.

Overseas Chinese prefer economic activities in which great gains can be made with little manpower, like commodity trading and real estate. They employ few professional managers, except their sons and sometimes daughters who have been sent to prestigious business schools abroad, but who upon return continue to run the family business the Chinese way.

The origin of this system, or—in the Western view—this lack of system, is found in the history of Chinese society, in which there were no formal laws, only formal networks of powerful people guided by general principles of Confucian virtue. The favors of the authorities could change daily, so nobody could be trusted except one's kinfolk—of whom, fortunately, there used to be many, in an extended family structure. The overseas Chinese way of doing business is also very well adapted to their position in the countries in which they form ethnic minorities, often envied and threatened by ethnic violence.

Overseas Chinese businesses following this unprofessional approach command a collective gross national product of some 200 to 300 billion US dollars, exceeding the GNP of Australia. There is no denying that it works.

## Management Transfer to Poor Countries

Four-fifths of the world population live in countries that are not rich but poor. After World War II and decolonization, the stated purpose of the United Nations and the World Bank has been to promote the development of all the world's countries in a war on poverty. After forty years it looks very much like we are losing this war. If one thing has become clear, it is that the export of Western-mostly American-management practices *and* theories to poor countries has contributed little to nothing to their development. There has been no lack of effort and money spent for this purpose: students from poor countries have been trained in this country, and teachers and Peace Corps workers have been sent to the poor countries. If nothing else, the general lack of success in economic development of other countries should be sufficient argument to doubt the validity of

Western management theories in non-Western environments.

If we examine different parts of the world, the development picture is not equally bleak, and history is often a better predictor than economic factors for what happens today. There is a broad regional pecking order with East Asia leading. The little dragons have passed into the camp of the wealthy; then follow South-East Asia (with its overseas Chinese minorities), Latin America (in spite of the debt crisis), South Asia, and Africa always trails behind. Several African countries have only become poorer since decolonization.

Regions of the world with a history of large-scale political integration and civilization generally have done better than regions in which no large-scale political and cultural infrastructure existed, even if the old civilizations had decayed or been suppressed by colonizers. It has become painfully clear that development cannot be pressure-cooked; it presumes a cultural infrastructure that takes time to grow. Local management is part of this infrastructure; it cannot be imported in package form. Assuming that with so-called modern management techniques and theories outsiders can develop a country has proven a deplorable arrogance. At best, one can hope for a dialogue between equals with the locals, in which the Western partner acts as the expert in Western technology and the local partner as the expert in local culture, habits, and feelings.

## Russia and China

The crumbling of the former Eastern bloc has left us with a scattering of states and would-be states of which the political and economic future is extremely uncertain. The best predictions are those based on a knowledge of history, because historical trends have taken revenge on the arrogance of the Soviet rulers who believed they could turn them around by brute power. One obvious fact is that the former bloc is extremely heterogeneous, including countries traditionally closely linked with the West by trade and travel, like Czechia, Hungary, Slovenia, and the Baltic states, as well as others with a Byzantine or Turkish past; some having been prosperous, others always extremely poor.

The industrialized Western world and the World Bank seem committed to helping the ex-Eastern bloc countries develop, but with the same technocratic neglect for local cultural factors that proved so unsuccessful in the development assistance to other poor countries. Free market capitalism, introduced by Western-style management, is supposed to be the answer from Albania to Russia.

Let me limit myself to the Russian republic, a huge territory with some 140 million inhabitants, mainly Russians. We know quite a bit about the Russians as their country was a world power for several hundreds of years before communism, and in the nineteenth century it has produced some of the greatest writers in world literature. If I want to understand the Russians—including how they could so long support the Soviet regime—I tend to re-read Lev Nikolayevich Tolstoy. In his most famous novel *Anna Karenina* (1876) one of the main characters is a landowner, Levin, whom Tolstoy uses to express his own views and convictions about his people. Russian peasants used to be serfs; serfdom had been abolished in 1861, but the peasants, now tenants, remained as passive as before. Levin wanted to break this passivity by dividing the land among his peasants in exchange for a share of the crops; but the peasants only let the land deteriorate further. Here follows a quote:

> (Levin) read political economy and socialistic works . . . but, as he had expected, found nothing in them related to his undertaking. In the political economy books—in (John Stuart) Mill, for instance, whom he studied first and with great ardour, hoping every minute to find an answer to the questions that were engrossing him he found only certain laws deduced from the state of agriculture in Europe; but he could not for the life of him see why these laws, which did not apply to Russia, should be considered universal. . . . Political economy told him that the laws by which Europe had developed and was developing her wealth were universal and absolute. Socialist teaching told him that development along those lines leads to ruin. And neither of them offered the smallest enlightenment as to what he, Levin, and all the Russian peasants and landowners were to do with their millions of hands and millions of acres, to make them as productive as possible for the common good.

In the summer of 1991, the Russian lands yielded a record harvest, but a large share of it rotted in the fields because no people were to be found for harvesting. The passivity is still there, and not only among the peasants. And the heirs of John Stuart Mill (whom we met before as one of the early analysts of "management") again present their universal recipes which simply do not apply.

Citing Tolstoy, I implicitly suggest that management theorists cannot neglect the great literature of the countries they want their ideas to apply to. The greatest novel in the Chinese literature is considered Cao Xueqin's *The Story of the Stone,* also known as *The Dream of the Red Chamber* which appeared around 1760. It describes the rise and fall of two branches of an aristocratic family in Beijing, who live in adjacent plots in the capital. Their plots are joined by a magnificent garden with several pavilions in it, and the young, mostly female members of both families are allowed to live in them. One day the management of the garden is taken over by a young woman, Tan-Chun, who states:

> I think we ought to pick out a few experienced trust-worthy old women from among the ones who work in the Garden—women who know something about gardening—already and put the upkeep of the Garden into their hands. We needn't ask them to pay us rent; all we need ask them for is an annual share of the produce. There would be four advantages in this arrangement. In the first place, if we have people whose sole occupation is to look after trees and flowers and so on, the condition of the Garden will improve gradually year after year and there will be no more of those long periods of neglect followed by bursts of feverish activity when things have been allowed to get out of hand. Secondly there won't be the spoiling and wastage we get at present. Thirdly the women themselves will gain a little extra to add to their incomes which will compensate them for the hard work they put in throughout the year. And fourthly, there's no reason why we shouldn't use the money we should otherwise have spent on nurserymen, rockery specialists, horticultural cleaners and so on for other purposes.

As the story goes on, the capitalist privatization—because that is what it is—of the Garden is carried through, and it works. When in the 1980s Deng Xiaoping allowed privatization in the Chinese villages, it also worked. It worked so well that its effects started to be felt in politics and threatened the existing political order; hence the knockdown at Tienanmen Square of June 1989. But it seems that the forces of privatization are getting the upper hand again in China. If we remember what Chinese entrepreneurs are able to do once they have become Overseas Chinese, we shouldn't be too surprised. But what works in China—and worked two centuries ago—does not have to work in Russia, not in Tolstoy's days and not today. I am not offering a solution; I only protest against a naive universalism that knows only one recipe for development, the one supposed to have worked in the United States.

## A Theory of Culture in Management

Our trip around the world is over and we are back in the United States. What have we learned? There is something in all countries called "management, but its meaning differs to a larger or smaller extent from one country to the other, and it takes considerable historical and cultural insight into local conditions to understand its processes, philosophies, and problems. If already the word may mean so many different things, how can we expect one country's theories of management to apply abroad? One should be extremely careful in making this assumption, and test it before considering it proven. Management is not a phenomenon that can be isolated from other processes taking place in a society. During our trip around the world we saw that it interacts with what happens in the family, at school, in politics, and government. It is obviously also related to religion and to beliefs about science. Theories of management always had to be interdisciplinary, but if we cross national borders they should become more interdisciplinary than ever.

Cultural differences between nations can be, to some extent, described using first four, and now five, bipolar *dimensions.* The position of a country on these dimensions allows us to make some predictions on the way their society operates, including their management processes and the kind of theories applicable to their management.

As the word culture plays such an important role in my theory, let me give you my definition, which differs from some other very respectable definitions. Culture to me is *the collective programming of the mind which distinguishes one group or category of people from another.* In the part of my work I am referring to now, the category of people is the nation.

Culture is a *construct,* that means it is "not directly accessible to observation but inferable from verbal statements and other behaviors and useful in predicting still other observable and measurable verbal and nonverbal behavior." It should not be reified; it is an auxiliary concept that should be used as long it proves useful but bypassed where we can predict behaviors without it.

The same applies to the *dimensions* I introduced. They are constructs too that should not be reified. They do not "exist"; they are tools for analysis which may or may not clarify a situation. In my statistical analysis of empirical data the first four dimensions together explain forty-nine percent of the variance in the data. The other fifty-one percent remain specific to individual countries.

The first four dimensions were initially detected through a comparison of the values of similar people (employees and managers) in sixty-four national subsidiaries of the IBM Corporation. People working for the same multinational, but in different countries, represent very well-matched samples from the populations of their countries, similar in all respects except nationality.

The first dimension is labeled *Power Distance,* and it can be defined as the degree of inequality among people which the population of a country considers as normal: from relatively equal (that is, small power distance) to extremely unequal (large power distance). All societies are unequal, but some are more unequal than others.

The second dimension is labeled *Individualism,* and it is the degree to which people in a country prefer to act as individuals rather than as members of groups. The opposite of individualism can be called *Collectivism,* so collectivism is low individualism. The way I use the word it has no political connotations. In collectivist societies a child learns to respect the group to which it belongs, usually the family, and to differentiate between in-group members and out-group members (that is, all other people). When children grow up they remain members of their group, and they expect the group to protect them when they are in trouble. In return, they have to remain loyal to their group throughout life. In individualist societies, a child learns very early to think of itself as "I" instead of as part of "we." It expects one day to have to stand on its own feet and not to get protection from its group any more; and therefore it also does not feel a need for strong loyalty.

The third dimension is called *Masculinity* and its opposite pole *Femininity.* It is the degree to which tough values like assertiveness, performance, success and competition, which in nearly all societies are associated with the role of men, prevail over tender values like the quality of life, maintaining warm personal relationships, service, care for the weak, and solidarity, which in nearly all societies are more associated with women's roles. Women's roles differ from men's roles in all countries; but in tough societies, the differences are larger than in tender ones.

The fourth dimension is labeled *Uncertainty Avoidance,* and it can be defined as the degree to which people in a country prefer structured over unstructured situations. Structured situations are those in which there are clear rules as to how one should behave. These rules can be written down, but they can also be unwritten and imposed by tradition. In countries which score high on uncertainty avoidance, people tend to show more nervous energy, while in countries which score low, people are more easy-going. A (national) society with strong uncertainty avoidance can be called rigid; one with weak uncertainty avoidance, flexible. In countries where uncertainty avoidance is strong a feeling prevails of "what is different, is dangerous." In weak uncertainty avoidance societies, the feeling would rather be "what is different, is curious."

The fifth dimension was added on the basis of a study of the values of students in twenty-three countries carried out by Michael Harris Bond, a Canadian working in Hong Kong. He and I had cooperated in another study of students' values which had yielded the same four dimensions as the IBM data. However, we wondered to what extent our common findings in two studies could be the effect of a Western bias introduced by the common Western background of the researchers: remember Alice's croquet game. Michael Bond resolved this dilemma by deliberately introducing an Eastern bias. He used a questionnaire prepared at his request by his Chinese colleagues, the *Chinese Value Survey* (CVS), which was translated from Chinese into different languages and answered by fifty male and fifty female students in each of twenty-three countries in all five continents. Analysis of the CVS data produced three dimensions significantly correlated with the three IBM dimensions of power distance, individualism, and masculinity. There was also a fourth dimension, but it did not resemble uncertainty avoidance. It was composed, both on the positive and on the negative side, from items that had not been included in the IBM studies but were present in the Chinese Value Survey because they were rooted in the teachings of Confucius. I labeled this dimension: *Long-term* versus *Short-term Orientation.* On the long-term side one finds values oriented towards the future, like thrift (saving) and persistence. On the short-term side one finds values rather oriented towards the past and present, like respect for tradition and fulfilling social obligations.

Table 1 lists the scores on all five dimensions for the United States and for the other countries we just discussed. The table shows that each country has its own configuration on the four dimensions. Some of the values in the table have been estimated based on imperfect replications or personal impressions. The different dimension scores do not "explain" all the differences in management I described earlier. To understand management in a country, one should have both knowledge of and

**Table 1** Culture Dimension Scores for Ten Countries PD = Power Distance; ID = Individualism; MA = Masculinity; UA = Uncertainty Avoidance; LT = Long Term Orientation, H = Top Third, M = Medium Third, L = Bottom Third (among 53 countries and regions for the first four dimensions; among 23 countries for the fifth)

| | *PD* | *ID* | *MA* | *UA* | *LT* |
|---|---|---|---|---|---|
| USA | 40 L | 91 H | 62 H | 46 L | 29 L |
| Germany | 35 L | 67 H | 66 H | 65 M | 31 M |
| Japan | 54 M | 46 M | 95 H | 92 H | 80 H |
| France | 68 H | 71 H | 43 M | 86 H | 30*L |
| Netherlands | 38 L | 80 H | 14 L | 53 M | 44 M |
| Hong Kong | 68 H | 25 L | 57 H | 29 L | 96 H |
| Indonesia | 78 H | 14 L | 46 M | 48 L | 25*L |
| West Africa | 77 H | 20 L | 46 M | 54 M | 16 L |
| Russia | 95*H | 50*M | 40*L | 90*H | 10*L |
| China | 80*H | 20*L | 50*M | 60*M | 118 H |

SOURCE: Academy of Management Executive by Hofstede, G. Copyright 1993 by Academy of Management. Reproduced with permission of Academy of Management via Copyright Clearance Center.

*estimated

empathy with the entire local scene. However, the scores should make us aware that people in other countries may think, feel, and act very differently from us when confronted with basic problems of society.

## Idiosyncracies of American Management Theories

In comparison to other countries, the U.S. culture profile presents itself as below average on power distance and uncertainty avoidance, highly individualistic, fairly masculine, and short-term oriented. The Germans show a stronger uncertainty avoidance and less extreme individualism; the Japanese are different on all dimensions, least on power distance; the French show larger power distance and uncertainty avoidance, but are less individualistic and somewhat feminine; the Dutch resemble the Americans on the first three dimensions, but score extremely feminine and relatively long-term oriented; Hong Kong Chinese combine large power distance with weak uncertainty avoidance, collectivism, and are very long-term oriented; and so on.

The American culture profile is reflected in American management theories. I will just mention three elements not necessarily present in other countries: the stress on market processes, the stress on the individual, and the stress on managers rather than on workers.

## The Stress on Market Processes

During the 1970s and 80s it has become fashionable in the United States to look at organizations from a "transaction costs" viewpoint. Economist Oliver Williamson has opposed "hierarchies" to "markets." The reasoning is that human social life consists of economic transactions between individuals. We found the same in d'Iribarne's description of the U.S. principle of the contract between employer and employee, the labor market in which the worker sells his or her labor for a price. These individuals will form hierarchical organizations when the cost of the economic transactions (such as getting information, finding out whom to trust etc.) is lower in a hierarchy than when all transactions would take place on a free market.

From a cultural perspective the important point is that the *"market"* is the point of *departure or base model,* and the organization is explained from market failure. A culture that produces such a theory is likely to prefer organizations that internally resemble markets to organizations that internally resemble more structured models, like those in Germany or France. The ideal principle of control in organizations in the market philosophy is *competition* between individuals. This philosophy fits a society that combines a not-too-large power distance with a not-too-strong uncertainty avoidance and individualism; besides the USA, it will fit all other Anglo countries.

## The Stress on the Individual

I find this constantly in the design of research projects and hypotheses; also in the fact that in the U.S. psychology is clearly a more respectable discipline in management circles than sociology. Culture however is a collective phenomenon. Although we may get our information about culture from individuals, we have to interpret it at the level of collectivities. There are snags here known as the "ecological fallacy" and the "reverse ecological fallacy." None of the U.S. college textbooks on methodology I know deals sufficiently with the problem of multilevel analysis.

Culture can be compared to a forest, while individuals are trees. A forest is not just a bunch of trees: it is a symbiosis of different trees, bushes, plants, insects, animals and micro-organisms, and we miss the essence of the forest if we only describe its most typical trees. In the same way, a culture cannot be satisfactorily described in terms of the characteristics of a typical individual. There is a tendency in the U.S. management literature to overlook the forest for the trees and to ascribe cultural differences to interactions among individuals.

A striking example is found in the otherwise excellent book *Organizational Culture and Leadership* by Edgar H. Schein (1985). On the basis of his consulting experience he compares two large companies, nicknamed "Action" and "Multi." He explains the differences in culture between these companies by the group dynamics in their respective boardrooms. Nowhere in the book are any conclusions drawn from the fact that the first company is an American-based computer firm, and the second a Swiss-based pharmaceutics firm. This information is not even mentioned. A stress on interactions among individuals obviously fits a culture identified as the most individualistic in the world, but it will not be so well understood by the four-fifths of the world population for whom the group prevails over the individual.

One of the conclusions of my own multilevel research has been that culture at the national level and culture at the organizational level—corporate culture—are two very different phenomena and that the use of a common term for both is confusing. If we do use the common term, we should also pay attention to the occupational and the gender level of culture. National cultures differ primarily in the fundamental, invisible values held by a majority of their members, acquired in early childhood, whereas organizational cultures are a much more superficial phenomenon residing mainly in the visible practices of the organization, acquired by socialization of the new members who join as young adults. National cultures change only very slowly if at all; organizational cultures may be consciously changed, although this isn't necessarily easy. This difference between the two types of culture is the secret of the existence of multinational corporations that employ, as I showed in the IBM case, employees with extremely different national cultural values. What keeps them together is a corporate culture based on common practices.

## The Stress on Managers Rather Than Workers

The core element of a work organization around the world is the people who do the work. All the rest is superstructure, and I hope to have demonstrated to you that it may take many different shapes. In the U.S. literature on work organization, however, the core element, if not explicitly then implicitly, is considered the manager. This may well be the result of the combination of extreme individualism with fairly strong masculinity, which has turned the manager into a culture hero of almost mythical proportions. For example, he not really she is supposed to make decisions all the time. Those of you who are or have been managers must know that this is a fable. Very few management decisions are just "made" as the myth suggests it. Managers are much more involved in maintaining networks; if anything, it is the rank-and-file worker who can really make decisions on his or her own, albeit on a relatively simple level.

An amusing effect of the U.S. focus on managers is that in at least ten American books and articles on management I have been misquoted as having studied IBM *managers* in my research, whereas the book clearly describes that the answers were from IBM *employees*. My observation may be biased, but I get the impression that compared to twenty or thirty years ago less research in this country is done among employees and more on managers. But managers derive their *raison d'être* from the people managed: culturally, they are the followers of the people they lead, and their effectiveness depends on the latter. In other parts of the world, this exclusive focus on the manager is less strong, with Japan as the supreme example.

## Conclusion

This article started with *Alice in Wonderland.* In fact, the management theorist who ventures outside his or her own country into other parts of the world is like Alice in Wonderland. He or she will meet strange beings, customs, ways of organizing or disorganizing and theories that are clearly stupid, old-fashioned or even immoral yet they may work, or at least they may not fail more frequently than corresponding theories do at home. Then, after the first culture shock, the traveler to Wonderland will feel enlightened, and may be able to take his or her experiences home and use them advantageously. All great ideas in science, politics and management have traveled from one country to another, and been enriched by foreign influences. The roots of American management theories are mainly in Europe: with Adam Smith, John Stuart Mill, Lev Tolstoy, Max Weber, Henri Fayol, Sigmund Freud, Kurt Lewin and many others. These theories were re-planted here and they developed and bore fruit. The same may happen again. The last thing we need is a Monroe doctrine for management ideas.

The issues explored here were presented by Dr. Hofstede, the Foundation for Administrative Research Distinguished International Scholar at the 1992 Annual Meeting of the Academy of Management, Las Vegas, Nevada, August 11, 1992.

# Reading 1.3

## WHATEVER HAPPENED TO MASCULINITY AND FEMININITY?

GEERT HOFSTEDE

The new eight-volume *Encyclopedia of Psychology* which appeared in March 2000 contains an 800-word entry on "Masculine and Feminine Cultures," so the cultural dimension of Masculinity and Femininity is alive and well. Yet this dimension had a more difficult youth than its twin, Individualism and Collectivism.

In a 1977 working paper I reported that in factor-analyzing country mean scores (rather than individual scores) on the importance of 14 work goals for 40 countries from an IBM employees database, I had found two clear orthogonal factors which I called "individual-collective" and "social-ego." The former corresponded to an "Individualism-Collectivism" dimension. The latter mainly consisted of goals on which men and women tended to differ, so I labeled the corresponding dimension "Femininity-Masculinity." In a subsequent 1978 working paper I validated the two dimensions against data from other populations and collected with other instruments. I also reported that the value differences between women and men in a country were positively correlated with that country's Masculinity dimension scores: values of men and women in the same occupations in the more "masculine" countries tended to be more different than in "feminine" ones.

Shortly afterwards I discovered in the 1969 second edition of the *Handbook of Social Psychology* an article on "National Character" by two U.S. social scientists, the sociologist Alex Inkeles and the psychologist Daniel Levinson. As I found out later, this article had already appeared in the 1954 first edition; much later it has been reprinted in Inkeles (1997). Inkeles and Levinson proposed: "To concentrate, for purposes of comparative analysis, on a limited number of psychological issues . . . that meet at least the following criteria. First, they should be found in adults universally, as a function both of maturational potentials common to man and of sociocultural characteristics common to human societies. Second, the manner in which they are handled should have functional significance for the individual personality as well as for the social system, in that their patterning in the individual will affect his readiness to establish, accept, maintain or change a given sociocultural pattern" (1954:989–90). From a broad literature review Inkeles and Levinson distilled three "standard analytic issues" that met these criteria:

1. Relation to authority;
2. Conception of self; and
3. Primary dilemmas or conflicts, and ways of dealing with them, including the control of aggression and the expression versus inhibition of affect.

---

SOURCE: Reprinted with permission from the *Cross-Cultural Psychology Bulletin, 34*(4), 14-19. 

Inkeles and Levinson's "standard analytic issues" were amazingly similar to the dimensions of national culture I had empirically derived from the IBM employee database. The first and third related to the dimensions of Power Distance and Uncertainty Avoidance which I had identified earlier. Both Individualism-Collectivism and Masculinity-Femininity related to the second standard analytic issue, the conception of self. About this issue Inkeles and Levinson wrote: "Pervading the overall conception of self will be the individual's concept of masculinity and femininity . . ."; further on, following the psychologist Kardiner, they referred to ". . . the self characteristics, such as modes of impulse control and social adaptation, by means of which the individual strives to achieve a secure, meaningful position in society and a correspondingly meaningful inner identity" (1954: 991). Thus Inkeles and Levinson split "conception of self" into two components; the prime component to them was Masculinity-Femininity; the second component was related to the individual's position in society, corresponding to the dimension of Individualism-Collectivism.

The two working papers were part of a series of 18 written between 1974 and 1979 which together were turned into my 1980 book *Culture's Consequences;* the book also paid due attention to Inkeles and Levinson's prediction. It represented the first operationalization of the "culture" variable in cross-cultural studies. From 1980 to 1999, according to the *Social Science Citation Index,* it was cited in over 2,000 journal articles in a broad variety of disciplines.

The identification of a Masculinity-Femininity dimension, based on a social-ego factor in national values differences, implied that values which differ between females and males within countries differ also between females and females, and between males and males, across countries. Many psychologists implicitly assume the values, role and behavior differences according to gender in all societies to be similar. As most English-language publications on gender issues are produced in the U.S.A., the dominant gender role model in the psychological literature is American. Gender roles in other countries, if different, are supposed to be developing towards the U.S. model, and this assumption is not only made by Americans. The Mas-Fem dimension shows that and how gender-related values vary among countries, even affluent "Western" ones.

From the four national culture dimensions found empirically in the IBM employee database, Mas-Fem is the only one entirely unrelated to national wealth (GNP per capita). Individualism is strongly correlated with wealth, Small Power Distance moderately, and weak Uncertainty Avoidance marginally. Mas-Fem shows zero correlations with wealth; feminine and masculine cultures are equally likely to be found in wealthy and in poor countries. In cross-country studies, "cultural" differences often hide economic causes. If national wealth is included as a variable in the analysis, it frequently predicts more variance in the results than, for example, Ind-Col, therewith making a cultural explanation redundant. Mas-Fem is the only dimension without a hidden economic component; the only one which is purely cultural. In multiple regression studies, Mas-Fem often becomes the main explanatory variable after controlling for wealth differences.

Yet the Mas-Fem dimension has been less easily accepted in the literature than its twin the Ind-Col dimension which was incredibly eagerly received, especially by the psychological profession. There was an evident taboo about using the Mas-Fem dimension, especially in countries which my research placed on the masculine side, like Britain and the U.S.A. At first I thought this was because of the "sexy" label I gave to the dimension which in these countries is politically incorrect, but this label can easily be circumvented and replaced by, for example, the original ego versus social. I later noticed that the very notion of a non-economic source of cultural differences between countries arouses resistance. In spite of disclaimers, cross-cultural studies often want to know what the better and what the worse culture is; and economic development is an implicit legitimization of the associated cultural traits: Individualism, small Power Distance, and weak Uncertainty Avoidance. But what about differences which lack such legitimization?

In my classes I always warned my students that culture is in our guts, not only in our minds. Cultural issues arouse emotions. Culture as cross-cultural psychologists use the concept is associated with basic values, deep feelings of evil and good. Social scientists are human, I assume, so we have emotions too. Reason to mistrust cross-cultural research that is too "hygienic," that lacks evidence of emotions. Far from invalidating the dimension, the taboo in some countries around the Mas-Fem dimension proves its relevance. It arouses emotions, so it is about real value issues. Some of these are the trade-off between a tough and a tender approach to others, and between the quantity and the quality of life.

Technically the validity of this dimension was first shown in the 1978 working paper and, more extensively, in the 1980 book. In this book each of the four dimensions was found to be significantly correlated with about 20 external measures, results of comparative cross-national studies by others.

Validation of Mas-Fem was for example found in percents of the Gross National Product spent by the governments of wealthy countries on aid to poor countries (associated with Femininity) and gender segregation in higher education (women and men studying different subjects, associated with Masculinity).

Over time the number of studies validating and explaining the dimensions kept growing. Studies using the Mas-Fem dimension were bundled in Hofstede et al. (1998). A chapter by Van Rossum, for example, showed differences in the socialization of children. The issue was what importance children of around 10 claimed to attach to different goals in the games they played. In the U.S.A. (a masculine culture) boys more than girls stressed performance, and girls more than boys stressed establishing positive and avoiding negative relationships. In the Netherlands (a feminine culture) the same research approach repeatedly produced no difference in goals between girls and boys. Another chapter (Hofstede, 1998a) showed across 22 democracies in 1995 the percentages of women in parliament and the percentages of female cabinet ministers to be significantly correlated with both low Uncertainty Avoidance and Femininity.

The last part of the 1998 book illustrated the taboo nature of the Mas-Fem dimension by proving its association with two highly sensitive areas of human behavior, religion and sexuality. A chapter by Verwey reported on differences in secularization (loss of religiosity) among 16 industrialized Christian countries and found that none of the current theories of secularization predicted the outcome; instead, cultural Femininity proved a strong and consistent predictor of secularization, in spite of the paradoxical fact that within countries, women were consistently more religious than men. In another chapter (Hofstede, 1998b) I collected evidence of differences in sexual attitudes and behavior across countries, including acceptance of abortion, contraception, masturbation and homosexuality. Consistently, feminine cultures stood for more lenient attitudes. For 22 industrialized countries the frequency of teenage pregnancies was also significantly correlated with cultural Masculinity, but the correlation was positive in low Uncertainty Avoidance countries and negative in high Uncertainty Avoidance countries. A summary chapter (Hofstede, 1998c) pointed to the association across very different human societies of the areas of religion and of sexuality, and the modification of both according to the society's cultural Masculinity of Femininity. In sexual behavior, masculine cultures tend to stress sex as performance; feminine cultures tend to stress sex as a way of relating to the other person. In (Christian) religion, masculine cultures focus on God, the Father; feminine cultures focus on one's Neighbor, that is on fellow human beings—which doesn't necessarily need the context of a Church and of formal religiousness.

A re-written second edition of *Culture's Consequences* has gone to press and should be out by early 2001. The number of external measures validating each of the four dimensions increased fivefold to over 100. The new book also validates the additional fifth dimension of Long versus Short-Term Orientation, albeit with a lower number of correlations. New validations of Mas-Fem were found in market research data (De Mooij, 1998). At the 2000 IACCP Congress in Poland, Marieke De Mooij showed that across European countries the percentages of women, but especially of men, working part-time were correlated with Femininity, and that worldwide the use of mobile telephones and the Internet, after controlling for national wealth, was also correlated with Femininity. De Mooij's interpretation was that the use of these new communication media reflects among other things the relative importance attached to maintaining rapport between people.

In the 1970s a common criticism of cross-cultural studies was that the major variable, culture, was not operationalized. My 1980 book changed this. Since then other operationalizations have appeared, the most important being the one by Shalom Schwartz, based upon surveys of students and of elementary school teachers (1994). One of Schwartz' dimensions, "Mastery," is significantly correlated with my Mas-Fem. Schwartz' dimensions, however, still await a more extensive validation against external measures.

Inkeles and Levinson's message from 1954 has lost nothing of its relevance for cross-cultural psychology. A major component of "national character"—we now say "national culture"—is our conception of ourselves. Pervading this is the individual's concept of masculinity and femininity. Any attempt to compare national cultures that ignores this component is incomplete.

## References

De Mooij, M. (1998). *Global Marketing and Advertising: Understanding Cultural Paradoxes.* Thousand Oaks, CA: Sage.

Hofstede, G. (1977). *Comparative Measurements of Work Goal Importance.* Working Paper 77–31,

Brussels: European Institute for Advanced Studies in Management, December.

Hofstede, G. (1978). *Cultural Determinants of Individualism and Masculinity in Organizations.* Working Paper 78–4, Brussels: European Institute for Advanced Studies in Management, February.

Hofstede, G. (1980). *Culture's Consequences: International Differences in Work-Related Values.* Beverly Hills, CA: Sage.

# Reading 1.4

# BUILDING COMPETITIVE ADVANTAGE FROM *UBUNTU*

## *Management Lessons From South Africa*

MZAMO P. MANGALISO

### Executive Overview

Much of management theory is based on the writings of early 20th-century Western scholars whose disciplinary orientations were heavily grounded in economics and classical sociology. These writings depict homo sapiens as an individualistic, utility-maximizing, transaction-oriented species. In contrast, recent scholarship has revealed the gender and racio-ethnic biases of these theories, and shown them to be invalid models of human nature. Humans are social and communal beings. Along with rationality, we are guided by emotions such as anxiety, hope, disappointment, fear, anger, excitement, pity, and remorse. By acknowledging the importance of emotions, world management discourse can evolve more holistic, inclusive, and emancipatory theories. South Africa offers a unique opportunity for understanding the African concept of *ubuntu* or humaneness. *Ubuntu* is rich with consideration for compassion and communality. This article discusses the characteristics of *ubuntu,* explores situations in which it manifests itself in the workplace, and argues that *ubuntu* can give competitive advantage to companies that incorporate its principles and practices.

### The High Costs of Ignoring *Ubuntu*

The workers of a South African mining company had a dispute with management. When they invited the top management to publicly address them on the issue, their request was turned down. Instead, management responded by sending messages through envoys and written statements posted on bulletin boards. Frustrated, the employees decided on a strike. The strike, which lasted for over two weeks, resulted in several hundreds of the employees' being fired, and several million dollars worth of losses due to serious underground rock convergence. The effects of the strike were so damaging that, even six months afterwards, production output had not quite recovered to pre-strike levels. But the most interesting thing is that the strike could have been avoided if senior management had just addressed the employees. One of the employee representatives was reported to have said, "The only thing the employees wanted was for the top management to come and address us. Just to speak to us."

The strike action described in this incident demonstrates the costs of failing to fully appreciate the underlying values that inform other people's decisions. For the group of African employees in the

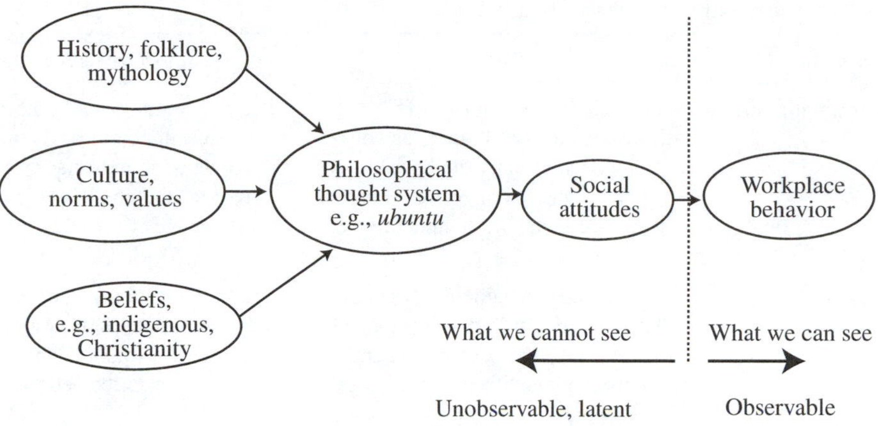


**Figure 1** Philosophical Thought System and Workplace Behavior

SOURCE: Academy of Management Executive by Mangaliso, M.P. Copyright 2001 by Academy of Management. Reproduced with permission of Academy of Management via Copyright Clearance Center.

case, face-to-face communication was an important aspect of dispute resolution. To them, addressing someone in person is a sign that you respect and care for them. By honoring this cardinal belief, the management could have easily averted the strike and saved the company lots of money. The company failed in this case because it neglected *ubuntu.*

## *Ubuntu* and Competitiveness

The dismantling of apartheid in the 1990s was a watershed of historic development for South Africa. The world watched as the country charted its course toward the establishment of a democratic, nonracial, nonsexist system of government. With democratic processes now firmly in place, the spotlight has shifted to economic revitalization. South Africa has shown steady economic progress since the days of apartheid, and stands 42nd in the 2001 IMD world competitiveness rankings.[1] This recovery is a welcome sign that South Africa has turned the corner. Now it can focus on those practices that will allow it to excel domestically and globally. An important step will be to understand the culture, values, norms, and beliefs held by the largest segment of the population, the Africans. The premise of this article is that observable workplace behavior is strongly influenced by latent, unobservable social attitudes. Such social attitudes manifest the philosophical thought system of the group from which the individual comes. The philosophical thought system itself is a product of various factors including history, folklore, mythology, culture, norms, values, and religious beliefs. These relationships are represented schematically in Figure 1.

There are important lessons to be learned from understanding the philosophical thought system known as *ubuntu,* which embodies the beliefs, values, and behaviors of a large majority of the South African population. Whether it is a critical issue that needs to be interpreted or a problem that needs to be solved, *ubuntu* is invariably invoked as a scale for weighing good versus bad, right versus wrong, just versus unjust. It is the contention of this article that *ubuntu* can guide development of managerial practices for healthy competitive advantage. Following are instructive examples of *ubuntu* in the workplace, and explanations of what can be learned.

## Competitive Advantages From *Ubuntu*

*Ubuntu* can be defined as humaneness—a pervasive spirit of caring and community, harmony and hospitality, respect and responsiveness—that individuals and groups display for one another. *Ubuntu* is the foundation for the basic values that manifest themselves in the ways African people think and behave toward each other and everyone else they encounter. One of the most important attributes of *ubuntu* is the high degree of harmony and continuity throughout the system. Unfortunately, with all the talk about *ubuntu,* the philosophy has not been fully embraced in the workplace since its strategic advantages are not fully appreciated by managers. Traditional management systems are guided by

**Table 1** Competitive Advantages from *Ubuntu*

| *Assumptions about* | *Ubuntu* | *Competitive advantages* |
|---|---|---|
| Relationships with others | Relationships are reciprocal vs instrumental. Treat others as your brother/sister. Individual predicated on belonging to collective. "I belong, therefore I am."* Extended family is important. | People are intrinsically motivated to contribute more when they are valued members. Mutual respect and empathy are *ubuntu* advantages. |
| Language and communication | Oral tradition. To name is to create. Meaning of words strongly related to context. Poetic expression and ability to play with words are signs of wisdom. | Shared understanding of deeper meanings supports complex consensus. *Ubuntu* communication means concerted action that is adaptable. |
| Decision making | Decisions by consensus. Dissenters compensated for. Process is circular. Polyocular vision. Dispute resolution to restore harmony. | *Ubuntu* might be slow to action, but greater commitment to goals means more long-run effectiveness and efficiency. |
| Time | Not a finite commodity; it is the healer; allow enough of it for important issues before arriving at a decision. | Punctuality is a virtue, but time's healing dimension is a hidden competitive advantage for *ubuntu*. |
| Productivity | Must be optimized. Solidarity, social harmony important. Rewards are shared, so is suffering. | Sustainable competitive advantage comes from strong loyalty to group goals in *ubuntu*. |
| Age and leadership | Age is an ongoing process of maturing and acquiring wisdom. Older people are respected. Gray hair is a sign of wisdom. | Older workers bring experience, wisdom, connections, informal networks. Competitive advantage from *ubuntu*. |
| Belief systems | Belief in the Creator, *uNkulunkulu*, and the existence of the *mesocosmos*. The mediating role of the *isangoma*. Christianity is now prevalent. | Spirituality brings out the best qualities in humans. *Ubuntu* has the edge. |

*SOURCE: Hampden-Turner, C. & Trompenaars, A. 1993. *The seven cultures of capitalism*. New York: Currency/Doubleday.

misapplied economic assumptions about human nature: that self-interest is the ultimate determinant of behavior, and it is maximized when employees earn as much as possible from contributing as little as possible.[2] The focus in this article will be on the various aspects of *ubuntu* as they relate to relationships with others, language, decision making, attitudes toward time, productivity and efficiency, leadership and age, and belief systems. These will each be discussed in turn, with implications for competitive advantage. (See Table 1.)

## Relationships With Others

An organizing concept of *ubuntu* is human interdependence. The driving norms are reciprocity, suppression of self-interest, and the virtue of symbiosis.[3] Hence it is often repeated that *umntu ngumntu ngabanye* [a person is a person through others]. This statement conveys the notion that a person becomes a person only through his/her relationship with and recognition by others. This recognition has far-reaching implications for day-to-day interactions among people and for an individual's status in society.

The preeminence of the collective can be observed more closely in the extended family as a unit of organization. Here the emphasis is on the unity of the whole rather than the distinction of the parts. This holistic approach is supported by an ideology that reveres the concentric linkages of individual to family, to extended family, to clan, to village, and ultimately to the entire community. The individual is a member not just of the nuclear family, but also of the extended family or clan. This has often presented problems to companies that offer paid leave of absence for the death of immediate family members. A white manager of a large multinational corporation once alleged that an employee was being dishonest when he requested a few days off for the death of his father. Company records indicated that, two years before, the same employee had already taken three days' paid leave for the death of his father. In the Western understanding, an uncle is not considered to be a father. However, under *ubuntu,* he is. If your mother has an older and a younger sister, then you have three mothers: a mother, an older mother, and a younger mother. Kinship ties also play an important part in hiring. Modern organizations usually frown on the hiring of relatives because of the negative stereotypes associated with nepotism. However, the opposite is true under *ubuntu,* which considers kinship ties within the organization to be a plus. After all, who can be trusted more than one's own relatives? Kinship is also formed with people who graduated from the same school, and with people whose origins can be traced to the same home town or village, commonly known as the "homeys." The presence of these kinship ties in the workplace provides a layer of emotional and psychological support to workers.

An equally important aspect of relationships with others is teamwork. The solidarity spirit of *ubuntu* simultaneously supports cooperation and competitiveness by allowing individuals to contribute their best efforts for the betterment of the entire team. Everyone understands that together the team can accomplish more than if each individual worked alone. The notion of synergy, i.e., the creation of a whole that is larger than the sum of the individual parts, is an integral part of *ubuntu.* Organizations can ensure that individuals continue to uphold this spirit, by linking their reward systems to team performance.

The similarities between *ubuntu* and its related social traditions and some of the recent writings on management theory are striking. For example, recent research in leadership uses the word "fusion" to characterize a style of management that achieves a sense of unity. Fusion offers a view of others as part of the same whole, recognition of similarities rather than differences, and an identification of common ground and a sense of community with shared vision, norms, and outcomes.[4] This may sound revolutionary to classically trained managers who emphasize individuality, competition, and control. In the context of *ubuntu,* fusion is merely the recognition of social reality and traditional relationship patterns.

Two imperatives can be delineated from the foregoing. First, it is important to treat others as members of one's own family, i.e., with kindness, compassion, and humility. Such a cordial regard will likely engender respect, deference, and compliance from those with whom a manager works. This is strikingly similar to Chester Barnard's notion that authority resides with those to whom it is directed.[5] If people sense that they are being treated with respect and dignity, they will respond by showing greater commitment to organizational goals. Second, it is important to recognize and acknowledge the significance of kinship ties in the workplace. If kinship ties result in harmony and commitment to the workplace, then companies ought to consider it positively in their hiring decisions. Whenever practical, these relationships should be taken into account in formulating company policies such as recruitment, placement, promotion, transfer, reward, discipline, and even retirement. In the new millennium, it is those organizations that can match their corporate strategies, policies, and procedures with the values and beliefs of local communities that will enjoy sustainable competitive advantage.

## Language and Communication

Communication is to the organization as blood is to the body. However, major ontological differences exist in communication between the linguistic world of the African and that of the Westerner.[6] In the African milieu, children are socialized from birth to listen to the context and nuances of language in conversation. The importance of language in establishing a sense of community, belonging, shared heritage, and common welfare is emphasized. Words are woven in dense fabrics of association that may be unwittingly activated by mere mention.[7] The pervasive axiom is that to talk and to name is to create experience, to construct reality. Until the middle of the 19th century, it was through oral tradition that African folk proverbs, ballads, legends, and mythology were sustained and kept alive, rather than through written history. These intergenerationally transmitted stories formed the bedrock of reason, wisdom, and morality.[8] A mastery of the art and skill of oratory is still a prerequisite for leadership. This becomes even more so during celebrations when skillful orators take center stage with their poetry and praise singing.

Traditional management training places greater emphasis on the efficiency of information transfer. Ideas must be translated quickly and accurately into words, the medium of the exchange must be appropriate, and the receiver must accurately understand the message. In the *ubuntu* context, however, the social effect of conversation is emphasized, with primacy given to establishing and reinforcing relationships. Unity and understanding among affected group members is valued above efficiency and accuracy of language. A premium is placed on personal rapport, i.e., the general sense of what is being said, which can easily get lost in translation. That is why it is encouraging to see that many white South Africans are learning to speak African languages as an important means of understanding the indigenous culture and patterns of interaction.[9]

In many organizations, work is divided into individually structured jobs and tasks, with performance evaluation and accountability being directed at the individual. This is consistent with the ideas of Frederick Taylor at the beginning of the last century, and Adam Smith before him.[10] Concerned more with efficiency than with healthy relationships, supervisors may discourage conversation and other forms of socializing in the workplace. What they fail to recognize is that this creates tension among employees and produces social distance between them. Needless to say, this contradicts the core values of *ubuntu.* Isolation results in a psychic conflict in the worker's mind, which eventually manifests itself in lowered morale, reduced productivity, and an environment that impedes the realization of the worker's full potential.[11]

One way to break this psychological impasse is to periodically hold company-sponsored events and ceremonies. Ceremonies are commonplace in many cultures for punctuating major accomplishments. *Ubuntu* boasts an extremely rich repertoire of rituals and attending forms of music and singing, dance, and the eloquent verbal expressions of praise singers. Western-style year-end socials, and celebrations of important anniversaries of service with the company conveniently satisfy the need for ceremony. Many companies hold ceremonies to celebrate people with 10, 15, 20, and 25 years of service with the company. *Ubuntu*-style ceremonies can also be witnessed in trailblazing American companies such as Southwest Airlines. These practices are fun while at the same time promoting a sense of trust and belonging, which supports the basic human values in *ubuntu.* It is not surprising, therefore, that employees of companies like Southwest Airlines exhibit a great degree of loyalty to their company.

Even at work, people enjoy interacting with each other. Work environments where appropriate interaction is discouraged may lead to dysfunctional behaviors and ultimately to an alienated workforce. Allowing workers to establish relationships, even when not required by the task structure, improves effectiveness and decreases antagonistic feelings toward the organization. Above all, a periodic celebration of the milestones accomplished goes a long way in building a sense of belonging and commitment to organizational goals and objectives. Here again, the culture of *ubuntu* can provide sustenance. *Ubuntu* is about what people value and what they aspire to be. Peter Drucker notes that organizational effectiveness results when both individual and organizational needs are harmonized.[12] Organizations that provide an opportunity for their employees to give expression to their values and beliefs in the course of carrying out their corporate responsibilities are likely to gain competitive advantage over those that do not. The lesson here: Provide opportunities for self-expression, achievement, and self-fulfillment, consistent with employee values.

## Decision Making

Decision-making processes followed under *ubuntu* differ markedly from those found in classical management textbooks where decision making is defined as the conscious choice of a course of action from available alternatives. The textbook process is linear: problem definition, determination of causes of the problem, generation of alternate solutions, choice of the best solution, implementation of the decision. Speed to closure is taken to be meritorious. Vision is usually monocular because unity of vision is idealized. Under *ubuntu* the decision-making process is a circular, inclusive one, proceeding at a deliberate speed, and often given to deviations in order to delve into other matters, however remotely related to the issue at hand. Vision tends to be polyocular. In other words, those who look at issues from different angles are seen as interesting and as providing valuable insights. Diversity of vision is not only permitted but also protected and encouraged. Before closure, considerable time is allowed to assure that all voices have been heard, and that a consensus has been reached. The goal of decision making in this context is to preserve harmony and achieve consensus. A decision that is supported is considered superior to the "right" decision that is resented or resisted by many. Unity is more valued than the utility of the decision reached.

Nowhere are these differences better demonstrated than in the way negotiations were conducted between the white South African government and the various black political movements during the CODESA (Convention for a Democratic South Africa) talks held near

Johannesburg in the early 1990s.[13] Although they outnumbered the government representatives by far, not once did the ANC-led national liberation organizations call for a vote on any of the critical decisions. Major decisions were made by consensus, often after a lot of behind-the-scenes discussions to bring other parties into agreement. These talks resulted in the formation of a Government of National Unity, which went on to govern the country peacefully for the next five years.

The success of the CODESA experience is not to suggest that decision making by majority has no place. However, because of the large base of support it enjoys, a solution based on African *ubuntu*-style consensus decision making will usually be more successful at the implementation stage. Equally important is that the new spirit of democracy that is prevailing around the world today requires that management be willing to negotiate with workers. Prior to the recognition of labor unions during the years of apartheid, management had been reluctant to enter into collective bargaining with employee representatives for fear of eroding their power. The reality that they found once they entered into negotiation with workers surprised them. They found employees not only willing to find the middle ground, but, as an executive of a large corporation in KwaZulu-Natal once noted, "Blacks have taken to negotiation as ducks take to water."[14] He had just discovered something he should have known long ago, that negotiation is an intrinsic component of *ubuntu.*

The distinctions between the classical management and ubuntu decision approaches suggest that paying heed to the latter will result in more effective implementation. By imposing control over employees and limiting their involvement, the classical management approach often leads to ineffective organizational outcomes and dysfunctional behaviors in the workplace. Consensus-based decision making, although initially costly in terms of time and effort, is more likely to result in improved commitment to organizational goals. The results will be seen in reduced supervisory requirements, decreased turnover and absenteeism, and increased efficiency.

## Time

Differences in attitudes toward time often present a problem when people conduct business across cultures. For instance, researchers in sociolinguistics have demonstrated that there is a level of discomfort in the different ways that Western and African cultures interpret pauses and silences during conversations.[15] The discussion here refers mostly to how the available time is allocated. Westerners are inclined to fill the pauses with words; Africans appreciate periodic gaps of silence within a conversation.

A case in point involves a sales representative who had secured an hour-long appointment with a Zulu customer at her home near Stanger in KwaZulu-Natal. When the salesperson arrived punctually, he was upset that his host was not ready. It took a while before the host finally came out to meet him and begin the scheduled discussion. The salesman found out later that, in the Zulu culture, when you have an appointment at someone's home, it means he/she has control over what happens in that time period. By agreeing to meet at the home of the client, the salesperson was tacitly agreeing that it was up to his host how she would prioritize her time between family activities and business discussion.

Unlike the classical management context in which time is a strategic commodity to be prudently used, in the *ubuntu* context it is treated as a healer. Time is not a commodity to be frugally consumed, a tool to be carefully utilized, or a regulator to be dutifully observed. Instead, it is a reference that locates communities with respect to their collective past and shared future; it assigns significance to patterns of events; and it orders relationships and affairs. Time is not an independent quantity that can be divided into ever-smaller units; it is a continuum that has meaning only as it is experienced. In the context of *ubuntu,* time is reflected as a unifying and integrating construct that emphasizes interdependence, shared heritage, regularity, and congruity. Furthermore, time is not experienced only in the present; it also heals past experiences and allows for reflection. The world saw this healing aspect in action in the truth and reconciliation hearings that were chaired by Archbishop Tutu, when the victims' relatives were told to "take your time" while giving testimony, often during prime-time TV. There is a saying: "God gave the African time, and the Westerner a watch."[16]

Misunderstandings over time are often a source of friction in cross-cultural interactions. They arise not because of different priorities assigned to time commitments, but because of fundamentally different meanings attached to time. This is a difficult gulf to span because it requires adopting a different worldview, or at a minimum, accepting the validity and reasonableness of a different worldview. Modern people understand the merits of punctuality and deadlines, when it comes to the corporate context. But when Western timing conflicts with

African timing (e.g., in task completion, healing, reconciliation), where expectations regarding speed to closure differ, traditional management may have something to learn. The Western concept of time management will be ineffective at best, and dysfunctional at worst, if it is carelessly pitted against the African conception of time.

## Productivity and Efficiency

Efficiency—the ratio of output value to input cost—is assumed to be a critical determinant of organizational viability. Maximizing efficiency is the sine qua non of traditional management theory. In the *ubuntu* context, on the other hand, the emphasis is on social well-being rather than on technical rationality. The objective is to optimize efficiency rather than to maximize it, and that allows higher priority for peaceful and harmonious relationships. In this context, an optimized solution is one that leads to the most favored outcome by a much wider group of stakeholders in the long run. In the short run, this will yield lower efficiencies than the maximized solution.[17] Attempts to maximize efficiency often incur the cost of fractured relationships, and social disruption can have unintended consequences.

Traditional training often emphasizes "denominator management." A cutback in the number of employees is a means to increased productivity.[18] Under *ubuntu,* the numerator and denominator in the productivity equation cannot be seen as independent variables. Employee layoffs (denominator reduction) would have a significant negative impact on output, likely resulting in reduced, not increased, productivity. This is especially so when a highly valued "output" is employee well-being and community. Multinational corporations often resort to between-country productivity comparisons and overlook the national contexts of the countries being compared. In most multinational corporations, it is commonplace to hear comparisons between headquarters operations and those of overseas subsidiaries. In those comparisons the subsidiary's production lines often come across as overmanned, implying that some of the "extra" workers should be removed from the line (eventually to be laid off). Workers in the West might accept the rationale behind the decision to downsize, even though many would struggle to understand its logic when the top management of the same companies receives hefty pay raises. Under ubuntu, such an action would constitute a direct affront to the norm of fairness. Believers in ubuntu trust that humans take care of each other, and violating that trust runs the risk of alienating the entire workforce and might result in a decrease in productivity as well as other disruptions. In a culture that is high on collectivism, ubuntu dictates the sharing of burdens during hard times because, in so doing, the suffering is diminished.[19] In that sense, across-the-board pay reductions would be much preferred to targeted layoffs. A good example comes from a recently reported case.[20] A company had initiated a program for building immaculate three-bedroom, carpeted houses for its black workers in one of the South African black townships. But the CEO was surprised when he learned that the employees would have preferred the money be used instead to upgrade a greater number of existing dwellings, so that more of the company's employees could benefit.

The unfortunate legacy of apartheid is that it systematically discriminated against blacks to the point that they are now grossly underrepresented in the key decision-making positions in many organizations. A recent report on employment equity in South Africa indicated that, although African males constituted 39 percent of the workforce, they made up 10 percent of management. By contrast, white males, who constituted 13 percent of the workforce, made up 52 percent of management.[21] Corresponding figures for females would probably indicate even wider disparities. Thus there is an urgent need to identify, attract, recruit, and promote capable blacks into management positions.

This case demonstrates the dilemma facing managers of Western-based firms in developing countries such as South Africa. The performance criteria of the organization—productivity, efficiency, increased output—may be in direct conflict with the indigenous values of the country's people solidarity, group well-being, social harmony. The two are not necessarily incompatible, and, if some consideration is given to protocols and proprieties, change can be introduced with minimal disruption. In fact, as with decision making, when properly communicated and deliberated, even the most difficult changes can be implemented effectively. The lesson can be summed up in the following way: blind application of traditional management notions of productivity and efficiency in the African context might unleash a number of complex problems. Attempts to increase efficiency without consideration of concomitant social impacts might end up actually reducing organizational productivity and efficiency at the same time. If important changes are to be introduced, this must be done using consultation and inclusive decision processes. Otherwise, implementation will be fraught with disruptions.

## Age and Seniority in Leadership

The context within which leadership choice and style operate is equally important to understand. In Africa, leadership is easier to accept from a more experienced (read, older) individual. This means that rarely would a younger person be comfortable leading a group of people he/she regards as his/her seniors. Equally, it would be awkward for older employees to take instructions from a supervisor whom they perceived to be their junior. This would be particularly difficult in an environment with highly structured tasks, where compliance is expected without question and the leader is required to be more directive. Such a requirement goes against the grain of African culture, particularly if carried out by a junior (younger) member of the community. The following example illustrates the point.

One senior manager at a major industrial firm in South Africa reported that, when the company initiated a black advancement program, the first blacks promoted to supervisory positions were young men (20–24 years old) who had performed very well. The workers of the group these men were assigned to supervise refused to work for them. When senior managers probed, they found that, within the culture of those workers, older men do not work for 11 youngsters. Management then revised their promotion criteria to include age as well as capability.[22]

Sometimes the "professionalism" displayed by young, Western-trained managers is misinterpreted and resented by other employees, as in the case of an African manager who was summoned before his family elders because he did not treat the workers as brothers and sisters but as employees.[23] An older person might not necessarily possess all the expertise for the task at hand, but through wisdom, vision, and ability to maintain harmonious working relations, he/she can get others to perform well.

The role of the leader is to show by example, yet the best operatives often do not become the best managers. The manager's job is to get things done through others, to integrate the various factors that contribute to organizational effectiveness.[24] The manager in an African work environment must have the appropriate balance between the demand for technical competence and social savvy. This approach to managing is gaining acceptance in more contemporary management thinking. More successful managers are seen to act as coaches, cheerleaders, and "nurturers of champions," rather than as cops, experts, and naysayers.[25] The lesson is that, in the African thought system, age is regarded as an ongoing process of maturing and acquiring wisdom. Gray hairs are respected. Organizations that understand this difference in their selection and promotion of people into leadership positions are bound to have competitive advantage over organizations that do not.

All things being equal, in choosing someone for a leadership position from among equally qualified employees, the *ubuntu* ethos would tip the scales in favor of the candidate with more seniority in terms of either chronological age, service to the company, or experience in the position. The corollary is that the more junior employee will get his/her turn in the future. The Nguni idiom, "*Zisina zidedelana,*" signifies that in a dance everyone will eventually get his/her turn on center stage.[26] Criteria for selecting employees into leadership positions must not be limited to demonstrated mastery of technical skills. Age must be taken into account as an asset, not as a liability associated with senility. After all, older workers do have wisdom, experience, and strong informal networks. They can use these characteristics to the company's competitive advantage. Often *ubuntu* has it right, and the West misses the point.

## Belief Systems

Christianity is the dominant faith for most South Africans, including over 90 percent of the African population. But prior to the arrival of Christian missionaries, indigenous people believed in the existence of the omnipotent, the creator, whom they called *uQamata, uNkulunkulu,* or *Modimo.* But not everyone could communicate with the creator, only those with special qualities. It is also believed that people who die join the ancestors in the *mesocosmos* to become mediators to the Creator on behalf of the living. Among the living are those who are anointed with special gifts of being able to communicate with the *mesocosmos.* It is from this ability that the *isangoma* or the traditional healer derives his/her power of healing and seeing things that other humans cannot. Hence when there is a medical problem, it is not uncommon, especially for rural Africans, to consult an *isangoma.* Although over 80 percent of the black labor force consult the *isangoma,* company managers have tended to downplay their centrality, or ridicule their involvement in their employees' health maintenance.[27] Other companies have taken full advantage of the power of the *isangoma* as the following real-life case illustrates.[28]

Faced with large-scale pilfering, one company tried everything—including peer monitors, fingerprinting, and police investigations—to stop it. After all efforts to stop the pilfering had failed, the CEO finally called in an *isangoma.* The *isangoma* told the employees that the person who had stolen the goods would die from a spell cast on all employees if he/she did not confess within 24 hours. Within eight hours, an employee confessed.

In this case, foreign-evolved management tactics, such as peer control, police investigations, and fingerprinting, did not work. Here we see that management and the workers came from entirely different worldviews. The successful strategy engaged employees in their own worldview. In general, if a large proportion of the workforce believes in the existence of *mesocosmic* spirits, why not formally retain the services of a company *isangoma?* This would result in mutually beneficial outcomes for both the company and its employees (and the *isangoma*). Of course, it would be necessary to orient the *isangoma* in the company's vision and mission for him/her to have sufficient appreciation of the symbiotic relationship between community values and the continued viability and competitiveness of the company. He/she would not just finger-point wrongdoers, but could also suggest appropriate remedial action that would accommodate both worldviews. After all, companies do hire company lawyers, company public relations officers, and consultants to solve ad hoc problems as they arise. The concurrent belief in the *mesocosmos* and the role of the *isangoma* makes him/her a key player in the process of mediation and arbitration.

The importance of *ubuntu* is clear. South Africa—and the world—consists of an array of peoples with diverse cultures and traditions, woven together in a colorful fabric of folklore. Until recently, Western norms were accepted as the modus operandi in business. But other traditions are increasingly gaining commonplace acceptance, for example the *isangoma* in the above case. The best strategic posture for companies is flexibility and willingness to learn from local cultures. Successful companies will treat each cultural exigency with caution, care, and understanding. Flexibility and accommodation will go a long way toward creating an atmosphere of mutual respect and an increased sense of company identity among employees. Companies that stick rigidly to the traditional Western management value system should be prepared to face major disruptions like the work stoppage discussed above.

## Implications for Management

Before discussing the implications of *ubuntu* in South Africa, it is important to offer some disclaimers. The first is a caution against wholesale acceptance of all African customs and practices. Several customs and practices carried out in the name of *ubuntu* are based on erroneous superstitions. Such practices can be oppressive and sexist, and often stifle individual aspirations and progress.[29] In the contemporary African milieu, the conventional wisdom is that customs will only be endorsed to the extent that they serve the common good. Otherwise, they will be challenged and changed.

Another caution is against the assumption that culture is static and that there is a one-way causal relationship between culture and behavior. Changing behaviors also causes changes in culture through feedback and reinforcement over time. Differences between the behaviors of younger and older generations contribute to the generation gap. Also, through years of contact with non-African cultures, the majority population has adapted the principles of *ubuntu.* There are differences between the cultural practices of urban and rural people, between college-educated and semiliterate people, and between migrant workers and middle-class people. In general, *ubuntu* helps in affirming universal human values, like humaneness, dignity, empathy, and compassion for others.

What are the management implications of *ubuntu* in the transformation process now taking place in South Africa? To start off, foreign and local white-controlled companies must be willing to work in partnership with indigenous people, with the understanding that they will listen to and learn from them. There have been several cases of successful collaborations. One example is the partnership between the giant American advertising company, McCann-Erickson, and the South African black company, HerdBuoys, to form HerdBuoys McCann-Erickson. McCann-Erickson contributes to the partnership its years of experience in advertising around the world, and HerdBuoys contributes its intimate knowledge of the South African market, and the marketing savvy of its founder, Peter Vundla. The result is a dynamic company that has risen from 14th to the top five in South Africa. Another example is the joint venture formed by American Express and the black company, PulaNala, in the travel and tourism industry. As a result of this partnership, American Express has become highly responsive to shifts in the travel industry. According to CEO Mike Mohohlo, the relationship benefits PulaNala through the transfer of business skills and the accelerated development of personnel into areas of executive responsibility.[30] To sum up, *ubuntu* is an important legacy from South Africa that can be parlayed into the practice of management for competitive advantage.

## Guidelines for Implementing *Ubuntu*

Several South African companies have begun to embrace the guidelines of *ubuntu* and to introduce them in their corporate practice with notable success.[31] Also, more writings are coming forth from authors giving advice ranging from corporate governance to marketing.[32] Some guidelines for helping managers in the process of incorporating the philosophy of *ubuntu* in their organizations are discussed next. Though not exhaustive, the guidelines are meant to provide a good starting point for managers wishing to incorporate the principles of *ubuntu* in their organizations.

- **Treat others with dignity and respect.** This is a cardinal point of *ubuntu.* Everything hinges on this canon, including an emphasis on humility, harmony, and valuing diversity. Helpfulness toward others creates an environment of collegiality based on caring and sharing. After all, who would not like to be appreciated, valued, and respected for their contributions for what they bring to the workplace?

- **Be willing to negotiate in good faith.** Take time to listen with empathy, especially in conflict resolution. Being listened to is tantamount to being acknowledged. In *ubuntu,* being acknowledged is a very important first step toward agreement and cooperation. Transparency and trust replace suspicion and hostility.

- **Provide opportunities for self-expression.** Honoring achievement, self-fulfillment, and affirmation of values are all important aspects of creating goodwill among employees. Periodic celebrations to punctuate achievement are one way to fulfill this need.

- **Understand the beliefs and practices of indigenous people.** Carefully incorporate into standard corporate policies the indigenous practices and beliefs discussed above. If employing people who are relatives has been successful, use it. Learn more about the belief systems that employees subscribe to. Engaging them in their own belief system will go a long way toward ensuring employee self-fulfillment and thus smooth-running operations.

- **Honor seniority, especially in leadership choices.** All things being equal, seniority adds value through experience, connections, and the wisdom that older employees have from their record of past experiences.

- **Promote equity in the workplace.** Fairness is a value that is upheld in most cultures. But it takes a special significance in countries such as South Africa, where there has been a history of sociopolitical inequities. Recruiting and promoting into senior management ranks qualified individuals from previously disadvantaged groups, i.e., blacks and women, is essential. This is not reverse discrimination. There is no room for discriminatory practices in the *ubuntu* philosophy.

- **Be flexible and accommodative.** Applying the recommendations above will require a careful balancing act by management between the imperatives of *ubuntu* and other tried and tested management principles. A carefully balanced blending, with flexibility and accommodation, holds the promise of greater value added to corporate performance.

## Appreciating the Value of Indigenous Cultures

In order to be effective, management principles and practices must receive the embrace of their host cultures. Effective management in South Africa and elsewhere will hinge on the successful harnessing and harmonizing of both indigenous and traditional corporate cultures. Unfortunately, the emphasis up to now has been on suppressing indigenous cultures rather than appreciating their added value. Traditional management—based on Western corporate culture—has been allowed to freely dominate corporate life around the world at the expense of indigenous cultures. With democracy beginning to dominate around the world, formerly marginalized cultures will increasingly want to publicly express themselves in the workplace. For managers, the challenge is to become familiar with these values, incorporate them into their policies, or run the risk of being outperformed by rivals who do.

Incorporating *ubuntu* principles in management holds the promise of superior approaches to managing organizations. Organizations infused with humaneness, a pervasive spirit of caring and community, harmony and hospitality, respect and responsiveness will enjoy more sustainable competitive advantages.

## Acknowledgment

Versions of this article were presented at the 1998 National Academy of Management Meetings in San Diego, CA; and the 1999 EAM Conference on Managing in a Global Economy in Prague, Czech Republic, with Zengie Mangaliso of Westfield State

College and John Bruton of the University of Massachusetts, Amherst. I wish to thank both for their insightful ideas. I also thank Bradford Knipes of Westfield State College and the reviewers of The Executive for their constructive comments.

## Notes

1. The world competitiveness scoreboard. *http://www.imd.chl/wcy/ranking/pastresults.html.*

2. Greenhalgh, L. 2001. *Managing strategic relationships: The key to business success.* New York: The Free Press.

3. Mangaliso, M. P. 1992. Entrepreneurship and innovation in a global context. *Entrepreneurship, Innovation, and Change.* 1: 437–450.

4. Daft, R. L. & Lengel, R. H. 1998. *Fusion leadership: Unlocking the subtle forces that change people and organizations.* San Francisco: Berret-Koehler.

5. Barnard, C. I. 1938. *The functions of the executive.* Cambridge, MA: Harvard University Press.

6. See Kiggundu, M. N., Jorgensen, J. J. & Hafsi, T. 1983. Administrative theory and practice in developing countries: A synthesis. *Administrative Science Quarterly,* 28: 66–84; and Mangaliso, M. P. 1991. Whose knowledge matters? The case for developing multicultural theories of management. In J. D. Jansen (Ed.), *Knowledge and power in South Africa: Critical perspectives across the disciplines.* Johannesburg: Skotaville.

7. Comaroff, J. & Comaroff, L. J. 1989. The colonization of consciousness in South Africa. *Economy and Society,* 8(3): 267–296.

8. See Ahiauzu, A. I. 1986. The African thought-system and the work behavior of the African industrial man. *International Studies of Management and Organizations,* 16(2): 37–58.

9. Crowe, S. White South Africans learn Zulu and much more. *Christian Science Monitor,* 13 November 1995: 1, 13.

10. Frederick Taylor is known as the father of time and motion studies. He was the first to proclaim that management can be made into an exact science. According to him, if you divided work into discrete, wholly programmed pieces, and then put the pieces together in a truly optimal way, you can have a truly top-performing unit. Taylor, F. W. 1911. *Principles of scientific management.* New York: Harper & Row. See also Peters, T. & Waterman, R. 1982. *In search of excellence: Lessons from America's best-run companies.* New York: Harper & Row.

11. Terkel, S. 1974. *Working.* New York: Pantheon.

12. Drucker, P. 1993. *The effective executive.* New York: HarperCollins.

13. The Convention for a Democratic South Africa (CODESA) provided the forum for talks between South African political movements led by the ANC and the South African government. Held from 1991 to 1993, these talks defined South Africa's new constitutional structure. All About South Africa. *http://www.southafricatravel.20m.com/splash/all about south africa.htm.*

14. Mangaliso, M. P. 1988. The relationship of environmental turbulence, strategy preference, and performance: A study of the preferences of North American and South African corporate executives. Unpublished Ph.D. dissertation. University of Massachusetts, Amherst.

15. Chick, J. K. 1990. The interaction accomplishment of discrimination in South Africa. In D. Carbaugh (Ed.), *Cultural communication and intercultural contact.* Hillsdale, NJ: Lawrence Erlbaum.

16. See Fadiman, J. A. 2000. *South Africa's black market: Doing business with Africans.* Yarmouth, ME: Intercultural Press.

17. For another perspective, see Cohen, K. J. & Cyert, R. M. 1975. *The theory of the firm.* Englewood Cliffs, NJ: Prentice Hall.

18. The typical measures of company productivity are return on investment (ROI), return on net assets (RONA), or return on capital employed (ROCE). These measures have two components, the numerator—net income, and the denominator—investment, and net assets, capital employed. Raising net income has proved to be a lot harder than cutting assets and headcount. So under pressure to improve ROI, executives often reach for the lever that will bring about the quickest, surest improvement in ROI—the denominator. However, just as any firm that cuts the denominator will reap productivity, so too will a company that grows its revenue stream atop a rising or constant capital and employment base. The first approach may be necessary, but in the *ubuntu* philosophical thought, the second is preferable. For further discussion, see Hamel, G. & Prahalad, C. K. 1994. *Competing for the future.* Boston: Harvard Business School Press.

19. From his empirical research, Hofstede found that national cultures differ on four dimensions, viz., *individualism-collectivism* (the supremacy of the needs of the individual over those of the group); *uncertainty avoidance* (the presence of systems to deal with anxiety created by uncertainty); *power distance* (acceptance of inequality in power among people); and *masculinity* (endorsement of traditional gender differences among its members). Hofstede, G.

1980. *Culture's consequences: International differences in work-related values.* Newbury Park, CA: Sage.

20. See Beaty, D. T. & Mangaliso M. P. 1999. New lessons on management transformation from South Africa. Paper presented at the Conference on Managing in a Global Economy, Prague, Czech Republic.

21. Department of Labor. Employment Equity Report: Executive Summary. Pretoria. 2 October 2000.

22. Beaty & Mangaliso, op. cit.

23. Ahiauzu, op. cit.

24. Greenhalgh, op. cit.

25. See Peters & Waterman, op. cit.

26. In this regard, it made sense that President Nelson Mandela and the African National Congress selected Thabo Mbeki to be the deputy president in 1994 since, aside from his many other skills and talents, the deputy president also enjoyed seniority over Cyril Ramaphosa, who had demonstrated impressive negotiation skills during the transitional talks.

27. This claim was made by a traditional healer based in Khayelitsha, Cape Town, during an interview for Public Broadcasting Service. See Ustinov, P. 1999. On the trail of Mark Twain. PBS Home Video, No B8074–2.

28. Beaty, D. Eurocentric or Afrocentric? In *Mastering management* (Part 2). Business Day Supplement. Johannesburg, 1996, 15.

29. An example among the Botswana is the custom of *mogaga,* which requires a widow to sprinkle leaves each time she leaves her homestead for a 12-month period of mourning. This custom is based on the belief that mourning and respecting the dead this way is vital for the protection of livestock against infertility. Many, including human rights advocates, have criticized this custom as sexist and archaic: it applies only to widows, and its connection with the protection of livestock against infertility is tenuous. HRC to indict if chief expels Christian widow. *http://www.dispatch.co.za/1998/06/29/southafrica/HRC.HTM.*

30. Mkhuma, Z. Happy landings. *Enterprise* (South Africa). January 1998, 87.

31. Wolmanrans, S. 1995. Ubuntu means to SAA what "putting people first" meant to BA. *http://www.pgw.orglvgc/mtl vhr95418.htm.*

32. Shonhiwa, S. African values for business. Financial Mail. 4 May 2001. *http://www.fm.co.za/cgi-bin/pp-print.pl.*

# Reading 1.5

# THE JAPANESE MANAGER'S TRAUMATIC ENTRY INTO THE UNITED STATES

## *Understanding the American-Japanese Cultural Divide*

RICHARD G. LINOWES

**Executive Overview**

Japanese executives routinely travel to the United States for business for periods extending up to several years. Their visits typically begin as a jarring experience for them and their families due to the substantial cultural differences they encounter. Despite the success of Japanese business worldwide and the growing presence of Japanese communities in many U.S. cities, Japanese individuals routinely face disorienting experiences in their dealings with Americans, encounters that impede their effectiveness and hamper the business they come here to manage. Such confrontations mirror in microcosm the tensions of contemporary U.S.-Japan relations. They reveal the presence of built-in cultural barriers to Japanese firms in the U.S. that constitute structural impediments every bit as real as the more widely criticized constraints on foreign business in Japan. They also highlight patterns of behavior that Americans must learn to bridle if they are to serve as key players in global institutions in the future.

Around a conference table in a large U.S. office tower, three American executives sat with their new boss, Mr. Akiro Kusumoto, the newly appointed head of a Japanese firm's American subsidiary, and two of his Japanese lieutenants. The meeting was called to discuss ideas for reducing operating costs. Mr. Kusumoto began by outlining his company's aspiration for its long-term U.S. presence. He then turned to the current budgetary matter. One Japanese manager politely offered one suggestion, and then an American proposed another. After gingerly discussing the alternatives for quite some time, the then exasperated American blurted out: "Look, *that* idea is just not going to have much impact. Look at the numbers! We should cut this program, and I think we should do it as soon as possible!" In the face of such bluntness, uncommon and unacceptable in Japan, Mr. Kusumoto fell silent. He leaned back, drew air between his teeth, and felt a deep longing to "return East." He realized his life in this country would be filled with many such jarring encounters, and lamented his posting to a land of such rudeness.

## The Newcomer's Surprise

This scenario illustrates one of the disagreeable surprises Akiro Kusumoto encountered when he first came to the United States a few years ago. As an officer of a Japanese financial services firm, he was dispatched to serve a multi-year tour of duty with his firm's American operation. That assignment began a most uncomfortable period of adjustment. In his new role, he faced a round of challenges that far exceeded what his travel books and corporate training programs had led him to anticipate. Though he had been engulfed with pictures and tales of America throughout his life, his experience of living and working with Americans as neighbors and employees proved to be far more unsettling than expected.

There were surprises in nearly all walks of life. City streets were a constant reminder that he lived in a strange and hostile environment, posing risks much more frightening than anything he had known before. He was startled and alienated by Yankee assertiveness and bluntness. Though most Americans were friendly, he had trouble understanding routine conversations and serious difficulty knowing whom to trust. He longed for the structure, clarity, security, and peace of Japanese society.

Eventually Mr. Kusumoto learned to live well in America. He grew to enjoy its freedoms, diversity, comforts, and conveniences. But his U.S. experience was definitely a transforming experience, one that made his ultimate return to Japan both psychologically taxing and socially problematic for him and his entire family.

Mr. Kusumoto is not alone. Every year thousands of Japanese business professionals come to the United States to pursue business interests. Many have made the trip innumerable times, gaining invaluable experience in American styles of business, while others are relative newcomers. The newcomers' trials and tribulations shed light on the strengths and weaknesses of American society, and highlight ways in which Americans bear some responsibility for contemporary strains in American-Japanese relations.

Forward-looking American managers are well advised to learn from Mr. Kusumoto's experience two key lessons that might improve their effectiveness in international dealings:

(1) *There exist significant American cultural impediments to Japanese business.* Americans need to be more sensitive to the challenges faced by Japanese when they tailor their traditional ways to the American experience. Difficulties between Americans and Japanese are in large measure the product of American conduct and habits of mind. A newfound awareness of American cultural impediments might temper their critique of Japanese ways, and form the basis for an improved, mutually respectful American-Japanese relationship. There is clearly room for improvement. According to a recent survey, only eighteen percent of Japanese believe Americans respect the Japanese, and only thirty-one percent of Americans think Japanese respect Americans.[1] Such suspicions do not bode well for multinational business, or any form of bilateral cooperation.

(2) *Some conventional American ways should be tempered in overseas dealing.* Japanese impressions of Americans are relevant to matters that go well beyond Japanese trade, for in overseas settings American business people are being compared increasingly to Japanese people. From Malaysia to Thailand to Venezuela to Spain, local business people deal with both Americans and Japanese, sometimes choosing between the two. In such settings, relative differences between American and Japanese are most apparent. Since America future in international business depends in part on the quality of these overseas relationships, it is time to hold up a mirror to American ways, warts and all. In this article, trouble spots in "the American way" are examined by listing the disappointments faced by recently arrived Japanese business people. Their positive impressions are overlooked to highlight factors that make their American business dealings both awkward and uncomfortable. Drawing on the author's research on the cross-cultural encounters inside the U.S. subsidiaries of Japanese firms, this article offers a new synthesis of recognized differences between American and Japanese ways.[2] It then examines how these differences undermine the effectiveness of visiting Japanese business people. Though the presentation paints a more critical portrait of America than most Japanese might wish to convey, the findings are instructive for all engaged in global commerce.

## Comparing American and Japanese Ways

To appreciate the shock of entry, the discussion begins with a pictorial summary of known differences between American and Japanese ways. Though Japanese and Americans share many similarities, they are different in critically important ways. Cultural traditions from each national heritage yield behavioral norms that are sometimes at odds with those from the other culture.

Exhibit 1 synthesizes these contrasts in visual form. Japanese values and behaviors appear on the left, while American values and behaviors appear on the right. Down the center appear the key contrasts reported over the years by keen observers, scholars, and the press.[3] The boldface print on both sides highlights fundamental differences: Japanese hold harmony as a social ideal, patience as a personal virtue, and hierarchy as an essential organizing principle. Americans, in contrast, hold freedom as a social ideal, action-orientation as a personal virtue, and equality as a fundamental organizing principle. Associated with each of these broad differences are the more specific paired contrasts appearing down the center. These contrasts are grouped by broad theme, but they are also linked sequentially from top to bottom. The key contrast appears across the middle, once again in boldface print: Japanese focus on maintaining the group, whereas Americans focus on protecting the individual. The other contrasts illuminate areas where each society's traditionally sanctioned conduct differs markedly from that prescribed by the other culture.

Exhibit 1 helps one visualize the American-Japanese cultural divide. It can be considered an "Intercultural Reference Card," identifying memorable patterns in the contrasts between different cultural ways. It clarifies how the distinct social ideals of these two societies produce a known set of contrasting social behaviors.

The roots of these differences lie in the different historical and cultural traditions of each country. The amazing cultural and ethnic diversity of the United States was produced by waves of immigrants who came in search of better opportunities (though some were brought as slaves). They arrived in a country shaped by Judeo-Christian thinking that emphasized individual choice and clearly distinguished spiritual from commercial life. The founding heroes of this country declared their independence in a rebellion against authority, an act still esteemed as model behavior by succeeding generations. Americans recite the belief that personal dreams can be achieved through individual effort.

Japanese society, in contrast, evolved in a self-contained fashion from a large, homogeneous population based in communal villages and urban settings. Its thinking was shaped by the combination of Shintoism, Confucianism, and Buddhism, which taught a love for natural forms, social order, and self-denial, respectively. Through much of its history, it preserved social order by maintaining strict codes of social conduct and a rigorously observed sense of social hierarchy (See Exhibit 1). Japanese recite the motto that "the nail that stands up gets hammered down."

Both countries are undergoing significant change today, but the essential facets of each society remain resilient. "The general character of Japan cannot be changed, should not be changed and will not be changed," declared Yoh Kurosawa, chairman of Japan's largest bank.[4] Even though Japan has adopted many of the cultural trappings of the United States over the years, there remain inherent cultural barriers that limit the effective interaction of American and Japanese people. These barriers can be overcome—indeed, many have done so successfully—but the path is difficult and not commonly taken. It involves much more than a "quick fix" of overseas travel and business protocol training. Improved relations will require significant willful adjustments by people from both sides of the Pacific.

The discussion that follows examines the contrasts shown in Exhibit 1 as they are experienced by the Japanese newcomer. By sampling vicariously the confusing and sometimes embarrassing situations encountered, we gain insight into the workings of American society.

## Coming to America

Mr. Kusumoto is one of a large and growing number of Japanese people who come to the United States every year as corporate executives, investors, and entrepreneurs. Accompanying these more senior individuals are legions of junior executives who come for their tour of duty—their "American experience"—learning English, building relationships, and developing insight into the ways of American business and government. To date, nearly all executives dispatched overseas by Japanese companies have been men.

Each person has a story to tell.[5] For some, adjustment goes smoothly, while for others it is stressful. To be sure, there are positive experiences, such as superstores and inexpensive merchandise. However, there are also telltale negative surprises, which fall into two broad classes: those facets of American society that are jarring in and of themselves, versus those sometimes "astonishing" ways that Americans react to Japanese conduct. The former surprises, termed here impression shock, identify well-established parts of American life that fall outside the accustomed experience of most Japanese business professionals and that prove disorienting when first encountered.

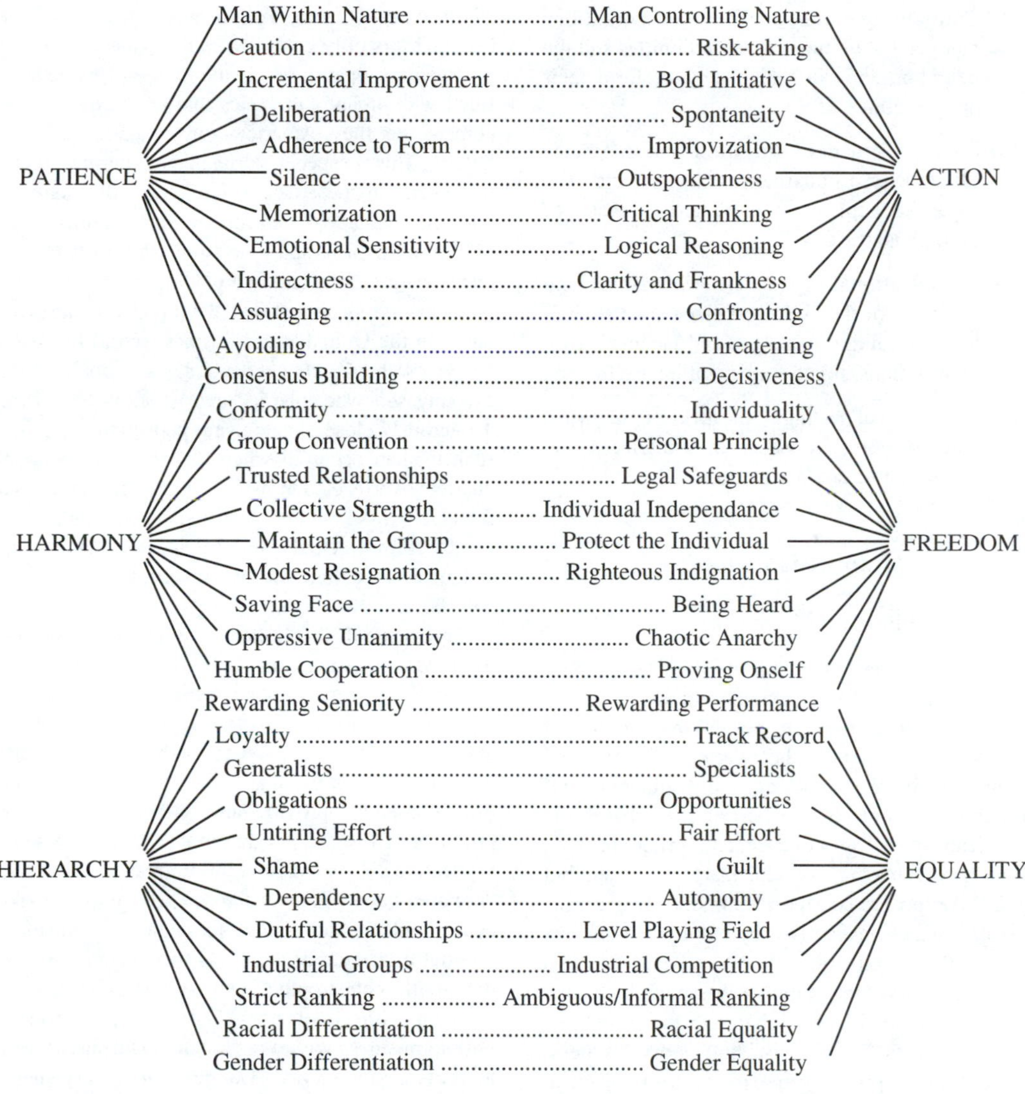


**Exhibit 1**

SOURCE: Academy of Management Executive by Linowes, Richard G. Copyright 1993 by Academy of Management. Reproduced with permission of Academy of Management via Copyright Clearance Center.

The latter, termed here integration shock, are surprises that surface after further involvement in American life when the Japanese executive has settled in and taken hold of the reins of his business. At that time, the Americans he encounters hear his words and watch his actions, but they develop their own interpretations of his behavior and react accordingly. These interpretations are often so far afield from intended meanings that Japanese visitors are occasionally shocked and dismayed by the American response.

Using these categories, Table 1 lists the disheartening surprises Japanese experience when they arrive in the United States. These surprises are further grouped by the context in which they arise:

(1) Community life—the living conditions enjoyed by visiting Japanese families and the neighborhoods in which they perform their daily routines;

(2) Business practice—the form and substance of Japanese business activity and the Japanese adjustment to American ways of doing business;

(3) Organizational dynamics—the nature and character of the U.S. workplace and the challenge of mixing American and Japanese work expectations in U.S. organizational settings;

(4) Interpersonal dealings—the awkward moments that sometimes arise when Americans and Japanese interact face to face.

## Impression Shock

### Community Life

Japanese never fail to be amazed by the diversity of American life. Television and movies may have readied visitors for the perplexing reality of American cities, but the sheer variety of people and cultures is both fascinating and frightening. Of greater concern are the social problems that riddle American life. The violence and crime of U.S. urban environments are legendary in Japan, but firsthand exposure is usually traumatic. Tragic murders of Japanese executives by unknown assailants in several U.S. cities have made Japanese visitors especially wary. One stabbing was done by a man who claimed he "lost his job due to Japanese business practices."[6] Poverty and homelessness, although now appearing in Tokyo, are rampant in the U.S., leading visiting Japanese to wonder, "How can the richest country in the world let such a thing happen!?!?" The U.S. educational system reportedly is in disarray, and Americans are shockingly ignorant of foreign ways (See Table 1). Some Japanese are so troubled by this American self-absorption that a Japanese foundation recently funded the painting of world maps on the floors of basketball courts in New York City.

### Business Practice

Arriving Japanese managers must choose between emulating American business practice and continuing Japanese ways. Most attempt American ways, but they find the process taxing since it requires that they replace entrenched behaviors with foreign practices that seem rather unattractive. Tight control from Tokyo or Osaka corporate headquarters only complicates the issue.

Business operations in the U.S. are sometimes filled with arcane intricacies that are hard for newcomers, be they American or Japanese, to fully fathom. This is especially true in the securities industry, where Japanese lack of knowledge of American business ways has led one chief administrative officer in their employ to suggest that Japanese managers are "like children playing on the freeway; they have no idea what they have gotten themselves into." In the United States business world for just a few years, they rarely get beyond being rookies. Like a young son who inherits great wealth, they come dangerously close to exercising poor judgment. One such mishap occurred when a firm's Tokyo headquarters overreacted to its U.S. subsidiary's reported financial "loss." After a year-end accounting adjustment deferred actual gains till the following year, headquarters called for an unnecessary round of layoffs.

Operational differences aside, Japanese are troubled by American ways of managing. The famed shortsightedness of American management is very frustrating and disappointing to Japanese associates. Americans seem unable to appreciate how business relationships can grow over time. Too often companies provide lackluster service and sell products of insufficient quality. Too often blase or inattentive sales personnel fail to treat customers as "honored guests." Americans are too quick to make deals, and too untrusting to engage in business without a brigade of attorneys to navigate through potentially catastrophic legal situations. Instead of working with people they know well, Americans will do business with most anyone—hiring lawyers to protect themselves.[7] Dangers lurk everywhere. Doing business in the U.S. can be very difficult.

### Organizational Dynamics

Within organizational contexts, entry problems are magnified. United States work settings resemble those in Japan, but American employees and Japanese managers hold very different work and career expectations. It is here that visiting Japanese businessmen often encounter their most unexpected and painful surprises.

In Japanese eyes, American work settings lack a spiritual quality. The feeling of "collective specialness" carefully bred in Japanese organizations is largely absent in U.S. businesses. Gone is the sea of

**Table 1** Negative Surprises Facing the Newly Arrived Japanese Manager

| | *IMPRESSION SHOCK Japanese Perceptions of American Ways* | *INTEGRATION SHOCK American Responses to Japanese Ways* |
|---|---|---|
| COMMUNITY LIFE | Social Diversity | All of/Clannish Community |
| | Violence and Crime | Misunderstood Customs |
| | Poverty and Homelessness | Economic Takeover |
| | Education Problems | Lingering Resentment |
| | Ignorance of Foreign Ways | Sell-Serving Conduct |
| BUSINESS PRACTICE | Different operations | Vagueness and Delay |
| | Shortsightedness | Overworked Employees |
| | Lackluster Service | Unfair Industrial Groups |
| | Hasty Dealmaking | Ethical Violations |
| | Legal Minefields | Influence Peddling |
| ORGANIZATIONAL DYNAMICS | No Spiritual Quality | Management Inexperience |
| | Individual Careerism | Avoided Accountability |
| | Narrow Job Focus | Closed Inner Circle |
| | Political Conifrontation | Stifled Employees |
| | Employee Disloyalty | Discriminatory Practices |
| INTERPERSONAL DEALINGS | Assertiveness | Distrust/Secrecy |
| | Frankness | Arrogance/Hubris |
| | Egoism | Withheld Sentiments |
| | Glibness | Cautious Intimacy |
| | Impulsiveness | Excessive Sensitivity |

NOTE: the rows of Table 1 are not symmetrical like Exhibit 1: they merely list the major surprises experienced by visitors.



dutiful, talented subordinates who work without complaint to accomplish whatever management requests. American managers pursue personal careers and are willing to jump from place to place to obtain their next promotion. People are more concerned with personal job performance and compensation in narrowly defined jobs than overall organizational mission and success. People engage in political confrontations to protect their own interests, producing nasty turmoil and dissension in the ranks. In Japanese eyes, it is tragic the way harmony is so wantonly violated.

Japanese are also surprised by the lack of loyalty in American institutions. Their experience has taught them that effective management depends on the richly woven, internal network of trusted relationships that take years to develop. In Japan, people who moved from one company to another at an advanced stage in their working lives are traditionally viewed as difficult to mold and suspect in their loyalties. Today, lateral movement is much more common, but the U.S. situation is markedly different. This difference was dramatically illustrated by a Japanese executive's motivational talk that resoundingly backfired. Speaking to a group of American employees, the Japanese visitor informed them that the firm was losing money, and he admonished all present to redouble their efforts. An audience of dutiful Japanese would have responded with renewed diligence, but Americans heard the news differently. In the next few weeks, most sent out resumes seeking jobs elsewhere. Senior American and Japanese managers watched with dismay as many talented employees walked out the door.

### Interpersonal Dealings

On an interpersonal level, Japanese newcomers face awkward moments relating to Americans. Many struggle just to communicate in a language not their own, but beyond this challenge lie the strains caused by broader cultural differences. Americans appreciate Japanese politeness, but they are rarely aware how their conduct strikes the Japanese.

Among Japanese people, many things are left unsaid. Elaborate rituals of social reciprocity build trust and "institutionalize thoughtfulness."[8] People are taught to be indirect in conversation, carefully editing their remarks to reflect both good form and the concerns and status of their listeners. Ideally, superiors do not give orders, subordinates are sensitive enough to understand exactly what is wanted and to act accordingly.

In contrast, Americans are usually forceful in their interactions. Rather than subtly reading interpersonal cues, Americans express their thoughts and feelings in frank, unencumbered ways. They have learned that through confrontation they can uncover truth and generate new ideas. Such bluntness is an effrontery to most Japanese. They have heard stories about American assertiveness all their lives, but they are still surprised to encounter it.

This impression is exacerbated when Japanese meet Americans who are particularly glib or egotistical. The free-flowing style of debate widely practiced in the U.S. is overwhelming to the Japanese. They cannot keep pace. They are largely unpracticed at such contests because they prefer to avoid the risk of offending other people. They further believe that especially talkative people cannot be competent. American displays of over-confidence seem shameless and contemptible to the Japanese. All displays of ego are severely punished in Japanese upbringing, and those of higher social standing are expected to display even greater modesty. Finally, Americans are impulsive, some frightfully so. They change direction and relationships much too easily. Impatient for the realization of their hopes and desires, they refuse to wait for developments to unfold naturally.

Taken together, American assertiveness and whimsy confuse the Japanese. Though most Americans are cooperative and trustworthy, trust is inhibited because Americans flagrantly violate Japanese social rules—even though as "foreigners" they are formally exempt from compliance. One Japanese executive described his quandary this way: "Eighty percent of Americans are wonderful people, but twenty percent are not, and I cannot tell the difference."

Impression shock, then, whether felt in communities, business dealings, inside organizations, or in personal relationships, encompasses the first round of surprises faced by newly arrived Japanese. As visitors to a foreign land, they witness the behavior patterns listed on the right side of Exhibit 1, and these violate the precious Japanese values and behaviors shown on the left.

## Integration Shock

Once Japanese commence a daily routine in the United States, they experience a new round of surprises as Americans react to them in unexpected ways. American interpretations of Japanese behavior are often so different from Japanese intent that visitors are sometimes astonished by the American response.

### Community Life

The suburban communities in which many Japanese managers choose to make their homes are often the same bedroom communities in which upwardly mobile, prosperous American executives live with their families. In Japan, these towns are portrayed on Japanese television as the symbols of wealth and comfort of the American lifestyle. They represent much of the best that America has to offer—spacious homes, beautiful parks, cordial neighbors, and impressive shopping malls. With an automobile, everything becomes convenient and accessible.

But life in these communities can be extremely lonely for the Japanese. Accustomed as they are to close group relations, Japanese newcomers find themselves desperately seeking forms of group involvement not routinely felt by their American neighbors. In some locations, such as Scarsdale, New York; Fort Lee, New Jersey; and Grosse Ile, Michigan, the Japanese community has become a substantial force in and of itself, developing a very visible presence in schools and stores, on tennis courts and golf courses. Wary of the corrosive influences of American life—which can seriously jeopardize a child's reassimilation into Japanese society—Japanese parents sometimes establish special Japanese schools to teach Japanese language and formal social manners. Such groupish behavior in nearly all walks of life leads many Americans to criticize their Japanese neighbors as excessively aloof and clannish.

Though American reactions to Japanese newcomers are usually cordial, some Japanese ways seem a bit too strange, enough to trigger the concern and reprimand of the local community. Japanese-style parenting sometimes involves locking misbehaving children outside the home to punish their selfish behavior. The miscreant offspring children outside the house begging his parents' forgiveness. Imported to the U.S., this technique has led well-intended neighbors to suspect child abuse. The resulting police intervention has proved very embarrassing for the authorities and most unsettling for the Japanese family.

There is also a less than admirable side of life in these communities. Public outbursts decrying Japanese corporate acquisitions and visible real estate purchases galvanize fears of economic takeover. Many people feel resentment about Japanese business prowess and its presumed impact on the lagging American economy.[9] Some express latent hostility to *any* Japanese presence in the U.S., vestiges of wartime animosity and pockets of racism.

To address these problems, and to build better relations with American people, Japanese firms now offer their own versions of corporate American "good citizenship" programs, offering generous gifts to many U.S. communities. Japanese are then shocked to find these philanthropic gestures sometimes disparaged in the American press, where cynics overlook the spirit of these acts and see them only as self-serving conduct.

## Business Practice

Americans react very emotionally to Japanese business practices. Over the years, some have felt annoyed and even deceived by vague Japanese communications, and others have felt frustrated and even manipulated by Japanese time-consuming decision making. These reactions once seemed warranted from an American perspective, but today they are regarded as unfortunate and inappropriate responses to the natural workings of Japanese organizations. Some U.S. subsidiaries now move quite nimbly, but in general, slowness to act is a natural consequence of the Japanese consensus-building process.

Sometimes, however, it signals a polite refusal. Japanese traditionally avoid offending others to almost any degree possible, even if that means skimping on the truth occasionally. Differences of opinion are usually downplayed to maintain good relations, often leaving associates without the whole story. Ironically, it is exactly this kind of conduct that makes Americans feel most offended or wronged.

Popular U.S. conceptions of Japanese business focus on overworked employees toiling away long after more family-minded Americans have headed home. Japanese do spend long hours at work, but largely out of work group devotion rather than blind ambition or fear of dismissal. Work relationships play a primary role in their lives. Forever attentive to their social obligations, they avoid being the first to break from the group at day's end. After-work soirées provide important opportunities to exchange information and nourish relationships. Americans have criticized Japanese "work obsession," and many Japanese firms are trying to modify their U.S. ways. Some distribute information to their U.S.-based Japanese employees on "enjoying a weekend, American-style." Some Japanese leaders even call for shorter work hours in Japan.[10]

Many Americans believe Japanese firms compete unfairly through their industrial groups.[11] Keiretsu members deal with each other extensively, reflecting the Japanese tendency to respect and honor long-established, trusted business relationships. Americans find fault with such cozy relations, and some get angry and demand market access. Ironically, their threats and arm-twisting create exactly the kind of tense emotional climate that is anathema to Japanese business relationships.

Japanese firms also appear to engage in the worst sorts of ethical violations: bribing officials, price fixing, paying off customers, and stealing industrial secrets. In Japan, such scandals routinely plague business as usual, for in some sense they are ill-fated extensions of traditional customs. Traditionally there were no "principles" that could not be compromised on occasion to build goodwill or maintain the group, even when moral issues might be involved.[12] The group's or leader's opinion more strongly influenced conduct than personal conscience. Individuals simply ignored their own ethical impulses for the sake of the group.[13] Depending on the situation, "bribery" and "pay offs" were justified to help solidify relationships; "rigged bidding" preserved interfirm harmony: "patent infringement" and "industrial espionage" protected a corporate group, or even the whole Japanese nation. However justified, such conduct today is roundly criticized in the industrialized world, and increasingly in Japan itself. Many Japanese now recognize that some of their traditional behavior patterns must be brought into alignment with Western ways if they are to be well received in international circles.[14]

Even so, Japanese feel jolted by American condemnation of Japanese political activities in the United States. In an effort to dissipate dark clouds of cultural misunderstanding, many Japanese feel they must make sincere efforts to educate American opinion makers and policymakers. Regrettably, these efforts are then sometimes denounced by American journalists and the public at large who condemn such attempts to influence officialdom.

## Organization Dynamics

The conflict between Japanese expatriate staff and local employees is actually the greatest concern Japanese managers face in globalizing their firms.[15] A closer look inside these firms shows why.

The career paths of Japanese managers typically build broad generalist perspectives rather than in-depth operational knowledge. As managers progress in their careers, they assume responsibility for tasks over which they have limited understanding and no direct experience. In Japan, such transitions rarely pose a problem since managers can rely confidently on a devoted and diligent staff in the new setting to, in effect, "run" the business.

In the U.S., the same kind of organization is not in place. Many American employees are accustomed to traditional top-down decision making where they expect the man or woman in charge to more or less "run the show" and "call the shots." In this context, Japanese executives' limited operational knowledge can be problematic, even embarrassing. Some of the most basic elements of American management experience are missing from their background. Most likely they have never acted decisively, never hired or fired anyone, never given frank performance reviews, never resolved internal disputes—all standard practice in the U.S. They are surely not familiar with the challenges of working with a racially and ethnically diverse workforce. These gaps produce many painful experiences. Senior Japanese executives sometimes make suggestions that their experienced American subordinates know to be incorrect or inappropriate.

Consensus decision making further exposes these gaps in experience. U.S. managers usually develop expertise in a functional area where they are granted autonomy to act decisively. Thus, when Americans join a Japanese management team, their contributions sometimes seem undervalued. They become just one voice in a group decision process, blending their advice with that of others who may have much less experience. Americans see this as a waste of time and talent.

In American eyes, most Japanese are not "hands on." They avoid accountability. No one wants to make a decision. They forever send faxes to and from Japan. Americans feel excluded from the closed inner circle of Japanese management. Sometimes their decisions are overturned by Japanese superiors. They feel stifled by the lack of personal challenge at work and frustrated by the ambiguity of their career path. One U.S. executive complained that promotions in his Japanese company are like "waiting for a subway door to open exactly where you are standing."[16]

Career-oriented Americans seek professional challenges and a chance to grow in their jobs, and they seek out organizations that provide that kind of opportunity. Japanese employees are accustomed to organizational life where people blend together in harmony. They serve collectively. Individual differences are suppressed and managers are punished for their errors. People are obedient to supervisors who care for them paternalistically. Promotions come in recognition of maturity. There is little room to express personal feelings or to search for personal challenge. In such a work environment, unfettered American career ambitions seem awkwardly out of place. It is hard to pursue the American dream inside a Japanese bureaucracy.

Some problems end up in court. Japanese are shocked by accusations of racial and gender discrimination filed by angry employees who demand their rights. At recent Congressional hearings, Japanese firms were blasted as "outrageous and disgusting" because they "flout our values and principles" by "violating our labor, civil rights, and nondiscriminational laws." Asking Japanese firms to offer in-house EEO training seminars "is like having Leona Helmsley instruct people on how to prepare a tax return. . . . We are opening up an ugly chapter in Japanese-American relations. It won't close until this discrimination ends."[17]

## Interpersonal Dealings

Japanese are further shocked by some American interpretations of their interpersonal encounters. Americans often feel offended by Japanese clannishness and apparent disdain. Yet this Japanese aloofness is partially a reaction to American assertiveness. That is, Americans in some sense induce or evoke from the Japanese the behavioral qualities they find least attractive. Consider the following.

Rigid social hierarchies play a prevailing role in Japanese society. Language richly affirms them through an elaborate system of verb conjugations that communicate distinctions of rank. Years of service within an organization usually mirror hierarchical position. Obedience to seniors helps maintain social order, and maintaining social order is of paramount importance.

Americans violate this order regularly. They routinely speak their minds and pursue personal agendas. To the Japanese, therefore, Americans generally seem to be noisy, disruptive, and confrontational, often airing views that are better left unsaid. Americans may even walk out the door at a moment's notice. Such conduct is acceptable—even entertaining—among Americans, but once Japanese enter the picture it becomes problematic. In Japanese minds, socially unruly Americans must be dealt with cautiously and sometimes excluded from the group altogether. Since they are non-Japanese, such arms-length treatment is acceptable in Japanese eyes. It takes a long time to develop trust with these foreigners.

Americans see the situation differently.[18] Some find the Japanese secretive, unwilling and unable to trust Americans. Others find them arrogant and conceited, quite willing to humiliate those of lower rank. Some get upset by the way Japanese hide their feelings and refrain from sharing personal thoughts. Japanese acquaintances seem overly cautious, and Japanese friends seem overly sensitive—too easily hurt by differences of opinion, and too fearful that disagreements will jeopardize friendships.

Most Japanese are probably unaware of these American perceptions. When they first learn of them, they are baffled and uncertain how to respond.

Integration shock, then, whether felt in communities, business dealings, organizations, or personal relationships, forms the second round of surprises Japanese face in America. Once they begin operating in this land of "foreigners," their well-entrenched values and behavior patterns listed on the left side of Exhibit 1 are often challenged and condemned as violations of American values and behaviors shown on the right.

Over time, Japanese visitors become more familiar with American ways. Events once shocking begin to lose potency. Japanese grow more accepting of America's great qualities, and some truly thrive in the new environment. America becomes a fertile ground for personal development. At some time in the future, however, when these individuals return home to Japanese society, they will most likely experience another painful and challenging transition. This readjustment to Japan is also worthy of study,[19] but we choose here to revisit Table 1 to suggest how Americans and Japanese can manage past their differences.

## Accepting Differences

Table 1's portrait of negative surprises provides a starting point for celebrating differences. Impression shock lists unattractive qualities of American life as seen through Japanese eyes. Integration shock underscores the unattractive qualities of Japanese life as seen through American eyes. Thus, Table 1 provides the "raw data" of Japanese and American mutual frustration. Brief summaries of their critiques follow.

In the eyes of the Japanese, American society is chaotic and dangerous. Communal problems are hard to manage and too often neglected. American businesses are too quick to act and too changeable to build trust. American organizations are fraught with dissension stirred up by self-seeking careerists. American people are too blunt and aggressive and disrespectful of authority.

Japanese society, on the other hand, appears to Americans to be closed to outsiders and bent on common missions. Japanese businesses are slow-moving and unfair because questionable practices cement interlocked relationships. Japanese organizations are oppressive and abusive and obsessed with saving face. Japanese people are timid, risk averse, and too easily embarrassed.

Confusion occurs when these different sets of socially sanctioned behaviors, each with considerable social utility in its own society, come together in the same work setting. As Exhibit 1 suggests, the conflicts inherent in American-Japanese cross-cultural encounters might be viewed as a clash of social ideals. In effect, when Americans and Japanese meet each other in work settings, they unwittingly offend each other's most sacred social principles.

The situation need not remain a standoff. People can learn to understand each other and appreciate enough of the fine points of the other culture to make room for its ideals in their professional lives. Americans can take steps to show respect and appreciation for the ideals of harmony, patience, and hierarchy in the workplace. Likewise, Japanese can take steps to show respect and appreciation for the ideals of freedom, action, and equality in the workplace. By modifying some routine behaviors to show courtesy and respect for the concerns of the other culture, people can develop cross-cultural associations that are more comfortable and effective.[20]

The recurring problems of cross-cultural encounters are seen daily by human resources professionals inside American subsidiaries of Japanese firms. The wisdom of one deserves our attention: "Most anger and frustration evolves more from misunderstandings and/or cultural differences than poor intent or indifference. Neither Americans nor Japanese can force a 'be like me' strategy. Cooperation and respect must prevail in the end."[21]

## Moving Forward

Americans who have lived their lives immersed in American society should now develop appreciation for life lived another way. They should discover what it is like to be part of a system where work and careers derive meaning from a different set of ideals than the ones that have patterned their lives. Armed with that awareness, Americans might review their customary ways to reassess the effectiveness in international dealings. Interactions with Japanese professionals demonstrate all too clearly that some American cultural norms produce displays of behavior that in Japanese eyes are totally socially unacceptable.

Americans should explore ways to broaden their repertoire to incorporate conduct that appears less offensive to Japanese people, which will also appeal less trying to those others who have begun to embrace Japanese ways. In particular, American bluntness, assertiveness, and self-righteousness should be reined in to win friends and influence people from some other cultural backgrounds. With a willful spirit, most Americans are capable of modifying this conduct. They are especially qualified to "engineer" such changes: Yankee ingenuity, openness, and improvisational talents are invaluable assets for making adjustments to overseas encounters. Numerous American firms, such as Apple Computers, have learned to tailor their ways to operate in Japan.[22]

Similarly, as Japanese expand their role in global commerce, finance, and diplomacy, they are becoming increasingly aware of the need to adjust their ways to work with people from other nations. "The global manager operates as an 'insider' in every market."[23] But that requires competence at business practices found outside Japan and, as the traumas described above clearly demonstrate, developing that competence can be difficult and painful.

Japanese corporate chieftains are now increasingly outspoken about the steps Japanese should take to respond to foreign criticism. They call for nontraditional forms of conduct to conform to the demands of overseas partners. If and when put into practice, their words are most welcome. But then are additional changes that might be encouraged, ones that extend the current fashionable idea of kyosei, or symbiosis. ". . . Normally complacent, the Japanese go to the other extreme of overaccommodation whenever criticism becomes too loud to ignore. . . . We try too hard to calm down others' anger, rather than solve the underlying problems."[24] A better approach would see Japanese adjust their ways to welcome and accommodate others, while learning to play a new leadership role in shaping the conduct of others. By encouraging more spiritual-mindedness and harmonious dealings in the workplace, Japanese can team up with people from other cultures while promoting accommodation to Japanese social ideals. In that way, just as Americans take a stand for freedom on the world stage, Japanese can become champions of social harmony, spreading that gospel among their foreign associates.

## Conclusion

At a time when the American and Japanese economies are increasingly interlinked, little is served by a rise of xenophobia in either country. Trade imbalances may raise concerns that warrant business cooperation and joint government intervention across the Pacific, but the accompanying acrimony heard on both sides is ill-considered and terribly incendiary. It is hoped that this examination of American and Japanese culturally bred differences—seen from the viewpoint of the Japanese newcomer—will make people more aware and respectful of systemic differences and prevent their being hoodwinked by negative passions.

Most important, it is time for Americans to end the conversation of resentment. Negative mental habits beget negative results. It is unfair to condemn the Japanese for being unfair if they really harbor no unfair intentions. If they are just being Japanese—complying with the social tenets of their society that regrettably inadvertently smell of "foul play"—then Americans should not rush to become confrontational. They should instead explain and encourage all necessary adjustments in the U.S. arena, maintaining goodwill toward Japanese associates throughout their rocky effort to learn American ways.

Similarly, in international settings, when questions arise over rules of trade, negotiators should consider using Japanese-style harmonious relations to move all parties towards mutual accommodation. Contentious issues should be resolved while working to nurture relationships; opponents should see themselves as partners in search of common long-term benefits. Action-oriented, American-style threats and deadlines are often not the best option. Overseas partners find them annoying and short-sighted, and Americans risk squandering their hard-earned goodwill.

One thing is clear. In the words of Akio Morita, chairman of Sony, "both Americans and Japanese are being denied the benefits that could be gained from our unique and complementary relationship because it is fraught with political posturing and suspicion. This is a loss for our two countries, certainly, but even more, it is a loss for the world. . . . Japan is committed to a genuine partnership with the United States—one that has real, tangible benefits for both sides. . . . Our goals are to cooperate and to gain and grow together."[25] To this, the chairman of Mitsubishi Electronics adds, "the cultural and social distance between Americans and Japanese remains huge, [but] it needn't be. . . . Americans and Japanese need to do more together. . . . Business relations [can grow. We must] aim for the highest goals and reach them one [step] at a time."[26]

A Final Word

What became of Mr. Kusumoto? After his initial, painful adjustment period, he learned to appreciate his life in America. He grew to enjoy its freedoms and spontaneity and love its spacious homes and gracious neighborhoods. He came to admire America's tolerance and even demand for independence in nearly all walks of life, and he now cherishes opportunities to act that way himself. In the office, he encourages subordinates to take bold initiatives, and he counts among his inner circle a few talented, modest Americans. In the community, he speaks out on matters that touch his interests and immerses himself in local affairs.[27] In modern parlance, Akiro Kusumoto came to America and "cut loose." Rumor has it he even joined a neighborhood amateur theatre group.

One hopes that he now displays the courage and confidence to share with others the social wisdom long developed in his native land. For if he can breed among his American colleagues the kind of mutually supportive, cooperative spirit so devoutly nurtured in Japanese organizations, then his U.S. sojourn will do more than just advance his business interests. He will make a social contribution to all those he meets, demonstrating the sense of peace and security that can be found in a network of harmonious relationships. In that way, he can inspire us to enrich our workplaces, our families, and our communities—even encourage us to strive more fervently to manage the world harmoniously. This then might become the real Japanese legacy.

## Notes

1. David E. Sanger, "Gloom Lifts in U.S. and Falls on Japan." *New York Times,* December 29, 1992, A4.

2. Tomasz Mroczkowski, Richard G. Linowes, and Masao Hanaoka, "Working for the Japanese Corporation: The View of American Professionals," in Anant R. Negandhi and Manuel G. Serapio, Jr. (eds.), *Japanese Direct Investments in the United States: Trends, Development, and Issues* (Greenwich, CT: JAI Press, 1992), 287–307. A brief summary appears in the article by Mroczkowski and Linowes entitled "Inside the Japanese Corporation Abroad: Views of American Professionals." in the autumn 1990 issue of *Management Japan* (Vol. 23, No. 2), 28–30. The study involved interviews with American and Japanese senior executives of Japanese firms in both the U.S. and Japan, and a survey of their American professional employees in the U.S.

3. References that support the contrasts noted in the figure include the following: Edwin O. Reischauer, *The Japanese Today* (Cambridge, MA: Harvard University Press, 1988); Takeo Doi, *The Anatomy of Self: the Individual Versus Society* (Tokyo: Kodansha International, 1986); Chie Nakane, *Japanese Society* (Berkeley, CA: University of California, 1970); E. Ohnuki-Tierney, *The Monkey as Mirror: Symbolic Transformations in Japanese History and Ritual* (Princeton, NJ: Princeton University Press, 1987); Thomas P. Rohlen, *For Harmony and Strength: Japanese White-collar Organization in Anthropological Perspective* (Berkeley, CA: University of California Press, 1974); Mark E. Mendenhall and Gary Oddou, "The Cognitive, Psychological and Social Contexts of Japanese Management," *Asia Pacific Journal of Management,* Vol. 4, No. 1, September 1986, 24–37; Robert C. Christopher, *The Japanese Mind: The Goliath Explained* (New York, NY: Simon & Schuster, 1983); Edward T. Hall and M. Hall, *Hidden Differences: Doing Business with the Japanese* (New York, NY: Prentice-Hall, 1988); Mark A. Zimmerman, *Dealing with the Japanese* (New York, NY: Random House, 1985); John C. Condon, *With Respect to the Japanese: A Guide for Americans* (Yarmouth, ME: Intercultural Press, 1984); Dean C. Barnlund, *Communicative Styles of Japanese and Americans: Images and Realities* (Belmont, CA: Wadsworth Publishing Company, 1989).

4. Richard Meyer, "Inside the World's Most Powerful Bank," *Financial World,* Vol. 160, No. 9, April 30, 1991, 36.

5. For those preferring fictional accounts, an interesting short story about a Japanese businessman in California appeared in *Made in Japan and other Japanese "Business Novels,"* edited by Tamae K. Prindle (Armonk, NY: M.E. Sharpe, 1990).

6. This incident was reported in "Executive Lived in Fear," *The Washington Post,* February 27, 1992, A16. On Halloween that same year a Japanese teenager was killed when he failed to understand the English expression "Freeze!" while walking from house to house for trick-or-treat. See T.R. Reid, Journey Into Fear: Japanese Courses Teach Travelers How to Guard Against U.S. Crime," *The Washington Post,* December 19, 1992, Al, A12. In a follow-up article, a Japanese professor claimed that "Americans spend their lives full of anger and fear," while another compared American

suburbs to war zones in Third World countries. A well-known Japanese television commentator said "Japan has always looked up to America. But now, which society is more mature? The idea that you protect people by shooting guns is barbarian." See T.R. Reid, "Japanese Medic Disparage Acquittal in 'Freeze Case,'" *The Washington Post,* May 25, 1993, A14.

7. "There are the Anglo-Saxons, who cut deals with anyone on a moment's notice and use a room full of lawyers to protect themselves. Then there are the Germans, Japanese, and others who do business only with people they know," noted the chairman of Industrial Bank Japan, in Meyer, *op. cit.,* 36.

8. Condon, *op. cit.,* 24.

9. See, for example, Frederick Rose, "Made in America: How a U.S. Company Used Anti-Japan Mood to Help Reverse a Loss," *The Wall Street Journal,* April 22, 1992, Al, A6. Some of these attitudes are expressed clearly in the popular murder mystery *Rising Sun* by Michael Crichton (New York, NY: Ballantine Books, 1992).

10. See J. Nemoto, Y. Tanaka, E. Washio, K. Yamamoto, and T. Ohio, "Seeking a Better Balance Between Leisure and Work" and other articles in a special issue on the topic "Working in Japan" in *Economic Eye,* 13 (1), Spring 1992. Also, Yumiko Ono and Jacob M. Schlesinger, "Land of Rising Fun: With Careful Planning, Japan Sets Out to Be Life Style Superpower." *The Wall Street Journal,* October 2, 1992, Al, A10. Dramatic pictures of this new lifestyle orientation can be found in Richard Phalon, "Enjoy, Enjoy!" *Forbes,* December 12, 1988, 144–5, 14B, 150; and Howard G. Chua-Eoan, "Welcome to the Great Indoors: The Japanese Slave Away on Enclosed Beaches and Slopes" *Time,* August 2, 1993, 46–47.

11. An informed but critical look is presented in K.M. Chrysler's "Master of the Game: Business by Whose Rules?—Japan's Inimitable *Keiretsu,*" *The Journal of the American Chamber of Commerce in Japan,* July 1991, 11–18. Forty percent of Americans think the Japanese compete unfairly with their American counterparts, while seventeen percent of Japanese hold the same opinion, according to the survey cited in Sanger, *op. cit.* But *keiretsu* restrict access for Japanese companies, as well. See Kuniyasu Sakai, "The Feudal World of Japanese Manufacturing," *Harvard Business Review,* Vol. 68, No. 6, November-December 1990, 38–49.

12. Chie Nakane, *op. cit.*

13. Such ethical issues were clearly discussed in the roundtable discussion "When Will the Individual Come First?" *Japan Update,* February 1992, 20–23.

14. Takashi Oka, "Japan's Own Version of Glasnost" (*The Christian Science Monitor,* August 9, 1991, 18) reported there is "wide agreement on the direction in which Japan must go: a fairer, more transparent society, a society ruled by laws applicable to all and not by a government of winks and nods." This is signaled clearly by the prestigious Japanese business association's recent "Keidanren Charter for Good Corporate Behavior" specifying principles of good corporate conduct. "So as not to give grounds for the criticism that Japanese business practices are exclusionary and opaque, it is urgent for us to work to achieve a free, transparent, fair market and establish international confidence in Japan's economic system." (*Keidanren Review,* No. 132, December 1991, 2–3). This charter followed their "Keidanren Resolution: Our Determination to Live with the World," which stated: "It is feared that the conduct of Japan's economic activities in the future could meet with unwanted friction, even to the detriment of our national aspiration to win an honorable place as a trusted and respected member of the international community." (*Keidanren Review,* No. 130, August 1991, 5–7). The chairman of the Keidanren recently added: "The scandals have given . . . foreign countries the impression that a structure of mutual dependence or unfairness is deeply imbedded in Japan's market economy. This is indeed a matter of great regret. . . . Economic activities based not on fair rules but on Japanese customs and practices . . . no longer hold water even in Japan." ("Establishment of a New Code of Ethics," in *Keidanren Review,* No. 131, October 1991, 2).

15. "Labor Letter," *The Wall Street Journal,* November 24, 1992, Al.

16. Mroczkowski et al., *op. cit.*

17. Quotations from Congressman Lantos in "House Hearing Probes of Discrimination Against Americans at Japanese-Owned Firms." *BNA International Business Daily*, No. 142, July 24, 1991. A-4.

18. Mroczkowski et al., *op. cit.*

19. Merry I. White, *Japanese Overseers: Can They Go Home Again?* (New York, NY: Free Press, 1988).

20. For a framework for building such cooperative relationships, see Richard G. Linowes, "The Design of American and Japanese Bicultural Work Teams," Best Paper Proceedings of the Sixth Annual Meeting of the Association for Japanese Business Studies, January 1993, 77–88.

21. Mroczkowski, et al., *op. cit.* Other works examining the cultural clash inside the U.S. subsidiaries of Japanese firms include Jeremiah J. Sullivan, *Invasion of the Salarymen*: *The Japanese*

*Business Presence in America* (Westport, CT: Praeger, 1992); Dennis Laurie, *Yankee Samurai: American Managers Speak Out About What It's Like to Work for Japanese Companies in the U.S.* (New York, NY: Harper Business, 1992); Alison R. Lanier, *The Raising Sun on Main Street: Working with the Japanese* (2nd edition) (Glendale, IL: Irwin, 1992) and Robert M. March, *Working for a Japanese Company: Insights into the Multicultural Workplace* (Tokyo: Kodansha International, 1992). Some interesting management lessons to be learned from experience with a Japanese firm are described in John E. Rehfeld, "What Working for a Japanese Company Taught Me," *Harvard Business Review*, Vol. 68, No. 6, November-December 1990, 167–176.

22. Edward W. Desmond, "Byting Japan," *Time*, October 5, 1992, 68, 69. Case studies of American assimilation into Japanese companies in Japan can be found in Patricia Gercik, *On Track with the Japanese: A Case-by-Case Approach to Building Successful Relationships* (Tokyo: Kodansha, 1992).

23. Kenichi Ohmae, "Managing in a Borderless World." *Harvard Business Review*, Vol. 67, No. 3, May-June 1989, 152.

24. Kenichi Ohmae, "Japan's Role in the World Economy: A New Appraisal." *California Management Review*, Vol. 29, No. 3, Spring 1987, 47.

25. Akio Morita, "Partnering for Competitiveness: The Role of Japanese Business." *Harvard Business Review*, Vol. 70, No. 3, May-June 1992, 77, 78, 83.

26. Tachi Kiuchi, chairman and CEO of Mitsubishi Electronics America, in his letter to the editor, "How Japanese Can Speak to Americans," *The Wall Street Journal*, March 4, 1992, A16. The Chairman of the Keidanren asserts that Japan and the United States must be linked not through a common threat, but through common aspirations and dreams. Let us both ask what we can do for the world. Then, let us join forces and work to reach our goals." (Gaishi Hiraiwa, "The World in Flux and Japan's Course in the Future." *Keidanren Review*, No. 140, June 1993, 1, 3–7). President Clinton remarked in Japan that "the post-Cold War relationship between our two nations is one of the great success stories of the latter half of the 20th Century. We have built a vital friendship . . . Our first international economic priority must be to create a new and stronger partnership between the United States and Japan." ("The Changes I Advocate Will Benefit Both of Us." *The Washington Post*, July 8, 1993, A14).

27. A recent American-style cultural event was produced in suburban New York. See Roberta Hershenson, "Scarsdale Japan Festival to Bridge East and West." *The New York Times*, January 17, 1993, Westchester Section, 6–8. The event's organizer described his life in the United States as "fantastic and . . . fabulous. There is nothing to compare it with anywhere in the world." See Louise Wollman, "Scarsdale Says 'Sanyonara' to Matsuo. A Brief Stay (24 Years) and Back to Japan." *The Scarsdale Inquirer*, July 9, 1993, 1, 5.

# Reading 1.6

# BEYOND SOPHISTICATED STEREOTYPING

## *Cultural Sensemaking in Context*

JOYCE S. OSLAND AND ALLAN BIRD

**Executive Overview**

Much of our cross-cultural training and research occurs within the framework of bipolar cultural dimensions. While this sophisticated stereotyping is helpful to a certain degree, it does not convey the complexity found within cultures. People working across cultures are frequently surprised by cultural paradoxes that do not seem to fit the descriptions they have learned. The authors identify the sources of cultural paradoxes and introduce the idea of value trumping. In a specific context, certain cultural values take precedence over others. Thus, culture is embedded in the context and cannot be understood fully without taking context into consideration. To decipher cultural paradoxes, the authors propose a model of cultural sensemaking, linking schemas to contexts. They spell out the implications of this model for those who teach culture, for people working across cultures, and for multinational corporations.

If U.S. Americans are so individualistic and believe so deeply in self-reliance, why do they have the highest percentage of charitable giving in the world and readily volunteer their help to community projects and emergencies?

In a 1991 survey, many Costa Rican customers preferred automatic tellers over human tellers because "at least the machines are programmed to say 'good morning' and 'thank you.'"[1] Why is it that so many Latin American cultures are noted for warm interpersonal relationships and a cultural script of *simpatia* (positive social behavior),[2] while simultaneously exhibiting seeming indifference as service workers in both the private and public sectors?

Based on Hofstede's[3] value dimension of Uncertainty Avoidance, the Japanese have a low tolerance for uncertainty while Americans have a high tolerance. Why then do the Japanese intentionally incorporate ambiguous clauses in their business contracts, which are unusually short, while Americans dot every i, cross every t, and painstakingly spell out every possible contingency?

Many people trained to work in these cultures found such situations to be paradoxical when they first encountered them. These examples often contradict and confound our attempts to neatly categorize cultures. They violate our conceptions of what we think particular cultures are like. Constrained, stereotypical thinking is not the only problem, however. The more exposure and understanding one gains about any culture, the more paradoxical it often becomes. For example, U.S. Americans are individualistic in some situations (e.g., "the most comprehensive of rights and the right most valued is the right to be left alone"[4]) and collectivist in others (e.g., school fundraising events).

Long-term sojourners and serious cultural scholars find it difficult to make useful generalizations since so many exceptions and qualifications to the stereotypes, on both a cultural and individual level, come to mind. These cultural paradoxes are defined as situations that exhibit an apparently contradictory nature.

Surprisingly, there is little mention of cultural paradoxes in the management literature.[5] Our long-term sojourns as expatriates (a combined total of 22 years), as well as our experience in teaching cross-cultural management, preparing expatriates to go overseas, and doing comparative research, has led us to feel increasingly frustrated with the accepted conceptualizations of culture. Thus, our purpose is to focus attention on cultural paradoxes, explain why they have been overlooked and why they exist, and present a framework for making sense of them. Our intent is to initiate a dialogue that will eventually provide teachers, researchers, and people who work across cultures with a more useful way to understand culture.

A look at the comparative literature reveals that cultures are described in somewhat limited terms.[6] There are 22 dimensions commonly used to compare cultures, typically presented in the form of bipolar continua, with midpoints in the first examples, as shown in Table 1. These dimensions were developed to yield greater cultural understanding and allow for cross-cultural comparisons. An unanticipated consequence of using these dimensions, however, is the danger of stereotyping entire cultures.

## Sophisticated Stereotyping

In many parts of the world, one hears a generic stereotype for a disliked neighboring ethnic group—"The (fill in the blank) are lazy, dirty thieves, and their women are promiscuous." This is a low-level form of stereotyping, often based on lack of personal contact and an irrational dislike of people who are different from oneself. Professors and trainers work very hard to dispel such stereotypes. Rarely, however, do we stop to consider whether we are supplanting one form of stereotyping for another. For example, when we teach students and managers how to perceive the Israelis using Hofstede's[7] cultural dimensions, they may come to think of Israelis in terms of small power distance, strong uncertainty avoidance, moderate femininity, and moderate individualism. The result is to reduce a complex culture to a shorthand description they may be tempted to apply to all Israelis. We call this sophisticated stereotyping, because it is based on theoretical concepts and lacks the negative attributions often associated with its lower-level counterpart. Nevertheless, it is still limiting in the way it constrains individuals' perceptions of behavior in another culture.

Do we recommend against teaching the cultural dimensions shown in Table 1 so as to avoid sophisticated stereotyping? Not at all. These dimensions are useful tools in explaining cultural behavior. Indeed, cultural stereotypes can be helpful—provided we acknowledge their limitations. They are more beneficial, for example, in making comparisons between cultures than in understanding the wide variations of behavior within a single culture. Adler[8] encourages the use of "helpful stereotypes," which have the following limitations: They are consciously held, descriptive rather than evaluative, accurate in their description of a behavioral norm, the first best guess about a group prior to having direct information about the specific people involved, and modified based on further observations and experience. As teachers, researchers, and managers in cross-cultural contexts, we need to recognize that our original characterizations of other cultures are best guesses that we need to modify as we gain more experience.

For understandable, systemic reasons, business schools tend to teach culture in simple-minded terms, glossing over nuances and ignoring complexities. An examination of the latest crop of organizational behavior and international business textbooks revealed that most authors present only Hofstede's cultural dimensions, occasionally supplemented by Hall's theory of high- and low-context cultures.[9] Although these disciplines are not charged with the responsibility of teaching culture in great depth, these are the principal courses in many curricula where business students are exposed to cross-cultural concepts. Another handicap is that many business professors do not receive a thorough grounding in culture in their own disciplines and doctoral programs. One could further argue that we are joined in this conspiracy to give culture a quick-and-dirty treatment by practitioners and students who are looking for ways to simplify and make sense of the world.

The limitations of sophisticated stereotyping become most evident when we confront cultural paradoxes. This is the moment we realize our understanding is incomplete, misleading, and potentially dangerous. Perhaps because cultural paradoxes reveal the limitations in our thinking, they are often left unmentioned, even though virtually anyone with

**Table 1** Common Cultural Dimensions

| | | |
|---|---|---|
| Subjugation to nature | Harmony | Mastery of nature |
| Past | Present | Future |
| Being | Containing and controlling | Doing |
| Hierarchical relationships | Group | Individualistic |
| Private space | Mixed | Public |
| Evil human nature | Neutral or mixed | Good |
| Human nature as changeable | | Human nature as unchangeable |
| Monochronic time | | Polychronic time |
| High-context language | | Low-context language |
| Low uncertainty avoidance | | High uncertainty avoidance |
| Low power distance | | High power distance |
| Short-term orientation | | Long-term orientation |
| Individualism | | Collectivism |
| Masculinity | | Femininity |
| Universalism | | Particularism |
| Neutral | | Emotional |
| Diffuse | | Specific |
| Achievement | | Ascription |
| Individualism | | Organization |
| Inner-directed | | Outer-directed |
| Individualism (competition) | | Group-organization (collusion) |
| Analyzing (reductivist) | | Synthesizing (larger, integrated wholes) |

SOURCE: Academy of Management Executive by Osland, J.S., & Bird, A. Copyright 2000 by Academy of Management. Reproduced with permission of Academy of Management via Copyright Clearance Center.

experience in another culture can usually identify one or two after only a moment's reflection.

## Why Don't We Know More About Cultural Paradoxes?

With one exception,[10] the cross-cultural literature contains no mention or explanation of cultural paradoxes. This absence can be explained by:

- Homegrown perceptual schemas that result in cultural myopia
- Lack of cultural experience that leads to misinterpretation and failure to comprehend the entire picture
- Cultural learning that plateaus before complete understanding is achieved
- Western dualism that generates theories with no room for paradox or holistic maps
- Features of cross-cultural research that encourage simplicity over complexity
- A between-culture research approach that is less likely to capture cultural paradoxes than a within-culture approach.

### Perceptual Schemas

When outsiders look at another culture, they inevitably interpret its institutions and customs using their own lenses and schemas; cultural myopia and lack of experience prevent them from seeing all the nuances of another culture.

In particular, a lack of experience with the new culture creates difficulties for new expatriates trying to make sense of what they encounter. The situation is analogous to putting together a jigsaw puzzle. Though one may have the picture on the puzzle box as a guide, making sense of each individual piece and understanding where and how it fits is exceedingly difficult. As more pieces are put into place, however, it is easier to see the bigger picture and understand how individual pieces mesh. Similarly, as one acquires more and varied experiences in the new culture, one can develop an appreciation for how certain attitudes and behaviors fit the puzzle and create an internal logic of the new culture.

The danger with sophisticated stereotyping is that it may lead individuals to think that the number of shapes that pieces may take is limited and that pieces fit together rather easily. As Barnlund notes:

"Rarely do the descriptions of a political structure or religious faith explain precisely when and why certain topics are avoided or why specific gestures carry such radically different meanings according to the context in which they appear."[11]

Expatriates and researchers alike tend to focus first on cultural differences and make initial conclusions that are not always modified in light of subsequent evidence.[12] Proactive learning about another culture often stops once a survival threshold is attained, perhaps because of an instinctive inclination to simplify a complex world. This may lead us to seek black-and-white answers rather than tolerate the continued ambiguity that typifies a more complete understanding of another culture.

One of the best descriptions of the peeling away of layers that characterizes deeper cultural understanding is found in a fictionalized account of expatriate life written by an expatriate manager, Robert Collins.[13] He outlines ascending levels on a Westerner's perception scale of Japanese culture that alternate, in daisy-petal-plucking fashion, between seeing the Japanese as significantly different or not really that different at all:

The initial Level on a Westerner's perception scale clearly indicates a "difference" of great significance. The Japanese speak a language unlike any other human tongue . . . they write the language in symbols that reason alone cannot decipher. The airport customs officers all wear neckties, everyone is in a hurry, and there are long lines everywhere.

Level Two is represented by the sudden awareness that the Japanese are not different at all. Not at all. They ride in elevators, have a dynamic industrial/trade/financial system, own great chunks of the United States, and serve Cornflakes in the Hotel Okura.

Level Three is the "hey, wait a minute" stage. The Japanese come to all the meetings, smile politely, nod in agreement with everything said, but do the opposite of what's expected. And they do it all together. They really are different.

But are they? Level Four understanding recognizes the strong group dynamics, common education and training, and the general sense of loyalty to the family—which in their case is Japan itself. That's not so unusual, things are just organized on a larger scale than any social unit in the West. Nothing is fundamentally different.

Level Five can blow one's mind, however. Bank presidents skipping through streets dressed as dragons at festival time; single ladies placing garlands of flowers around huge, and remarkably graphic, stone phallic symbols; Ministry of Finance officials rearranging their bedrooms so as to sleep in a "lucky" direction; it is all somewhat odd. At least, by Western standards. There is something different in the air.

And so on. Some Westerners, the old Japan hands, have gotten as far as Levels 37 or 38.[14]

The point of Collins's description is that it takes time and experience to make sense of another culture. The various levels he describes reflect differing levels of awareness as more and more pieces of the puzzle are put into place. Time and experience are essential because culture is embedded in the context. Without context it makes little sense to talk about culture. Yet just as its lower-order counterpart does, sophisticated stereotyping tends to strip away or ignore context. Thus, cognitive schemas prevent sojourners and researchers from seeing and correctly interpreting paradoxical behavior outside their own cultures.

## Theoretical Limitations

Another reason for the inattention to cultural paradoxes stems from the intersection between cognitive schemas and theory. Westerners have a tendency to perceive stimuli in terms of dichotomies and dualisms rather than paradoxes or holistic pictures.[15] The idea of paradox is a fairly recent wrinkle on the intellectual landscape of management theorists[16] and has not yet been incorporated into cultural theories in a managerial context.

Cross-cultural research is generally held to be more difficult than domestic studies. Hofstede's[17] work represented a major step forward and launched a deluge of studies utilizing his dimensions. Hundreds of studies have used one or more of Hofstede's dimensions to explore similarities and differences across cultures regarding numerous aspects of business and management. However, Hofstede himself warned against expecting too much of these dimensions and of using them incorrectly. For example, he defended the individualism-collectivism dimension as a useful construct, but then went on to say: "This does not mean, of course, that a country's Individual Index score tells all there is to be known about the backgrounds and structure of relationship patterns in that country. It is an abstraction that should not be extended beyond its limited area of usefulness."[18]

When we fail to specify under what conditions a culture measures low or high on any of the common cultural dimensions, or to take into consideration the impact of organizational culture, it misleads rather than increases our understanding of comparisons of culture and business practices. Such an approach prevents rather than opens up opportunities for learning and exploration.

A final explanation for the failure to address cultural paradoxes can be traced to the emic/etic distinction commonly used in the cultural literature. An emic perspective looks at a culture from within its boundaries, whereas an etic perspective stands outside and compares two or more cultures. To make between-culture differences more prominent, the etic approach minimizes the inconsistencies within a culture. Most cultural approaches in management adopt a between-culture approach, playing down the within-culture differences that expatriates must understand in order to work successfully in the host country.

Anthropologist Claude Levi-Strauss warned that explanation does not consist of reducing the complex to the simple, but of substituting a more intelligible complexity for one that is less intelligible.[19] In failing to acknowledge cultural paradoxes or the complexity surrounding cultural dimensions, we may settle for simplistic, rather than intelligently complex, explanations.

## Sources of Paradox in Cultural Behavior

Behavior that looks paradoxical to an expatriate in the initial stages of cultural awareness may simply reflect the variance in behavioral norms for individuals, organizational cultures, subcultures, as well as generational differences and changing sections of the society. In addition, expatriates may also form microcultures[20] with specific members of the host culture. The cultural synergy of such microcultures may not be reflective of the national culture. These false paradoxes need to be discarded before more substantive paradoxes can be evaluated.

Based on an analysis of all the paradoxes we could find, we have identified six possible explanations for cultural behaviors that appear truly paradoxical. They are:

- The tendency for observers to confuse individual with group values
- Unresolved cultural issues
- Bipolar patterns
- Role differences
- Real versus espoused values
- Value trumping, a recognition that in specific contexts certain sets of values take precedence over others

Confusing individual with group values is exemplified by the personality dimension labeled allocentrism versus idiocentrism, which is the psychological, individual-level analog to the individualism-collectivism dimension at the level of culture.[21] Allocentric people, those who pay primary attention to the needs of a group, can be found in individualistic cultures, and idiocentric people, those who pay more attention to their own needs than to the needs of others, in collectivist cultures. What we perceive as cultural paradox may not reflect contradictions in cultural values, but instead may reveal the natural diversity within any culture that reflects individual personality and variation.

Unresolved cultural issues are rooted in the definition of culture as a learned response to problems. Some paradoxes come from problems for which there is no clear, happy solution. Cultures may manifest a split personality with regard to an unresolved problem.[22] As a result, they shuttle back and forth from one extreme to the other on a behavioral continuum. U.S. Americans, for example, have ambivalent views about sex, and, as one journalist recently noted: "Our society is a stew of prurience and prudery."[23] Censorship, fears about sex education, and sexual taboos coexist uncomfortably with increasingly graphic films and TV shows and women's magazines that never go to press without a feature article devoted to sex. This melange is more than a reflection of a diverse society that has both hedonists and fundamentalists with differing views of sex; both groups manifest inconsistent behaviors and attitudes about sex, signaling an enduring cultural inability to resolve this issue.

Bipolar patterns make cultural behavior appear paradoxical because cultural dimensions are often framed, perhaps inaccurately, as dualistic, either-or continua. Cultures frequently exhibit one of these paired dimensions more than the other, but it is probable that both ends of the dimensions are found in cultures—but only in particular contexts. For example, in Latin America, ascribed status, derived from class and family background, is more important than its polar opposite, achieved status, which is based on talent and hard work. When it comes to professional soccer, however, achieved status trumps class and ascription.

Often some groups and roles appear to deviate from cultural stereotypes. For example, in the United States, autocratic behavior is frequently tolerated in CEOs, even though the United States is characterized as an egalitarian culture. Such behavior may also be an example of a high power distance context in a low power distance culture: We accept that CEOs possess an unequal degree of power and that they will behave in a different manner than most U.S. Americans.

There is also a difference between real versus espoused values. All cultures express preferences

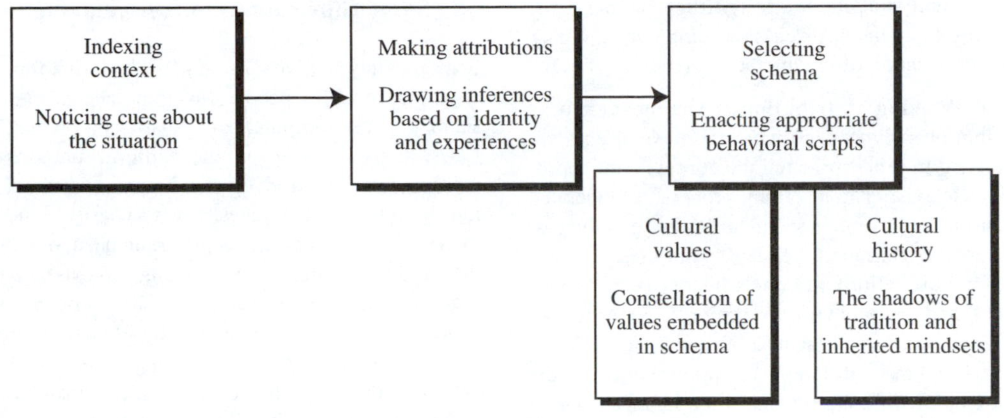


**Figure 1** Cultural Sensemaking Model

SOURCE: Academy of Management Executive by Osland, J.S., & Bird, A. Copyright 2000 by Academy of Management. Reproduced with permission of Academy of Management via Copyright Clearance Center.

for ideal behaviors—for what should be valued and how people should act. Nevertheless, people do not always act consistently with ideal behaviors and values. For example, U.S. Americans may simultaneously pay lip service to the importance of equality (an espoused value), while trying to acquire more power or influence for themselves (a real value).

A final possible explanation of cultural paradoxes derives from a holistic, contextual view of culture in which values co-exist as a constellation, but their salience differs depending on the situation. Using the Gestalt concept of figure-ground, at times a particular value becomes dominant (figure), while in other circumstances, this same value recedes into the background (ground).[24] In India, for example, collectivism is figural when individuals are expected to make sacrifices for their families or for the larger society—such as Hindu sons who postpone marriage until their sisters marry, or daughters who stay single to care for their parents. In other circumstances, however, collectivism fades into the background and individualism comes to the fore and is figural when Indians focus more upon self-realization—for example, elderly men who detach themselves from their family to seek salvation.[25] Taking the figure-ground analogy a step further, depending on the context, one cultural value might trump another, lessening the influence another value normally exerts.[26] For example, we find it useful to view culture as a series of card games in which cultural values or dimensions are individual cards. Depending on the game, previous play, and the hand one is dealt, players respond by choosing specific cards that seem most appropriate in a given situation. Sometimes a particular card trumps the others; in another round, it does not. In a given context, specific cultural values come into play and have more importance than other values. To a foreigner who does not understand enough about the cultural context to interpret why or when one value takes precedence over another, such behavior looks paradoxical. Members of the culture learn these nuances more or less automatically. For example, children learn in what context a socially acceptable white lie is more important than always telling the truth. A true understanding of the logic of another culture includes comprehending the interrelationships among values, or how values relate to one another in a given context.

## A Model of Cultural Sensemaking

To make sense of cultural paradoxes and convey a holistic understanding of culture, we propose a model of cultural sensemaking. The model shown in Figure 1 helps explain how culture is embedded in context.[27]

Cultural sensemaking is a cycle of sequential events:

- **Indexing Context.** The process begins when an individual identifies a context and then engages in indexing behavior, which involves noticing or attending to stimuli that provide cues about the situation. For example, to index the context of a meeting with a subordinate, we consider characteristics such as prior events (recent extensive layoffs), the nature of the boss-subordinate relationship within and without work (golfing partner), the specific topic under discussion (employee morale), and the location of the interaction (boss's office).

• **Making Attributions.** The next step is attribution, a process in which contextual cues are analyzed in order to match the context with appropriate schema. The matching process is moderated or influenced by one's social identity (e.g., ethnic or religious background, gender, social class, organizational affiliation) and one's history (e.g., experiences and chronology). A senior U.S. American manager who fought against the Japanese in World War II will make different attributions about context and employ different schema when he meets with a Japanese manager than will a Japanese-American manager of his generation, or a junior U.S. manager whose personal experience with Japan is limited to automobiles, electronics, and sushi.

• **Selecting Schema**. Schemas are cultural scripts, a pattern of social interaction that is characteristic of a particular cultural group.[28] They are accepted and appropriate ways of behaving, specifying certain patterns of interaction. From personal or vicarious experience, we learn how to select schema. By watching and working with bosses, for example, we develop scripts for how to act when we take on that role ourselves. We learn appropriate vocabulary and gestures, which then elicit a fairly predictable response from others.

• **The Influence of Cultural Values**. Schemas reflect an underlying hierarchy of cultural values. For example, people working for U.S. managers who have a relaxed and casual style and who openly share information and provide opportunities to make independent decisions will learn specific scripts for managing in this fashion. The configuration of values embedded in this management style consists of informality, honesty, equality, and individualism. At some point, however, these same managers may withhold information about a sensitive personnel situation because privacy, fairness, and legal concerns would trump honesty and equality in this context. This trumping action explains why the constellation of values related to specific schema is hierarchical.

• **The Influence of Cultural History**. When decoding schema, we may also find vestiges of cultural history and tradition. Mindsets inherited from previous generations explain how history is remembered.[29] For example, perceptions about a colonial era may still have an impact on schemas, particularly those involving interactions with foreigners, even though a country gained its independence centuries ago.

## Some Illustrations of Sensemaking

Sensemaking involves placing stimuli into a framework that enables people "to comprehend, understand, explain, attribute, extrapolate, and predict."[30] Let's analyze each of the cultural paradoxes presented in the introduction using the sensemaking model. In the United States, when a charity requests money, when deserving people are in need, or when disaster hits a community (indexing contexts), many U.S. Americans (e.g., religious, allocentric people making attributions) respond by donating their money, goods, or time (selecting schema). The values underlying this schema are humanitarian concern for others, altruism,[31] and collectivism (cultural values). Thus, individualism (a sophisticated stereotype) is moderated by a communal tradition that has its roots in religious and cultural origins (cultural history).

Fukuyama[32] writes that U.S. society has never been as individualistic as its citizens thought, because of the culture's relatively high level of trust and resultant social capital. The United States "has always possessed a rich network of voluntary associations and community structures to which individuals have subordinated their narrow interests."[33] Under normal conditions, one should take responsibility for oneself and not rely on others. However, some circumstances and tasks can overwhelm individual initiative and ingenuity. When that happens, people should help those in need, a lesson forged on the American frontier (cultural history). To further underscore the complexity of culture, in the same contexts noted above, the tax code and prestige associated with philanthropy (cultural history) may be the primary motivations for some citizens (e.g., idiocentric, upwardly ambitious people making attributions) to act charitably (selecting schema), but the value underlying the schema would be individualism.

The Costa Rican example is illustrated in Figure 2. When bank tellers interact with clients (indexing context) many of them (e.g., members of various in-groups, civil servants making attributions) do not greet customers and make eye contact, but concentrate solely on their paperwork (selecting schema). The values that underlie this schema are in-group-out-group behavior[34] and power (cultural values). In collectivist cultures such as Costa Rica, members identify strongly with their in-group and treat members with warmth and cooperation. In stark contrast, out-group members are often treated with hostility, distrust, and a lack of cooperation. Customers are considered as strangers and out-group members who do not warrant the special treatment given to in-group members (family and friends). One

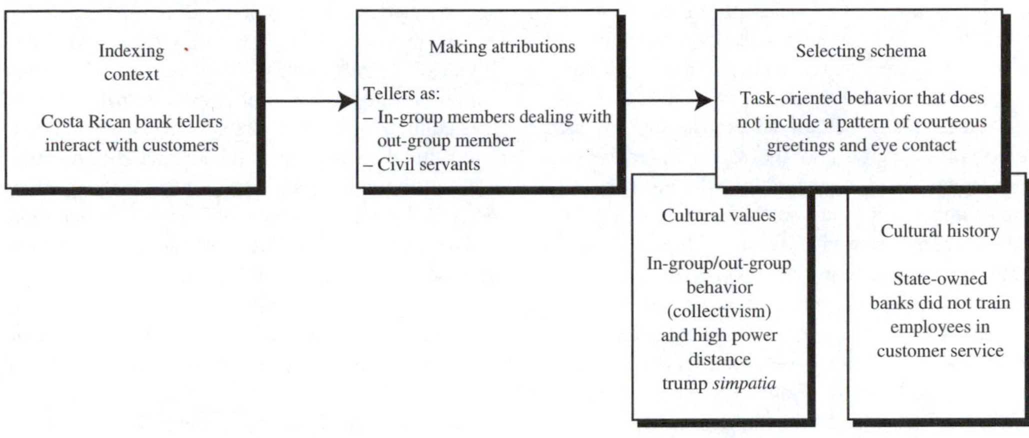


**Figure 2** Making Sense of Paradoxical Behavior: Seemingly Indifferent Customer Service in a Culture Characterized by Positive, Warm Relations

SOURCE: Academy of Management Executive by Osland, J.S., & Bird, A. Copyright 2000 by Academy of Management. Reproduced with permission of Academy of Management via Copyright Clearance Center.

of the few exceptions to *simpatia* and personal dignity in Costa Rica, and Latin America generally, is rudeness sometimes expressed by people in positions of power.[35] In this context, the cultural value of high power distance (the extent to which a society accepts the fact that power in institutions and organizations is distributed unequally)[36] trumps *simpatia.* Whereas *simpatia* lessens the distance between people, the opposite behavior increases the distance between the powerful and the powerless. Unlike many other contexts in Costa Rica, bank telling does not elicit a cultural script of *simpatia,* and state-owned banks did not have a history of training employees in friendly customer service (cultural history) at this time.

In the third cultural example, when Japanese business people make contracts (indexing context), they (e.g., business people making attributions) opt for ambiguous contracts (selecting schema). The dominant value underlying this schema is collectivism (cultural value). In this context, collectivism is manifested as a belief that those entering into agreement are joined together and share something in common; thus, they should rely on and trust one another. Collectivism trumps high uncertainty avoidance (sophisticated stereotype) in this context, but uncertainty avoidance is not completely absent. Some of the uncertainty surrounding the contract is dealt with upstream in the process by carefully choosing and getting to know business partners, and by using third parties. An additional consideration is that many Japanese like flexible contracts, because they have a greater recognition of the limits of contracts and the difficulties of foreseeing all contingencies (cultural history). Even though U.S. Americans are typically more tolerant of uncertainty (sophisticated stereotype), they value pragmatism and do not like to take unnecessary risks (cultural values). If a deal falls through, they rely on the legal system for a resolution (cultural history).

## Working From a Sensemaking Approach

Sophisticated stereotypes are useful in the initial stages of making sense of complex behaviors within cultures. However, rather than stereotyping cultures somewhere along a continuum, we can advance understanding by thinking in terms of specific contexts that feature particular cultural values that then govern behavior. Geertz maintains that "culture is best seen not as complexes of concrete behavior patterns—customs, usages, traditions, habit clusters—as has by and large been the case up to now, but as a set of control mechanisms—plans, recipes, rules, instructions (what computer engineers call 'programs')—for the governing of behavior."[37]

Understanding the control mechanisms within a culture requires the acquisition of attributional knowledge, the awareness of contextually appropriate behavior.[38] This is in contrast to factual knowledge and conceptual knowledge. Factual knowledge consists of descriptions of behaviors and attitudes. For example, it is a fact that Japanese use small groups extensively in the workplace. Conceptual knowledge consists of a culture's views and values about central concerns. Sophisticated stereotyping operates in the realm of conceptual knowledge. This category of knowledge is an organizing tool, but it is not sufficient for true cultural understanding. Knowing that the Japanese are a communal society (conceptual knowledge) does not explain the noncommunal activities that exist in Japanese organizations or when the Japanese will or will not be communal. For example, why are quality control circles used in some work settings and not in others? Factual and conceptual knowledge about Japanese culture cannot answer that question; only attributional knowledge can.

Managers can acquire attributional knowledge from personal experience, vicariously from others' experience, and from cultural mentoring. The personal experience method involves carefully observing how people from another culture act and react, and then formulating and reformulating hypotheses and cultural explanations for the observed behavior. When expatriates test their hypotheses and find them valid, they form schemas about specific events in the host culture.

One can learn vicariously by reading about other cultures, but the best form of vicarious learning is via cultural assimilator exercises.[39] These are critical incidents of cross-cultural encounters, accompanied by alternative explanations for the behavior of people from the foreign culture. After choosing what they perceive as the most likely answer, trainees then read expert opinions relating why each answer is adequate or inadequate. These opinions are validated by cross-cultural experts and include information about the relative importance of cultural dimensions or context-specific customs in the culture in question.

A cultural mentor can be viewed as a hybrid of vicarious and personal acquisition of attributional knowledge a sort of live cultural assimilator. Cultural mentors are usually long-term expatriates or members of the foreign culture. The latter are often helpful souls who have lived abroad themselves and understand the challenge of mastering another culture or people not totally in step with their own culture.[40] "They interpret the local culture for expatriates and guide them through its shoals, as well as providing them with the necessary encouragement when it feels like the expatriates will never 'break the code' of another culture and fit in comfortably."[41] Reading an explanation from a book or working through a series of cultural assimilators is different from receiving an explanation of an experience the expatriate has personally lived through and now wishes to understand. Cultural mentors can correct inaccurate hypotheses about the local culture. Expatriates who had cultural mentors overseas have been found to fare better than those who did not have such mentors: They were more fluent in the foreign language; they perceived themselves as better adapted to their work and general living conditions abroad; they were more aware of the paradoxes of expatriate life, indicating a higher degree of acculturation and understanding of the other culture; and they received higher performance appraisal ratings from both their superiors and themselves.[42]

In spite of the benefits of mentoring, few multinationals formally assign a cultural mentor to their expatriates. Yet another way of developing an expatriate's attributional knowledge is to provide more training in the host country rather than relying solely on predeparture culture "inoculations."

Admittedly, there are trade-offs to developing attributional knowledge. The acquisition of cultural knowledge takes a good deal of time and energy, which is not available to all managers. Nor is it reasonable to expect employees who work with people from various cultures on a daily basis to master each culture. Nevertheless, organizing the knowledge they do acquire as context-specific schemas can speed up cultural learning and prevent confusion and errors in making sense of cultural paradoxes.

If we accept that cultures are paradoxical, then it follows that learning another culture occurs in a dialectical fashion—thesis, antithesis, and synthesis. Thesis entails a hypothesis involving a sophisticated stereotype; antithesis is the identification of an apparently oppositional cultural paradox. Synthesis involves making sense of contradictory behavior—understanding why certain values are more important in certain contexts. Behavior appears less paradoxical once the foreigner learns to index contexts and match them with the appropriate schemas in the same way that members of the host culture do. Collins's description of the Westerner's Perception Scale in comprehending Japanese culture[43] illustrates one form of dialectical culture learning, an upwardly spiraling cycle of cultural comprehension.

## Using the Model

Because this cultural sensemaking model provides a more complex way of understanding culture, it has clear implications for those who teach culture, for those who work across cultures, and for organizations that send expatriates overseas.

## Teaching About Cultural Understanding

Sophisticated stereotyping should be the beginning of cultural learning, not the end, as is so often the case when teaching or learning about culture. Recognition of a more complex, holistic, sensemaking model of culture allows us to respond more effectively when students or trainees provide examples of paradoxes that seem to contradict cultural dimensions. The model also requires a somewhat different teaching approach. We have developed a sequential method that has been effective in our teaching:

- **Help students understand the complexity of their own culture.** To acquaint students with the vast challenge of comprehending culture, we begin with a thorough understanding of the internal logic of one's own culture and its socioeconomic, political, and historical roots. We add complexity by pointing out paradoxes as well as identifying regional, ethnic, religious, organizational, and individual variations in behavior. For example, when Thai students describe their culture as friendly, we ask the following series of questions: "Are all Thais friendly? Are Thais always friendly? Under what circumstances would Thais not exhibit friendly behavior? Why?"

- **Give students cultural dimensions and values as well as sophisticated stereotypes as basic tools.** These dimensions, including the values listed in Table 1, can then be used to explain contrasting behavior from two or more different cultures (e.g., What can sample obituaries from the United States and Mexico reveal about cultural values? What is the typical response of businesses in both countries when a member of an employee's family dies?). Students practice recognizing cultural dimensions in cross-cultural dialogues and cases and learn sophisticated stereotypes. This helps them gain conceptual knowledge about different cultures so they can make between-culture distinctions.

- **Develop students' skills in cultural observation and behavioral flexibility.** One of the difficulties expatriates confront in making sense of a new culture is the contradiction between the expected culture, the sophisticated stereotype taught in predeparture training or gleaned from others, and the manifest culture, the one actually enacted in a situation.[44] To help students become skilled at observing and decoding other cultures, teach them to think more like anthropologists and give them practice in honing observational and interpretive skills. To help students develop the behavioral flexibility needed to adapt to unanticipated situations, role-playing and videos of cross-cultural interactions can be used.

- **Have students do an in-depth study or experience with one culture.** To go beyond sophisticated stereotypes, students learn the internal logic and cultural history of a single culture. They acquire attributional knowledge from cultural mentors and/or cultural immersion, in addition to extensive research.

- **Focus on learning context-appropriate behavior in other cultures and developing cultural hypotheses and explanations for paradoxical behavior.** Once students have mastered the preceding steps, the emphasis changes to learning schemas for different contexts. For example, student teams are instructed to deliberately demonstrate incorrect behavior; they ask others to point out the mistakes and then replay the scene using correct behavior. To model the crucial behavior of asking for help in understanding cultural mysteries,[45] students use cultural mentors to explain situations they choose to learn about (e.g., "How do managers in _______ encourage employees to perform at high levels? Why does that work for them?") The variation in the mentors' answers ("Some managers are successful doing this while others . . .") and the qualified answers ("This seems to work unless . . . it depends on . . .") helps students develop more complex understandings of the other culture. To highlight the message of moving beyond cultural stereotypes, use language that focuses on forming and testing hypotheses about contextual behavior: "What are your hypotheses about why a French employee behaves this way in this situation? How can you find out if these hypotheses are correct?"

## Sensemaking for Individuals Working Across Cultures

After the training program, and once on assignment in a new culture, this cultural sensemaking approach has other practical implications.

- **Approach learning another culture more like a scientist who holds conscious stereotypes and hypotheses in order to test them.** One of the key differences between managers who were identified by their fellow MBA students as the "most internationally effective" and the "least internationally effective" is that the former changed their stereotypes of other nationalities as they interacted with them while the latter did not.[46]

- **Seek out cultural mentors and people who possess attributional knowledge about cultures.** Perhaps one of the basic lessons of cross-cultural interaction is that tolerance and effectiveness result from greater understanding of another culture. Making sense of a culture's internal logic and decoding cultural paradoxes is easiest with the aid of a willing and knowledgeable informant.

- **Analyze disconfirming evidence and instances that defy cultural stereotypes.** Even people with a great deal of experience in another culture can benefit from analyzing cultural paradoxes. For instance, the question, "In what circumstances do Latin Americans fail to exhibit *simpatia?*" led to a more complex cultural understanding for one of the authors, who had already spent nine curious years in that region. Once expatriates can function reasonably well in another culture, it is easy for them to reach plateaus in their cultural understanding and mistakenly assume that they comprehend the entire puzzle. This presents a danger when expatriates inadvertently pass on inaccurate information about the local culture, or make faulty, and even expensive, business decisions based on partial understandings.

- **Learn cultural schemas that will help you be effective.** Knowing how to act appropriately in specific cross-cultural settings results in self-confidence and effectiveness. One cannot memorize all the rules in another culture, but understanding the values that underlie most schemas can often prevent us from making serious mistakes.

### How Multinational Organizations Can Use the Sensemaking Model

The cultural sensemaking model also has practical implications for multinational organizations.

- **Use cognitive complexity as a selection criterion for expatriates and people in international positions.** Avoid black-and-white thinkers in favor of people who exhibit cognitive complexity, which involves the ability to handle ambiguity and multiple viewpoints. This skill is better suited to a thesis-antithesis approach to understanding the paradoxical nature of culture.

- **Provide in-country cultural training for expatriates that goes beyond factual and conceptual knowledge.** Predeparture cultural training is complemented by on-site training, which has the advantage of good timing. In-country culture training takes place when expatriates are highly motivated to find answers to real cultural dilemmas and when they are ready for greater complexity.[47]

- **Gauge the cultural knowledge possessed by expatriates within a country.** The accuracy and depth of one's cultural understanding is not always linked to the time one has spent in another country; it depends on the degree of involvement with the other culture as well as cultural curiosity and desire to learn. Nevertheless, when companies determine the optimum length of overseas assignments, they should consider how much time is generally necessary to function effectively in a particular culture. If a firm's expatriates stay abroad for only two years, it is less likely that a deep understanding of the culture will be shared among them than if they were to stay for longer periods. As long as the longer-term expatriates do not stop at a low-level plateau of cultural learning, mixing short-term (2–3 years) with longer-term expatriates (6–7 years) with permanent expatriates could produce more shared organizational learning about the culture. It is also essential to recognize that expatriates working for the same organization may be at different levels of cultural understanding.

- **Act like learning organizations with regard to cultural knowledge.** Multinationals benefit from formal mechanisms to develop a more complex understanding of the cultures where they do business through such methods as cultural mentors and in-country cultural training. There should also be mechanisms for sharing cultural knowledge. For example, having returned expatriates give formal debriefing sessions in which they report what they learned in their assignment increases the company's collective cultural knowledge and eases the expatriates' transition home by helping them make sense of a highly significant experience.[48]

## Acknowledgment

The authors would like to thank the UCLA CIBER Cross Cultural Collegium for its contributions to the article. Dr. Osland's research is partially funded by a grant from the Robert B. Pamplin Jr. Corporation.

## Notes

1. This was one of the findings of a class research project on the acceptance of ATMs by Dr. Osland's graduate students at INCAE's (Central American Institute of Business Administration) Banking Program in 1991.

2. Triandis, J. C., Marin, G., Lisansky, J., & Betancourt, H. 1984. *Simpatia* as a cultural script of hispanics. *Journal of Personality and Social Psychology,* 47(6): 1363–1375.

3. Hofstede, G. 1980. *Culture's consequences: International differences in work related values.* Beverly Hills, CA: Sage.

4. Olmstead v. United States, 277 U.S. 438, 478 (1928) (Brandeis, J., dissenting).

5. The descriptions of cultural metaphors in *Understanding global cultures: Metaphorical journeys through 17 countries* (Thousand Oaks, CA: Sage, 1994) by Martin Gannon and his associates, contain passing references to paradoxes, but do not address the issue directly.

6. Parsons, T. & Shils, E. 1951. *Toward a general theory of action.* Cambridge: Harvard University Press; Kluckhohn, F. & Strodtbeck, F. L. 1961. *Variations in value orientations.* Evanston, IL: Row, Peterson; Hofstede, op.cit.; Triandis, H. C. 1982. Dimensions of cultural variations as parameters of organizational theories. *International Studies of Management and Organization,* 12(4): 139–169; Ronen, S. & Shenkar, 0. (1985). Clustering countries on attitudinal dimensions: A review and synthesis. *Academy of Management Review,* 10: 435–454; Hall, E. T. & Hall, M. R. 1990. *Understanding cultural differences.* Yarmouth, ME: Intercultural Press; Fiske, A. P. 1992. The four elementary forms of sociality: Framework for a unified theory of social relations. *Psychological Review,* 99(4), 689–723; Schwartz, S. 1992. Universals in the content and structure of values: Theoretical advances and empirical tests in 20 countries. In M. Zanna (Ed.), *Advances in experimental social psychology,* 25: 1–66. New York: Academic Press; Trompenaars, F. & Hampden Turner, C. 1993. *The seven cultures of capitalism.* New York: Doubleday.

7. Hofstede, op. cit.

8. Adler, N. 1997. *International dimensions of organizational behavior,* 3' ed. Cincinnati: South-Western, 75–76.

9. Hall & Hall, op. cit.

10. Gannon, op. cit.

11. Barnlund, D. 1975. *Public and private self in Japan and the United States.* Yarmouth, ME: Intercultural Press, 6.

12. Osland, J. S. 1995. *The adventure of working abroad: Hero tales from the global frontier.* San Francisco: Jossey-Bass.

13. Collins, R. J. 1987. *Max Danger: The adventures of on expat in Tokyo.* Rutland, VT: Charles E. Tuttle Co.

14. Ibid., 14–15.

15. Tripathi, R. C. 1988. *Aligning development to values in India.* In D. Sinha & H. S. R. Kao (Eds.), Social values and development: Asian perspectives: 315–333. New Delhi: Sage; Wilbur, J. 1995. *A brief history of everything.* New York: Shambala.

16. Quinn, R. & Cameron, K. S. (Eds.) 1988. *Paradox and transformation.* Cambridge, MA: Ballinger, Smith, K. K. & Berg, D. N. 1987. *Paradoxes of group life.* San Francisco: Jossey-Bass.

17. Hofstede, op. cit.

18. Hofstede, G. 1994. In U. Kim, H. S. Triandis, C. Kagitribasi, S. Choi & G. Yoon (Eds.), *Individualism and collectivism.* Thousand Oaks, CA: Sage, xi.

19. Levi-Strauss, C. 1962. *La pensée sauvage.* Paris: Adler's Foreign Books, Inc.

20. Fontaine, G. 1989. *Managing international assignments: The strategy for success.* Englewood Cliffs, NJ: Prentice Hall.

21. Triandis, H. C., Bontempo, B., Villarreal, M. J., Asai, M., & Lucca, N. 1988. Individualism and collectivism: Cross-cultural perspectives on self-ingroup relationships. *Journal of Personality and Social Psychology,* 54(2): 323–338.

22. Bateson, G. 1973. *Steps to an ecology of mind.* London: Paladin Books.

23. Haught, J. 1993, What does sex have to do with it? *Oregonian,* December 29,1993, D7.

24. Tripathi, Marin, op. cit.

25. Ibid.

26. Bird, A., Osland, J. S., Mendenhall, M., & Schneider, S. 1999. Adapting and adjusting to other cultures: What we know but don't always tell. *Journal of Management Inquiry,* 8(2): 152–165.

27. Context is also embedded in culture, so one could argue that the entire model is situated within the broader culture. For simplicity's sake, however, we chose to focus only on the sense-making that occurs in deciphering cultural paradoxes.

28. Triandis, Marin, et. al, op. cit.

29. Fisher, G. 1997. *Mindsets: The role of culture and perception in international relations.* Yarmouth, ME: Intercultural Press.

30. Starbuck, W. H. & Milliken, F. J. 1988. *Executives' personal filters: What they notice and how they make sense.* In D. Hambrick (Ed.), The executive effect: Concepts and methods for studying top managers. Greenwich, CT: JAI Press, 51.

31. Barnlund, op. cit.

32. Fukuyama, F. 1996. *Trust.* New York: Penguin Books.

33. Ibid., 29.

34. Triandis, et al., op. cit.

35. Osland, J. S., De Franco, S., & Osland, A. 1999. Organizational implications of Latin American culture: Lessons for the expatriate manager. *Journal of Management Inquiry,* 8(2): 219234.

36. Hofstede, *Culture's consequences,* op. cit.

37. Geertz, C. 1973. *The interpretation of cultures.* New York: HarperCollins Basic Books, 44.

38. Bird, A., Heinbuch, S., Dunbar, R. & McNulty, M. 1993. A conceptual model of the effects of area studies training programs and a preliminary investigation of the model's hypothesized relationships. *International Journal of Intercultural Relations,* 17(4): 415–436.

39. The original cultural assimilators were developed by Harry Triandis at the University of Illinois. A recent collection is found in *Intercultural interactions: A practical guide,* by R. Brislin, K. Cushner, C. Cherrie, & Yong, M., Thousand Oaks, CA: Sage, 1986 and 1996 (second edition).

40. Osland, *Working abroad,* op. cit.

41. Ibid., 68.

42. Ibid., 74.

43. Collins, op. cit.

44. Schermerhorn, Jr., J. & Bond, M. H. 1997. Cross-cultural leadership dynamics in collectivism and high power distance settings. *Leadership & Organization Development Journal,* 18(4): 187–193.

45. On occasion we have heard frustrated cross-cultural trainers grumble that some expatriates view seeking out cultural explanations with the same disdain they reserve for stopping to ask for driving directions.

46. Ratiu, I. 1983. Thinking internationally: A comparison of how international students learn. *International Studies of Management and Organization,* 13:139–150.

47. Bird, Osland, et al., op. cit.

48. Osland, *Working Abroad,* op. cit.

# Case 1.1

# MERCK & COMPANY, INC.

## *Having the Vision to Succeed*

STEPHANIE WEISS AND DAVID BOLLIER

### An Expensive Care for a Poor Market

In 1978, Dr. P. Roy Vagelos, then head of the Merck research labs, received a provocative memorandum from a senior researcher in parasitology, Dr. William C. Campbell. Dr. Campbell had made an intriguing observation while working with ivermectin, a new antiparasitic compound under investigation for use in animals.

Campbell thought that ivermectin might be the answer to a disease called river blindness that plagued millions in the Third World. But to find out if Campbell's hypothesis had merit, Merck would have to spend millions of dollars to develop the right formulation for human use and to conduct the field trials in the most remote parts of the world. Even if these efforts produced an effective and safe drug, virtually none of those afflicted with river blindness could afford to buy it. Vagelos, originally a university researcher but by then a Merck executive, had to decide whether to invest in research for a drug that, even if successful, might never pay for itself.

### River Blindness

River blindness, formally known as onchocerciasis, was a disease labeled by the World Health Organization (WHO) as a public health and socioeconomic problem of considerable magnitude in over 35 developing countries throughout the Third World. Some 85 million people in thousands of tiny settlements throughout Africa and parts of the Middle East and Latin America were thought to be at risk. The cause: a parasitic worm carried by a tiny black fly that bred along fast-moving rivers. When the flies bit humans—a single person could be bitten thousands of times a day—the larvae of a parasitic worm, *Onchocerca volvulus*, entered the body.

These worms grew to more than two feet in length, causing grotesque but relatively innocuous nodules in the skin. The real harm began when the adult worms reproduced, releasing millions of microscopic offspring, known as microfilariae, which swarmed through body tissue. A terrible itching resulted, so bad that some victims committed suicide. After several years, the microfilariae caused lesions and depigmentation of the skin.

SOURCE: This case was prepared as the basis for class discussion rather than to illustrate either effective or ineffective handling of an administrative situation. Reprinted with permission of the authors.

Eventually they invaded the eyes, often causing blindness.

The World Health Organization estimated in 1978 that some 340,000 people were blind because of onchocerciasis, and that a million more suffered from varying degrees of visual impairment. At that time, 18 million or more people were infected with the parasite, though half did not yet have serious symptoms. In some villages close to fly-breeding sites, nearly all residents were infected and a majority of those over age 45 were blind. In such places, it was said, children believed that severe itching, skin infections, and blindness were simply part of growing up.

In desperate efforts to escape the flies, entire villages abandoned fertile areas near rivers, and moved to poorer land. As a result, food shortages were frequent. Community life disintegrated as new burdens arose for already impoverished families.

The disease was first identified in 1893 by scientists and in 1926 was found to be related to the black flies. But by the 1970s, there was still no cure that could safely be used for community-wide treatment. Two drugs, diethylcarbamazine (DEC) and Suramin, were useful in killing the parasite, but both had severe side effects in infected individuals, needed close monitoring, and had even caused deaths. In 1974, the Onchocerciasis Control Program was created to be administered by the World Health Organization, in the hope that the flies could be killed through spraying of larvacides at breeding sites, but success was slow and uncertain. The flies in many areas developed resistance to the treatment, and were also known to disappear and then reinfest areas.

## Merck & Co., Inc.—A Summary of Operations

Merck & Co., Inc. was, in 1978, one of the largest producers of prescription drugs in the world. Headquartered in Rahway, New Jersey, Merck traced its origins to Germany in 1668 when Friedrich Jacob Merck purchased an apothecary in the city of Darmstadt. Over three hundred years later, Merck, having become an American firm, employed over 28,000 people and had operations all over the world.

In the late 1970s, Merck was coming off a 10-year drought in terms of new products. For nearly a decade, the company had relied on two prescription drugs for a significant percentage of its approximately $2 billion in annual sales: Indocin, a treatment for rheumatoid arthritis, and Aldomet, a treatment for high blood pressure. Henry W. Gadsden, Merck's chief executive from 1965 to 1976, along with his successor, John J. Horan, were concerned that the 17-year patent protection on Merck's two big moneymakers would soon expire, and began investing an enormous amount in research.

Merck management spent a great deal of money on research because it knew that its success ten and twenty years in the future critically depended upon present investments. The company deliberately fashioned a corporate culture to nurture the most creative, fruitful research. Merck scientists were among the best-paid in the industry, and were given great latitude to pursue intriguing leads. Moreover, they were inspired to think of their work as a quest to alleviate human disease and suffering world-wide. Within certain proprietary constraints, researchers were encouraged to publish in academic journals and to share ideas with their scientific peers. Nearly a billion dollars was spent between 1975 and 1978, and the investment paid off. In that period, under the direction of head of research, Dr. P. Roy Vagelos, Merck introduced Clinoril, a painkiller for arthritis; a general antibiotic called Mefoxin; a drug for glaucoma named Timoptic; and Ivomec (ivermectin, MSD), an antiparasitic for cattle.

In 1978, Merck had sales of $1.98 billion and net income of $307 million. Sales had risen steadily between 1969 and 1978 from $691 million to almost $2 billion. Income during the same period rose from $106 million to over $300 million.

At that time, Merck employed 28,700 people, up from 22,200 ten years earlier. Human and animal health products constituted 84% of the company's sales, with environmental health products and services representing an additional 14% of sales. Merck's foreign sales had grown more rapidly during the 1970s than had domestic sales, and in 1978 represented 47% of total sales. Much of the company's research operations were organized separately as the Merck Sharp & Dohme Research Laboratories, headed by Vagelos. Other Merck operations included the Merck Sharp & Dohme Division, the Merck Sharp & Dohme International Division, Kelco Division, Merck Chemical Manufacturing Division, Merck Animal Health Division, Calgon Corporation, Baltimore Aircoil Company, and Hubbard Farms.

The company had 24 plants in the United States, including one in Puerto Rico, and 44 in other countries. Six research laboratories were located in the United States and four abroad.

While Merck executives sometimes squirmed when they quoted the "unbusinesslike language" of George W. Merck, son of the company's founder and its former chairmen, there could be no doubt that Merck employees found the words inspirational. "We try never to forget that medicine is for the people," Merck said. "It is not for the profits. The profits follow, and if we have remembered that, they have never failed to appear. The better we have remembered it, the larger they have been." These words formed the basis of Merck's overall corporate philosophy.

## The Drug Investment Decision

Merck invested hundreds of millions of dollars each year in research. Allocating those funds among various projects, however, was a rather involved and inexact process. At a company as large as Merck, there was never a single method by which projects were approved or money distributed.

Studies showed that, on the average, it took 12 years and $200 million to bring a new drug to market. Thousands of scientists were continually working on new ideas and following new leads. Drug development was always a matter of trial and error; with each new iteration, scientists would close some doors and open others. When a Merck researcher came across an apparent breakthrough—either in an unexpected direction, or as a derivative of the original lead—he or she would conduct preliminary research. If the idea proved promising, it was brought to the attention of the department heads.

Every year, Merck's research division held a large review meeting at which all research programs were examined. Projects were coordinated and consolidated, established programs were reviewed and new possibilities were considered. Final approval on research was not made, however, until the head of research met later with a committee of scientific advisors. Each potential program was extensively reviewed, analyzed on the basis of the likelihood of success, the existing market, competition, potential safety problems, manufacturing feasibility, and patent status before the decision was made whether to allocate funds for continued experimentation.

## The Problem of Rare Diseases and Poor Customers

Many potential drugs offered little chance of financial return. Some diseases were so rare that treatments developed could never be priced high enough to recoup the investment in research, while other diseases afflicted only the poor in rural and remote areas of the Third World. These victims had limited ability to pay even a small amount for drugs or treatment.

In the United States, Congress sought to encourage drug companies to conduct research on rare diseases. In 1978, legislation had been proposed that would grant drug companies tax benefits and seven-year exclusive marketing rights if they would manufacture drugs for diseases afflicting fewer than 200,000 Americans. It was expected that this "orphan drug program" would eventually be passed into law.

There was, however, no U.S. or international program that would create incentives for companies to develop drugs for diseases like river blindness, which afflicted millions of the poor in the Third World. The only hope was that some Third World government, foundation, or international aid organization might step in and partially fund the distribution of a drug that had already been developed.

## The Discovery of Ivermectin

The process of investigating promising drug compounds was always long, laborious, and fraught with failure. For every pharmaceutical compound that became a "product candidate," thousands of others failed to meet the most rudimentary preclinical tests for safety and efficacy. With so much room for failure, it became especially important for drug companies to have sophisticated research managers who could identify the most productive research strategies.

Merck had long been a pioneer in developing major new antibiotic compounds, beginning with penicillin and streptomycin in the 1940s. In the 1970s, Merck Sharp & Dohme Research Laboratories were continuing this tradition. To help investigate for new microbial agents of potential therapeutic value, Merck researchers obtained 54 soil samples from the Kitasato Institute of Japan in 1974. These samples seemed novel and the researchers hoped they might disclose some naturally occurring antibiotics.

As Merck researchers methodically put the soil through hundreds of tests, Merck scientists were pleasantly surprised to detect strong antiparasitic activity in Sample No. OS3153, a scoop of soil dug up at a golf course near Ito, Japan. The Merck labs quickly brought together an interdisciplinary team to try to isolate a pure active ingredient from the microbial culture. The compound eventually isolated—avermectin—proved to have an astonishing potency and effectiveness against a wide range of parasites in cattle, swine, horses, and other animals. Within a year, the Merck team also began to suspect that a group of related compounds discovered in the same soil sample could be effective against many other intestinal worms, mites, ticks, and insects.

After toxicological tests suggested that ivermectin would be safer than related compounds,

Merck decided to develop the substance for the animal health market. In 1978, the first ivermectin-based animal drug, Ivomec, was nearing approval by the U.S. Department of Agriculture and foreign regulatory bodies. Many variations would likely follow: drugs for sheep and pigs, horses, dogs, and others. Ivomec had the potential to become a major advance in animal health treatment.

As clinical testing of ivermectin progressed in the late 1970s, Dr. William Campbell's ongoing research brought him face-to-face with an intriguing hypothesis. Ivermectin, when tested in horses, was effective against the microfilariae of an exotic, fairly unimportant gastrointestinal parasite, *Onchocerca cervicalis*. This particular worm, while harmless in horses, had characteristics similar to the insidious human parasite that causes river blindness, *Onchocerca volvulus*.

Dr. Campbell wondered, could ivermectin be formulated to work against the human parasite? Could a safe, effective drug suitable for community-wide treatment of river blindness be developed? Both Campbell and Vagelos knew that it was very much a gamble that it would succeed. Furthermore, both knew that even if success were attained, the economic viability of such a project would be nil. On the other hand, because such a significant amount of money had already been invested in the development of the animal drug, the cost of developing a human formulation would be much less than that for developing a new compound. It was also widely believed at this point that ivermectin, though still in its final development stages, was likely to be very successful.

A decision to proceed would not be without risks. If a new derivative proved to have any adverse health effects when used on humans, its reputation as a veterinary drug could be tained and sales negatively affected, no matter how irrelevant the experience with humans. In early tests, ivermectin had had some negative side effects on some specific species of mammals. Dr. Brian Duke of the Armed Forces Institute of Pathology in Washington, D.C. said the cross-species effectiveness of antiparasitic drugs are unpredictable, and there is "always a worry that some race or sub-section of the human population might be adversely affected."

Isolated instances of harm to humans or improper use in Third World settings might also raise some unsettling questions: Could drug residues turn up in meat eaten by humans? Would any human version of ivermectin distributed to the Third World be diverted into the black market, undercutting sales of the veterinary drug? Could the drug harm certain animals in unknown ways?

Despite these risks, Vagelos wondered what the impact might be of turning down Campbell's proposal. Merck had built a research team dedicated to alleviating human suffering. What would a refusal to pursue a possible treatment for river blindness do to morale? Ultimately, it was Dr. Vagelos who had to make the decision whether or not to fund research toward a treatment for river blindness.

# Case 1.2

# UNOCAL AND THE YADANA GAS PIPELINE PROJECT[1]

ANNE T. LAWRENCE AND HOWARD TOLLEY, JR.

John F. Imle, Jr., president of Unocal Corporation, was seated in his spacious office at the firm's corporate headquarters in El Segundo, California. The date was January 4, 1995. Across from him sat a delegation of human rights activists concerned about the company's involvement in a controversial gas pipeline then under construction across the southern panhandle of Burma. A longtime Unocal veteran, Imle had spent much of his career in Asia. Described by his colleagues as an "experienced international deal-maker," the fifty-three year old petroleum engineer had been promoted to president just six months earlier.

In 1992, Unocal had entered into a joint venture with the governments of Burma and Thailand and a French oil company, Total. Their goal was to construct and operate a pipeline to deliver natural gas from a field in the Andaman Sea, across the southern panhandle of Burma, to a power plant near Bangkok. The Burmese government had agreed to provide security for the project, known as the Yadana gas pipeline. Human rights activists had charged that the government had used brute military force to clear the pipeline area, relocating entire villages and terrorizing the civilian population. Many civilians, including women, children and the elderly, had been forcibly conscripted to clear land and build roads, barracks, and helipads. Although Unocal had not engaged in these acts directly, the company's critics felt that as the government's business partner, it shared responsibility. Now, under mounting pressure, Imle had agreed to meet with a group of activists face-to-face.

"What is happening in the exact pipeline area," said Paula Wellner of Greenpeace, an environmental organization, "is increased forced labor, increased relocation of villagers. And so the situation there is getting much worse . . . Your project is fostering massive human rights violations in the area," she asserted.

"Well, I would suggest if there were fewer threats . . ." Imle began. The pipeline was being laid through a region controlled by ethnic rebels, and there had been reports of armed attacks on work crews.

"It has nothing to do with threats," Wellner interjected. "These are just people going about their day-to-day business."

"People are threatening physical damage to the pipeline, do you agree with that?" Imle asked.

"I agree with that, but it has nothing to do with taking people out of their villages and forcing them to work."

---

SOURCE: Reprinted by permission from the *Case Research Journal,* Volume 22, Issue 2. 

"I'm sorry," Imle persisted. "It has a lot to do with the military presence there, and an increasing military presence."

"And using people as forced labor has to do with threats? Are you saying if they didn't threaten to blow up the pipeline or to disrupt it . . ."

"You are taking what I am saying completely out of context, and you understand that," Imle interjected. "Let's be reasonable about this. What I'm saying is that if you threaten the pipeline there's going to be more military. If forced labor goes hand in hand with the military, yes, there will be more forced labor. For every threat to the pipeline, there will be a reaction."[2]

## Union Oil of California[3]

At the time of this contentious conversation, Unocal was in the midst of a difficult transformation from a West Coast operator of refineries and gas stations to a global energy exploration and production company with a focus on Asia.

The Union Oil Company of California, or Unocal as it later became known, had been founded in 1890 in Santa Paula, California by Lyman Stewart and Wallace Hardison. Both men were wildcatters who had launched their careers speculatively drilling for oil in the industry's early days in northeastern Pennsylvania. The partners had been drawn to southern California in 1883 both by the promise of plentiful crude and by the chance to escape the monopolistic business practices of John D. Rockefeller, who had already driven many competing oil men out of business in the eastern fields. Things had not gone smoothly at first. Western oil was heavy, soils were rocky, and money was short. But eventually the fledgling venture developed productive fields near Los Angeles and, later, elsewhere in the state.

Recognizing early the value of vertical integration, Union expanded its operations into research, refining, distribution and marketing. The company founded the first petroleum research facility on the West Coast, built one of its first refineries, and launched one of its first steel oil tankers. Union opened its original gas station in downtown Los Angeles in 1913, the same year that Henry Ford introduced the moving assembly line to produce the Model T. During the post-World War II period, the company acquired Pure Oil, with service stations in the southeast and Midwest, enabling it to spread the *Union 76* brand name across much of the country. The company promoted full-service stations, high-octane fuel, clean rest rooms, and auto repair service in a bid to attract upscale motorists and to build strong brand loyalty.

## A New World, A New Unocal

Although it had gradually acquired properties elsewhere in the United States and abroad, Unocal remained known through most of its century-long history as a cautious, regional player closely identified with its West Coast refineries, transportation network, and *Union 76* gas stations. During the postwar period, when most oil companies were aggressively expanding their global operations, Unocal remained, in the words of one historian, "tucked into its geographical niche."[4] By the mid-1990s, it was clear that this strategy could no longer deliver for stockholders. The company's retail operations were earning just two cents on the dollar, and shareholder returns were among the lowest in the industry.[5] Roger C. Beach, who became CEO in 1994 and Chairman the following year, later recalled in an interview:

> It was becoming increasingly apparent to us that our West Coast downstream [retail] operations—in which we had a great deal of capital tied up—were going to continue as a low-margin, low-return-on-asset business, limiting our ability to take on global upstream [exploration and production] projects which allow much higher rates of return—in the 15% to 25% range.[6]

The California oil fields were close to played out, and opportunities for exploration in the lower 48 states were diminishing. Moreover, a well-publicized oil spill at a Unocal platform off the coast of Santa Barbara in 1969 had led to a public outcry and increasingly strict environmental regulations, including a ban on offshore drilling in California. The company was also still suffering from a heavy debt load incurred during a failed takeover bid for the company by famed corporate raider T. Boone Pickens in the 1980s.

In March 1997, Unocal's new management team took a bold and formerly unthinkable action: they sold off the company's core assets—all of its U.S. refineries, tankers, and gas stations—to Tosco Corporation for around $2 billion. The company used some of the proceeds to buy back stock and to pay down a portion of its debt. Then, it took most of the rest and invested in exploration and development projects overseas, mostly in Asia, where executives hoped the company could earn significantly higher returns. That same year, Unocal underscored its commitment to Asia by opening a twin corporate headquarters in Kuala Lumpur, Malaysia. President Imle relocated there from California.

Of particular interest to the company's management team were vertically integrated projects, where the company could develop a resource, build the infrastructure to deliver it, and market it directly to fast-growing markets. In an interview with *Petroleum Economist* in 1998, a company executive explained:

> Our market-to-resource approach is what sets us apart. Other companies typically want to go out and find oil and gas, with little thought given to the market. We're looking at opportunities in proven resource basins where there are new markets. We want to participate in those markets, not only in energy resource production, but possibly also in pipeline and power plant projects.[7]

Chairman Beach and other top executives believed that this integrated approach would distinguish the company from its competition when negotiating with foreign countries. "What every government likes about Unocal," he told a reporter for the *Wall Street Journal,* "is one-stop shopping—one group able to take the whole project from development to the marketing end."[8]

Unocal envisioned itself as a growing "super independent," the provider of choice for integrated energy projects throughout Asia. Project Energy Renaissance, unveiled in December 1997, envisioned a trans-Asia network of natural gas pipelines connecting resources to markets throughout the region, including Bangladesh, Azerbaijan, China, Thailand, Turkmenistan, Vietnam, Thailand, and Burma.[9] In a 1998 briefing for security analysts, Beach summed up the company's transformation:

> Over the past two years, we have created a new Unocal, with exploration and production making up more than 75% of our net property and equity investment. We are now the world's largest non-state-owned E&P [exploration and production] company—one that combines [the] global reach, technical expertise and financial muscle of a major with the agility, aggressiveness and creativity of a small independent.[10]

In a sense, Unocal had returned to its original culture: like its founders Stewart and Hardison, the oil company was once again wildcatting, this time on a new frontier.

## The Yadana Gas Pipeline Project

One of the initiatives that figured prominently in the "new Unocal" was the Yadana gas pipeline. This project, already underway, gained importance as the company shifted its strategic focus to Asia.

In 1982, natural gas deposits were discovered in the Andaman Sea off the western coast of Burma, also known as Myanmar (Exhibit 1). In 1992, the government of Burma, seeking to develop these assets, formed a state-owned company, the Myanma Oil and Gas Enterprise (MOGE) and initiated negotiations with several international oil companies, including Unocal, over rights to these gas fields. Total, a French oil company, won the first bid, for which it paid MOGE around $15 million.

Total entered into two contracts with MOGE, a Production Sharing Contract (PSC) and a Memorandum of Understanding (MOU). These agreements clearly stated, in writing, the mutual obligations of the parties. Total agreed to be the contractor on the project, that is, first to explore the field and then to construct the gas drilling platforms and the pipeline itself. MOGE agreed to supply the rights to the gas and to provide security and rights of way for the pipeline project, as indicated in the following clause in the MOU:

> MOGE shall assist and expedite Contractor's execution of the Work Program by providing . . . security protection and rights of way and easements as may be requested by Contractor.[11]

The joint venture participants envisioned a several-stage project. First, the seabed gas field would be fully explored. If it were found to have adequate reserves, Total would formally announce a commercial discovery. At that point, the field would be developed and a pipeline constructed to deliver gas to a power plant to be built by the government of Thailand. The 36-inch diameter pipeline would run underwater from the Yadana field to landfall (215 miles), then on land across Burma's Tenasserim panhandle (39 miles), and finally through Thailand to Ratchiburi, near the capital city of Bangkok (161 miles) (Exhibit 2). There, the gas would be used to fuel a 2,800-megawatt electric power plant operated by the Thai government. Once the project was operational, gas sales to the Thai government would, it was conservatively estimated at the time, produce around $200 million a year in revenue for the Myanmar government.[12]

When it was initially involved in negotiations over the Andaman gas rights, Unocal contracted with a consulting firm, the Control Risk Group, to assess the political and other risks involved in investment in Burma. The CRG's report to the company stated:

> Throughout Burma the government habitually makes use of forced labour to construct roads. In [the] Karen and Mon states the army is forcing villagers to move to more secure sites (similar to the "strategic hamlets" employed by the US Army in Vietnam) in the hope of cutting off their links with the guerillas. There are credible reports of military attacks on civilians in the regions. In such circumstances UNOCAL and its partners will have little freedom of maneuver. The local community is already terrorized: it will regard outsiders apparently backed by the army with extreme suspicion.[13]

Although it had lost out in the initial bidding over the Andaman gas rights, Unocal remained interested and entered into negotiations directly with Total to purchase a share of its interest in the project. In December 1992, Unocal purchased a 49 percent share of Total's rights under the Agreements from the French company for $8.6 million. In their negotiations over this sale, the two companies discussed the issues raised by the risk analysis report concerning the role of the Burmese military. According to a deposition later given by Unocal's vice president of international affairs:

> In our discussions between Unocal and Total, we said that the option of having the military provide protection for the pipeline construction and operation of it would be they might proceed in the manner that would be out of our control and not be in the manner that we would like to see them proceed, I mean, going to the excess. So that was the hazard we were talking about. It was out of our control if that kind of full relinquishment of security was given to the government.[14]

Nevertheless, Unocal decided to proceed. In a further set of agreements between Unocal and Total, the French company agreed to act as "operator." Each company would pay expenses according to its share and could vote on joint venture operations through an operating committee. Unocal formed a wholly owned subsidiary, the Unocal Myanmar Offshore Co. Ltd. (UMOC), to hold the company's interest in the Yadana project.

In February 1995, Total declared a commercial discovery. Shortly thereafter, the joint venture partners formed a separate corporation, the Moattama Gas Transportation Company (MGTC), to build and operate the natural gas pipeline. After both MOGE and the Petroleum Authority of Thailand (PTTEP), a state agency, exercised their options to acquire a share of MGTC, ownership shares in the pipeline project were: Total, 31%; Unocal, 28%; PTTEP, 26%; and MOGE, 15%.

## A Rogue State

Burma, the nation with which Unocal had entered into a business partnership, was widely regarded in the international community as a rogue state.

Located on the Andaman Sea between Bangladesh and Thailand, Burma shared inland borders with India, China, and Laos. Slightly smaller than the state of Texas, the country consisted of a central, tropical lowlands ringed by a semicircle of rugged hills. Among the nation's 42 million people, the dominant ethnic group was the Burman, comprising 68 percent of the population, who mainly populated the lowlands. Several minority ethnic groups, including the Shan, Karen, Kachin, Mon, Wa, and Rakhine, mainly inhabited the highlands. Most of the Burmese people lived in poverty; in the early 1990s, per capita income was between $200 and $300 a year.

For fourteen years after the country had become independent from Britain in 1948, Burma had enjoyed a constitutional democracy. However, in 1962 General Ne Win had seized power and launched the "Burmese Road to Socialism." The regime had nationalized all property, including foreign businesses, and had isolated the country by expelling all international correspondents and limiting tourist visas. Ne Win consolidated his control in a 1974 constitution that combined executive, legislative and judicial power in a one-party system. The regime detained opposition politicians without trial and shut down the universities for years at a time. Inadequate energy resources produced regular blackouts, and the country spun into economic decline.

In 1988, opponents of the regime staged massive pro-democracy demonstrations. The opposition was brutally crushed by the junta, and full martial law was imposed. At that time, the military government assumed the title of the State Law and Order Restoration Council (SLORC) and renamed the country Myanmar. Elections were held in 1990. But after the National League for Democracy, an opposition coalition, won 82 percent of the seats in parliament, the military nullified the elections and placed many of the party's leaders, including Nobel laureate Aung San Suu Kyi, under arrest.

In the wake of the 1990 military crackdown, the Myanmar regime had apparently stepped up its reign of terror against the civilian population. The government of Burma was widely criticized by the U.S. State Department, the United Nations, Amnesty International and many other public and private organizations for escalating human rights violations. A 1995 report on human rights practices in Burma issued by the U.S. State Department summarized these concerns:

> The Government's severe repression of human rights continued . . . There continued to be credible reports, particularly from ethnic minority dominated areas, that soldiers committed serious human rights abuses, including extra-judicial killings and rape. Disappearances continued, and members of the security forces beat and otherwise abused detainees. Prison conditions remained harsh, and the judiciary [was] not independent of the executive. The use of porters by the army—with attendant mistreatment, illness, and even death for those compelled to serve—remained a standard practice. The military continued to force ordinary Burmese on a massive scale (including women and children) to "contribute" their labor, often under harsh working conditions, on construction projects throughout the country . . . The SLORC continued to restrict severely the basic rights to free speech, press, assembly, association, and privacy. Workers' rights [were] also severely limited. Political party activity remained severely restricted, and citizens do not have the right to change their government.[15]

A major concern of human rights advocates was SLORC's practice of forcibly conscripting the labor of its own citizens. Thousands of Burmese were compelled to work without pay, under threat of violence, in government-sponsored development projects, building roads, railroads, dams, and canals and toiling as porters for the army. In fact, the value to the economy of "peoples' contributions" was so significant that it was regularly reported as a separate line in government budget figures. Human Rights Watch/Asia estimated in 1995 that at least two million people had been forcibly conscripted. The government was quite open about these practices, defending them as a continuation of the age-old practice in Burma of contributing labor for the public good (in fact, both Buddhist kings and later British colonists had required unpaid community service).

Many in the drug enforcement community believed that SLORC was also deeply involved in the heroin trade. The hilly area of northeastern Burma, sometimes called the Golden Triangle, was a major poppy-growing region (poppies provide the raw material for the production of heroin). Satellite surveillance showed a sharp increase in areas under poppy cultivation after the SLORC took power. By the mid-1990s, Burma provided more than half of the world's supply of heroin, and according to U.S. State Department estimates, more than 60 percent of street heroin sold in the United States. Burma was also a significant source of methamphetamine. The U.S. Embassy in Thailand issued a report in 1996 that stated that at least half of Myanmar's economy was "unaccounted for and extralegal."

Profits from the heroin trade appeared to be funding the government's own activity. The International Monetary Fund reported that from 1991 to 1993, the Burmese government had purchased $1.2 billion worth of arms—although its foreign exchange reserves for the period were a mere $300 million. Research by the nonprofit Geopolitical Drug Watch of Paris suggested, moreover, that MOGE—the state-run oil company and Unocal's partner—was "the main channel for laundering the revenues of heroin produced and exported under the control of the Burmese army."[16]

## Securing the Pipeline Route

In the early 1990s, the Burmese government moved decisively to fulfill its contractual commitment to provide security protection and rights of way for the Yadana pipeline.

The pipeline was projected to pass through a remote, mountainous, and underdeveloped region of Burma politically controlled by a rebel group, the Karen National Union (KNU). The Karen, a distinct ethnic group of about perhaps four million with their own language and culture, were descendants of Mongolians who had entered present-day Burma around the eighth century BC.[17] Later, the Burman invaded, and the Karen retreated to the narrow, mountainous coastal region of the Malay Peninsula, beginning centuries of conflict between the two ethnic groups. After World War II, the Karen appealed to the British to grant them a separate state; this appeal was denied, and upon independence their district became a part of Burma.[18] (The location of the Karen state is shown in Exhibit 2.)

In the early-1990s, the KNU was allied with the National Democratic Front (the pro-democracy coalition) and advocated a "genuine Federal Union comprised of all the states of the nationalities on the basis of equality and self-determination."[19] The

KNU's position was that although it was not on principle opposed to construction of a gas pipeline through Karen territory, it *was* opposed to "any business venture that strengthens the illegal SLORC's hold on power and hence fuels the civil war." Thus, although it was not opposed to *any* pipeline, it was opposed to *this* pipeline, because it would benefit the military junta.

What exactly happened in the Tenasserim region in the mid-1990s is a matter of factual dispute. The area was closed to the foreign press, and the government routinely denied visas to human rights organizations. The military itself saw no reason to justify, or report on, its own behavior. One young man, however, made extraordinary sacrifices to help this story be told. In 1988, Ka Hsaw Wa, an 18-year old Karen student, had participated in the pro-democracy demonstrations. He was tortured by SLORC officers and fled across the border to Thailand. Wa later joined with two young law students from the University of Virginia to establish EarthRights International in Thailand. With financial support from the Soros and other foundations, the former Burmese student activist and several associates made numerous trips across the border to his homeland during the 1992–96 period to collect evidence of human rights abuses from villagers in the pipeline region. In 1996, EarthRights and the Southeast Asian Information Network published Wa's findings under the title *Total Denial.*[20] In addition to Wa's evidence, reports published by Amnesty International, Human Rights Watch/Asia, Southeast Asia Information Network; writings by Karen activists and refugees; and depositions later given by Karen villagers from the area provide a partial view of a chaotic situation.

In 1992, the Burmese military began to build up the presence of light infantry battalions (of 400–800 soldiers each) in the pipeline area. A villager told EarthRights International:

> Before 1991, we saw Burmese soldiers very seldom, only Karen soldiers. But after 1991, light infantry battalions 408, 409, and 410 led by Major Han Htin started to base their outpost in our area . . . In 1992, we saw [government] soldiers almost every day.[21]

Over the next four years, these Burmese troops asserted military control in the region. They also organized the construction of support facilities along the pipeline corridor. These facilities included a fortified base camp for Total's use, with 60 buildings and two underground bunkers surrounded by three rings of barbed-wire fences; a nearby landing strip; a second, smaller base camp near the mid-point of the proposed route; and a dozen helicopter landing pads. The army also supervised the construction of service roads and the clearing of right of way for the pipeline.

To recruit labor for these construction projects and to serve the battalions themselves, the army forcibly conscripted local Karen villagers. One Tenasserim resident later described this process in a sworn deposition:

> When the government needs porter[s], well, the soldier will inform the police, and the police will inform the head of the village. And the head of the village will tell the villagers to go for forced labor. And those who can give money and those who are rich, they can give money and stay at home, because they are afraid that they would be killed. And those who were very poor, as they cannot afford to pay money, they have to go by themselves.[22]

Often, families sent the young and elderly to fulfill their forced labor obligations, because the more able-bodied members of the family, particularly young men, were needed to maintain their farms. Conditions in the conscripted labor gangs were brutal. Workers who could not keep up were summarily executed. Amnesty International reported the following incident:

> I heard Tun Shwe say to the soldier behind him, a private from Battalion 531, "Sir, don't kill me. I will try to do my best to reach your destination. Now I cannot carry, cannot walk, but I will try. Don't punish me, don't kill me." After Tun Shwe exclaimed "I cannot carry, cannot walk" the soldier shot him dead, one bullet from a G-4 at a distance of about four meters, in his back so his insides came out. After the shooting nothing happened, no one could say anything. The soldiers just said to the other porters "complete your duty, go on, go on" as if he was driving cows.

Soldiers in the area routinely confiscated food and property and exhorted money from villagers to support their operations. One villager described the theft of his pig:

> They [soldiers from Light Infantry Battalion 407] said, "what are you doing with these two pigs?" They said, "we will send you and your pigs to jail tomorrow." Another soldier said, "send them to their graves." I thought the troops were going to kill us. Then I told them, "wait a

> minute, let me pray to God." When I said that, one of the soldiers pushed me very hard making me fall down. The next morning, one of the troops came and told me, "We are not going to kill you or send you jail, if you give us one of your pigs." I said, "Please, I want to celebrate Christmas." But, finally they took one of my pigs. I paid 4,000 kyat per pig. That was quite a lot.

Another villager reported having to pay what he called a "pipeline tax."

> About the pipeline construction, none of us know exactly about that, except that we have to pay money for building it. The soldiers came to our village and informed the village and asked for the donation. For our house, we have to pay 500 kyat. The villagers are getting poorer and poorer. Some are selling their own things like cattle to pay the forced labor fees, porter fees, and other forced donations, like donations for all the buildings and so many things. So many villagers are easily getting sick, like diarrhea and oh, I can't think of it all. A lot of them are suffering. So many villagers are trying to leave and come to the border . . . If I mention all of the atrocities of SLORC, I'll not be finished in two days.

Rapes and assaults were used to intimidate and terrorize civilians. In one such incident, a 54-year old Karen woman had been travelling on foot with her granddaughter in December 1993, when they encountered a light infantry battalion patrolling the area immediately south of the pipeline route.

> [The commander] said, "Old woman, tell me the truth. How old is your granddaughter?" I responded, "Seventeen years old." Then he said, "go and tell your granddaughter to come here." I took my granddaughter to him. As soon as he saw me, he yelled at me: "Why did you come with her? I'll kill you with a hoe." . . . He also took out his knife and threatened me . . . I heard my granddaughter screaming "Grandma! Grandma!" But I dared not go. I was so scared. After fifteen minutes they freed my granddaughter. My granddaughter said he told her to sleep with him. She refused. Finally, he raped her . . . Before they released us, they told us not to tell anyone about what happened. And the commander said, "Old woman, if you tell anyone about that, I'll kill you and your relatives."

The army was also alleged to have forcibly relocated civilians whose villages lay in the path of the proposed pipeline. The practice of forcible relocation by the army had escalated in Burma after 1988, according to human rights reports; the number of Burmese compelled to move was estimated from 100,000 to 1.5 million.[23] Critics of the Yadana project charged that several villages that stood in the path of the proposed pipeline were forcibly relocated in the early 1990s. Unocal vigorously denied that that *any* village relocations had occurred in the area after 1992, when the Agreement was signed. However, the company did pay local villagers about around $1 million to reimburse them for 525 acres of land used by the project. In 1995, the Thai government ran an advertisement in the *Bangkok Post* that stated that "Myanmar has recently cleared the way by relocating 11 Karen villages that would otherwise obstruct the passage of the gas resource development project."[24] The company charged that this report was in error.

Although outmanned and outgunned by the army, the KNA and the Karen National Liberation Army, its military wing, carried out a series of attacks against the pipeline project. In March 1995, Karen rebels fired on a convoy of three trucks carrying Total employees and armed SLORC soldiers. Reportedly, several Burmese employees of Total were killed. In December 1995, rebels attempted an attack on Total's fortified base camp, which failed. In February 1996, a second attack on the base camp occurred; this time, six employees were wounded. EarthRights International reported:

> The retaliation from SLORC for these attacks was swift . . . [Several infantry battalions] marched into Shin Byn village . . . The troops seized Saw Kyi Lwin, the village headman. He was accused of collaborating with the KNLA, interrogated and tortured. He was later executed by the SLORC soldiers.

During this period, thousands of villagers fled the area and sought sanctuary as refugees along the Thai border.

In 1996, the International Federation of Human Rights Leagues (FIDH), in a review of evidence collected by its member organizations, reported that the Yadana pipeline had given "occasion to large-scale, repeated and documented violations of human rights . . . [W]ithout the pipeline, all, or at least some, of these violations would not have occurred."[25]

## Monitoring the Situation

During the period prior to pipeline construction, Unocal monitored its investment closely. A

Singapore-based Unocal executive, Joel Robinson, was assigned to oversee the company's interest in the Yadana joint venture. At least half a dozen times prior to January 1996, Robinson and his associates visited the pipeline area to evaluate the situation first hand. He reported his findings to his superiors in a series of reports and letters.[26] During this period, Robinson was also in communication with Total officials and with the U.S. Embassy in Thailand.

In March 1994, Robinson met with Total officials to discuss the threat to the pipeline posed by Karen rebels. He reported:

> The Myanmar Army claims that, despite these people [Karen rebels], they have an area secured only along the proposed pipeline route and within +/–10 kilometers of the proposed pipeline route . . . The Burmese Army claims to have many battalions in the area, based in Kaleinaung, with up to 200 troops in the mountain jungle area near the border along the pipeline route.

Over the following year, Robinson learned more about the activities of the Myanmar Army, and he seemed worried about his findings. In March 1995, Robinson wrote:

> [I have received] more of the publications of the "Karen press" which depicted in more detail than I have ever seen before the increased encroachment of SLORC activities into the villages of the pipeline area. Our assertion that the SLORC has not expanded and amplified its usual methods around the pipeline on our behalf may not withstand much scrutiny.

His report two months later, however, was more positive.

> Unocal's observer in Myanmar spent four days in early May [1995] visiting 11 villages along the pipeline route, meeting with over 160 villagers. . . . It is clear that there is strong local support for the project. Local people welcome the jobs, the training, and the benefits to the local economy.

That same month, Robinson met with U.S. embassy officials in Thailand. A confidential cable later sent by embassy personnel summarized their conversation.

> On the general issue of the close working relationship between Total/Unocal and the Burmese military, Robinson had no apologies to make. He stated forthrightly that the companies have hired the Burmese to provide security for the project and pay for this through the Myanmar Oil and Gas Enterprise (MOGE). He said that three truckloads of soldiers accompany project officials as they conduct survey work and visit villages. He said Total's security officials meet with military counterparts to inform them of the next day's activities so that soldiers can ensure the area is secure and guard the work perimeter while the survey team goes about its business.[27]

In late 1995, perhaps in response to concerns raised by Robinson and by external human rights groups, Unocal commissioned another consultant's report on conditions in the area, apparently in an effort to learn more about the army's activities. The resulting document was hardly reassuring. The consultant, a former military attaché to the U.S. Embassy in Burma, wrote the company:

> My conclusion is that egregious human rights violations have occurred, and are occurring now, in southern Burma. The most common are forced relocations without compensation to families from land near/along the pipeline route; forced labor to work on infrastructure projects supporting the pipeline (the SLORC calls this government service in lieu of payment of taxes); and imprisonment and/or execution by the army of those opposing these actions. Unocal, by seeming to have accepted SLORC's version of events, appears at best naïve and at worst a willing partner in the situation.

## Forced Labor

One of the issues that clearly concerned Robinson, and his contacts at Total, was the military's use of conscripted labor. The two companies agreed that forced labor was unacceptable. In April 1994, he reported to his superiors:

> Total and Unocal will insist upon western style construction practices including fair labor rates and the use of an internationally recognized contractor. I specifically asked if Total would ever agree to allow Myanmar to build a road or some other facilities as a partial contribution to the partnership knowing that they might use impressed labor. Mr. Madeo [from Total] assured us that would be unacceptable to Total.

A year later, Robinson wrote Total with his "general thoughts." By this time, Robinson had apparently abandoned the idea that the oil companies could prevent the military from conscripting labor. His comments focused, rather, on keeping these practices clearly at arm's length from the pipeline project. He stated:

> [F]rom Unocal's standpoint, probably the most sensitive issue is "what is forced labor" and "how can you identify it." I am sure that you will be thinking about the demarcation between work done by the Project and work done "on behalf of" the Project. Where the responsibility of the Project ends is very important.

Total and Unocal continued to discuss the matter of forced labor, and how to draw a line between the military's actions and those of the operator. A few months later, Total's construction manager, Herve Chagnoux, wrote Robinson:

> By stating that I could not guarantee that the army is not using forced labour, I certainly imply that they might (and they might), but I am saying that we do not have to monitor army's behavior: We have our responsibilities; they have their responsibilities; and we refuse to be pushed into assuming more than what we can really guarantee. About forced labour used by the troops assigned to provide security on our pipeline project, let us admit between Unocal and Total that we might be in a gray zone.

By September 1996, Total had apparently decided that the best course of action would be to pay conscripted workers directly in situations where they were arguably providing services to the pipeline project. Chagnoux wrote Robinson, "when we had knowledge of such occurrences [forced labor supporting pipeline operations], the workers have been compensated." Total also began to provide food rations for both the army and "project helpers" "hired" by the army. Clearly, both oil companies felt uncomfortable in the "gray zone," and Total made a point to pay wages and provide rations for local workers provided by the army to assure they were properly compensated.

## Challenges at Home and Abroad

As Unocal struggled to draw a clear "demarcation" between their sphere of responsibility and the Army's, external pressures on the company from critics in both the United States and abroad were mounting. Human rights organizations continued to express to Unocal their concerns about government abuses in the pipeline area. In January 1995, Greenpeace, EarthRights International, and other activists met with president Imle. In June 1995, Amnesty International sent Unocal their most recent human rights report on Burma. It was accompanied by a cover letter that drew the company's attention to the use of "voluntary labor" in the pipeline area. The letter pointed out, "We know from long experience with this regime that what they call 'voluntary' labor is called forced labor in other parts of the world; and, forced labor not only for convicts, but of ordinary citizens. Myanmar forced labor conditions have been documented to be brutal and even deadly."

At the state and local level, activists lobbied for selective purchasing laws that denied contracts to firms doing business in Burma.[28] Four states and nearly thirty municipalities adopted selective purchasing measures before corporate litigation derailed the campaign.[29]

Unocal's challengers also took their campaign to service station managers, state governments, and company shareholders. Feminist organizations joined the growing anti-Unocal coalition to protest a proposed pipeline in Afghanistan where Taliban fundamentalists denied equal rights to women. A coalition petitioned the California attorney general to revoke Unocal's charter because of crimes against humanity, an effort that failed to persuade the state government but attracted considerable press coverage.[30] Dissident shareholder resolutions calling on Unocal to investigate and disclose information about the Yadana gas pipeline project never won more than 15 percent of votes cast, but attracted some support, including that of the powerful California Public Employees Retirement System (CalPERS). Ka Hsaw Wa visited the U.S. as part of a "Free Burma" campaign, spreading a message of human rights abuses.

Government and nongovernmental organizations also became involved in the debate. Delegates to the International Labor Organization initiated a formal investigation of coerced labor in June 1996. The U.S. Department of Labor also launched an inquiry, and the United Nations continued to assign a special rapporteur to Burma. In 1997, the U.S. Congress imposed new sanctions on Burma, adopting legislation that allowed completion of existing agreements but foreclosed future corporate investments in the rogue nation. As Congress debated sanctions, a number of other corporations withdrew from Burma, giving wide publicity to their human rights concerns.

In October 1996, Burmese plaintiffs brought a class action lawsuit in U.S. District Court under the

Alien Torts Act, charging the pipeline consortium with using forced labor conscripted by the military government. Unocal's Beach and Imle were personally named as defendants. The court granted sovereign immunity to SLORC and MOGE, and also dismissed Total as a defendant, but allowed discovery to proceed against Unocal on claims of forced labor and related human rights violations.

## Through Thick and Thin

On a number of occasions, Unocal executives attempted to persuade activists and the public of the company's determination to proceed in an ethical manner in Burma. For example, in one letter to activists, CEO Beach wrote:

> I want to state unequivocally that Unocal does not tolerate human rights violations in connection with any of our business activities. It is our policy only to do business in countries where we can operate ethically and responsibly. Myanmar is no exception. We are monitoring issues in Myanmar very closely, both on our own and through continuing dialog with international organizations.[31]

Sometime in 1995, by its own report, Unocal launched a $6 million community assistance program in 13 villages in the vicinity of the pipeline.[32] Funded projects included building or renovating health centers and schools; immunizing children; constructing roads, water systems, and power lines; and supporting local enterprises such as poultry, cattle, and pig farms. The company stated that it worked with representative committees in each village to help determine how community development funds would be spent.

Outside observers noted many benefits. In its 1997 report, for instance, the World Health Organization noted that infant mortality rate in the villages in the pipeline vicinity had dropped to about half the national average—to 46 deaths per 1,000 live births, compared with 95 deaths per 1,000 live births for the country overall. The U.S. State Department reported that school attendance was also up in the pipeline region, where 77 percent of children were enrolled, compared with around 60 percent elsewhere.

The company also set out to correct what it viewed as false accusations. On its Web site, in letters to the editor of leading newspapers, and in press releases, it set forth its defense of its involvement in the Yadana project. The company stated that while human rights abuses might have taken place, it was not responsible for the actions of the Burmese government.

> We have always acknowledged the challenges of working in a country under authoritarian rule. We have also acknowledged that it is quite possible that human rights abuses have occurred in Myanmar . . . [However,] foreign companies like Unocal have no control over the actions of the military forces of Myanmar, a sovereign nation.

Moreover, Unocal insisted that it had not directly participated in forced labor, or other abusive practices. It asserted that the pipeline contractor had always paid market wages.

> We are . . . confident that no such [forced labor] abuses have taken place at our work sites or in activities directly related to the Yadana project. We have met with the government numerous times to express our concerns about such abuses.

Total hired an international contractor, Spie-Capag, to carry out the actual construction of the pipeline, which occurred between October 1996 and April 1997. The consortium asserted that it had hired many Burmese, including villagers from the area, and paid wages above the local prevailing rate. The U.S. State Department appeared to confirm this when it reported in 1998: "If charges are made that the pipeline itself was built with forced labor, we would find such charges very difficult to believe."

With respect to its relationship with the Burmese military, company executives described military security in the pipeline area as the type of protection a police would routinely provide to any private business. "We cannot and I cannot personally take responsibility for the conduct of the government of Burma any more than I can take responsibility for the conduct of the Los Angeles Police Department," Imle told a reporter for ABC's Nightline. "I can take responsibility for what goes on in our pipeline area."[33]

In 1998, Unocal commissioned its own "Humanitarian Report on the Yadana Natural Gas Development Project," by the Reverend Richard W. Timm and Justice K.M. Subhan of the Bangladeshi Commission on Justice and Peace. After a visit to the project and nearby villages, the factfinders concluded, "Not only are [the project operators] paying fair wages, well above the market price, but they are keeping their employees happy and the inhabitants of the 13 villages near the pipeline have experienced great improvement in their lives."[34]

**Exhibit 1** Map of Burma

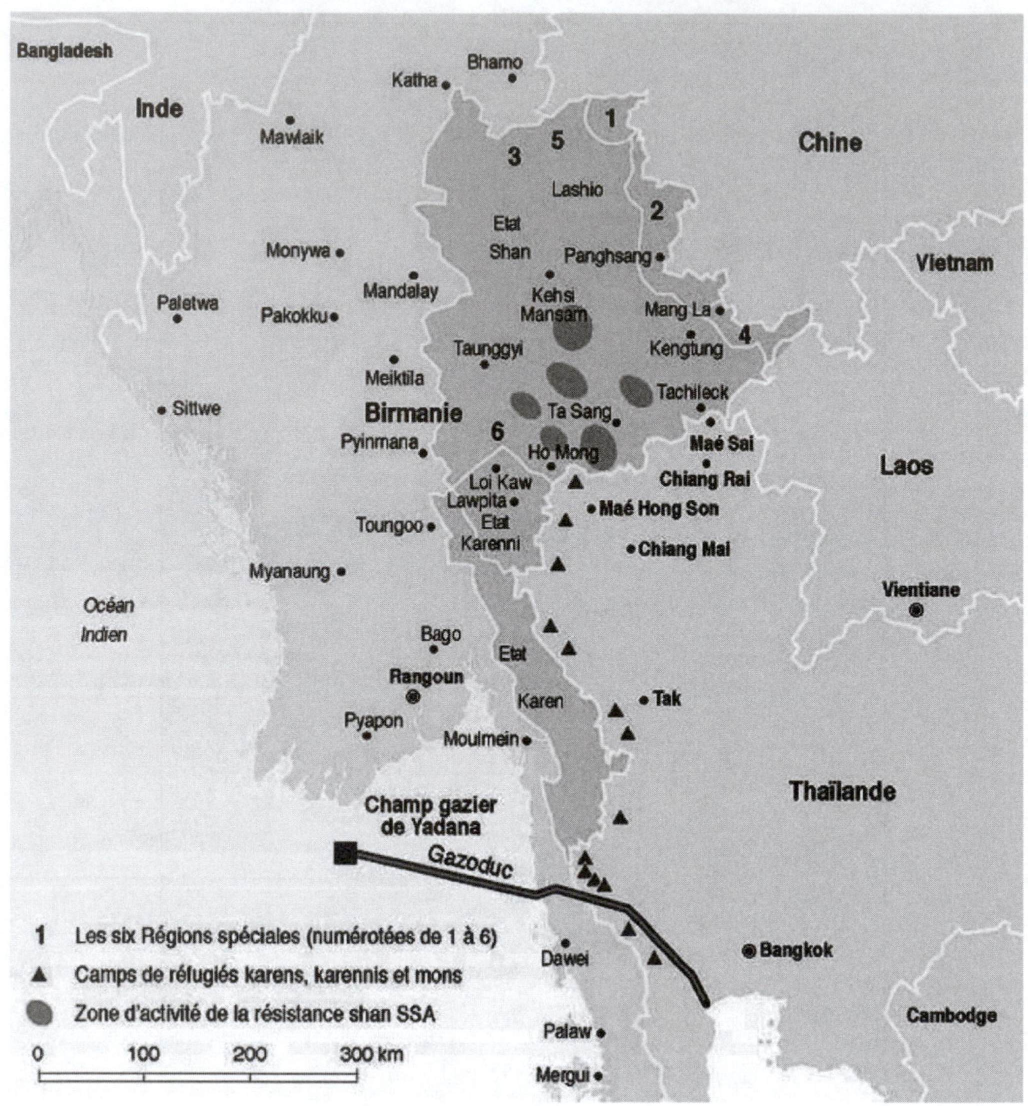


**Exhibit 2** Detailed Map Showing Site of Yadana Gas Pipeline, Relative to Refugee Sites and Resistance Zones

SOURCE: Le Monde Diplomatique (French*), http://www.monde-diplomatique.fr/cartes/thailandedp12000*
Date: January,

On the issue of the impact of foreign investment, Unocal staunchly defended the principle of *constructive engagement.* The company argued that "engagement is by far the more effective way to strengthen emerging economies and promote more open societies." In particular, Unocal asserted that the Yadana project had brought economic opportunity to the people of the Tenasserim region:

Unocal is proud of its involvement in the Yadana project and the tangible benefits it has brought to the people of Myanmar. This has included high-paying jobs, technical training, and medical care, schools, and socioeconomic programs. Throughout the construction phase, Total and Unocal insisted on maintaining a high level of business standards and construction practices, including fair labor rates and use of an internationally recognized contractor. At all times, the project was conducted in accordance with Unocal's guiding principles and values.

Moreover, the company maintained, natural gas supplied by the pipeline would provide a relatively clean source of power in a developing region that already suffered from severe air pollution. Low-cost energy would contribute to the emergence of an Asian middle class and, with it, democratic reform. "The culture of Asia is [based on] long-term relationships," Beach told a reporter for *Forbes* in 1998. "You have to be there through thick and thin."[35]

## Appendix A: Chronology

**1962** General Ne We seizes power in Burma and launches the Burmese "Way to Socialism."

**1982** Natural gas discovered in the Andaman Sea; Total invests $15 million.

**1988** Pro-democracy demonstrations in Burma crushed.

**1990** SLORC imposes harsh military rule and negates elections.

**Dec. 1992** Unocal purchases 49% of Total's share in the Yadana project.

**Feb. 1995** Commercial discovery declared. The Burmese and Thai governments sign a thirty-year contract; Thailand agrees to purchase of gas from the Yadana field.

**1993–1996** Military clears pipeline route, establishes base camp, and builds support infrastructure. Complaints of forced labor and relocation made to ILO, Unocal, and U.S. State Department. Karen rebels attack base camp and construction workers.

**1995** Unocal launches $6 million community assistance program in pipeline area.

**Oct. 1996** Pipeline construction begins. Two U.S. lawsuits are filed against Unocal, Beach, Imle, Total, SLORC and MOGE on behalf of Burmese villagers.

**1997** U.S. Congress adopts economic sanctions against Burma, bars future investment; Massachusetts and other states adopt sanctions; Protesters introduce resolutions at Unocal shareholder meetings; U.S. court dismisses all defendants except Unocal, Beach and Imle; Unocal sells off U.S. assets, launches Project Energy Renaissance.

**June 1998** Pipeline completed on schedule. Critical reports by ILO, U.S. Department of Labor, U.S. State Department.

## Appendix B: Glossary

Andaman Sea West of Burma's Tenasserim region, site of Yadana oil and gas field

Aung San Suu Kyi National League for Democracy party leader; Nobel laureate

Beach, Roger Chairman, CEO of Unocal

CRG Control Risk Group

EarthRights International Non-governmental organization opposed to pipeline

ILO International Labour Organization, Geneva

Imle, John F. President of Unocal

Ka Hsaw Wa Karen refugee, co-founder Earth Rights International

Karen Ethnic minority group in pipeline region

KNU Karen National Union

MGTC Moattama Gas Transportation Company

MOGE Myanma Oil and Gas Exploration (Burmese state owned)

MOU Memorandum of Understanding

Myanmar Burma, country name change made by SLORC in 1988

Ne Win General who seized power in Burma in 1962

PSC Production Sharing Contract

PTTEP Petroleum Authority of Thailand (Thai state owned)

SLORC State Law and Order Restoration Council, military government after 1990; later renamed the State Committee for Peace and Development

Tenasserim Panhandle region of Southern Burma on the Andaman Sea

Total, S.A. French corporation; world's eighth largest energy company

UMOC Unocal Myanmar Offshore Co. Ltd. (Unocal subsidiary)

Unocal Multinational corporation with offices in California and Malaysia

Yadana Natural gas pipeline project linking Andaman Sea field to Thailand

## References

### Books and Articles

Aceves, William J. and Bernard H. Oxman, *Doe v. Unocal, 92 American Journal of International Law,* 309, 1997.

Benson, Robert, *Challenging Corporate Rule: Petition to Revoke Unocal's Charter as a Guide to Citizen Action,* New York: Apex Press, 1999.

Bernstein, Dennis, and Leslie Kean, "People of the Opiate: Burma's Dictatorship of Drugs," *The Nation,* December 16, 1996.

Bowerset, Laura, "Casenote: Doe v. Unocal: Tortuous Decision for Multinationals Doing Business in Politically Unstable Environments," *Transnational Lawyer* v. 11, no. 1 (Spring, 1998), p. 361–82.

Branigin, William, "Unocal 'Smoking Gun' Alleged; Burmese Refugees Claim Cable Supports Abuse Charges," *Washington Post,* May 2, 2000, p. E1.

Branigin, William, "Rights Victims in Burma Want a U.S. Company to Pay; Suit Alleges Army Abuses While Pipeline Was Built," *The Washington Post,* April 13, 1999, p. A13.

Brunnstrom, David, "Risks Foreseen in Total's $1 Billion Burma Venture," *Reuters,* October 27, 1992.

"Business in Politically Unstable Environments," Spring, 1998, 11 *The Transnational Lawyer* 361.

Compa, Lance and Stephen Diamond, eds., *Human Rights, Labor Rights, and International Trade,* Philadelphia: University of Pennsylvania Press, 1996.

"Company Profile: Unocal: Three-Pronged Turnaround," *Petroleum Economist,* July 21, 1998, pp. 23 ff.

Cox, Gail D. "A 'Low Tech' Guy In High-Stakes Job: Dennis P. R. Codon, Unocal Corp." *The National Law Journal,* November 10, 1997.

EarthRights International and Southeast Asian Information Network, *Total Denial: A Report on the Yadana Pipeline Project in Burma,* 10 July 1996. http://www.burmafund.org/Research_Library/yadana_natural_gas_pipeline_proj.htm

"Getting the Lead Out," *Forbes,* July 17, 1995, pp. 106–107.

Greer, Jed, "U.S. Petroleum Giant to Stand Trial for Burma Atrocities," *The Ecologist,* January/February, 1998; available online at: http://www.irn.org/burma/news/ecologist.html.

Hast, Adele, Ed., "Unocal Corporation," pp. 569–571 in *International Directory of Company Histories,* Chicago: St. James Press, 1991.

Hoover's Online, "Unocal Corporation," available online at: http://www.hoovers.com/co/capsule/9/0,2163,11569,00.html.

Human Rights Watch, "New Burma Policy Needed After Decade of No Results," August 6, 1998.

Imle, John F. Jr., "Pipeline Project in Myanmar," *Los Angeles Times,* June 7, 1996, Letters, Metro; Part B; p. 8.

International Commission of Jurists, *The Burmese Way: To Where? Report of a Mission to Burma,* December 1991.

International Energy Agency, *South East Asia Gas Study* OECD/IEA Paris, 1999.

International Federation of Human Rights Leagues (FIDH), *Burma, Total and Human Rights: Dissection of a Project,* Nov. 1996.

Iritani, Evelyn, "Feeling the Heat: Unocal Defends Myanmar Gas Pipeline Deal," *Los Angeles Times,* February 20, 1995, Monday, Home Edition Business, p. D1.

Iritani, Evelyn, "Myanmar Project Fueling International Controversy," *Los Angeles Times,* November 24, 1996, p. 1.

Iritani, Evelyn, "Coalition Challenges Burma Trade Ban," *Los Angeles Times.* May 1, 1998, p. D1.

"Justices Overturn a State Law on Myanmar," *The New York Times,* June 20, 2000, p. A23.

Lothrop, Gloria Ricci, "A Centennial Salute: UNOCAL," *Southern California Quarterly,* 72(2), pp. 173–187, 1990.

Mergui Tavoy Information Service, Karen National Union, Report the Facts: The Yadana Gas Pipeline Construction in Tavoy District, Tennasserim Division, 1995.

"Myanmar Pipeline Project Hits Major Snag," *Oil & Gas Journal,* Mar 1, 1999; p. 42.

"Myanmar: Trouble in the Pipeline," *The Economist,* January 18, 1997, p. 39.

Nyberg, Maurice, "At Risk from Complicity with Crime." *Financial Times.* July 28, 1998, Inside Track, p.15.

Oo, Maw May, "Ethnic Issues in the Politics of Burma: A Karen Perspective," paper presented at the University of California, Los Angeles, at the Free Burma '97 conference, October 4–6, 1997, available online at: *http://karen.org/history/docs/may.htm.*

Palmeri, Christopher, "Through Thick and Thin," *Forbes,* June 15, 1998.

Pederson, Barbara L., *Unocal 1890–1990: A Century of Spirit,* Los Angeles: Unocal Corp., 1990.

Pizzurro, Joseph and Nancy Delaney, "New Peril for Companies Doing Business Overseas: Alien Tort Claims Act Interpreted Broadly," *The New York Law Journal* November 24, 1997. http://www.ljx.com/ practice/ intrade/ 11240versea.html.

Plate, Tom, "Capitalism vs. Moralism in Burma," *Los Angeles Times,* September 24, 1996, p. B7.

Prussel, Deborah, "Feminists Take on UNOCAL," *The Progressive,* October 1998, pp. 1–15.

"Reinventing Unocal" [interview with Roger C. Beach], *Oil and Gas Investor,* Sept. 1998, pp. 45–48.

Schoenberger, Karl, "The Human Rights Pipeline; Charges of Slave Labor in Myanmar Lead to Ballot at Unocal," *Los Angeles Times,* April 11, 1994, p. D1.

Shelton, Anna, "Storyteller for Human Rights," *The Progressive,* September 1999, p. 13.

Silverstein, Ken, "Beyond Rangoon," *The Village Voice;* New York; Apr 22, 1997.

Stegemeier, Richard J., *A Century of Spirit: The History of Unocal,* New York: The Newcomen Society, 1990.

Stevens, Jane, "Myanmar Military's Rule by Repression," *Los Angeles Times,* February 22, 1993, p. 1.

Timm, Rev. Richard W., CSG, and Justice K.M. Subhan, "Humanitarian Report on the Yadana Natural Gas Development Project," Bangladeshi Commission on Justice and Peace, January, 1998.

"Unocal Is Shifting Strategy to International Operations," *Wall Street Journal,* Nov. 20, 1996, p. B4.

"Unocal Plans Major Gas Grid in South Asia," *Oil & Gas Journal;* Dec. 15, 1997; pp. 24–25.

"Unocal Sees Strong Growth From International Projects and Prospects," *PR Newswire,* July 14, 1998.

"Unocal Unveils South Asia Integrated Gas Project," *http://www.unocal.com* (press release dated 12/9/97).

Unocal, *http://www.unocal.com/myanmar/index. htm.*

Unocal, *A New World A New Unocal,* Unocal 1996 Annual Report.

Unocal, *Unocal in Myanmar (Burma): The Yadana Project,* March 1997.

Wells, Leslie, "A Wolf in Sheep's Clothing: Why Unocal Should be Liable Under U.S. Law for Human Rights Abuses in Burma," 32 *Colum. J.L. & Soc. Probs.* Fall, 1998, p. 35.

Welty, Earl M., and Frank J. Taylor, *The 76 Bonanza: The Fabulous Life and Times of the Union Oil Company of California,* Menlo Park, CA: Lane Book Co., 1966.

Winston, Morton, "U.S. Litigation and Corporate Responsibility for Human Rights," *http://www.corpwatch.org/trac/feature/ humanrts/resistance/winston.html.*

Winston, Morton, "John Doe vs. Unocal: The boardroom/courtroom battles for ethical turf," *Whole Earth;* San Rafael; Summer 1999; pp. 17–19.

Zia-Zarifi, Saman, "Suing Multinational Corporations in the U.S. for Violating International Law," 4 UCLA *Journal of International Law and Foreign Affairs.* 81 Spring/Summer, 1999.

**International Labor Organization**

*Forced Labour in Myanmar (Burma).* Report of the Commission of Inquiry appointed under article 26 of the Constitution of the International Labour Organization to examine the observance by Myanmar of the Forced Labour Convention, 1930 (No. 29). Geneva, 1998, http://www.ilo.org/public/english/bureau/inf/pr/

Memorandum of the Government of Myanmar on the Report of the Director-General to the Members of the Governing Body, May 21, 1999, http://www.ilo.org/public/english/standards/relm/gb/docs/gb276/gb-6-a2.htm

**United Nations**

Development and International Economic Co-operation: Transnational Corporations, U.N. ESCOR, 2d Sess., U.N. Doc. E/1990/94.

Interim Report of the Special Rapporteur on Burma, (1997), UN Doc. A/52/484.

Interim Report of the Special Rapporteur on Burma, (1996), UN Doc. A/51/466.

Report of the Special Rapporteur on Burma, (1997), UN Doc. E/CN.4/1997/64.

Report of the Special Rapporteur on Burma, (1995), UN Doc. E/CN.4/1995/65.

Yozo Yokota, Report of the Special Rapporteur of the Commission on Human Rights on the Situation of Human Rights in Myanmar, A/50/568, October 16, 1995.

**United States**

U.S. Department of State, Burma Country Reports on Human Rights Practices, *http://www.state.gov/www/global/human_rights/ 1997_hrp_report.html*

Department of Labor, Bureau of International Labor Affairs, Report on Labor Practices in Burma, September 1998.

**U.S. Cases**

*Doe v Unocal,* 110 F.Supp.2d 1294 (C.D. Cal.2000)

*John Doe I v. Unocal,* 963 F. Supp. 880 (C.D. Cal. 1997) http://diana.law.yale.edu/diana/db/31198–1.html

*John Doe I v. Unocal,* 27 F. Supp. 2d 1174; (C.D. Cal. 1998)

*John Doe I v. Unocal,* 67 F. Supp. 2d 1140, (C.D. Cal. 1999)

*National Coalition Gov't of the Union of Burma v. Unocal, Inc.,* 176 F.R.D. 329 (C.D. Cal. 1997)

**Appeals Briefs**

Appellants' Opening Brief, *Doe v. Unocal* No. 00–56603 in the U.S. Court of Appeals for the Ninth Circuit, February 26, 2001.

Brief of Amici Curiae in support of Plaintiffs-Appellants Urging Reversal , *Doe v. Unocal* No. 00–56603 and Roe v. Unocal, No. 00–56628 in the U.S. Court of Appeals for the Ninth Circuit (submitted by Center for International Environmental Law, Global Exchange, Rainforest Action Network, Sierra Club).

Defendants/Appellees' Consolidated Answering Brief, *Doe v. Unocal* No. 00–56603 and Roe v. Unocal, No. 00–56628 in the U.S. Court of Appeals for the Ninth Circuit, May 7, 2001

**Videotapes**

"The Opium Kings," PBS/Frontline, first aired May 20, 1997. A transcript is available at *www.pbs.org/wgbh/frontline/shows/heroin/etc/script.html*.

"Unocal in Burma," ABC Nightline, aired March 28, 2000. A transcript is available at *http://abcnews.go.com/onair/nightline/transcripts/n1000328_trans_1.html.*

## Notes

1. This case was written on the basis of publicly available information and of trial records provided by attorneys solely for the purpose of stimulating student discussion. All individuals and events are real. An earlier version of this case was presented at the 2001 annual meeting of the North American Case Research Association. The comments of reviewers at that meeting are greatly appreciated. Research for this case was supported, in part, by San Jose State University and the University of Cincinnati; this support is gratefully acknowledged.

2. Transcript of meeting, from the trial transcript, quoted by Judge Ronald S. W. Lew in his decision of August 31, 2000, *Doe v. Unocal,* 110 R. Supp.2nd 1294 (C.D. Cal.2000).

3. This account of the history of Union Oil Company of California is based on Barbara L. Pederson, *Unocal 1890–1990: A Century of Spirit* (Los Angeles: Unocal Corp., 1990); Gloria Ricci Lothrop, "A Centennial Salute: UNOCAL," *Southern California Quarterly,* 72(2), pp. 173–187, 1990; Richard J. Stegemeier, "A Century of Spirit: The History of Unocal" (New York: The Newcomen Society, 1990); Adele Hast, ed., "Unocal Corporation," pp. 569–571 in *International Directory of Company Histories* (Chicago: St. James Press, 1991), v. 4; Earl M. Welty and Frank J. Taylor, *The 76 Bonanza: The Fabulous Life and Times of the Union Oil Company of California* (Menlo Park, CA: Lane Book Co., 1966); "Unocal Corporation," in "Houston: Simply Spectacular," in *Houston Magazine,* online at: http://www.towery.com/relocation/tapes-try-houston/profiles/e.pdf; and Hoover's Online, "Unocal Corporation," http://www.hoovers. com/co/capsule/9/0,2163,11569,00.html.

4. "Unocal Corporation," in Adele Hast, op. cit., p. 570.

5. "Getting the Lead Out," *Forbes,* July 17, 1995, pp. 106–107.

6. "Reinventing Unocal" [interview with Roger C. Beach], *Oil and Gas Investor,* Sept. 1998, pp. 45–48.

7. Barry Lane, quoted in "Company Profile: Unocal: Three-Pronged Turnaround," *Petroleum Economist,* July 21, 1998, pp. 23 ff.

8. "Unocal Is Shifting Strategy to International Operations," *Wall Street Journal,* Nov. 20, 1996, p. B4.

9. "Unocal Unveils South Asia Integrated Gas Project" (press release dated 12/9/97).

10. "Unocal Sees Strong Growth From International Projects and Prospects," *PR Newswire,* July 14, 1998.

11. Memorandum of Understanding, dated July 9, 1992, quoted by Judge Ronald S. W. Lew in his decision of Aug. 31, 2000, from the trial record, *Doe v. Unocal,* 110 R. Supp.2nd 1294 (C.D. Cal.2000).

12. "Myanmar: Trouble in the Pipeline," *The Economist,* January 18, 1997, p. 39. Other estimates put the figure as high as $400 million a year.

13. Control Risk Group report to Unocal Corp., dated May 1992, quoted by Judge Ronald S. W. Lew from the trial record in his decision of Aug. 31, 2000, *Doe v. Unocal,* 110 R. Supp.2nd 1294 (C.D. Cal.2000).

14. Deposition of Stephen Lipman, quoted by Judge Ronald S.W. Lew from the trial record in his decision of Aug. 31, 2000, *Doe v. Unocal,* 110 R.Supp.2nd 1294 (C.D. Cal.2000).

15. U.S. Department of State, "1995 Country Report on Human Rights Practices: Burma."

16. Dennis Bernstein and Leslie Kean, "People of the Opiate: Burma's Dictatorship of Drugs," *The Nation,* December 16, 1996. This topic was also treated in a Frontline documentary, "The Opium Kings," aired May 20, 1997. A transcript is available at *www.pbs.org/wgbh/frontline/shows/heroin/etc/script.html.*

17. No accurate population census has been conducted in Burma since 1939. The KNU has claimed a population of 7 million; Human Rights Watch has estimated the Karen to number between 3 and 4 million.

18. The KNU's interpretation of the history of the Karen people may be found at: http://karen.org/history.

19. Maw May Oo, "Ethnic Issues in the Politics of Burma: A Karen Perspective," paper presented at the University of California, Los Angeles, at the Free Burma '97 conference, October 4–6, 1997, available at: *http://karen.org/history/docs/may.htm.*

20. The entire text of *Total Denial* is available online at: www.burmafund.org/Research_ Library/yadana_natural_gas_pipeline_proj.html. The Web site for EarthRights International is at: www.earthrights.org. In 1999, Wa received the Reebok Human Rights Award for his work.

21. The quotations in this section are taken from *Total Denial,* unless otherwise noted.

22. Deposition of John Doe IX, quoted in testimony given by Katharine J. Redford of EarthRights International, available online at: http://www.irn.org/burma/news/testimony.html.

23. U.S. Dept. of Labor, Bureau of International Affairs, *Report on Labor Practices in Burma,* September 1998, p. 7.

24. April 17, 1995, *Bangkok Post.*

25. International Federation of Human Rights Leagues, *Burma, Total, and Human Rights: Dissection of a Project,* November 1996.

26. Unless otherwise noted, all quotations in this section and the following section are drawn from the deposition of Joel Robinson, as quoted by Judge Ronald S.W. Lew from the trial record in his decision of Aug. 31, 2000, *Doe v. Unocal,* 110 R.Supp.2nd 1294 (C.D. Cal.2000).

27. Quoted in Appellants' Opening Brief, *Doe v. Unocal* No. 00–56603 in the U.S. Court of Appeals for the Ninth Circuit, February 26, 2001, p. 8. This cable was produced through a Freedom of Information Act request by plaintiffs' attorneys.

28. Silverstein, Ken, "Beyond Rangoon," *The Village Voice,* April 22, 1997.

29. "Justices Overturn a State Law on Myanmar," *The New York Times*, June 20, 2000, p. A23.

30. Robert Benson, *Challenging Corporate Rule: The Petition to Revoke Unocal's Charter as a Guide to Citizen Action* (New York: Council on International and Public Affairs, Apex Press), 1999.

31. Quoted by Judge Ronald S.W. Lew from the trial record in his decision of Aug. 31, 2000, *Doe v. Unocal,* 110 R.Supp.2nd 1294 (C.D. Cal.2000).

32. This figure and the subsequent quotations are taken from Unocal's Web site, at www.unocal.com, unless otherwise noted.

33. "Unocal in Burma," Nightline, March 28, 2000.

34. "Humanitarian Report on the Yadana Natural Gas Development Project," January, 1998.

35. "Through Thick and Thin," *Forbes,* June 15, 1998, pp. 46–47.

# Case 1.3

# COMMON BOND VALUES AT THE NEW ZEALAND OFFICE OF AT&T

DEBORAH SHEPHERD

*"What I really wanted in the organisation was a group of responsible, interdependent workers, similar to a flock of geese flying in the "V" formation . . . [with] every goose being responsible for getting itself to wherever the gaggle was going, changing roles whenever necessary . . . And whenever the task changed, the geese would be responsible for changing the structure of the group to accommodate, similar to the geese that fly in a "V" but land in waves.*

[from Belasco & Stayer, 1993, "Flight of the Buffalo"]

It was writings such as these that inspired Jerre Stead, former Executive Vice President and Chief Executive Officer at Corporate Office in America's AT&T Global Information Solutions (GIS). Jerre Stead, a Belasco admirer and follower, was one of the key change agents wanting to bring the former NCR into alignment with AT&T following the AT&T take-over. And while Stead had a clear vision and ideology which supported the views and ideas in the book "Flight of the Buffalo," the question plaguing Una Diver's mind was how could this metaphor of the geese and the many other ideas fed down from AT&T's American Corporate Office be translated into tangible practices and policies to assist the 210 people who work in the New Zealand office of AT&T GIS.

## Una Diver, Human Resources, AT&T GIS, New Zealand

How would the "down-to-earth," practical Kiwis working in the New Zealand offices respond to these types of ideas? The reason Una Diver, from Human Resources in AT&T GIS NZ, was contemplating these issues was that in a couple of days, she would be hosting Kim Rose, a visiting Australian AT&T trainer. Rose was coming to New Zealand to introduce and implement a host of ideas from Corporate Office in America. Specifically during this visit he was going to facilitate workshops on the values called *"Our Common Bond"* and the new *"Vision and Direction"* workshops that everyone in AT&T GIS throughout the world were required to

SOURCE: This case was prepared as a basis for classroom discussion only. No part of this case may be reproduced in any form without the permission of the author. Originally published in *Cross-Cultural Management: Case study development and delivery.* The Research Institute for Asia and Pacific Economic Co-operation (APEC), 153-161. Reprinted with permission.

attend. This included both employees and everyone in a management position although interesting at AT&T the terms managers and employees had been replaced with the terms "coaches" and "associates" respectively.

This was May 1994. As Una pondered on the upcoming workshops, she also reflected on her brief time with the company since joining in October 1993. Una had joined when AT&T GIS was still called NCR as the Human Resource assistant. In the 8 months until the following May she had witnessed and been part of a huge number of changes as NCR was integrated into the AT&T stable of businesses.

## The Old NCR

NCR was an established company that had been operating in New Zealand since 1907 and during that time had successfully managed three generations of technological change from cash registers, to accounting machines, to computers, the market it was currently operating within. In September 1991, NCR merged with AT&T. However, when Una joined the company, the guaranteed two-year "hands-off" period was still in place (until November, 1993) and so while there were pockets of change occurring and senior management knew change was imminent, for a few short months, Una was part of NCR. The AT&T acquisition of NCR had apparently been aggressive and NCR had resisted the change for some time. Consequently, many people believed that the "hands off" two-year period was agreed to as a way of assisting NCR to adjust to the inevitable widespread changes.

In her short time with NCR, Una could see that it was a company that appeared to foster traditional values such as being caring and family-like. This was evidenced by the fact that there were people in the organisation who had worked for NCR as engineers since leaving school and have never left NCR—some individuals had worked for the company for over 30 years when AT&T came into the picture. For many NCR people working for another company was undoubtedly going to be a real challenge. This uncertainty and concern about change was especially heightened when the first wave of restructuring occurred soon after the official take-over period. At this time staff retrenchment was achieved through non-replacement, redundancies, and early retirement options. However, such practices had not been seen very often in the NCR "good old days." In one year (from December 1993 to December 1994) the total number of staff went from 260 to 204. But as Una thought about the reduced head count, she accepted that AT&T could not be solely "blamed," if that is the right word, for the redundancies. Prior to the take-over, NCR had started to change albeit slowly with the inevitable recognition that the status quo could no longer prevail in an increasingly competitive and global industry.

Well before AT&T initiated any changes, there was a group of people, many of whom were reasonably new to NCR, who considered the company too conservative and traditional. There was concern about the overly inward focus on internal issues and the lack of focus on customers and other external matters. It was seen as a company made up of "too much dead wood" which was slow to make critical decisions. Even amongst the most loyal NCR supporters, people were aware that the company would need to change if it was going to survive in the face of the changing market and altered business style within the Information Technology industry. As a result, some restructuring had already begun in NZ prior to November 1993 when NCR officially became the computing arm of AT&T. For example, the Customer Support Services (CSS) division, the largest group in NCR, had undergone an extensive Business Process Re-engineering exercise in which the way the division conducted its business was analysed. Changes were then implemented aimed at focusing more explicitly on delivering quality services to the customer. Furthermore, NCR New Zealand had also acknowledged that quality was going to be an integral part of the success of their business at a company wide level. Consequently, the company had been through the process of becoming ISO900036 accredited by Telarc prior to the merger with AT&T.

## Life After the AT&T Takeover

However, as Una now realised, compared to what lay ahead, these changes were merely tinkering within the established parameters of the NCR way. The changes that followed the AT&T take-over were wide reaching and the implications for the way work would be conducted in the future, profound. As Una reflected on her time since the AT&T presence had been felt she decided that it was definitely far more competitive, market driven, and customer focused with an overt and explicit concern for the bottom line dollar profit compared to NCR.

However, despite the many changes that have been implemented since AT&T acquired NCR, some of the old legacies of the NCR days have nevertheless continued. For example, the sales people continue to be the ones who are recognised and rewarded for company successes while the customer support services (CSS) division, primarily field engineers, frequently feel forgotten and ignored. This group of engineers has historically felt an under-valued part of the corporation, despite the fact that they are an integral part of the business model in New Zealand. As Una notes, she is fully aware that CSS is the bread and butter of the organisation, but because it is the less glamorous side of the business it is easily and often overlooked by certain groups of people (including those in senior positions). The engineers themselves are acutely aware of this. They watch as the sales people are rewarded financially as well as through benefits including cars and trips to overseas destinations for sales conventions because sales figures have been met-targets to which the field engineers believe they also contribute. In Auckland these differences are further heightened by the fact that the sales and administration people are based in the Head Office location while the CSS division is across town in a separate, less plush, location.

Although some of the old NCR ways still exist in GIS, AT&T has overtly attempted to abolish the NCR culture and replace it with something more akin to the way AT&T as a whole operates. One of the most obvious attempts to change the old NCR culture has been through the staff composition changes to the American Corporate Office GIS Quality Council. When NCR became AT&T GIS, many of NCR's most senior executives were still part of the company. However, since 1991 this American Corporate Quality Council (the equivalent to a senior management team) has slowly but surely changed so that it is now composed of mainly AT&T people or people from outside either the AT&T or NCR networks. In fact, the former CEO of GIS, Jerre Stead, fits this latter category. He was new to both NCR and AT&T although not to the computer industry (and has since left himself). While arguably this head office change had little immediate impact on the New Zealand office, the flow-on effect was such that eventually the changes initiated at the US head-quarters were filtered out to all of the GIS offices world-wide.

## AT&T's Customer Focused Teams

One such initiative, which resulted in fundamental change for previous NCR people, was the shift in focus with respect to the way the organisation was structured and business conducted. A customer-focused business model was introduced aimed at grouping individuals in the company together to focus on discrete markets or customers. The corporate focus for AT&T GIS is in niche marketing of products and services. Although GIS has six-target markets world wide (Financial and Insurance, Retail, Communications, Public Sector, Manufacturing of Consumer Goods, and Transportation), the New Zealand division only concentrates on three of these markets; retail, financial, and communications (see Appendix 1, the organisational structure). For each of these three markets, there is a Customer Focused Team (CFT) that is responsible for delivering complete solutions to their customers in the form of hardware, software and services. These cross-functional teams were designed to better understand customer needs and interests, interpret them and then work with marketing and support teams to provide smart, deliverable solutions that fit the unique profile of every customer. This reorganisation of the way work was conducted and by whom was a deliberate strategy by AT&T GIS to assist it to reach its newly articulated Vision and Mission.

## AT&T's Vision

"Together, always delighting the customer."

## AT&T's Mission

"To be the world's best at bringing computing and communication solutions together to provide people easy access to information and to each other—anytime, anywhere."

While AT&T world-wide has grown, diversified, and altered the way it conducts business, it has, all the while, continued to be a highly successful international company. The combined company has annual revenues of approximately US$67 billion dollars and employs more than 300,000 people around the globe. It ranks in the "top three" of the computer industry which ever way it is measured—be it size, operating income (profit), or revenue. AT&T GIS New Zealand is also a very successful company. It is one of the nation's largest and most successful suppliers of information processing products and services with annual revenues of over NZ$50 million and employing over 200 people in 16 locations.

Yet despite these successes, Bob Allen, the Chief Executive Officer and Chairman of the Board for the entire AT&T Corporation, along with others in senior management positions at AT&T Corporate Office in the USA, were feeling some concern and starting to ask some far-reaching questions. How could they maintain and strengthen AT&T's success? How could they assist AT&T associates to adjust to the changes, continue to work hard towards the company goals, and increase, or in the case of the recently taken over NCR associates instill, loyalty to AT&T?

## Development of a Values Set at AT&T

In answering some of these critical questions, it was decided that there was a need for a shared value set that would guide behaviour, decision-making, internal and external interactions and essentially govern the way AT&T people conducted business with both their internal and external customers. As a result of the many organisational changes, Bob Allen perceived a sense of confusion around what the company stood for amongst associates and was concerned that people in AT&T were struggling to adjust. He had hearing through his network that some associates had concerns about the company. He then began reflecting on the question: "If everyone is working fairly independently in their customer-focused teams (CFTs) then what is the glue that holds the company together?" In response to this, and other similar questions, Allen and members from the US Quality Council began work on what he called "The Common Bond."

However, recognising the importance of getting people's input, Bob Allen didn't develop AT&T's values alone. He encouraged and received plenty of assistance. From meetings that spawned the original ideas, through surveys and then focus groups, hundreds of associates, mainly Americans, helped produce what later became *"Our Common Bond"*— a set of five values for AT&T world-wide.

The process began with senior executives outlining seven values upon which associates from many different offices were asked to comment. It was associates who suggested that one of the original values, citizenship, not be a separate value. Similarly, while many associates acknowledged the importance of shareowners receiving a competitive return on investment, they successfully argued that if AT&T people behaved in accordance with all of the other values, benefits to the shareholders would accrue automatically. Both of these changes were accepted.

It was Bob Allen's intention that the values would reflect what critical success elements for AT&T, what differentiates AT&T from its competitors, what would make AT&T a superior place to work, and a set of statements that AT&T people around the globe would embrace. By the end of the process, 16 groups of associates at all job levels, from 8 states and 4 countries (the United States, the Netherlands, the United Kingdom, and Singapore), representing all parts of the business, had voiced their views in focus groups. Following these discussions, the list of values was reduced to the "final five" and the last alteration was to change the title from "The Common Bond" to "Our Common Bond."

## "Our Common Bond"

The following values and brief description now make up "Our Common Bond":

Respect for Individuals

"We treat each other with respect and dignity, valuing individual and cultural differences. We communicate frequently and with candor, listening to each other regardless of level or position."

Dedication to Helping Customers

"We truly care for each customer. We build enduring relationships by understanding and anticipating our customers' needs and by serving them better each time than the time before."

Highest Standards of Integrity

"We are honest and ethical in all our business dealings, starting with how we treat each other. We keep our promises and admit our mistakes. Our personal conduct ensures that AT&T's name is always worthy of trust."

Innovation

"We believe innovation is the engine that will keep us vital and growing. Our culture embraces creativity, seeks different perspectives and risks pursuing new opportunities."

Teamwork

"We encourage and reward both individual and team achievements. We freely join with colleagues across organizational boundaries to advance the interests of customers and shareowners."

During the workshop in which the values were introduced and their meaning and implications discussed, every AT&T member was given a foldout business/information card that included the values and summaries as above. Under the heading "*Our Common Bond*" is the following statement: *"We commit to these values to guide our decisions and behavior."*

After the five value descriptions the concluding statement is: "By living these values, AT&T aspires to set a standard of excellence world-wide that will reward our shareowners, our customers, and all AT&T people."

## Responses to the Values

Una recalls the first time she saw the values and their descriptions. There was no way that you could disagree with their intention, there was no doubt that the values were admirable and worth pursuing but Una wondered whether the values might be "too idealistic to make practical and be of use in the everyday workplace?" Particularly she questioned how New Zealand associates would cope with the very American style of the values and the idea of having them written down and displayed to the public.

Prior to launching the value set to associates across the entire company, sixty senior officers from Corporate devoted a full day to understanding the values and the connections between the values and behaviour and desired business results. These officers engaged in a lively discussion of corporate versus business unit and division values. Should there be a single value set for *all* AT&T people who represent an extremely diverse group of people around the world, or should different groups of people develop or continue to endorse the values that are meaningful to them? One side argued the need for a common bond across all of AT&T, the other argued to maintain other values that some people had worked long and hard to embrace and personally commit to their group's values.

It was Bob Allen who made the final call. He stated that "while we must respect and honour the work already done on values by AT&T people in their business units and divisions, *"Our Common Bond*" must become the core, the corporation's 'glue.'" Bob Allen believed that with these values, "we preserve the best of our past and define the framework for our future success."

Now, almost one year since the values were introduced to NZ, along with many other directives from America, Una considers if Bob Allen was right in his decision. Una could only reflect on the implications for the NZ office, but certainly she had experienced some resistance and difficulty implementing US directives amongst the strong-minded and independent NZ associates. "Are HR coaches in other countries experiencing similar resistance?" wondered Una.

## Values Workshops

The values were introduced to every associate of AT&T via training sessions by specially trained facilitators for this role from within AT&T. Each workshop discussed the five values in detail, including what behaviours reflected the spirit of each value and which behaviours violated the underlying meaning and intention of each value. Issues such as harassment, acknowledging and valuing diversity in the workplace, managing change, giving and receiving feedback and personal development were addressed during these sessions. In New Zealand Kim Rose and Una Diver facilitated these workshops during the first six months of 1994. All NZ associates attended a two-day workshop that not only addressed *"Our Common Bond"* values but also included sessions on Opportunity and Change, and Vision and Direction.

Interestingly, the people least committed to these sessions were senior management personnel, the senior coaches. During one workshop, one of the NZ quality council members was never seated for more than 15 minutes without leaving to take or make telephone calls on a cellular phone. Another was required to give part of a seminar and, seemingly, from nonchalance and a lack of preparation, read straight from the manual and seemed totally disinterested and, perhaps, even cynical about the material. Yet another coach was part of a discussion group during the workshop and said something derogatory to one of the other discussants. When the offended individual chastised the manager by saying that the remark was "a common bond violation" the manager replied with "tell someone who cares."

Kim Rose saw many incidents that indicated that it was frequently more difficult getting people in senior positions to adopt the values and align their behaviour to them than people further down the organisational hierarchy. Rose pondered that "perhaps the values were more threatening for senior people if associates under them could challenge their behaviour."

## Tony Bradley, CEO, AT&T GIS, NZ Division

For New Zealander Tony Bradley, the chief executive officer of AT&T GIS New Zealand, he was certainly prepared to champion the values as a desirable and worthwhile contribution to the way AT&T should operate. He believed that having a single organisational culture and single values set for *all* AT&T people world-wide could potentially remove the corridors of power and give people a set of behaviours within which to work.

As Tony Bradley reflected on the current business environment, he pictured a world of retrenchment, downsizing, re-engineering and constant change—all the more reasons, in his opinion, for the common bond values to be useful. Furthermore, being in a senior coach position in a company that is being explicit about valuing integrity and respecting individuals has assisted him and the people he works with to make decisions and manage effectively the people around them. According to Bradley, there was no denying that the values, like other directions for AT&T GIS came top-down from the American Corporate Office. However, because he had been managing in Singapore at the time the values were devised, he felt that he had an opportunity to be involved in the development and introduction of the values. The GIS office in Singapore had a close relationship with Corporate Office in America due to the size of AT&T's presence in Singapore and because the Singapore office was one of the first offices to have the values introduced. Tony had seen their usefulness in a non-western culture as well as in New Zealand, a mostly Western culture. Although he acknowledges that *"Our Common Bond"* can, and will, be interpreted in a variety of ways depending on individuals' own agendas, as a behavioural guide and an avenue for opening otherwise difficult discussions (for example on diversity issues), Bradley is pleased AT&T has their values statement.

## Our Common Bond Values in AT&T GIS NZ

As Tony reflects on the Systemedia coach who has given time off work on Friday afternoons to a particular ethnic group for religious beliefs, their practical use is clearly apparent. The value of "Respect for Individuals" assisted this manager in making the decision. In Bradley's view, along with those in senior positions at the USA corporate office, it is especially important that people at the coach level are seen to act and work in accordance with the common bond values. To facilitate this end AT&T have left nothing to chance.

Twenty five percent of the performance appraisal system for senior coaches is based on the way each coach endorses and acts in accordance with the five Common Bond values. Tony Bradley rates each member of the NZ quality council and poor scores on this part of the appraisal impact on the overall appraisal, which is then directly related to the coach's remuneration package. Low scores result in smaller merit pay increases. At present it is only at the coach level, but it is envisaged that eventually all people in AT&T will be appraised and evaluated in relation to the Common Bond values.

The risk of course with the values is that people may use it as a way of trying to get advantage over others, or for people in positions of power to use the values as a way of maintaining their power. As Una Diver points out, when people are given information they don't want to hear or when something happens that was not what they individually wanted, the Common Bond can be used as a tool to challenge the decision by suggesting a "Common Bond Violation."

On reflection though, Tony Bradley believes that probably 90% of the individuals in the New Zealand subsidiary accept the values at a common sense level but he is aware that there are some individuals who are cynical about their usefulness. Furthermore, Tony acknowledges that for some New Zealanders, being told how to behave by Americans can be insulting, and the hype that was part of the rollout of *"Our Common Bond"* and other related workshops did not necessarily fit with the New Zealand style of work. Una Diver also shares this last sentiment, as she is the one most often responsible for running the workshops or training sessions or disseminating the information sent from the United States Corporate Office.

Una believes that the USA Corporate Office should give information and ideas but there should be some flexibility so any necessary adjustments to the material, the language, the style of the presentation or the activities to be included can be made so that it fit more closely with the way a particular subsidiary organisation operates. However, Una is in favour of having tight controls in place to ensure that the workshops, training, celebrations etc are held. She knows it would otherwise be too easy to get caught up with day-to-day business and overlook such activities or avoid them because some New Zealand associates may be cynical. For example, it didn't take very long for Our Common Bond to be labelled "A Common Blond" amongst NZ associates and for the jokes to spring up. However, Una wonders whether this was not just an attempt to use humour as a way of coping with some serious issues such as harassment or diffusing the awkwardness some NZ associates may have felt explicitly discussing values in the workplace.

## Appendix 1: AT&T Organisational Structure

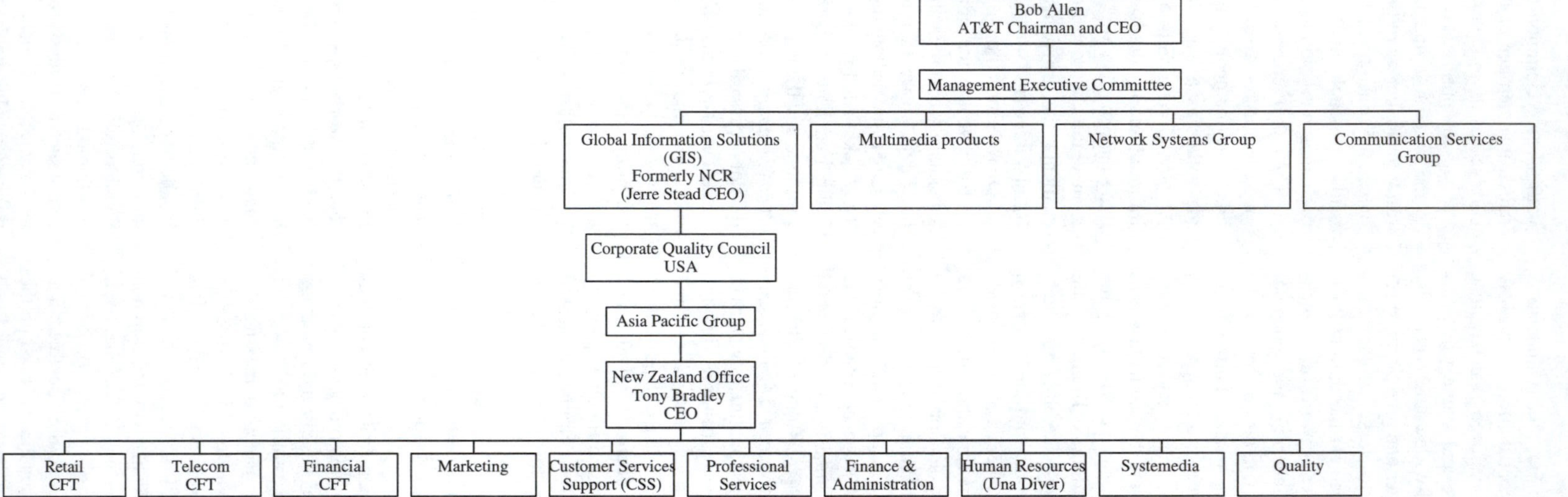

Una recalls the feedback from staff about the Common Bond and other workshops, as being too American, too full of hype and overly drawn out for what were considered to be "general common sense ideas" according to some associates. Even the vision which includes the phrase 'delighting the customer' draws a response from New Zealanders who do not usually use the adjective 'delight' in response to delivering customer service and feel that it is just "too over-the-top" and not the way business is conducted in New Zealand. New Zealanders, it would seem to Una, have a real 'get on and do it' attitude and are not interested in sitting around celebrating and speculating as much as their American counterparts.

Now almost one year later, all of these issues are still highly relevant to Una. Since August 1994 she has been the Human Resources manager and change initiatives continue at AT&T in an ongoing fashion. Jerre Stead has left GIS, but the Common Bond and Vision that he championed in GIS are now embedded in the company. Furthermore, Bob Allen is still CEO of AT&T and he continues to push for the values to be the basis of all decision-making and actions in all divisions of AT&T. There is still plenty of information and ideas coming to Una from the USA Corporate Office that she is expected to either implement or disseminate to the NZ associates.

## The 1994 "Values Fest"

Una's concerns about how applicable the American "way" of operating for the NZ division were heightened again in recent times as the latest Corporate Office initiative landed on her desk. This time it was for a Common Bond celebration called a "Values Fest." A directive came from Dayton, Ohio outlining the "Values Fest" to be held on the 7th of November. As usual, the material only arrived on her desk a few days before the actual required action date—the celebration day. The timeframe and her immediate and strong reservations about the content of the directive forced her to make a decision at short notice. The manuals instructed her to show a video, to get associates to complete a quiz and some written exercises, to get involved in discussion groups on the values, to make a "call to action" in relation to each of the five values outlined in the Common Bond, and to get people to sign a Common Bond poster as a celebration of the values. All of this would have taken half a day. Una knew that such sessions just would not go down very well with the NZ associates because they would see it as both a waste of time and, more importantly, that the content and style was just not relevant to them in the New Zealand office. Instead, she chose the 45 minute option for companies that "did not have sufficient time for the full agenda and who could give Corporate Office a serious reason for adopting this option." Una felt she had a very definite reason. She describes her decision for the short version as "a cultural decision." The material and session exercises and activities outlined in the manual from the United States were not appropriate for AT&T's New Zealand associates. It appeared to Una that following the 45 minutes of formality, everyone gathered around for refreshments and food and seemed to thoroughly enjoy themselves.

## Appropriateness of American Directives for the NZ Division

This Common Bond Celebration again raised the issue of how and when does the NZ office need to adapt Corporate directives to suit the NZ working style. Following the celebrations, Una believed that she had made the right decision to alter the American format and use the shortest possible version for the NZ organisation. As the Human Resources manager she knew she had to make a judgement decision and she decided in this case that if all of the material was taken and used literally from the documentation she received, "it would go down like a lead balloon."

The telephone rings in the Human Resources reception area. Enough daydreaming thinks Una. She chuckles her notorious laugh that has helped her and others keep these issues in perspective. It is time to get back to work and deal with the mounting 'in-tray' of work. She knows the company will get through the difficult times and that change is now just an inevitable and constant part of life. Although that makes her HR role difficult at times, there is no denying that this is a dynamic, well-known, ambitious and successful company which makes her life at AT&T interesting, rewarding and above all challenging.

## Note

1. ISO (International Standards Organisation) is the accreditation body which certifies companies following an extensive audit to ensure that the company has systems and procedures in place that indicate that the company's product(s) and/or

service(s) will be consistently delivered in line with the standards indicated by the company. ISO9000 specifies quality process and quality outcome standards for each industry and appoints agents in each country to inspect organisations applying for accreditation against rigorous standards. Accreditation not only helps organisations focus their quality initiatives, being certified by ISO9000 has become a necessity for many companies if they want to attract and retain customers.

# Case 1.4

# THE ROAD TO HELL

GARETH EVANS

John Baker, Chief Engineer of the Caribbean Bauxite Company of Barracania in the West Indies, was making his final preparations to leave the island. His promotion to production manager of Keso Mining Corporation near Winnipeg—one of Continental Ore's fast-expanding Canadian enterprises—had been announced a month before and now everything had been tidied up except the last vital interview with his successor, the able young Barracanian, Matthew Rennalls. It was vital that this interview be a success and that Rennalls should leave his office uplifted and encouraged to face the challenge of his new job. A touch on the bell would have brought Rennalls walking into the room but Baker delayed the moment and gazed thoughtfully through the window considering just exactly what he was going to say and, more particularly, how he was going to say it.

John Baker, an English expatriate, was forty-five years old and had served his twenty-three years with Continental Ore in many different places: in the Far East; several countries of Africa; Europe; and, for the last two years, in the West Indies. He hadn't cared much for his previous assignment in Hamburg and was delighted when the West Indian appointment came through. Climate was not the only attraction. Baker had always preferred working overseas (in what were termed the developing countries) because he felt he had an innate knack—better than most other expatriates working for Continental Ore—of knowing just how to get on with regional staff. Twenty-four hours in Barracania, however, soon made him realize that he would need all of this "innate knack" if he was to deal effectively with the problems in this field that now awaited him.

At his first interview with Hutchins, the production manager, the whole problem of Rennalls and his future was discussed. There and then it was made quite clear to Baker that one of his most important tasks would be the "grooming" of Rennalls as his successor. Hutchins had pointed out that, not only was Rennalls one of the brightest Barracanian prospects on the staff of Caribbean Bauxite—at London University he had taken first-class honors in the B.Sc. Engineering Degree—but, being the son of the Minister of Finance and Economic Planning, he also had no small political pull.

The company had been particularly pleased when Rennalls decided to work for them rather than for the government in which his father had such a prominent post. They ascribed his action to the effect of their vigorous and liberal regionalization program which, since the Second World War, had produced eighteen Barracanians at mid-management level and given Caribbean Bauxite a good lead in this respect over all other international concerns operating in Barracania. The success of this timely regionalization policy has led to excellent relations with the government—a relationship that had been given an added importance when

Barracania, three years later, became independent, an occasion which encouraged a critical and challenging attitude toward the role foreign interests would have to play in the new Barracania. Hutchins had therefore little difficulty in convincing Baker that the successful career development of Rennalls was of the first importance.

The interview with Hutchins was now two years old and Baker, leaning back in his office chair, reviewed just how successful he had been in the "grooming" of Rennalls. What aspects of the latter's character had helped and what had hindered? What about his own personality? How had that helped or hindered? The first item to go on the credit side would, without question, be the ability of Rennalls to master the technical aspects of his job. From the start he had shown keenness and enthusiasm and had often impressed Baker with his ability in tackling new assignments and the constructive comments he invariably made in departmental discussions. He was popular with all ranks of Barracanian staff and had an ease of manner which stood him in good stead when dealing with his expatriate seniors. These were all assets, but what about the debit side?

First and foremost, there was his racial consciousness. His four years at London University had accentuated this feeling and made him sensitive to any sign of condescension on the part of expatriates. It may have been to give expression to this sentiment that, as soon as he returned home from London, he threw himself into politics on behalf of the United Action Party who were later to win the preindependence elections and provide the country with its first Prime Minister.

The ambitions of Rennalls—and he certainly was ambitious—did not, however, lie in politics for, staunch nationalist as he was, he saw that he could serve himself and his country best (for was not bauxite responsible for nearly half the value of Barracania's export trade?) by putting his engineering talent to the best use possible. On this account, Hutchins found that he had an unexpectedly easy task in persuading Rennalls to give up his political work before entering the production department as an assistant engineer.

It was, Baker knew, Rennalls's well-repressed sense of race consciousness which had prevented their relationship from being as close as it should have been. On the surface, nothing could have seemed more agreeable. Formality between the two men was at a minimum; Baker was delighted to find that his assistant shared his own peculiar "shaggy dog" sense of humor so that jokes were continually being exchanged; they entertained each other at their houses and often played tennis together—and yet the barrier remained invisible, indefinable, but ever present. The existence of this "screen" between them was a constant source of frustration to Baker since it indicated a weakness which he was loath to accept. If successful with all other nationalities, why not with Rennalls?

But at least he had managed to "break through" to Rennalls more successfully than any other expatriate. In fact, it was the young Barracanian's attitude—sometimes overbearing, sometimes cynical—toward other company expatriates that had been one of the subjects Baker had raised last year when he discussed Rennalls's staff report with him. He knew, too, that he would have to raise the same subject again in the forthcoming interview because Jackson, the senior draftsman, had complained only yesterday about the rudeness of Rennalls. With this thought in mind, Baker leaned forward and spoke into the intercom. "Would you come in Matt, please? I'd like a word with you," and later, "Do sit down," proffering the box, "have a cigarette." He paused while he held out his lighter and then went on.

"As you know, Matt, I'll be off to Canada in a few days' time, and before I go, I thought it would be useful if we could have a final chat together. It is indeed with some deference that I suggest I can be of help. You will shortly be sitting in this chair doing the job I am now doing, but I, on the other hand, am ten years older, so perhaps you can accept the idea that I may be able to give you the benefit of my longer experience."

Baker saw Rennalls stiffen slightly in his chair as he made this point so added in explanation, "You and I have attended enough company courses to remember those repeated requests by the personnel manager to tell people how they are getting on as often as the convenient moment arises and not just the automatic 'once a year' when, by regulation, staff reports have to be discussed."

Rennalls nodded his agreement, so Baker went on. "I shall always remember the last job performance discussion I had with my previous boss back in Germany. He used what he called the 'plus and minus' technique. His firm belief was that when a senior, by discussion, seeks to improve the work performance of his staff, his prime objective should be to make sure that the latter leaves the interview encouraged and inspired to improve. Any criticism must, therefore, be constructive and helpful. He said that one very good way to encourage a person—and I fully agree with him—is to tell him about his good points—the plus factors—as well as his weak ones—the minus factors—so I thought, Matt, it would be a good idea to run our discussion along these lines."

Rennalls offered no comment, so Baker continued: "Let me say, therefore, right away, that, as far as your own work performance is concerned, the plus far outweighs the minus. I have, for instance, been most impressed with the way you have adapted your considerable theoretical knowledge to master the practical techniques of your job—that ingenious method you used to get air down to the fifth-shaft level is a sufficient case in point—and at departmental meetings I have invariably found your comments well taken and helpful. In fact, you will be interested to know that only last week I reported to Mr. Hutchins that, from the technical point of view, he could not wish for a more able man to succeed to the position of chief engineer."

"That's very good indeed of you, John," cut in Rennalls with a smile of thanks. "My only worry now is how to live up to such a high recommendation."

"Of that I am quite sure," returned Baker, "especially if you can overcome the minus factor which I would like now to discuss with you. It is one which I have talked about before so I'll come straight to the point. I have noticed that you are more friendly and get on better with your fellow Barracanians than you do with Europeans. In point of fact, I had a complaint only yesterday from Mr. Jackson, who said you had been rude to him—and not for the first time either.

"There is, Matt, I am sure, no need for me to tell you how necessary it will be for you to get on well with expatriates because until the company has trained up sufficient people of your caliber, Europeans are bound to occupy senior positions here in Barracania. All this is vital to your future interests, so can I help you in any way?"

While Baker was speaking on this theme, Rennalls had sat tensed in his chair and it was some seconds before he replied. "It is quite extraordinary, isn't it, how one can convey an impression to others so at variance with what one intends? I can only assure you once again that my disputes with Jackson—and you may remember also Godson—have had nothing at all to do with the color of their skins. I promise you that if a Barracanian had behaved in an equally peremptory manner I would have reacted in precisely the same way. And again, if I may say it within these four walls, I am sure I am not the only one who has found Jackson and Godson difficult. I could mention the names of several expatriates who have felt the same. However, I am really sorry to have created this impression of not being able to get on with Europeans—it is an entirely false one—and I quite realize that I must do all I can to correct it as quickly as possible. On your last point, regarding Europeans holding senior positions in the Company for some time to come, I quite accept the situation. I know that Caribbean Bauxite—as they have been doing for many years now—will promote Barracanians as soon as their experience warrants it. And, finally, I would like to assure you, John—and my father thinks the same too—that I am very happy in my work here and hope to stay with the company for many years to come."

Rennalls had spoken earnestly and, although not convinced by what he had heard, Baker did not think he could pursue the matter further except to say, "All right, Matt, my impression *may* be wrong, but I would like to remind you about the truth of that old saying, 'What is important is not what is true but what is believed.' Let it rest at that."

But suddenly Baker knew that he didn't want to "let it rest at that." He was disappointed once again at not being able to "break through" to Rennalls and having yet again to listen to his bland denial that there was any racial prejudice in his makeup. Baker, who had intended ending the interview at this point, decided to try another tack.

"To return for a moment to the 'plus and minus technique' I was telling you about just now, there is another plus factor I forgot to mention. I would like to congratulate you not only on the caliber of your work but also on the ability you have shown in overcoming a challenge which I, as a European, have never had to meet.

"Continental Ore is, as you know, a typical commercial enterprise—admittedly a big one—which is a product of the economic and social environment of the United States and Western Europe. My ancestors have all been brought up in this environment for the past two or three hundred years and I have, therefore, been able to live in a world in which commerce (as we know it today) has been part and parcel of my being. It has not been something revolutionary and new which has suddenly entered my life. In your case," went on Baker, "the situation is different because you and your forebears have only had some fifty or sixty years' experience of this commercial environment. You have had to face the challenge of bridging the gap between fifty and two or three hundred years. Again, Matt, let me congratulate you—and people like you—once again on having so successfully overcome this particular hurdle. It is for this very reason that I think the outlook for Barracania—and particularly Caribbean Bauxite—is so bright."

Rennalls had listened intently and when Baker finished, replied, "Well, once again, John, I have to thank you for what you have said, and, for my part, I can only say that it is gratifying to know that my own personal effort has been so much appreciated.

I hope that more people will soon come to think as you do."

There was a pause and, for a moment, Baker thought hopefully that he was about to achieve his long awaited "breakthrough," but Rennalls merely smiled back. The barrier remained unbreached. There remained some five minutes' cheerful conversation about the contrast between the Caribbean and Canadian climate and whether the West Indies had any hope of beating England in the Fifth Test before Baker drew the interview to a close. Although he was as far as ever from knowing the real Rennalls, he was nevertheless glad that the interview had run along in this friendly manner and, particularly, that it had ended on such a cheerful note.

This feeling, however, lasted only until the following morning. Baker had some farewells to make, so he arrived at the office considerably later than usual. He had no sooner sat down at his desk than his secretary walked into the room with a worried frown on her face. Her words came fast. "When I arrived this morning I found Mr. Rennalls already waiting at my door. He seemed very angry and told me in quite a peremptory manner that he had a vital letter to dictate which must be sent off without any delay. He was so worked up that he couldn't keep still and kept pacing about the room, which is most unlike him. He wouldn't even wait to read what he had dictated. Just signed the page where he thought the letter would end. It has been distributed and your copy is in your 'in tray.'"

# Case 1.5

# CAFÉ MAM AND ISMAM

RONALD NIGH

ANN D. WALSH

DAHINDA MEDA

## Introduction

The ISMAM (Indigenous Peoples of the Sierra Madre of Motozintla) cooperative grows and markets organic coffee, Café Mam (sounds like "mom"). This cooperative of native Mayan farmers lives in the highlands of Chiapas, Mexico. Emphasizing responsibility to the coop, hard work and standards of excellence, ISMAM built its cooperative on a foundation of egalitarian democratic ideals. Within a period of less than 10 years, the cooperative became a world exporter of gourmet coffee and is currently diversifying into other food processing ventures and ecotourism. Unlike some other groups, ISMAM did not succumb to the "postmodern condition" characterized by homogenization of culture and domination by big capital (Jameson 1990). Instead ISMAM sought specific markets for their products. In these markets they have been able to capitalize on their cultural identity and maintain a competitive advantage.

## Mam Maya

The members of ISMAM, who live in Chiapas, are part of the Mam Tzetal and Moche peoples. The ethnic group's demographic center is in Guatemala and is home to approximately half a million Guatemalan Mames. The Mames inhabit traditional communities established in colonial times. The Chiapas Mam also date back to the colonial period; however, in the 16th century they migrated to join the workforce of the Spanish cacao plantations. The current Mam population in Chiapas (estimated at around 8,000) came later toward the end of the 19th century. They were fleeing from the policies of the Guatemalan government, which was passing laws to expropriate communal lands and forcing Indians to work for ladino land owners (Hernandez 1995).

After migrating to Chiapas, the Mam experienced more repression. Around the turn of the century, many Mames were forced to serve as laborers on coffee plantations owned by German and foreign investors. Much of the best coffee lands were taken from the natives before the Mexican Revolution of 1910. What was left was *ejido* (common community) land or private land, both of which were divided into small parcels. Even though the Mam gained control of small parcels of poor land, their marketing outlets were still controlled by middlemen or "coyotes." The prices that they received for their coffee were kept low.

---

SOURCE: Previously published in *Multinational Management: A Strategic Approach* (1999), edited by John B. Cullen (pp. 399-406). South-Western College Publishing. Reprinted with permission.

During the past two decades, the Mam society experienced further disruption as Guatemalan braceros, those who work far below the Mexican minimum wage, flooded local labor markets. These and other economic trends stimulated large migrations to other lands and various social changes such as widespread conversion to Protestantism (Hernandez 1994). But since the 1970s the Mexican government has reversed some of its policies in favor of Mam ethnic identity and has developed programs that support the recovery of Mam culture and language. Also, during this period the government has opened alternative coffee markets for the small producers.

Coinciding with these developments, the Catholic Church reoriented its policies toward indigenous people in this area. Historically, the Catholic Church in Mexico has been much farther to the left than its counterpart in Rome. In the Revolution, the Roman Church backed the wrong side and subsequently lost much of its land and many of its churches. Under the distrustful eye of the government, the Mexican Catholic Church adapted its symbolism to the natives and directed its efforts to the indigenous people. As political advocates of the oppressed native American classes, many bishops promoted liberation by economic, political and theological means. In this context, some church sectors began to look more sympathetically on Mam culture and ethnic identity. In attempts to address the needs of the poor, the local priest of Motozintla, Father Jorge Aguilar, assumed a social activist role and greatly influenced the formation of the ISMAM cooperative. Father Aguilar literally went from community to community to convince farmers that with cooperation and hard work they could free themselves from the downward spiral that was threatening their culture and their ability to support themselves.

## The Organic Coffee Market

The organic food market appears to be growing due to the changes in consumer behavior in developed countries. Between 1994 and 1995, total sales of organic foods grew from $2.31 billion to $2.8 billion. This 20% increase surpassed that of other food categories (Mergintine and Emerich 1994). Sloan (1994) estimated that U.S. sales of organic food will increase nine times in the next ten years.

Organic coffee contributes to this growth. According to 1994 estimates, 71 million sacks of coffee were produced worldwide. Of the total, nearly 500,000 sacks of organic coffee were produced by 20 countries. Mexico's share of the organic coffee market was about 20%, which is less than Peru's, but twice that of Guatemala and Kenya. Demand for organically grown coffee is a relatively recent phenomenon with the first exportation of organic coffee from the Finca Irlanda Plantation in Chiapas in 1967. Recently, Lucas (1997) reported that modest sales interest in organic coffee is noted in a study by the Specialty Coffee Association of America.

Meeting the needs of this market poses a number of challenges. On the market side, the world consumers of organic coffee seek much more than a commodity. They want a product that is produced according to internationally established methods and free of chemicals, in a "socially responsible" manner, and one that meets their taste expectations. On the production side, farmers must have access to the information and possess the skills to produce coffee that meets the strict standards of organic certification. As Santoyo et al. (1995, 133) point out:

> . . . it should be emphasized that the production of organic coffee requires impeccable discipline in cultivation and marketing, which is not easy for an organization that only seeks economic benefit. For this reason, the organizations that have been successful in this market establish rules that go beyond mere production and commerce, orienting organic production to an entire way of life.

Thus, the argument evolves, if neither the consumer market nor the production process lends itself to commodity production, organic coffee production may be a viable option for only those who are willing to make it a way of life.

## Associative Corporations

In Mexico, as elsewhere, populations divide themselves on a number of different lines such as religions, political parties, and organizational lines, as well as on typical territorial-based communities. Some organizations operate on regional levels, often cutting across ethnic and religious ties. Agriculture coops like ISMAM are examples of regional organizations. To describe this type of regional organization, Batra (1991) coined the term "associative corporations." On the surface, associative corporations resemble traditional cooperatives. They base their collective organizations on Indian concepts of communitarian democracy and reciprocity, yet, they share commonalties with modern corporations with clearly defined administrative structures and well-established financial controls. While they practice voluntary working relations, common property management, and horizontal decision-making processes, they focus on making a profit. Overall, associative corporations reflect "hybrid" cultural institutions, which Garcia Canclini (1991) claimed are typical for postmodern Latin America.

## The Mam Organic Coffee Cooperative ISMAM

From its humble beginnings with 59 members in 1979–80, ISMAM has grown to its current size of over 1,300 members from 34 regions. Most of the members are Mames, though not exclusively. The cooperative's present-day structure grew out of reorganization and extensive discussion and workshops conducted over a two-year period in 1986–87. In the reorganized structure, farmers elect officers and members to nine standing committees: executive-administration, finance, education, vigilance, solidarity, technical, advisory, membership admission, and the representative congress. Officers and committee members are elected for two-year terms and in accordance with Mayan tradition they cannot be reelected. The two-year rule places emphasis on process and cooperation rather than on personal power and personalities. Even though the transition of officers and committee members temporarily weakens the cooperative, it also strengthens it. Rotation of officers and committee members increases the depth of talent and knowledge.

Communication among members is carried out by monthly representative assemblies and a general assembly of all members. At the general assemblies, members make major decisions and elect officers and heads of committees in charge of coop business. In addition, assemblies serve as a vehicle for conveying and getting information, especially information of a technical nature. At times the current structure, which is highly dynamic, appears somewhat random. For instance, if the members dislike leaders, they oust them and elect others.

In the field, members work together in groups of ten *socios* (there are no hired laborers). Each group selects on representative who coordinates with ISMAM's nine-person technical staff and serves in the coop congress. Often the groups function as teams farming the combined land of all ten owners. However, each farmer must provide an equal work-share and insure that his own farm meets all standards of fertilization, pruning, harvesting, and postharvest treatment of the crop. Equality of human work over the randomness of parcel size and distribution are emphasized. Cash prizes are awarded for highest production per acre and highest quality grown in each district. Working together results in higher yields and sharing of knowledge.

## ISMAM's Strategy

The cooperative based its strategy on the assumption that with cooperative effort ISMAM could achieve a high enough volume of coffee production, which would permit direct export without intermediaries. The elimination of intermediaries would generate greater return for the small growers. From the start, the coop was determined to produce high-quality gourmet coffee for an exclusive, upscale market, even though the market potential for organic coffee was unknown at the time.

In the first workshops, ISMAM's founding members faced a gloomy situation. Small farmer production was much lower relative to that of the larger private growers. In addition, production costs were rising due to increasing costs of agrochemicals, while profits were being absorbed by ladino intermediaries who controlled the market channels and forced the farmers to accept low prices. ISMAM members realized that they had to do something about the low levels of production and the channels of distribution.

Eliminating the intermediaries proved to be a difficult task. The political mechanism of expropriating the peasants' products and transferring the value to the regional and extraregional economy was a traditional feature of the Chiapas regional economy. Intermediaries, who enjoyed the full repressive support of regional, oligarchic political structures, were not about to turn over their lucrative control of the marketing channels. As a result farmers' initial attempts to assume more control of the marketing channels were met with repression from local and state governments. Repression was further compounded by the imposition of a military man as state governor. Policies aimed at neutralizing agrarian claims and obstructing independent farmer organizations resulted in systematic violation of human rights.

Apart from the political difficulties associated with "appropriation of the productive process," the new cooperative encountered a number of technical and economic problems. To address these challenges, the coop turned to outsider advisors and financial support of several kinds. Two key people in the field were Robert Soto, an agronomist and organic specialist, and Jose Caballero, a specialist in composting, erosion, and annual crops for higher altitudes. Also, Guatemalan agronomists, who were fleeing their country's repression of Indian coops, brought technical expertise and workshop methodology experience to the ISMAM cooperative. Together, these advisors and ISMAM members developed a methodology for collective analysis and problem solving. The methodology evolved into a group discussion workshop called *trabajo comun organizado* (TCO), "organized work together." Now all new ISMAM members are required to participate. In these workshops, members continue to analyze their socioeconomic situation, its causes, and the possible solution to their severe problems of poverty and social marginality.

## The Importance of Organic Farming

ISMAM's decision to adopt organic farming methods proved to be a critical element in production and marketing strategies. But, before the collective decision was made, ISMAM members carefully weighed the pros and cons of organic methods. In their discussions, members noted that organic methods were more harmonious with Indian traditional agriculture. For centuries the Mayan people of Chiapas and Guatemala practiced polycultural farming on loosely scattered farms in the jungles. They also experimented with canals and terraces. Their methods were sustainable and organic, and so effective that Pre-Columbian Mexican agriculture has been cited as a model of sustainability, the most productive and least erosive in the world. Not until they abandoned their native ways did they encounter the problem of massive erosion caused by mismanagement and use of large machinery on environmentally sensitive lands. Therefore, when the concept of organic farming was discussed as a possible alternative, ISMAM members were already favorably disposed toward it.

Besides being more harmonious with Indian traditional agriculture, organic farming opened the door to a highly specialized market in Europe, the type that ISMAM was seeking. At that time the Western European market was supported by a network of 300 "social solidarity" shops that carried products from indigenous communities and cooperatives of the Third World. To help consolidate indigenous organizations, the shops collected a surcharge of around 10% on all products sold. In turn, the surcharge was returned to the producers. For ISMAM the surcharge from the sales of organic coffee provided critical support during the years of development and allowed the cooperative to circumvent the trading monopolies of conventional products. Today, the direct solidarity market accounts for a little over 15% of ISMAM's annual sales.

Transition to organic methods profoundly affected ISMAM's internal organization and the technological development of coffee production among the growers. To enter the organic market, ISMAM had to insure that all phases of their coffee production (i.e., growing, cleaning, drying, milling, bagging, shipping import customs, transporting, warehousing, and roasting) met the guidelines for "organic labeling." The label not only meant that no synthetic chemicals were used in growing or processing but that a long-term fertility management system had to be put into place. In the case of Mexican organic coffee, fertility management involved maintenance of a diversified population of composts, ecological pest control, and crop diversification. Organic products are certified by recognized certification organizations who carry out yearly inspections in the fields and who may contract laboratory analyses to determine levels of pesticide residues in products, all at the growers' expense. National and state legislation in the United States, the EC, and in many other countries including Mexico currently regulate organic production.

ISMAM had to implement strict internal controls on all phases of their coffee production; postharvest processing (carried out by each grower on his farm), transportation of dried coffee to the final processing plant, and selection of lots for export. To insure that all farmers would comply, ISMAM's agronomists had to establish an inspection plan. They set up monthly visits with each grower to check on progress in fertility management and to provide advice and assistance. All visits were recorded and entered into a computer bank in the central office in Motozintla. The coop also established a system for labeling bags of coffee so that any single bag could be traced to its origin.

Switching to organic farming also helped solve the technical problems identified by ISMAM members in their early workshops. First, productivity increased as much as fivefold or more in three to five years as a direct result of the long-term fertility program required for certification. Second, organic methods such as production of compost and biological controls eliminated the need for agrochemicals, thereby significantly lowering the production costs. Third, organic methods resulted in a much higher quality product, which could be exported directly to European and U.S. gourmet markets. Furthermore, organic methods helped insulate ISMAM from fluctuations in the commodity coffee market. For instance, in 1989 when the price of coffee collapsed on the international market, ISMAM's organic strategy paid off. While many other Mexican producers, large and small, left their coffee crops unharvested in the fields, ISMAM members received premium prices for their organic coffee. To further stabilize their position, coop members agreed to retain profits to contract their own agronomists and for harvest-time credit to members. Retaining profits helped strengthen ISMAM's independence from government, banks, and middlemen in matters of technology and marketing.

## The Policy Context of the New Agrarian Movement

Traditionally, peasants have been expected to assume the roles of providers of raw materials and/or cheap labor. Political force has been used to insure that other sectors of regional society can appropriate the value added by marketing peasant products or exploiting peasant labor. The "appropriation of the productive process" (including marketing) by intermediaries has been the cornerstone of the political economy systems related to peasants. Without access to global information and communication structures, peasants remain captured in this traditional structure.

In contrast with the ISMAM Mam, most rural Mexican societies are unable to access new information and communication structures. Social disorganization and anomie tend to prevail. ISMAM's ability to utilize global structures to create alliances outside the region help explain why the coop has been able to successfully consolidate; whereas, Indian members of many sister organizations in the Selva Lacondona have not been successful and have had to seek other options to solve their political problems.

Thus, while the ISMAM experience is atypical of Indian and peasant organizations in Mexico, it is not unique. ISMAM's organizational structure reflects a general process that is taking place in Mexican rural society. The traditional communities and the political and economic organizations associated with those identities are giving way to new organizations based on cross-community and cross-ethnic ties. The new organizations promote Indian identity in a regional, national, and even transnational context. These organizations demand more than land, technical assistance, and credit; they expect cultural and political autonomy, and multilingual and intercultural education as well. As demonstrated in the political program of the Zapatista movement in Chiapas today, political freedom, democracy, and local autonomy are fundamental demands of the new peasant organizations. Land reform is simply not enough.

Overall, the new organizational structures can be seen as a response of Indian communities to changes in three fundamental links between global and local processes: (1) changes in national government policies as versions of a neoliberal ideology promoted by global financial brokers, (2) changes in the relations of power within regional society, in this case in Chiapas, and (3) new relationships between local Indian societies and other global forces, such as the growing demand for organic foods and Indian solidarity movements in the First World.

## ISMAM Diversification

ISMAM recently own a multimillion dollar grant to develop an ecotourism model coffee farm. The 700-acre farm will be located in the Sierra Madre mountains at an altitude of 1,300 meters and will be large enough for mountain biking, hiking, bird watching, and organic farmwork. With its own electrical system, the farm will become the new home of 120 native families. All visitors and inhabitants will find themselves in a lush, tropical, chemical-free environment.

Other coop projects include a new cultural center in Tapachula. The center, a gift of a German church group, is in the final stages of construction. ISMAM has also entered into a joint venture with a fishing cooperative on an island surrounded by a 4,700-square-mile ecological preserve. In addition, ISMAM has expanded its product lines, adding organic honey and cacao (chocolate), and it will soon add cinnamon and hibiscus tea. Other projects under consideration involve a joint venture with U.S. partners to form a company that will market all ISMAM products and tourism options.

ISMAM's current products and most recent undertakings can be found on the Internet, at *http://cafemam.com*.

## References

Batra, Armando. 1991. Pros, contras y asegunes de la "appropriacion del proceso productivo." *Cuademos desarollo de base* 2:5–22.

Garæia Canclini, Nestor. 1991. *Culturás hibridas. Estratgias para entrar y salir de la modermidad,* Los noventa #50. Editorial Grijalbo, Mexico City.

Hernandez Castillo, Rosalva Aida. 1994. Identidades colectivas en los márgenes de la nacion: etnicidad y cambio religioso entre los mames de Chiapas. *Nueva Antropologia,* No. 45.

_____. 1995. Inventando tgradiciones: encuentros y desencuentros de los mames con el indigenismo mexicano. *America Indigena* (special volume on Chiapas).

Jameson, Frederic. 1990. *Post-modernism or the Cultural Logic of Late Capitalism.* Durham, NC: Duke University Press.

Lucas, Eric. 1997. "Socially responsible coffee." Downloaded from *http://www.coffeetalk.com/html/current_issue.html.*

Mergintine, K., and M. Emerich. 1994. NFM's organic market overview, 1993. *Natural Food Merchandiser,* 15, No. 6: 48–50.

Santoyo, Cortés, V. Horacio, Salvador Diaz Cardenas, and Benigno Rodriguez Padron. 1995. *Sistema Agroindustrial Café en Mexico: Diagnostico, Problematica y Alternativas.* Universidad Autonoma Chapingo, Mexico.

Sloan, A. E. 1994. Top ten trends to watch and work on, *Food Technology,* July: 89–100.

# Case 1.6

# GOLD STAR PROPERTIES

## *Financial Crisis*

JOSEPH J. DISTEFANO

### Background

Gold Star Properties had started as a small construction company during the early growth periods in Hong Kong back in the early 1970s. Gold Star had enjoyed steady success over the next three decades and grew in size and reputation. By the 1990s it was a sizable organization with a very good reputation in the construction industry in Hong Kong. As it had grown as a main contractor, Gold Star had outsourced most of its work to smaller subcontractors, which had grown along with Gold Star. The most valuable assets of the company were its staff of experienced engineers and quantity surveyors.

### Decision to Diversify in Property—and Its Aftermath

As the company built its financial success and took part in the boom of the mid-1990s in Hong Kong, the directors decided to diversify the company's activities from the core business of construction by making related investments in a wide range of properties throughout mainland China. As the People's Republic of China had opened up to investment and economic development, Gold Star had developed good relationships with key government officials when it took on several construction contracts in the mainland, starting with the expansion of factories and related infrastructure (such as the toll road) in the Guangdong area adjoining Hong Kong.

Between 1994 and 1997, largely employing funds borrowed from Hong Kong-based financial institutions, the company made property investments, primarily in Shanghai, Beijing, Chengdu, Chongching and Hainan. Unfortunately, immediately after this investment expansion, the Asian financial crisis struck with full force, starting with Thailand's devaluation in mid-1998. This hit the property industry particularly hard and most of the companies in which Gold Star had recently invested were struggling to make ends meet. To make matters worse, the banks that had been so generous loaning capital in boom times were now calling in loans. Gold Star was servicing debt of HK$800 million,[1] which the banks indicated they would not roll over when it matured in the coming months. In order to survive, Gold Star turned its attention back to its core business in construction.

AUTHOR'S NOTE: Professor Joseph J. DiStefano prepared this case as a basis for class discussion rather than to illustrate either effective or ineffective handling of a business situation. The cooperation of an anonymous business executive is gratefully acknowledged. Names of people, companies and mainland cities have been disguised.

However, by 2000 the construction business was in rapid decline as large projects left over from the boom were being completed and planned construction was put on hold. Competition was fierce and had driven margins down to around 3%. With such small margins, the company was struggling to maintain its operations and still repay its debt. Joseph, Zhang Jinfu had failed in his attempts to convince Gold Star's bankers to roll over the maturing loan. He had also sought, in vain, new funds. Many of the foreign banks, particularly those from Japan whose head offices were having serious problems of their own, had called in their loans and pulled out of Hong Kong. In addition to causing crises for their own customers, this development, combined with the general decline, meant that capital was in short supply. Gold Star, with its own financial performance deteriorating, was therefore forced to find alternative sources of cash.

## Decision to Divest

In early 2000, with the company feeling the cash squeeze and the situation projected to worsen by mid-year, William Cheng, in discussion with Joseph's predecessor, had decided to divest its investments in a power plant in Chongching, a prized entertainment complex in Chengdu and a five-star hotel in Shanghai. The executive committee approved the sale, which was expected to generate about HK$900 million. They planned to use the proceeds to increase working capital and repay the matured debt. Since the end of the first quarter of 2000, Gold Star had been trying to close the deals and realize the proceeds from the sales. But between the bureaucracy of the mainland officials and the market slump, the company had been unable to recover the money. Halfway through the final quarter of the year William and Joseph met again to assess the probabilities of getting the cash by year-end. Despite the good relationships they had with the mainland officials, they were not optimistic. So they concluded that it was time to decide how to deal with the crisis, which they expected to peak in the first quarter of 2001.

## The People

William Cheng joined Gold Star Properties in 1998 as managing director. He was from China and had a civil engineering degree and was experienced in construction. He was hired for a combination of his knowledge of the industry and his experience with senior PRC officials.

Joseph, Zhang Jinfu had adopted the English name of Joseph when he started traveling in the West in the early 1990s. He had joined Gold Star in January 2000 as assistant finance director and took over as director when his predecessor resigned in September. Prior to coming to Hong Kong, he had earned his doctorate in engineering at Shanghai Jiao Tong University and joined The Industry Investment Corporation of China as a project director. Two years later he was promoted to deputy divisional director. In 1994 Joseph joined The Industry Bank of China and gained experience in finance. In 1996 he transferred to the bank's international business department, where he took charge of the credit division and was responsible for client lending and borrowing from foreign banks. He moved to Hong Kong in the late 1999.

Eric Osborne, the technical director, was from England. He was an experienced architect with an exceptional knowledge of the engineering aspects of construction. He was the longest-serving member of the executive committee, having joined the company 20 years earlier. He had earned a strong reputation in Hong Kong as a man of exceptional integrity and technical expertise.

The other two directors were both from Hong Kong and had joined the company about the same time in 1990. One was responsible for sales and marketing; the other was head of the project managers, who were the company's representatives responsible for managing the budgets and schedules at each construction site. *(Refer to **Exhibit 1** for the organization chart of the executive committee of Gold Star.)*

## The Meeting and Eric Osborne's Reactions

The day before the executive committee was scheduled to meet, William asked Joseph to join him in his office to discuss how to deal with the situation. Both agreed that while working on obtaining the cash from the divestment of the assets, they must place financial stability and continuous operation of the company as their top priorities. They reached consensus on three general principles:

1. Try to balance paying off the debt service and making subcontractor payments
2. Avoid triggering the banks' calling in their loans: as far as possible, meet the demands of those that were most likely to do so
3. Use the company's good relationships with subcontractors to help resolve the cash shortage

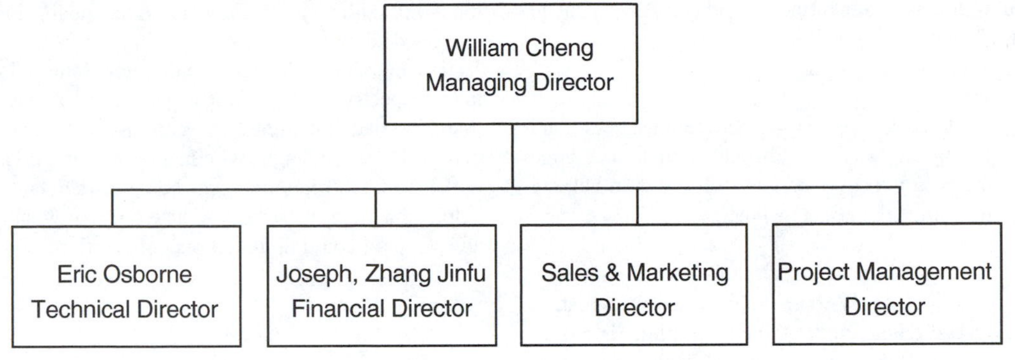


**Exhibit 1** Organization Chart of Gold Star's Executive Committee

by, as far as possible, deferring payments to those with whom they had the best relationships and who they also thought were in better financial shape of others.

The next day William laid out the priorities he and Joseph had developed and explained the thinking behind them to the executive committee. Joseph was taken aback by the way the meeting went, noting:

> I was really surprised by Eric's reaction. He asked one question after another to both William and me, acting as if he knew little about the precarious position we were facing. Eric said that he knew that our financial performance from 1988 wasn't great, but it hadn't affected our project bidding.

Joseph described Eric's position in the meeting.

> He said that if we needed more working capital, then we needed to do more contract work. He proposed that we should put first priority on completing projects on time, because doing so was the only way to get more contracts. He strongly demanded that we pay our subcontractors according to the contract schedules, because he worried about possible penalties resulting from work delays. He was convinced that otherwise there would be negative impacts in future contract bidding.

William and Joseph explained that most of the subcontractors had excellent long-term relations with Gold Star and that they needed to use those relationships now:

> We told him that we thought some delay in payments wouldn't cause them to stop or slow work because they valued their relationship with us. We emphasized that the subcontractors should believe that their help to Gold Star would bring more business to them in the future.

The project management director added that Gold Star had lent money to some of these subcontractors in the past, when they couldn't get working capital from the banks. "These people don't forget favors like that," he stressed.

Joseph tried to provide more financial data to Eric to underline the seriousness of the situation:

> I told him that the bankers were already very nervous and if we defaulted on the debt service they would be very upset. But I wasn't sure that he really heard me.

When Eric finally realized that the other directors supported William's strategy, he turned to Joseph again and pressed for clarity on how much money he could use to pay subcontractors in the following months before the cash from the divestment of assets arrived.

Joseph replied:

> Here's a cash flow projection that I prepared so we can plan how to proceed. But remember, we might adjust the fund allocations differently as time goes on. We need to treat the bankers and the subcontractors dynamically, based on the actual situation at any given time.

Obviously frustrated and dissatisfied with Joseph's response, Eric started to get angry. "If you can't give me a fixed number month by month, then how can I do my work!!??" He ended his remarks with repeated exclamations about the importance of his credibility with the subcontractors and his subordinates. Joseph and the others were silent in the face of his intensity.

William stepped in:

> Look, Eric, I appreciate your feelings, but we are facing an extremely difficult situation. I hope that you will give us your full effort in helping to resolve the crisis together.

Eric paled and did not reply. As the meeting came to a close, William summarized the situation again and reiterated the three principles. He closed by asking all the directors not to disclose the situation to their subordinates in order to avoid further instability. All except Eric promised to maintain the confidentiality. Ominously, once again Eric remained silent.

The meeting ended and the directors returned to their respective offices. But it was clear to Joseph that Eric had not joined the consensus. He wondered why his colleague who had been so important to the firm's development was being so reluctant to help at this time of crisis. And he wondered what he and William could do to get his cooperation.

## Note

1. The Hong Kong dollar was pegged to the US$ at the rate of HK$7.799 = US$1.

# Case 1.7

## CHIBA INTERNATIONAL, INC.

NINA HATVANY AND VLADIMIR PUCIK

Ken Morikawa, the general manager for administration of a Japanese manufacturing plant under construction in rural Georgia, was troubled. This morning his American personnel manager, John Sinclair, had walked eagerly across the temporary open-plan office and announced: "I've found a professor of Japanese at Georgia State University who is willing to help translate our corporate philosophy. I would like to hire him for the job."

Ken felt pressured. He thought that John Sinclair, like many Americans, was expecting too much of Japanese companies. The company philosophy that he, Ken, had learned to live by in Tokyo would continue to guide him, but he did not feel that Americans would welcome or even understand a Japanese company philosophy.

Ken had a very large task to do in supervising the building of a plant that might ultimately provide jobs for up to 2,000 employees in the area where very few workers had any industrial experience. He wished to show that his was a company that cared about the welfare of its workers and their job security and could be trusted to treat them fairly and not to lay them off. He believed that such a philosophy, if it could be properly explained to workers and carefully implemented, would help to build a high morale among the employees and consequently improve productivity.

Ken also wanted to ensure that high morale would be maintained as the workforce expanded to full capacity. Indeed, aside from issues of ease of transportation and distribution, the characteristics of the local workforce, their "Japanese" work ethic, had been one of the primary reasons for establishing the plant here. He believed that the training costs involved in transforming very "green" workers were well worth it to avoid people who had picked up "bad habits" or had had their morale lowered in prior industrial jobs. In Japan, teaching company philosophy is an important part of the company's introductory training program. But will it work here?

Ken wondered if his new administrative duties were lowering his concern for personnel matters. Ever since he had had to read Alfred Sloan's *My Years with General Motors* during the company training program and had written a review that focused on human resource issues, he had held positions related to his field. Even though he had majored in mathematical economics in college, his first assignment had been in the personnel "design center," which controlled training and salary administration for white-collar employees. After two years he was sent to a district office as a salesman. He returned after 13 months to the employee welfare section of the personnel department at the head office, administering such programs as house loans and recreational activities. Eight years with the company had passed by the time he was sent to an American college to study personnel-related subjects and improve his English.

After receiving his MBA, he returned to the head office. His most recent assignment before coming to Georgia was in personnel development research, planning new wage systems. It was expected that in his new job in Georgia he would eventually hand the reins over to an American general manager and remain only in an advisory capacity. However, he felt that it was at this vital stage that the corporation depended on his human relations expertise to set the scene for future success. Was he neglecting an area in which he had been trained to be sensitive?

He brought the subject up at lunch with John Sinclair. "Let me tell you something, John. I have a hunch why the Japanese are more successful in achieving high quality and productivity than Americans have been recently. It has to do with application, rather than ideas. Many great ideas have come from the United States, but the Japanese concentrate on applying them very carefully. Americans emphasize creating something new and then moving on. The Japanese meticulously analyze a problem from all angles and see how a solution might be implemented.

"As they say, Rome wasn't built in a day. I'm not sure our American workers will understand what it really means to have a company philosophy. Let's take it slowly and see what kind of people we hire and then see what best meets their needs."

John, who had worked at a rather traditional U.S. company for 11 years and had become increasingly interested in how Japanese companies managed their U.S. employees, had been eager to join a Japanese company. He wanted to see in action such "Japanese" strategies to long-term employment, the expression of a company philosophy and careful attention to integrating the employees into the company. He answered comfortingly, "Ken, I know you hate conflict. But I also know that you think it is important to gather information. One of our purchasing agents, Billy, told me about a Japanese company that he recently visited, Chiba International. Apparently, they already have a fully developed company philosophy and I understand that they're doing very well with it. Why don't we go out to California and talk with their management and try and understand how and why they concentrated on communicating their philosophy."

"And soak up some sun, too," beamed Ken. "You're on!"

## The Company

Chiba International, Inc., in San Jose, California, makes high-precision, sophisticated electronics parts used in the final assembly of customized and semi-customized integrated circuits—particularly the expensive memory chips used in computers and military hardware. In such products, reliability is everything, price a lesser consideration. The similar but cheaper parts that manufacturers use once a product reaches a high volume are left for others to make.

Chiba International is a subsidiary of Chiba Electronics Company. *Nihon Keizai Shimbun,* Japan's preeminent business paper, recently ranked Chiba Electronics as one of the foremost companies in Japan on the basis of its management earnings stability and performance, ahead of such better-known giants as Sony, Matshushita Electric and Toyota Motor. Chiba Electronics Co. has 70% of the $250-million-a-year world market for its products. Chiba International likewise has a 70% share of the $250-million-a-year U.S. market.

Chiba International started in the United States 12 years ago, with a small sales office. A manufacturing plant that had been losing $100,000 to $200,000 a month was acquired from an American competitor. The American management was terminated, and a team of Japanese, headed by a Canadian-born Japanese-reared executive, succeeded in turning it around within two years.

Today 14 of the 24 top executives and 65 of 70 salesmen at Chiba are Americans. All the employees in other categories are also American.

## Chiba's Philosophy

As the sun rises brilliantly in the sky,
Revealing the size of the mountain, the
market,
Oh this is our goal.
With the highest degree of mission in our
heart we serve our industry,
Meeting the strictest degree of customer
requirement.
We are the leader in this industry and our
future path
Is ever so bright and satisfying.

"That's a translation of our company song," said a high-ranking Japanese executive, one of the group of Japanese and American managers who had agreed to meet with Ken and John. "But we haven't introduced it to our employees yet. That's typical of the way we brought the company philosophy to our employees—slowly and carefully. Every line worker gets a leaflet explaining our company philosophy when he or she starts work. We don't have a specific training session on it, and we don't force them to swallow it. It's up to them to digest and understand it."

"What about when you acquire a company as you have done over the past few years?" asked John.

"The same thing. It's very gradual. If we force it, it causes nothing but indigestion. Here it has been easy; the work is very labor intensive, repetitive, tedious assembly. In other places the soil is different. At one, for example, almost all the employees are exempts. They understand the philosophy but won't necessarily go by it. Engineers and technical people also seem to be less receptive than people in sales, personnel, and administration. In other sites, though, where the technology is more similar to this, we have had no problem at all."

One of the other managers present in the group, this one American, interrupted to show Ken and John a copy of the leaflet. It was quite rhetorical in tone, and a few paragraphs struck them as particularly interesting.

*Management Philosophy*

*Our goal is to strive toward both the material and spiritual fulfillment of all employees in the Company, and through this successful fulfillment, serve mankind in its progress and prosperity.*

*Management Policy*

*(. . .) Our purpose is to fully satisfy the needs of our customers and in return gain a just profit for ourselves. We are a family united in common bonds and singular goals. One of these bonds is the respect and support we feel for our fellow family coworkers.*

Also, the following exhortation:

*When there is a need, we all rally to meet it and consider no task too menial or demeaning; all that matters is that it should be done! We are all ready to sweep floors, sort parts, take inventory, clean machines, inspect parts, load trucks, carry boxes, wash windows, file papers, run furnaces, and do just about anything that has to be done.*

## Meetings

"Daily meetings at the beginning of each shift are held in the courtyard," explained the group. "All the workers stand in lines (indicated by metal dots in the asphalt). Each day, a different member of management speaks for about five minutes. On Mondays executives speak, on Tuesdays, personnel and administration are represented, Wednesdays are about safety concerns, and on Thursdays and Fridays, members of production and sales speak. They are all free to say whatever they like. The shift workers tend to develop favorites, especially among the more extroverted sales managers.

"Then a personnel coordinator delivers news about sports events and so on, and perhaps a motivational message, and goes on to lead the group in exercises for one minute. These calisthenics are voluntary, but most of the employees join in. After that, the large group breaks up for brief departmental meetings."

"Again, in the departmental meetings, a speaker is chosen for the day and speaks for about five minutes. Even people at the lowest exempt level find themselves speaking.

Then the department manager discusses yesterday's performance, today's schedule and any other messages, such as that housekeeping is inadequate or that certain raw materials are in short supply.

"Once a month, there is an announcement of total company performance versus plans. This is important, as all company employees share at the same rate in the annual company bonus, which is based on profitability and usually equals about one month's salary or wages."

Another Japanese manager continued, "Years ago, there were complaints about having so many meetings, but I haven't heard any for a long time now. The employees like to hear important announcements and even less important ones, such as who is selling theater tickets, bowling league reports, and tennis match dates."

The American personnel manager chimed in: "I was the one who came up with the idea of exercises. I saw it on my visit to Japan. They are just a part of the rituals and symbols that you need in order to get better mutual understanding. The atmosphere was right and the timing was good. Even so, because they weren't mandatory, it took about one-and-a-half years until everyone joined in. Now most people understand the meaning behind it. If we were to stop it now, we'd get complaints.

"Besides the morning meeting, we have several other meetings. On Mondays, we have a very large liaison meeting for information sharing. All the executives attend: sales managers and staff managers, the plant manager and the assistant plant manager. On Tuesdays, we have a production meeting attended by the production managers and any staff involved with their problems. On Monday at four o'clock every second week we have a supervisors' meeting, mainly for one-way communication to them. On the alternating weeks we have a training meeting. The whole personnel department also meets every week.

"Less formally, we have many sales meetings about, for example, new products. We have combination sales and production meetings, which are called on an asneeded basis. Team meetings on the production line are also called whenever needed."

"All these formal meetings are supplemented by many company-sponsored activities. We have a company bowling league, tennis matches, softball, fishing, and skiing. We often organize discount tickets. We're planning the Christmas party. Each employee can bring a guest, so it costs us about $40,000. Our company picnic costs $29,000."

"It sounds very well worked out for the non-exempts," commented John. "How about for the exempts?"

## Sales Force

They started with the largely American sales force.

"They're a very different species. They have tremendous professional pride. Most American sales engineers have a very arrogant take-it-or-leave-it attitude. Our attitude is almost the complete opposite. We try to serve our customers' needs, almost like a geisha girl, who makes her customer feel that he is the only one served by her.

"We try to communicate the following motto to them:

| | |
|---|---|
| S | incerity |
| A | bility |
| L | ove |
| E | nergy |
| S | ervice |

*Sincerity is the basic attitude you need to have, as well as the ability to convince the customer. You must love the products that you sell or you can't convince the customer. You must have energy because at the end of the day it's always the case that you could have done one more thing or made one more sales call. Finally, the mentality of serving the customer is the most important.*

"We communicate that to our sales force and they like it, especially when they don't have to tell white lies to customers or put up with harassment from customers. We also want them to be honest with us, even about their mistakes. Quite often we depend on the salesmen's input for our understanding of customers, so an objective daily report by fax or phone is very important to us.

"No one in our company works on a commission basis, not even salesmen. We would lose market share for products that are difficult to promote. Also, the nature of different sales territories would make commissions unfair.

"Although we pay on straight salary only, we don't just have a unilateral sales quota. The salesman discusses his targets with his boss. They are purposely set high, so good performance against goals is grounds for a merit increase the next year."

"We don't really have a marketing department. We feel that it is an expensive luxury and while we have a vice president in charge of marketing, his is almost a corporate sales staff function."

## U.S. Management

John was curious about how American line managers reacted to working in a Japanese company.

A Japanese manager explained: "When Americans join us, they expect the usual great deal of internal politicking. They scan people in meetings, looking for those with real power, looking, to use our expression, for whose apple they should polish. It takes time for them to realize that it's unnecessary.

"When we interview American executives for a job, we do it collectively so five to ten interviewers are present. This usually puzzles the interviewee. He wonders whom he will report to. We reply that he will be hired by the company, although he may report to one individual. As in Japan, the company will take care of him, so it does not depend on his loyalty to one individual."

What about your company criteria for hiring managers?

"His way of thinking, not necessarily his ability. Although a Harvard MBA is welcomed, it is not essential. In fact, no one here has one. We don't provide an elegant fit to his social elite. There are no private offices. Salary and benefits are up to par for the location (and industry) but not especially high. We work long hours.

"We're looking for devotion and dedication as well as an aggressive attitude. We conduct two or three long interviews for an important position. We ask questions like 'What is your shortcoming?' We're interested not in the answer itself but in the kind of thinking behind it. We do make mistakes sometimes, but our batting average is good.

"Sometimes there's a very deep communication gap between Japanese management and U.S. management because we believe in dedication and devotion to the company. They do, too, but only to a certain point. We often tell them that the joy of working for the company can be identical to personal happiness with the family. I ask my wife for her understanding of that, and I work six days a week, from seven o'clock to ten o'clock. Their wives place demands on them to come home at six o'clock. U.S. executives put personal and family happiness first. I'm not telling you which is right. But it is second nature for me to think about the future of the company. So long as I have challenging assignments and job opportunities, I will put the company before my personal happiness."

What do American interviewees feel about all this?

"One problem is that they ask, 'What's my real future? Can I be considered for president?' There's no real answer because it probably will be a Japanese. However, we don't like to close those doors to a really capable American.

"The issue of communication between Japanese and Americans is still a problem. After the Americans go home, the Japanese get together at seven or eight o'clock and talk in Japanese about problems and make decisions without the Americans present. Naturally this makes the Americans feel very apprehensive. We're trying to rectify it by asking the Japanese managers not to make decisions alone and asking the Americans to stay as late as possible.

"More important, if we could really have our philosophy permeate the American managers, we Japanese could all go back to Japan and not worry about it. Our mission is to expedite that day by education and training.

"So far, however, there is a gap. Americans are more interested in individual accomplishment, remuneration and power. When they are given more responsibility, they don't feel its heavy weight, rather they feel that it extends their sovereign area so that they have more of a whip. That creates power conflicts among U.S. managers."

"Let me tell you, though" summarized the American personnel manager, "I like it. I was recruited by a headhunter. Now, I've been with the company five years and the difference from my former employer is astounding. I don't have to get out there and be two-faced, fudging to keep the union out, hedging for the buck. In general, it's hard to find an American employer that really sincerely cares for the welfare of the low-level employee. This company went almost too far in the opposite direction at first. They wanted to do too much for the employees too quickly, without their earning it. That way, you don't get their respect."

## Financial People

"Our financial people throughout the company are proud because of our impressive company performance. Only 20% of our financing is through debt, in contrast to many Japanese companies. We also have a rather unique way of treating some of our raw materials internally. We try to expense everything out. It's derived from our founder's very conservative management. We ask the question: 'If we closed down tomorrow, what would our liquid assets be?' In line with that, for example, internally we put our inventory at zero.

"We follow the 'noodle peddler theory.' The noodle peddler is an entrepreneur. He has to borrow his cart, his serving dishes and his pan to make ramen. He has to be a good marketer to know where to sell. He has to be a good purchasing director and not overbuy noodles, in case it rains. He could buy a fridge but he would need a lot of capital, the taste of noodles would deteriorate, and he would need additional manpower to keep an inventory of the contents of the fridge. The successful noodle peddler puts dollars aside at the end of the day for depreciation and raw materials for tomorrow. Only then does he count profits. That's also why we don't have a marketing department. The successful peddler doesn't have time to examine opportunities in the next town."

"This is the way a division manager has to operate. In order to maximize output with minimum expenditure, every effort is made to keep track on a daily basis of sales, returns, net shipment costs and expenses."

## Open Communications

"I understand all that you've said so far," mused John, "but how exactly do you take all these abstract philosophical ideas and make them real?"

"Oh, open communications is the key. We have a fairly homogeneous workforce. Most are intelligent, some are even college graduates. Most are also very stable types with dependents or elderly parents they send money to."

"We're lucky, but of course it's not as homogeneous as in Japan, where everyone has experienced one culture. So here, the philosophy has to be backed up by a great deal of communication."

"We mentioned the meetings. We also have a suggestion box and we answer all the suggestions in print in the company newspaper. Also, one person from personnel tours the plant all day, for all three shifts, once a week, just chatting and getting in touch with any potential problems as they arise. It's kind of a secondary grievance system. We're not unionized and I guess we'd rather stay that way as it helps us so much with flexibility and job changes among our workforce.

"In the fall, when work is slow, we have many kompas. You may not know about this, John. A kompa is a small gathering off-premises after work. Eight to eighteen people participate, and the company pays for their time and refreshments. They're rarely social, they have an objective. For example, if two departments don't get along and yet they need to work together, they might hold a kompa. A kompa can take place at all levels of the company. Those groups that do it more frequently tend to move on from talking about production problems to more philosophical issues."

## Appraisal and Reward Systems

"It all sounds great," sighed Ken, "just as good as Japan. But tell me, how does it tie in with wages and salaries, because people here are used to such different systems."

"Well, we don't have lifetime employment, but we do have an explicit no-layoff commitment. We are responsible for our employees. This means that employees also have to take responsibility and have broad job categories so we don't have to redo paperwork all the time. We have tried to reduce the number of job classifications to the raw minimum, so we have two pay grades covering 700 workers. At the higher levels, we have three pay grades for craftsmen and two for technicians."

John ventured, "I guess an example of your job flexibility in action is the mechanic you mentioned when we toured the plant."

"Yes, the person you spoke with was a dry press mechanic. He's doing menial labor this week, but his pay hasn't been cut, and he knows he wouldn't be taken off his job if it weren't important."

"We don't hire outside, if we can avoid it," added the personnel manager. "Only if the skill is not available in-house. The bulk of our training is on-the-job. We don't utilize job postings. We promote when a person's skills are ripe or when there is a need.

"The job of a 'lead' or team leader is the steppingstone to supervisor. It's not a separate job status within our system, but the lead is given a few cents an hour extra and wears a pink, not a yellow, smock. The lead is carefully groomed for his or her position, and although a lead might be demoted because a specific need for them no longer existed, a lead would rarely be demoted for lack of skills or leadership ability.

"Rewards are for service and performance. Plant workers, unskilled and semiskilled, are reviewed every six months. The lead completes the evaluation form (see Exhibit 1). This is checked or confirmed by the supervisor and the overall point score translates into cents per hour. There are two copies, one for the supervisor and one for the employee. Depending on the supervisor, some employees get a copy, some don't.

"The office clerical staff are all reviewed on April 1st and October 1st. A similar review form for managers is used to determine overall letter scores. All the scores are posted on a spread sheet and compared across departments, through numerous meetings of managers and personnel people, until the scores are consistent with one another. Then the scores are tied to dollars. Some managers feed back, some don't.

"Exempt staff are reviewed on April 1st, and as a separate process, the spreadsheet procedure just outlined is carried out. At least two managers review any exempt employee, but feedback is usually minimal. The reason is that we encourage feedback all year. If there are no surprises for your subordinate at review time, then you've managed well.

"Agreements on reviews for exempt personnel take place in many meetings at various levels. The process is very thorough and exceptionally fair, and contributes to the levels of performance we get."

## Quality and Service

A question from John as to how Chiba International was doing as a result of all this elicited much pride.

"Turnover is 2½% a month, which is very satisfactory for our kind of labor, given a transient society. We rarely have to advertise for new employees now. The community knows about us. But we do select carefully. The personnel department does the initial screening, and then the production managers and supervisors get together and interview people.

"The lack of available technically trained people used to be a big problem, but over the years we've developed the expertise internally. Our productivity is now almost as high as in Japan."

Ken and John asked what other aspects of the company they had not yet discussed. They were told that quality, and, hence, customer service, was another central part of the philosophy.

"Our founder, Mr. Amano, firmly believes in zero defect theory. Doctor Deming taught us the concept of quality control. Unfortunately, many

<table>
<tr><td rowspan="2">Employee's Name</td><td rowspan="2">Clock No.</td><td rowspan="2">Dept.</td><td rowspan="2">shift</td><td colspan="4">Over Last 6 Month Period</td></tr>
<tr><td>Days Absent</td><td>Number Tardies</td><td>Number Early Exit</td><td>Work Days Leave of Absences</td></tr>
<tr><td>Employee's Job Title</td><td>Anniversary</td><td></td><td></td><td></td><td></td><td></td><td></td></tr>
</table>

| Rate on Factors Below: | | Numerical Score L | S | M | F |
|---|---|---|---|---|---|
| 1. LOYALTY/EDUCATION | Faithful to the company cause, ideals, philosophy, customers; a devoting or setting aside for company purposes. | | | | |
| 2. SPIRIT/ZEAL | Amount of interest & enthusiasm shown in work; full of energy, animation & courage; eagerness & ardent interest in the pursuit of company goals. | | | | |
| 3. COOPERATION | A willingness & ability to work with leaders & fellow employees toward company goals. | | | | |
| 4. QUANTITY OF WORK | Volume of work regularly produced; speed & consistency of output. | | | | |
| 5. QUALITY OF WORK | Extent to which work produced meets quality requirements of accuracy, thoroughness & effectiveness. | | | | |
| 6. JOB KNOWLEDGE | The fact or condition of knowing the job with familiarity gained through experience, association & training. | | | | |
| 7. SAFETY ATTITUDE | The willingness & ability to perform work safely. | | | | |
| 8. CREATIVENESS | The ability to produce through imaginative skill. | | | | |
| 9. ATTENDANCE | Includes all types of absence (excused or unexcused), tardies, early exits, L.O.A's from scheduled work. | | | | |
| 10. LEADERSHIP | The ability to provide direction, guidance & training to others. | | | | |
| OVERALL EVALUATION OF EMPLOYEE PERFORMANCE: | | | | | |

<table>
<tr><td>Supervisor's Approval</td><td colspan="2"></td><td>Personnel Dept. Approval</td></tr>
<tr><td colspan="4">Do Not Write Below This Line—For Human Resource Department Use Only</td></tr>
<tr><td>Present Base Rate</td><td>New Base Rate</td><td>Effective Date of Increase</td><td>Refer to instructions on the back side of this paper</td></tr>
</table>

**Exhibit 1**

American companies did not emphasize this. During World War II, the concept of acceptable quality level was developed in the United States. The idea was that with mass production there will be some defects. Rather than paying for more inspectors on the production line, real problems, for example, with cars, could be identified by the consumer in the field and repaired in the field.

"We don't allow that. We have 100% visual inspection of all our tiny parts. They only cost $50 per 1,000 units. We inspect every finished package under a microscope, so we have 130 inspectors, which is about one-sixth of our production staff.

"The company's founder, Amano, has said to us, 'We try to develop every item our customers want. Being latecomers, we never say no, we never say we can't.' Older ceramic manufacturers would evaluate a proposal on a cost basis and say no. Yet we have been profitable from the start."

As the interview drew to a close, one Japanese manager reflected that Mr. Suzuki has a saying:

$$\text{Ability} \times \text{philosophy} \times \text{zeal} = \text{performance.}$$

If the philosophy is negative, performance is negative because it's a multiplicative relationship.

"But in our company, which now numbers 2,000, we must also start to have different kinds of thinking. The Japanese sword is strong because it is made of all different kinds of steel wrapped around one another. The Chinese sword is also very strong, but because it's all one material, it's vulnerable to a certain kind of shock. We must bear that in mind so that we have differences within a shared philosophy.

"We're thinking of writing a book on our philosophy, addressing such issues as what loyalty is, by piecing together events and stories from our company history. This would be a book that would assist us in training."

Ken and John walked out into parking lot. "Whew!" sighed John. "It's more complicated than I had thought."

"Oh, yes! You need a great deal of patience," responded Ken paternally.

"So we'd better get started quickly," enthused John. "Where shall we begin? Perhaps I should call the translator."

# Case 1.8

# FOOTWEAR INTERNATIONAL

R. WILLIAM BLAKE

John Carlson frowned as he studied the translation of the front page story from the afternoon's edition of the Meillat, a fundamentalist newspaper with close ties to an opposition political party. The story, titled "Footwear's Unpardonable Audacity," suggested that the company was knowingly insulting Islam by including the name of Allah in a design used on the insoles of sandals it was manufacturing. To compound the problem, the paper had run a photograph of one of the offending sandals on the front page. As a result student groups were calling for public demonstrations against Footwear the next day. As Managing Director of Footwear Bangladesh Carlson knew he would have to act quickly to defuse a potentially explosive situation.

## Footwear International

Footwear International is a multinational manufacturer and marketer of footwear. Operations span the globe and include more than 83 companies in 70 countries. These include shoe factories, tanneries, engineering plants producing shoe machinery and moulds, product development studios, hosiery factories, quality control laboratories and approximately 6300 retail stores and 50,000 independent retailers.

Footwear employs more than 67,000 people and produces and sells in excess of 270,000,000 pairs of shoes every year. Head office acts as a service center and is staffed with specialists drawn from all over the world. These specialists, in areas such as marketing, retailing, product development, communications, store design, electronic data processing and business administration, travel for much of the year to share their expertise with the various companies. Training and technical education, offered through company run colleges and the training facility at headquarters, provide the latest skills to employees from around the world.

Although Footwear requires standardization in technology and the design of facilities it also encourages a high degree of decentralization and autonomy in its operations. The companies are virtually self-governing, which means their allegiance belongs to the countries in which they operate. Each is answerable to a board of directors which includes representatives from the local business community. The concept of "partnership" at the local level has made the company welcome internationally and has allowed it to operate successfully in countries where other multinationals have been unable to survive.

## Bangladesh

With a population approaching 110,000,000 in an area of 143,998 square kilometres (Exhibit 1),

SOURCE: Previously published in *International Management Behavior* (2000), edited by H. Lane, J. J. DiStefano, and M. Maznevski (pp. 165-172). Blackwell Business. Reprinted with permission.

Bangladesh is the most densely populated country in the world. It is also among the most impoverished with a 1987 per capita Gross National Product of $160 US and a high reliance on foreign aid. Over 40% of the Gross Domestic Product is generated by agriculture and more than 60% of its economically active population works in the agriculture sector. Although the land in Bangladesh is fertile, the country has a tropical monsoon climate and suffers from the ravages of periodic cyclones. In 1988 the country experienced the worst floods in recorded history.

The population of Bangladesh is 85% Moslem and Islam was made the official state religion in 1988. Approximately 95% of the population speaks Bengali with most of the remainder speaking tribal dialects.

Bangladesh has had a turbulent history in the 20th century. Most of the country was part of the British ruled East Bengal until 1947. In that year it joined with Assam to become East Pakistan, a province of the newly created country of Pakistan. East Pakistan was separated from the four provinces of West Pakistan by 1600 kilometres of Indian territory and, although the East was more populous, the national capital was established in West Pakistan. Over the following years widespread discontent built in the East whose people felt that they received a disproportionately small amount of development funding and were under-represented in government.

Following a period of unrest starting in 1969 the Awami League, the leading political party in East Pakistan, won an overwhelming victory in local elections held in 1970. The victory promised to give the league, which was pro independence, control in the National Assembly. To prevent that happening the national government suspended the convening of the Assembly indefinitely. On March 26th, 1971, the Awami League proclaimed the independence of the Peoples republic of Bangladesh and civil war quickly followed. In the ensuing conflict hundreds of thousands of refugees fled to safety across the border in India. In December India, which supported the independence of Bangladesh, declared war and twelve days later Pakistan surrendered. Bangladesh had won its independence and the capital of the new country was established at Dhaka. In the years immediately following independence industrial output declined in major industries as the result of the departure of many of the largely non-Bengali financier and managerial class.

Throughout the subsequent years political stability proved elusive for Bangladesh. Although elections were held, stability was threatened by the terrorist tactics resorted to by opposition groups from both political extremes. Coups and counter coups, assassinations and suspension of civil liberties became regular occurrences.

Since 1983 Bangladesh had been ruled by the self proclaimed President General H.M. Ershad. Despite demonstrations in 1987, that led to a state of emergency being declared, Ershad managed to retain power in elections held the following year. The country remains politically volatile, however. Dozens of political parties continually manoeuvre for position and alliances and coalitions are the order of the day. The principal opposition party is the Awami League, an alliance of eight political parties. Many of the parties are closely linked with so called "opposition newspapers" which promote their political positions. Strikes and demonstrations are frequent and often result from co-operation among opposition political parties, student groups and unions.

## Footwear Bangladesh

Footwear became active in what was then East Bengal in the 1930's. In 1962 the first major investment took place with the construction of a footwear manufacturing facility at Tongi, an industrial town located 30 kilometres north of Dhaka. During the following years the company expanded its presence in both conventional and unconventional ways. In 1971 the then Managing Director became a freedom fighter while continuing to oversee operations. He subsequently became the only foreigner to be decorated by the government with the "Bir Protik" in recognition of both his and the company's contribution to the independence of Bangladesh.

In 1985 Footwear Bangladesh went public and two years later spearheaded the largest private sector foreign investment in the country, a tannery and footwear factory at Dhamrai. The new tannery produced leather for local Footwear needs and the export market while the factory produced a variety of footwear for the local market.

By 1988 Footwear Bangladesh employed 1800 employees and sold through 81 stores and 54 agencies. The company introduced approximately 300 new products a year to the market using their in house design and development capability. Footwear managers were particularly proud of the capability of the personnel in these departments, all of whom were Bangladeshi.

Annual sales in excess of 10,000,000 pairs of footwear gave the company 15% of the national market in 1988. Revenues exceeded $30 million US and after tax profit was approximately $1 million. Financially, the company was considered a medium contributor within the Footwear organization. With a population approaching 110,000,000, and per capita consumption of one pair of shoes every two years, Bangladesh was perceived as offering Footwear enormous potential for growth both through consumer education and competitive pressure.

The Managing Director of Footwear Bangladesh was John Carlson, one of only four foreigners working for the company. The others were the managers of production, marketing and sales. All had extensive and varied experience within the Footwear organization.

## The Incident

On Thursday, June 22nd 1989, John Carlson was shown a copy of that day's **Meillat**, a well known opposition newspaper with pro Libyan leanings. Under the headline "Footwear's Unpardonable Audacity," the writer suggested that the design on the insole of one model of sandal produced by the company included the Arabic spelling of the word "Allah" (Exhibit 2). The story went on to suggest that Footwear was under Jewish ownership and to link the alleged offense with the gunning down of many people in Palestine by Jews. The story highlighted the fact that the design was on the insole of the sandal and, therefore, next to the foot, a sign of great disrespect to Moslems.

Carlson immediately contacted the supervisor of the design department and asked for any information he could provide on the design on the sandals. He already knew that they were from a medium-priced line of women's footwear known as "Chappels" which had the design on the insole changed often as a marketing feature. Following his investigation the supervisor reported that the design had been based on a set of Chinese temple bells that the designer had purchased in the local market. Pleased by the appearance of the bells she had used them as the basis for a stylized design which she submitted to her supervisor for consideration and approval (Exhibit 3).

All of the employees in the development and marketing department were Moslems. The supervisor reported that the woman who had produced the offending design was a devout Bengali Moslem who spoke and read no Arabic. The same was true of almost all of the employees in the department. The supervisor confirmed to Carlson that numerous people in the department had seen the new design prior to its approval and no one had seen any problem or raised any objection to it. Following the conversation Carlson compared the design to the word Allah which he had arranged to have written in Arabic (Exhibit 4).

Carlson was perplexed by the article and its timing. The sandals in question were not new to the market and had not been subject to prior complaints. As he reread the translation of the **Meillat** article he wondered why the Jewish reference had been made when the family that owned Footwear International were Christian. He also wondered if the fact that students from the university had taken the sandals to the paper was significant.

As the day progressed the situation got worse. Carlson was shown a translation of a proclamation that had been circulated by two youth groups calling for demonstrations against Footwear to be held the next day (Exhibit 5). The proclamation linked Footwear, Salman Rushdie and the Jewish community and, ominously, stated that "even at the cost of our lives we have to protest against this conspiracy."

More bad news followed. Calls had been made for charges to be laid against Carlson and four others under a section of the criminal code that forbade "deliberate and malicious acts intended to outrage feelings of any class by insulting its religion or religious believers" (Exhibit 6). A short time later Carlson received a copy of a statement that had been filed by a local lawyer, although no warrants were immediately forthcoming (Exhibit 7).

While he was reviewing the situation Carlson was interrupted by his secretary. In an excited voice she informed him that the Prime Minister was being quoted as calling the sandal incident an "unforgivable crime." The seriousness of the incident seemed to be escalating rapidly and Carlson wondered what he should do to try to minimize the damage.

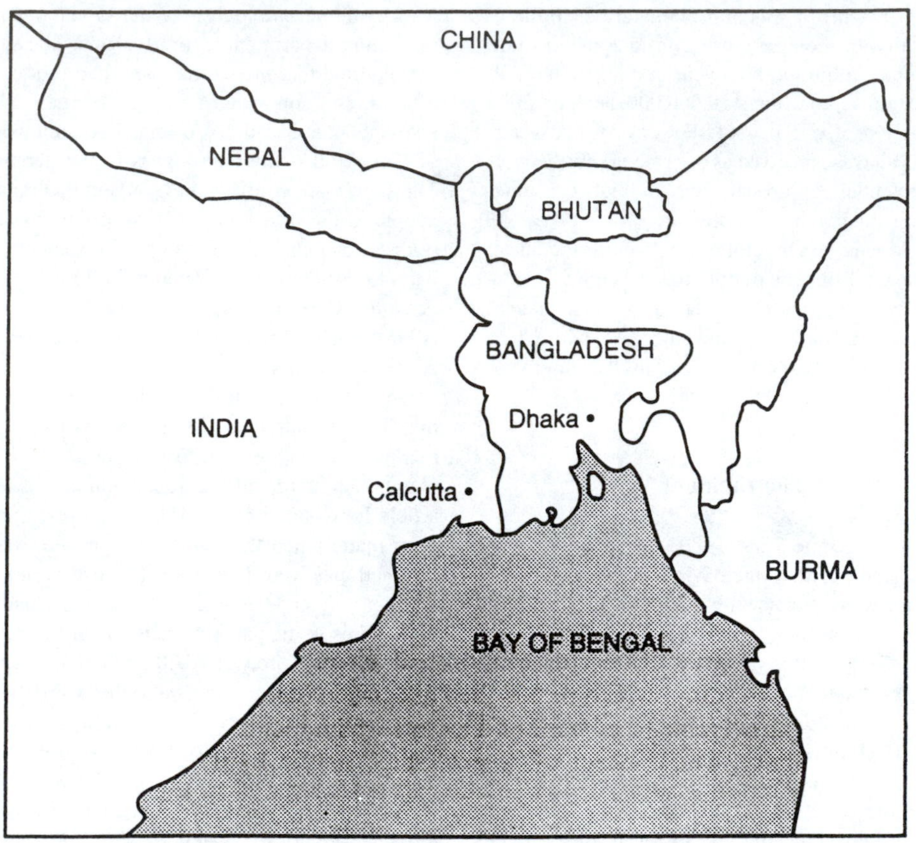


**Exhibit 1** Bangladesh

## UNPARDONABLE AUDACITY OF FOOTWEAR

In Bangladesh a Sandal with Allah as Footwear trade mark in Arabic designed in calligraphy has been marketed although last year Islam was made the State Religion in Bangladesh. The Sandal in black and white contains Allah in black. Prima facie it appears it has been designed and the Alif "the first letter in Arabic" has been jointly written. Excluding Alif it reads LILLAH. In Bangladesh after the Salman Rushdies[2] Satanic Verses which has brought unprecendented demonstration and innumerable strikes (Hartels). This International shoe manufacturing organization under Jewish ownership with the design of Allah has made religious offence. Where for sanctity of Islam one million people of Afganistan have sacrificed their lives and wherein occupied Palestine many people have been gunned down by Jews for sanctity of Islam in this country the word Allah under this guise has been put under feet.

Last night a group of students from Dhaka university came to **Meillat** office with a couple of pairs of Sandal. The management staff of Footwear was not available over telephone. This sandal has got two straps made of foam.

1. The translation is identical to that which Carlson was given to work with.
2. Salman Rushdie was the author of the controversial book, "The Satanic Verses." The author had been sentenced to death, in absentia, by Ayatollah Khomenei, the leader of Iran, for crimes against Islam.

**Exhibit 2** Translation of the **Meillat** Story[1]

**Exhibit 3** The Temple Bells and the Design Used on the Sandal

SOURCE: Redrawn from a facsimile sent to headquarters by John Carlson.

**Exhibit 4** The Arabic Spelling of Allah

SOURCE: Redrawn from a facsimile sent to headquarters by John Carlson.

The audacity through the use of the name "Allah" in a sandal

Let Rushdies Jewish Footwear Company be prohibited in Bangladesh.

Dear people who believe in one God It is announced in the holy Quran Allahs name is above everything but shoe manufacturing Jewish Footwear Shoe Company has used the name Allah and shown disrespect of unprecedented nature and also unpardonable audacity. After the failure of Rushdies efforts to destroy the beliefs of Moslems in the Quran, Islam and the prophet (SM) who is the writer of Satanic verses the Jewish People have started offending the Moslems. This time it is a fight against Allah. In fact Daud Haider, Salman Rushdie Viking Penguin and Footwear Shoe Company all are supported and financed by Jewish community. Therefore no compromise with them. Even at the cost of our lives we have to protest against this conspiracy.

For this procession and demonstration will be held on 23rd. June Friday after Jumma prayer from Baitul Mukarram Mosque south gate. Please join this procession and announce we will not pardon Footwear Shoe Companys audacity. Footwear Shoe Company has to be prohibited, don't buy Jewish products and Footwear shoes. Be aware Rushdies partner.

Issued by Bangladesh Islamie Jubashibir (Youth Student Forum) and Bangladesh Islamic Satrashbir (Student Forum)

1. The translation is identical to that which Carlson was given to work with.

**Exhibit 5** Translation of the Student Groups Proclamation[1]

[295-A. *Deliberate and malicious acts intended to outrage religious feelings of any class by insulting its religion or religious believers.* Whoever, with deliberate and malicious intention of outraging the religious feelings of any class of [the citizens . . . .], by words, either spoken or written, or by visible representations insults or attempts to insult the religion or religious beliefs of that class, shall be punished with imprisonment. . . .

. . . In order to bring a matter under S. 295-A it is not the mere matter of discourse or the written expression but also the manner of it which has to be looked to. In other words the expressions should be such as are bound to be regarded by any reasonable man as grossly offensive and provocative and maliciously and deliberately intended to outrage the feelings of any class of citizens. . . . If the injurious act was done voluntarily without a lawful excuse, malice may be presumed.

**Exhibit 6** Section 295 of the Criminal Code

The plaintiff most respectfully states that:

1) The plaintiff is a lawyer, and a Bangladeshi Citizen and his religion is Islam. He is basically a devout Moslem. According to Islamic tradition he regularly performs his daily work.

2) The first accused of this . . . is the Managing Director of Footwear Shoe Company, the second accused is the Production Manager of the said company, the third accused is the Marketing Manager, the fourth accused is the Calligrapher of the said company and last accused is the Sales Manager of the said company. The said company is an international organization having shoe business in different countries.

3) The accused persons deliberately wanted to outrage the religion of Muslims by engraving the calligraphy of "Allah" in Arabic on a sandal thereby to offend the Religion of majority this Muslim Country. By marketing this sandal with the calligraphy of "Allah" they have offended the religious feelings of millions of Muslims. It is the solemn religious duty and responsibility of every devout Muslim to protect the sanctity of "Allah." The plaintiff first saw the sandal with this calligraphy on 22nd June 1989 at Elephant road shop.

The accused persons collectively and deliberately wanted this calligraphy under the feet thereby to offend the religion of mine and many other Muslims and have committed a crime under provisions of section 295A of the Penal Code. At the time of hearing the evidence will be provided.

Therefore under the provisions of section 295A of the Penal Code the accused persons be issued with warrant of arrest and be brought to court for justice.

The names of the Witnesses

1)

2)

3)

**Exhibit 7** The Statement of the Plaintiff

# PART II

## Roles of the International Manager

This section presents material that examines what international managers do. Managerial work has been categorized in a variety of ways. Undeniably though, much of what managers do involves interpersonal interactions. In the articles and cases in this section, managers can be seen acting out their roles as communicator and negotiator, as decision maker, as organizer and resource allocator, and as organization builder, change agent, and leader. In the international context these roles are played out across national boundaries, with people from different cultures who have different values and standards of ethical behavior.

# Reading 2.1

## VALUES IN TENSION

### *Ethics Away From Home*

THOMAS DONALDSON

When we leave home and cross our nation's boundaries, moral clarity often blurs. Without a backdrop of shared attitudes, and without familiar laws and judicial procedures that define standards of ethical conduct, certainty is elusive. Should a company invest in a foreign country where civil and political rights are violated? Should a company go along with a host country's discriminatory employment practices? If companies in developed countries shift facilities to developing nations that lack strict environmental and health regulations, or if those companies choose to fill management and other top level positions in a host nation with people from the home country, whose standards should prevail?

Even the best-informed, best-intentioned executives must rethink their assumptions about business practice in foreign settings. What works in a company's home country can fail in a country with different standards of ethical conduct. Such difficulties are unavoidable for businesspeople who live and work abroad.

But how can managers resolve the problems? What are the principles that can help them work through the maze of cultural differences and establish codes of conduct for globally ethical business practice? How can companies answer the toughest question in global business ethics: What happens when a host country's ethical standards seem lower than the home country's?

#### Competing Answers

One answer is as old as philosophical discourse. According to cultural relativism, no culture's ethics are better than any other's; therefore there are no international rights and wrongs. If the people of Indonesia tolerate the bribery of their public officials, so what? Their attitude is no better or worse than that of people in Denmark or Singapore who refuse to offer or accept bribes. Likewise, if Belgians fail to find insider trading morally repugnant, who cares? Not enforcing insider-trading laws is no more or less ethical than enforcing such laws.

#### Section II: Roles of the International Manager

This section presents material that examines what international managers do. Managerial work has

SOURCE: Reprinted with permission from Harvard Business Review. From "Values in Tension: Ethics Away From Home" by Donaldson, T., Sept/Oct 1996, pp. 48-62. 

been categorized in a variety of ways. Undeniably though, much of what managers do involves interpersonal interactions. In the articles and cases in this section managers can be seen acting out their roles as communicator and negotiator, as decision maker, as organizer and resource allocator, and as organization builder, change agent, and leader. In the international context these roles are played out across national boundaries, with people from different cultures, and who have different values and standards of ethical behavior.

The cultural relativist's creed—When in Rome, do as the Romans do—is tempting, especially when failing to do as the locals do means forfeiting business opportunities. The inadequacy of cultural relativism, however, becomes apparent when the practices in question are more damaging than petty bribery or insider trading.

In the late 1980s, some European tanneries and pharmaceutical companies were looking for cheap waste-dumping sites. They approached virtually every country on Africa's west coast from Morocco to the Congo. Nigeria agreed to take highly toxic polychlorinated biphenyls. Unprotected local workers, wearing thongs and shorts, unloaded barrels of PCBs and placed them near a residential area. Neither the residents nor the workers knew that the barrels contained toxic waste.

We may denounce governments that permit such abuses, but many countries are unable to police transnational corporations adequately even if they want to. And in many countries, the combination of ineffective enforcement and inadequate regulations leads to behavior by unscrupulous companies that is clearly wrong. A few years ago, for example, a group of investors became interested in restoring the SS *United States,* once a luxurious ocean liner. Before the actual restoration could begin, the ship had to be stripped of its asbestos lining. A bid from a U.S. company, based on U.S. standards for asbestos removal, priced the job at more than $100 million. A company in the Ukrainian city of Sevastopol offered to do the work for less than $2 million. In October 1993, the ship was towed to Sevastopol.

A cultural relativist would have no problem with that outcome, but I do. A country has the right to establish its own health and safety regulations, but in the case described above, the standards and the terms of the contract could not possibly have protected workers in Sevastopol from known health risks. Even if the contract met Ukrainian standards, ethical businesspeople must object. Cultural relativism is morally blind. There are fundamental values that cross cultures, and companies must uphold them. . . .

At the other end of the spectrum from cultural relativism is ethical imperialism, which directs people to do everywhere exactly as they do at home. Again, an understandably appealing approach but one that is clearly inadequate. Consider the large U.S. computer-products company that in 1993 introduced a course on sexual harassment in its Saudi-Arabian facility. Under the banner of global consistency, instructors used the same approach to train Saudi Arabian managers that they had used with U.S. managers: the participants were asked to discuss a case in which a manager makes sexually explicit remarks to a new female employee over drinks in a bar. The instructors failed to consider how the exercise would work in a culture with strict conventions governing relationships between men and women. As a result, the training sessions were ludicrous. They baffled and offended the Saudi participants, and the message to avoid coercion and sexual discrimination was lost.

The theory behind ethical imperialism is absolutism, which is based on three problematic principles. Absolutists believe that there is a single list of truths, that they can be expressed only with one set of concepts, and that they call for exactly the same behavior around the world.

The first claim clashes with many people's belief that different cultural traditions must be respected. In some cultures, loyalty to a community—family, organization, or society—is the foundation of all ethical behavior. The Japanese, for example, define business ethics in terms of loyalty to their companies, their business networks, and their nation. Americans place a higher value on liberty than on loyalty; the U.S. tradition of rights emphasizes equality, fairness, and individual freedom. It is hard to conclude that truth lies on one side or the other, but an absolutist would have us select just one.

The second problem with absolutism is the presumption that people must express moral truth using only one set of concepts. For instance, some absolutists insist that the language of basic rights provide the framework for any discussion of ethics. That means, though, that entire cultural traditions must be ignored. The notion of a right evolved with the rise of democracy in post-Renaissance Europe and the United States, but the term is not found in either Confucian or Buddhist traditions. We all learn ethics in the context of our particular cultures, and the power in the principles is deeply tied to the way in which they are expressed. Internationally accepted lists of moral principles, such as the United Nations' Universal Declaration of Human Rights, draw on many cultural and religious traditions. As philosopher

Michael Walzer has noted. "There is no Esperanto of global ethics."

The third problem with absolutism is the belief in a global standard of ethical behavior. Context must shape ethical practice. Very low wages, for example, may be considered unethical in rich, advanced countries, but developing nations may be acting ethically if they encourage investment and improve living standards by accepting low wages. Likewise, when people are malnourished or starving, a government may be wise to use more fertilizer in order to improve crop yields, even though that means settling for relatively high levels of thermal water pollution.

When cultures have different standards of ethical behavior—and different ways of handling unethical behavior—a company that takes an absolutist approach may find itself making a disastrous mistake. When a manager at a large U.S. specialty-products company in China caught an employee stealing, she followed the company's practice and turned the employee over to the provincial authorities, who executed him. Managers cannot operate in another culture without being aware of that culture's attitudes toward ethics.

If companies can neither adopt a host country's ethics nor extend the home country's standards, what is the answer? Even the traditional litmus test—What would people think of your actions if they were written up on the front page of the newspaper?—is an unreliable guide, for there is no international consensus on standards of business conduct.

## Balancing the Extremes: Three Guiding Principles

Companies must help managers distinguish between practices that are merely different and those that are wrong. For relatives, nothing is sacred and nothing is wrong. For absolutists, many things that are different are wrong. Neither extreme illuminates the real world of business decision making. The answer lies somewhere in between.

When it comes to shaping ethical behavior, companies must be guided by three principles.

- Respect for core human values, which determine the absolute moral threshold for all business activities.
- Respect for local traditions.
- The belief that context matters when deciding what is right and what is wrong.

Consider those principles in action. In Japan, people doing business together often exchange gifts—sometimes expensive ones—in keeping with long-standing Japanese tradition. When U.S. and European companies started doing a lot of business in Japan, many Western businesspeople thought that the practice of gift giving might be wrong rather than simply different. To them, accepting a gift felt like accepting a bribe. As Western companies have become more familiar with Japanese traditions, however, most have come to tolerate the practice and to set different limits on gift giving in Japan than they do elsewhere.

Respecting differences is a crucial ethical practice. Research shows that management ethics differ among cultures; respecting those differences means recognizing that some cultures have obvious weaknesses—as well as hidden strengths. Managers in Hong Kong, for example, have a higher tolerance for some forms of bribery than their Western counterparts, but they have a much lower tolerance for the failure to acknowledge a subordinate's work. In some parts of the Far East, stealing credit from a subordinate is nearly an unpardonable sin.

People often equate respect for local traditions with cultural relativism. That is incorrect. Some practices are clearly wrong. Union Carbide's tragic experience in Bhopal, India, provides one example. The company's executives seriously underestimated how much on-site management involvement was needed at the Bhopal Plant to compensate for the country's poor infrastructure and regulatory capabilities. In the aftermath of the disastrous gas leak, the lesson is clear: companies using sophisticated technology in a developing country must evaluate that country's ability to oversee its safe use. Since the incident at Bhopal, Union Carbide has become a leader in advising companies on using hazardous technologies safely in developing countries.

Some activities are wrong no matter where they take place. But some practices that are unethical in one setting may be acceptable in another. For instance, the chemical EDB, a soil fungicide, is banned for use in the United States. In hot climates, however, it quickly becomes harmless through exposure to intense solar radiation and high soil temperatures. As long as the chemical is monitored, companies may be able to use EDB ethically in certain parts of the world.

## Defining the Ethical Threshold: Core Values

Few ethical questions are easy for managers to answer. But there are some hard truths that must guide managers' actions, a set of what I call *core human values,* which define minimum ethical standards for all companies. The right to good health and the right to economic advancement and an improved standard of living are two core human values. Another is what Westerners call the Golden Rule, which is recognizable in every major religious and ethical tradition around the world. In Book 15 of his *Analects,* for instance, Confucius counsels people to maintain reciprocity, or not to do to others what they do not want done to themselves.

Although no single list would satisfy every scholar, I believe it is possible to articulate three core values that incorporate the work of scores of theologians and philosophers around the world. To be broadly relevant, these values must include elements found in both Western and non-Western cultural and religious traditions. Consider the examples of values in Exhibit 1, "What Do These Values Have in Common?"

At first glance, the values expressed in the two lists seem quite different. Nonetheless, in the spirit of what philosopher John Rawls calls *overlapping consensus,* one can see that the seemingly divergent values converge at key points. Despite important differences between Western and non-Western cultural and religious traditions, both express shared attitudes about what it means to be human. First, individuals must not treat others simply as tools; in other words, they must recognize a person's value as a human being. Next, individuals and communities must treat people in ways that respect people's basic rights. Finally, members of a community must work together to support and improve the institutions on which the community depends. I call those three values *respect for human dignity, respect for basic rights,* and *good citizenship.*

Those values must be the starting point for all companies as they formulate and evaluate standards of ethical conduct at home and abroad. But they are only a starting point. Companies need much more specific guidelines, and the first step to developing those is to translate the core human values into core values for business. What does it mean, for example, for a company to respect human dignity? How can a company be a good citizen?

I believe that companies can respect human dignity by creating and sustaining a corporate culture in which employees, customers, and suppliers are treated not as means to an end but as people whose intrinsic value must be acknowledged, and by producing safe products and services in a safe workplace. Companies can respect basic rights by acting in ways that support and protect the individual rights of employees, customers, and surrounding communities, and by avoiding relationships that violate human beings' rights to health, education, safety, and an adequate standard of living. And companies can be good citizens by supporting essential social institutions, such as the economic system and the education system, and by working with host governments and other organizations to protect the environment.

The core values establish a moral compass for business practice. They can help companies identify practices that are acceptable and those that are intolerable—even if the practices are compatible with a host country's norms and laws. Dumping pollutants near people's homes and accepting inadequate standards for handling hazardous materials are two examples of actions that violate core values.

Similarly, if employing children prevents them from receiving a basic education, the practice is intolerable. Lying about product specifications in the act of selling may not affect human lives directly, but it too is intolerable because it violates the trust that is needed to sustain a corporate culture in which customers are respected.

Sometimes it is not a company's actions but those of a supplier or customer that pose problems. Take the case of the Tan family, a large supplier for Levi Strauss. The Tans were allegedly forcing 1,200 Chinese and Filipino women to work 74 hours per week in guarded compounds on the Mariana Islands. In 1992, after repeated warnings to the Tans, Levi Strauss broke off business relations with them.

## Creating an Ethical Corporate Culture

The core values for business that I have enumerated can help companies begin to exercise ethical judgement and think about how to operate ethically in foreign cultures, but they are not specific enough to guide managers through actual ethical dilemmas. Levi Strauss relied on a written code of conduct when figuring out how to deal with the Tan family. The company's Global Sourcing and Operating Guidelines, formerly called the Business Partner Terms of Engagement, state that Levi Strauss will "seek to identify and utilize business partners who aspire as individuals and in the conduct of all their businesses to a set of ethical standards not incompatible with our own." Whenever intolerable business situations arise, managers should be guided by precise statements that spell out the behavior and operating practices that the company demands.

Ninety percent of all *Fortune 500* companies have codes of conduct, and 70% have statements of vision and values. In Europe and the Far East, the percentages are lower but are increasing rapidly. Does that mean that most companies have what they need? Hardly. Even though most large U.S. companies have both statements of values and codes of conduct, many might be better off if they didn't. Too many companies don't do anything with the documents; they simply paste them on the wall to impress employees, customers, suppliers, and the public. As a result, the senior managers who drafted the statements lose credibility by proclaiming values and not living up to them. Companies such as Johnson & Johnson, Levi Strauss, Motorola, Texas Instruments, and Lockheed Martin, however, do a great deal to make the words meaningful. Johnson & Johnson, for example, has become well known for its Credo Challenge sessions, in which managers discuss ethics in the context of their current business problems and are invited to criticize the company's credo and make suggestions for changes. The participants' ideas are passed on to the company's senior managers. Lockheed Martin has created an innovative site on the World Wide Web and on its local network that gives employees, customers, and suppliers access to the company's ethical code and the chance to voice complaints.

Codes of conduct must provide clear direction about ethical behavior when the temptation to behave unethically is strongest. The pronouncement in a code of conduct that bribery is unacceptable is useless unless accompanied by guidelines for gift giving, payments to get goods through customs, and "requests" from intermediaries who are hired to ask for bribes.

Motorola's values are stated very simply as "How we will always act: [with] constant respect for people [and] uncompromising integrity." The company's code of conduct, however, is explicit about actual business practice. With respect to bribery, for example, the code states that the "funds and assets of Motorola shall not be used, directly or indirectly, for illegal payments of any kind." It is unambiguous about what sort of payment is illegal: "the payment of a bribe to a public official or the kickback of funds to an employee of a customer. . . ." The code goes on to prescribe specific procedures for handling commissions to intermediaries, issuing sales invoices, and disclosing confidential information in a sales transaction—all situations in which employees might have an opportunity to accept or offer bribes.

Codes of conduct must be explicit to be useful, but they must also leave room for a manager to use his or her judgment in situations requiring cultural sensitivity. Host-country employees shouldn't be forced to adopt all home-country values and renounce their own. Again, Motorola's code is exemplary. First, it gives clear direction: "Employees of Motorola will respect the laws, customs, and traditions of each country in which they operate, but will, at the same time, engage in no course of conduct which, even if legal, customary, and accepted in any such country, could be deemed to be in violation of the accepted business ethics of Motorola or the laws of the United States relating to business ethics." After laying down such absolutes, Motorola's code then makes clear when individual judgment will be necessary. For example, employees may sometimes accept certain kinds of small gifts "in rare circumstances, where the refusal to accept a gift" would injure Motorola's "legitimate business interests." Under certain circumstances, such gifts "may be accepted so long as the gift inures to the benefit of Motorola" and not "to the benefit of the Motorola employee."

Striking the appropriate balance between providing clear direction and leaving room for individual judgment makes crafting corporate values statements and ethics codes one of the hardest tasks that executives confront. The words are only a start. A company's leaders need to refer often to their organization's credo and code and must themselves be credible, committed, and consistent. If senior managers act as though ethics don't matter, the rest of the company's employees won't think they do, either.

## Conflicts of Development and Conflicts of Tradition

Managers living and working abroad who are not prepared to grapple with moral ambiguity and tension should pack their bags and come home. The view that all business practices can be categorized as either ethical or unethical is too simple. As Einstein is reported to have said, "Things should be as simple as possible—but no simpler." Many business practices that are considered unethical in one setting may be ethical in another. Such activities are neither black nor white but exist in what Thomas Dunfee and I have called *moral free space.* In this gray zone, there are no tight prescriptions for a company's behavior. Managers must chart their own courses—as long as they do not violate core human values.

Consider the following example. Some successful Indian companies offer employees the opportunity for one of their children to gain a job with the company once the child has completed a certain level in school. The companies honor this commitment even when other applicants are more qualified than an employee's child. The perk is extremely valuable in a country where jobs are hard to find, and it reflects the Indian culture's belief that the West has gone too far in allowing economic opportunities to break up families. Not surprisingly, the perk is among the most cherished by employees, but in most Western countries, it would be branded unacceptable nepotism. In the United States, for example, the ethical principle of equal opportunity holds that jobs should go to the applicants with the best qualifications. If a U.S. company made such promises to its employees, it would violate regulations established by the Equal Employment Opportunity Commission. Given this difference in ethical attitudes, how should U.S. managers react to Indian nepotism? Should they condemn the Indian companies, refusing to accept them as partners or supplies until they agree to clean up their act?

Despite the obvious tension between nepotism and principles of equal opportunity, I cannot condemn the practice for Indians. In a country, such as India, that emphasizes clan and family relationships and has catastrophic levels of unemployment, the practice must be viewed in moral free space. The decision to allow a special perk for employees and their children is not necessarily wrong—at least for members of that country.

How can managers discover the limits of moral free space? That is, how can they learn to distinguish a value in tension with their own from one that is intolerable? Helping managers develop good ethical judgment requires companies to be clear about their core values and codes of conduct. But even the most explicit set of guidelines cannot always provide answers. That is especially true in the thorniest ethical dilemmas, in which the host country's ethical standards not only are different but also seem lower than the home country's. Managers must recognize that when countries have different ethical standards, there are two types of conflict that commonly arise. Each type requires its own line of reasoning.

In the first type of conflict, which I call a *conflict of relative development,* ethical standards conflict because of the countries' different levels of economic development. As mentioned before, developing countries may accept wage rates that seem inhumane to more advanced countries in order to attract investment. As economic conditions in a developing country improve, the incidence of that sort of conflict usually decreases. The second type of conflict is a *conflict of cultural tradition.* For example, Saudi Arabia, unlike most other countries, does not allow women to serve as corporate managers. Instead, women may work in only a few professions, such as education and health care. The prohibition stems from strongly held religious and cultural beliefs; any increase in the country's level of economic development, which is already quite high, is not likely to change the rules.

To resolve a conflict of relative development, a manager must ask the following question: Would the practice be acceptable at home if my country were in a similar stage of economic development? Consider the difference between wage and safety standards in the United States and in Angola, where citizens accept lower standards on both counts. If a U.S. oil company is hiring Angolans to work on an offshore Angolan oil rig, can the company pay them lower wages than it pays U.S. workers in the Gulf of Mexico? Reasonable people have to answer yes if the alternative for Angola is the loss of both the foreign investment and the jobs.

Consider, too, differences in regulatory environments. In the 1980s, the government of India fought hard to be able to import Ciba-Geigy's Entero Vioform, a drug known to be enormously effective in fighting dysentery but one that had been banned in the United States because some users experienced side effects. Although dysentery was not a big problem in the United States, in India, poor public sanitation was contributing to epidemic levels of the disease. Was it unethical to make the drug available in India after it had been banned in the United States? On the contrary, rational people should consider it unethical not to do so. Apply our test: Would the United States, at an earlier stage of development, have used this drug despite its side effects? The answer is clearly yes.

But there are many instances when the answer to similar questions is no. Sometimes a host country's standards are inadequate at any level of economic development. If a country's pollution standards are so low that working on an oil rig would considerably increase a person's risk of developing cancer, foreign oil companies must refuse to do business there. Likewise, if the dangerous side effects of a drug treatment outweigh its benefits, managers should not accept health standards that ignore the risks.

When relative economic conditions do not drive tensions, there is a more objective test for resolving ethical problems. Managers should deem a practice permissible only if they can answer no to both of the following questions: Is it possible to conduct business successfully in the host country without undertaking the practice? and Is the practice a violation of a core human value? Japanese gift giving is a perfect example of a conflict of cultural tradition. Most experienced businesspeople, Japanese and non-Japanese alike, would agree that doing business in Japan would be virtually impossible without adopting the practice. Does gift giving violate a core human value? I cannot identify one that it violates. As a result, gift giving may be permissible for foreign companies in Japan even if it conflicts with ethical attitudes at home. In fact, that conclusion is widely accepted, even by companies such as Texas Instruments and IBM, which are outspoken against bribery.

Does it follow that all nonmonetary gifts are acceptable or that bribes are generally acceptable in countries where they are common? Not at all. . . . What makes the routine practice of gift giving acceptable in Japan are the limits in its scope and intention. When gift giving moves outside those limits, it soon collides with core human values. For example, when Carl Kotchian, president of Lockheed in the 1970s, carried suitcases full of cash to Japanese politicians, he went beyond the norms established by Japanese tradition. That incident galvanized opinion in the United States Congress and helped lead to passage of the Foreign Corrupt Practices Act. Likewise, Roh Tae Woo went beyond the norms established by Korean cultural tradition when he accepted $635.4 million in bribes as president of the Republic of Korea between 1988 and 1993.

## Guidelines for Ethical Leadership

Learning to spot intolerable practices and to exercise good judgment when ethical conflicts arise requires practice. Creating a company culture that rewards ethical behavior is essential. The following guidelines for developing a global ethical perspective among managers can help.

*Treat corporate values and formal standards of conduct as absolutes.* Whatever ethical standards a company chooses, it cannot waver on its principles either at home or abroad. Consider what has become part of company lore at Motorola. Around 1950, a senior executive was negotiating with officials of a South American government on a $10 million sale that would have increased the company's annual net profits by nearly 25%. As the negotiations neared completion, however, the executive walked away from the deal because the officials were asking for $1 million for "fees." CEO Robert Galvin not only supported the executive's decision but also made it clear that Motorola would neither accept the sale on any terms nor do business with those government officials again. Retold over the decades, this story demonstrating Galvin's resolve has helped cement a culture of ethics of thousands of employees at Motorola.

*Design and implement conditions of engagement for suppliers and customers.* Will your company do business with any customer or supplier? What if a customer or supplier uses child labor? What if it has strong links with organized crime? What if it pressures your company to break a host country's laws? Such issues are best not left for spur-of-the-moment decisions. Some companies have realized that. Sears, for instance, has developed a policy of not contracting production to companies that use prison labor or infringe on workers' rights to health and safety. And BankAmerica has specified as a condition for many of its loans to developing countries that environmental standards and human rights must be observed.

*Allow foreign business units to help formulate ethical standards and interpret ethical issues.* The French pharmaceutical company Rhône-Poulenc Rorer has allowed foreign subsidiaries to augment lists of corporate ethical principles with their own suggestions. Texas Instruments has paid special attention to issues of international business ethics by creating the Global Business Practices Council, which is made up of managers from countries in which the company operates. With the overarching intent to create a "global ethics strategy, locally deployed," the council's mandate is to provide ethics education and create local processes that will help managers in the company's foreign business units resolve ethical conflicts.

*In host countries, support efforts to decrease institutional corruption.* Individual managers will not be able to wipe out corruption in a host country, no matter how many bribes they turn down. When a host country's tax system, import and export procedures, and procurement practices favor unethical players, companies must take action.

Many companies have begun to participate in reforming host-country institutions. General Electric, for example, has taken a strong stand in India, using the media to make repeated condemnations of bribery in business and government. General Electric and others have found, however, that a single company usually cannot drive out entrenched corruption. Transparency International, an organization based in Germany, has been effective in helping coalitions of companies, government officials, and others work to reform bribery-ridden bureaucracies in Russia, Bangladesh, and elsewhere.

*Exercise moral imagination.* Using moral imagination means resolving tensions responsibly and creatively. Coca-Cola, for instance, has consistently

| *Non-Western* | *Western* |
|---|---|
| Kyosei (Japanese): Living and working together for the common good. | Individual liberty |
| Dharma (Hindu): The fulfillment of inherited duty. | Egalitarianism |
| Santutthi (Buddhist): The importance of limited desires. | Political participation |
| Zakat (Muslim): The duty to give alms to the Muslim poor. | Human rights |

**Exhibit 1** What Do These Values Have in Common?

turned down requests for bribes from Egyptian officials but has managed to gain political support and public trust by sponsoring a project to plant fruit trees. And take the example of Levi Strauss, which discovered in the early 1990s that two of its suppliers in Bangladesh were employing children under the age of 14—a practice that violated the company's principles but was tolerated in Bangladesh. Forcing the suppliers to fire the children would not have ensured that the children received an education, and it would have caused serious hardship for the families depending on the children's wages. In a creative arrangement, the suppliers agreed to pay the children's regular wages while they attended school and to offer each child a job at age 14. Levi Strauss, in turn, agreed to pay the children's tuition and provide books and uniforms. That arrangement allowed Levi Strauss to uphold its principles and provide long-term benefits to its host country.

Many people think of values as soft; to some they are usually unspoken. A South Seas island society uses the word *mokita,* which means, "the truth that everybody knows but nobody speaks." However difficult they are to articulate, values affect how we all behave. In a global business environment, values in tension are the rule rather than the exception. Without a company's commitment, statements of values and codes of ethics end up as empty platitudes that provide managers with no foundation for behaving ethically. Employees need and deserve more, and responsible members of the global business community can set examples for others to follow. The dark consequences of incidents such as Union Carbide's disaster in Bhopal remind us how high the stakes can be.

## Notes

1. In other writings, Thomas W. Dunfee and I have used the term *hypernorm* instead of *core human value.*

2. Thomas Donaldson and Thomas W. Dunfee, "Toward a Unified Conception of Business Ethics: Integrative Social Contracts Theory," *Academy of Management Review,* April 1994; and "Integrative Social Contracts Theory: A Communication Conception of Economic Ethics," *Economics and Philosophy,* Spring 1995.

# Reading 2.2

## WHEN ETHICS COLLIDE

### *Managing Conflicts Across Cultures*

PAUL F. BULLER, JOHN J. KOHLS, AND KENNETH S. ANDERSON

Nike—one of the fastest-growing companies in the world—has been stymied recently due in part to consumer reaction to conflicts involving management practices in its suppliers' factories in the Far East. Among the accusations—poor working conditions, low wages, enforced overtime, and harsh, sometimes brutal, discipline and corporal punishment.

Levi Strauss & Co. was recently confronted with the challenge of how to deal with contractors in Bangladesh that employed young children, a legal practice in Bangladesh, but one contrary to Levi's company policy. The fact that these children were often a sole or significant source of their family income further complicated the matter.

Tony Anderson, Chairman and CEO of H. B. Fuller Company, was faced with a decision regarding the company's responsibility for illegitimate use of one of its products. Resistol, a toluene-based glue, has become an addictive drug of choice for many Central American street children. These "Resistoleros" inhale the glue and often experience violent reactions and serious health problems, including kidney failure and brain damage.

Today's businesses operate in a dynamic global community rife with potential conflicts due to differences in values and practices across cultures. As these introductory incidents suggest, many conflicts involve questions of business ethics—that is, the rightness or wrongness of certain business practices. Ethical conflicts may involve a variety of issues:

- **Bribery and extortion,** as in the highly publicized case of Lockheed, which made $12.5 million in payments to Japanese agents and government officials to secure an important order from Nippon Air. This incident was a major impetus for the passage of the Foreign Corrupt Practices Act in 1977.

- **Human rights** concerns, like those now being debated in the apparel industry involving companies such as Nike and Gap. Cross-cultural differences in employment practices and work values have led to a number of ethical issues in this and other industries.

- **Financial reporting,** illustrated by the Daiwa Bank Ltd. fiasco, in which Toshida Iguchi, a bank employee, was found guilty by the U.S. Federal Reserve (Fed) on six counts of fraud, including falsifying bank documents, embezzling money for his own use, and misappropriating $1.1 billion in unauthorized trades. Through the investigation of this case, it was revealed that

SOURCE: Reprinted from *Journal of World Business, Vol. 34*, Buller et al., "When Ethics Collide," pp. 52-66. 

Japanese banks operate under different accounting rules based, in part, on cultural differences. Japanese rules allowed banks to keep their affiliates' results private, in the interest of "family affairs." Thus, regulators can examine the financials of a bank and miss problems that may have been moved to the affiliates. There is no way of knowing the true performance of the bank.

- **Product safety,** as demonstrated by Nestle's infant formula debacle in Africa. Among other charges, the company was accused of attempting, without justification, to change indigenous behavior to the detriment of the health of the babies affected. Part of the problem was that Nestle used marketing practices that, although appropriate for developed Western countries, were very misleading to African consumers.

- **Responsibility for the environment,** illustrated by Shell Oil's tragic experience in Nigeria. Shell discovered and developed a major oil reserve in the Niger River delta, home of the Ogoni people, among the poorest in Nigeria. Ogoni activists, led by writer Ken Saro–Wiwa, protested what they believed to be serious environmental degradation of the delta. Protests became violent, eventually resulting in the internationally denounced trial and execution of Saro–Wiwa and several other activists.

Differences regarding these and other ethical issues are largely due to different social, cultural and economic factors. These cross-cultural differences in ethics raise challenging questions for managers in the multinational corporation. For example, when ethical perspectives, values, and behaviors conflict, whose ethics are right? How does one resolve the differences?

This chapter presents a pragmatic, yet ethical framework that can assist managers in addressing cross-cultural ethical conflicts. First, we provide a brief rationale for and description of the framework. We then demonstrate how the model can be applied using several case incidents. We conclude with a discussion of the implications of the model for organizations and managers operating in a global context.

## Global Business Ethics

Global business ethics is the application of moral values and principles to complex cross-cultural situations. Multinational companies have paid increasing attention to global ethics in recent years. For example, a recent survey conducted by Texaco Inc. in conjunction with the Ethics Officer Association (EOA), found that 61% percent of the EOA member companies responding had compliance and ethics programs that had been implemented internationally. Further, of companies with international operations, 81% have distributed a global ethics code of conduct to international-based employees.

Despite the move to develop global ethics guidelines, no strong consensus exists regarding the appropriate ethics of multinational companies. Indeed, although there are certainly common ethical beliefs and practices across cultures, the preponderance of the research on global ethics suggests strongly that different national cultures have different perspectives regarding ethical values and practices. The question is—when is being different wrong?

A number of business ethicists have developed frameworks and guidelines to address the unique challenges of global ethics. Some frameworks, like the Caux roundtable principles (i.e., ethical principles developed jointly by business leaders from Japan, Europe, and the U.S.), emphasize universal international moral principles. Other approaches argue that, although universal principles are important, they also may be too constricting, and even inappropriate, under certain circumstances. In general, recent writing on global ethics suggests that there is no simple answer to the question of what is right and wrong ethical behavior across different national cultures. Thomas Donaldson, in a *Harvard Business Review* article, summarized the current situation well by observing that U.S. businesses have tended to adopt one of two extreme positions when faced with cross-cultural ethical questions: relativism or absolutism. The relativist perspective takes the familiar position, "When in Rome, do as the Romans do." At the other extreme, the absolutist view argues that the home country ethical values must be applied everywhere the multinational corporation operates. Donaldson argues that neither extreme accurately reflects the realities of the global business environment and that a range of possible ethical responses is more appropriate.

Thus, the emerging conclusion of international business ethicists is that making appropriate ethical decisions in the multinational corporation is a complex and, sometimes, highly ambiguous process. Although there may be situations in which managers facing cross-cultural ethical differences can rightfully insist on universal moral principles, there may be other instances in which the decision-maker should adopt the local ethical norms. An example of the first may be Levi Strauss' decision to leave China due to human rights issues and, particularly, the

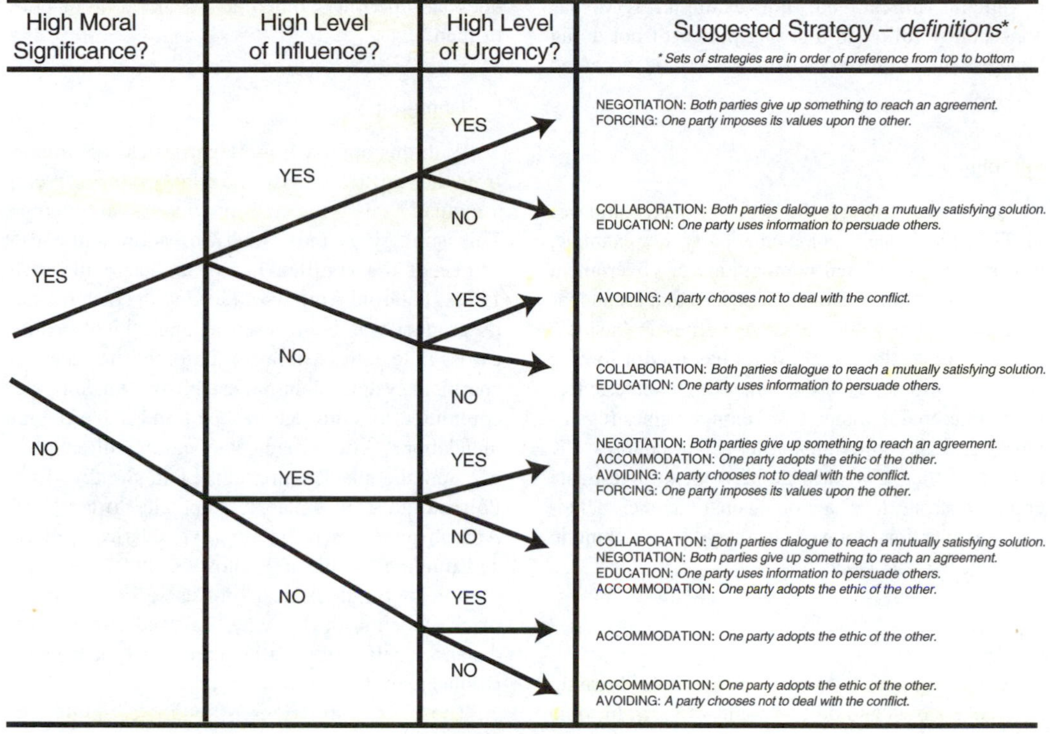
High Moral Significance?
High Level of Influence?
High Level of Urgency?
Suggested Strategy – definitions*
* Sets of strategies are in order of preference from top to bottom
YES
NO
YES
NO
YES
NO
YES
NO
YES
NO
YES
NO
YES
NO
NEGOTIATION: Both parties give up something to reach an agreement.
FORCING: One party imposes its values upon the other.
COLLABORATION: Both parties dialogue to reach a mutually satisfying solution.
EDUCATION: One party uses information to persuade others.
AVOIDING: A party chooses not to deal with the conflict.
COLLABORATION: Both parties dialogue to reach a mutually satisfying solution.
EDUCATION: One party uses information to persuade others.
NEGOTIATION: Both parties give up something to reach an agreement.
ACCOMMODATION: One party adopts the ethic of the other.
AVOIDING: A party chooses not to deal with the conflict.
FORCING: One party imposes its values upon the other.
COLLABORATION: Both parties dialogue to reach a mutually satisfying solution.
NEGOTIATION: Both parties give up something to reach an agreement.
EDUCATION: One party uses information to persuade others.
ACCOMMODATION: One party adopts the ethic of the other.
ACCOMMODATION: One party adopts the ethic of the other.
ACCOMMODATION: One party adopts the ethic of the other.
AVOIDING: A party chooses not to deal with the conflict.

**Exhibit 1** A Decision Tree Framework for Managing Cross-Cultural Ethical Conflicts

expectation that the company would be involved in enforcing China's "reproduction" policies. On the other hand, respecting local traditions, many companies, such as Motorola, have adopted the widespread practice of gift giving (within certain limits) in Asian countries. There are also other situations in which the manager may be obligated, through collaboration and/or moral imagination, to develop a unique response to a cross-cultural ethical dilemma, one that attempts to find common ground among different ethical views. As will be described later, Levi Strauss' response to child labor practices among its contractors in Bangladesh is an example of this type of imaginative resolution.

## A Model for Addressing Ethical Conflict

Our approach to addressing cross-cultural ethical conflict is based upon the research in conflict management. We use a decision-tree framework, shown in Exhibit 1, that recommends specific strategies based on particular characteristics of the situation. This model is intended to provide a conceptually sound, yet pragmatic aid to managers who are facing cross-cultural ethical conflicts. We believe that the use of this framework can assist managers and employees to make better ethical decisions. Below, we provide a brief explanation of the model and then demonstrate how it applies to several cross-cultural situations.

## Relevant Strategies

Alternative strategies for responding to cross-cultural ethical conflicts are similar to those available in most conflict situations. They range on a continuum from complete adaptation to the host country's ethical standards (accommodation) to complete insistence on the application of the home country's standards (forcing). We have identified six basic strategies:

### Avoiding

With this approach, the decision-maker simply chooses to ignore or not deal with the conflict, so it remains unresolved. For example, IBM has consistently followed a strong policy of not doing business in countries where bribery is accepted practice.

Forcing

Using this strategy, the decision-maker imposes his/her ethical views on the other party. For example, powerful multinational corporations or government officials sometimes demand practices that are inconsistent with the values of other parties in business transactions. Calvin Klein (CK) has used a forcing strategy to protect its brand name from counterfeiters in international markets. Even though values regarding patents and copyrights differ across cultures, CK has established a worldwide network to investigate and take strong legal action against anyone, including street vendors, found to be illegally trafficking in goods bearing its label.

Education

This approach attempts to facilitate learning about one's own and others' points of view. In some cases, education is intended to convert others to one's own position. For example, Shell International has launched an initiative to educate its partners and customers around the world about the concept and practice of sustainable development. According to Jeroen van der Veer, Royal Dutch/Shell Group managing director, "this initiative is a social investment program that aims to help society build a sustainable energy future."

Negotiation

With this strategy, both parties give up something to reach a settlement. The resulting compromise usually leads one party or the other (or both) to feel dissatisfied with the outcome and to feel that the basic conflict has not been resolved. An example is the trade discussions that took place several years ago between the CEOs of the big three U.S. auto companies and Japanese auto executives and government officials.

Accommodation

Here, one party merely adapts to the ethics of the other party. An example is Burns and McCallister, an international consulting company, which, despite criticism at home, has implemented a policy prohibiting women partners from being assigned to account negotiations in countries whose culture does not permit women to speak in a meeting of men.

Collaboration

With this approach, both parties choose to confront the conflict directly and collaborate to develop a mutually satisfying solution: a win-win outcome. This strategy is most likely to address the root source of the conflict. For example, in the early 1970s, Polaroid Corp. was faced with concerns that its product was being used to make identification cards in South Africa to enforce the detested apartheid system. Polaroid established an employee committee to study the problem and make recommendations. After broad consultation with employees and the black communities in South Africa, Polaroid adopted a plan to stop sales to the South African government, to improve salaries, benefits and training for black employees, and to devote a portion of South African profits to education for black students. In this way, Polaroid attempted to distance itself from apartheid and meet the needs of its black employees.

These six strategies, though certainly not exhaustive, represent a broad range of possible approaches for responding to cross-cultural ethical conflicts. Our assumption is that no one particular strategy is always best, and that the appropriate response depends upon the particular ethical situation. Below, we describe three specific factors that help determine the best strategy to use.

## Key Factors in Selecting a Strategy

Three factors are central in determining the appropriate strategy for addressing ethical conflicts: moral significance, power, and urgency.

Moral Significance

This is the importance or significance of the moral values at stake. Moral significance is characterized by values that are central to an individual, company, or society, and that are widely shared. All ethical conflicts are not of the same importance. For example, gift giving, which is an accepted business practice in many cultures, is greatly restricted in the United States and is perceived as setting up a potential conflict of interest. In some cultures, the giver and receiver of the gift take it as a sign of respect and an expected way of building the relationship. In the U.S., the receiver is likely to be offended, or at least suspicious of the gift giver's motives. In some instances, the ethical conflict may be interpreted as minor, because the intention of the gift giver is not to sway the other party's business decisions. On the other hand, a gift designed to influence the decision-maker toward making a judgment in one's favor is definitely a bribe. The first conflict, when fully understood, is more an issue of business etiquette; the second conflict, when fully understood, deals with more fundamental issues of fairness in business dealings.

Obviously, strong consensus around moral values provides a basis of support for the decision-maker's actions consistent with those values. For example, U.S. culture strongly discourages employing young children. The high level of societal consensus on this issue suggests that it would have high moral significance for a U.S. manager operating in a foreign subsidiary. Corporate culture also can influence perceptions of consensus around moral values. Organizations that have strong, ethical cultures may influence managers to act at a higher level of ethics, even when the prevailing national culture norms are not as strong. Multinational companies like Johnson & Johnson Inc., Motorola Inc., Levi-Strauss, and Texas Instruments Inc. have been widely recognized for their strong ethical corporate cultures. Similarly, if a company has a strong unethical or amoral culture, its value priorities would also strongly influence managers' perceptions of what is important.

Power

We define power as the decision maker's ability to influence the outcomes of a conflict, ranging from complete control to no influence at all. With a high degree of power, a decision-maker can readily impose her or his own values or insist on concessions from the other party. Certainly, U.S. companies and other international organizations used their individual and collective powers, with some success, in an effort to end the apartheid system in South Africa. In general, the greater the difference in power between two conflicting parties, the easier it is for the party with the greater power to use more directive strategies. However, it may or may not be ethical to use force. If the decision maker has little or no power, she or he may have fewer options and may feel forced to give in, to compromise her or his values, or to avoid the situation altogether. IBM's policy to avoid doing business in countries that condone bribery is an example.

Some ethicists have argued that, in cases where decision makers feel powerless to act, they still have a moral obligation to initiate the development of policies, procedures, incentives, systems, institutions, or other means to support appropriate moral values. An example is the discussions among international business and government leaders leading to two recent international treaties on bribery: the Inter American Convention against Corruption, signed in 1996, and the Convention on Combating Bribery of Foreign Public Officials in International Business Transactions, signed in 1997.

Urgency

Urgency reflects the need for immediate action and can range from highly urgent to not at all urgent. Research on conflict resolution indicates that managers faced with a conflict situation tend to take the expedient action (e.g., forcing or avoiding), even when they recognize that collaboration or problem solving might lead to more positive outcomes. However, decision-makers in a conflict situation can have both short-term and long-term goals. In the short term, they often select more expedient strategies to resolve the immediate concern. They also may seek long-term resolution of the conflict, perhaps by changing the conditions that produce the conflict in the first place.

## A Tool for Decision Making

The framework in Exhibit 1 prescribes a feasible set of appropriate strategies based upon an assessment of moral significance, power, and urgency. To use the model effectively, it is important to make the following assumptions. First, we assume that the decision-maker wants to do the right thing. The model does not address the problem of individuals who manipulate the decision tree to justify unethical actions. We assume that the ethically motivated person will attempt to be as objective as possible in evaluating what are admittedly complex factors. Second, we assume that the decision-maker has already completed an investigation of the facts and an ethical analysis to determine the moral significance of the issues involved. The model does not address the issue of what ethical frameworks are used or how the decision-maker makes this determination.

The model is based on three critical questions concerning the levels of moral significance, power and urgency characterizing the conflict situation. Responses to these questions guide the decision-maker to appropriate actions for addressing the ethical conflicts. The determination of appropriate strategies is based on the following pragmatic and ethical considerations.

### Pragmatic Considerations

1. Strategies that take some time to implement (e.g., collaboration, education) cannot generally be used in urgent situations. (Of course, it requires some judgment to determine how urgent the situation really is.) Frequently, short-term and long-term strategies will be different.

2. Generally, only strategies that one has the power to implement are feasible. (Again, this requires judgment.) In situations of very low power, forcing, negotiating, and collaboration may not be feasible.

### Ethical Considerations

1. The higher the moral significance of the values at stake in the conflict, the more one is justified in pressing for conformity with one's views (when they are consistent with core or central values), especially when it appears that the moral issues have less significance to the other party.

2. The less the moral significance of the values at stake, the more one is justified in accommodating or negotiating, especially when the moral issues are highly significant to the other party.

3. As far as possible, the position of the other party, especially when it reflects fundamental values of the culture, must be treated respectfully. This requires listening, empathy, and attempting to understand the values, beliefs, and assumptions of the other party.

4. As far as possible, the freedom and autonomy of those who differ should be respected.

### Ethical Corollaries

There are some additional corollaries to these ethical principles regarding particular strategies. These corollaries help the decision-maker to select the preferred strategy from a set of feasible options. If all strategies were possible, ethical considerations would suggest the following:

1. Whenever possible, use collaborative problem-solving approaches, especially when the moral issues at stake are highly significant to both parties. This strategy provides the best environment for encouraging mutual respect and concern for each party's position. If a win-win solution can be found, neither party must sacrifice ethical values or standards important to them.

2. Negotiation and compromise may be considered second in preference, especially when parties make concessions on values of less moral significance and preserve values of higher moral significance. Often, it is not the same concerns that have high moral significance to both parties in a cross-cultural conflict.

3. Avoiding, forcing, and accommodation are usually only short-term or low-power solutions. Avoidance is sometimes necessary to keep from supporting perceived unethical activity. But it has the possible disadvantage of withholding economic activity and potentially significant benefits from the local people. Forcing may be justified when collaboration and negotiation are not possible due to time constraints, or when those efforts have failed, especially when the practice with which one is in conflict is not consistent with fundamental moral norms. Forcing should be a last resort, however, as this strategy clearly interferes with others' free decision making, is destructive to the relationship, and encourages the other party to circumvent one's demands. Accommodation is permissible only in situations of low moral significance to the decision-maker. In these circumstances, the decision maker may even be morally obligated to accommodate, especially if the issue is of high moral significance to the other party.

4. Education is a long-term strategy that often accompanies other shorter-term strategies like forcing, accommodation or negotiation. Education involves sharing values that are important and explaining why they are important. Education can be used almost any time it is feasible. It respects the other party and leaves choices in her/his hands.

### Some Illustrations

Now let's apply the model to three different case examples. We evaluate each of the following cases from the point of view of a U.S. decision maker facing the situation.

---

### Case A: Nepotism Versus Equal Employment Opportunity

*A new American expatriate manager of a U.S. subsidiary in India has learned that some of the subsidiary's Indian-owned suppliers practice nepotism. Specifically, one of the supplier's Indian managers recently hired one of his own sons to fill an open supervisory position, even though there were other job candidates more qualified. In investigating the action, the U.S. manager learned that it is common practice for Indian employers to hire their family members, reflecting the strong cultural value placed on family relationships, as well as the exceedingly high unemployment rate in the country. The U.S. manager feels strongly that the ethical principle of fairness, made explicit in American equal opportunity policies, is also important. He ponders how to respond.*

Applying the model to this case, the first question is: Is the situation high in moral significance? Certainly, current U.S. employment regulations and practices are based on principles of fairness. The Equal Employment Opportunity guidelines are clear in stating that selection decisions must be based on job-related criteria. There is strong consensus in U.S. companies regarding these issues of fairness. In addition, a manager's responsibility to make decisions that contribute most to improved performance is also broadly accepted. Thus, for the U.S. manager in this case, the moral significance is quite high. So too, however, for the manager of the Indian subsidiary. Moral norms in India place a high value on family relationships. Equal employment laws are virtually nonexistent in Indian companies. In the context of a struggling economy, many Indian companies traditionally have placed more emphasis on preserving family cohesiveness than on providing equal opportunities for employment. Consequently, the moral significance of the issues at stake is high for both parties.

The second question is: Does the manager have a high level of influence over the outcome of the ethical situation? the extent to which the U.S. manager can control this situation is not clear. The supplier is a wholly owned Indian company that has historically operated in the context of Indian culture and laws. Since the U.S. subsidiary contracts with local suppliers, it is probable that the manager can insist on a change in the supplier's policies to emphasize equal employment opportunity. If the supplier refuses to comply with this directive, it is possible for the U.S. subsidiary to terminate the supplier contract. However, because many Indian companies practice nepotism and are not concerned about equal employment, it may be difficult for the U.S. manager to find a suitable new supplier. In general then, we would argue that the manager has some, but not complete, control over the outcome of this situation.

The third question in the model asks: Is there a high level of urgency to resolve this situation? The U.S. manager may feel some sense of urgency to address this situation. Certainly, the manager believes that the supplier's actions are unethical, and something should be done about it. However, given that the supplier is Indian-owned, any response by the manager is likely to take some time. At the very least, he will have to consult with his corporate superiors and subsidiary staff before making a decision. Further, because nepotism is widely practiced in many Indian companies and is a reflection of Indian cultural values, the manager must reasonably conclude that he can't change this practice soon, except perhaps by finding a new supplier that will adhere to U.S. employment norms. In general then, the situation will take some time to resolve.

Using the decision model (high moral significance, high power, low urgency) leads to the strategies of education and/or collaboration. Note that in our evaluation we were somewhat tentative about the level of power the manager actually had in this case. One could argue that the manager has relatively low power. In this situation (high moral significance, low power, low urgency) the feasible options are the same: education and/or collaboration. The model suggests that the manager should engage the supplier in a process of education and collaborative problem solving in an effort to resolve the conflicting cross-cultural values. This is a case that might require some moral imagination to create a set of principles or practices acceptable to both parties. Such a solution might include an effort to help the supplier to recruit and select individuals, including family members, who are best qualified for each job. It may also include assistance in establishing training and development programs with the supplier to improve the skills of all employees, including family members. The goal of this collaborative effort would be to mutually satisfy the needs and values of both parties.

---

### Case B: Child Labor Versus Economic Subsistence

*An operations manager of Levi-Strauss becomes aware that two of the company's contractors in Bangladesh are employing children younger than 14 years of age. Although this is acceptable under Bangladesh law, it violates International Labor Organization standards that bar employment of children under age 14. Further, the company has a well-developed code of ethics that explicitly prohibits child labor violations by its contractors. If a violation occurs, the company policy requires the contractor to fire the children younger than age 14 or lose the company business. After studying the issue, however, the manager discovers that the underage children are often the sole source of economic support for their families.*

Applying the model, the first question is: Is this situation high in moral significance? Child labor involves issues of basic human rights, and there is reasonably strong consensus worldwide against employment of young children. This conclusion is supported by the fact that the International Labor Organization has developed standards prohibiting employment of children under age 14. In addition, Levi-Strauss has strong norms against this practice. However, there are certainly cross-cultural differences regarding this value. In Bangladesh, local norms are more tolerant of child labor practices, and the Bangladesh society appears to place a greater value on basic sustenance needs of their families. Given the above considerations, we would conclude that the level of moral significance of the issues in this case is fairly high, even though U.S. and Bangladesh decision-makers would disagree on which values are most important.

The second question asks: Does the decision-maker have a high level of influence over the outcomes of the ethical situation? Levi Strauss is a large multinational corporation operating in a developing country. It is in a relatively powerful position and it can demand that the contractor fire the underage workers, or else it will terminate the contract.

The third question is: Is there a high level of urgency to resolve the situation? Because the contractors' behavior is against International Labor Organization standards and Levi's code of ethics, it is rather urgent that the company ceases this practice as soon as possible. Additionally, media scrutiny of multinational labor practices has been intense and it would be difficult to explain a delay in taking action. Because the company has the power to do so in this case, it can demand that the contractor change its practices immediately or face the consequences.

Following Exhibit 1 (high moral significance, high power, high urgency), either forcing or negotiation is a feasible option in this case. Forcing would simply mean requiring the contractor to fire all of the children under the age of 14, or face termination of the contract. As explained earlier, negotiation is more desirable if there is sufficient time. Collaboration would be best, but in most urgent situations there is not sufficient time for collaboration. In any case, negotiation (or collaboration) does not often take place between parties of unequal power. Effective negotiation or collaboration occurs only to the extent that the stronger party empowers the weaker.

Interestingly, Levi Strauss negotiated a compromise with the contractors, primarily because it learned that many of the underage children were the sole breadwinners for their families. The company asked the contractor to have the children quit work and go back to school. The contractor was to continue paying regular wages to the underage children while they attended school and offer each child a job at age 14. Levi Strauss in turn, funded the children's schooling, including books, uniforms, and tuition. This outcome is consistent with the model and demonstrates the need for moral imagination in reaching the highest ethical action in a given case.

---

## Case C: Economic Development Versus Human Rights

*Telex, a large multinational corporation in the telecommunications industry, has developed a leading edge product (XE-2000) with the combined features of user-friendliness, portability, durability, versatility and affordability. The company believed that this product would revolutionize economic development around the world, especially in developing countries, because it allowed entrepreneurs to get timely, accurate business information at a distance. Early international sales of the XE-2000 were highly promising.*

*However, the company became alarmed when it was informed by several international human rights groups that the new product was being used extensively in Amrubia, a developing country governed by a new oppressive military regime. This controlling regime had developed an extensive network of informers throughout Amrubian villages and towns. The informers used the XE-2000 to report to government officials any "subversive" talk or actions on the part of Amrubian citizens. These reported subversives were often jailed and sometimes tortured for their actions. Amnesty International has condemned the Amrubian government, as has the U.S. State Department, although the latter organization has not yet prohibited business transactions in Amrubia.*

*In investigating the situation, Telex discovers that the XE-2000 product has not produced the anticipated positive economic results in Amrubia to date. In addition, one of the international human rights groups has demanded that Telex address this situation immediately or face a worldwide boycott of all its products. The Vice President of International Marketing at Telex must decide what to do.*

In analyzing this situation, the first question is: Is this situation high in moral significance? Clearly, Telex's product, XE-2000, is being used extensively to aid oppressive regimes in violating standards of human rights. This is definitely a matter of high moral significance. Obviously, Telex could argue that the product is also a potentially important tool for economic development in developing countries like Amrubia. But all indications are that the product is not having a positive economic impact in Amrubia to date.

The second question is: Does the manager have a high level of influence over the outcome of the situation? Although Telex can probably do little to recover the products it has already sold in Amrubia, it can stop selling and supporting all product sales immediately. Of course, the company cannot completely control the smuggling of its products purchased outside of Amrubia, nor can it control the inhumane government regime. However, as a large multinational corporation, it can enlist the cooperation of other companies and governments to help control the problem and perhaps create some ways to sanction the oppressive Amrubian government. In general, although the V.P. of International Marketing has considerable control over Telex actions in Amrubia, she has minimal control over eliminating the human rights problems in Amrubia.

The third question asks: Is there a high level of urgency to resolve the situation? The human rights violations are serious and, even though it will take time to eliminate the entire problem, Telex can act quickly to stop the sales and support of XE-2000s to Amrubia. In addition, an international human rights group has threatened a worldwide boycott of Telex products. Although this should not be the only (or primary) justification for stopping sales to Amrubia, it definitely adds to the urgency of the situation.

The decision model (high moral significance, low power, high urgency) leads to one basic option—avoiding the situation. This outcome suggests that, as a minimum ethical requirement, Telex should withdraw from Amrubia and cease all sales and support operations. Beyond this basic action, Telex could take a proactive stance in alerting other companies and industry and government officials about the abuse of Telex products in Amrubia. In addition, Telex could develop an ethical policy specifying conditions for initiating and continuing sales of the XE-2000 and other similar products in markets around the world, particularly those in developing nations.

## Putting the Model Into Practice

These examples illustrate how the model can be used to guide managers through the decision process. As demonstrated, the framework encourages contingency thinking and points to plausible courses of action in situations where ethics collide across cultures. It should be noted that, in some cases in which the level of moral significance, power and urgency are not clearly high or low, the decision tree analysis may lead to different possible strategies. Even in these more ambiguous cases, however, the model provides a framework for thinking through viable solutions. In any case, it is important to emphasize that the decision tree is not a substitute for careful evaluation of the full range of factors that may be involved in a particular situation. As the Levi Strauss example demonstrates, the model provides an aid, but moral imagination is often needed to find the most ethical course of action.

Of course, the model by itself will do little to increase the ethical decision making of managers. To be most effective, the model should be implemented in an organizational climate that supports ethical behavior. Such a climate is characterized by the following conditions.

- **Top managers value ethics** as an integral part of the company's mission, strategy, and culture. Effective leaders articulate a vision that includes ethical principles, communicate the vision in a compelling way, and demonstrate consistent commitment to the vision over time. The reputation for strong ethical cultures in companies like Johnson & Johnson (CEO James Burke), Motorola (CEO Robert Galvin), and U.S. Shell (CEO Phil Carroll) can be traced directly to inspirational leaders who consistently, by their words and deeds, signaled the importance of and commitment to high moral standards.

- **The organization engages in a collaborative learning process** with its international employees, suppliers, customers and other partners to develop an understanding of and sensitivity to cross-cultural perspectives on ethics. An ongoing process of organizational learning is essential to developing a global corporate code of ethics and operational policies that are sensitive and responsive to cross-cultural similarities and differences. Motorola's *Ethics Renewal Process* provides an example of such a process. With a trained core of senior executives, Motorola is engaged in a process of building ethical awareness, skill development, and team building in diverse teams of managers across the company's international operations. These transnational teams identify ethical issues and collaborate on possible solutions. Particular attention is paid to creating dialogue on local ethical perspectives that may differ from the Motorola corporate code of ethics. Local ethics committees, created in this process, are trained in various ethical frameworks and authorized to develop policies and guidelines that address local ethical issues. As noted previously, Motorola has developed specific guidelines on gift giving in Japan that differ from the company's guidelines on gift giving in other countries. The products of these local ethics committees are then shared with other similar committees around the world.

- **The organization's human resource management practices are designed to build and sustain an ethical climate.** Managers, employees, and human resource and ethics professionals collaborate to ensure that selection, training and development, performance appraisal and compensation activities are clearly linked to ethical behavior. For example:

- **Selection and performance appraisal** criteria should include cross-cultural awareness, flexibility, capacity to learn, and ethical behavior. Multinational corporations such as IBM and Unilever have developed sophisticated databases that enable managers and human resource professionals to identify qualified job candidates from across their international operations. At Wetherill Associates, Inc., the company takes special care to hire people it believes will support ethical behavior. Competence and suitability for employment are determined by considering both ethics and specific job skills. In addition, international companies such as Ben & Jerry's Homemade Inc. and Royal Dutch/Shell base executive appraisals in part on the results of annual social audits, which include performance on a number of social responsibility and ethics indices.

- **Training and development** activities should educate employees about the corporate code of ethics and the various international codes and regulations. Training should also include a variety of frameworks for ethical analysis as well as opportunity to understand and apply the decision tree model to cross-cultural situations. As noted earlier, some companies, like Motorola and Royal Dutch/Shell, incorporate ethics training in a cross-cultural, team-building process. By developing work processes and policies that integrate diverse ethical perspectives of their members, these transnational teams can play a central role in managing cross-cultural ethical conflicts.

- **Compensation and recognition systems** must be directly tied to employees' ethical behaviors and outcomes. Motorola, Olin, Texaco and other companies explicitly link rewards to ethical behavior. For example, Texas Instrument's *Ethics Vision* states that: "TIers are empowered to make ethics and integrity primary considerations in all actions and decisions. And they are recognized internally and externally for consistently achieving that objective."

These contextual factors—top management values and leadership, organizational learning processes, and human resource management practices—help to shape and support an organization's ethical climate. Although they do not guarantee that there will never be ethical mistakes, they do help ensure that appropriate ethical standards and expectations are defined and communicated, that employees are encouraged and supported in making ethical decisions, and that they are provided the tools to do so.

## Summary and Conclusions

With increasing global interactions, managers are more frequently confronted with conflicts of ethics across cultures. Often these situations are complex, and appropriate solutions are not readily apparent. In this article we have proposed a framework to help managers consider a wide range of possible responses to cross-cultural ethical conflicts, depending upon specific characteristics of the situation. When implemented in a supportive organizational context, we believe this model can be a useful tool for addressing conflicting ethics across cultures. It provides a framework that is teachable, practical, and is readily applied to a broad range of ethical challenges in multinational business interactions.

# Reading 2.3

## KEY CONCEPTS

### *Underlying Structures of Culture*

EDWARD T. HALL AND MILDRED REED HALL

#### Culture Is Communication

In physics today, so far as we know, the galaxies that one studies are all controlled by the same laws. This is not entirely true of the worlds created by humans. Each cultural world operates according to its own internal dynamic, its own principles, and its own laws—written and unwritten. Even time and space are unique to each culture. There are, however, some common threads that run through all cultures.

It is possible to say that the world of communication can be divided into three parts: *words, material things,* and *behavior.* Words are the medium of business, politics, and diplomacy. Material things are usually indicators of status and power. Behavior provides feedback on how other people feel and includes techniques for avoiding confrontation.

By studying these three parts of the communication process in our own and other cultures, we can come to recognize and understand a vast unexplored region of human behavior that exists outside the range of people's conscious awareness, a "silent language," that is usually conveyed unconsciously (see Edward T. Hall's *The Silent Language*). This silent language includes a broad range of evolutionary concepts, practices, and solutions to problems which have their roots not in the lofty ideas of philosophers but in the shared experiences of ordinary people. In the words of the director of a project on cross-cultural relations, understanding the silent language "provides insights into *the underlying principles that shape our lives.*" These underlying principles are not only inherently interesting but eminently practical. The readers of this book, whether they be German, French, American, or from other countries, should find these principles useful at home and abroad.

Culture can be likened to a giant, extraordinarily complex, subtle computer. Its programs guide the actions and responses of human beings in every walk of life. This process requires attention to everything people do to survive, advance in the world, and gain satisfaction from life. Furthermore, cultural programs will not work if crucial steps are omitted, which happens when people unconsciously apply their own rules to another system.

During the three years we worked on this book, we had to learn two different programs for our office computer. The first was quite simple, but mastery did require paying close attention to every detail and several weeks of practice. The second was a much more complex program that required weeks of intensive practice, hours of tutoring, and days of depression and frustration when "the darn thing didn't work." Learning a new cultural program is infinitely more complicated and requires years of practice, yet there are many similarities in the learning process.

---

SOURCE: "Key Concepts: Underlying Structures of Culture" from *Understanding Cultural Differences* by Edward T. Hall and Mildred Reed Hall. Reprinted with permission.

Cultural communications are deeper and more complex than spoken or written messages. The essence of effective cross-cultural communication has more to do with releasing the right responses than with sending the "right" messages. We offer here some conceptual tools to help our readers decipher the complex, unspoken rules of each culture.

## Fast and Slow Messages: Finding the Appropriate Speed

The speed with which a particular message can be decoded and acted on is an important characteristic of human communication. There are fast and slow messages. A headline or cartoon, for example, is fast; the meaning that one extracts from books or art is slow. A fast message sent to people who are geared to a slow format will usually miss the target. While the content of the wrong-speed message may be understandable, it will not be received by someone accustomed to or expecting a different speed. The problem is that few people are aware that information can be sent at different speeds.

**Examples of Fast and Slow Messages**

| Fast Messages | Slow Messages |
|---|---|
| *Prose* | *Poetry* |
| Headlines | Books |
| A communiqué | An ambassador |
| Propaganda | Art |
| Cartoons | Etchings |
| TV commercials | TV documentary |
| Television | Print |
| Easy familiarity | Deep relationships |
| Manners | Culture |

Almost everything in life can be placed somewhere along the fast/slow message-speed spectrum. Such things as diplomacy, research, writing books, and creating art are accomplished in the slow mode. Buddha, Confucius, Shakespeare, Goethe, and Rembrandt all produced messages that human beings are still deciphering hundreds of years after the fact. Language is a very slow message; after 4,000 years, human beings are just beginning to discover what language is all about. The same can be said of culture, which incorporates multiple styles of "languages" that only release messages to those who are willing to spend the time to understand them.

In essence a person is a slow message; it takes time to get to know someone well. The message is, of course, slower in some cultures than in others. In the United States it is not too difficult to get to know people quickly in a relatively superficial way, which is all that most Americans want. Foreigners have often commented on how "unbelievably friendly" the Americans are. However, when Edward T. Hall studied the subject for the U.S. State Department, he discovered a worldwide complaint about Americans: they seem capable of forming only one kind of friendship—the informal, superficial kind that does not involve an exchange of deep confidences.

Conversely, in Europe personal relationships and friendships are highly valued and tend to take a long time to solidify. This is largely a function of the long-lasting, well-established networks of friends and relationships—particularly among the French—that one finds in Europe. Although there are exceptions, as a rule it will take Americans longer than they expect to really get to know Europeans. It is difficult, and at times may even be impossible, for a foreigner to break into these networks. Nevertheless, many businesspeople have found it expedient to take the time and make the effort to develop genuine friends among their business associates.

## High and Low Context: How Much Information Is Enough?

*Context* is the information that surrounds an event; it is inextricably bound up with the meaning of that event. The elements that combine to produce a given meaning—events and context—are in different proportions depending on the culture. The cultures of the world can be compared on a scale from high to low context.

A high context (HC) communication or message is one in which *most* of the information is already in the person, while very little is in the coded, explicit, transmitted part of the message. A low context (LC) communication is just the opposite; that is, the mass of the information is vested in the explicit code. Twins who have grown up together can and do communicate more economically (HC) than two lawyers in a courtroom during a trial (LC), a mathematician programming a computer, two politicians drafting legislation, two administrators writing a regulation. (Edward T. Hall, 1976)

Japanese, Arab, and Mediterranean peoples, who have extensive information networks among family, friends, colleagues, and clients and who are involved in close personal relationships, are high-context. As a result, for most normal transactions in daily life they do not require, nor do they expect, much in-depth, background information. This is because they keep themselves informed about everything having to do with the people who are important in their lives. Low-context people include Americans, Germans, Swiss, Scandinavians, and other northern Europeans; they compartmentalize their personal relationships, their work, and many aspects of day-to-day life. Consequently, each time they interact with others they need detailed background information. The French are much higher on the context scale than either the Germans or the Americans. This difference can affect virtually every situation and every relationship in which the members of these two opposite traditions find themselves.

Within each culture, of course, there are specific individual differences in the need for contexting—the process of filling in background data. But it is helpful to know whether the culture of a particular country falls on the high or low side of the scale since every person is influenced by the level of context.

Contexting performs multiple functions. For example, any shift in the level of context is a communication. The shift can be up the scale, indicating a warming of the relationship, or down the scale (lowering the context), communicating coolness or displeasure—signaling something has gone wrong with a relationship. In the United States, the boss might communicate annoyance to an assistant when he shifts from the high-context, familiar form of address to the low-context, formal form of address. When this happens the boss is telling the subordinate in no uncertain terms that she or he has stepped out of line and incurred disfavor. In Japan moving the direction of the context is a source of daily feedback as to how things are going. The day starts with the use of honorifics, formal forms of address attached to each name. If things are going well the honorifics are dropped as the day progresses. First-naming in the United States is an artificial attempt at high-contexting; it tends to offend Europeans, who view the use of first names as acceptable only between close friends and family. With Europeans, one is always safe using a formal form of address, waiting for the other person to indicate when familiarity is acceptable.

Like their near relations the Germans, many Anglo-Americans (mostly those of northern European heritage) are not only low-context but they also lack extensive, well-developed information networks. American networks are limited in scope and development compared to those of the French, the Spanish, the Italians, and the Japanese. What follows from this is that Americans, unless they are very unsophisticated, will feel the need for contexting, for detailed background information, any time they are asked to make a decision or to do something. The American approach to life is quite segmented and focused on discrete, compartmentalized information; Americans need to know what is going to be in what compartment before they commit themselves. We experienced this in Japan when we were asked on short notice to provide names of well-placed Japanese and Americans to be participants in a small conference. Like most prudent Americans, we were reluctant to provide names until we knew what the conference was about and what the individuals recommended would be expected to do. This seemed logical and reasonable enough to us. Nevertheless, our reluctance was read as obstructionist by our Japanese colleagues and friends responsible for the conference. In Japan the mere presence of certain individuals endows the group and its activities with authority and status, which is far more important than the topic of the conference. It is characteristic of high-context, high-information societies that attendance at functions is as much a matter of the prestige associated with the function as anything else. This in turn means that, quite frequently, invitations to high-level meetings and conferences will be issued on short notice. It is taken for granted that those invited will eschew all previous commitments if the meeting is important enough. As a general rule Americans place greater importance on how long ago a commitment was made, on the agenda, and on the relevance of the expertise of different individuals to the agenda. . . .

Another example of the contrast between how high- and low-context systems work is this: consider a top American executive working in an office and receiving a normal quota of visitors, usually one at a time. Most of the information that is relevant to the job originates from the few people the executive sees in the course of the day, as well as from what she or he reads. This is why the advisors and support personnel who surround the presidents of American enterprises (as well as the president of the United States) are so important. They and they alone control the content and the flow of organizational information to the chief executive.

Contrast this with the office of virtually any business executive in a high-context country such as France or Japan, where information flows freely and from all sides. Not only are people constantly coming and going, both seeking and giving information, but the entire form and function of the organization is centered on gathering, processing, and disseminating information. Everyone stays informed about every aspect of the business and knows who is best informed on what subjects.

In Germany almost everything is low-context and compartmentalized. The executive office is both a refuge and a screen—a refuge for the boss from the distractions of day-to-day office interactions and a screen for the employees from continual supervision. Information communicated in the office is not shared except with a select few—the exact antithesis of the high-information cultures.

High-context people are apt to become impatient and irritated when low-context people insist on giving them information they do not need. Conversely, low-context people are at a loss when high-context people do not provide *enough* information. One of the great communications challenges in life is to find the appropriate level of contexting needed in each situation. Too much information leads people to feel they are being talked down to; too little information can mystify them or make them feel left out. Ordinarily, people make these adjustments automatically in their own country, but in other countries their messages frequently miss the target.

The other side of the coin when considering context level is the apparent paradox that high-context people, such as the French, want to see *everything* when evaluating a *new* enterprise to which they have not been contexted. Annual reports or tax returns are not enough. Furthermore, they will keep asking until they get the information they want. Being high-context, the French are driven to make their own synthesis of the meanings of the figures. Unlike Americans, they feel uncomfortable with someone else's synthesis, someone else's "bottom line."

## Space

Every living thing has a visible physical boundary—its skin—separating it from its external environment. This visible boundary is surrounded by a series of invisible boundaries that are more difficult to define but are just as real. These other boundaries begin with the individual's personal space and terminate with her or his "territory."

### Territoriality

Territoriality, an innate characteristic whose roots lie hundreds of millions of years in the past, is the act of laying claim to and defending a territory and is a vital link in the chain of events necessary for survival. In humans, territoriality is highly developed and strongly influenced by culture. It is particularly well developed in the Germans and the Americans. Americans tend to establish places that they label "mine"—a cook's feeling about a kitchen or a child's view of her or his bedroom. In Germany this same feeling of territoriality is commonly extended to all possessions, including the automobile. If a German's car is touched, it is as though the individual himself has been touched.

Space also communicates power. A corner office suite in the United States is conventionally occupied by "the brass," and a private office in any location has more status than a desk in the open without walls. In both German and American business, the top floors are reserved for high-ranking officials and executives. In contrast, important French officials occupy a position in the *middle,* surrounded by subordinates; the emphasis there is on occupying the central position in an information network, where one can stay informed and can control what is happening.

### Personal Space

Personal space is another form of territory. Each person has around him or her an invisible bubble of space which expands and contracts depending on a number of things: the relationship to the people nearby, the person's emotional state, cultural background, and the activity being performed. Few people are allowed to penetrate this bit of mobile territory and then only for short periods of time. Changes in the bubble brought about by cramped quarters or crowding cause people to feel uncomfortable or aggressive. In northern Europe, the bubbles are quite large and people keep their distance. In southern France, Italy, Greece, and Spain, the bubbles get smaller and smaller so that the distance that is perceived as intimate in the north overlaps normal conversational distance in the south, all of which means the Mediterranean Europeans "get too close" to the Germans, the Scandinavians, the English, and those Americans of northern European ancestry. In northern Europe one does not touch others. Even the brushing of the overcoat sleeve used to elicit an apology.

### The Multisensory Spatial Experience

Few people realize that space is perceived by *all* the senses, not by vision alone. Auditory space is perceived by the ears, thermal space by the skin, kinesthetic space by the muscles, and olfactory space by the nose. As one might imagine, there are great cultural differences in the programming of the senses. Americans to some extent and Germans to a greater extent rely heavily on auditory screening, particularly when they want to concentrate. High-context people reject auditory screening and thrive on being open to interruptions and in tune with what goes on around them. Hence, in French and Italian cities one is periodically and intrusively bombarded by noise.

### Unconscious Reactions to Spatial Differences

Spatial changes give tone to communication, accent it, and at times even override the spoken word. As people interact, the flow and shift of distance between them is integral to the communication process. For example, if a stranger does not maintain "normal" conversational distance and gets too close, our reaction is automatic—we feel uncomfortable, sometimes even offended or threatened and we back up.

Human beings in the course of a lifetime incorporate literally hundreds of spatial cues. They imbibe the significance of these cues like mother's milk, in the context of their own culture. Just as a fragrance will trigger a memory, these cues and their associated behaviors release unconscious responses, regulating the tone, tempo, and mood of human transactions.

Since most people don't think about personal distance as something that is culturally patterned, foreign spatial cues are almost inevitably misinterpreted. This can lead to bad feelings which are then projected onto the people from the other culture in a most personal way. When a foreigner appears aggressive and pushy, or remote and cold, it may mean only that her or his personal distance is different from yours.

Americans have strong feelings about proximity and the attendant rights, responsibilities, and obligations associated with being a neighbor. Neighbors should be friendly and agreeable, cut their lawns, keep their places up, and do their bit for the neighborhood. By contrast, in France and Germany, simply sharing adjacent houses does not necessarily mean that people will interact with each other, particularly if they have not met socially. Proximity requires different behavior in other cultures.

## Time

Life on earth evolved in response to the cycles of day and night and the ebb and flow of the tides. As humans evolved, a multiplicity of internal biological clocks also developed. These biological clocks now regulate most of the physiological functions of our bodies. It is not surprising, therefore, that human concepts of time grew out of the natural rhythms associated with daily, monthly, and annual cycles. From the beginning humans have been tied to growing seasons and were dependent on the forces and rhythms of nature.

Out of this background two time systems evolved—one as an expression of our biological clocks, the other of the solar, lunar, and annual cycles. These systems will be described under the headings "Time as Structure" and "Time as Communication." In the sections that follow, we restrict ourselves to those manifestations of time that have proved to be stumbling blocks at the cultural interface.

### Monochronic and Polychronic Time

There are many kinds of time systems in the world, but two are most important to international business. We call them monochronic and polychronic time. Monochronic time means paying attention to and doing only one thing at a time. Polychronic time means being involved with many things at once. Like oil and water, the two systems do not mix.

In monochronic cultures, time is experienced and used in a linear way—comparable to a road extending from the past into the future. Monochronic time is divided quite naturally into segments; it is scheduled and compartmentalized, making it possible for a person to concentrate on one thing at a time. In a monochronic system, the schedule may take priority above all else and be treated as sacred and unalterable.

Monochronic time is perceived as being almost *tangible:* people talk about it as though it were money, as something that can be "spent," "saved," "wasted," and "lost." It is also used as a classification system for ordering life and setting priorities: "I don't have time to see him." Because monochronic time concentrates on one thing at a time, people who are governed by it don't like to be interrupted. Monochronic time seals people off from one another and, as a result, intensifies some relationships while shortchanging others. Time becomes a room which some people are allowed to enter, while others are excluded.

Monochronic time dominates most business in the United States. While Americans perceive it as almost in the air they breathe, it is nevertheless a learned product of northern European culture and is therefore arbitrary and imposed. Monochronic time is an artifact of the industrial revolution in England; factory life required the labor force to be on hand and in place at an appointed hour. In spite of the fact that it is *learned,* monochronic time now appears to be natural and logical because the great majority of Americans grew up in monochronic time systems with whistles and bells counting off the hours.

Other Western cultures—Switzerland, Germany, and Scandinavia in particular—are dominated by the iron hand of monochronic time as well. German and Swiss cultures represent classic examples of monochronic time. Still, monochronic time is not natural time; in fact, it seems to violate many of humanity's innate rhythms.

In almost every respect, polychronic systems are the antithesis of monochronic systems. Polychronic time is characterized by the simultaneous occurrence of many things and by a *great involvement with people.* There is more emphasis on completing human transactions than on holding to schedules. For example, two polychronic Latins conversing on a street corner would likely opt to be late for their next appointment rather than abruptly terminate the conversation before its natural conclusion. Polychronic time is experienced as much less tangible than monochronic time and can better be compared to a single point than to a road.

Proper understanding of the difference between the monochronic and polychronic time systems will be helpful in dealing with the time-flexible Mediterranean peoples. While the generalizations listed below do not apply equally to all cultures, they will help convey a pattern:

### The Relation Between Time and Space

In monochronic time cultures, the emphasis is on the compartmentalization of functions and people. Private offices are sound-proof if possible. In polychronic Mediterranean cultures, business offices often have large reception areas where people can wait. Company or government officials may even transact their business by moving about in the reception area, stopping to confer with this group and that one until everyone has been attended to.

Polychronic people feel that private space disrupts the flow of information by shutting people off from one another. In polychronic systems, appointments mean very little and may be shifted around even at the last minute to accommodate someone more important in an individual's hierarchy of family, friends, or associates. Some polychronic people (such as Latin Americans and Arabs) give precedence to their large circle of family members over any business obligation. Polychronic people also have many close friends and good clients with whom they spend a great deal of time. The close links to clients or customers create a reciprocal feeling of obligation and a mutual desire to be helpful.

### Polychronic Time and Information

Polychronic people live in a sea of information. They feel they must be up-to-the-minute about everything and everybody, be it business or personal, and they seldom subordinate personal relationships to the exigencies of schedules or budgets.

It is impossible to know how many millions of dollars have been lost in international business because monochronic and polychronic people do not understand each other or even realize that two such different time systems exist. The following example illustrates how difficult it is for these two types to relate:

> A French salesman working for a French company that had recently been bought by Americans found himself with a new American manager who expected instant results and higher profits immediately. Because of the emphasis on personal relationships, it frequently takes years to develop customers in polychronic France, and, in family-owned firms, relationships with customers may span generations. The American manager, not understanding this, ordered the salesman to develop new customers within three months. The salesman knew this was impossible and had to resign, asserting his legal right to take with him all the loyal customers he had developed over the years. Neither side understood what had happened.

These two opposing views of time and personal relationships often show up during business meetings. In French meetings, the information flow is high, and one is expected to read other people's thoughts, intuit the state of their business, and even garner indirectly what government regulations are in the offing. For the French and other polychronic/high-context people, a tight, fixed agenda can be an encumbrance, even an insult to one's intelligence. Most, if not all, of those present have a pretty good idea of what will be discussed beforehand. The purpose of the meeting is to create consensus. A rigid agenda and consensus represent opposite goals and do not mix. *The importance of this basic dichotomy cannot be overemphasized.*

### Past- and Future-Oriented Countries

It is always important to know which segments of the time frame are emphasized. Cultures in countries such as Iran, India, and those of the Far

| *Monochronic People* | *Polychronic People* |
|---|---|
| Do one thing at a time | Do many things at once |
| Concentrate on the job | Are highly distractible and subject to interruptions |
| Take time commitments (deadlines, schedules) seriously | Consider time commitments an objective to be achieved, if possible |
| Are low-context and need information | Are high-context and already have information |
| Are committed to the job | Are committed to people and human relationships |
| Adhere religiously to plans | Change plans often and easily |
| Are concerned about not following rules of privacy and consideration | Are more concerned with those who are closely related (family, friends, close business associates) than with privacy |
| Show great respect for private property; seldom borrow or lend | Borrow and lend things often and easily |
| Emphasize promptness | Base promptness on the relationship |
| Are accustomed to short-term relationships | Have strong tendency to build lifetime relationships |

East are past-oriented. Others, such as that of the urban United States, are oriented to the present and short-term future; still others, such as those of Latin America, are both past- and present-oriented. In Germany, where historical background is very important, every talk, book, or article begins with background information giving a historical perspective. This irritates many foreigners who keep wondering, "Why don't they get on with it? After all, I am educated. Don't the Germans know that?" The Japanese and the French are also steeped in history, but because they are high-context cultures, historical facts are alluded to obliquely. At present, there is no satisfactory explanation for why and how differences of this sort came about.

## Time as Communication

As surely as each culture has its spoken language, each has its own *language of time;* to function effectively in France, Germany, and the United States, it is essential to acquaint oneself with the local language of time. When we take our own time system for granted and project it onto other cultures, we fail to read the hidden messages in the foreign time system and thereby deny ourselves vital feedback.

For Americans, the use of appointment-schedule time reveals how people feel about each other, how significant their business is, and where they rank in the status system. Treatment of time can also convey a powerful form of insult. Furthermore, because the rules are informal, they operate largely out of awareness and, as a consequence, are less subject to conscious manipulation than language.

It is important, therefore, to know how to read the messages associated with time in other cultures. In France almost everything is polychronic whereas in Germany monochronic promptness is even more important than it is in the United States.

### Tempo, Rhythm, and Synchrony

Rhythm is an intangible but important aspect of time. Because nature's cycles are rhythmic, it is understandable that rhythm and tempo are distinguishing features of any culture. Rhythm ties the people of a culture together and can also alienate them from members of other cultures. In some cultures people move very slowly; in others, they move rapidly. When people from two such different cultures meet, they are apt to have difficulty relating because they are not "in sync." This is important because synchrony—the subtle ability to move together—is vital to all collaborative efforts, be they conferring, administering, working together on machines, or buying and selling.

People who move at a fast tempo are often perceived as "tailgating" those who move more slowly, and tailgating doesn't contribute to harmonious interaction—nor does forcing fast-paced people to move too slowly. Americans complain that the Germans take forever to reach decisions. Their time is out of phase with American time and vice versa.

One must always be contexted to the local time system. There will be times when everything seems to be at a standstill, but actually a great deal is going on behind the scenes. Then there will be other times when everything moves at lightning speed and it is necessary to stand aside, to get out of the way.

### Scheduling and Lead Time

To conduct business in an orderly manner in other countries, it is essential to know how much or how little lead time is required for each activity: how far ahead to request an appointment or schedule meetings and vacations, and how much time to allow for the preparation of a major report. In both the United States and Germany, schedules are sacred; in France scheduling frequently cannot be initiated until meetings are held with concerned members of the organization to permit essential discussions. This system works well in France, but there are complications whenever overseas partners or participants are involved since they have often scheduled their own activities up to two years in advance.

Lead time varies from culture to culture and is itself a communication as well as an element in organization. For instance, in France, if the relationship is important, desks will be cleared when that person arrives, whether there has been any advance notice or not. Time will be made to work together, up to twenty-four hours a day if necessary. In the United States and to some extent in Germany, on the other hand, the amount of lead time can be read as an index of the relative importance of the business to be conducted, as well as of the status of the individuals concerned. Short lead time means that the business is of little importance; the longer the lead time, the greater the value of the proceedings. In these countries, two weeks is the minimum advance time for requesting appointments. In Arab countries, two weeks may be too long—a date set so far in advance "slides off their minds"; three or four days may be preferable. In Japan, lead time is usually much shorter than in the United States, and it is difficult to say how many conferences on important subjects, attended by all the most competent and prestigious Japanese leaders in their fields, fail to attract suitable counterparts from the United States because of the short lead time. Although misunderstandings are blameless artifacts of the way two very different systems work, accidents of culture are seldom understood for what they are.

Another instance of time as communication is the practice of setting a date to end something. For example, Americans often schedule how long they will stay in a foreign country for a series of meetings, thus creating the psychological pressure of having to arrive at a decision by a certain date. *This is a mistake.* The Japanese and, to a lesser degree, the French are very aware of the American pressure of being "under the gun" and will use it to their advantage during negotiations.

### The Importance of Proper Timing

Choosing the correct timing of an important event is crucial. Politicians stake their careers on it. In government and business alike, announcements of major changes or new programs must be carefully timed. The significance of different time segments of the day also must be considered. Certain times of the day, month, or year are reserved for certain activities (vacations, meal times, and so on) and are not ordinarily interchangeable. In general in northern European cultures and in the United States, anything that occurs outside of business hours, very early in the morning or late at night, suggests an emergency. In France, there are times when nothing is expected to happen, such as national holidays and during the month of August, when everything shuts down for *vacances.* Culturally patterned systems are sufficiently complex so that it is wise to seek the advice of local experts.

In the United States, the short business lunch is common and the business dinner rarer; this is not so in France, where the function of the business lunch and dinner is to create the proper atmosphere and get acquainted. Relaxing with business clients during lunch and after work is crucial to building the close rapport that is absolutely necessary if one is to do business.

### Appointments

The way in which time is treated by Americans and Germans signals attitude, evaluation of priorities, mood, and status. Since time is highly valued in both Germany and the United States, the messages of time carry more weight than they do in polychronic countries. Waiting time, for example, carries strong messages which work on that part of the brain that mobilizes the emotions (the limbic system). In the United States, only those people with very high status can keep others waiting and get away with it. In general, those individuals are the very ones who know enough of human relations to avoid "insults of time" whenever possible. It is the petty bureaucrat who likes to throw his weight around, the bully who takes pleasure in putting people down, or the insecure executive with an inflated ego who keeps visitors waiting. The waiting-room message is a double-edged sword. Not only does it communicate an attitude towards the visitor, but it reveals a lot about the individual who has kept a visitor waiting. In monochronic cultures such as those in the United States and Germany, keeping others waiting can be a deliberate putdown or a signal that the individual is very disorganized and can't keep to a schedule. In polychronic cultures such as those of France or Hispanic countries, no such message is intended. In other words, one's reading of the message should be tempered by the context, the realities of the situation, and not with an automatic projection of one's own culture.

Clearly, interactions between monochronic and polychronic people can be stressful unless both parties know and can decode the meanings behind each other's language of time. The language of time is much more stable and resistant to change than other cultural systems. We were once involved in a research project in New Mexico, conducting interviews with Hispanics. Our subjects were sixth- and seventh-generation descendants of the original Spanish families who settled in North America in the early seventeenth century. Despite constant contact with Anglo-Saxon Americans for well over a hundred years, most of these Hispanics have remained polychronic. In three summers of interviewing, we never once achieved our scheduled goal of five interviews each week for each interviewer. We were lucky to have two or three. Interviews in Hispanic homes or offices were constantly interrupted when families came to visit or a friend dropped by. The Hispanics seemed to be juggling half a dozen activities simultaneously, even while the interviews were in progress.

Since we are monochronic Anglo-Saxons, this caused us no little concern and considerable distress. It is hard not to respond emotionally when the rules of your own time system are violated. Nor was an intellectual understanding of the problem much help at first. We did recognize, however, that what we were experiencing was a consequence of cultural differences and was, therefore, a part of our data. This led us to a better understanding of the importance as well as the subtleties of information flow and information networks in a polychronic society.

## Information Flow: Is It Fast or Slow and Where Does It Go?

The rate of information flow is measured by how long it takes a message intended to produce an action to travel from one part of an organization to another and for that message to release the desired response. Cultural differences in information flow are often, the greatest stumbling blocks to international understanding. Every executive doing business in a foreign land should know how information is handled—where it goes and whether it flows easily through the society and the business organization, or whether it is restricted to narrow channels because of compartmentalization.

In low-context countries, such as the United States, Germany, and Switzerland, information is highly focused, compartmentalized, and controlled, and, therefore, not apt to flow freely. In high-context cultures, such as the French, the Japanese, and the Spanish, information spreads rapidly and moves almost as if it had a life of its own. Those who use information as an instrument of "command and control" and who build their planning on controlling information are in for a rude shock in societies where people live in a sea of information.

In high-context cultures, interpersonal contact takes precedence over everything else; wherever people are spatially involved with each other, information flows freely. In business, executives do not seal themselves off behind secretaries and closed doors; in fact in Japan senior executives may even share offices so that each person knows as much about the entire base of operations as possible, and in France an executive will have ties to a centrally located bureau chief to keep a finger on the pulse of information flow. In these cultures most people are already highly contexted and therefore do not need to be briefed in much detail for each transaction; the emphasis is on stored rather than on transmitted information. Furthermore, channels are seldom overloaded because people stay in constant contact; therefore, the organizational malady of "information overload" is rare. Schedules and screening (as in the use of private offices) are minimized because they interfere with this vital contact. For high-context people, there are two primary expectations: to context everybody in order to open up the information channels and determine whether the group can work together and to appraise the chances of coming to an agreement in the future. The drive to stay in touch and to keep up to date in high-context cultures is very strong. Because these cultures are also characteristically high-information flow cultures, being out of touch means to cease to exist as a viable human being.

Organizations where information flows slowly are familiar to both Americans and northern Europeans because low-flow information is associated with both low-context and monochronic time resulting from the compartmentalization associated with low-context institutions and of taking up one thing at a time. In the United States, information flows slowly because each executive has a private office and a secretary to serve as a guard so that the executive is not distracted by excessive information. Since executive territory is jealously guarded, American executives often do not share information with their staff or with other department heads. We were once hired as consultants to a large government bureaucracy in which there were problems. Our study revealed multiple causes, the most important of which was a bottleneck created by a high-ranking bureaucrat who managed to block practically all the information going from the top down and from the bottom up. Once the problem had been identified, an agency staff director remarked, "I see we have a blockage in information." In a high-context situation everyone would have already known that this was the case. In a low-context system, however, it was necessary to call in outside consultants to make explicit what some people had suspected but were unable or unwilling to identify.

## Action Chains: The Importance of Completion

An action chain is an established sequence of events in which one or more people participate—and contribute—to achieve a goal. It's like the old-fashioned ritual of courtship with its time-honored developmental stages. If either party rushes things too much, omits an important procedure, or delays too long between steps, the courtship grinds to a halt.

Business is replete with action chains: greeting people, hiring and training personnel, developing an advertising campaign, floating a stock offering, initiating a lawsuit, merging with or taking over other companies, even sinking a golf putt. Many bureaucratic procedures are based unconsciously on the action-chain model. Because of the diversity of functions, it may be difficult for some people to link all these activities in their minds, but the common thread of underlying, ordered sequence ties each case to the others.

Because the steps in the chain are either technical (as in floating a stock offering or completing a merger) or else so widely shared and taken for granted that little conscious attention is paid to the details, the need to reexamine the entire pattern has largely gone unrecognized in the overseas setting.

There are important rules governing the structure, though not the content, of action chains. If an important step is left out, the action must begin all over again. Too many meetings and reports, for example, can break the action chains of individual projects, making it difficult for people to complete their work. In fact the breaking of an action chain is one of the most troublesome events with which human beings have to contend in our speeded-up technological twentieth century.

All planning must take into account the elaborate hierarchy of action chains. Monochronic, low-context cultures, with their compartmentalized approach and dependence on scheduled activities, are particularly sensitive to interruptions and so are more vulnerable to the breaking of action chains than high-context cultures. Most Americans are brought up with strong drives to complete action chains. High-context people, because of their intense involvement with each other and their extensive, cohesive networks, are more elastic; there is more "give" in their system. Some polychronic peoples will break an action chain simply because they don't like the way things are going or because they think they can "get a better deal." For instance, we once knew a monochronic architect in New York who was designing a building for a polychronic client. The client continually changed the specifications for the building. With each change, the building design had to be revised, even down to alterations in the building's foundations. The architect found this process particularly devastating because designing and constructing a building is an incredibly complex and elaborate collection of action chains. Changing one thing is likely to throw everything else out of gear.

The relationship between action chains and disputes is important. All cultures have built-in safeguards—even though they may not always work—to prevent a dispute from escalating to an out-and-out battle. Keep in mind, however, that these safeguards apply only within the context of one's own culture. In any foreign situation where a dispute appears imminent, it is essential to do two things immediately; proceed slowly, taking every action possible to maintain course and stay on an even keel; and seek the advice of a skillful, tactful interpreter of the culture.

## Interfacing: Creating the Proper Fit

The concept of interfacing can be illustrated by a simple example: it is impossible to interface an American appliance with a European outlet without an adaptor and a transformer. Not only are the voltages different, but the contacts on one are round; on the other, thin and flat. The purpose of this [article] is to serve as an adaptor for business executives operating at the interfaces between American, French, and German cultures.

The problems to be solved when interfacing vary from company to company, but some generalizations are possible.

First, it is more difficult to succeed in a foreign country than at home.

Second, the top management of a foreign subsidiary is crucial to the success of interfacing. Therefore, it is important to send the very best people available, take their advice, and leave them alone. Expect that your foreign manager or representative will start explaining things in terms of the local mentality which may sound alien and strange.

Cultural interfacing follows five basic principles:

1. The higher the context of either the culture or the industry, the more difficult the interface;
2. The greater the complexity of the elements, the more difficult the interface;
3. The greater the cultural distance, the more difficult the interface;
4. The greater the number of levels in the system, the more difficult the interface;
5. Very simple, low-context, highly evolved, mechanical systems tend to produce fewer interface problems than multiple-level systems of great complexity that depend on human talent for their success.

An example of an easy-to-interface business would be the manufacture of small components for microscopes by two divisions, one in Germany, the other in Switzerland. The cultural distance in this case is not great since both cultures are low-context as well as monochronic, and the business operation itself does not involve different levels of complexity.

A difficult-to-interface enterprise would be a newspaper or magazine in two countries that are vastly different, such as France and the United States. Publishing is a high-context enterprise which must be neatly meshed at literally dozens of points, including writing, advertising, and editorial policy. The success of newspapers and magazines depends on writers and editors who understand their audience's culture and know how to reach their readers.

## Releasing the Right Responses

### The Importance of Context and Following the Rules

The key to being an effective communicator is in knowing the degree of information (contexting) that must be supplied. If you're communicating with a German, remember she or he is low-context and will need lots of information and all the details, in depth. If you're communicating with someone from France, she or he is high-context and won't require as much information. Here are two examples from our interviews:

> One German manager working for a French firm was fired after his first year because he didn't perform as expected. The German manager was stunned. His response was, "But nobody told me what they wanted me to do."

> The opposite problem was encountered by a Frenchman who resigned from a German firm because he was constantly being told what he already knew by his German superior. Both his intelligence and his pride were threatened.

In both situations, the executives were inept at releasing the right response from their subordinates.

One of the factors that determines whether one releases the right response includes observing the rules of the other culture, including the time system. In Germany a salesman can have a very fine presentation, but if he arrives late by even a few minutes, no one will be impressed, no matter how good it is. Indeed, in all probability, the Germans will not even wait around to hear it. In France form is preeminent; without it, no message can release the right response. Americans must take great care not to alienate the French by being casual and informal in their manners; if Americans are not meticulously polite and formal, their message will not get through to the French, and they and their product will suffer.

### The Importance of the Right Interpreter

Releasing the right response will also depend on choosing the right interpreter. An interpreter's accent or use of the local dialect can cause a negative reaction. The importance of this facet of communication cannot be overstressed, yet it is one of the most frequent violations of the unwritten laws of communication abroad. For example, if you are trying to communicate with a Japanese executive using an interpreter who is not well educated nor extremely polite and proper, the desired response from the Japanese will not be forthcoming. A well-educated and well-mannered interpreter whose use of the language reflects a good background is also highly desirable in France and Germany.

## Summary

Speed of messages, context, space, time, information flow, action chains, and interfacing are all involved in the creation of both national and corporate character. In organizations everything management does communicates; when viewed in the cultural context, all acts, all events, all material things have meaning. Some organizations send strong, consistent messages that are readily grasped by employees and customers alike. Other organizations are less easy to interpret; they do not communicate clearly, or their messages are incongruent. Sometimes one part of the organization communicates one thing and another part communicates something else. The cues around which these corporate and cultural messages are organized are as different as the languages with which they are associated. Most important, their meaning is deeply imbedded and therefore harder for management to change when making the transition from one country to another.

Many messages are implied or have a cultural meaning, and there is a tacit agreement as to the nature of that meaning which is deeply rooted in the context of the communication. There is much that is taken for granted in culture that few people can explain but which every member of the culture accepts as given. Remember that messages come in many forms (most of them not in words) which are imbedded in the context and in the choice of channels.

Within all cultures there are important unstated differences as to what constitutes a proper *releaser.* Our research over the years in choosing the correct releaser has indicated that people cluster around preferences for "words," "numbers," and "pictures." Using the wrong format (sending numbers when words are wanted, words when the recipient only feels comfortable with numbers, or words and/or numbers to the visually oriented person) can only release a negative, frustrated response. The fascinating thing is that the message can be the same in every case. Furthermore, it is quite evident that each culture has its own preferences in this regard.

A television ad that is effective in the United States will have to be translated into a print media message to reach Germans. Germans are print-oriented, which explains in part why there is so little advertising on German TV. Also, Germans are always looking for what is "true" and to them numbers are a way of signaling that a product is exactly as it has been represented. Germans demand facts, facts, and more facts.

It is not uncommon for Americans to experience difficulty getting the French—even those whom they know and have done business with—to reply to inquiries, even urgent ones. This can be exasperating. The reasons are many but most have to do with the importance of immediate human contacts to the French. A solution that succeeds when other methods fail is to use a surrogate to relay messages rather than relying on a letter or a phone call. Why? Because letters and telephone calls aren't personal enough. If you send a properly placed emissary, one whom the individual you are trying to reach likes and trusts and considers important, you add the necessary personal touch to your message and will thereby release the right response.

The French also stress the importance of observing the many rituals of form. If you don't use the right form, the message conveyed is that you are ignorant or ill-mannered or do not care. In any event, the response that is released is almost certain to be negative. Remember that the French deplore casualness and informality. Paying attention to the details and being correct in everything you do is the only tactic that releases the right response in France.

It is not necessary to solve every problem at once, only to show a genuine desire to do so and to take one step at a time, even if it seems to take a lifetime. The rewards are not only material but psychological and mental as well. New frontiers are not only to be found in outer space or in the microworld of science; they are also at the interfaces between cultures.

# Reading 2.4

## NEGOTIATING WITH THE CHINESE

### *A Socio-Cultural Analysis*

PERVEZ GHAURI
TONY FANG

The People's Republic of China (PRC) started to open up its economy to the rest of the world in December 1978. Since then, Western business communities have been enthusiastic about China—the world's largest emerging market with more than one billion consumers. The Western enthusiasm for China decreased somewhat during a period following the Tienanmen Square incident in June 1989. But it rebounded and increased even more vigorously in the 1990s. China's rank in world trade rose from 32nd in 1978 to 9th today. By the end of 1995, China already approved a total of 258,000 foreign-invested enterprises with contractual foreign investment of US$395.7 billion and actual invested capital of US$135.4 billion. By the year 2000, China was recipient of more than 20% of the total FDI in developing countries and more than 5% of total FDI in the world. This makes China the largest recipient of foreign direct investment among developing countries and the second largest in the world next only to the U.S.A.

However, China is also a difficult and risky market for Western business communities to operate in. The surprises, disappointment, and frustration on the part of Western business people are not strange. China is a special challenge: it is the world's largest emerging market, largest Communist bureaucracy, and oldest culture. These unique features make China a unique case in international business that calls for special academic and managerial attention. Now that China has reached an agreement with the European Union and the United States of America about its membership in the World Trade Organization (WTO), the importance of China as a trade partner is going to increase further.

Sino-Western business negotiation is a key dynamic of the Sino-Western business relationship. Knowledge about the Chinese negotiating practices in the Sino-Western business negotiation process will generate insight into the Chinese business mindset, increase the success rate of Western businesses with China, and ultimately, strengthen the Sino-Western business relationship. Based on our in-depth personal interviews, this paper aims to study Chinese negotiating style in the Sino-Western business negotiation process. We are particularly interested in a process view of how the Chinese negotiate and how the Chinese negotiating style can be explained from the Chinese culture. The study intends to answer these questions: What are the meaningful stages of the Sino-Western business negotiation process? What are the main contentious issues in the formal negotiation sessions? How can we understand Chinese negotiating style observed in various stages from the Chinese culture point of view? We also attempt to generate managerial implications for negotiating effectively with the Chinese.

---

SOURCE: Reprinted from *Journal of World Business, Vol. 36,* Ghauri and Fang, "Negotiating With the Chinese," pp. 303-325.

## Empirical Base

The empirical base of this paper is our investigation of the negotiations of the Swedish multinational corporation Ericsson with Chinese customers in the early and mid 1990s. These negotiations concerned Ericsson's mobile systems selling and joint venture establishment and operations in China. Ericsson is a world leader in telecommunications. In 1999, it had net sales of US$26 billion and a global market share for mobile infrastructure of 30%, while in China it had 40% market share. Ericsson's history in China dates back to 1894 when the company made its first shipment of 2000 desk telephone handsets to Shanghai. Ericsson re-entered into the Chinese market in 1984 by delivering its AXE-10 exchange to the Beijing post and telecommunications authorities. In 1985, Ericsson opened its first representative office in China. Since then, Ericsson's China activities have experienced an explosive growth and the company is now a major foreign player in the Chinese telecommunications infrastructure. Ericsson is particularly advanced in mobile system technology and has had a major market share in China. At the time of the study, it had 53% market share in China's mobile telecommunications market, while its main competitor Nokia had 15%.

The first author followed one China area manager at Ericsson Radio Systems AB in Stockholm for three years in the early 1990s; a series of in-depth interviews were conducted with him and with one of his colleagues who was functioning as a liaison officer between Ericsson and its Chinese customers. The liaison officer, a native Chinese, was employed by Ericsson and, at the time of the study, was residing in Sweden. The second author conducted, both in Sweden and China, interviews with more than forty Ericsson managers (Swedes and Westerners) and their Chinese negotiating counterparts during 1995 through 1996. The interviews were unstructured or semistructured and were designed to maximize the understanding of how the Chinese negotiate in the Sino-Western business negotiation process. The rich empirical materials collected from these negotiation processes, events, and situations make it possible for us to use cross-sectional data to synthesize, structure, and describe the Sino-Western business negotiation process to best achieve the aim of this research. While reporting contrasting statements, we will discuss negotiation within the same project and issues.

One specific project that was studied thoroughly was Beijing Ericsson Mobile Communication Co. Ltd. (BMC), a joint venture (JV) agreement between Ericsson and China National Post and Telecommunications Industry Corporation (PTIC), signed in 1995. For the BMC project, Ericsson was competing with Motorola and Nokia. For this case, both Chinese officials and Ericsson managers involved in the negotiation were interviewed. This was the first joint venture in which Ericsson managed to team up with the then most powerful government telecommunications authority, the Ministry of Posts and Telecommunications (MPT). However, the relationship between the parties developed fast, as stated by Dr. Lars Ramqvist, Ericsson President and CEO:

> "We have also established a JV for digital mobile telephone systems and in total we have six JV companies in China."

BMC manufactures and sells products in mobile telecommunications, including GSM (Global System for Mobile Communications) and TACS (Total Access Communication Systems). It is a 50/50 JV and took two years to negotiate. From March 1993 [the signing of Memorandum of Understanding (MOU)] to July 1995 [the BMC contract was approved by the Ministry of Foreign Trade and Economics Cooperation (MOFTEC)].

## Literature Review

Since the early 1980s, a special area of inquiry has been gradually developed in the literature that deals with international business negotiations between Western firms and the PRC organizations (Blackman, 1997; Chen, 1993; Davidson, 1987; Deverge, 1986; Fang, 1999; Frankenstein, 1986; Hendryx, 1986; Kirkbride, Tang, & Westwood, 1991; Lee & Lo, 1988; Pye, 1982, 1986; Seligman, 1990; Shenkar & Ronen, 1987; Stewart & Keown, 1989; Stone, 1992; Tung 1982, 1989; Warrington & McCall, 1983). The central concern of these works is to arrive at an in-depth socio-cultural understanding of Chinese business negotiating style.

Pye (1982) lays the foundation of the area by publishing his seminal work *Chinese Commercial Negotiating Style.* Three major sources of difficulty in Sino-Western business negotiations are identified: problems that arise from the newness of the relations and the lack of experience on both sides, problems inherent in capitalist enterprises seeking to do business with the socialist economy in uncertain transition and reform, and problems that arise from the differences between the Chinese and Western cultures. Pye characterizes the Chinese negotiation process into the opening moves and the substantive negotiating session. During opening moves, the Chinese insist on opening negotiation with some

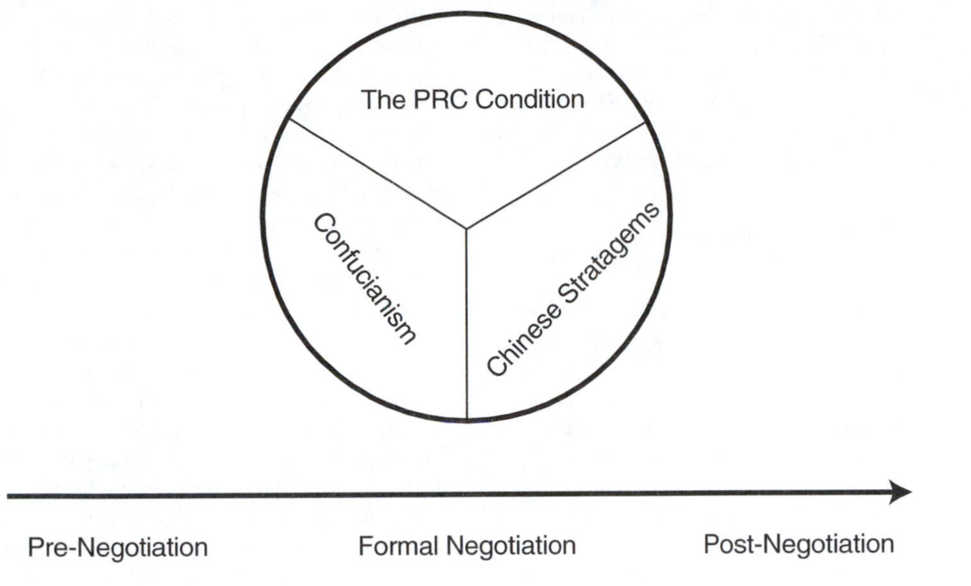


**Figure 1** A "Ping-Pong" Model

general principles which will later be utilized by the Chinese to their own advantage. They manipulate various kinds of negotiating tactics to induce the other party into showing their hand first and then cause "the long wait." The substantive negotiating session is a stage where the Chinese often display a fascination for tactics and issues are bargained over, discussions held, and agreement reached. In the post agreement stage, Pye cautions that nothing is ever final in negotiating with the Chinese who believe in "continuous negotiations."

Tung (1982) finds that the differences between the Chinese and American negotiating styles are among the most important factors responsible for the failure of business with China. Her follow-up study (Tung, 1989) suggests that despite the considerably increased contacts between American and Chinese negotiators during 1979 through 1987, marked differences in the Chinese and American negotiating styles still persist and are believed to be "culture-based." Blackman (1997) also provides insightful cases of Western business negotiations with the PRC. Hoon–Halbauer (1999) studied Shanghai Volkswagen Automobile Co. and the Beijing Jeep Corporation and provided with an excellent account of daily management process of Sino-foreign joint ventures. Although more generic models of international business negotiations (see e.g., Weiss 1994a,b; Ghauri & Usunier, 1996) and negotiating with East Asians and Chinese (see e.g., Tung 1982, 1996) are available, there is hardly any study on specific negotiation process between Chinese and Western firms. We identify five weaknesses in the existing literature: (1) lack of a systematic model; (2) lack of a cultural study of Chinese negotiating tactics; (3) lack of a presence of the Chinese voices in the debates; (4) weak empirical description; and (5) predominance of U.S.-China negotiation literature. To overcome these weaknesses, we propose a model of Chinese business negotiation process to analyze Chinese negotiating style.

The literature review suggests that although reports on Sino-Western business interactions appear rather regularly, empirically based analyses of the Chinese negotiating style in the Sino-Western business negotiation process are still few. This study therefore sets out to look at the Chinese negotiating style from a process view.

## A "Ping-Pong" Model

Given the aim of this paper, we developed a model to structure our analysis of the Sino-Western business negotiation process. Figure 1 presents our "Ping-Pong" model. The model is based on a number of previous studies of international business negotiation and Chinese business negotiating style (Fang, 1999; Frankenstein, 1986; Ghauri & Usunier, 1996; Graham & Lin, 1987; Pye, 1982) as well as our own observations from the empirical studies. The model comprises two major constructs: (1) stages of the Sino-Western business negotiation process and (2) dimensions of Chinese business culture. Using the "Ping-Pong" (table-tennis game) metaphor, we intend to emphasize the continuous back and forth bargaining feature (the Chinese ping-pong style) in the Chinese negotiating style and the Sino-Western business negotiation process (as a result, the negotiation process is bouncing back and forth).

### Sino-Western Business Negotiation Process

Negotiation process is a process by which the negotiating parties interact with one another to reach mutual agreements to provide terms, conditions, and guidelines for future behavior. For the sake of analysis, a negotiation process is usually divided into several stages. Ghauri (1996) structures the international business negotiation process in terms of the pre-negotiation, negotiation, and post-negotiation stages. These three stages are influenced by factors such as culture, strategy, background, and atmosphere. Graham and Lin's (1987) model opens a space for discussion of cultural factors and is considered useful for our study. However, their model does not cover the post-negotiation phase that is particularly relevant for the analysis of the Sino-Western business negotiation process as suggested by the Chinese business negotiating style literature. Combining these two international business negotiation process models with our own investigations, we divide the Sino-Western business negotiation process into three stages from the Western marketers' perspective; (1) *pre-negotiation* (lobbying, presentation, informal discussion, and trust building); (2) *formal negotiation* (task-related exchange of information, persuasion, concessions and agreement); and (3) *post-negotiation* (implementation and new rounds of negotiations).

### Chinese Business Culture

Furthermore, we adopt Fang's (1999) Chinese business culture framework to analyze Chinese negotiating style in the Sino-Western business negotiation process. This framework consists of three distinctive and interrelated components: the *PRC condition, Confucianism,* and *Chinese stratagems.*

#### *The PRC Condition*

The PRC condition (guoqing) is a contemporary social and institutional factor influencing the PRC. This is parallel to environmental conditions reported by other authors (Fayerweather & Kapoor, 1976; Ghauri, 1996). It is comprised of eight variables. (1) Politics. China is a socialist state with the Chinese Communist Party as the ruling party. Chinese politics has an all pervasive influence on every aspect of Chinese life; Chinese business and politics can hardly be separated under the current Chinese social system. (2) Economic planning. Chinese economic structure is rather centralized, which is characterized by strong state planning and government control. Chinese enterprises are essentially not independent economic entities, but rather "factories" of the Chinese government who is the "biggest boss." For sure, reforms have brought decentralization in many industries. But in all the key industries, like telecommunications and now IT, foreign direct operations are rather restricted. A more open and transparent Chinese economic system is emerging in pace with China's forthcoming entry into the WTO. (3) Legal framework. China's legal system is still young, unstable; law is invariably subjected to ideology and influenced by a great deal of human factors. (4) Technology. China is short of modern technology. To import and attract foreign technologies to modernize China and enhance the people's living standard is the reason why China opened its economy in 1978. (5) Great size. China's population boasts the world's largest one. To exchange the large Chinese market for advanced foreign technologies is China's state policy. (6) Backwardness. China is still a relatively poor country with some 300 million people living under the U.N.-poverty level (one U.S. dollar per day). (7) Rapid change. Reform and importation of foreign technology since the late 1970s have brought about great changes in Chinese society. Maoist ideology, traditional Chinese cultural values, and Western lifestyle exist side by side in today's Middle Kingdom. (8) Chinese bureaucracy. At the center of the PRC condition lies the theme of Chinese bureaucracy which features red tape (more often, decision making requires consensus at various levels crossing various departments) as well as quick buying (e.g., when politics requires a quick deal and when your products fit in with the government's priority categories). Chinese negotiators follow the Chinese government's policies and plans to do business.

#### *Confucianism*

Confucianism is a 2500-year-old Chinese philosophical tradition that has exerted a fundamental influence on the Chinese and East Asian modes of thinking and ways of behaving. The influence of Confucianism on the Chinese style of business can be studied from the six basic Confucian values. (1) *Moral cultivation.* Confucianism emphasizes people's self-moral cultivation and lifelong learning.

Trust and sincerity are among the most important qualities for being human. In Confucian terms, a ruler should govern his state and people by means of moral persuasion and rules of propriety instead of law. (2) *Importance of interpersonal relationships.* Confucianism is a practical teaching of interpersonal relationships and conducts. It sees the human world through the Five Cardinal Relationships *(Wulun),* which is, the relationships between the ruler and subject, father and son, spouse and spouse, elder and younger brothers, and senior and junior friends. The seniors must be loving and benevolent to gain the respect and loyalty from the juniors, and vice versa. *Guanxi* (the Chinese term for relationships, connections, or contacts) is a major mechanism in the Chinese social psychology. *Guanxi* is closely related to *renqing* (favor), and *li* (etiquette, propriety, and rules of conduct) in regulating relationships. (3) *Family and group orientation.* In the Chinese society, family is the most basic and important social unit. In China where there has been lack of a well functioning legal system for thousands of years, the Chinese family shoulders much of the social responsibility. In the PRC, *danwei* or *zuzhi* ("work unit" or "organization") plays some of the roles traditionally played by the family (e.g., allocation of housing, arrangement of pensions and other welfare programs). (4) *Respect for age and hierarchy.* In the Confucian tradition, age is wisdom and must be respected. Hierarchy is honored through ordered relationships in which every person does his duty to contribute to social harmony and stability. (5) *Avoidance of conflict and need for harmony.* Confucianism stresses the need to achieve harmony in society through moral conduct in all kinds of relationships. Confucius says that a gentleman has no squabbles. When a gentleman is forced to compete, he will then compete like a gentleman. The Confucian ideal is to achieve harmony between Heaven, Earth, and Man. (6) *The concept of Chinese face (mianzi, lian).* Although face is a universal human nature, it is particularly salient for the Chinese culture. Behind the Chinese concept of face, lies the Confucian notion of shame. Confucius teaches a kind of statesmanship that advocates governing people by instilling "a sense of shame" into their mind. Face as a self-regulating moral mechanism has fundamental impact on the Chinese way of life (for interesting discussion on this issue see for example, Early, 1997; Ting–Toomey, 1994; Weldon, 1997).

From the Confucian perspective, the Chinese negotiators are "Confucian gentlemen" who look more for long-term working relationships to solve problems that may crop up at any time in than for a one-off legal deal. However, given the family centered Confucian tradition, the "Confucian gentlemen" may also appear to be formidable negotiators, when they bargain for the interest and face of their "family" or "group."

## Chinese Stratagems

Chinese stratagems, or *ji* in Chinese, refer to a long-lasting Chinese cultural tradition that shapes the strategic Chinese business behavior. *Ji* is probably the single most important word in the world's earliest treatise on military strategy—*Art of War*—written 2300 years ago by the most famous ancient Chinese military strategist Sun Tzu. Chinese stratagems can be understood as carefully devised Chinese schemes that deal with various kinds of situations and gain psychological and material advantage over one's adversary. A variety of Chinese stratagems can be found in the *Art of War,* such as deception, conquering by strategy, creating a situation, focus, espionage, benchmarking, shared vision, extraordinary troops, flanking, prudence, flexibility, leadership, and so forth. At the center of all the Chinese stratagems lies Sun Tzu's aphorism (Sun Tzu, 1982: 77)[1]:

> "To win one hundred victories in one hundred battles is not the acme of skill. To subdue the enemy without fighting is the acme of skill."

Hence, the Chinese assert the superiority of using human wisdom rather than engaging in pitched battles to conquer the opponent. This traditional Chinese strategic thinking is diametrically different from its Western counterpart as shown in von Clausewits's *On War* published in 1832. Whereas the former advocates gaining victory without fighting, the latter teaches winning by applying "absolute forces."

The Chinese have summarized their thousands of years of experience in dealing with various kinds of people and situations into a 138-character compendium titled *The Thirty-Six Stratagems* (The 36 *Ji's*) (see Table 1)[2]. The compendium was compiled by an anonymous Chinese in the late Ming (1368–1644) or early Qing (1644–1911) dynasties. These thirty-six ancient Chinese stratagems are theoretically grouped into six categories: Numbers 1 through 6 to be used when being superior; Numbers 7 through 12 for confrontation; Numbers 13 through 18 for attack; Numbers 19 through 24 for confused situations; Numbers 25 through 30 for gaining ground; and Numbers 31 through 36 to be used when being put in an inferior situation. In practice, however, the stratagems may be flexibly used in any possible situation. The 36 stratagems all appear in the popular form of Chinese idioms, each of which is made up of less than four (inclusive) Chinese characters, arranged so that when recited they produce a rhythmic effect, making it easy even for school children to remember them. These stratagems provide vivid examples of how the Chinese "subdue the enemy without fighting." Chiao (1981) shows that Chinese stratagems are a strategic force driving the Chinese mind in all Chinese societies the world over, regardless of whether they are Communist or non-Communist. The Chinese can use Chinese stratagems intentionally or unintentionally given the great influence of the stratagem culture on the Chinese socialization process.

The 36 Chinese stratagems provide a useful guide for Western business people to diagnose Chinese negotiating tactics. Linking the concept of Chinese stratagems with the Chinese business negotiating style literature, we find an amazing fit between the patterns of Chinese negotiating tactics and the recipes of the 36 Chinese stratagems: Attacking the opponent's vulnerabilities ✓Stratagem 2 ("Besiege Wei to rescue Zhao"); Playing home court ✓Stratagem 4 ("Await leisurely the exhausted enemy"); Manipulating friendship and hospitality ✓Stratagem 10 ("Hide a knife in a smile"); and Stratagem 31 ("The beautiful woman stratagem"); Playing the competitors against each other ✓Stratagem 3 ("Kill with a borrowed knife"), and so forth. From the Chinese stratagems perspective, the Chinese negotiator is Sun Tzu-like strategist who seldom wages a physical business war but rather is keen on a psychological wrestling of wit to create a favorable situation to manipulate his counterpart into doing business his way.

The Chinese are intensely practical people. For them, Confucianism, Taoism, and Buddhism, often regarded by many Westerners as the three religions of china, are more of philosophies than religions. Chinese business culture framework suggests that the Chinese negotiators have a "three-in-one" negotiating style; they negotiate like "bureaucrats," "gentlemen," and "strategists." Trust is a prime indicator showing which role the Chinese are going to play. When mutual trust between the business partners is high, the Chinese will negotiate as "gentlemen"; when it is low, they will negotiate as strategists! The PRC negotiators also negotiate as "bureaucrats," particularly so when the political wind blows.

## Analysis of the Sino-Western Business Negotiation Process

In this section, we use the "Ping-Pong" model to analyze the Sino-Western business negotiation process based on our empirical investigations of business negotiations between the foreign firm Ericsson and its Chinese customers.

### Pre-Negotiation

The Chinese negotiation process starts with early contacts with the Chinese government authorities. The Chinese show keen interests in getting to know the other party during these initial contacts. They try to ascertain whether or not the foreign firm has (1) the most advanced technology required for the project; (2) the willingness to sell or transfer it to the Chinese side by way of, for example, joint venture; and (3) the capacity of delivering the products on time. As one of the Chinese negotiators explained:

> "Our intention is to import the most advanced technology and to cooperate with large, world-famous foreign companies, because the life cycle of a technology is short. We pay even more attention to the supplier's *houjing* (reserve strength) for continuous technological development."

#### *Lobbying*

Lobbying before the Chinese government authorities is one of the most important marketing activities facing foreign firms that want to sell large industrial projects in Chinese key industries like telecommunications. Foreign firms must convince the Chinese that they have cutting-edge technologies that suit Chinese government's priorities, that they have long-term commitment to the Chinese market, and that they are financially strong. They must present a highly reliable image before the Chinese, making them feel safe to do business with them. The Chinese said that they liked to do business with "big mountains" like Ericsson that they could trust and rely on in the long run. One Ericsson manager (local Chinese) emphasized that lobbying, though existing in all countries, is particularly important in China. Lobbying must occur not only in Beijing but also in all large cities, both coastal and inland. Lobbying channels include visits to government authorities (e.g., MPT), presentations, technical seminars, advertising in Chinese professional journals and informal channels such as dinner parties.

#### *Presentation*

Giving attractive and reliable presentations to let potential Chinese partners know the company,

**Table 1** The Thirty-Six Ancient Chinese Stratagems

| | |
|---|---|
| Stratagem 1 | Cross the sea without Heaven's knowledge—*Man Tian Guo Hai* |
| Stratagem 2 | Besiege Wei to rescue Zhao—*Wei Wei Jiu Zhao* |
| Stratagem 3 | Kill with a borrowed knife—*Jie Dao Sha Ren* |
| Stratagem 4 | Await leisurely the exhausted enemy—*Yi Yi Dai Lao* |
| Stratagem 5 | Loot a burning house—*Chen Huo Da Jie* |
| Stratagem 6 | Clamour in the east but attack in the west—*Sheng Dong Ji Xi* |
| Stratagem 7 | Create something out of nothing—*Wu Zhong Sheng You* |
| Stratagem 8 | Openly repair the walkway but secretly march to Chen Cang—*An Du Chen Cang* |
| Stratagem 9 | Watch the fire burning from across the river—*Ge An Guan Huo* |
| Stratagem 10 | Hide a knife in a smile—*Xiao Li Cang Dao* |
| Stratagem 11 | Let the plum tree wither in place of the peach tree—*Li Dai Tao Jiang* |
| Stratagem 12 | Lead away a goat in passing—*Shun Shou Qian Yang* |
| Stratagem 13 | Beat the grass to startle the snake—*Da Cao Jig She* |
| Stratagem 14 | Borrow a corpse to return the soul—*Jie Shi Huan Hun* |
| Stratagem 15 | Lure the tiger to leave the mountains—*Diao Hu Li Shan* |
| Stratagem 16 | In order to capture, first let it go—*Yu Qin Gu Zong* |
| Stratagem 17 | Toss out a brick to attract a piece of jade—*Pao Zhuan Yin Yu* |
| Stratagem 18 | To capture bandits, first capture the ringleader—*Qin Zei Qin Wang* |
| Stratagem 19 | Remove the firewood from under the cooking pot—*Fu Di Chou Xin* |
| Stratagem 20 | Muddle the water to catch the fish—*Hun Shui Mo Yu* |
| Stratagem 21 | The golden cicada sheds its shell—*Jin Chan Tuo Qiao* |
| Stratagem 22 | Shut the door to catch the thief—*Guan Men Zhuo Zei* |
| Stratagem 23 | Befriend the distant states while attacking the nearby ones—*Yuan Jiao Jin Gong* |
| Stratagem 24 | Borrow the road to conquer Guo—*Jia Dao Fa Guo* |
| Stratagem 25 | Steal the beams and change the pillars—*Tou Liang Huan Zhu* |
| Stratagem 26 | Point at the mulberry tree but curse the locust tree—*Zhi Sang Ma Huai* |
| Stratagem 27 | Play a sober-minded fool—*Jia Chi Bu Dian* |
| Stratagem 28 | Lure the enemy onto the roof, then take away the ladder—*Shang Wu Chou Ti* |
| Stratagem 29 | Flowers bloom in the tree—*Shu Shang Kai Hua* |
| Stratagem 30 | The guest becomes the host—*Fan Ke Wei Zhu* |
| Stratagem 31 | The beautiful woman stratagem—*Mei Ren Ji* |
| Stratagem 32 | The empty city stratagem—*Kong Cheng Ji* |
| Stratagem 33 | The counter-espionage stratagem—*Fan Jian Ji* |
| Stratagem 34 | The self-torture stratagem—*Ku Rou Ji* |
| Stratagem 35 | The stratagem of interrelated stratagems—*Lian Huan Ji* |
| Stratagem 36 | Running away is the best stratagem—*Zho Wei Shang Ji* |

*Source:* Fung (1999: 166).

products and negotiating team members, is an important step toward formal negotiation sessions. Presentations aim to convince the Chinese of the sincerity of the company in doing business with China and show the Chinese that the company's products are an advanced technology with high quality and reasonable price. Foreign firms need to present themselves and their technologies to a number of authorities. Very often one has to endlessly repeat the same things to different negotiators who may suddenly, without explanation, be replaced by another team. From the Chinese point of view, it is done to check the reliability and firmness of the supplier. One Ericsson negotiator said:

> "You have to learn how to make presentations . . . you have to present your technology and company many times to different groups . . . and sometimes the same group comes back, but of course, they do not remember anything from the earlier presentation . . . they ask the same questions . . . I think they do this to check you."

Ericsson provided all the presentation material in English and Chinese, since most Chinese decision-makers were above 50 years of age and did not speak English. Sometimes the foreign team of 3 to 4 persons had to meet a Chinese team of 10 to 15 people; one interpreter on the foreign team was not enough to help communicate efficiently with the Chinese. As people ask many questions, especially in between the formal sessions, you need to have a couple of people to handle bigger groups. The presentation materials were made available for both potential end-users (e.g., the local post and telecommunication administration, the MPT affiliated plants) and various Chinese government authorities (e.g., State Planning Commission, MPT, and Ministry of Foreign Trade and Economic Cooperation—MOFTEC). It was at times a problem to duplicate high quality presentation materials quickly in China. A portable PC and printer, along with all the information and calculations when visiting Chinese customers is a necessity.

*Informal Discussion*

Initial and informal discussions with Chinese organizations often occur directly after the presentations. At this early stage, the Chinese already showed a keen concern for *technology* and *price.* For example, they were interested in not only the price but also in comparing the price with competitors. In one case, Ericsson succeeded in convincing the Chinese that although its price was much higher than that of the Japanese, its system capacity was more powerful; and its technology was better and would facilitate future expansions.

*Trust Building*

The Chinese attach great importance to trust building in business negotiations. One of the Chinese negotiators explained:

> "They [Western firms] want to come and sign the contract quickly and do not know that [if] we do not understand each other . . . there is no business relationship. First, we have to know and trust each other, then we sign the contract."

Nevertheless, an Ericsson manager observed that it was rather difficult to develop close social relationships with the Chinese. For example, the Chinese seldom invited foreigners to their homes. During the pre-negotiation phase, Chinese organizations sent delegations abroad for fact-finding tours. Being the host, the foreign firm could get many insights into Chinese priorities in industrial policies and development plans. In several instances, the Swedes invited the Chinese to come to Sweden to inspect the technical systems in operation. It proved to be much easier to understand the Chinese priorities and concerns during such visits, because decision-makers were, more often than not, included in the trip. Hosting a Chinese delegation also provides a good opportunity for foreign firms to strengthen friendship with the Chinese. For example, Ericsson invited the Chinese to Sweden not only to show them plants, facilities and technologies, but also to take them sight-seeing and have them participate in social activities such as, inviting them to private houses for dinner and taking them to "midsummer" celebrations. During these negotiations, Swedish pop Group Roxette visited Beijing, and Ericsson invited the Chinese negotiators to go and see them together, which was highly appreciated. These gestures of hospitality turned out to be greatly valued by the Chinese.

We can link the Chinese negotiating style in the pre-negotiation stage with the Chinese business culture discussed earlier. The Chinese change of negotiating team members was seen in this case as maneuvering a typical Chinese stratagem "Steal the beams and change the pillars" (Stratagem 25, see Table 1). In Chinese culture, trust is high within but low outside family and kinship borders. The Chinese constantly find themselves in such a quandary: business can only be done between people who have a high level of mutual respect and trust; however, business partners cannot always be immediate or extended family members. The Chinese "relying on big mountains" mentality also reflects the deep-seated Chinese psychological craving for face: doing business with second-class, technologically weaker, firms would make the Chinese lose face. This behavior can also be explained from the Chinese stratagems perspective: teaming up with a strong foreign partner will help breath new life into "dying" Chinese firms that have many technological, financial and management problems, a stratagem called "Borrow a corpse to return the soul" (Stratagem 14, see Table 1). The Chinese sensitivity to price is well known; the average living standard in the PRC and Chinese companies' lack of foreign exchange, are main reasons. That the Chinese do not invite foreigners to their homes should not be blamed on a lack of hospitality. In the PRC, every state employee belongs to a *danwei,* which controls much of the employee's life. Internal regulations generally do not encourage individuals to receive foreign visitors alone.

### Formal Negotiation

*Task-Related Exchange of Information*

Formal negotiation starts when the Chinese show a strong interest in "further discussions" and both parties sign a "letter of intent." The Chinese tend to send a formal document, informing the foreign party of the composition of the Chinese team and ideas for future meetings. In all cases, the following Chinese organizations were involved in the formal negotiation sessions: Managers from national industrial corporations under MPT, managers from MPT-affiliated plants (end users of the technology to be transferred), officials from the Bank of China (foreign exchange controlling organization), design staff from research institutes and sometimes local government officials. On the Swedish side, the negotiators were Ericssons' China area manager, product/technology manager, in-house lawyer, technical support and an intermediary (a liaison officer). An obvious contrast between the Chinese and the foreign teams was that the Chinese lawyers never participated in the formal negotiation sessions. Five major contentious issues during the formal negotiation sessions are singled out from our investigations: equity share, contribution of each party, management control, technology, price and other financial issues:

- Equity share. The Chinese were sensitive to their equity holdings and to start with, they wanted to have a majority share. However, after realizing that they could not achieve that, they insisted on having at least 50% holding, because they believed that majority ownership would lead to management control. The Chinese also considered the equity share a matter of "state sovereignty" having political importance.

- Contribution of each party. The Chinese side contributed tangible resources like production premises, existing machinery and equipment, labor, and so forth; while the foreign side, besides initial capital, provided intangible resources like technology, managerial training, marketing know-how, international networking, and so forth. It was relatively easy to estimate the tangible costs but difficult to assess the intangible costs.

- Management control. While the Swedes wanted to "teach" the Chinese modern technical know-how through keeping as many senior management positions in the joint venture as possible, the Chinese wanted to share senior management positions with the Swedes exactly in proportion to the parties' equity share. The Chinese were very interested in acquiring financial manager and administrative (or human resource) manager positions.

- Technology. The Chinese wanted absolutely to obtain the most up-to-date technology. They were deeply concerned about the Western firms' willingness to transfer the technology and to train the local Chinese. The foreign side was, on the other hand, very concerned about how to protect its technology and patents. Ericsson spends 18% of its sales on R&D annually. According to one Ericsson negotiator, it was difficult to make the Chinese understand the R&D cost incurred by the foreign firm; they believed that once they had paid for the project they would automatically be entitled to use whatever technologies they pleased. The term "rolling technology" (*gun doing ji shu*) is coined by the Chinese to refer to the newer generations of the technology being "rolled" constantly into the joint venture.

- Price. The Chinese demanded very low technology transfer prices, royalty fees, documentation fees, and so on. They thought prices offered by the foreign party were always too high. The Swedes, on the other hand, considered the Chinese the "only take, never give" type. However, the Chinese side considered that they had already given too much—a huge Chinese market—to the foreigners. It seemed that the Chinese keenly knew the value of the Chinese market as well as the value of foreign technology. What the Chinese did was to "trade" the Chinese market for foreign technology. The financial issues such as financing of the project, terms of payment, definition of net sales, countertrade or buy-back tend also to be a bone of contention between the parties. As pointed out by the Swedish negotiator:

> "The Chinese were all the time using this tactic and saying. "You know that we are poor and lag behind. We have no technology and you must help us. You will get an enormous market here. China is a vast country with huge buying power, you will sell in huge volume here."

*Persuasion*

The Chinese use a variety of negotiating tactics to persuade the other party to do business their way during the formal negotiation sessions: flattery, identifying the opponent's problems, shaming, deception and pitting competing foreign companies against one another. But you must be firm on your offer and build credibility. This can be done in the sessions and also in between sessions. One Ericsson manager gave an example:

> "Once one of the Chinese negotiators insisted that our project in Thailand had some problems and that our technology did not work well. I did not say anything, but when I came back to the hotel, I called the head office and asked our office in Bangkok to check . . . there was no problem. Next day, in a private meeting, over the dinner, I told the Chinese Manager that his statement about Thailand was not correct and that I did not say anything in yesterday's meeting not to embarrass him . . . I gave him the telephone number of our Thai counterpart and asked him to check for himself. After that he became very friendly and even helped us to get that order."

In another case, the Chinese were driving parallel negotiations with Ericsson and Nokia. These two Nordic "brothers" had a hard time in those days: they not only took their turns to court the same "bride," but also happened to stay in the same hotel in Beijing, looking into each other's heavy hearted eyes over the breakfast tables every morning.

*Concessions and Agreement*

The formal negotiation ends with an agreement by the negotiating parties through their concessions or compromise. In this stage, the Chinese show a strong inclination to settle all suspending issues in a "package deal." The Chinese made concessions too; however, their concessions very often turned out to be a disguised gesture devised to attract the counterpart into making real concessions. For every concession, they wanted a counter concession. As Ericsson, negotiator for BMC recalled:

> "They [the Chinese] often make threats, "You answer yes or no. If no, we will talk with Nokia. Nokia is right here in the hotel, but we do not want to talk to them, we want to talk to you first."

When drafting the contract, the Chinese weighed words meticulously when it came to the clauses that would affect the Chinese, while treating issues of concern to the foreign party as generally as possible. Agreement was almost always signed in the presence of high ranking officials from the government authorities and followed by a series of lavish banquets and ceremonies. While enjoying the Chinese hospitality and etiquette, one Swedish negotiator also described a Chinese negotiating tactic:

> "A tactic which I believe that the Chinese employ is that . . . they set the deadline on a certain week and arrange a banquet long before the contract is actually ready. They told us that things must be ready on Saturday when the mayor would come to the banquet. In this way, the Chinese applied pressure on us to reach an agreement. This was common. . . . You became a little disappointed the first time you came across such a situation. But, after a while, when you recognized the same thing happening again in other places, you knew that it was a tactic."

In analyzing the formal negotiation stage, we find that Chinese negotiating teams tend to be large; people from many organizations and departments take part in negotiations and ask many questions. From the PRC condition point of view, Chinese companies are not companies in Western terms; rather, they are "factories" of the Chinese government. "Collective participation"—a large number of people are involved in negotiations and keep asking questions—facilitates communication among the Chinese and in case something goes amiss, the "collective responsibility" would also allow individuals to escape punishment. The Chinese propensity to ask many questions seems necessary given China's relatively new involvement in international business and their curiosity about foreign technologies. But the same behavior may also be understood from the Chinese stratagems perspective as a tactical move to stimulate the other party to show their hand first: "Beat the grass to startle the snake" (Stratagem 13). The absence of Chinese lawyers at the face-to-face negotiation table could be viewed as a typical Confucian business behavior; legal power does not feature at all in Confucianism. From the PRC condition vantage point, the legal framework of the PRC was still young and Chinese lawyers did not have the same status and respect compared with their Western counterparts (though the situation is improving in the recent years). In BMC case we found that Chinese negotiators did communicate with their internal lawyers beyond the negotiation table, but they never showed up during the face-to-face negotiations sessions.

In terms of management control, the Chinese wanted to acquire financial manager and administration manager positions. The PRC condition provides the answer: in state-owned Chinese enterprises, financial and administration/personnel departments assume the most power. Also, the Chinese believed some of the Western management practices would not be applicable in China.

The persuasion tactics used by the Chinese were all of this type: using external forces to influence instead of direct confrontation. For example, the Chinese reference to the Thailand project (a third party) was aimed at attacking the foreign party's weakness (e.g., quality) to gain more bargaining power in other issues (e.g., price). The prototype of this tactic can be found in the Thirty-Six Chinese Stratagems: "Besiege Wei to rescue Zhao" (Stratagem 2) and "Clamour in the east but attack in the west" (Stratagem 6). It turned out that the Chinese attack was groundless, probably because they had not carefully ascertained their source of information. But "Create something out of nothing" (Stratagem 7) is a Chinese stratagem which serves to gain advantage by conjuring illusions. The Swedish manager did not argue with the Chinese in the formal sessions but rather explained to him informally. This proved to work well; the Chinese certainly felt the Swede was honest and sincere and, most important of all, helped the Chinese save face. Therefore, he also became friendly, helpful, and did favors in return.

The Chinese way of making concessions is to "Toss out a brick to attract a piece of jade" (Stratagem 17) or to exchange their "small things" with the opponent's "big things" as the Swedish negotiator remarked. In wording the contract, the Chinese style of dealing with details is a direct outcome of the Chinese bureaucracy. In the bureaucratic system, the Chinese are punished if they make mistakes but they are rarely rewarded for their outstanding performance; this rule of the Chinese bureaucratic game prods the Chinese to prefer doing nothing to doing one hundred things with one mistake.

## Post-Negotiation

### *Implementation and New Rounds of Negotiations*

Our empirical findings reveal that problems in negotiating with China also exist after the formal negotiations are finished, that is, during the phase of implementation of the agreement. Generally speaking, the Chinese honor their contract; however, cases of Chinese nonfulfilment of their obligations do occur. In one case, the Swedish firm entered a joint-venture agreement with the Chinese. It was agreed by the parties that the joint venture would have a Swedish managing director (MD) and that he would be provided with a Western-standard residence in China. Later, when the Swedish MD arrived in China, he was offered a Chinese-standard residence similar to those of other Chinese senior executives, closer to MD's rank. The Swedish side asked the Chinese to observe what was stipulated in the contract but the Chinese did not agree. The Chinese argued that providing a Western-standard residence for the Swedish MD was unfair to the Chinese senior executives who worked in the same joint venture. The conflict deteriorated to the point that the Swedish side was about to calculate the consequences of terminating the contract. However, the Chinese were stubborn on their stand, reasoning that the Western-style residence demanded by the MD would cost about US$70,000 per year equal to the salaries of some 200 ordinary Chinese workers altogether and the joint venture could not bear such a cost. Finally, a compromise solution was reached through new rounds of negotiations.

The Chinese attitude toward contracting is problem solving based on the changing situations instead of contracts. We believe that the Chinese, in this case, must have known what the Western-style residence meant when signing the agreement. Flatly rejecting the implementation of the agreement certainly violated the "law of Chinese face." The Chinese side might probably have been "forced" by their superiors to make a "fair" adjustment of the contract based on the market conditions, feelings of the Chinese executives, and the joint venture's interests. One Swedish negotiator recalls:

> "I have worked with Ericsson in different places for 20 years. I have quite a broad negotiating experience with European, Middle Eastern and African countries. The difference between Chinese and these countries [negotiators] was that although one also has tough negotiations there, once an agreement was made the issue was clear and over. Negotiators did not call the old issue into question again. But this was not the case with Chinese. The Chinese could take up and renegotiate whatever whenever they wanted. They did not stand by what they had already said."

### Managerial Implications

Based on the foregoing discussions, we can draw some managerial implications for negotiating effectively with the PRC. Our advice is organized by way of 4 P's: Priority, Patience, Price, and People.

#### Priority

Driven by "China fever" and the belief that China needs foreign technologies, Western business people rushed into the Chinese market with various advanced technological solutions. Many succeeded but many others failed. An important reason for the failure is that the PRC condition has not been paid sufficient attention: Chinese government is the "biggest boss" and all Chinese state enterprises do business according to the government's priorities, policies and plans. Our research suggests that in negotiating large industrial projects with the PRC, foreign firms should above all, be sensitive to the guiding principles of China's social and economic development set forth by the Chinese Communist Party and the Chinese government, and also, should make a careful study of the Chinese government's priorities and implementation policies. These policies are often stated in five-year plans and official plans for different provinces and sectors. The priorities are also available in some Western statistics, such as the US Department of State's Country Commercial Guide. The priorities are also important indicators of what the Chinese want to spend their foreign exchange on. Therefore, it is vitally important for a Western firm to determine whether its project comes into the priority project category or not. If the project is included in the Chinese priority categories, it will interest the Chinese side and negotiations will proceed relatively quickly; if not, there may be problems in everything. Energy, transportation and telecommunications are among the traditional Chinese priorities. Recently, revitalizing China's deficit-ridden state-owned enterprises is also added to the list of Chinese priorities. Before priorities become public knowledge, foreign firms may still be able to glimpse much of the picture. For example, this can be done by establishing good relationships with the counterpart (Chinese negotiators) and by asking questions about the status of the particular project. The middleman can also be helpful in this case. This study suggests that Chinese delegations' visits to foreign firms help to provide valuable opportunities for the latter to receive insights into Chinese priorities and preferences.

### Patience

Patience is the most important qualification for successful negotiations with the Chinese. From the PRC condition point of view, China is large with many yet underdeveloped areas ranging from infrastructure to living facilities and problems of various types are bound to happen. Negotiations in China often take time because different Chinese organizations and different departments within one organization tend to be involved in negotiation processes and decision-making within the Chinese bureaucracy often takes time. From the vantage point of Confucianism, the Chinese will not rush into any serious meetings with someone whom they do not know; trust and a certain feeling of closeness must be in place for any negotiation to start. The Confucian notions of relationship, face, etiquette, harmony, and so forth, are all time-consuming qualifications. Therefore, it takes time to negotiate with the Chinese because it takes time to communicate with the "Confucian gentlemen." From the Chinese stratagems perspective (see Stratagem 4 . . . await leisurely the exhausted enemy), the Chinese are deceptive negotiators who can use, deliberately or inadvertently, a variety of Chinese stratagems to achieve their objectives. When mutual trust is not very high and the Chinese are exposed to solutions to the problems. However, they do compare your price to that of the competitors. In one case, where Ericsson was competing with Motorola, the Chinese negotiator recalled:

> "We asked both companies to provide their total offer including the price for the system, hand phones, components, kits, and parts. It turned out that Motorola's offer was really lower than Ericsson's was. For example, Ericsson offered the license fee at US$1.5 million, compared to Motorola's US$0.5 million, Ericsson's price for hand phones was one thousand and several hundred dollars, while Motorola's price was US$1050 . . . We at PTIC were for Ericsson, but at the factory, people were for Motorola, mainly because of the price."

### People

Because of the deep Confucian aversion to law and orientation toward interpersonal relationships, the Chinese believe in people more than contracts. Foreign firms need to take a people-oriented approach and try to establish a high level of trust with their Chinese partners. A trusting relationship is also the best way to neutralize the Chinese stratagems. Chinese teams' foreign visits are probably the best time for the foreign party to develop rapport and *guanxi* with the Chinese decision-makers. Traveling in Western countries is still considered by many Chinese a privilege and, if offered with special hospitality, will be greatly appreciated by the Chinese. According to the Confucian rules of relationships, the Chinese will reciprocate your hospitality when you visit China next time. Relationship marketing with the focus on people has become a buzzword in Western marketing theory since the late 1980s and a competitive advantage sought by many Western firms recently. In China, everyone will answer the question of what marketing is all about without hesitation: *Guanxi.* Therefore, we highly appreciate the business philosophy of a senior Ericsson executive in China (local Chinese) who said: "To do things in China, you must do people first." In the case of Ericsson, a middleman, a liaison officer, was used to enhance this understanding to establish a relationship with the Chinese. As one Chinese negotiator reported:

> "Another very important reason why we finally chose Ericsson was that they had a *zhongjianren* [middleman], that is, Ericsson's Chinese employee, a Shanghainese working for Ericsson. He was a very good friend of ours, and had a good guanxi with both sides. He contributed a lot to the success of this project. He was like the matchmaker in a marriage. You know, we are all people that have feelings. Whenever the negotiation deadlocked, he explained to the parties. A friend coming to us to explain is always better than the same work performed by a *laowai* [foreigner]. This is in fact a question of trust."

## Conclusion

This chapter has proposed a "Ping-Pong" model to analyze Chinese negotiating style in the Sino-Western business negotiation process which is divided into three stages: pre-negotiation (lobbying, presentation, informal discussion, and trust building), formal negotiation (task-related exchange of information, persuasion, concessions, and agreement), and post-negotiation (implementation and new rounds of negotiations). The Ping-Pong model is focused on the process of Chinese business negotiation analyzed from the Chinese socio-cultural perspective. As compared to most other "generic" models of international business negotiations, this model provides a more "emic" understanding of negotiating with the Chinese. That is, using indigenous components of Chinese culture to explain Chinese negotiation behavior and tactics. Another feature of this model is that it is process oriented. Few studies have used that approach earlier. We believe Ericsson's negotiation experience is relevant for all that seek to deal with the Chinese business people and extremely valuable for those that negotiate in Chinese key industries (such as; telecommunication, IT, energy, agriculture, and environment) where government has strong control.

Five major contentious issues in the formal negotiation sessions are identified: equity share, contribution of each party, management control, technology, price, and other financial issues. The Chinese negotiating behaviors observed in the negotiation process are explained from the perspectives of the PRC condition, Confucianism, and Chinese stratagems. We have demonstrated that the "Ping-Pong" model developed by us really works well and captures the essence of the Chinese negotiation behavior while negotiating with Western parties. However, we believe there is a need for further studies on Chinese negotiation behavior and perhaps studies where the model can be statistically tested.

The chapter has also drawn managerial implications for effective negotiation with the PRC in terms of 4p's: Priority, Patience, Price, and People. These 4P's should be considered in all the three stages of the Sino-Western business negotiation process; yet, some are more stage-specific. For example, a Western firm has to find out, in the pre-negotiation stage, whether or not its China project falls into the Chinese priority category. Patience is required throughout the entire process. Price needs to be calculated as early as the pre-negotiation stage, and to be negotiated carefully in the formal negotiation sessions. Although people and trust building are most critical in the pre-negotiation stage, they should be handled and further developed during the later stages of negotiations.

## Notes

1. In Sun Tzu (1982), *ji* is translated by Samuel B. Griffith as "strategy."

2. For a detailed historical and legendary account of *The Thirty-Six Stratagems,* readers are referred to Chu (1991), Gao (1991), Sun (1991), and von Senger (1991).

## References

Blackman, C. (1997). *Negotiating China: Case studies and strategies.* St. Leonards, Australia: Allen & Unwin.

Chen, M. (1993). Tricks of the China trade. *The China Business Review, 20*(2): 12–16.

Chiao, C. (1981). Chinese strategic behaviours: A preliminary list. In *Proceedings of the International Conference on Sinology.* Taipei, August 15–17, 1980. Academia Sinica, Taipei, pp. 429–440.

Chu, C. N. (1991). *The Asian mind game.* New York: Rawson Associates.

Davidson, W. H. (1987). Creating and managing joint ventures in China. *California Management Review, 29*(4): 77–95.

Deverge, M. (1986). Negotiating with the Chinese. *Euro-Asia Business Review, 5*(1): 34–36.

Earley, P. (1997). *Face, harmony, and social structure: An analysis of organizational behavior across cultures.* New York: Oxford University Press.

Fang, T. (1999). *Chinese business negotiating style.* Sage: Thousand Oaks, CA.

Fayerweather, J., & Kapoor, A. (1976). *Strategy and negotiation for the international corporation: Guidelines and cases,* Cambridge, MA: Ballinger.

Frankenstein, J. (1986). Trend in Chinese business practice: Change in the Beijing wind. *California Management Review, 29*(1): 148–160.

Gao, Y. (1991). *Lure the tiger out of the mountains: The thirty-six stratagems of ancient China.* New York: Simon & Schuster.

Ghauri, P. N. (1996). Introduction. In P. N. Ghauri & J. C. Usunier (Eds.), *International business negotiations* (pp. 3–20). Oxford: Pergamon.

Ghauri, P. N. & Usunier J.-C. (1996). *International Business Negotiations.* Oxford: Pergamon.

Graham, J. L., & Lin, C.-Y. (1987). A comparison of marketing negotiations in the Republic of China (Taiwan) and the United States. In Cavusgil, T. (ed.) *Advances in international marketing* (Vol. 2, pp. 23–46). Greenwich, CT: JAI Press.

Hendryx, S. R. (1986). The Chinese trade: Making the deal work. *Harvard Business Review,* July-August: 75–84.

Hoon-Halbauer, S. K. (1999). Managing relationships within sino-foreign joint ventures. *Journal of World Business, 34*(4): 344–371.

Kirkbride, P. S., Tang, S. F. Y., & Westwood, R. I. (1991). Chinese conflict preferences and negotiating behavior: Cultural and psychological influences. *Organization Studies, 12*(3): 365–386.

Lee, K.-H. H., & Lo, T. W.-C. (1988). American business people's perceptions of marketing and negotiating in the People's Republic of China. *International Marketing* Review, *5*(2): 41–51.

Pye, L. W. (1982). *Chinese commercial negotiating style.* Cambridge, MA: Oelgeschlager, Gunn & Hain.

Pye, L. W. (1986). The China trade: Making the deal. *Harvard Business Review,* July-August: 74–80.

Seligman, S. D. (1990). *Dealing with the Chinese: A practical guide to business etiquette.* London: Mercury.

von Senger, H. (1991). *The book of stratagems.* New York: Viking Penguin.

Shenkar, O., Ronen, S. (1987). The cultural context of negotiations: The implications of Chinese interpersonal norms. *The Journal of Applied Behavioral Science, 23*(2): 263–275.

Stewart, S., & Keown, C. F. (1989). Talking with the dragon: Negotiating in the People's Republic of China. *Columbia Journal of World Business, 24*(3): 68–72.

Stone, R. J. (1992). Negotiating with China is not easy. *Hong Kong Business, 11*(125): 64–65.

Sun H. C. (1991). *The wiles of war: 36 military strategies from ancient China.* Beijing: Foreign Languages Press.

Sun Tzu. (1982). *Sun Tzu: The art of war* (translated by Samuel B. Griffith). London: Oxford University Press.

Ting-Toomey, Stella (Ed.). (1994). *The challenge of facework, SUNY series in Human Communication Processes.* Albany, NY: State University of New York Press.

Tung, R. L. (1982). US-China trade negotiations. *Journal of International Business Studies,* Fall: 25–38.

Tung, R. L. (1989). A longitudinal study of United States-China business negotiations. *China Economic Review, 1*(1): 57–71.

Tung, R. L. (1996). Negotiations with East Asians. In P. N. Ghauri & J. C. Usunier (Eds.), *International business negotiations* (pp. 369–381). Oxford: Pergamon.

Warrington, M. B., & McCall, J. B. (1983). Negotiating a foot into the Chinese door. *Management Development, 21*(2): 3–13.

Weiss, S. E. (1994a). Negotiating with the 'Romans'—Part 1. *Sloan Management Review, 35*(2): 51–61.

Weiss, S. E. (1994b). Negotiating with the 'Romans'—Part 2. *Sloan Management Review, 35*(3): 85–99.

Weldon, Elizabeth J. (1994). Intercultural interaction and conflict management in US-Chinese joint-ventures. In S. Stewart (Ed.), *Advances in Chinese industrial studies* (Vol. 4). Greenwich, CT: JAI.

# Reading 2.5

## UNDERSTANDING THE BEAR

### *A Portrait of Russian Business Leaders*

SHEILA M. PUFFER

Consider the following descriptions of individuals who made *Moscow Magazine's* 1992 list of the Top 50 business people in Russia:

*Evgenii Alekseevich Brakov—Fifty-four years old, married with one daughter and a granddaughter. General Director of the huge ZIL Automobile Factory. Rags-to-riches story: Brakov began as a humble mechanic at ZIL (top-of-the-line Russian limousine) and worked his way to the top. No time for hobbies, he is utterly devoted to turning ZIL into a successful company.*

*Dmitrii Vladimirovich Liubomudrov—Financial director of the industrial finance firm Profiko, founded in August 1990. Thirty years old, married with one child. Hobbies include horseback riding and Amateur Song Club. One of the founders of MosInkomBank. Director of brokers office of Moscow Central Stock Exchange and the Russian Commodity Exchange. Among Soviet and foreign bankers is well-known for being meticulous and hard working. An outstanding horseman, at one time he even trained horses for professional competition. He is also an excellent electrician; a large part of the everyday appliances in his home were made with his own hands.*[1]

In some ways North Americans may feel they already know such people. They possess the same hard-driving ambition, boundless energy, and keen ability that are associated with successful business leaders in the United States. Yet, by probing a little deeper, some important differences emerge that, if not well understood, could interfere with Russian and U.S. managers' efforts to work effectively together.

This chapter draws upon interviews and surveys of Russian managers that I have conducted since 1979 while living and working periodically in Russia and collaborating with a number of Russian and American colleagues. In part, we will explore how the traits that made managers successful under communism compare with those that are needed in the nascent market economy.[2] The framework for this portrait of Russian business leaders will consist of four leadership traits that researchers have identified in effective leaders in the U.S.: (1) leadership motivation; (2) drive; (3) honesty and integrity; and (4) self-confidence.[3] As shown in Exhibit 1, I will first describe how historical influences in traditional Russian society have shaped these traits, and then discuss how these traits apply to Russian managers in two eras: the "Red Executive"[4] of the communist regime which prevailed from 1917 to 1991,[5] and the market-oriented manager who had emerged in the market economy which began to develop after the breakup of the Soviet Union at the end of 1991.[6]

Leadership Motivation

> *Leadership requires first and foremost the strong desire to lead. Leadership motivation includes: (1) the desire to exercise power and be recognized as influential and occupying a position superior to others; and (2) the willingness to assume responsibility.*

*Traditional Russian Society.* The image of Russian leaders as powerful autocrats is legendary.[7] Centralization of authority and responsibility in Russia has a long history. In the peasant village communes of medieval Russia, the board of village elders was entrusted to "find the common will."[8] Villagers would discuss issues in an open forum in such a way that suggestions and criticisms were lost in the din and could not be pinned on any individual. According to a proverb, "No one is responsible for the *mir*" (village commune).[9] It was the elders' task to sort through the comments, define the consensus of the group, and make recommendations to the chief elder (*starosta*). Group members believed that it was not possible to anticipate the elders' wishes, and would wait to be told what to do rather than initiate action themselves. In sum, the village elders who were the leaders in traditional Russian society wielded unchallenged power and bore full responsibility for the welfare of the group. In addition, they behaved paternalistically toward the members of the community, and were addressed as *batiushka* (little father).

One-person leadership, which denoted the unquestioned authority of the leader, had predominated in the army and in public administration under Emperor Paul I in the late eighteenth century, and was legalized under Lenin in 1923 as the basic management tenet of Soviet enterprises.

*The Red Executive.* Traditional Russian attitudes toward power and responsibility found their way into work organizations in the communist period and resulted in practices that hampered the effectiveness of enterprise managers and their subordinates. According to communist principles, managers were supposed to balance two types of leadership reminiscent of the village communes and the board of elders: one-person leadership (*edinonachalie*) and collective leadership (*kollegial'nost'*). One-person leadership, which denoted the unquestioned authority of the leader, had predominated in the army and in public administration under Emperor Paul I in the late eighteenth century, and was legalized under Lenin in 1923 as the basic management tenet of Soviet enterprises.[10] A few years later, managers were instructed by the party to combine one-person leadership with collective leadership. The leader's task was to identify issues and set goals. The collective was then expected to discuss the issues and submit a proposal to the leader, who in turn made the decision and instructed the collective to implement it. This alternating wave pattern, that our research team labelled "centralized leadership/grass-roots democracy,"[11] was short-lived. Stalin's totalitarian oppression and managers' critical roles in the rapid industrialization of the country in the 1930s resulted in centralized leadership stifling grass-roots democracy as enterprise managers became more autocratic. During *perestroika,* the 1987 Law on the Soviet State Enterprise was intended to redress the imbalance of power and improve economic performance by granting greater participation in decision making to the collective. The law mandated the election of line managers by the workers and the creation of an elected council of the workers' collective in each enterprise to oversee organizational decision making. However, neither initiative had a lasting effect. In 1989, the Soviet government abolished the election of managers in response to protests by influential enterprise managers who argued that the policy was undermining organizational effectiveness. Managers cited instances in which workers elected bosses who made life easy for them rather than those who made tough decisions in the interests of productivity and efficiency. Furthermore, the workers' council was essentially an advisory body to top management who retained final decision-making authority in enterprises.

Wielding virtually all the power within their enterprises, heads of enterprises also bore all the responsibility. They became thoroughly overburdened, and enterprises became paralyzed because no one took action without authorization from their superior as a way of avoiding blame if something went wrong. In fact, Russian executives have marveled at the way Western executives delegate many tasks, freeing themselves to concentrate on strategic decision making.[12] In contrast, Russian executives were micro managers and macro puppets.

*The Market-Oriented Manager. Many enterprise managers have endeavored to retain the autocratic grip on power that they have enjoyed for decades. Now, however, in an attempt to save their enterprises from bankruptcy, they are forced to share power with*

| Leadership Trait | Traditional Russian Society (1400s to 1917) | The Red Executive (1917 to 1991) | The Market-Oriented Manager (1991 to Present) |
|---|---|---|---|
| **Leadership Motivation** | | | |
| Power | Powerful autocrats | Centralized leadership stilled grass-roots democracy | Shared power and ownership |
| Responsibility | Centralization of responsibility | Micro managers and macro puppets | Delegation and strategic decision making |
| **Drive** | | | |
| Achievement Motivation | Don't rock the boat | Frustrated pawns | The sky's the limit |
| Ambition | Equal poverty for all | Service to party and collective good | Overcoming the sin of being a winner |
| Initiative | Look both ways | Meticulous rule following and behind-the-scenes finessing | Let's do business |
| Energy | Concentrated spasms of labor | "8-hour day," 8 to 8, firefighting | 8-day week, Chasing opportunities |
| Tenacity | Life is a struggle | Struggling to accomplish the routine | Struggling to accomplish the new |
| **Honesty and Integrity** | | | |
| Dual ethical standard | Deception in dealings, fealty in friendship | Two sets of books, personal integrity | Wild capitalism, personal trust |
| Using connections (blat) | Currying favor with landowners | Greasing the wheels of the state | Greasing palms, but learning to do business straight |
| Self-Confidence | From helplessness to bravado | From inferior quality to "big is beautiful" | From cynicism to over-prompting |

**Exhibit 1** Russian Leadership Traits in Three Eras

*employees who have become owners, as well as with outside investors and stockholders. These established managers, therefore, must learn to use their power in a more collegial way in order to survive in the new economic environment.*

The urgent requirements for restructuring state enterprises and creating new business ventures in Russia call for individuals who have a high need for power and who are willing to assume a high level of responsibility for their work. Some promising signs come from surveys that my colleagues and I have conducted. Many of the forty Moscow entrepreneurs we surveyed in 1992 had created their businesses in order to be their own boss, and were willing to share power and create an atmosphere of participation in their organizations, particularly in small firms staffed by talented professionals.[13] We also found that 120 managers at all hierarchical levels of state-owned enterprises felt considerable responsibility for their work,[14] attitudes that were confirmed by government economic officials.[15] Yet, managers must continue to push responsibility down the hierarchy and teach subordinates to solve problems themselves.[16] Besides delegating routine tasks, senior executives need to learn and practice strategic decision making to make their enterprises competitive and economically viable.

### Drive

*The second cluster of leadership traits is drive, a set of the following five characteristics associated with expending a high level of effort: (1) achievement motivation, (2) ambition, (3) initiative, (4) energy, and (5) tenacity. High achievers gain satisfaction from performing challenging tasks, meeting high standards, and finding better ways of doing things. Ambitious people have a strong desire to advance in their careers and to demonstrate their abilities. Having initiative means being proactive in making choices and pressing for change. Energetic leaders have great physical, mental, and emotional vitality and stamina. Lastly, tenacity refers to persevering under adversity and pursuing goals that may take many years to accomplish.*

According to egalitarian principles, no one was supposed to sink too low, nor was anyone to rise too high. People who strived to be better than others were seen as taking away the rightful share of others.

*Traditional Russian Society.* In the communal living and farming conditions of traditional Russian society, the well-being of the collective was highly valued, and individuals who showed signs of making themselves better than the group were viewed with suspicion and contempt. Consequently, such individualistic traits as achievement striving, ambition, and initiative were considered to be socially undesirable and destructive for group harmony. The norm was to blend into the group and avoid challenging the standard way of doing things. In fact, farming techniques in Russia remained primitive for so long that grain yields were the lowest in all the long-settled countries, including India.[17] There was an anti-achievement attitude that could be summarized as, "Don't rock the boat."

In a similar vein, ambitious people have long been viewed with resentment, suspicion, and envy, feelings that stem from the deeply rooted view that social justice consists of everyone subsisting at the same level. According to egalitarian principles, no one was supposed to sink too low, nor was anyone to rise too high. People who strived to be better than others were seen as taking away the rightful share of others.[18] One anecdote about Russians' preoccupation with envy involves a peasant to whom God would grant any wish, but would also give his neighbor twice as much. After much thought, the peasant asked God to strike out one of his eyes along with both of his neighbor's eyes.[19] In place of ambition, then, Russians substituted envy, creating "the syndrome of equal poverty for all."[20]

Russians are a tenacious people. Their ability to endure hardship and survive under adverse conditions is a hallmark of their character.

Another characteristic often associated with Russians is caution. The peasant admonition dating from the fifteenth century, "to look both ways," is thought to be associated with the rough terrain and harsh environment.[21] With such a high value placed on cautious behavior, it is little wonder that initiative was not a common feature of traditional Russian society.

The last two elements of drive, energy and tenacity, also bear a unique Russian stamp. Russians are notorious for their bursts of energy, followed by long periods of lethargy. Historians have traced this behavior to peasants who would work feverishly during the spring and summer to bring in the harvest, and then lie idle throughout the long, cold winter months. A nineteenth-century Russian historian boldly concluded: "No other nation in Europe can put forward such concentrated spasms of labor as the Russian."[22]

Russians are a tenacious people. Their ability to endure hardship and survive under adverse conditions is a hallmark of their character. They have persevered through brutally harsh winters, the ravages of war, and severe shortages of basic material goods and comforts that the Western world takes for granted. Many believe that their destiny, reinforced by the teachings of the Russian Orthodox Church, is to endure suffering as a means to a brighter future. Two often-heard refrains are that life is a struggle, and that one must be patient.

*The Red Executive.* Conditions in most enterprises during the communist period were frustrating for managers who had high levels of drive. For instance, their achievement strivings were channeled toward meeting unrealistic deadlines and manufacturing products specified in the plan using insufficient or inferior raw materials, unsuitable equipment, and unmotivated workers. While standards for production volume were often unrealistically high, quality standards were often abysmally low or easily subverted.[23] In short, achievement-oriented managers were frustrated pawns of the central planning authorities.

During the communist regimes initiative was not only discouraged, but was often punished.

To be successful, upwardly striving managers had to direct their ambition toward service to the party and advancement of their enterprise's collective good. Their success depended on both talent and political factors, including party membership, protection, connections, and loyalty to superiors.[24] In addition, it was common for managers advancing to top management ranks in enterprises to spend several years on leave working in a communist party organization before returning to a line management position in their enterprise.

During the communist regime initiative was not only discouraged, but was often punished. Officially, managers were rewarded for meticulously following rules and demonstrating loyalty to communist party principles. However, behind the scenes, many managers showed exceptional initiative and creativity by finessing problems in order to meet planned targets. For example, at an electric motor manufacturing plant we studied in 1988, a multimillion-dollar computerized machine tool ordered from Europe by ministry officials turned out to be incompatible with the existing machine tools on the assembly line.

Several dozen workers were assigned to perform the operation by hand using outmoded tools—an expensive and labor-intensive process.[25]

During the communist period, conscientious managers had to have the energy to work long hours and be all things to all people. Managers whom our team interviewed in 1988 would joke that they worked an "eight-hour day"—from 8 A.M. to 8 P.M., that is.[26] Heads of enterprises spent most of their time "fighting fires." They were "hands-on" managers who would tour their plants once or twice a day and become involved in operational problems. Unfortunately, the amount of energy required to be successful took its toll on the health of many Russian managers. Heads of Soviet enterprises have been diagnosed as experiencing more stress and health problems than managers in the United States, Japan, and India.[27]

Managers during the communist period struggled tenaciously to accomplish routine tasks. Effective managers persevered under adversity and fulfilled their enterprise's plans in spite of shortages and bureaucratic obstacles. For example, a successful materials manager we interviewed in 1988 had chronic problems getting a supplier to provide copper wire for a new model of motor. First, the manager went several hundred miles to see the supplier. When this attempt failed, the plant used economic sanctions against the supplier who paid them several thousand rubles in fines, yet still sent no wire. Finally, the manager had higher authorities force his counterpart to meet with him at the ministry in charge of wire production. The motor plant finally began receiving the wire, but shipments were consistently at least five percent short.[28]

Although there is no longer any legal restriction on realizing one's personal ambition by starting a private enterprise, there is still tremendous social pressure against ambitious entrepreneurs.

*The Market-Oriented Manager.* A growing number of managers and entrepreneurs are exhibiting the five elements of drive that are associated with success in a market economy. For example, according to one recent study, Russian entrepreneurs have as much achievement motivation as their American counterparts.[29] My colleagues and I also found that entrepreneurs sought challenging tasks and had high standards. Many in our study had left the security of the state sector to start new businesses that would allow their scientific and technical expertise to flourish. Moreover, they rated the high quality of their products and services as the number one factor contributing to their firms' success.[30] The spirit of these achievement-oriented individuals is that the sky's the limit.

Although there is no longer any legal restriction on realizing one's personal ambition by starting a private enterprise, there is still tremendous social pressure against ambitious entrepreneurs.

Although there is no longer any legal restriction on realizing one's personal ambition by starting a private enterprise, there is still tremendous social pressure against ambitious entrepreneurs. As one American journalist observed: "In America, it's a sin to be a loser, but if there's one sin in Soviet society, it's being a winner."[31] In essence, "blind, burning envy of a neighbor's success . . . has become (virtually at all levels) a most powerful brake on the ideas and practice of restructuring [the economy]."[32] Ambitious business people, therefore, must deal with the problem of overcoming the sin of being a winner, and being the object of envy and resentment. The new economic conditions have also sparked a heated debate about social justice in the press, including the legitimacy and morality of private enterprise. In some articles entrepreneurs have been portrayed as latter-day Nepmen (entrepreneurs encouraged for a few short years during Lenin's New Economic Plan) and kulaks (prosperous peasants who were often accused of exploiting other peasants). Many entrepreneurs recall how such people were persecuted in earlier times and fear they will suffer the same fate. According to Oleg Smirnov, a Russian representative of Pepsi-cola: "There is no tradition of law in this country, so some powerful official can strangle a cooperative [private business] in five minutes—there are sixty-four thousand ways to do it."[33]

Many new Russian entrepreneurs are also demonstrating a great deal of initiative, although one study has found them to be more risk averse and less innovative than Americans.[34] Nevertheless, hordes of entrepreneurs, brimming with initiative, have been unleashed in Russia. Their attitude is, "Let's do business." Claimed Herman Sterligov, president of the computerized commodity exchange, The Alysa System, in Moscow: "Every day we have a thousand people who come to our Moscow office saying, 'Please privatize us' or 'I have this idea and I need funding.'"[35]

The new entrepreneurs must also possess energy and stamina to start their own businesses and foster their growth. Some people are pursuing so many opportunities that they seem to work eight days a week. An outstanding example is Sviatoslav Fedorov, who was named Businessman of the Year in 1991 by Moscow Magazine in recognition of his ventures that include eye surgery clinics, medical manufacturing plants, and hotels and casinos.[36] Among the most energetic entrepreneurs are young people who have little experience with the communist regime. In Moscow, for example, teenagers could be found recently washing cars and fetching hamburgers for customers unwilling to wait in line. The most enterprising were earning as much as 300,000 rubles a month when the average monthly wage was less than 10,000. Such individuals "were not tainted by all those years of 'Glory to the Communists'" and they represent "the first generation that will have no doubts about the need for a market economy."[37]

Whereas communist managers struggled tenaciously to accomplish the routine, market-oriented managers, who face immense obstacles, struggle to accomplish the new. There is virtually no legal or economic infrastructure to support private enterprise, and venture capital is extremely limited. The Moscow entrepreneurs, my colleagues and I queried in 1992 cited the unstable political situation and government regulation as the biggest obstacles to doing business.[38] For example, some laws are so ambiguous or rewritten so frequently that it is difficult for firms to develop long-term business strategies.

Honesty and Integrity

> *Effective leaders are viewed as credible and trustworthy because they behave ethically and exhibit honesty and integrity. Honesty means telling the truth, and integrity refers to being consistent in words and actions.*

*Traditional Russian Society.* While there are many basic similarities in the ethical and value systems of Western and Russian people, two important differences stand out. The first one, the dual ethical standard, refers to the way ethics is construed in different situations. In the West, particularly in America, people are expected to employ the same set of ethical standards regardless of the situation. In contrast, in Slavic cultures two sets of ethical standards have developed—one for impersonal or official relationships, and one for personal relationships.[39] In short, there is deception in business dealings, but fealty in friendship. Thus, in Russia, while it would not necessarily be considered unethical to deceive someone in a business transaction to achieve a worthy goal, it would be considered unethical to deceive a friend or trusted colleague. In contrast, in the United States, deception would be considered unethical in both business and personal relationships.

The second feature of the Russian ethical system is the use of blat, informal influence or connections to obtain favors. This practice probably stems from the era of serfdom and bondage that began under Ivan III in 1440 and lasted until The Emancipation Act of 1861. Peasants worked land they did not own, and would curry favor with landowners by bringing them food they had grown.

*The Red Executive.* The dual ethical standard was evident in the distinction made between personal and professional honesty by the managers with whom I studied in Moscow in 1979. They contended that honesty was essential in personal conduct, such as keeping one's word, but that honesty in terms of managing by the rules was considered unrealistic, and even undesirable. The managers agreed that if they tried to abide by all the 80,000 rules and regulations in an average enterprise, they would not accomplish much and would not be successful in their jobs.[40] This duality of ethics helps explain why, under communism, a great many people routinely engaged in behavior that was in violation of the 1961 twelve-point moral code of the communist party.[41] For instance, the relatively common practice of stealing state property from the workplace was certainly not condoned, but it was viewed by most people as less serious than stealing possessions from an individual. Moreover, workers and professionals would deceive managers about production quality and output, and the managers in turn would deceive ministry officials. Enterprises typically would keep two sets of books, one containing actual results for their own records, the other containing information prepared for the ministry. In this way the enterprise would receive its bonuses, while protecting itself from receiving a tight plan or fewer resources. It was a game in which virtually everyone tacitly participated. Such deception was often a matter of survival, and was viewed as a necessary evil.

Another questionable practice stemmed from the use of blat to break through bureaucratic bottlenecks and grease the wheels of the state. Managers would make informal deals to get things done, such as obtain scarce spare parts or obtain authorization for an activity. Personal gifts or needed goods or services produced by the enterprise were the customary methods. Good managers knew the boundary between using blat for the legitimate benefit of the organization as opposed to abusing it for personal gain or other corrupt purposes.

In the communist system, then, a good manager was skilled in manipulating the truth as well as in using blat for the benefit of the enterprise and the individuals who worked in it. At the same time, a good manager did not betray employees and developed a relationship based on personal trust and honesty with them. Managers and employees were like a family with mutually dependent members whose personal and professional lives were intertwined.

*The Market-Oriented Manager.* Ethics and morality have come under much public scrutiny since perestroika and disintegration of the Soviet Union. People have expressed their dismay at the decline in moral values which occurred under the communist regime. Professor Dmitrii Likhachev, considered by many to be the spiritual and moral leader of perestroika, said that a fundamental failing of the Soviet people is "we became used to a double life: we say one thing, but we do the other. We have unlearned how to tell the truth, the full truth."[42] Professor Likhachev attributes this society of deception to the fact that traditional Russian culture was shown disrespect and even destroyed by the communists.[43]

To run their businesses, people are forced to grease the palms of government officials to obtain licenses and permits, as well as of criminal figures who threaten violence if they do not receive a portion of the profits.

Corruption and unethical behavior are rampant in both business and government. Some entrepreneurs are tenaciously trying to hold onto their businesses and keep them from being overtaken by the criminal element. For instance, some private business owners have formed associations to find ways to deal with threats by organized crime. Similarly, a few years ago, one thousand taxi drivers staged a meeting at Vnukovo Airport to discuss how to avoid paying protection money.[44] Still other entrepreneurs have rebuilt their businesses that were sabotaged or closed down by government officials.[45] Yet, most businesses are at the mercy of the mafia, and murders of business people have been reported in the press.[46]

The pervasiveness of corruption associated with "wild capitalism" in Russia makes it extremely difficult for ethically-minded business people to function. To run their businesses, people are forced to grease the palms of government officials to obtain licenses and permits, as well as of criminal figures who threaten violence if they do not receive a portion of the profits. Furthermore, ethical business people frequently endure unfounded criticism from the general public, many of whom hold the stereotype that all entrepreneurs are dishonest and exploitative. Finally, some people who want to conduct business in an ethical manner are prisoners of their experience in the communist period. According to Ira Tatelbaum, an American partner in a Moscow clothing factory, some of his Russian employees still want to do business the old convoluted, underhanded way. Out of habit they use blat, but are learning to appreciate the relative simplicity and straightforwardness associated with standard Western business practices.[47]

## Self-Confidence

*The many demands placed upon leaders require them to have self-confidence in making decisions under uncertainty, directing the work of others, overcoming obstacles, taking risks, and accepting responsibility for mistakes.*

*Traditional Russian Society.* Throughout their history, Russians have been portrayed as having self-confidence that ranged from helplessness to bravado. At one extreme, writers such as Dostoyersky and Gogol have depicted Russians as a pessimistic people who see life as gloomy and hopeless and beyond their control. Some scholars believe this mentality has its origins in religious beliefs that a savior will deliver the people from their plight. At the other extreme are writers who portray Russians as highly confident and adept at outsmarting others. For example, in the nineteenth-century short story by Leskov, The Left-Handed Man, a cross-eyed left-handed Russian craftsman outdid British metalworkers by making shoes for a steel flea they had made for the Tsar.

*The Red Executive.* As in literature and folklore, extremes of self-confidence can also be found among Russian business leaders. During the communist period managers' self-confidence took a blow from the inferior quality of products they produced, yet they took pride in the "big is beautiful" phenomenon of running some of the biggest factories in the world. Russian managers were also the target of sharp criticism by the public. One frustrated citizen even proposed that the entire power structure be replaced by foreigners in the following letter to the editor of a popular magazine:

> Where, for heaven's sake, is there a sensible distribution? When are we going to be well off? With bosses like we've got now—never. I therefore propose that we sack all the apparatchiks from leading posts, all the various factory managers, and all the sundry farm chairman . . . and invite managers and administrators from West Germany, asking them to take over. I figure the situation would improve immediately. If we don't, it's no use anticipating any improvements in three years or even ten. If you remember, in Peter the Great's time we invited plenty of foreigners to Russia to serve and work, and they successfully replaced the arrogant grandees and bureaucrats. It worked great.[48]

*The Market-Oriented Manager.* Among market-oriented managers self-confidence ranges from cynicism about their ability to solve problems, to over-promising what they can actually deliver to their business partners and clients. Low self-confidence may account for the wish that some managers have for others, particularly foreigners, to solve their problems for them. As Vladimir Kachenuyk, a Russian executive, explained:

Low self-confidence may account for the wish that some managers have for others, particularly foreigners, to solve their problems for them.

> [T]he people in the Soviet Union in general have an almost fanatic belief in the United States . . . All the American goods, American experience and ideas, American organization and production management, American technology—outstanding! All of these are being perceived as a panacea which will prove to be the salvation of the Soviet Union.[49]

A call for help from foreigners was expressed more seriously by Eduard Shevarnadze, former Soviet foreign minister, in an appeal for Western investment following the dissolution of the Soviet Union: "We are sure that Russia can be saved by foreign business."[50]

In contrast, the power that high self-confidence has in improving managerial performance is illustrated by the success story of the Cheremushkii Sewing Factory. In the late 1980s, with a boost of self-confidence derived from increased pride in their product, enterprise officials succeeded in having Russian women actually purchase some of the 22 million brassieres they manufactured annually, rather than continue to produce them "for the warehouse." The brassieres had been of high quality, but women refused to wear them because of the stigma of Russian-made goods. A retired American businessperson, Harold Willens conducted an experiment in Moscow whereby he had 50 identical brassieres made in the United States, and then switched half the labels. Those with Russian labels were disparaged by consumers. When the factory managers and ministry officials realized that they offered a high-quality product, they launched a marketing campaign about their "world-class bras" and received an increase in orders as a result.[51]

The music of the market is playing, and many North Americans may find themselves dancing with the bear.

Despite such successes, some highly ambitious entrepreneurs need to guard against becoming overly confident. With many attractive opportunities to explore, and few laws and regulations to control their business dealings, a number of entrepreneurs have adopted a "Wild West" attitude towards doing business. By cutting corners and acting unscrupulously for quick gains, they tarnish the reputation of private enterprise for everyone.

## No More Dancing in the Dark: Some Guidelines

The fall of communism and the reconfiguration of the Russian political and economic system have created many promising opportunities for doing business with Russians. This trend is likely to continue. The music of the market is playing, and many

North Americans may find themselves dancing with the bear. Whether Russian partners come from established state enterprises or from fledging entrepreneurial firms, I hope this portrait describes them sufficiently to avoid the feeling of dancing in the dark. However, for those still unsure about taking the first step, let us look at ways that this portrait of Russian leaders can help Western firms build effective business partnerships. The following guidelines should help create a favorable impression on Russians by showing sensitivity to the way Russians perceive themselves and do business. In addition, these guidelines should enable Westerners to develop the appropriate responses and behaviors to make interactions with Russian business leaders go smoothly.

**First, relieve Russians of responsibility for unforeseen negative consequences.** Power, responsibility, and decision making are typically centralized in Russian organizations, and many executives have difficulty delegating authority. Russian managers at all levels are accustomed to exercising power without being challenged by subordinates, but they hesitate to act, even on trivial matters, if they fear being held responsible for decisions that have not been explicitly approved by the head of the organization or not been prescribed in standard procedures. Consequently, it is easier for Russians to take action if their partners relieve them of responsibility for unforeseen negative consequences. They should be assured that someone else will bear the responsibility. This unconventional approach is part of the risk associated with doing business with Russian partners, and it is important to exercise judgment about the particular situations in which it is appropriate.

**Second, avoid appearing exploitative, and respect collectivistic attitudes.** Russian business leaders have had much of their drive suppressed by communal traditions and attitudes passed on from peasant society, as well as by the egalitarian principles of communist ideology and the stultifying bureaucracy of the centrally planned economic system. Three of the five components of drive—achievement, ambition, and initiative—have been denigrated in Russia. People with a high need for achievement have been condemned for being individualistic, antisocial, and enemies of the people. Personal ambition has been met with envy, vindictiveness, and derision. And initiative has usually been received with indifference, at best, and punishment, at worst. Negative attitudes towards these characteristics are so deeply ingrained in the Russian psyche that many Russians who want to realize their ambitions feel pressure from two sources—public scorn and their own guilt from violating the values they were raised with.

Foreign joint ventures have also been the target of such criticism. Some Russians view them as "a convenient front for those trying to make money . . . as fast as possible."[52] Therefore, when working with Russians, foreign firms should avoid presenting an image that could be construed as exploitative of individual Russians or of their society. In addition, foreign firms should respect their Russian colleagues' requests to avoid publicizing their achievements, material possessions, or privileges. They simply don't want to arouse feelings of envy or guilt, since the egalitarian norm of social justice is still strong. However, Western firms should take their cues from their Russian colleagues because some of them may be more open about their accomplishments and may want recognition and approval.

**Third, stress the importance and urgency of taking action.** Russian leaders have two components of drive in abundance: energy and tenacity. They are used to hard work, can call upon large reserves of energy when required, and they are capable of persevering in spite of immense obstacles. In the words of Sviatoslav Fedorov, the highly successful surgeon-cum-entrepreneur: "The notion that all Russian workers are stupid or lazy is nonsense. But what can you expect if the government takes away property and forces them to live like domestic animals?"[53]

> Westerners should consider it their duty to uphold the highest standards of business practice as a service to Russians who are learning the ways of the world economy.

To spur Russian partners to action, then, Westerners should emphasize the importance and urgency of the situation, and stress that the Russians' utmost effort is needed to ensure success. This appeal should also be accompanied by valuable material rewards. The noted Russian economist, Pavel Bunich, commented that Russians who work in Western joint ventures will work hard as long as they are rewarded sufficiently to compensate for the absence of security and benefits they had enjoyed without exerting much effort in state-owned enterprises. Says Bunich, "Who would otherwise want to lose benefits more or less guaranteed by the state?"[54]

**Fourth, forge personal relationships.** As in any interpersonal interaction, integrity and honesty are crucial for developing a lasting and rewarding relationship with Russian business colleagues. Developing mutual trust and respect with them presents special challenges in light of some Russian practices that violate Western ethical sensibilities. One way to shape ethical behavior is by effectively using the Russian concept of dual ethics. This involves making a genuine and serious effort to forge a strong personal relationship with Russian colleagues, rather than maintaining an arms-length, formal business relationship. An approach of strengthening personal ties is more likely to trigger the ethical behavior, loyalty, and trust that Russians show their closest friends, family members, and colleagues. The tendency, if it existed at all, for Russians to see foreigners as simply impersonal business contacts to be duped and exploited, should be greatly reduced.

**Fifth, uphold the highest standards of business practice.** Another approach to developing an ethically sound business relationship with your Russian counterparts is to instill respect for business ethics, protocol, and accepted business practices. The market economy is such a new phenomenon in Russia that few people have a complete understanding of its complexities. Furthermore, many otherwise sophisticated Russians are unaware of the official legislation, as well as the unofficial accepted business practices, that keep a potentially destructive free market in check. Westerners should consider it their duty to uphold the highest standards of business practice as a service to Russians who are learning the ways of the world economy. For example, it would be useful to demonstrate how standard Western business procedures eliminate the need to use connections (blat) and underhanded methods of doing business.

**Sixth, encourage joint problem solving.** It is important to have an awareness of the two extremes of self-confidence that Russian colleagues might exhibit. In some cases, low self-confidence may lead them to look to their Western partners to solve problems and provide needed resources. To develop a mutually beneficial long-term relationship, however, it is better for all concerned to take the time to make decisions and resolve issues together. Such an approach, while time consuming, provides a stronger foundation for developing expertise and commitment of both sides.

**Seventh, develop a concrete action plan.** On some occasions Russians may engage in seemingly impulsive or reckless behavior resulting from overconfidence or bravado. Because of inexperience they may not fully understand the complexities of a situation, and may overestimate their ability to deal with it successfully, or overlook the steps involved in putting an idea into practice. In such cases it would be helpful to develop a concrete action with them to ascertain the feasibility of their ideas.

## Notes

1. "Moscow magazine's top 50," *Moscow Magazine,* December 1991/January 1992, 52–57.

2. Many Russians believe that there are specific traits characterizing successful women managers. These traits are discussed in S. M. Puffer, "Women managers in the former USSR: A case of 'too much Equality'?" in N. J. Adler and D. N. Izraeli, eds., *Competitive frontiers: Women managers in a global economy* (Cambridge, MA: Blackwell, 1993).

3. S. A. Kirkpatrick and E. A. Locke, "Leadership: Do traits matter?" *The Academy of Management Executive, 5*(2), 1991, 48–60. Two cognitive traits identified by these researchers, cognitive ability and knowledge of the business, are not discussed in this article, which focuses on motivational traits.

4. This term is taken from D. Granick, *The red executive* (Garden City, NY: Doubleday Anchor, 1962).

5. The discussion of the communist period will focus mostly on senior executives in manufacturing organizations, since the industrial sector was the most emphasized and the most prestigious. Conditions in other sectors such as services and R&D were largely comparable.

6. We will look at executives who are transforming their state-owned enterprises into various forms of private and employee ownership, as well as entrepreneurs who have founded start-up businesses. In 1992, 46,000 enterprises were wholly or partially privatized, bringing the total to six percent of Russian industry (*Economic Newsletter, Russian Research Center, 16*(6), February 20, 1993). Despite this small percentage, privatization efforts are expected to increase dramatically over the next few years. For a comparison of managers in the former Soviet Union with Eastern European managers, see A. Shama, "Management under fire: The transformation of managers in the Soviet Union and Eastern Europe," *The Academy of Management Executive, 7*(1), 1993, 22–35.

7. M. Mead, *Soviet attitudes toward authority* (New York, NY: William Morrow and Company, 1955); G. Gorer and J. Rickman, *The people of Great Russia: A psychological study* (New York, NY: Norton, 1949/1962).

8. N. Vakar, *The taproot of Soviet society* (New York, NY: Harper, 1962), 47.

9. Vakar, *ibid.*

10. H. Kuromiya, "Edinonachalie and the Soviet Industrial Manager 1928–1937," *Soviet Studies, 36*(2), 1984, 185–204.

11. C. A. Vlachoutsicos, "Key Soviet management concepts for the American reader," in

P. R. Lawrence and C. A. Vlachoutsicos, eds., *Behind the factory walls: Decision making in Soviet* and *U.S. enterprises* (Boston, MA: Harvard Business School Press, 1990), 76.

12. N. A. Kaniskin. "The Western executive and the Soviet executive: A talk with Nikolai A. Kaniskin," in S. M. Puffer, ed., *The Russian management revolution: Preparing managers for the market economy* (Armonk, NY: M. E. Sharpe, 1992), 41–51.

13. D. McCarthy, S. M. Puffer, and S. V. Shekshnia, "The resurgence of an entrepreneurial class in Russia," *Journal of Management Inquiry, 1993, 2*(2), 125–137.

14. D. J. McCarthy and S. M. Puffer, "Perestroika at the plant level: Managers' job attitudes and views of decision making in the former USSR," *Columbia Journal of World Business, 1992, 27*(1), 86–99.

15. P. R. Gregory, "Soviet bureaucratic behavior: Khozyaistvenniki and Apparatchiki," *Soviet Studies,* October 1989, 511–525.

16. J. B. Shaw, C. D. Fisher, and W. A. Randolph, "From maternalism to accountability: The changing cultures of Ma Bell and Mother Russia," *The Academy of Management Executive, 5*(1), 1991, 7–20.

17. L. Maynard, *Russia in flux* (New York, NY: Macmillan, 1948), 30.

18. W. D. Connor, "Equality of opportunity," in A. Jones, W. D. Connor, and D. E. Powell, eds., *Soviet social problems.* Boulder, CO: Westview, 1991), 137-153.

19. A. Sobchak, cited in H. Smith, *The New Russians* (New York, NY: Random House, 1990), 204.

20. N. Shmelev, speech to the Third Congress of People's Deputies, March 12, 1990, reported in *Foreign Broadcast Information Service* (FBIS). March 14, 1990.

21. V. O. Kliuchevskii, *Collected works.* Vol. 1 (Moscow: Mysl, 1987), 312.

22. Kliuchevskii, *op. cit.,* 315.

23. L. B. Forker, "Quality: American, Japanese, and Soviet perspectives*," The Academy of Management Executive, 5*(4), 1991, 63–74.

24. P. R. Gregory, "Productivity, slack, and time theft in the Soviet economy," in J. R. Millar ed., *Politics, work, daily life in the USSR: A survey of former Soviet citizens* (Cambridge: Cambridge University Press, 1987), 241–275.

25. S. M. Puffer and V. I. Ozira, Capital investment decisions, in P. R. Lawrence and C.A. Vlachoutsicos, eds., *op. cit.,* 1990, 183–226.

26. P. R. Lawrence and C. A. Vlachoutsicos, "Managerial patterns: Differences and commonalities," in P. R. Lawrence and C. A. Vlachoutsicos, eds., *op. cit.,* 1990, 271–286.

27. J. M. Ivancevich, R. S. DeFrank, and P. R. Gregory, "The Soviet enterprise director: An important resource before and after the coup." *The Academy of Management Executive, 6*(1), 1992, 42–55.

28. S. M. Puffer, Unpublished field notes for *Behind the factory walls: Decision making in Soviet and U.S. enterprises* (Boston, MA: Harvard Business School Press, 1990). Notes dated 1988.

29. W. L. Tullar, "Cultural transformation: democratization and Russian entrepreneurial motives." Paper presented at the Academy of Management meetings. Las Vegas, 1992.

30. D. J. McCarthy, S. M. Puffer, and S. V. Shekshnia, *op. cit.,* 1993.

31. F. Barringer, Comment at the conference, Chautauqua at Pitt: The Fifth General Chautauqua Conference on U.S. and Soviet Relations, October 30, 1989. Cited in H. Smith. *The new Russians* (New York: Random House, 1990), 203.

32. N. Shmelev, "New Anxieties," in A. Jones and W. Moskoff, eds., The great market debate in Soviet economics (Armonk, NY: M.E. Sharpe, 1991), 3–35; quote from p. 34.

33. O. Smirnov, cited in H. Smith, *op. cit.,* 1990, 285.

34. W. L. Tullar, *op. cit.,* 1992.

35. H. Sterligov, cited in P. Klebnikov, "A market grows in Russia," *Forbes,* June 8, 1992. 79–82: quote from p. 79.

36. P. Hotheinz. "The Pied Piper of capitalism," *Moscow Magazine,* December 1991/January 1992, 50, 51; R. I. Kirkland, *op. cit.,* 1990.

37. A. Lasov, cited in J. Auerbach, "Coming of age in capitalistic Russia*," The Boston Globe,* January 4, 1993, 20, 21.

38. D. J. McCarthy, S. M. Puffer, and S. V. Shekshnia, *op. cit.,* 1993.

39. V. D. Lefebvre, *Algebra of conscience: A comparative analysis of Western and Soviet ethical systems* (Boston, MA: D. Reidel Publishing Company, 1982).

40. S. M. Puffer, "Inside a Soviet management institute," *California Management Review, 24*(1), 1981, 90–96.

41. R. T. DeGeorge, *Soviet ethics and morality* (Ann Arbor, MI: The University of Michigan Press, 1969).

42. D. S. Likhachev, "Trevogi sovesti" ("Pangs of conscience"), *Literaturnaia Gazeta,* January 1, 1987.

43. D. S. Likhachev, "Ot Pokaianiia—K Deistviiu" ("From repentance—to action"),

*Literaturnaia Gazeta,* September 9, 1987. For a summary in English of these two articles by Likhachev, see V. Krasnov, "Dmitrii Likhachev on morality, religion, and Russian heritage," *Russia beyond Communism: A chronicle of national rebirth* (Boulder, CO: Westview Press, 1991), 81–86.

44. P. C. Roberts and K. LaFollette, *Meltdown: Inside the Soviet economy* (Washington, DC: Cato Institute, 1990), 97.

45. A. Jones and W. Moskoff, *Ko-ops: The rebirth of entrepreneurship in the Soviet Union* (Bloomington, IN: Indiana University Press, 1991), 66–70.

46. V. Volokhov, "Ubivaiut Vsekh Podriad" ("People Are Being Murdered One After the Other"), *Novoe Russkoe Slovo,* 13–14 February, 1993, 15.

47. I. Tatelbaum, unpublished interview by Kara Danehy, Northeastern University, Boston, August, 1992.

48. A. Kononov, Letter to the editor of *Sobesednik,* 31, August 1990. Translated in J. Riordan and S. Bridger, eds., *Dear comrade editor: Readers' letters to the Soviet Press under Perestroika* (Bloomington, IN: Indiana University Press, 1992), 230.

49. V. A. Kachenuyk, cited in C. M. Vance and A. V. Zhuplev, "Myths About Doing Business in the Soviet Union: An Interview with Vladimir A. Kachenuyk, Deputy Director, Moscow Personnel Center," *Journal of Management Inquiry, 1*(1), 1992, 66–69.

50. E. Shevardnadze, cited in "The Dark Forces are Growing Stronger," *Time,* October 5, 1992, 64, 65.

51. R. Parker, "Inside the Collapsing Soviet Economy," *The Atlantic Monthly,* June 1990, 68–76.

52. B. Alexseyev, "Joint Ventures: Is the Formula Right?" *Soviet Life,* October 1991, 41.

53. S. Fedorov, cited in R. I. Kirkland, "Curing Communism," *Moscow Magazine,* October 1990, 64–68. Quote from p. 67.

54. P. Bunich, cited in B. Alexseyev, *op. cit.,* October 1991, p. 41.

# Reading 2.6

# CONTRASTS IN CULTURE

## *Russian and Western Perspectives on Organizational Change*

SNEJINA MICHAILOVA


### Executive Overview

When Westerners enter Russian companies, either by acquiring shares in existing ones or by making greenfield investments, they plan, initiate, carry out, and manage ambitious and fundamental organizational changes. In the complex process of planning change, they often face serious difficulties and experience clashes with the local managers and employees.

This article focuses on planning change in Russian companies with foreign participation. Based on extensive interviews with Russians and Westerners in five companies, it identifies four major obstacles arising in that process: the variety of roles in the change process, the need for developing common understandings, the manner in which vision is communicated in the organization, and the importance of symbols and signals in the process of planning and carrying out organizational changes. The article addresses these themes from both Russian and Western perspectives. It presents a number of practical lessons and guidelines for Western owners, managers, and expatriates in Russian companies.


After the break-up of the Soviet Union and the collapse of communism in 1991, Russia began to open its economy and attract the interest of foreign investors. As the country with the largest territory in the world, with a population of approximately 150 million, and a wealth of attractive natural resources, Russia offers enormous opportunities that might have a significant influence on future international business. At the same time, however, with a weak legal system, an unpredictable economy, and short-lived governments, Russia has the reputation as a country with paradoxical realities and shocking experiences, a country that is in a systematic collapse and general chaos, and is one of the most difficult markets to enter.[1] In the words of Marshall Goldman, an expert on the Russian economy, Russia is predictable in the sense that it will continue to be unpredictable. Others describe it as a combination of contradictions and a unity of opposites.[2] There is the need to know how these phenomena are reflected in Russian management practice and what that would imply for Westerners[3] engaged in Russian enterprises.

Significant contrasts between cultures do exist[4] and do indeed make a difference, often substantial, in the way managers and workers behave in organizations.[5] The cultures of some countries, such as Russia, are especially difficult for Westerners to understand: Westerners and Russians differ not merely in terms of national culture, but also in the economic, political, ideological, religious, and social systems from which they come.

When a company establishes itself in a foreign country, the new organization will reflect certain features of both host and foreign country elements.[6] The interface between foreign and host country personnel, on the one hand, and between the foreign company and the host country environment, on the other, are of critical importance for the organization exposed to a variety of intercultural issues. Although the debate on whether Western management principles and practices are applicable in an alien environment is not new,[7] a substantial number of management models implicitly assume that Western management approaches and techniques can easily be transferred across borders.

The findings in this article support the argument that managerial knowledge and practices are contextually embedded. They reflect attitudes, values, and norms of the society where they have been developed, and might, therefore, be limited in their applicability elsewhere. Even though Western managerial practices have proved to be superior in a number of countries with developed market economies, they do not suggest the one best way for managing organizations-even less so in societies such as those in the former Soviet Union.[8] The uncritical application of Western management philosophies and practices in alternative cultural settings neglects cultural diversity and ignores the potential for learning and development processes rooted in national, business, and management cultures.[9]

This article looks predominantly at differences in perceptions, understandings, work patterns, and behaviors adopted by Russians and Westerners in Russian-Western organizational settings. It emphasizes the contrasts, although certain similarities between these two groups also exist. The intention is not merely to focus on obvious differences, but to discover underlying intents. Since Russia is an extremely diverse country in terms of races, cultures, regions, religions, and languages, the conclusions drawn here are valid mainly for the specific settings analyzed in the article. However, the findings and conclusions can be extrapolated to a larger sample of organizations where Westerners and Russians work together.

From 1996 to 1999, I collected data from five Russian companies with Western participation. Written and video material about the companies, observations, informal conversations, and interviews were among the instruments applied. I carried out 37 open-ended, face-to-face interviews with organizational members, 24 of them with Russians and 13 with Westerners. Most of the respondents were top and middle managers, since these constitute the most important and potentially most influential and powerful organizational subpopulation in terms of planning and initiating change.[10] The following section introduces the five companies by providing contextual details relevant for understanding the process of planning change.

## Five Russian Organizations

Established in the 1920s, Oilgas[11] is a Russian project organization operating in the oil and gas industry. Following changes in Russian legislation, it was transformed into a joint stock company in 1992. After 70 years of existence, the company's prospects were rather negative. The problems on the Soviet market were grave and the year-long practice of delivering to nonpaying clients was discouraging. The most probable outcome at that maturity stage of the life cycle would have been destruction,[12] whereby the company would go bankrupt, be taken over, or merge with another company. But in 1996, a large multinational enterprise with West European origins acquired shares in Oilgas. The majority of Oilgas's shares belonged to the Russian state. The company employed 750 people with an average age of 45. The average age at the management level was over 55, and 160 organizational members were pensioners—women over 55 and men over 60. Six expatriates from various Western countries were assigned to key management positions in Oilgas. The CEO was a Russian who occupied the position for the last 10 years. In 1996, only nine employees in Oilgas spoke English and only one of the six Western expatriates spoke Russian. The long-term aim, as formulated by the Westerners in Oilgas, was to transform the company into an engineering organization, able to deliver to Western clients.

Teleon is a five-year-old Russian company in the telecommunications sector. A minor part of its shares belonged to a Western company with long-term activities in the Russian market and a major part to a Russian shareholder. Teleon employed 70 people with an average age of 30. A Westerner was assigned to work in Teleon as a controller. He was present in the company full time for the first three years and half time for the following year. By 2000, the Western presence in the everyday life of Teleon was almost nonexistent. The CEO, who joined the company one year after it was established, was Russian, as was his management team. The managers in Teleon spoke English.

**Table 1** Overview of the Companies

| *Firm* | *Industry* | *Firm's age (years)* | *Western shareholder's years in Russia* | *Number of employees* | *CEO's nationality* | *Top management team* | *Main shareholders* |
|---|---|---|---|---|---|---|---|
| Oilgas | Oil and gas | 79 | 4 | 745 | Russian | Westerners and Russians | Russian government |
| Teleon | Telecommunications | 5 | 5 | 70 | Russian | Russians | Russian organization |
| Construct | Construction | 30 | 1 | 560 | Western | Westerners | Western company |
| Trans | Transport | 7 | 7 | 25 | Western | Westerners | Western company |
| Equip | Equipment | 6 | 6 | 100 | Western | Westerners | Western company |

Construct is the result of the takeover of part of a Russian factory in the construction industry by a large Western company. Construct employed 560 people. A team of six Westerners occupied the key management positions—the CEO and the vice-CEO posts and the positions of production, financial, marketing, and personnel directors. One of the Westerners spoke Russian fluently and the others were learning Russian. None of the Russians in Construct spoke English, except a few secretaries hired after the takeover.

Trans was established when a large Western company with international operations started its activities in Russia in 1992. Trans operated in the transport industry and employed 25 people in two Russian cities. The largest office employed 16 people with an average age of 26. The key management positions were occupied by four Westerners who did not speak Russian. All Russian employees spoke English, as this was one of the selection criteria for their employment.

Equip was started in 1993 as a greenfield investment by an internationally operating Western company in the equipment industry. Approximately 100 people were employed in Equip's production unit and sales office. The CEO was a Westerner, as were the members of the management team. Equip presented a mixed picture in terms of English language abilities—some spoke English and some did not. An overview of the five companies and their key characteristics is presented in Table 1.

Two of the Russian companies, Oilgas and Construct, had been operating as state-owned organizations in the centrally planned economy. They were stable, formalized, and bureaucratic. Their cultures were monolithic and dominated by the managers. Conformity contributed to their repeating past experiences. Top-down management and one-man authority were combined with strong and lasting relationships among organizational members. In 2000, these two companies were in the process of rebirth, and their struggle to survive was aided by a strong injection of capital and know-how by the respective Western partners. Teleon, Trans, and Equip were established after the collapse of the centrally planned economic system and, consequently, did not bear the burden of the socialist past. However, many of the managers and employees working for these companies had been influenced by the experiences of a socialist past, and some relied heavily on these experiences.

In the cases of Oilgas and Construct, the investors considered the rich experience of the respective Russian partner in the particular industry, the partner's reputation and position in the Soviet market, and the importance of existing personal networks and relationships. In the cases of Trans and Equip, the Western investors preferred that the Russian employees have no considerable previous experience, were young, well-educated, and able to speak English. Teleon was formed at the outset of the business in which the company operated. In this case, the Western investor relied mainly on the Western managers' personal contacts in Russia.

## Critical Issues in Planning Change

Based on the data generated in these companies, Figure 1 proposes a model of planning change in Russian companies with Western participation.

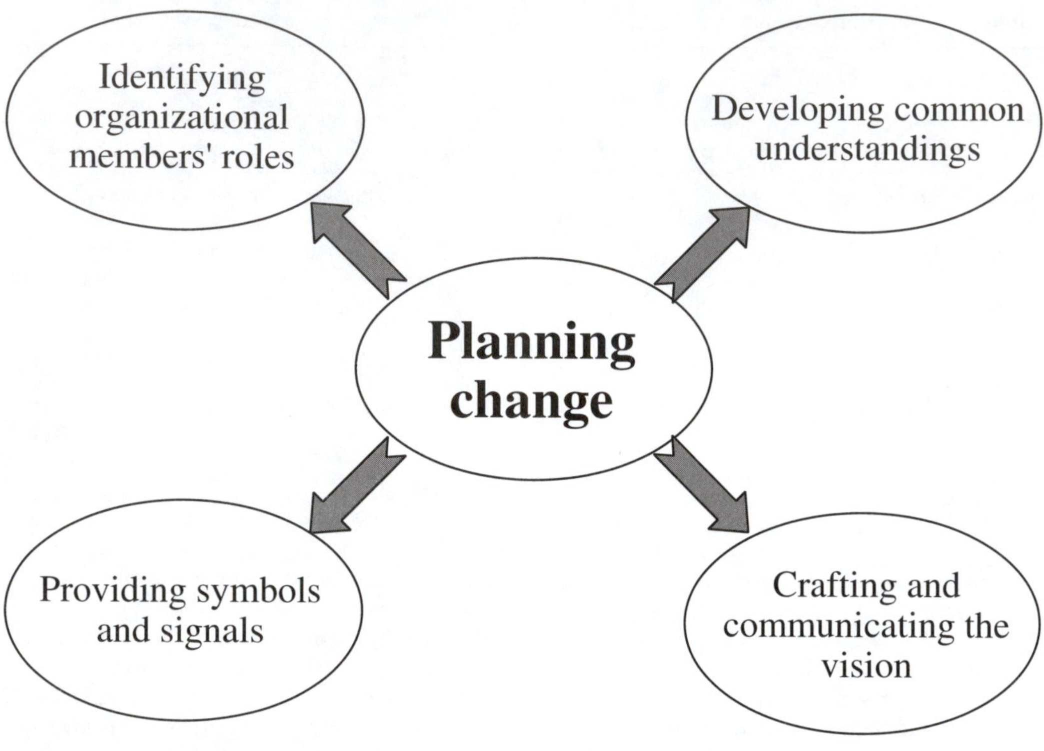


**Figure 1** Planning Change in Russian Companies With Western Partners

The model identifies the major issues that appear to be most problematic in these Western-Russian organizational settings.

The four issues illustrated in Figure 1 are not iterative stages in the change process. The emphasis on issues varies in different cases and over time. Additionally, since change is complex, nonlinear and unfolding in nature, organizations move back and forth between these issues, some of which are likely to occur simultaneously or stop and start again. Moreover, the processes of planning change cannot be separated from those of implementation: the managers' task is also to ensure that the planned changes actually occur.[13]

The following sections provide an analysis of the variety of roles in the organizational change process, examine difficulties in developing common understandings, focus on key features related to crafting and communicating the vision of the organization, and point out the relevance of symbols and signals sent and received. Examples let the reader hear some of the voices of Russians and Westerners from the five companies. Each section concludes with action-oriented guidelines addressed mainly to Westerners.

## Identifying Roles in the Change Process

Planned change is associated with transformational rather than incremental change. Whereas the former refers to major shifts in the strategy of the organization, the latter refers to gradual change within the routines and paradigms of those in the organization.[14] Planning and managing change is related to organizational politics and the various roles played by organizational members.[15] The following three subsections analyze the roles of Western expatriates, Russian managers, and Russian employees in the process of planning change in the five companies.

### *Western Expatriates: Change Strategists*

In each of the companies, the Western expatriates established strong coalitions among themselves soon after they were assigned to work in Russia. They form a kind of clan culture,[16] although lasting relationships among them were rare. The clan consisted of enthusiasts united around the potential of an idea or vision, and respected diversity, complexity, and fluidity. The Western expatriates identified the need for change, crafted the vision, defined the nature of the change, and decided on its feasibility. They developed specific work plans, schedules, and budgets.

In Construct, Trans, and Equip, the top manager was a Westerner, as were the members of the top management team. In the case of Oilgas, where the CEO was Russian, the change vision and strategy was developed by the Westerners working there. Teleon had a Russian management team, but the main initiative and the key concepts in terms of further change and development were designed by the foreign investor. When the Russian team in Teleon came up with more strategically oriented suggestions, these were discussed with and approved by the Westerners in a dialogue with the Russian shareholder. The transformation activities in all five Russian organizations were heavily financed by the Western partners.

One of the main obstacles to identifying roles in the change process was the way Western expatriates were perceived by Russian employees and managers. Westerners were viewed as capital deliverers, consultants, or outsiders, even in the cases where the companies were started by Westerners. This reinforced the us-versus-them attitude, made the communication links within the respective organization fragile, jeopardized the integrity of joint actions, and left a significant imprint on future cooperation.

Another concern shared by the Western respondents was that, even if they took the opportunity to demonstrate and implement their transformation vision at the organizational level, the company environment did not change, at least not with the same speed as the organization's. Their frustration was caused by the discrepancy between their strong belief that the environment could be transformed and the reality they encountered in Russia. According to the field data, Russians seemed to prefer adapting to the environment instead of trying to transform it. Russians have been found to perceive their physical and social environment as having a narrow zone of assured safety (where the environment is considered friendly and secure), a larger zone of uncertainty (containing a mixture of good and danger), and a huge zone of danger (the part of the environment that primarily contains hazards).[17] Both Westerners and Russians in the companies seemed to have accepted the existence of the different realities, their organizations and the outside environment, and to have learned their intricate rules.

A related problem was handling the organization-environment relationship. One of the change strategist's main tasks is to deal with the environment. However, this is exactly what the Western expatriates found difficult in Russia: they defined the environment as very different, alien, sometimes impossible, and absolutely unpredictable. They needed to have the insiders' view and knowledge of a number of issues when dealing with other Russian organizations, authorities, or the public. At the same time, the Russian top managers' perspective on developing the change vision and strategy was not as refined as that of the Westerners. Only one company in the study, Teleon, successfully integrated the advantages of the locals and the foreigners.

Identifying key persons in the change process and clarifying the distribution of tasks and responsibilities are critical in the process of planning change. At Oilgas, the Western expatriates applied an approach that functioned very well in the Russian context, appointing a person from the expatriates' group as transformation director, although he and the Russians defined his functions and responsibilities in completely different ways. The Russians claimed that they would know whom to blame if the transformation did not work, which was in line with the centralization approach and the one-man authority style. In contrast, the transformation director saw his own role and responsibility as an enthusiastic, positive thinker who dealt mainly with relationships and who, of course, could not be solely responsible for Oilgas's transformation.

Since planning change is related to the issue of power and coalitions, a meaningful question would be: with whom should the Western expatriates establish coalitions? In the cases where the CEO was a Russian, it was important to convince him to work for the change initiated by the Western expatriates. Westerners in Oilgas adopted this approach from the very beginning, as did Westerners in Construct before they took over part of the existing Russian factory. The Western controller in Teleon, however, who spoke Russian, started at the bottom of the organization and made his way up to the CEO gradually: "The Russians prepared a nice office for me at the end of the corridor, but I asked them to move me to one that had a much worse design but a more central location. This is how I got to know the people quite well. Then gradually, I worked my way up to the management level. But before I reached the top people, they were quite impressed by my relationship and contacts with the shop-floor employees."

Once the potential partners in the coalition have been identified, the question arises: how to establish the coalition? To assume that the formal organizational chart reflects the real power distribution would be wrong. The problem for the Westerners in these companies was that they were hardly involved in the informal life of the organization. Participating in company parties or other social events would give the Westerners much more information about which individuals and groups set agendas at critical junctures and really make the decisions; who among the Russians is more influential; who is more respected; who communicates with whom; who is avoiding whom; what rumors are circulating. In terms of establishing coalitions, this would be highly relevant information, but information difficult to obtain formally at the meeting table.

A number of authors highlight the importance of personal relationships and trust in the Russian context,[18] and these issues often cause another difficulty for Western expatriates, who typically do not interact with Russian managers in other Russian companies. Westerners establish very good relationships among themselves within the companies as well as across them. They tend to share problems and exchange experiences, however, only among themselves, not with Russians. Friendships between Westerners and Russians would be of great benefit and value in the Russian organizational context.[19] Although establishing intimate friendships is a long, energy-consuming and difficult process, investing in friendships is worthwhile, especially since Russians regard friends[20] as people whom they can trust fully.

### *Russian Managers: Change Implementers in an Ambiguous Position*

Russians and Westerners view change differently, as illustrated by the following comments:

> I often say that each general director should be sent to the Canary Islands for three to four months and be left there without connection to his company. If the company changes in a negative direction, the director must be fired. If the company develops positively, he must also be fired. If everything goes on without any changes, he must receive a bonus, because this would mean that he has established standards and procedures that work effectively.
>
> —Russian CEO, Teleon

> They [Western expatriates] only talk about changes. How about not changing, and maintaining what we already have?
>
> —Russian middle manager, Construct

> There is so much that needs to be changed, actually everything—from the reconstruction of the building, introduction of new qualifications and skills, to changing attitudes and values.
>
> —Western expatriate, Construct

They also differ about their roles in the change process:

> I do not like the Western-Russian separation, but it is there. It goes in various aspects. We work together in terms of space, but that is it. We are very, very different. They [Westerners] have the power, because they have money. They invest in our company according to contract and that is fine.
>
> —Russian middle manager, Oilgas

> My role as transformation director is internal. I am a change agent, but I am somehow treated as a consultant. My clients are people from the organization, mainly from the top.
>
> —Western expatriate, Oilgas

The Russian top and middle managers acted mainly as change implementers[21] in the day-to-day change process. Since the Russian managers were not actually involved in developing the change strategy, they were motivated to implement it either because they believed in it or because they were told to. While both motivations were found in the studied companies, the data strongly suggest that the main motivation for implementing change came from following orders.

In Oilgas and Construct, the Western management teams forced the Russian managers to change the roles in which they had been trapped for years and which shaped their identities as managers. The Western managers demanded radical changes in their Russian colleagues' leadership style and ways of communicating and motivating. The Russian employees, however, preferred that their managers preserve the long-term alliances they had built with them in the socialist past.[22] This created a great deal of ambiguity for Russian managers—"should they serve the tsar or should they serve the people?"[23] The older Russian managers and employees in Equip and Teleon dealt with the same dilemma, incorporating experiences from previous work places into the organization. The mentality and spirit of paternalism remained very strong. A CEO of a traditional Russian organization can still be compared with the largest matrioshka doll who holds all the other managers and workers,[24] and enjoys the support and trust of the workers on many different occasions.[25] As a result, Russian managers in companies with foreign participation are not completely sure of their roles, and how they should meet the various expectations from their Western colleagues and superiors and their Russian colleagues and subordinates.[26]

Moreover, the very idea of change is alien to many of the interviewed Russian managers. They explicitly claimed that the manager's task is to establish procedures that ensure continuity. They defined the change projects initiated by the Westerners as "losing the ground, because there are so many changes at the same time," or "not understandable, since the managers' task is to secure the stability of the organization."

#### *Russian Employees: Forced to Change But Choosing to Resist*

The majority of Russian employees in the studied companies regarded openness as inappropriate behavior. Afraid of how their superiors would understand and interpret what they said, they preferred to keep their opinions to themselves. Their initiative and ambition had been denigrated for decades by a system that tolerated gray, drab, and conventional people, and excluded those oriented towards personal achievement. Disobedient and independently thinking employees were regarded as conflict-prone, or as antisocial personalities, and were often called "enemies of the people."[27]

Russian employees in the studied companies were not involved in planning change. They felt uncomfortable and claimed they were being forced to change. If the Western expatriates had been removed from the management groups, it is likely that organizational change in all five companies would have either stopped completely or slowed down considerably. The employees' participation in decision making was relatively limited.[28] Some of them agreed ostensibly with the change, but since they did not commit to it, they were only passively in favor of it. Many employees were partly dissatisfied with the former management system; however, they did not consider the new alternatives proposed by the Western investors to be much more promising. Therefore, it is difficult to draw a clear distinction between passive resistance to change and passive support for change. Passive and covert resistance to change is the most serious problem for Western expatriates to cope with: employees may agree to change, but their agreement is, in truth, rejection, and they cannot be counted on.[29]

Actions for Westerners in
Developing Roles in the Change Process

- Create a coalition with the Russian top managers based on trust and oriented towards a long-term friendship.
- Get actively involved in the social life of the company. Attend the parties organized by Russian colleagues. Establish good informal relationships with people who may be strong supporters of the change activities, and do not form coalitions merely by following the formal organizational chart.
- Expand the circle of interactions beyond the relationships with other Western colleagues and establish contacts with Russian managers in Russian companies without foreign participation. This will help gain a deeper understanding of the Russians' behavior in a Westerner's own organization.
- Remember that Russian managers are in a highly ambiguous situation. What a Westerner wants from them is often the opposite of what their Russian subordinates expect them to do. Be sensitive to the fact that Russian managers greatly value stability and continuity.
- Remember that Russian employees have been subject to ideological changes with no substantive basis in the past and tend to extrapolate these experiences into the present. Therefore, be prepared for passive resistance to change from shop-floor employees.

### Developing Common Understandings

The diversity of meanings generated by the same words is a highly significant issue in organizational life. People's understandings are not uniform, and notions and terms are not used in a vacuum. They involve different associations in different cultural environments. In that sense, notions themselves might be viewed as cultural artifacts and language as a means of communication in a particular culture rather than a universal means of communication. Where different cultures interact, language is a guide for classifying reality into perceptual units that make a difference for people in the culture.[30] Russians and Westerners note major differences in the meanings of a number of words and phrases. Significantly, many words in the Western management vocabulary, such as planning, decision making, and teamwork, evoke different mental images. Terms like market, profit, and money often sound

**Table 2** Views of Time

| *Russians* | *Westerners* |
|---|---|
| Value the past and admire history | Value the present and the future |
| Have a very high respect for traditions | Believe that traditions slow down the pace of progress |
| Refer frequently to previous experiences | Focus on action and prefer exploring new things |

negative in Russia, since they connote social injustice and chaos.[31] The variety of meanings as such does not lead to a quandary: The problem is the failure to clarify and agree on the meanings and the consequent failure to reach a common understanding. This causes a great deal of uncertainty in interactions, often with a heavy impact on organizational life.

The following examples from the field are important in planning change. They focus particularly on how time, planning, and control were interpreted by Russians and Westerners in the studied companies.

Understanding of Time

> The past is there and we cannot simply eliminate it, even though some try to do so. The past is a fact and we have to deal with it.
>
> —Russian CEO, Oilgas

> One should not forget that this company has been existing for years. It may be fine to change, and restructure, but we should look back more often and remember how it was.
>
> —Russian middle manager, Construct

> In order to develop, one should look forward. We are oriented towards the future and this helps us survive.
>
> —Western expatriate, Trans

Time is perceived differently by the Russians and Westerners who participated in the study. (See Table 2).

The Russian respondents frequently referred to their experiences and the traditional Russian way of handling situations. Whereas efficiency, predictability, professionalism, and modernity are seen as key forces for rationality in the West,[32] belief in fate and destiny reflect an underlying faith in the Russian context. While a professionally oriented and modern Western society provides little room for traditions and regards them as slowing down progress, Russians tend to value them very highly. They perceive the future orientation and focus on action and achievement in the Western context as not very appropriate, and admire history and traditions instead.

Understanding of Planning

> A plan is a plan. Once you get it, you have to execute it. This is very serious.
>
> —Russian middle manager, Teleon

> There is no discipline without an exactly defined plan. And if there is no discipline, there is no success.
>
> —Russian middle manager, Equip

> There are jumps back and forth. We continue diagnosing, since we find new surprises every day. The diagnosis phase is never ending. We do not know how it is going to be—it might be worse, it might be better. We will not know until we go through it; everything else is pure speculation.
>
> —Western expatriate, Oilgas

Another concept that exemplifies the variety of meanings interpreted by Russians and Westerners is planning.[33] (See Table 3.)

Westerners view the plan as a document that articulates alternative courses of action. For them, planning is a long-term activity of continuous reassessment and readjustment. It is a management tool that they use actively in evaluating work progress and in implementing a major new course of action. To formulate a plan means to commit initially to the goal. However, this is only a starting point; continuously reformulating the plan is a significant part of their managerial job.

Soon after Westerners enter a Russian company and start working with Russian colleagues, they often realize that their perception of planning is alien to the Russian understanding of setting and executing goals. Although Russia had a planned economy for more than 70 years and managers had been planning all the time, most are actually not

**Table 3** Views of Planning in Organizations

| *Russians* | *Westerners* |
|---|---|
| The plan is an ultimate end-task. | The plan is only a starting point and articulates alternative courses of action. |
| The plan must be executed by all means in the way that it was initially defined. | The plan needs to be adjusted continuously. |
| Only short-term planning is meaningful. | Planning is a long-term activity. |
| Success is measured according to whether the plan has been executed. | In order to be successful, one needs to reassess and readjust the plan. |

interested in long-term planning and consider it useless. They prefer small and sure steps: any sizable move might bring them into the dark area of the totally unknown.[34] Russians generally perceive short-term oriented plans as ultimate end-tasks, the execution of which they associate with success. Oilgas provides an extreme case in that sense. According to the Russian CEO, his perspective for thinking and acting was 24 hours, while the plans of some Western expatriates in the same company were 10 years ahead. The Russian managers concentrated their thoughts and actions on the survival of their companies and their own positions. Because of that perspective, as well as unpredictable changes in the environment, they did not see much room for strategic thinking or long-term plans.

Russians are committed to the goal, expect more rigidity,[35] and resist changing plans at a later time. Planning understood as an ultimate value might be seen as a legacy of the socialist system, where a planned economy, on a societal level, reinforced the execution of the plan by all means, including manipulations and massive collective overtime work. It might also take its roots centuries back in history, in the times of the village communes. The members of the communes "openly and uninhibitedly exercised their right to articulate their interests and opinions before decisions were made. However, once a decision had been reached, they were obliged to abide by it."[36] Two specific considerations were made at that point. First, the decision was taken by one single person who did not necessarily respect the opinions and voices of the others. Second, even if new and unpredicted circumstances appeared, the plan had to be executed and the decision had to be followed as formulated initially.

## Understanding of Control

When asked questions concerning feedback mechanisms in their organizations, many of the Russians asked if the author meant how control was exercised in the company. When they elaborated, it was clear that they perceived control as a top-down and discrete activity. The Russian notion assumes that top managers periodically check on the activities of employees at lower levels. The underlying understanding is that formal reward and punishment systems are most effective in getting employees to perform their tasks. This differs tremendously from the understanding of the Western respondents, who prefer the concept of feedback rather than control. When speaking of control, Westerners mean a continuous activity intrinsic to the actions of all organizational members. To them, control focuses on involvement, not on formalized bureaucracy. (See Table 4.)

The variety of meanings and understandings that single words can generate sometimes has serious and expensive consequences. In Oilgas, for example, the Western expatriates and Russian managers had several discussions on how to organize the control activities after a new information technology system was installed. Every time, both groups left the meeting room frustrated and confused. Each group thought the other was "blocking us and our activities" and "not willing to cooperate." They never asked each other how the other party understood the term "control." Instead, each assumed that the interpretations were identical; therefore, they discussed only operational issues.

One of the ways to overcome this type of misunderstanding is to employ a cultural catalyst,[37] who has a bicultural background and is aware of different representations of the same phenomenon. Two of the companies, Construct and Oilgas, have applied this approach. Construct hired a Westerner who had been living in Russia for 10 years, spoke the language fluently, and acted, in his words, as "a bridge between the understandings of the Russians and the Westerners." One of the Western expatriates in Oilgas was born in Russia. Although he left the country in his childhood, he was very helpful as a cultural catalyst during his assignment.

**Table 4** Views of Control in Organizations

| *Russians* | *Westerners* |
|---|---|
| Prefer the notion of control instead of feedback. | Prefer the notion of feedback instead of control. |
| Control is top-down. | Control is intrinsic to all organizational members' actions. |
| Control is focused on formalized bureaucracy. | Control is oriented towards involvement. |
| Control is exercised by using rewards and punishments. | Control is related to monitoring processes. |
| Control is a discrete activity. | Control is continuous. |

In a cross-cultural setting in which different languages are used, one encounters frequent reports of confusion and misunderstanding unless two interpreters are used—one to translate, and the other to monitor and feed back the extent to which the intended meaning has been conveyed. During the fieldwork, several misinterpretations occurred. In eight of the interviews with Russians at Construct, the interviewing team of two researchers worked with the company's interpreter. Had the researchers not understood Russian, they would not have been aware that on a number of occasions the interpreter completely modified the meaning of the questions or the answers. It would not be surprising if such mistranslations also occurred in the everyday communication of the company.

Actions for Westerners to
Develop Common Understandings

- Assume as few things as possible. Listen carefully and ask clarifying questions. Before discussing how to do things, make sure that you and your Russian counterparts are talking about the same things. Time, planning, and control are only a few examples of how different people's understandings might be.
- Do not ignore the importance of traditions, history, and past experiences. Russians value them highly.
- When introducing strategic plans, formulate short-term tasks with achievable and observable results and assign Russians to work on them.
- Do not be afraid of applying formalized top-down control techniques. Russians respect them and, therefore, expect them.
- Invest in a cultural catalyst who has a bicultural background and is aware of different representations of the same phenomenon. Or hire an interpreter with these qualifications. This should be someone who does not merely translate words, but effectively conveys the intended meanings.

## Crafting and Communicating the Vision

What direction an organization should take, why it should do so, and how it can proceed are components of a vision. A vision is an articulation of the possible and the desirable under given circumstances. It is the larger picture that needs to be kept in mind, in order to avoid the preoccupation with daily operational activities at the cost of the overall organizational goals.[38]

In the five companies studied, the Western expatriates elaborated a vision, but in a number of cases communicated it poorly or not at all. Consequently, employees neither understood nor shared. The Western expatriates in Oilgas, for instance, developed both an overall and a detailed version of a transformation plan; however, only a few Russian managers in the company were told about its content. Employees at the lower levels did not even know of its existence and were convinced that the Western managers did not have a clear idea of what to do and where to lead them. The real power of a vision is unleashed only when most of those involved in an enterprise or activity have a common understanding of its goals and direction. That shared sense of the desirable future can help motivate and coordinate the kinds of actions that create transformation.[39]

Communicating the vision is especially important in Russia, since Russian employees are accustomed to a high level of certainty about the direction of the organization, the concrete organizational goals, and the means of achieving them. Failing to clearly transmit the vision creates a vacuum in terms of responsibility. Since managing is, in a very general sense, directing others' work, vision must be communicated to those working at the lower levels where the everyday work is performed. Making the vision explicit and ensuring its diffusion throughout the organization can provide a shield against anxiety in a period of change, can boost morale, and sustain self-esteem.[40]

An important aspect of communicating the vision is the way it is verbalized. Using formulations that Russian employees associate with those used in the centrally planned economy could have the opposite effect to that intended by Westerners. The following extract from an interview with a Russian middle manager in Oilgas is indicative:

> This happened shortly after our Western colleagues came here. They arranged a meeting in the big room where we used to have communist party meetings and various celebrations. We all were there, 750 people. The first shock was when the Westerners announced that they called this meeting because they wanted to give us the opportunity to ask questions, put forward concerns, in other words, give us the stage to share with them whatever we thought was important. I found that completely meaningless and so did my colleagues. How can you put hundreds of people together without a clear agenda? What are we discussing here? Give us the topic, then we can maybe discuss.
>
> After long minutes of complete silence, one of us, a 55-year-old woman, had a question about our Western colleagues' office hours. She asked when their office hours would be, but they understood the question to be about their working hours. After the Westerners understood that she was asking about the hours when employees are allowed to go to the managers' offices, one of them said: "Thank you very much for this question. I am happy and proud to tell all of you that we will not have any office hours. All the time we will be here only for you." All the time here only for you. This we have heard so many times before. Westerners use the same nice words like our communist leaders did. What the Westerners said sounded very much like the socialist phrase "everything for the person and his well-being."

Using expressions that can easily be associated with the communist past increases the risk that Russian employees will evaluate the vision as just words, or just another change project like those that never worked in the past.

Actions for Westerners to Communicate the Vision

- Tell employees about the vision. Communicate it explicitly and clearly. Russian employees sometimes have difficulties dealing with ambiguity about the organization's direction and the main goals to be achieved.
- Be aware that stability and certainty are highly valued by Russian managers and employees. When planning change, make sure that Russian organizational members understand what will be maintained and reproduced.
- Be very careful when phrasing ideas. Do not use words and sentences that can be easily associated with the communist period and that may seem laden with meaningless ideology.

## Providing Symbols and Signals

Much of organizational change is symbolic and based on signals. The need to understand the signals is crucial, since mundane tools for creating and manipulating symbols over time can reshape beliefs and expectations.[41] Symbols and signals are embedded in the structure, relationships, and language of the everyday life of an organization. It is important that the verbal signals sent by managers are consistent with their actions. This is even more important in cross-cultural settings, where people are more sensitive and more careful in observing each other's behavior and interpreting signals.

Two stories from Oilgas illustrate the difficulties of interpreting symbols and signals. The source of inconsistency in the first story is the Russian CEO and in the second the Western expatriates. Both cases had serious negative consequences for planning change.

### The Russian CEO's Last-Second Block

After long negotiations with the Russian CEO, the Western expatriates in Oilgas reached agreement that the company needed to appoint a young, well educated and highly professional person to be responsible for introducing and managing the new information technology system in the organization. They also agreed that this person would receive a salary corresponding to her or his qualifications and not to age, and that the salary would be funded by the Western investor's budget. The recruitment and selection procedure turned out to be very time-consuming. The Russian CEO took part and was continuously informed about progress.

After several weeks of announcements, meetings, and interviews a "brilliant" candidate was selected. A contract was prepared, but before it was signed the Russian CEO, the Russian middle managers, and the Western expatriates met. The Russian CEO announced to everybody: "After several months of procedures, we finally have selected a person who will be in charge of the IT department. He has been studying at [ . . . ] and has [ . . . ] qualifications. He is 26 years old and will start by the beginning of next month with a salary of [ . . . ] rubles." The CEO knew perfectly well that his middle managers, who had been working in the company for decades, would never accept and allow a situation where a newcomer, half their age, received a salary twice their own. Told informally by the Russian CEO and middle managers that he would not get the job, the candidate phoned and informed the company that he would not be taking the position.

The Russian CEO claimed throughout that he agreed with the terms suggested by the Western expatriates. He even participated actively in the selection and appointment of the new candidate. However, this did not actually mean that he supported the decision. According to the Western vice-CEO and a number of middle Russian managers, mentioning the salary was a deliberate act that blocked the decision and put an end to a time-consuming and complicated process without achieving the result expected by the Westerners.

### Westerners' Actions Contradict Talk of Teamwork

The Western expatriates in Oilgas simultaneously did two things that contradicted each other. Soon after they joined the company, they started working hard on introducing the teamwork idea at the management level, conducting meetings and initiating discussions devoted to the topic. They also offered psychological training in group work and team leadership for the whole management group aimed at solving some of the problems between Russians and Westerners. At the same time, however, the Westerners redesigned and ordered new furniture for their own offices, but not for the uncomfortable and poorly furnished offices of the Russian CEO and their Russian colleagues.

Upgrading the furniture for the Russian managers would have been a very small investment in terms of money, but it would have gone a long way in demonstrating that the Westerners meant what they said about being a team. The Russian respondents in the company repeatedly cited this example of the discrepancy between Westerners' statements and actual behavior. The inconsistency between claims and actions led to postponing or never reaching mutual trust, which is vitally important in planning and carrying out organizational change. In Oilgas, both incidents led to deep frustration and tensions.

Another important and sensitive topic is the way in which rewards are handled in Russian companies with foreign participation, and how the rewards relate to the notion of contributing equally and working as a team at the management level. There is often a huge difference between the salaries of the Russian managers and their Western colleagues in companies where they work together. Expatriates typically receive a base salary, benefits, allowances, and tax equalization. The immense differences in salaries are often expected by Westerners, but is seriously demoralizing for Russian managers. This additionally complicates the relationship between the two groups. When local employees begin to learn about the much higher benefits people working next to or sometimes under them enjoy and compare them to their own compensation, they may feel underpaid, betrayed, or discriminated against. According to one expert:

> When local people do not see super performance by extremely well-paid expatriates (which often is the case due to various reasons), they begin to question the relation between expatriates' costs and the value they add to the company, as well as the fairness of the compensation system itself. So far this problem has not caused any major revolts on the Russian side, only silent disapproval, but it could be a time-bomb.[42]

### Actions for Westerners to Provide Symbols and Signals

- Be consistent in terms of statements and actual behavior. Their signals should clearly indicate that they mean what they say. During transformational change, organizational members are extremely sensitive towards discrepancies between words and actions, and need as much coherence as possible. The significance increases in a cross-cultural setting where the different parties are generally more sensitive and more careful in observing each other's behavior.
- Do not assume that Russian colleagues and subordinates will act according to what they say. If Western managers' actions contradict their basic attitudes and understandings, the Russians will often find ways to surprise them.

- Take up the salary issue. Present the picture honestly and explain that there are reasons why expatriates receive higher salaries than the locals in the company. This helps to avoid rumors and establish a good basis for trust.

## Toward Greater Cooperation

Organizational change is related to a variety of different needs—financial, psychological, and social. It evokes strong feelings that are often deeply ambivalent: change is both needed and not needed, expected and unexpected, constructive and destructive. Unless these meanings are taken into serious consideration, planning organizational change may bring about negative consequences.

No one seems to dispute the fact that differences in perceptions, values, attitudes, and relational systems make the application of standard managerial systems and practices inappropriate. What is in dispute, however, is how and to what extent to localize management approaches and techniques. Western investors and managers need to develop deeper insights and understandings of Russian organizational and managerial assumptions, traditions, attitudes, and values if they are to do business with Russians successfully. Neither side should subscribe to the other's way of doing things. Both parties must be willing to work at developing understandings of each other's values and experiences, as well as organizational realities and processes. In doing so, they may develop an appreciation of why the other party behaves in certain ways, which could lead to greater cooperation.

## Acknowledgments

Part of the data used in this article are from the action-research project SODIAC (Sculpturing Organizational Dynamics in a Context) at Copenhagen Business School, Denmark. The author gratefully acknowledges the participation of the case organizations and the financial support of the funding companies and institutions.

## Notes

1. Oleynik, I. 1999. Dealing with Russia: A winning strategy for the future. *Journal of East-West Business,* 4(4): 81–90; Coleman, L. & Beaulieu, E. 1999. Marketing in Russia: A problem or opportunity? *Journal of East-West Business,* 4(4): 69–80; Driakhlov, N. 1996. Tradition versus modernity. In C. Williams, V. Chuprov, & V. Staroverov (Eds.), *Russian society in transition:* 75–83. Aldershot, UX: Dartmouth.

2. Hingley, R. 1981. *The Russian mind.* New York: Charles Scribner.

3. The terms "Western" and "Westerners" were frequently used by the respondents in this study, Russians as well as foreign expatriates. This ambiguous term has gained broad acceptance mainly in terms of dichotomies, such as West-East, Western Europe-Eastern Europe, or Europe-America. Western culture includes many national cultures, national identities, and sociocultural contexts, and reflects a wide variety of organizational practices and forms, management attitudes and behavior, leadership styles, and human resource policies and practices.

4. Kelley, L., Whatley, A. & Worthley, R. 1987. Assessing the effects of culture on managerial attitudes. *Journal of International Business Studies,* 18(2): 17–31; Griffeth, R., Hom, P., DeNisi, A. & Kirchiner, W. 1980. Multivariate multinational comparison of managerial attitudes. *Academy of Management Proceedings:* 63–67.

5. Steers, R., Bischoff, S. & Higgins, L. 1992. Cross-cultural management research: The fish and the fisherman. *Journal of Management Inquiry,* 1(4): 321–330; McDonald, G. & Pak, P. 1996. Ethical acculturation of expatriate managers in a cross cultural context. *Cross Cultural Management: An International Journal,* 3(3): 9–30.

6. Buono, J. & Bowditch, A. 1989. *The human side of mergers and acquisitions: Managing collisions between people and organizations.* San Francisco: Jossey-Bass; Kelley et al., op. cit.

7. Kanungo, R. & Jaeger, A. 1990. Introduction: The need for indigenous management in developing countries. In P. Kanungo & A. Jaeger, (Eds.), *Indigenous management in developing countries:* 1–19. London: Routledge; Boyacigiller, N. & Adler, N. 1991. The parochial dinosaur: Organizational science in a global context. *Academy of Management Review,* 16(2): 262–290.

8. Puffer, S. M., McCarthy, D. J. & Naumov, A. I. 2000. *The Russian capitalist experiment: From state-owned organizations to entrepreneurships.* Cheltenham, U.K. and Northampton, MA: Edward Elgar.

9. Culture is defined in a number of ways (see Usinier, J.-C. 1998. *International and cross-cultural management research.* London: Sage). Many difficulties exist in differentiating between

cultural and national factors (see Kelley, L. & Worthley, R. 1981. The role of culture in comparative management: A cross-cultural perspective. *Academy of Management Journal,* 16(1): 67–76) and between cultural, national, and situational effects (see Bhagat, R. & McQuaid, S. 1982. Role of subjective culture in organizations: A review and directions for further research. *Journal of Applied Psychology,* Monograph, 67, 5). The majority of studies implicitly assume national boundaries as operational definitions of culturally distinctive units (see Adler, N. 1983. A typology of management studies involving culture. *Journal of International Business* Studies, 14(2): 29–47). The present article adopts the view of culture as a shared system of representations and meaning (see Geertz, C. 1983. *Local knowledge.* New York: Basic Books; Goodenough, W. 1971. *Culture, language and society.* Reading, MA: Addison-Wesley) that is learned and used by people to interpret experience and to generate social behavior (see Terpstra, V. & David, K. 1991. *The cultural environment of international business,* 3rd edition. Cincinnati: South-Western Publishing Co.). This implies that culture is not necessarily associated with the whole of a particular society (see Ronen, S. 1986. *Comparative and multinational management.* New York: John Wiley & Sons), but is related to certain sets of activities and interactions within the boundaries of a specific group. When the article refers to cultural characteristics and features it assumes that these constitute key determinants of managerial practices and effectiveness (see Neghandi, A. & Prasad, B. 1971. *Comparative management.* New York: Appleton-Century-Crofts). These characteristics are of a more fundamental, pervasive nature in their capacity to induce valences for a broad variety of domains (see Wilpert, B. & Scharpf, S. 1990. Intercultural management—Joint ventures in the People's Republic of China. *International Journal of Psychology,* 25: 643–656).

10. Of the interviews with the Western expatriates, eight were conducted in English and five predominantly in the language (other than English) of the Western expatriate. The author conducted 15 of the interviews with the Russian respondents in Russian, one in English, and eight using a translator. In order to study the obstacles in the communication when using translators in the companies' everyday life, an interpreter was asked to translate the questions and responses in five of the interviews in one of the studied organizations. In these cases, the interview interpreter was an employee working as interpreter in the respective Russian company.

11. All company names in this article are disguised.

12. Schein, E. 1992. *Organizational culture and leadership,* 2nd edition. San Francisco: Jossey-Bass.

13. Senior, B. 1997. *Organizational change.* London: Pitman Publishing.

14. Johnson, G. & Scholes, K. 1999. *Exploring corporate strategy,* 5th edition. London: Prentice Hall.

15. Kanter, R., Stein, B. & Jick, T. 1992. *The challenge of organizational change: How companies experience it and leaders guide it.* New York: The Free Press; Hardy, C. 1994. *Managing strategic action, mobilizing change: Concepts, readings and cases.* London: Sage; Hardy, C. & Clegg, S. 1999. Some dare call it power. In S. Clegg & C. Hardy, (Eds.), *Studying organization: Theory & method.* London: Sage: 368–387.

16. Ouchi, W. 1980. Markets, bureaucracies, and clans. *Administrative Science Quarterly,* 25: 129–141.

17. Mikheyev, D. 1987. The Soviet mentality. *Political Psychology,* 8(4): 491–523.

18. Dabars, Z. & Vokhmina, L. 1995. *The Russian way.* Lincolnwood, IL: Passport Books; Holden, N., Cooper, C. & Carr, J. 1998. *Dealing with the new Russia: Management cultures in collision.* Chichester, UK: John Wiley & Sons; Kets de Vries, M. 1998. *The anarchist within: Clinical reflections on Russian character, leadership style, and organizational practices.* Working paper 98/96, Fontainebleau, France: INSEAD; Ledeneva, A. 1998. *Russia's economy of favors: Blat, networking and informal exchange.* Cambridge, UK: Cambridge University Press.

19. Puffer, S. M. 1994. Understanding the bear: A portrait of Russian business leaders. *The Academy of Management Executive,* 8(1): 41–54; Smith, H. 1976. *The Russians.* New York: Times Books/Quadrangle.

20. The Russian language offers a number of different words for friend.

21. Kanter et al., op. cit.

22. Puffer, S. M. & McCarthy, D. J. 1995. Finding the common ground in Russian and American business ethics. *California Management Review,* 37(2): 29–46; Richmond, Y. 1996. *From nyet to da: Understanding the Russians.* Yarmouth, ME: Intercultural Press.

23. A Russian proverb says: Who serves the tsar, cannot serve the people.

24. Vlachoutsicos, C. & Lawrence, P. 1990. What we don't know about Soviet management. *Harvard Business Review,* November-December: 50–63.

25. Puffer, S. M. 1993. A riddle wrapped in an enigma: Demystifying Russian managerial motivation. *European Management Journal,* 11(4): 473–480.

26. Ivancevich, J., DeFrank, R., & Gregory, P. 1992. The Soviet enterprise director: An important resource before and after the coup. *The Academy of Management Executive,* 6(1): 42–55.

27. Michailova, S. 1998. Interface between Western and Russian management attitudes: Implications for organizational change. In Lang, R., (Ed.), *Führungskräfte im osteuropäischen Transformationsprozeß (Executives in the East European transformation process):* 279–302. Munich: Hampp.

28. Wright, M., Hoskisson, R., Filatotchev, I., & Buck, T. 1998. Revitalizing privatized Russian enterprises. *The Academy of Management Executive,* 12(2): 74–85.

29. Ward, M. 1995. *50 essential management techniques.* Aldershot: Gower.

30. Whorf, B. 1956. *Language, thought, and reality.* New York: Wiley; Terpstra & David, *op. cit.*

31. Cattaneo, E. 1992. Managing joint-ventures in Russia: Can the problems be solved? *Long Range Planning,* 25(5): 68–72.

32. Adams, G. & Ingersol, V. 1990. Culture, technical rationality, and organizational culture. *American Review of Public Administration,* 20(4): 285–302.

33. Michailova, S. & Anisimova, A. 1999. Russian voices from a Danish company. *Business Strategy Review,* 10(4): 65–78.

34. Mikheyev, *op. cit.,* 521.

35. Lawrence, P. & Vlachoutsicos, C. 1990. Managerial patterns: Differences and commonalities. In P. Lawrence & C. Vlachoutsicos, (Eds.), *Behind the factory walls: Decision making in Soviet and U.S. enterprises:* 271–286. Boston: Harvard Business School Press.

36. Vlachoutsicos, C. 1998. The dangers of ignoring Russian communitarism. *Transition,* October: 13–14.

37. Lee, M. 1995. Working with choice in Central Europe. *Management Learning,* 26(2): 215–230.

38. Legge, K. 1984. *Evaluating planned organizational change.* London: Academic Press.

39. Kotter, J. 1996. *Leading change.* Boston: Harvard Business School Press.

40. Carnall, C. 1995. *Managing change in organizations.* 2nd edition. London: Prentice Hall.

41. Peters, T. 1987. Symbols, patterns and settings: An optimistic case for getting things done. *Organizational Dynamics,* 7(2): 3–23.

42. Shekshnia, S. 1996. Managing people in Russia. In S. M. Puffer & Associates, (Eds.), *Business and management in Russia:* 239–257. Cheltenham, U.K. and Brookfield, VT: Edward Elgar.

43. Mikheyev, *op. cit.,* 514.

44. Kets de Vries, *op. cit.*

# Case 2.1

## NIKE'S DISPUTE WITH THE UNIVERSITY OF OREGON[1]

REBECCA J. MORRIS AND ANNE T. LAWRENCE

On April 24, 2000, Philip H. Knight, CEO of athletic shoe and apparel maker Nike Inc., publicly announced that he would no longer donate money to the University of Oregon (UO). It was a dramatic and unexpected move for the high-profile executive. A former UO track and field star, Knight had founded Nike's predecessor in 1963 with his former UO coach and mentor, Bill Bowerman. Over the years, Knight had maintained close ties with his alma mater, giving more than $50 million of his personal fortune to the school over a quarter century. In 2000, he was in active discussion with school officials about his biggest donation yet—millions for renovating the football stadium. But suddenly it was all called off. Said Knight in his statement: "[F]or me personally, there will be no further donations of any kind to the University of Oregon. At this time, this is not a situation that can be resolved. The bonds of trust, which allowed me to give at a high level, have been shredded."[2]

At issue was the University of Oregon's intention, announced April 14, 2000 to join the Worker Rights Consortium (WRC). Like many universities, UO was engaged in an internal debate over the ethical responsibilities associated with its role as a purchaser of goods manufactured overseas. Over a period of several months, UO administrators, faculty, and students had been discussing what steps they could take to ensure that products sold in the campus store, especially university-logo apparel, were not manufactured under sweatshop conditions. The University had considered joining two organizations, both of which purported to certify goods as "no sweat." The first, the Fair Labor Association (FLA), had grown out of President Clinton's Apparel Industry Partnership (AIP) initiative and was vigorously backed by Nike, as well as several other leading apparel makers. The second, the Worker Rights Consortium, was supported by student activists and several United States-based labor unions that had broken from the AIP after charging it did not go far enough to protect workers. Knight clearly felt that his alma mater had made the wrong choice. "[The] University [has] inserted itself into the new global economy where I make my living," he charged. "And inserted itself on the wrong side, fumbling a teachable moment."

The dispute between Phil Knight and the University of Oregon captured much of the furor swirling about the issue of the role of multinational corporations in the global economy and the effects of their far-flung operations on their many thousands of workers, communities, and other stakeholders. In part because of its high-profile brand name, Nike had become a lightning rod for activists concerned about worker rights abroad. Like many U.S.-based

SOURCE: By Rebecca J. Morris and Anne T. Lawrence. Reprinted by permission from the *Case Research Journal*, Vol. 21, Issue 3 (Summer 2001), pp. 129-146. 

shoe and apparel makers, Nike had located its manufacturing operations overseas, mainly in Southeast Asia, in search of low wages. Almost all production was carried out by subcontractors rather than by Nike directly. Nike's employees in the United States, by contrast, directed their efforts to the high-end work of research and development, marketing, and retailing. In the context of this global division of labor, what responsibility, if any, did Nike have to ensure adequate working conditions and living standards for the hundreds of thousands of workers, mostly young Asian women, who made its shoes and apparel? If this was not Nike's responsibility, then whose was it? Did organizations like the University of Oregon have any business pressuring companies through their purchasing practices? If so, how should they best do so? In short, what were the lessons of this "teachable moment"?

## Nike, Inc.

In 2000, Nike, Inc., was the leading designer and marketer of athletic footwear, apparel, and equipment in the world. Based in Beaverton, Oregon, the company's "swoosh" logo, its "Just Do It!" slogan and its spokespersons Michael Jordan, Mia Hamm, and Tiger Woods were universally recognized. Nike employed around 20,000 people directly, and *half a million* indirectly in 565 contract factories in 46 countries around the world turning out Nike products.[3] Wholly owned subsidiaries included Bauer Nike Hockey Inc. (hockey equipment), Cole Haan (dress and casual shoes), and Nike Team Sports (licensed team products). Revenues for the 12 months ending November 1999 were almost $9 billion.[4] With a 45% global market share, Nike was in a league of its own.[5] Knight owned 34% of the company's stock and was believed to be the sixth-richest individual in the United States.[6]

Knight had launched this far-flung global empire shortly after completing his MBA degree at Stanford University in the early 1960s. Drawing on his first-hand knowledge of track and field, he decided to import low-priced track shoes from Japan in partnership with his former college coach. Bowerman would provide design ideas, test the shoes in competition, and endorse the shoes with other coaches; Knight would handle all financial and day-to-day operations of the business. Neither man had much money to offer, so for $500 a piece and a handshake, the company (then called Blue Ribbon Sports) was officially founded in 1963. The company took the name Nike in 1978; two years later, with revenues topping $269 million and 2,700 employees, Nike became a publicly traded company.[7]

From the beginning, marketing had been a critical part of Knight's vision. The founder defined Nike as a "marketing-oriented company." During the 1980s and early 1990s, Nike aggressively sought out endorsements by celebrity athletes to increase brand awareness and foster consumer loyalty. Early Nike endorsers included marathoners Alberto Salazar and Joan Benoit, Olympic gold medalist Carl Lewis, Wimbledon champion Andre Agassi, and six members of the 1992 Olympic basketball "Dream Team." Later Nike endorsers included tennis aces Pete Sampras and Monica Seles, basketball great Michael Jordan, and golf superstar Tiger Woods.

Nike became the world's largest athletic shoe company in 1991 when revenues soared to $3 billion, but that was only the beginning.[8] Continued development of "cool shoes," aggressive geographic expansion, and the world dominance of Nike-endorsing athletes resulted in record-breaking performance year after year. By 1998, Nike's total revenues exceeded $9.5 billion.[9] Although the Asian economic crisis and sluggish U.S. sales caused revenues to dip slightly in 1999, Nike easily led the athletic footwear industry, outpacing the number two firm (Adidas) by 1.5 times.[10] Key events in Nike's history are summarized in Exhibit 1.

## Cutting Edge Products

An important element in Nike's success was its ability to develop cutting-edge products that met the needs of serious athletes, as well as set fashion trends. Research specialists in Nike's Sports Research Labs conducted extensive research and testing to develop new technologies to improve the performance of Nike shoes in a variety of sports. Tom McQuirk, head of the company's Sports Research Labs stated, "Our job here in Sports Research is to define human movement in terms of biomechanics and physiology. Our job is to translate activities into a set of performance-enhancing and injury-reducing needs."[11] For example, research specialists studied the causes of ankle injuries in basketball players to develop shoes that would physically prevent injuries as well as signal information to the user to help him or her resist turning the ankle while in the air. Other specialists developed new polymer materials that would make the shoes lighter, more aerodynamic, or more resistant to the abrasions incurred during normal athletic use.

Findings from the Sports Research Labs were then passed on to design teams that developed the look and styling of the shoes. Drawing heavily from trends in popular culture, shoe designers in the Jordan Building of Nike's Beaverton, Oregon, corporate campus blended the technological with the "romance and imagery and all those subliminal characteristics that make an object important to people in less utilitarian ways."[12] Put more simply, the Nike designers took a technologically sophisticated piece of sporting equipment and gave it attitude.

## The Making of Athletic Shoes

Although it was the leading athletic footwear company in the world, Nike never manufactured shoes in any significant number. Rather, from its inception, the company had outsourced production to subcontractors in Southeast Asia, with the company shifting production locations within the region when prevailing wage rates became too high. In the early years, it had imported shoes from Japan. It later shifted production to South Korea and Taiwan, then to Indonesia and Thailand, and later yet to Vietnam and China, as shown in Exhibit 2.[13]

The reasons for locating shoe production mainly in Southeast Asia were several, but the most important was the cost of labor. The availability of component materials and trade policies were also factors. Modern athletic shoes were composed of mesh, leather, and nylon uppers that were hand-assembled, sewn and glued to composite soles.[14] Mechanization had not been considered effective for shoe manufacturing due to the fragile materials used and the short life spans of styles of athletic shoes.[15] Therefore, shoe production was highly labor-intensive. Developing countries, primarily in Southeast Asia, offered the distinct advantage of considerably lower wage rates. For example, in the early 1990s, when Nike shifted much of its shoe production to Indonesia, daily wages there hovered around $1 a day (compared to wages in the U.S. shoe industry at that time of around $8 an hour).[16]

Along with lower labor costs, Asia provided the additional advantage of access to raw materials suppliers.[17] Very few rubber firms in the United States, for example, produced the sophisticated composite soles demanded in modern athletic shoe designs. Satellite industries necessary for modern shoe production, plentiful in Asia, included tanneries, textiles, and plastic and ironwork moldings.[18]

A third factor in determining where to locate production was differential tariffs that applied to athletic shoes. The tariffs were determined by the manner in which the upper was attached to the sole of the shoe. The three types—non-molded, molded and fox-banded (where a strip of material was applied over the joint of the sole and upper, as in canvas sneakers)—were assessed different tariffs for importation. Variations in the materials used for the uppers also determined the tariff rate. In general, canvas sneakers were assessed higher tariffs than leather molded footwear, such as basketball or running shoes. As a result, differential tariffs prompted shoe companies to outsource higher margin high-tech athletic shoes while sometimes producing low-margin canvas shoes domestically.[19]

The economic reality for many firms in the athletic footwear industry involved balancing consumer demand for new and innovative styles with pressures to improve the profit picture. Manufacturing new high-technology styles in Southeast Asia permitted the firms to take advantage of lower labor costs, lower tariffs and a better-developed supplier network. Many of Nike's factories in Asia were operated by a small number of Taiwanese and Korean firms that specialized in shoe manufacturing, many owned by some of the wealthiest families in the region. When Nike moved from one location to another, often these companies followed, bringing their managerial expertise with them.

## Nike's Subcontractor Factories

In 2000, Nike contracted with over 500 different footwear and apparel factories around the world to produce its shoes and apparel.[20] Although there was no such thing as a typical Nike plant, a factory operated by the Korean subcontractor Tae Kwang Vina (TKV) in the Bien Hoa City industrial zone near Ho Chi Minh City in Vietnam provided a glimpse into the setting in which many Nike shoes were made.[21]

TKV employed approximately 10,000 workers in the Bien Hoa City factory. The workforce consisted of 200 clerical workers, 355 supervisors, and 9,465 production workers, all making athletic shoes for Nike. Ninety percent of the workers were women between the ages of 18 to 24. Production workers were employed in one of three major areas within the factory: the chemical, stitching, and assembly sections. Production levels at the Bien Hoa City factory reached 400,000 pairs of shoes per month; Nike shoes made at this and other factories made up fully 5 percent of Vietnam's total exports.[22]

A second-generation South Korean shoe worker employed by Nike described the challenges of work in the typical shoe factory as the "three D's." "It's dirty, dangerous, and difficult," explained T.H. Lee. "Making shoes on a production line is something people only do because they see it as an important and lucrative job. Nobody who could do something else for the same wage would be here. It's less dirty, dangerous, and difficult than it was in the past—but it's not an easy way to spend a day."[23]

*The Chemical Section:[24]* Over 1,000 natural and man-made materials were used in the factory to produce shoes from scratch. Workers in the chemical or polyurethane (PU) plant were responsible for producing the high-technology outsoles. Production steps in the chemical division involved stretching and flattening huge blobs of raw rubber on heavy-duty rollers and baking chemical compounds in steel molds to form the innovative three-dimensional outsoles. The chemical composition of the soles changed constantly in response to the cutting-edge formulations developed by the Beaverton, Oregon, design teams, requiring frequent changes in the production process.

The smell of complex polymers, the hot ovens, and the clanging of the steel molds resulted in a working environment that was louder, hotter and had higher concentrations of chemical fumes than allowed by Vietnamese law.[25] Chemicals used in the section were known to cause eye, skin, and throat irritations; damage to liver and kidneys; nausea; anorexia; and reproductive health hazards through inhalation or in some cases through absorption through the skin.[26] Workers in the chemical section were thought to have high rates of respiratory illnesses, although records kept at the TKV operations did not permit the tracking of illnesses by factory section.

Workers in the chemical section were issued gloves and surgical-style masks. However, they often discarded the protective gear, complaining that it was too hot and humid to wear them in the plant. Cotton masks and gloves also were ineffective in protecting workers from solvent fumes and exposure to skin-damaging chemicals.[27]

*The Stitching Section:[28]* In a space the size of three football fields, row after row of sewing machines operated by young women hummed and clattered. One thousand stitchers worked on a single floor of the TKV factory, sewing together nylon, leather and other fabrics to make the uppers. Other floors of the factory were filled with thousands of additional sewing machines producing different shoe models.

The stitching job required precision and speed. Workers who did not meet the aggressive production goals did not receive a bonus. Failing to meet production goals three times resulted in the worker's dismissal. Workers were sometimes required to work additional hours without pay to meet production quotas.[29] Supervisors were strict, chastising workers for excessive talking or spending too much time in the restrooms. Korean supervisors, often hampered by language and cultural barriers, sometimes resorted to hard-nosed management tactics, hitting or slapping slower workers. Other workers in need of discipline were forced to stand outside the factory for long periods in the tropical sun. The Vietnamese term for this practice was "phoi nang," or sun-drying.[30]

*The Assembly Section:*[31] Women worked side by side along an assembly line to join the uppers to the outersoles through the rapid manipulation of sharp knives, skivers,[32] routers, and glue-coated brushes. Women were thought to be better suited for the assembly jobs because their hands were smaller and more capable of the manual dexterity needed to fit the shoe components together precisely. During the assembly process, some 120 pairs of hands touched a single shoe.

A strong, sweet solvent smell was prominent in the assembly area. Ceiling-mounted ventilation fans were ineffective since the heavy fumes settled to the floor. Assembly workers wore cotton surgical masks to protect themselves from the fumes; however, many workers pulled the masks below their noses, saying they were more comfortable that way.[33]

Rows and rows of shoes passed along a conveyor before the sharp eyes of the quality control inspectors. The inspectors examined each of the thousands of shoes produced daily for poor stitching or crooked connections between soles. Defective shoes were discarded. Approved shoes continued on the conveyor to stations where they were laced by assembly workers and finally put into Nike shoeboxes for shipment to the United States.[34]

Despite the dirty, dangerous, and difficult nature of the work inside the Bien Hoa factory, there was no shortage of applicants for positions. Although entry level wages averaged only $1.50 per day (the lowest of all countries where Nike manufactured), many workers viewed factory jobs as better than their other options, such as working in the rice paddies or pedaling a pedicab along the streets of Ho Chi Minh City.[35] With overtime pay at one and a half times the regular rate, workers could double their salaries—generating enough income to purchase a motorscooter or to send money home to impoverished rural relatives. These wages were well above national norms. An independent study by researchers from Dartmouth University showed that the average annual income for workers at two Nike subcontractor factories in Vietnam was between $545 and $566, compared to the national average of between $250 and $300.[36] Additionally, workers were provided free room and board and access to on-site health care facilities.

Many Vietnamese workers viewed positions in the shoe factory as transitional jobs—a way to earn money for a dowry or to experience living in a larger city. Many returned to their homes after working for Nike for two or three years to marry and begin the next phase of their lives.[37]

## The Campaigns Against Nike

In the early 1990s, criticism of Nike's global labor practices began to gather steam. *Harper's Magazine,* for example, published the pay stub of an Indonesian worker, showing that the Nike subcontractor had paid the woman just under 14 cents per hour, and contrasted this with the high retail price of the shoes—and the high salaries paid to the company's celebrity endorsers.[38] The Made in the U.S.A. Foundation, a group backed by American unions, used a million dollar ad budget to urge consumers to send their "old, dirty, smelly, worn-out Nikes" to Phil Knight in protest of Nike's Asian manufacturing practices.[39] Human rights groups and Christian organizations joined the labor unions in targeting the labor practices of the athletic shoes firm. Many felt that Nike's anti-authority corporate image ("Just Do It") and message of social betterment through fitness were incompatible with press photos of slight Asian women hunched over sewing machines 70 hours a week, earning just pennies an hour.

By mid-1993, Nike was being regularly pilloried in the press as an imperialist profiteer. A CBS news segment airing on July 2, 1993, opened with images of Michael Jordan and Andre Agassi, two athletes who had multimillion dollar promotion contracts with Nike. Viewers were told to contrast the athletes' pay checks with those of the Chinese and Indonesian workers who made "pennies" so that Nike could "Just Do It."[40]

In 1995, the *Washington Post* reported that a pair of Nike Air Pegasus shoes that retailed for $70 cost Nike only $2.75 in labor costs, or 4% of the price paid by consumers. Nike's operating profit on the same pair of shoes was $6.25, while the retailer pocketed $9.00 in operating profits, as shown in Exhibit 3. Also that year, shareholder activists organized by the Interfaith Center on Corporate Responsibility submitted a shareholder proposal at Nike's annual meeting, calling on the company to review labor practices by its subcontractors; the proposal garnered 3% of the shareholder vote.

Things were to get worse. A story in *Life*[41] magazine documented the use of child labor in Pakistan to produce soccer balls for Nike, Adidas, and other companies. The publicity fallout was intense. The public could not ignore the photographs of small children sitting in the dirt, carefully stitching together the panels of a soccer ball that would become the plaything of some American child the same age.[42] Nike moved quickly to work with its Pakistani subcontractor to eliminate the use of child labor, but damage to Nike's image had been done.

In October 1996, CBS News *48 Hours* broadcast a scathing report on Nike's factories in Vietnam. CBS reporter Roberta Baskin focused on low wage rates, extensive overtime, and physical abuse of workers. Several young workers told Baskin how a Korean supervisor had beaten them with a part of a shoe because of problems with production.[43] A journalist in Vietnam told the reporter that the phrase "to Nike someone" was part of the Vietnamese vernacular. It meant to "take out one's frustration on a fellow worker." Vietnamese plant managers refused to be interviewed, covering their faces as they ran inside the factory. CBS news anchor Dan Rather concluded the damaging report by saying, "Nike now says it plans to hire outside observers to talk to employees and examine working conditions in its Vietnam factories, but the company just won't say when that might happen."[44]

The negative publicity was having an effect. In 1996, a marketing research study authorized by Nike reported the perceptions of young people aged 13 to 25 of Nike as a company. The top three perceptions, in the order of their response frequency, were: athletics, cool, and bad labor practices.[45] Although Nike maintained that its sales were never affected, company executives were clearly concerned about the effect of criticism of its global labor practices on the reputation of the brand they had worked so hard to build.

## The Evolution of Nike's Global Labor Practices

In its early years, Nike had maintained that the labor practices of its foreign subcontractors—like TKV—were simply not its responsibility. "When we started Nike," Knight later commented, "it never occurred to us that we should dictate what their factor[ies] should look like, which really didn't matter because we had no idea what a shoe factory should look like anyway."[46] The subcontractors, not Nike, were responsible for wages and working conditions. Dave Taylor, Nike's vice president of production, explained the company's position: "We don't pay anybody at the factories and we don't set policy within the factories; it is their business to run."[47]

When negative articles first began appearing in the early 1990s, however, Nike managers realized that they needed to take some action to avoid further bad publicity. In 1992, the company drafted its first Code of Conduct (Exhibit 4), which required every subcontractor and supplier in the Nike network to honor all applicable local government labor and environmental regulations, or Nike would terminate the relationship.[48] The subcontractors were also required to allow plant inspections and complete all necessary paperwork. Despite the compliance reports the factories filed every six months, Nike insiders acknowledged that the code of conduct system might not catch all violations. Tony Nava, Nike's country coordinator for Indonesia, told a *Chicago Tribune* reporter, "We can't know if they're actually complying with what they put down on paper."[49] In short, Nike required its subcontractors to comply with existing labor laws, but did not feel it was the firm's duty to challenge local policies that suppressed worker rights or kept wages low in order to attract manufacturing.

In 1994, Nike tried to address this problem by hiring Ernst & Young, the accounting firm, to independently monitor worker abuse allegations in Nike's Indonesian factories. Later, Ernst & Young also audited Nike's factories in Thailand and Vietnam. Although these audits were not made public, a copy of the Vietnam audit leaked to the press showed that workers were often unaware of the toxicity of the compounds they were using and ignorant of the need for safety precautions.[50] In 1998, Nike implemented important changes in its Vietnamese plants to reduce exposure to toxins-substituting less harmful chemicals, installing ventilation systems, and training personnel in occupational health and safety issues.

In 1996, Nike established a new Labor Practices Department, headed by Dusty Kidd, formerly a public relations executive for the company. Later that year, Nike hired GoodWorks International, headed by former U.S. ambassador to the United Nations Andrew Young, to investigate conditions in its overseas factories. In January 1997, GoodWorks issued a glossy report, stating that "Nike is doing a good job in the application of its Code of Conduct. But Nike can and should do better." The report was criticized by activists for its failure to look at the issue of wages. Young demurred, saying he did not have expertise in conducting wage surveys. Said one critic, "This was a public relations problem, and the world's largest sneaker company did what it does best: it purchased a celebrity endorsement."[51]

Over the next few years, Nike continued to work to improve labor practices in its overseas subcontractor factories, as well as the public perception of them. In January 1998, Nike formed a Corporate Responsibility Division, combining the Labor Practices, Global Community Affairs, and Environmental Action Teams under the leadership of former Microsoft executive Maria S. Eitel, hired to be Nike's new Vice President for Corporate and Social Responsibility. Nike subsequently doubled the staff of this division. In May of that year, Knight gave a speech at the National Press Club, at which he announced several new initiatives. At that time, he committed Nike to raise the minimum age for employment in its shoe factories to 18 and in its apparel factories to 16. He also promised to achieve OSHA standards for indoor air quality in all its factories by the end of the year, mainly by eliminating the use of the solvent toluene; to expand educational programs for workers and its microenterprise loan program; and to fund university research on responsible business practices. Nike also continued its use of external monitors, hiring PricewaterhouseCoopers to join Ernst & Young in a comprehensive program of factory audits, checking them against Nike's code. At the conclusion of his speech Knight said,

> At the end of the day, we don't have all the answers. Nobody has all the answers. We want to be the best corporate citizens we can be. If we continue to improve, and our industry colleagues and people interested in these issues join in our efforts, the workers are the ultimate beneficiaries.[52]

## Apparel Industry Partnership

One of Nike's most ambitious social responsibility initiatives was its participation in the Apparel Industry Partnership. It was this involvement that would lead, eventually, to Knight's break with the University of Oregon.

In August 1996, President Clinton launched the White House Apparel Industry Partnership on Workplace Standards (AIP). The initial group was comprised of 18 organizations. Participants included several leading manufacturers, such as Nike, Reebok, and Liz Claiborne. Also in the group were several labor unions, including the Union of Needletrades, Industrial, and Textile Employees (UNITE) and the Retail, Wholesale and Department Store Union; and several human rights, consumer, and shareholder organizations, including Business for Social Responsibility, the Interfaith Center on Corporate Responsibility, and the National Consumers League. The goal of the AIP was to develop a set of standards to ensure that apparel and footwear were not made under sweatshop conditions. For companies, it held out the promise of certifying to their customers that their products were "no sweat." For labor and human rights groups, it held out the promise of improving working conditions in overseas factories.[53]

In April 1997, after months of often-fractious meetings, the AIP announced that it had agreed on a Workplace Code of Conduct that sought to define decent and humane working conditions.[54] Companies agreeing to the code would have to pledge not to use forced labor—that is, prisoners or bonded or indentured workers. They could not require more than 60 hours of work a week, including overtime. They could not employ children younger than 15 years old, or the age for completing compulsory schooling, whichever was older—except they could hire 14-year-olds if local law allowed. The code also called on signatory companies to treat all workers with respect and dignity; to refrain from discrimination on the basis of gender, race, religion, age, disability, sexual orientation, nationality, political opinion, or social or ethnic origin; and to provide a safe and healthy workplace. Employees' rights to organize and bargain collectively would be respected. In a key provision, the code also required companies to pay at least the local legal minimum wage or the prevailing industry wage, whichever was higher. All standards would apply not only to a company's own facilities but also to their subcontractors or suppliers.

Knight, who prominently joined President Clinton and others at a White House ceremony announcing the code, issued the following statement:

Nike agreed to participate in this Partnership because it was the first credible attempt, by a diverse group of interests, to address the important issue of improving factories worldwide. It was worth the effort and hard work. The agreement will prove important for several reasons. Not only is our industry stepping up to the plate and taking a giant swing at improving factory conditions, but equally important, we are finally providing consumers some guidance to counter all of the misinformation that has surrounded this issue for far too long.[55]

### The Fair Labor Association

But this was not the end of the AIP's work; it also had to agree on a process for monitoring compliance with the code. Although the group hoped to complete its work in six months, over a year later it was still deeply divided on several key matters. Internal documents leaked to the *New York Times* in July 1998 showed that industry representatives had opposed proposals, circulated by labor and human rights members, calling for the monitoring of 30% of plants annually by independent auditors. The companies also opposed proposals that would require them to support workers' rights to organize independent unions and to bargain collectively, even in countries—like China—where workers did not have such rights by law. Said one nonindustry member, "We're teetering on the edge of collapse."[56]

Finally, a subgroup of nine centrist participants, including Nike, began meeting separately in an attempt to move forward. In November 1998, this subgroup announced that it had come to agreement on a monitoring system for overseas factories of U.S.-based companies. The AIP would establish a new organization, the Fair Labor Association (FLA), to oversee compliance with its Workplace Code of Conduct. Companies would be required to monitor their own factories, and those of their subcontractors, for compliance; all would have to be checked within the first two years. In addition, the FLA would select and certify independent external monitors, who would inspect 10 percent of each firm's factories each year. Most of these monitors were expected to be accounting firms, which had expertise in conducting audits. The monitors' reports would be kept private. If a company were found to be out of compliance, it would be given a chance to correct the problem. Eventually, if it did not, the company would be dropped from the FLA and its termination announced to the public. Companies would pay for most of their own monitoring.[57]

The Clinton administration quickly endorsed the plan. Secretary of Labor Alexis Herman said, "[We are] convinced this agreement lays the foundation to eliminate sweatshop labor, here and abroad. It is workable for business and creates a credible system that will let consumers know the garments they buy are not produced by exploited workers."[58]

Both manufacturers and institutional buyers stood to benefit from participation in the Fair Labor Association. Companies, once certified for three years, could place an FLA service mark on their brands, signaling both to individual consumers and institutional buyers that their products were "sweatshop-free." It was expected that the FLA would also serve the needs of institutional buyers, particularly universities. By joining the FLA and agreeing to contract only with certified companies, universities could warrant to their students and others that their logo apparel and athletic gear were manufactured under conditions conforming with an established code of fair labor standards.[59] Both parties would pay for these benefits. The FLA was to be funded by dues from participating companies ($5000 to $100,000 annually, depending on revenue) and by payments from affiliated colleges and universities (based on 1 percent of their licensing income from logo products, up to a $50,000 annual cap).

## Criticism of the Fair Labor Association

Although many welcomed the agreement—and some new companies signed on with the FLA soon after it was announced—others did not. Warnaco, a leading apparel maker that had participated in the AIP, quit, saying that the monitoring process would require it to turn over competitive information to outsiders. The American Apparel Manufacturing Association (AAMA), an industry group representing 350 companies, scoffed at the whole idea of monitoring. "Who is going to do the monitoring?" asked a spokesperson for the AAMA, apparently sarcastically. "Accountants or Jesuit priests?" The FLA monitoring scheme was also attacked as insufficient by some Partnership participants that had not been part of the subgroup. In their view, companies simply could not be relied upon to monitor themselves objectively. Said Jay Mazur, president of UNITE, "The fox cannot watch the chickens. If they want the monitoring to be independent, it can't be controlled by the companies."[60] FLA critics believed that a visit from an external monitor once every ten years would not prevent abuses. And in any case, as a practical matter, they stated that most monitors would be drawn from the major accounting firms that did business with the companies they were monitoring and were therefore unlikely to seek out lapses. Companies would not be required to publish a list of their factories, and any problems uncovered by the monitoring process could be kept from the public under the rules governing nondisclosure of proprietary information.

One of the issues most troubling to critics was the code's position on wages. The code called on companies to pay the minimum wage or prevailing wage, whichever was higher. But in many of the countries of Southeast Asia, these wages fell well below the minimum considered necessary for a decent standard of living for an individual or family. For example, the *Economist*[61] reported that Indonesia's average minimum wage—paid by Nike subcontractors—was only two-thirds of what a person needed for basic subsistence. An alternative view was that a code of conduct should require that companies pay a *living wage,* that is, compensation for a normal workweek adequate to provide for the basic needs of an average family, adjusted for the average number of adult wage earners per family. One problem with this approach, however, was that many countries did not systematically study the cost of living, relative to wages, so defining a living wage was difficult. The Partnership asked the U.S. Department of Labor to conduct a preliminary study of these issues; the results were published in 2000 (Exhibit 5).

The code also called on companies to respect workers' rights to organize and bargain collectively. Yet a number of FLA companies outsourced production to nondemocratic countries, such as China and Vietnam, where workers had no such rights. Finally, some criticized the agreement on the grounds it provided companies, as one put it, "a piece of paper to use as a fig leaf." Commented a representative of the needle trades unions, "The problem with the partnership plan is that it tinkers at the margins of the sweatshop system but creates the impression that it is doing much more. This is potentially helpful to companies stung by public condemnation of their labor practices, but it hurts millions of workers and undermines the growing antisweatshop movement."[62]

## The Worker Rights Consortium

Some activists in the antisweatshop movement decided to chart their own course, independent of the FLA. On October 20, 1999, students from more than 100 colleges held a press conference to announce formation of the Worker Rights Consortium (WRC), and called on their schools to withdraw from, or not to join, the FLA. The organization would be formally launched at a founding convention in April, 2000.[63]

The Worker Rights Consortium differed radically in its approach to eliminating sweatshops. First, the WRC did not permit corporations to join; it was comprised exclusively of universities and colleges, with unions and human rights organizations playing an advisory role. In joining the WRC, universities would agree to "require decent working conditions in factories producing their licensed products." Unlike the FLA, the WCA did not endorse a single, comprehensive set of fair labor standards. Rather, it called on its affiliated universities to develop their own codes. However, it did establish minimum standards that such codes should meet—ones that were, in some respects, stricter than the FLA's. Perhaps most significantly, companies would have to pay a living wage. Companies were also required to publish

| | |
|---|---|
| 1957 | Phil Knight and Coach Bill Bowerman met for the first time at the University of Oregon. |
| 1959 | Phil Knight graduated from the University of Oregon with a BBA degree in Accounting. |
| 1962 | Knight wrote the marketing research paper outlining the concept that became "Blue Ribbon Sports" (BRS). |
| 1963 | The first shipment of 200 Tiger shoes arrived from Japan. |
| 1966 | The first retail store was opened. |
| 1969 | Knight left the accounting field to devote his full time efforts to building the company. |
| 1970 | Nike's legal dispute with the Japanese supplier resulted in the exploration of manufacturing in Mexico, Puerto Rico and Canada. |
| 1971 | Nike contracted for the production of shoes in Mexico; however, the shoes were a disaster—cracking when used in cold weather. |
| 1972 | The first shoes bearing the Nike brand were sold. |
| 1977 | Nike contracted with factories in Taiwan and Korea, ending the manufacturing relationship with the Japanese firm. |
| 1978 | The split between Blue Ribbon Sports and their Japanese supplier became final. BRS changed to the Nike name for all operations. |
| 1980 | Nike sold the first shares of common stock to the public. |
| 1981 | Revenues were $457.7 million and Nike had 3,000 employees. |
| 1982 | Phil Knight received the Pioneer Award. The Pioneer Award was given annually by the University of Oregon to a person "whose character places him/her in a position of leadership." The award recognized individuals who led in business, philanthropy, communications, government or the arts. |
| 1986 | For the first time, Nike revenues surpassed the billion-dollar mark. |
| 1990 | Growth in international sales helped Nike reach $2 billion in revenues. Nike employed 5,300 employees in the United States. The Nike World Campus opened in Beaverton, Oregon. |
| 1991 | Revenues reached $3 billion with $869 million in international revenues. Michael Jordan wears Nike shoes while leading the Chicago Bulls to their first NBA championship. |
| 1995 | Nike's revenues were $4.8 billion. Nike shoes using the patented Nike-Air system were introduced, radically changing show design. |
| 1996 | Nike's revenues were $6.5 billion. In the Atlanta Olympics, Michael Johnson became the fastest man in the world wearing a pair of specially designed gold metallic Nike's. Phil Knight donated $25 million to the Oregon Campaign. His gift designated $15 million to the creation of endowed chairs. The remaining $10 million helped finance the construction of a new law school building that was named the William W. Knight Law Center after Phil Knight's father. The $25 million gift was the largest single gift to a university in the Pacific Northwest. Knight's earlier gifts to UO totaled $25 million. Knight funds supported athletics and the university library was named for his family in the 1980's. |

**Exhibit 1** Key Events in Nike's History[66]

| | |
|---|---|
| 1998 | Nike's revenues were $9.5 billion. Basketball shoes slumped as Michael Jordan retired and the NBA played a shortened season due to a labor dispute. Nike's international trading partner, Nissho Iwai of Japan, donated an undisclosed "generous" amount to the UO Knight Library to "honor Mr. Knight's great commitment to supporting the University of Oregon." Nissho Iwai had made a donation to the renovation of the library in 1990. One floor of the library was named for the Japanese company.[61] |
| 1999 | Nike's revenues dipped to $8.8 billion. Revenue decline was attributed to the "brown shoes" movement in the United States and the Asian economic slump. |
| 2000 | Phil Knight withdrew his pledge for a $30 million contribution for the University of Oregon's football stadium. |

**Exhibit 1** Continued

the names and addresses of all of their manufacturing facilities, in contrast to FLA rules. Universities could refuse to license goods made in countries where compliance with fair labor standards was "deemed impossible," whatever efforts companies had made to enforce their own codes in factories there.

By contrast with the FLA, monitoring would be carried out by "a network of local organizations in regions where licensed goods are produced," generally nongovernmental organizations, independent human rights groups, and unions. These organizations would conduct unannounced "spot investigations," usually in response to worker complaints; WRC organizers called this the "fire alarm" method of uncovering code violations. Systematic monitoring would not be attempted.

The consortium's governance structure reflected its mission of being an organization by and for colleges and universities. Its 12 person board was composed of 3 representatives of United Students Against Sweatshops, 3 university administrators from participating schools, and 6 members drawn from an Advisory Board of persons with "expertise in the issues surrounding worker abuses in the apparel industry and independent verification of labor standards in apparel factories." No seats at the table were reserved for industry representatives. The group would be financed by 1 percent of licensing revenue from participating universities, as well as foundation grants.

## The Universities Take Sides

Over the course of the spring semester 2000, student protests were held on a number of campuses, including the University of Oregon, to demand that their schools join the WRC. By April, around 45 schools had done so. At UO, the administration encouraged an open debate on the issue so that all sides could be heard on how to ensure that UO products were made under humane conditions. Over a period of several months, the Academic Senate passed a resolution in support of the WRC. In a referendum sponsored by the student government, three-quarters of voters supported a proposal to join the WRC. A committee of faculty, students, administrators, and alumni appointed by the president voted unanimously to join the consortium.[64] Finally, after concluding that all constituents had had an opportunity to be heard, on April 12, 2000, University of Oregon president David Frohnmayer announced that UO would join the WRC for one year. Its membership would be conditional, he said, on the Consortium's agreement to give companies a voice in its operations and universities more power in governance. Shortly after the University's decision was announced in the press, Phil Knight withdrew his philanthropic contribution. In his public announcement, he stated his main disagreements with the Worker Rights Consortium:

> Frankly, we are frustrated that factory monitoring is badly misconstrued. For us one of the great hurdles and real handicaps in the dialogue has been the complexity of the issue. For real progress to be made, all key participants have to be at the table. That's why the FLA has taken so long to get going. The WRC is supported by the AFL-CIO and its affiliated apparel workers' union, UNITE. Their main aim, logically and understandably, however misguided, is to bring apparel jobs back to the U.S. Among WRC rules, no company can participate in setting standards, or monitoring. It has an unrealistic living wage provision. And its "gotcha" approach to monitoring doesn't do what monitoring should—measure conditions and make improvements.

| | *1995* | *1996* | *1997* | *1998* | *1999* |
|---|---|---|---|---|---|
| China | 31 | 34 | 37 | 37 | 40 |
| Indonesia | 31 | 38 | 37 | 34 | 30 |
| South Korea | 16 | 11 | 5 | 2 | 1 |
| Thailand | 14 | 10 | 10 | 10 | 11 |
| Taiwan | 8 | 5 | 3 | 2 | 2 |
| Vietnam | | 2 | 8 | 11 | 12 |
| Philippines | | | 4 | 4 | 2 |
| Italy | | | | | 2 |

**Exhibit 2** Location of Shoe Production in Nike Subcontractor Factories, 1995–1999 Percent of Athletic Shoe Production by Country[67]

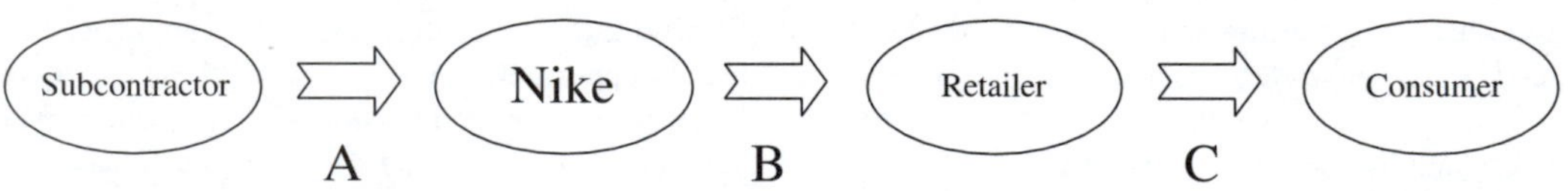


| A. COST TO NIKE | | B. COST TO RETAILER | | C. COST TO CONSUMER | |
|---|---|---|---|---|---|
| Materials | $9.00 | Nike's Operating Profit | $6.25 | Retail Sales Personnel | $9.50 |
| Tariffs | 3.00 | Sales, Distribution & Administration | 5.00 | Rent of Retail Space | 9.00 |
| Rent & Equipment | 3.00 | Promotion/Advertising | 4.00 | Retailer's Operating Profit | 9.00 |
| Production Labor | 2.75 | Research & Development | 0.25 | Other Expenses | 7.00 |
| Subcontractor's Operating Profit | 1.75 | | | | |
| Shipping | 0.50 | | | | |
| **Cost to Nike** | $20.00 | **Cost to Retailer** | $35.50 | **Cost to Consumer** | $70.00 |

**Exhibit 3** The Cost of a Pair of Nike "Air Pegasus" Shoes[68]

NIKE Inc. was founded on a handshake.

Implicit in that act was the determination that we would build our business with all our partners upon trust, teamwork, honesty and mutual respect. We expect all of our business partners to operate on the same principles.

At the core of the NIKE corporate ethic is the belief that we are a company comprised of many different kinds of people, appreciating individual diversity, and dedicated to equal opportunity for each individual.

NIKE designs, manufactures and markets sports and fitness products. At each step in that process we are dedicated to minimizing our impact on the environment. We seek to implement to the maximum extent possible the three "R's" of environmental action-reduce, reuse and recycle.

There is No Finish Line.

MEMORANDUM OF UNDERSTANDING

Wherever NIKE operates around the globe, we are guided by our Code of Conduct and bind our business partners to those principles with a signed Memorandum of Understanding.

**Government Regulation of Business** (Subcontractor/supplier) certifies compliance with all applicable local government regulations regarding minimum wage; overtime; child labor laws; provisions of pregnancy, menstrual leave; provisions for vacation and holidays; and mandatory retirement benefits.

**Safety and Health** (Subcontractor/supplier) certifies compliance with all applicable local government regulations regarding occupational health and safety.

**Worker Insurance** (Subcontractor/supplier) certifies compliance with all applicable local laws providing health insurance, life insurance and worker's compensation.

**Forced Labor** (Subcontractor/supplier) certifies that it and its suppliers and contractors do not use any form of forced labor—prison or otherwise.

**Environment** (Subcontractor/supplier) certifies compliance with all applicable local environmental regulations, and adhere to NIKE's own broader environmental practices, including the prohibition on the use of chloro-flouro-carbons (CFCs), the release of which could contribute to the depletion of the earth's ozone layer.

**Equal Opportunity** (Subcontractor/supplier) certifies that it does not discriminate in hiring, salary, benefits, advancement, termination or retirement on the basis of gender, race, religion, age, sexual orientation or ethnic origin.

**Documentation and Inspection** (Subcontractor/supplier) agrees to maintain on file such documentation as may be needed to demonstrate compliance with the certifications in this Memorandum of Understanding, and further agrees to make these documents available for NIKE's inspection upon request.

---

**Exhibit 4** Nike's 1992 Code of Conduct[69]

| *Country* | *Year (Latest Available)* | *National Poverty Line* | *Minimum Wage* | *Prevailing Wage in Apparel and Footwear Industries* |
|---|---|---|---|---|
| China | 1997 | \$21-\$27/cap/mo[71] | \$12-\$39/mo | \$115-\$191/mo |
| Indonesia | 1999 | \$5-\$6/cap/mo | \$15-\$34/mo | \$15-\$42/mo |
| South Korea | 1999 | \$182/mo | \$265/mo | \$727-\$932/mo |
| Thailand | 1999 | \$22/cap/mo | \$93-\$109/mo | \$106/mo |
| Taiwan | 1998 | \$214-\$344/mo | \$476/mo | \$690-\$742/mo |
| Vietnam[72] | 1997 | \$27-\$29/mo | \$35-\$45/mo | \$47-\$56/mo |
| Philippines | 1999 | \$26/cap/mo | \$150/mo | \$150/mo |
| Italy | 1998 | \$390/cap/mo | \$949-1,445/mo | \$1,280-\$1,285/mo |
| United States | 1998 | \$693/cap/mo | \$858/mo-\$1,083/mo | \$1,420-\$1,488/mo |

N*ational Poverty Line:* Poverty measures reflect an estimate of absolute poverty thresholds based on some specified set of basic needs. Opinions differ as to whether the poverty line should reflect mere physical subsistence levels or sufficient income to provide for a nutritious diet, safe drinking water, suitable housing, energy, transportation, health care, child care, education, savings and discretionary income. Comparability between countries is difficult because the basis for establishing the poverty level usually differs across countries.

*Minimum Wage:* The minimum wage fixing system differs according to the country's objectives and criteria. It is usually set by striking a balance between the needs of the worker and what employers can afford or what economic conditions will permit. A range for minimum wage indicates that the country has differential minimums based on the region, often differing for urban and rural regions.

*Prevailing Wage:* The prevailing wage reflects the "going rate" or average level of wages paid by employers for workers in the apparel or footwear industries. Positions requiring greater skills, supervisory responsibilities or workers with longer years of employment typically earn more than the wage reported. Non-wage benefits such as access to health care, paid vacations, supplementary pay or training are not included in the prevailing wage.

**Exhibit 5** Wages, Minimum Wages and Poverty Lines for Selected Countries[70] in U.S. Dollars

## Notes

1. This case was written on the basis of publicly available information solely for the purpose of stimulating student discussion. All individuals and events are real. An earlier version of this case was presented at the 2000 annual meeting of the North American Case Research Association. The comments of reviewers at that meeting and of three anonymous reviewers for the Case Research Journal are greatly appreciated.

2. "Knight's Statement," by Philip H. Knight, via press release, <http://www.oregonlive.com>.

3. Greenhouse, S. (January 26, 2000). "Anti-Sweatshop Movement is Achieving Gains Overseas," *The New York Times,* Section A, p. 10.

4. Lee, L. (February 21, 2000). "Can Nike Still Do It," *Business Week,* p. 120.

5. Martinson, J. (July 8, 2000). "Brand Values: Nike: The Sweet Swoosh of Success," *The Guardian* (London), Guardian City Pages, p. 26.

6. Anonymous. (October 11, 1999). "The Forbes 400: America's Richest People," *Forbes,* p. 296.

7. *Our History: BRS Becomes Nike.* (n.d). Nike, Inc. Accessed: February 3, 2000. <http://www.nikebiz.com/story/before.shtml>.

8. *Our History: In Our Own League.* (n.d.). Nike, Inc. Accessed: February 3, 2000. <http://www.nikebiz.com/story/chrono.shtml>.

9. Nike, Inc. (1999, May 31—filing date). *Form 10-K.* Securities and Exchange Commission. Accessed: February 5, 2000.

10. Gellene, D. (April 8, 1999). "Ad Reviews: Adidas," *The Los Angeles Times,* Part C, p. 6.

11. Katz, D. R. (1995), *Just Do It: The Nike Spirit in the Corporate World,* Holbrook, MA: Adams Media Corporation, p. 132.

12. *Just Do It,* p. 130.

13. Although Nike operated shoe factories in New England in the 1970s and 1980s, Nike's annual U.S. production never accounted for more than one week of demand annually. Later, these plants were closed, and Nike stopped producing shoes in the U.S., other than prototypes.

14. Nike, Inc. (1999, May 31—filing date). *Form 10-K.* Securities and Exchange Commission. Accessed: February 5, 2000.

15. Vanderbilt, T. (1998). *The Sneaker Book.* New York: The New Press, p. 77.

16. *Just Do It,* 162.

17. *The Sneaker Book,* p. 81.

18. *The Sneaker Book,* p. 90.

19. Austen, J. and Barff, R. (1993). "It's gotta be da shoes," *Environment and Planning,* 25, pp. 48–52.

20. Greenhouse, S. (January 26, 2000). "Anti-Sweatshop Movement is Achieving Gains Overseas," *The New York Times,* Section A, P. 10.

21. Descriptions of the Tae Kwang Vina factory in Bien Hoa City were derived from the following: Manning, J. (November 9, 1997). "Nike: Track's Across the Globe" [Three part newspaper series originally appearing in *The Oregonian*] online source <http://oregonlive.com/series/nike 11091.html>. Katz, D.R. (1995). *Just Do It: The Nike Spirit in the Corporate World,* Holbrook, MA: Adams Media Corporation. Vanderbilt, T. (1998), *The Sneaker Book,* New York: The New Press. Ernst & Young, (January 13, 1997). *Ernst & Young Environmental and Labor Practice Audit of the Tae Kwang Vina Industrial Ltd. Co., Vietnam.* [Copy of the audit available at <http://www.corpwatch.org/trac/nike/audit.html>].

22. Greenhouse, S. (November 8, 1997). "Nike Shoe Plant in Vietnam Is Called Unsafe for Workers," *The New York Times,* Section A, p. 1.

23. *Just Do It,* p. 161.

24. Manning, J. (November 9, 1997). "Nike: Track's Across the Globe" [Three part newspaper series originally appearing in *The Oregonian*] online source <http://oregonlive.com/series/nike 11091.html>.

25. Manning, J. (November 11, 1997). "Poverty's Legions Flock to Nike," *The Oregonian,* <http://www.oregonlive.com/series/nike11103.html>.

26. *Ernst & Young Audit.* (n.d.). Corporate Watch. Accessed: March 26, 2000. <http://www.corpwatch.org/trac/nike/audit.html>.

27. *Ernst & Young Audit.* (n.d.). Corporate Watch. Accessed: March 26, 2000. <http://www.corpwatch.org/trac/nike/audit.html>.

28. Manning, J. (November 9, 1997). "Nike: Track's Across the Globe" [Three part newspaper series originally appearing in *The Oregonian*] online source <http://oregonlive.com/series/nike 11091.html>.

29. Manning, J. (November 9, 1997). "Nike's Asian Machine Goes on Trial" Part 1 of a three part newspaper series originally appearing in *The Oregonian*] online source <http://oregonlive.com/series/nike11091.html>.

30. Manning, J. (November 10, 1997). "Poverty's Legions Flock to Nike" Part 2 of a three part newspaper series originally appearing in *The Oregonian*] online source <http://oregonlive.com/series/nike11091.html>.

31. *The Sneaker Book,* p. 84.

32. Skivers are cutting tools that are used to split leather. In athletic shoe manufacturing, skivers are used to cut away the excess leather when bonding the upper to the sole.

33. *Ernst & Young Audit.* (n.d.). Corporate Watch. Accessed: March 26, 2000. <http://www.corpwatch.org/trac/nike/audit.html>.

34. *Just Do It,* p. 160.

35. Lamb, D. (April 18, 1999). "Job Opportunity or Exploitation?," *The Los Angeles Times,* Part C. p. 1.

36. Baum, B. (August 27, 1999). "Study Concludes That Nike Workers Can More Than Make Ends Meet," *Athenaeum* [online version available at: <http://www.athensnewspapers.com/1997/101797/1017.a3nike.html>].

37. Manning, J. (November 10, 1997). "Poverty's Legions Flock to Nike" Part 2 of a three part newspaper series originally appearing in *The Oregonian*] online source [<http://oregonlive.com/series/nike11091.html>].

38. Ballinger, J. (August 1992). "Nike: The New Free Trade Heel," *Harper's,* p. 119.

39. *Just Do It,* p. 166.

40. *Just do It,* p. 187.

41. Schanberg, S. (June 1996). "Six Cents an Hour," *Life Magazine,* pp. 38–47.

42. Holstein, W.J., Palmer, B., Ur-Rehman, S. and Ito, T. (December 23, 1996). "Santa's Sweatshops," *U.S. News and World Report,* p. 50.

43. The *48 Hours* report, however, neglected to mention that supervisor had subsequently been fired and was later criminally convicted in Vietnamese court (*Just Do It,* p. 188.).

44. CBS News 48 Hours (October 17, 1996), transcript.

45. Manning, J. (November 10, 1997). "Poverty's Legions Flock to Nike," [Part 2 in Nike: Tracks Across the Globe Series]. *The Oregonian* <http://wwworegonlive.com/series/nike11101.html>.

46. Philip Knight, Speech to the National Press Club, May 12, 1998.

47. *Just Do It,* p. 191.

48. *Just Do It,* p. 191.

49. Goozner, M. (November 7, 1994). "Nike Manager Knows Abuses Do Happen," *The Chicago Tribune,* p. 6.

50. Hammond, K. (November 7, 1997). "Leaked Audit: Nike Factory Violated Worker Laws," *Mother Jones.* <http://www.motherjones.com/news_wire/nike.html>.

51. Glass, S. (August 25, 1997). "The Young and the Feckless," *The New Republic,* online source: <http://www.corpwatch.org/trac/feature/sweatshops/newprogressive.html>. Glass was later fired by *The New Republic,* which charged that Glass had fabricated some of his sources for this and other articles.

52. Federal News Service. (May 12, 1998). National Press Club Luncheon Address By Philip Knight, Chief Executive Officer, Nike. LEXIS-NEXIS Academic Universe, Category: News. Accessed: August 27, 2000 *<http://web.lexis-nexis.com/universe>.*

53. "Companies Agree to Meet on Sweatshops," *Washington Post,* August 3, 1996.

54. [For the full text of the Fair Labor Association Workplace Code of Conduct, see <http://www.fairlabor.org/html/amendctr.html#workplace>].

55. Philip H. Knight, statement released to the press April 14, 1997.

56. Steven Greenhouse, "Anti-Sweatshop Coalition Finds Itself at Odds on Garment Factory Code," *New York Times,* July 3, 1998.

57. [For a description of the monitoring process, see: <http://www.fairlabor.org/html/amendctr.html#monitoringprocess>].

58. "Plan to Curtain Sweatshops Rejected by Union," *New York Times,* November 5, 1998.

59. [For a list of signatory companies, universities, and other organizations, see: <http://www.fairlabor.org/html/affiliat.html>.]

60. *New York Times,* November 21, 1997.

61. Anonymous. (June 15, 1991). Indonesia: Staying Alive, *The Economist,* p. 38.

62. Alan Howard, "Partners in Sweat," *The Nation,* December 29, 1998.

63. The Web site for the WRC is: <http://www.workersrights.org>. Further material on disagreements within the FLA that led to the WRC's founding may be found at: <http://www.sweatshopwatch.org>.

64. Sarah Edith Jacobson, "Nike's Power Game" [editorial page letter], *New York Times,* May 16, 2000.

65. "Knight's Statement," by Philip H. Knight, via press release, <http://www.oregonlive.com>.

66. Based on the following sources: *Our History.* (n.d.). Nike, Inc. Accessed: February 3, 2000. <http://www.nikebiz.com/story/chrono.shtml>. Katz, D.R. (1995). Just Do It: The Nike Spirit in the Corporate World, Holbrook, MA: Adams Media Corporation. Nike, Inc. (1995–1999). *Form 10-K.* Securities and Exchange Commission. Accessed: February 5, 2000.

67. Nike 10-K statements, 1995–1999

68. Adapted from *Washington Post,* (May 3, 1995). "Why It Costs $70 for a Pair of Athletic Shoes."

69. Code of Conduct. (n.d.). Nike, Inc. Accessed: November 18, 2000. <http://www.nikebiz.com/labor/code.shtml>.

70. U.S. Department of Labor, (February, 2000). Wages, Benefits, Poverty Line and Meeting Workers' Needs in the Apparel and Footwear Industries of Selected Countries. <http://www.dol.gov/ilab/public/media/reports/ oiea/main.htm>.

71. Per capita per month.

72. Canada NewsWire, (October 16, 1997). Nike Factory Workers in SE Asia Help Support Their Families and Have Discretionary Income, According to Preliminary Findings of Study By MBA Team From Dartmouth's Tuck School.

# Case 2.2

# HOW MUCH SLEAZE IS TOO MUCH?

ASBJORN OSLAND

## Overview

Eric had returned to Africa as a field director assigned to Senegal after a failed rotation through the organization's headquarters. Now in Senegal, Eric was pleased that the program was going well but concerned that he had become too accommodating in his approach to ethical issues. Things that he would previously have judged as clearly wrong, he now tolerated. He wondered if his faded idealism had been supplanted by a realism that bordered on unethical. Should he continue to show flexibility in his handling of ethical dilemmas? Should he renew his youthful idealism and refuse to budge on behaviors that were clearly wrong by North American standards? Should he simply leave and no longer have to deal with the question of "how much sleaze is too much?"

## Development International

Development International was founded in the 1930s to assist war orphans of the Spanish civil war. It is a child sponsorship agency that markets its appeal through the personal identification of the donor with a sponsored child and family. The agency experienced rapid growth from the 1970s through the 1990s, primarily funded by donors from Canada, the United States, and the Netherlands. Given the need to enroll more poor families, the program was established in Senegal in 1982. Control over the donors' contributions, used to finance development projects in the Third World, was a critical value expressed by Development International; field directors were regularly fired for failing to exert sufficient control.

## Eric

Eric began his career in international service as a Peace Corps volunteer in his mid 20s. After he left Peace Corps, he worked for Development International in Latin America and French West Africa. In the process, he found that he enjoyed the process of building a new program more than managing one that was already established. He also enjoyed the autonomy of working thousands of miles away from the direct control of his superior. He liked the responsibility of establishing and managing a program without too much interference from his superiors. He felt that he was competent and experienced as a field director. Serving the needy of the Third World gave him a sense of meaning and he felt the development projects had a positive impact.

During Eric's rotation through headquarters, his superiors concluded that his political skills were better utilized overseas, where the challenge of dealing with different cultures obligated him to

SOURCE: Previously published in *Cases in International Organizational Behavior* (1998), edited by Gary Oddou and Mark Mendenhall, Blackwell Publishers. Reprinted with permission.

interact in a diplomatic manner. Eric had incorrectly assumed that while working in his home culture he could be himself and speak candidly to his bosses. They sometimes made assertions that reflected a lack of experience in the areas of the Third World where Eric had served (i.e., West Africa and Latin America), and Eric would correct them with less diplomacy than required. That, combined with the fact that Eric was used to running his own show, made it difficult for Eric to integrate into the headquarters. He lacked the political sensitivity to interact effectively in a headquarters environment. In contrast, while overseas he had learned to be very careful, as a rule, and present himself in a manner that was respectful of the foreign culture. Because Eric had insulted his superiors at headquarters and given them the impression that he regarded them as incompetent, the international director felt that Eric's skills could be utilized more effectively in Africa. He had previously served there and accomplished that which the organization desired—i.e., enrolled enough families so that contributions covered expenses as well as developed programs that were recognized by the host government officials as meeting the needs of the population served. Although he had enjoyed working in Africa, he was tired of working in the Third World. He found it exasperating and had lost his zeal or sense of mission for Development International. After the transfer had been announced, he saw the errors of his brutal candor but felt let down by his bosses whom he previously had admired a great deal. Therefore he tried to find another job but it proved impossible.

So off he went, first to negotiate the establishment of a program in Central Africa. However, the official with whom he had to arrange the details of the agreement repeatedly asked for substantial bribes. Eric refused to pay them and told his headquarters. Consequently, his boss arranged for him to go to Senegal where the central government proved highly cooperative and an agreement was signed in several weeks. Eric then returned to the U.S., reported to headquarters and received a conditional go ahead, subject to the international board's approval, to begin operations in Senegal. He then returned to Senegal with Jennifer and their children. Jennifer proved a good sport for the move, though she was saddened that Eric felt so badly about the exile. Eric was worried by the prospect of illness for his children, based on previous experience in Africa, and the work his wife would have to undertake to establish a home in conditions of great hardship.

In Senegal, his coping strategy for the stress he suffered proved self-destructive. He and his expatriate friends would get together once or twice a week and indulge themselves in long bouts of jogging followed by rewarding themselves with a beer for each of the many kilometers jogged. This caused his wife great dismay.

Eric was unsure of his status within the organization, given his forced transfer from the headquarters. He was close to completing his ten years with Development International, which would guarantee him some retirement benefits, at which time he and his wife Jennifer planned to return to graduate school. However, for the next two years, he would have to accomplish the organization's goals. He knew that he had to work closely with productive, though sometimes corrupt, indigenous leaders, such as Saidou.

## Saidou

Eric found the Senegalese government amenable to the establishment of a program and the preliminary arrangements with the central government went smoothly. Eric then requested the necessary tax exoneration on a vehicle and was awaiting the approval. This process generally took six to eight weeks. It was worth the wait as excise taxes on vehicles were several hundred percent of the landed value. He had been in contact with the local development office in northern Senegal and had made arrangements to visit the rural areas where the program would begin. He and his family took up temporary residence in a local hotel built during the colonial era on the Senegal River at the foot of the bridge crossing the river.

His contact, Saidou, had proven cooperative. Saidou was the assistant director of the regional office of the national government's ministry of social development, the branch of the national government with which Development International had signed its agreement. Eric enjoyed Saidou's company and his stories. Saidou was in his early 50's at that time. One morning, Eric entered his office, directly across from the hotel. In broken Wolof, the local African language spoken by many Senegalese, Eric said, "Good morning."

Saidou responded with a smile and a question that Eric didn't understand. Saidou noted that Eric hadn't understood and clarified, "I asked how your son was." Eric had noticed that Third World people always seemed to ask about his son but not his daughters.

Eric had been thinking about Saidou's stories of the post-independence period. "You once said you had been to Moscow. How did that come about?" he asked.

Saidou responded, "During the early years of independence we were fairly leftist in our sympathies. Also, there was lots of money available for training all over the place. I also went to Israel, before the boycott, and to France."

"How did you like France?" asked Eric. Eric noted that Saidou's demeanor changed, and he seemed to grow cold and distant.

Saidou looked away and said, "You have no idea how painful it was. People would run from me and point at me. They said I was a monkey."

Eric added, "I noticed that the waiters in the hotel treat the French guests with chilling distance. Yet with us, once they hear our American accents, they seem to warm up. Why is that?"

Saidou explained, "The Americans have a better reputation. During World War II, they provided relief, which was well received and is remembered by the older segment of the population. Also, Peace Corps Volunteers generally attempt to learn the local languages, something few French nationals do."

Saidou looked with warmth at Eric. He seemed to see some of that Peace Corps-like desire to assist in Eric. Over the next few months, Saidou guided Eric through the labyrinth of officialdom to get the program started. Eric often visited him in his office to consult about different concerns as they arose.

Saidou's assistance extended to the personal domain as well. Eric had fallen years before off a roof and suffered a herniated disc that became aggravated in Senegal, perhaps due to jogging. As it was evident that Eric was occasionally in great pain, Saidou thought he could best help his new friend by introducing him to a traditional healer. Eric was prepared to cooperate with incantations and dancing but was not about to drink the "prescribed" purgative that would provide the necessary "output," which the healer would then "read" to determine whether or not the problem had been cured. "How is it that a well-educated man like Saidou would trust such cures?" wondered Eric. However, Eric simply accepted this difference as one of many where he and Saidou clearly marched to a different drummer. Eric enjoyed these differences with Saidou, which made it interesting to work in Africa. He also respected Saidou a great deal as a development professional.

Eric wanted to hire Saidou to head the program. He found him extremely knowledgeable about development and well connected with the traditional leaders of the villages in the surrounding area. He had confidence in Saidou's commitment to serving his people. He saw Saidou as a man possessed with a desire to serve—it was his last chance to make the contribution he had dreamed of as a young man during the heady days of independence. Then his career had somehow been derailed, and he was relegated to spending his time smoking and waiting for the day to end in his office. Eric also knew Saidou had the ability to generate solid program results. One day Eric asked him if he wanted a job: "Saidou, you have all the experience one could ever hope for. I wonder if you could somehow get the government to assign you to Development International? We'd pay you a good salary and provide you with a vehicle."

Saidou put down his newspaper and placed his cigarette holder in the overflowing ashtray. He then pulled out a Kola nut (a source of caffeine) from his tunic top and broke off a piece and began to chew it. Eric noted the pair of stub fingers that had resulted from an accident Saidou had suffered as an apprentice carpenter working for a Frenchman during the colonial era. Saidou spoke with bitterness about the incident, describing the conditions as unsafe. After what seemed like a few minutes, Saidou responded, "It'll take some doing but, yes, I'm interested." He rose and they shook hands.

During a subsequent visit, Eric noted that Saidou appeared very anxious and quietly asked, "Is something bothering you?"

Saidou responded, "I don't know how I'm going to make ends meet. I can't go to work for you until the government gives its approval, yet I don't have the money at the moment to buy the rice I need to feed my two families next month." Saidou had two wives who lived in separate homes and he was short 100 kilograms of rice, the monthly ration for all the people he was expected to feed. Almost in the same breath, Saidou suggested, "Say, while we wait for your customs clearance on the vehicle to come through, we could repair a vehicle that the government has. It would only be about $75 dollars."

Eric was suspicious but agreed. Saidou looked away at the window and said, "God is great." Eric wondered what he meant, as the car never did appear, though it was always "almost" ready each time Eric questioned Saidou. Eventually Eric stopped asking.

After the government gave its approval and the customs clearance finally came through for Development International to purchase vehicles, Saidou went to work and proved to be an extremely industrious and effective program head. Since he was well connected to the informal network that ran the country, he could generally work out whatever problems occurred with the government. The official bureaucracy seemed to exist to provide jobs for the educated elite, in Eric's view. However, the informal network of kinship and collegial bonds was highly effective. With Saidou working the informal system, Eric and Development International were spared the onerous task of obtaining written approval for each specific project, though Saidou always obtained verbal approval from the local official.

### Budget Planning and Changes

While at headquarters, Eric had developed a planning format called the Situation Assessment and Goal Establishment, the SAGE report. This was the core document on which the budget would be based. Eric enjoyed this period of planning. He would obtain reports from the U.S. government in Senegal in which the development priorities and needs of the country were described and discussed, based on studies prepared by experts. Development International had also engaged the services of an American scholar who was an expert on Senegal. Armed with the information contained in such reports, Eric and Saidou would next speak with the various local officials and village leaders, conversations that generally proved very informative.

However, the villagers would present long lists of needs that were indeed apparent; education, health, infrastructure (i.e., public water sources, roads, schools, clinics, etc.) and jobs were all desperately needed. Nevertheless, Development International could not provide everything. This was also beyond the ability of the community to support and sustain. The communities that received assistance were generally asked to provide in-kind support—usually "sweat equity" (i.e., manual labor to complete the projects). The projects they were willing to support with hard work were the ones Saidou felt they should do. However, only future experience would show what villagers were willing to support. Because Eric had to present an annual budget and was unsure of what people would contribute their sweat equity toward, he included the lengthy list of requests made by the villagers. The budget had been approved and they were in the implementation phase, when the monthly financial statements would be monitored by the international controller.

Eric had experienced difficulty with the international controller in previous years when he had attempted to be responsive to changing development priorities due to natural disaster, political turmoil, and the need to substitute projects planned by Development International but then undertaken by other agencies. The controller had accused Eric of poor control and attempted to cause him to lose face with the international executive director. However, Eric's immediate supervisor had come to his aid and documented the approval he had given for such flexibility.

Eric enjoyed the flexibility of beginning a new program. One never knew what would occur. For example, while launching the program in Senegal, a drought occurred. The area served by Development International was at the northern-most limit of peanut cultivation in the country. Senegal depended on peanut exportation for foreign exchange. During the colonial era, the French had encouraged the country to switch from subsistence crops, such as millet, that were well suited to the soil and growing conditions, to peanuts, a cash crop. To compensate for the food deficiency brought about by the abandonment of subsistence crops, the French imported broken rice from Indochina, also then under French rule. However, peanut cultivation exhausted the sandy soils in northern Senegal. During the period Eric served in Senegal, there was virtually a total peanut crop failure in the area just south of St. Louis due to the drought. Many of the able-bodied men, and some women, left home to work in the capital or other major cities in labor-intensive jobs. Some men traveled to other African nations and France as well. They sent remittances home to avert the starvation of their families.

One morning Saidou entered Eric's office. He sat down and smoked several cigarettes while discussing varied concerns. Then he observed, "These are desperate times for the villagers. We need to help them and I believe their desperation could serve as motivation to work hard on suitable projects related to food. Why don't we take a drive to visit the site of a community garden so you can see what I mean?" Eric agreed. He had wanted to see what had become of the community gardens, two of which had been budgeted. Eric loved this part of his job, when he and Saidou would drive throughout the rural area they served.

On the way they stopped at a small store so that Saidou could get a pack of cigarettes. Eric enjoyed these small stores because they sold one cigarette at a time, thereby permitting him a taste of indulgence without the embarrassment of bumming one from Saidou. These tiny stores were found in every small town and neighborhood of larger towns or cities. Saidou explained that the owners were Mauritanians, Arabs working in Black Africa. They used relatives to operate and live in the store in a bondage-like arrangement. The boss, a patriarch of the clan, would travel from store to store in an aging Mercedes Benz collecting the day's revenues. He would then go to the bank to make a cash deposit. Bank patrons were often forced to await such deposits to cash their checks, since the bank seldom had cash. The Mauritanians came in daily with their shopping bags full of dirty small bills to replenish the coffers of the bank. Eric appreciated such cultural explanations provided by Saidou as to why things were the way they were.

During village visits, Eric watched Saidou speak with the villagers. They sat for long periods, sipping very strong sweetened green tea made in an elaborate ceremony. Beautiful young women often served the tea. Though scarcely eighteen years old, one of them caught Saidou's eye. He later took her as his third wife. Eric enjoyed watching Saidou and the girl's relatives laugh and talk.

Eric was always struck by the contrast of such joy with the pathetic image presented in the American press of Africa. He became convinced that the Africans he had known were generally happier than most of his compatriots, though lacking in material wealth and other objective measures of development (i.e., infant mortality, life expectancy etc.). Like Saidou said, "There's more to life than life expectancy."

As they approached the village in the car, Saidou told Eric, "Yesterday I came here and told the villagers that they would have to choose a site and fence it off. We would then put in the wells they need for water." When Saidou stopped the car at the top of the hill, both Eric and Saidou were stunned to see about 50 people, both men and women, completing the perimeter of the garden. They had planted a living fence, a type of shrub. One often finds such fencing material in the tropics, sometimes with barbed wire attached after the shrubs had grown tall enough. Here, they didn't have the money for barbed wire and relied instead on thorn bushes to fill in the holes in the fence. Saidou exclaimed, "Look at that! In 24 hours they've almost completed what I thought would take them several weeks." The villager elders approached and gathered around Saidou. He complimented them on their achievement and spoke with them about the next steps. They would have to house and feed the well diggers as well as assist them in their work.

Saidou and Eric drove back to St. Louis in the late afternoon after completing their work. At that time, the softer light brought out colors and shapes that the sun of mid-day seemed to suffocate in its blaze. Appreciative of the shifting light, Eric felt a sense of comfort. Eric returned from his day dreaming and asked, "Why do you think the villagers built the fence so quickly"

"They simply don't have much hope in the peanut harvest. These community gardens are a potential source of vegetables for the families as well as a likely supplement to their income," replied Saidou.

"Too bad we didn't budget more of these gardens. It looks like something all 20 villages could use," observed Eric.

"That's true. Why can't we do more of the gardens and fewer schools and health projects?" asked Saidou. "We'd finance the gardens with those funds."

"That's logical, but I don't know if our headquarters will go for it. Let me think about it," said Eric. They drove the rest of the way in silence, interrupted by occasional small talk. Eric was preoccupied with his thoughts about the gardens. He wanted to spend the funds allocated to other projects on the gardens but worried that the controller and others at headquarters would object to major changes in the budget at mid-year. Also, the health and education projects were important. However, Eric saw for himself the nearly desperate level of motivation displayed by the villagers for the gardens. He worried about his tentative status with the organization and if he had the political clout to get this budget change approved. He went to bed that night discussing the matter with his wife. His wife tried to help, but Eric found it difficult to believe in himself enough to feel influential. He didn't want to appear both disorganized (i.e., ask for a major change to the program budget) and too flexible in his response to the requests from the authorities for payments and Saidou's improper behavior.

## More Control Problems

In mulling over Saidou's proposals, Eric thought about some of the problems with Saidou. He noticed that when he sent Saidou to the capital with the accountant, another Senegalese, to make major purchases, they would always be charged more than Eric found he would be charged for comparable purchases. Eric brought this up to the accountant: "How is it that when I make purchases I pay less than what you and Saidou pay?" Eric noted the smile on the accountant's face.

"I think you should make the purchases," came the reply.

Saidou was also hypersensitive to Western style audits that Eric would periodically ask the accounting staff to perform. Saidou became extremely upset and indignant that Eric would have the "gall" to send a young female accountant to audit one of his projects. "How could you send a grandchild of mine to check on me?"

Eric didn't respond to Saidou but excused himself by saying he had to check on something in the donor services office. He didn't want to have this matter blow up into an argument. Besides, he thought to himself, "I don't see how Saidou is related to the accountant except as part of the same large clan."

Though he needed Saidou to get the job done, he wondered how an eventual successor would deal with Saidou. Eric made a mental note to himself: "It seems that Africans tolerate my audits and follow-up memos, yet go ballistic when a compatriot does the same thing."

Though Saidou was opportunistic in his behavior regarding the resources of Development International, he proved very helpful to Eric in dealing with the tremendous frustration one can encounter in such settings.

One such instance that Saidou helped resolve was a contract that had not been fulfilled by a local cabinet-maker. Eric had worked with the cabinet-maker, Alioune, for a year, during which time he had made good furniture for the office. When funding was approved for a school desk project, Eric asked Alioune and several other local cabinet-makers to bid on the project. Eric used other low bids and added the additional leverage of a substantial advance for materials to pressure Alioune into lowering his bid. Eric liked working with Alioune and wanted to help him raise the funds to purchase a power saw. Alioune agreed to Eric's terms without objection. He would likely have protested had a compatriot of comparable class and age coerced him in this way. However, Alioune was a poor man with limited capital and opportunities. He perceived Eric as representing power and money. It was the chance of a lifetime for Alioune—he would never be able to save enough money to purchase a table saw, given the intense competition from other artisans and the demands on his cash made by family members.

However, after the saw had been installed and materials stockpiled, deliveries failed to meet the schedule. Alioune had actually cut himself on the saw, which was an acceptable excuse for a time. Eric realized how mean-spirited he had become when he met with Alioune and noticed the bandage. Rather than immediately feeling sympathy, Eric had felt scorn when Alioune asked for an extension. Eric's granted the extension, but he was alarmed at his latent hostility. A few months passed, Alioune's wound healed and he still did not deliver the desks as promised.

Eric didn't know exactly how to proceed, but Alioune's failure to fulfill the contract signified a sizable control problem that the regional auditor from the international headquarters would have to be told of during his forthcoming visit. Directors were fired for such things. Saidou suggested that he apply family pressure on Alioune. He called a meeting of Alioune's family and used shame to get him to resume deliveries.

Eric feared the auditor's report regarding Alioune, as there was a potential loss of several thousand dollars. He wondered what a Western auditor would write in his or her report. It could read, "A seemingly reckless advance was made to an impoverished local cabinet-maker to fill a larger order than any he had ever delivered. He is now several months behind in deliveries. The field director claims to have taken appropriate action by holding a meeting with his father and other elders, a group of what appeared to be retired, frail men dressed in traditional garb." Eric winced at the thought of such a report reaching the international controller. On several occasions he had pushed the controller's limits and Eric felt the controller was waiting to nail him.

In Senegal, things just didn't work the same way they did in developed countries, Eric would mutter to himself. One day he had been summoned to the office of Amadou, the regional director of social development. Amadou accused Eric of being uncooperative and threatened to denounce him to the minister. Eric never found out what he had done. Perhaps he had been too demanding of a few local contractors who Eric had accused of incompetence for their inadequate services—the social network was tight and Amadou could have been told. At any rate, Eric concluded that he would have to satisfy Amadou to avoid difficulty since he could not afford to have the program fail in Senegal.

Thus, when Eric asked Amadou to go to the capital to speak with a visiting international board member of Development International, he decided to pay whatever expenses Amadou claimed, within reason. Eric knew that he needed to make a good impression on the board member—the go ahead for the village garden program depended on it. After the meeting between Eric, Amadou and the board member, Amadou informed Eric that he had "lost" the money and could not pay his hotel bill nor get back to St. Louis. Eric suspected that the funds would be used for his personal benefit. However, since Amadou could make it very difficult for Eric to manage his program and had given an excuse, Eric paid him and duly recorded the payments in the "Other Expenses" section of the monthly financial statement with a full explanation.

Another particularly galling situation, in Eric's view, involved the work inspector. All employees in Senegal had to be referred by the work inspector, a dubious legacy from the French. Given his position as a gatekeeper or channel to employers, the work inspector enjoyed considerable power over applicants. For example, all the initial candidates for secretarial positions were very attractive but none could type. Eric suspected they were required to perform sexual favors for the work inspector. One could keep rejecting candidates until a suitable one was sent, but this meant quite a number of rejections. The work inspector could also inspect an office at will and levy large fines for infractions, real or imagined. He would summon Eric to his office, make him wait all morning, and then extort gasoline coupons from Eric with the veiled threat of an inspection. The choice was pay or suffer an audit; Eric paid.

Though he succeeded in managing the relationship with the work inspector, Eric had become callused to the point where he wondered if he had not crossed the line from facilitation payments to bribery. According to the Foreign Corrupt Practices Act, Eric understood that a facilitation payment was a legal payment to speed the process for something that would eventually occur without the payment. On the other hand, a bribe was an illegal payment made so that something would happen that would otherwise not occur. "Were the gasoline coupons a bribe?" Eric wondered. He rationalized the incident to himself by concluding that he would have donated the coupons to the work inspector had he simply asked - he had done this before with another official and reported it as such in the financial statements. The work inspector's treatment left Eric with a bitter taste in his mouth but as time went on, the work inspector came to respect Eric as a decent employer and stopped calling on Eric for such assistance.

Once the local authorities had accepted him, Eric found that they didn't continue asking for favors. He asked Saidou about this.

Saidou responded in a fatherly tone, "You were kind of hard to get along with when you first came. You seemed bitter. However, over time you seem to have calmed down. Also, I think the authorities have recognized the contributions made to rural development by our programs. The other thing you always have to remember is that the French were very mean to us in school and when they were our colonial administrators. We've all grown up with tremendous hostility. Thus, when we can stick it to a white man, we are tempted to do so." Saidou smiled mischievously and they both laughed at this last statement.

Eric enjoyed such moments with Saidou. Saidou could always explain why things were the way they were. However, Eric wondered if he hadn't been too flexible with the authorities and Saidou. Their behavior had been unethical by North American standards. "Have I crossed the line into unethical behavior?" Eric asked himself. He felt his frequent explanations to the international controller for such dubious payments weakened his influence in attempting to push for approval of the mid-year budget change. Yet he felt tremendous pressure to perform and achieve the program results the organization wanted from him. He spoke with Jennifer about his plight: "I don't know if I'm being practical or being unethical in paying the authorities and putting up with Saidou's requests. Sometimes I think I should be tougher and draw the line more clearly? But, if I blow it and Saidou resigns, the program could stall or the authorities could shut us down. I suppose we could simply continue for a while and then leave once I'm vested with the company after 10 years service. Then you can attend grad school. I don't know. I'm just not sure what to do."

# Case 2.3

## MOTO: COMING TO AMERICA

PATRICIA GERCIK

Moto arrived in Chicago in the middle of winter, unprepared for the raw wind that swept off the lake. The first day he bought a new coat and fur lined boots. He was cheered by a helpful salesgirl who smiled as she packed his lined raincoat into a box. Americans were nice, Moto decided. He was not worried about his assignment in America. The land had been purchased, and Moto's responsibility was to hire a contracting company and check on the pricing details. The job seemed straightforward.

Moto's firm, KKD, an auto parts supplier, had spent 1½ years researching American building contractors. Allmack had the best record in terms of timely delivery and liaisons with good architects and the best suppliers of raw materials. That night Moto called Mr. Crowell of Allmack, who confirmed the appointment for the next morning. His tone was amiable.

Moto arrived at the Allmack office at nine sharp. He had brought a set of *kokeshi* dolls for Crowell. The dolls, which his wife had spent a good part of the day picking out, were made from a special maple in the mountains near his family home in Niigata. He would explain that to Crowell later, when they knew each other. Crowell also came from a hilly snowy place, which was called Vermont.

When the secretary ushered him in, Crowell stood immediately and rounded his desk with an outstretched hand. Squeezing Moto's hand he roared, "How are you? Long trip from Tokyo. Please sit down, please."

Moto smiled. He reached in his jacket for his card. By the time he presented it, Crowell was back on the other side of the desk. "My card," Moto said seriously.

"Yes, yes," Crowell answered. He put Moto's card in his pocket without a glance.

Moto stared at the floor. This could not be happening, he thought. Everything was on that card: KKD, Moto, Michio, Project Director.

KKD meant University of Tokyo and years of hard work to earn a high recommendation from Dr. Iwasa's laboratory. Crowell had simply put it away.

"Here." Crowell handed his card.

"Oh, John Crowell, Allmack, President," Moto read aloud, slowly trying to recover his equilibrium. "Allmack is famous in Japan."

"You know me," Crowell replied and grinned. All those faxes. Pleased to meet you, Moto. I have a good feeling about this deal."

Moto smiled and laid Crowell's card on the table before him.

"KKD is pleased to do business with Allmack," Moto spoke slowly. He was proud of his English. Not only had he been a top English student in high school and university, but he had also studied English in a *juku* (an after-school class) for five years. As soon as he received this assignment,

SOURCE: Reprinted with permission of the author.

he took an intensive six-week course taught by Ms. Black, an American, who also instructed him in American history and customs.

Crowell looked impatient. Moto tried to think of Ms. Black's etiquette lessons as he continued to talk about KKD and Allmack's history. "We are the best in the business," Crowell interrupted. "Ask anyone. We build the biggest and best shopping malls in the country."

Moto hesitated. He knew Allmack's record—that's why he was in the room. Surely, Crowell knew that. The box of *kokeshi* dolls pressed against his knees. Maybe he should give the gift now. No, he thought, Crowell was still talking about Allmack's achievements. Now Crowell had switched to his own achievements. Moto felt desperate.

"You'll have to come to my house," Crowell continued. "I live in a fantastic house. I had an architect from California build it. He builds for the stars, and for me." Crowell chuckled.

"Built it for my wife. She is the best wife, the very best. I call her my little sweetheart. Gave the wife the house on her birthday. Took her right up to the front door and carried her inside."

Moto shifted his weight. Perhaps if he were quiet, Crowell would change the subject. Then they could pretend the conversation never happened. "Moto-san, what's your first name? Here, we like to be on a first name basis."

"Michio," Moto whispered.

"Michio-san, you won't get a better price than from me. You can go down the block to Zimmer or Casey, but you got the best deal right here."

"I brought you a present," Moto said, handing the box of *kokeshi* dolls.

"Thanks," Crowell answered. He looked genuinely pleased as he tore open the paper. Moto looked away while Crowell picked up a *kokeshi* in each hand. "They look like Russian dolls. Hey, thanks a lot, my daughter will love them."

Moto pretended that he had not heard. I will help by ignoring him, Moto thought, deeply embarrassed.

Crowell pushed the *kokeshi* dolls aside and pressed a buzzer. "Send George in," he said.

The door opened, and a large heavyset man with a dark crew cut stepped inside the room.

"George Kubushevsky, this is Moto-san, Michio. . . ."

"How do you do?" Kubushevsky's handshake was firm.

Moto took out his card.

"Thanks," Kubushevsky said. Never carry those." He laughed and hooked his thumbs in his belt buckle. Moto nodded. He was curious. Kubushevsky must be a Jewish name—or was it Polish, or maybe German? In Japan, he'd read books about all three groups. He looked at Kubushevsky's bone structure. It was impossible to tell. He was too fat.

"George, make sure you show Michio everything. We want him to see all the suppliers, meet the right people, you understand?"

"Sure." George grinned and left the room.

Moto turned to Crowell. "Is he a real American?" Moto asked.

"A real American? What's that?"

Moto flushed. "Is he first generation?" Moto finished lamely. He remembered reading that Jews, Lebanese, and Armenians were often first generation.

"How do I know? He's just Kubushevsky."

During the next few weeks, Moto saw a great deal of Kubushevsky. Each morning he was picked up at nine and taken to a round of suppliers. Kubushevsky gave him a run down on each supplier before they met. He was amiable and polite, but never really intimate. Moto's response was also to be polite. Once he suggested that they go drinking after work, but Kubushevsky flatly refused, saying that he had to work early the next morning. Moto sighed, remembering his favorite bar and hostess in Tokyo. Yuko-san must be nearly fifty now he thought affectionately. She could make him laugh. He wished he was barhopping with his colleagues from his *ringi* group at KKD. Moto regretted that he had not brought more *kokeshi* dolls, since Kubushevsky had not seemed delighted with the present of the KKD pen.

One morning they were driving to a cement outlet.

"George."

"Yes, Michio-san."

Moto paused. He still found it difficult to call Kubushevsky by his first name. "Do you think I could have some papers?"

"What kind of papers?" Kubushevsky's voice was friendly. Crowell kept an even tone. Moto liked that.

"I need papers on the past sales of these people."

"We're the best."

"I need records for the past five years on the cement place we are going to visit."

"I told you, Michio-san, I'm taking you to the best! What do you want?"

"I need some records."

"Trust me, I know what I am doing."

Moto was silent. He did not know what to say. What did trust have to do with anything? His *ringi* group in Tokyo needed documentation so they could discuss the issues and be involved in the decision. If the decision to go with one supplier or the other was correct, that should be reflected in the figures.

"Just look at what's going on now," George said. "Charts for the last five years that's history."

Moto remained silent. George pressed his foot to the gas pedal. The car passed one truck, and then another. Moto looked nervously at the climbing speedometer. Suddenly Kubushevsky whistled and released his foot. "All right, Michio-san, I'll get you the dammed figures."

"Thanks," Moto said softly.

"After we see the cement people, let's go for a drink."

Moto looked uneasily at the soft red light bulb that lit the bar. He sipped his beer and ate a few peanuts. Kubushevsky was staring at a tall blonde at the other end of the bar. She seemed to notice him also. Her fingers moved across the rim of the glass.

"George," Moto said gently. "Where are you from, George?"

Here and there," Kubushevsky said idly, still eyeing the blonde.

Moto laughed. "Here and there."

Kubushevsky nodded. "Here and there," he repeated.

"You Americans," Moto said. "You must have a home."

"No home, Michio-san."

The blonde slid her drink down the bar and slipped into the next seat. Kubushevsky turned more toward her.

Moto felt desperate. Last week Crowell had also acted rudely. When Imai, KKD's vice-president, was visiting from Japan, Crowell had dropped them both at the golf course. What was the point?

He drained his beer. Immediately the familiar warmth of the alcohol made him buoyant. "George," he said intimately. "You need a wife. You need a wife like Crowell has."

Kubushevsky turned slowly on his seat. He stared hard at Moto. "You need a muzzle," he said quietly.

"You need a wife," Moto repeated. He had Kubushevsky's full attention now. He poured Kubushevsky another beer. "Drink," he commanded.

Kubushevsky drank. In fact, they both drank. Then suddenly Kubushevsky's voice changed. He put his arm around Moto and purred in his ear. "Let me tell you a secret, Moto-san. Crowell's wife is a dog. Crowell is a dog. I'm going to leave Allmack, just as soon as possible. Want to join me, Michio-san?"

Moto's inside froze. Leave Crowell. What was Kubushevsky talking about? He was just getting to know him. They were a team. All those hours in the car together. All those hours staring at cornfields and concrete. What was Kubushevsky talking about? Did Crowell know? What was Kubushevsky insinuating about joining him?

"You're drunk, George."

"I know."

Moto smiled. The blonde got restless and left the bar. Kubushevsky didn't seem too notice. For the rest of the night he talked about his first wife and his two children, whom he barely saw. He spoke of his job at Allmack and his hopes for a better job in California. They sat at a low table. Moto spoke of his distant children and distant wife. It felt good to talk. Almost as good as having Yoko next to him.

As they left the bar, Kubushevsky leaned heavily on him. They peed against a stonewall before getting in the car. All the way home Kubushevsky sang a song about a folk hero named Davy Crockett, who "killed himself a bear when he was only three." Moto sang a song from Niigata about the beauty of the snow on the rooftops in winter. Kubushevsky hummed along.

They worked as a team for the next four months. Kubushevsky provided whatever detailed documentation Moto asked for. They went drinking a lot. Sometimes they both felt a little sad, sometimes happy, but Moto felt entirely comfortable. Kubushevsky introduced him to Porter, a large, good natured man in the steel business who liked to hunt and cook gourmet food; to Andrews, a tiny man who danced the polka as if it were a waltz; and to many others.

Just before the closing, Kubushevsky took him to a bar and told him of a job offer in California. He had tears in his eyes and hugged Moto good-bye. Moto had long since accepted the fact that Kubushevsky would leave.

Two weeks later Moto looked around the conference room at Allmack. Ishii, KKD's president, and Imai had flown in from Tokyo for the signing of the contract for the shopping mall, the culmination of three years of research and months of negotiation. John Crowell stood by his lawyer, Sue Smith. Sue had been on her feet for five hours. Nike Apple, Moto's lawyer, slammed his fist on the table and pointed at the item in question. The lawyers argued a timing detail that Moto was sure had been worked out weeks before. Moto glanced nervously at Ishii and Imai. Ishii's eyes were closed. Imai stared at the table.

Moto shifted uneasily in his seat. Sue was smarter than Mike he thought. Perhaps a female lawyer wouldn't have been so terrible. While it was not usual to see females in professional positions in Japan, this was America. Tokyo might have understood. After all this is America, he repeated to himself. Internationalization required some adjustment.

A year ago he would have had total loss of face if confronted with the prolonged, argumentative closing. Today he did not care. He could not explain to Tokyo all he'd learned in that time, all the friends he'd made. When he tried to communicate about business in America, the home office sent him terse notes by fax.

Now the lawyers stood back. President Ishii opened his eyes. Crowell handed a pen to Ishii. They signed the document together. The lawyers smiled. Sue Smith looked satisfied. She should be pleased, Moto thought. Her extensive preparation for the case made him realize again that the Japanese stereotype of the lazy American was false. Sue's knowledge of the case was perfect in all the details. I'll have to use her next time, Moto thought. She's the smart one. Yes, he thought, his friend Kubushevsky had taught him many things. Suddenly he felt Kubushevsky's large presence. Moto lowered his head in gratitude.

# Case 2.4

# NEGOTIATING ACROSS THE PACIFIC

XIAOHUA LIN AND JIAN GUAN

Bill Wright, vice president of US Fortune, had just finished a telephone conversation with Edward Tang, general manager of Asia-Pacific Consulting Group, during which Tang had informed him that their stalled negotiations with BBT could lead to an international lawsuit. Eight months earlier, Beijing Bio-Tech (BBT), an animal feed manufacturer from China, asked Tang to help locate a supplier of feed grade lecithin in the US. Tang working with Wright as intermediaries initiated negotiations between NutriNex, a US lecithin producer, and BBT. The negotiation had been long and very difficult and the transaction was not completed as planned.

The evening of July 16, 1997, found Bill reflecting on what had happened during the past eight months. He felt trapped and did not know what to do, but knew that he had to deal with the situation quickly. Edward had suggested to him that he should get the negotiation back on track, but Bill did not know if that was possible. However, Bill realized that if negotiations were not successful the Chinese might launch a lawsuit against him.

## Background: Participants and Transaction

Asia-Pacific Consulting Group (APCG) was a Philadelphia-based company specializing in export management, cross-cultural training, and foreign language-related services such as translation. The company's clients were from all over the United States and a dozen foreign countries, especially in Asia. This was because APCG's two founding partners, Edward Tang and his wife Joyce, were originally from China and had maintained extensive relationships in Asia.

Beijing Bio-Tech Co. Ltd. (BBT) was a joint venture set up by a Taiwan-based multinational company and a Beijing-based company affiliated with China's Ministry of Agriculture. BBT specialized in research, development, and production of nutrition, feeding, and breeding products for aquaculture. Since its establishment in 1990, BBT had made substantial progress in product innovation and marketing, and became a leading aqua-biotech company in China. To recognize its accomplishment, the city government of Beijing named BBT a "Most Admirable Foreign-Funded Enterprise" for each of the last four years. Mrs. Ming Kuo, general manager of BBT, was featured in a publication as one of the "Outstanding Females in Contemporary China."

In November 1996, Ming Kuo contacted APCG and requested assistance in locating a supplier of feed-grade lecithin in the United States. The product was a core feed additive ingredient for fresh water fish and shrimp, which was BBT's main product line. In the past, BBT purchased lecithin from two sources, a Chinese manufacturer that operated in China, and a Hong Kong distributor that supplied US-made lecithin. BBT preferred the US

SOURCE: Reprinted by permission from *Case Research Journal*, Volume 21, Issue 4. 

products because they had more consistent quality. However, involving the Hong Kong distributor made the price very expensive. The average price of lecithin in the market was $3,700 per ton, ranging from $3,500 to 4,300. As far as the Asian markets were concerned, margins for middlemen could be as high as 40%. BBT currently purchased about 50 metric tons of lecithin annually. It intended to increase the purchase by 100% in the next year, and then by 10% in the subsequent years. Eliminating the middleman and establishing a direct relationship with a US supplier were important goals for BBT.

On November 12, 1996, Ming Kuo wrote a letter to APCG explaining the company's criteria for selecting the supplier: "We are looking for a long-term relationship with a reliable supplier. This means that we would consider the first purchase as a trial, hopefully both sides will be satisfied and decide to continue the relationship." While quality and price were important, on-time delivery was especially crucial. "Our season starts in late August and we must have the lecithin in our plants by that time," Mrs. Kuo stated.

As Edward Tang and his wife Joyce read the letter, they became excited. APCG had been involved in about a dozen international trade deals, but only a few of them had come through. This time the Tangs not only knew the Chinese company's reputation, they also interacted on several occasions with Mrs. Kuo and enjoyed a good personal relationship with her. In fact, it was the relationship that brought the business to APCG. As Mrs. Kuo stated: "As a Chinese, I like to do business with people I know." Access to hard currency usually posed a major challenge to foreign firms selling to China. The Chinese currency was not convertible and Chinese importers had to purchase the foreign currency necessary for authorized imports, which was always troublesome. However, hard currency would not be a problem in this case because, like all joint ventures with investment from Taiwan, BBT was given a Sino-foreign joint venture status and therefore was allowed to retain foreign currency contributed by the "foreign" (Taiwanese, in this case) partner or earned by the joint venture. As the Tangs knew, BBT enjoyed a high credit standing and never had payment problems in international trade. The Tangs also realized this might be a big deal, and if this transaction did succeed, it could evolve into a continuous business.

In 1996 the United States was the leading supplier of lecithin in the world due to its superior technology as well as its abundant domestic soybean supplies. Although China had made an effort to develop its own lecithin production, its technology was far behind. More importantly, lecithin was produced from soybean, but there was little room for China to expand its soybean production in order to manufacture lecithin on a large scale. With limited arable lands, China had to concentrate on grains more suitable for human consumption, such as wheat and rice.

To locate sources of lecithin, the Tangs started with the US Department of Agriculture, trade associations, and published industry directories. Then, with a short list of potential suppliers, they began calling companies. It was not too long, however, until they realized that these companies did not like to deal with middlemen. They said that they were definitely interested but would like to communicate directly with the buyer. With this concern, Edward called Bill Wright.

## Bill Wright and His Working Plan

Bill Wright was executive vice president and a director of US Fortune, an investment bank that had operations across the East Coast. US Fortune was a well-established company. Edward Tang had met Bill through a client who was Bill's close friend. Bill Wright had been with US Fortune for over twenty years, and because of this, he was very well connected in the business community. As a senior executive, he currently had little involvement in the company's daily operation and was able to develop other business interests outside US Fortune. Particularly, Bill held substantial stakes in several food and drug-related firms. To take care of these businesses, Bill frequently traveled to Europe. However, he had never dealt with Asian countries.

Bill Wright was thrilled with the opportunity. BBT was a reputable Chinese company and lecithin trade was a very profitable business. Most importantly, Bill had a long-time client, NutriNex, which happened to be a major manufacturer of lecithin.

NutriNex was located in the Midwest. It was a major player in the industry and had started exporting several years ago. Dr. Robert Fisher, NutriNex's CEO, knew the huge potential of the Chinese market. The company had been looking for an opportunity to enter the market at that time. However, NutriNex had been unsuccessful thus far because of the difficulties of establishing contacts in China. Therefore, when Bill called, Dr. Fisher could hardly believe it. "I am delighted to help," he said calmly. "Bill, just let me know what you want me to do." As they were talking, Bill already had a plan wherein he and the Tangs acted as middlemen between NutriNex and BBT (see Exhibit 1).

In practice, a middleman had two options in an export or import transaction. First, the middleman could work on a commission basis without taking title to the goods; his job was to provide a bridge between the buyer and seller. Second, the middleman could act as a real buyer and reseller and actually take title to the goods. In doing so, the middleman could be able to avoid the financial burden by means of back-to-back letters of credit (L/C). With this procedure, the buyer issued a L/C to the middleman who then issued another L/C to the supplier. The first L/C involved an amount larger than the second L/C; the middleman retained the difference as profits. Under the first option, the middleman's role was terminated after the buyer and seller were connected and a pre-determined amount of commission was paid to the middleman. Quite often, a middleman did not want the buyer and seller to interact directly so that they would depend on his mediation in any further transactions. This was the main reason why some middlemen, often the experienced ones, took the second option.

Bill sensed that the purchase of BBT was likely to become a repeat business. He did not want to just take a commission and go away. Over the phone, he told CEO Fisher that he would like to handle the transaction through the following process:

1. Bill Wright should negotiate with the Chinese buyer for a purchase agreement and appear in the agreement as the SELLER.
2. The Chinese buyer should issue a letter of credit to Bill Wright.
3. Upon receipt of the L/C from the Chinese buyer, Bill Wright should then issue another L/C to NutriNex.
4. NutriNex should make the shipment after receiving the L/C from Bill Wright.

In the next hour, Bill sent a fax to Dr. Fisher to confirm their conversation. "OK, if this is how you want to do it," replied Dr. Fisher over the phone.

Letters of credit (L/C) was a basic method of receiving payment for products sold abroad. A letter of credit added a bank's promise of paying the exporter to that of the foreign buyer when the exporter has complied with all the terms and conditions of the letter of credit. In a typical export process, only one letter of credit was necessary: the foreign buyer applied for issuance of the letter of credit to the exporter. The process specified in Bill Wright's working plan involved two letters of credit (see Exhibits 2 and 3).

As agreed upon by Bill Wright and Robert Fisher, NutriNex would arrange shipping of the goods from its manufacturing facility directly to Xin Gang, the Chinese port where BBT would pick up the goods. At NutriNex factories, the lecithin would be loaded in a container, which then was carried by a truck to a port in California. At the port, the container was put on an ocean carrier. In normal situations, it took three to four weeks for a container to get from a US port to China. At the Chinese port, BBT unloaded the goods to trucks. It took about an hour from the port to BBT's facilities in Beijing by trucks.

The Tangs had no problem with the arrangement. The only question was: Should they tell Ming Kuo everything? They knew that Mrs. Kuo intended to deal with a manufacturer, but they also knew that Bill did not want the buyer to establish direct contact with the supplier. In the end, the Tangs decided not to complicate the situation. "While the goods are not from Bill, Bill knows NutriNex's president. We should be OK," they said to each other. They did not tell BBT that the ultimate supplier was not Bill Wright but NutriNex.

## Economic and Cultural Environment in China

Bill Wright's past overseas experience was largely limited to Europe. He felt that he needed to gain a broad perspective about what was going on in China. He called the Tangs with many questions. He realized that China had been one of the fastest growing economies in the world in recent years. This dynamic growth could be attributed largely to China's policy of reforming its economy and opening up to the outside world, which began in 1979. One of the most striking features in the changing economic system was the steady growth in the number of foreign-funded enterprises. He was aware that BBT, which was his Chinese counterpart in the transaction, was one of many enterprises jointly owned by Taiwanese and Mainland Chinese companies.

Bill Wright had heard that China's rapid economic growth and bold reform measures pointed to enormous market potential in China, and particularly that the Chinese had a high regard for American products. However, he just now realized how large the Chinese market for American manufactured lecithin could be. According to the Tangs, the Chinese consumers, with increasing purchasing power, had been demanding more and better products from the aquacultural sectors. Because of this, a number of aqua-biotech companies had recently emerged in the areas of research and development, production of nutrition, feeding, and breeding products for aquaculture. These Chinese companies, however, had to face a major challenge posed by China's limited per capita natural resources. For instance, with scarce arable lands the Chinese had used soybean mainly for direct human consumption. Coupled with lack of advanced technologies, currently and probably in the foreseeable future, the Chinese aqua-biotech companies had to rely on imported lecithin to meet the growing needs for quality feed additive.

Having talked to the Tangs, Bill realized that the Chinese people had a cultural system that was quite different from that in the US and other Western countries. In conducting business, Chinese paid much attention to building *guanxi,* that is, the intricate and pervasive network of personal relations. The Chinese culture also emphasized "face," or a person's credit, honor, and reputation. Embarrassment, failure, or contradictions lead to loss of face. Importantly, the Chinese concepts of *guanxi* and face were not universal, but highly situational and reciprocal. When a Chinese acted, he normally anticipated a return. And a Chinese would deal with a party as that party dealt him. The Chinese would say: "If you are good to me, I will be ten times better to you; but if you are bad to me, I will be ten times worse to you!" Hence, Chinese were morally justified to either repay or retaliate upon another person depending how that person treated him.

Similarly, face could be traded. A person doing a favor for someone was said to be giving face and the person who had received a favor was expected to give face in return. The notions of *guanxi* and face were evident in a Chinese business negotiation context. As observed by many Western negotiators, the Chinese took longer to make decisions. They apparently were more concerned with long-term associations and invested time in building a good working relationship. Because of this, they attached great importance to sincerity and reputation on the part of the foreign party. The Chinese seldom used the word "no," because they tried to save face for both parties. They proceeded cautiously and slowly at the negotiation table, because they tried to avoid mistakes that would embarrass them.

Bill was especially amazed by the Chinese attitude toward legalistic approaches in business. Consistent with their attention to human relations and face, Chinese traditionally shunned legal considerations. Instead, they stressed the moral principles of everyday living and carefully managed relationships in business settings and among social groups. Even in today's international business environment, the Chinese preferred not to have lawyers involved in the negotiation process. To a large extent, they relied on personal trust instead of legal documents as the foundation of business relationships. For the Chinese, negotiation was an ongoing process and did not end with a signed contract. When disagreements occurred, they often sought compromise and consultation through a third party who was trusted by both sides. Legalistic measures were used only as a last resort.

While describing Chinese negotiation styles, the Tangs tried to illustrate some of the salient differences between the Chinese and Americans. Compared to Chinese emphasis on personal relationships, Americans took a factual approach toward negotiation and considered it as a place simply for problem solving. Unlike their Chinese counterparts, American negotiators separated people from issues and felt comfortable with confrontation. During the negotiation process, they were expected to give and take and even engage in hard bargaining. However, when a legal contract was signed, the negotiation reached the endpoint that both sides had to follow. The approaches toward conflict resolution were also different between the two people. While a typical Chinese approach was emotion-confounded, situational, and sometimes circuitous, a typical American approach was factual-based, legalistic, and generally straightforward.

### The Ball Was Rolling . . .

It did not take long for Bill to draft a purchase agreement. The only difficult part of the job was to determine the amount of commissions. In this transaction, there were two intermediaries: APCG and Bill Wright. Bill wanted to build in $20,000, which would be split equally between APCG and himself.

The total cost for a 40-foot container of lecithin, including insurance and freight, was $56,000. Edward figured that a commission over one-third of the sale-price, exactly 38%, was too high to be acceptable and expressed his concern immediately. After listening to Edward, Bill replied: "Well, this is the normal way we do business in this country. The best price is the maximum you can charge yet the buyer is willing to pay. Who knows, maybe the Chinese will think it's okay!" "What if the Chinese think it's too expensive?" asked Edward. He was afraid that this price would scare BBT away. He then suggested to reduce the commission and give a more generous offer that he believed would signal goodwill to the Chinese buyer. "I understand that," Bill insisted, "but why don't we just start with this price. We can always back off some if BBT thinks our price is too high."

On February 16, 1997, APCG sent a fax to inform BBT of the price quoted by Bill Wright. Four weeks passed, but there had been no answer from BBT. Edward decided to call Mrs. Kuo. Mrs. Kuo first apologized for not responding and then said: "You should know how I feel—when a price quote seems way too high, we don't believe the seller is serious."

Edward felt embarrassed and said: "I am sorry, but I thought you might know how Americans start a negotiation. Believe me, they are really serious about this transaction." "Why should I know how Americans negotiate, Edward? Ming Kuo replied. "You went to American school, but I didn't. So you have better understanding on how they deal with these matters than I do. Well, since you've said that, I don't mind giving them a try. But please—tell them this time is for real. By the way, I am now thinking of a 20-foot container, not the 40-foot. Do you think they will do that?" Edward replied: "Ok, let me talk to Bill."

"How can they change from a 40-foot to 20-foot container, and why did it take them a month to respond!" Bill was upset while talking to Edward over the phone. Edward replied: "Bill, I told you that we should lower the price to be real. Now, if you listen to me this time, this is what we should do—get back to them as quickly as possible, agree to take an order for a 20-foot container, and lower the price. What I'm suggesting is that we show them that we are flexible and try very hard to work with them. Remember I told you that BBT is not just looking at this single deal, they are trying to find a partner to work with for a long time."

On April 2, Bill sent a fax to Edward, informing him that Dr. Fisher from NutriNex agreed to take an order for a 20-foot container. Bill also agreed to quote a lower price to BBT, with the total commissions being reduced to $6,000. Edward was pleased with the news and sent a message to BBT on the same day. Twenty-four hours later, Ming Kuo called Edward. She was grateful for the effort made by APCG and agreed with the price. She promised that she would ask her Import Manager, Rong Zhang, to proceed immediately.

However, another week passed before Edward received the response from Rong Zhang of BBT. Mr. Zhang apologized for the delay and explained why. Since the tariff on lecithin was very high to manufacturing firms like BBT, the company had been negotiating with a licensed foreign trade company, Beijing International Trading Co. Ltd., to handle the import process. Under the Chinese government's import/export regulations, this trading company would pay lower tariffs for importing a product like lecithin than would BBT.

It was not until late May when Bill Wright and BBT could start serious discussions on the contractual terms. After several rounds of negotiation on items such as product name and packaging, the contract was finalized. Bill Wright signed the contract as "Executive Vice President, US Fortune, Inc." The contract followed rather standardized format in international trade. It stipulated "Shipment within 30 days upon receipt of Buyer's Irrevocable, Transferable L/C issued from a reputable international bank or equivalent."

## . . . But Finally Dropped

On June 9, 1997, Bill faxed the signed contract to BBT. BBT signed the contract and faxed it back to Bill two weeks later. On July 3, BBT opened a L/C from Bank of China. On July 7, Bill received the copy of the L/C.

As he called on NutriNex to arrange delivery, Bill could hardly believe what he heard from Dr. Fisher. He was told that the delivery time requested couldn't be met because something had happened, which was outside the control of NutriNex. According to Dr. Fisher, there had been heavy rains, which caused a serious flood in the mid-western states. The flood created delays in transportation and ultimately slowed down the manufacturing of lecithin. At that time the company was experiencing a backlog of orders. "When you first talked to me about the deal, I said we would ship the goods to the buyer within three weeks. Now, it is going to take at least two months," said Dr. Fisher. Bill said he understood the situation but insisted NutriNex should figure out a way to make the delivery. "I am sorry, Bill," replied Dr. Fisher. "But there is no way my company can deliver this time." He pointed out that if there was a signed contract between Bill and NutriNex, they would have had to ship the goods on time, but there was no contract.

Listening to Dr. Fisher, Bill was shocked by the plain fact that he, not NutriNex, was obligated to make the delivery according to his contract with BBT. In the contract, he himself was the seller. "Why did I dare to sign the contract?" he asked himself. Yes, he had the verbal promise from Dr. Fisher and he believed his friendship with Dr. Fisher provided the assurance, but he didn't have a signed contract with Dr. Fisher and NutriNex did not have to deliver.

Bill took the corporate jet to visit Dr. Fisher at NutriNex's headquarters. He believed that Dr. Fisher was able to help if he wanted to: NutriNex was so big that it should have no problem to fill a 20-foot container. However, Dr. Fisher offered no help.

NutriNex's new delivery schedule was two months and even this delivery time could not be guaranteed until "We've received the order," said Dr. Fisher.

## No Way Out?

When Bill came back to his office from the trip, he had several messages from Edward on his answering machine explaining that BBT had been waiting for the delivery. Bill sent a fax to BBT, informing the Chinese of the inevitable delay. He explained how the production was delayed by the weather and proposed to amend the contract with a new delivery time schedule.

It took only one day for Bill Wright to receive a fax from BBT. "We understand the difficulty due to the natural disaster," the fax stated. "However, our manufacturing season is approaching and we cannot afford a delay."

Bill Wright was now desperate, and decided to visit Dr. Fisher again. However, nothing had changed and NutriNex could not deliver to China at the moment. Bill sent another fax to BBT, indicating that he simply could not deliver on time.

BBT returned a fax to Bill the next day. It stated that Bill had violated the contract and caused the Chinese company a loss amounting to $13,450, as a result of an emergency purchase and the fund lockfee for the L/C in the bank. BBT therefore asked Bill to:1) apologize for the mistake, 2) compensate them for the loss, and 3) provide details of the amendment.

On July 21, Bill replied with a fax. He first stressed that the delay was unavoidable because of high demand and the rains and then gave another reason for the delay: "As you know, we have been dealing with you through our associates at APCG. . . . They have been out of town. . . . I did not feel that it was proper for me to contact you directly until I had spoken to them," and finally apologized for the delay. He suggested making an amendment to the original shipment time, 40–60 days instead of 30 days after receipt of an updated L/C from BBT. He did not mention the loss compensation issue.

Edward received a phone call from Mr. Zhang. He said Mrs. Kuo was very upset by Bill's response, he then asked Edward to pass the following message to Bill: BBT would initiate a lawsuit if it could not get a fair solution with Bill Wright.

## Cross-Cultural Agent at Work

Edward translated the message very carefully when he talked to Bill on the phone, but he did not mention the word "lawsuit." He still hoped Bill could realize the seriousness of the situation: "No matter what happened, the contract had a delivery date and you didn't deliver," said Edward. "Ed, you know what? When you first talked to me like this, I kind of blamed myself too, then I said wait a minute, if they moved reasonably fast when we started the negotiation, there wouldn't have been a delay," Bill argued. "Please understand that when we began this process, it was over 4 months ago. At that time shipment was 2 to 3 weeks after placing an order. As you know all commodities are subject to supply and demand forces." Finally, Bill replied: "Ed, I am sorry for their loss and I have apologized for the delay. But I have no control over the weather and I didn't ask them to lock funds at the bank."

While disappointed with what Bill had said, the Tangs decided to save the deal at any cost. That night, Joyce Tang called Mrs. Kuo at home. She told Mrs. Kuo that the responsibility was definitely Bill Wright's. However, she suggested that Mrs. Kuo try to get some good out of the bad since things had already happened: "See, you've already borne a loss. If you quit here, you've got nothing. Although this season's gone, if you don't give up, I am sure they will work very hard to deliver on time for your next season. Think about the time and money you've already spent. As long as their lecithin is good that means that you did not waste all your money, and I promise to help you work with the manufacturer directly next time."

After a long silence, Mrs. Kuo replied: "Well, you're probably right; but we just think this American is too arrogant, he's made a mistake but blamed the flood. You're asking me to look forward, but I haven't received a true apology from Bill Wright! He needs to change his attitude if we are to continue doing business together. By the way, Joyce, you should have told me if I was dealing with a real seller or not!"

Having talked with Mrs. Kuo, Edward was more frustrated than ever. He knew that for the problem to be settled, Bill had to do something. However, Bill was not listening to him. Edward decided to make a dramatic move as he started dialing Bill's phone number in the middle of the night.

"Bill, we need to talk. I know you're upset. You know this is not just your problem, don't you? I'm on the phone all the time and I realize I've already lost face with Mrs. Kuo. But I try to say to myself, 'things already happened, you've got to face it.' Now, no matter what really caused the problem, the fact is that we didn't deliver, so that means we broke the contract. Bill, I don't want tell you this, but I was told BBT is preparing a lawsuit."

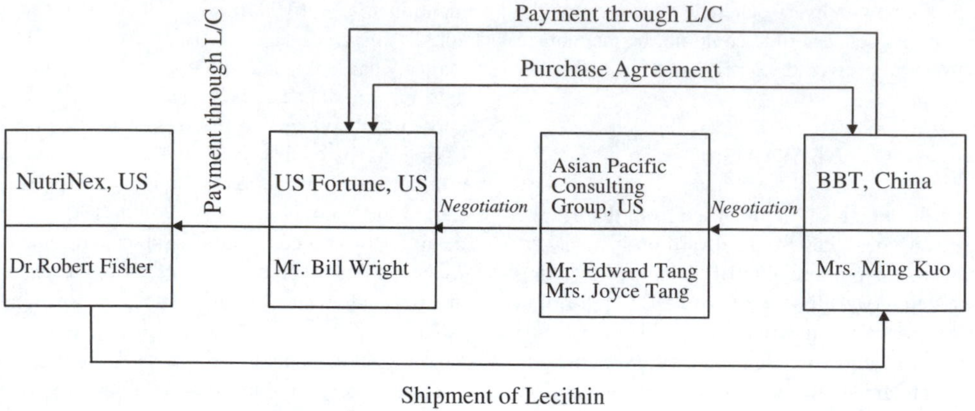


**Exhibit 1** Bill Wright's Working Plan

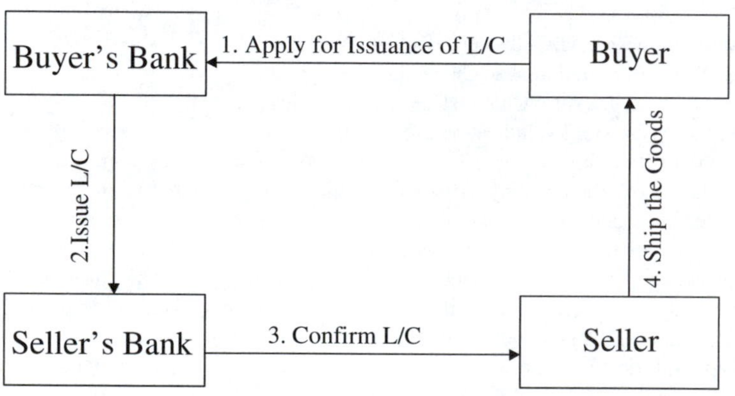


**Exhibit 2** Export Process Involving L/C

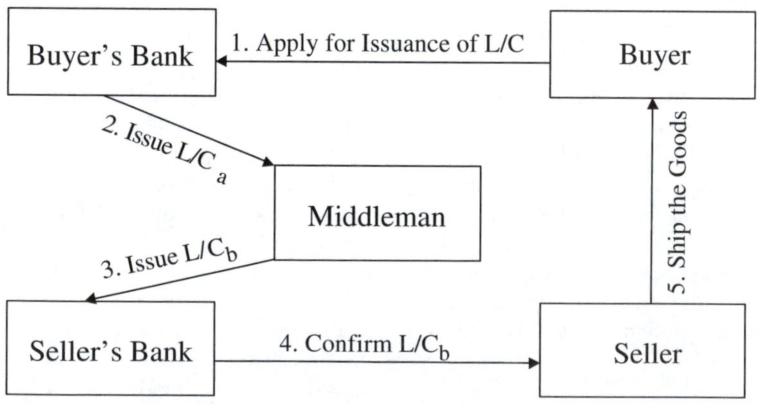


**Exhibit 3** Export Process Involving Back-to Back L/C

Note: These charts include only key paths; actual transactions can be more complicated.

"Fine. Tell them I will see them in court!" Bill reacted immediately.

"Wait a minute, Bill. You know I'm here to help. Remember I told you before that the Chinese don't like to go to court? I really don't believe Mrs. Kuo wants to take this step. What they want is a real apology, don't you ever understand this, Bill? Please! You've probably never dealt with the Chinese before. If you can show them that you are sorry about their loss and want to do something, you can calm them down and many times you'll make friends out of such situations. Bill, are you there?"

After another uncomfortable pause, Bill said, "Well, what exactly do you want me to do, Ed?"

"You know Bill, we are a team, and I made mistakes too. I'm thinking that we can offer to sign a new contract for next season. In the next contract, we could reduce the price, basically the commissions, yours and mine. Then we can say, 'Look, we're really sorry for what happened. We can't compensate you at this time, but we will help you by dropping all commissions in the new contract. We know this won't be enough to cover all your losses, but that's what we can do to help. We will work very hard to make sure things like this won't happen again in the future. And we would like to have a very productive working relationship.' I think that by doing this it would stop them from going through with the lawsuit."

## Lawsuit . . . Impossible?

Bill Wright was shocked to hear that BBT was going to sue. According to his notes, the Chinese culture deviated from a legalistic mentality. In resolving disagreements, Chinese used courts only as a last resort. "Are they really going to sue me just for this amount of money?" Bill asked himself. As this question came to his mind, Bill rushed to find the copy of the purchasing agreement. In the agreement, there was no mention of possible court procedures. Yet, the agreement stated that the seller should not be held responsible for any losses sustained by the buyer due to natural causes. Remembering all of this, Bill did not believe that BBT could win the case if they went to court in the United States. So, if BBT wanted to enter a lawsuit and win, they had to appeal to a court in China. If Bill did not agree to appear in a Chinese court, then the lawsuit would not take place.

# Case 2.5

# CONSOLIDATED ENGINEERING CO. GOES TO CHINA[1]

TRAVIS MAPLES AND PENELOPE B. PRIME

"Do I have to satisfy every set of eyes in China?" After more than a year since the contract had been signed, this was how Vice President of Operations and Project Manager, Travis Maples, felt about the deal that maybe wasn't. He had worked hard to find a business opportunity to open the doors to China for his company, Consolidated Engineering, but now wondered if it was worth it. He knew that he could still walk away from this deal, sell the equipment somewhere else, and go on. Many companies had given too much away to do business in China, and he was not going to be one of them.

CEC

**Mission 2000**

To achieve a consistent 25% growth rate by maximizing positive customer experience through continuous improvement and innovation of the highest quality thermal processing equipment and services.

**Figure 1** CEC Mission 2000

### The Company

Consolidated Engineering Company (CEC) was one of a number of major firms worldwide that produced heat processing equipment for metals to be used primarily in engines, automotive parts, and other aluminum casting components. They produced three major product categories: 1) A continuous heat treating system; 2) ovens & furnaces; and 3) coil coating products. CEC had their own research and development division, and held 33 patents worldwide. Their major customers included Mercedes Benz, Ford, Honda, GM, Chrysler, Jaguar, VW, Kaiser, Alcoa, and Reynolds Aluminum. CEC was a privately held company established in 1959, and did approximately $35 million worth of sales in 1998. Their projects ranged from a quarter of a million dollars to 11 million or more.

Based on their historical development, CEC established a goal of 25% annual sales growth in the 1990s and beyond. They believed so strongly in this goal that the company incorporated it into their mission statement (Figure 1). To achieve this target, management believed they needed to deal extensively

AUTHORS' NOTE: We would like to thank Volker Knoblock and Matt Westendorf for their help in preparing this case.

SOURCE: Reprinted with permission of the authors.

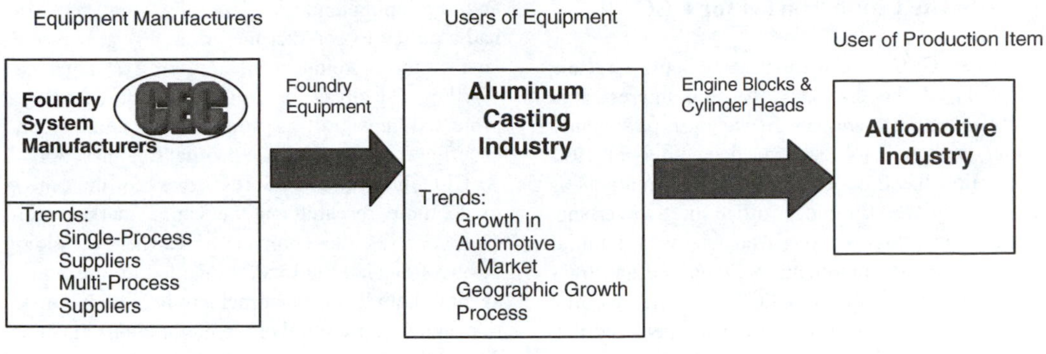


**Figure 2**

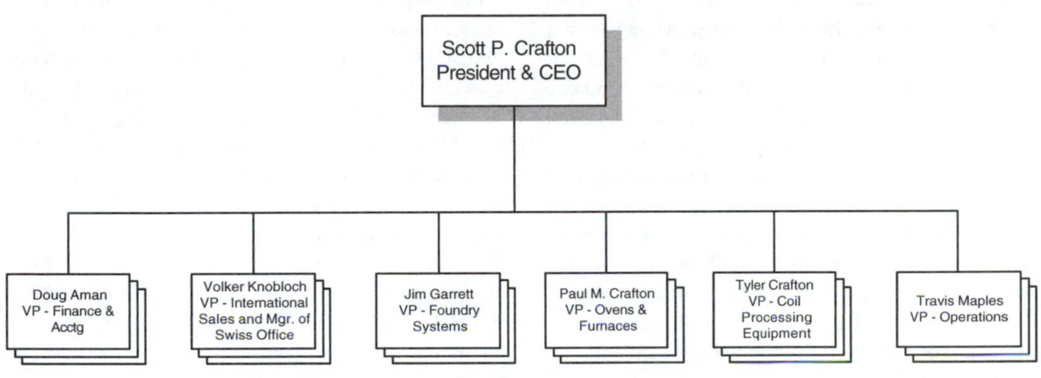


**Figure 3** Consolidated Engineering Company, Kennesaw, GA, 1998

with four key foreign markets: Germany, England, Mexico and China. They were doing business in the first three markets, but as of 1997 had not yet sought any sales in China. Approximately 30% of their sales were to the U.S. market.

As a result of the growth in the usage of aluminum, because of its weight advantages, nearly all new foundry facilities constructed in the world in recent years had been for the purpose of manufacturing aluminum castings (Figure 2). These have been state-of-the-art facilities, using the latest in proven technologies. This growth advanced technology usage in the foundry industry has been the source of CEC's greatest growth opportunities. There also had been a movement by the large automobile manufacturers to standardize engines and this standardization had created facility expansions all over the world. Mexico has been the country of choice for the North American manufacturers and Asia for the growing Pacific market.

The organization of CEC also had contributed greatly to its growth and ability to take advantage of sales opportunities. Due to the extensive experience of the upper management sales staff, they were given a lot of freedom in developing new markets and customers. Operations worked closely with all sales managers to assist in their sales efforts. It was the responsibility of the Sales Manager to keep the President informed as to the status of a potential order. Also, he had to keep Operations informed to allow the necessary capacity and schedule planning that would be required if the sales effort was successful (Figure 3).

After a sale was closed, the order was passed from Sales to Operations. At this time Operations became the primary customer contact and interface. It was Operation's responsibility to engineer, manufacture, deliver, and install (if required by the contract) the equipment covered by the sales order.

## The China Market for CEC

To meet CEC's growth target, Scott Crafton, President of the company, became interested in establishing a presence in the Far East, particularly China. Volker Knoblock had been hired in 1997 to develop the European and Far East markets as head of CEC's European office in Switzerland. With advice from Volker, who was very familiar with business development in China and had traveled there many times, CEC did some research about foreign foundry markets. They believed that China's industrial sector was expanding rapidly and would be in need of the type of equipment that CEC produced. In particular, China's auto industry was poised to develop rapidly. Already, as of 1995, 1.3 million cars were sold in China annually.[2] This was more than Thailand, Indonesia, Malaysia and the Philippines combined. After much debate by academics and policy makers, official Chinese policy changed in the mid-1990s to allow, and even encourage, family ownership of cars. And while foreign cooperation on developing this industry was welcomed, imports were not. Hence China was set on developing a substantial domestic automotive industry utilizing foreign technology from world class companies such as Chrysler, Ford, General Motors, Honda and Toyota, with an initial target of producing two and half million vehicles annually by the year 2000.[3]

Continuous heat treating systems were essential to that industry. If CEC didn't sell it to manufacturers in China, certainly one of its competitors would. Many auto parts require heat treatment. CEC's designs were for both ferrous and non-ferrous applications including roller hearth, pusher, and walking beam designs for castings, forgings, plant, bare and tube products. CEC believed that these processes would be increasingly demanded in the China market, and that few of its competitors had yet ventured very far into that market.

Travis knew there were risks involved in transferring technology to China. Many companies had found copies of their products being sold in China, often with a copied label as well. China's base of engineers and technical ability was substantial, and this talent was quite capable of reverse engineering. In addition, China's legal system was primitive at best. Because of these concerns, CEC planned a sales contract rather than a joint venture involving manufacturing in China. CEC believed this strategy made the technology transfer risks reasonable. In terms of political-financial risk, the Asia Crisis was just unfolding, giving companies more reason to be cautious when investing in Asia and developing countries generally. However, CEC had a policy to contract the price only in U.S. dollars, so there would be no foreign exchange risk. The key risk areas for CEC would be ensuring a protected transfer of its proprietary technology, and ensuring they completed a profitable transaction.

CEC did not have the resources—or the time—to do more research on the China market itself. Therefore, as the company did whenever doing business outside the U.S., it decided to hire a local agent to help locate customers, to help with translation, and to represent them in negotiations in China. As project sales manager, Volker made a contact in mid-1997 with a Chinese company interested in serving as an agent. This agent helped Volker identify Shenyang Aerospace-Mitsubishi Motors Engines Manufacturing Co., LTD. (SAME), which was looking to purchase heat treatment processes like CEC's. SAME was a joint venture between Mitsubishi of Japan and the Shenyang Aerospace Bureau. They were beginning to produce parts that would be assembled into an engine to be initially exported to Japan and later used in domestic auto production. The engine parts needed to be heat treated, which is where CEC's system would come in.

Volker and his agent met with SAME four times to hammer out the details of a contract. When SAME called Volker to say they were ready to sign, there was only one caveat—they wanted CEC to change agents. Representatives from SAME said they believed CEC's agent was not translating accurately, had not properly registered with the Chinese government as CEC's agent, and could not be fully trusted. They recommended Charles Yang of Freeson Company. Surprised, Volker approached both agents to ask if either of them could provide a confirmation of SAME's readiness to sign in writing. Only Charles Yang could. Feeling he did not have much choice, Volker hired Charles and together they met SAME and signed the contact in January, 1998, for CEC to build two furnace systems for SAME. The Chinese side conveyed to Volker that although late payment was a critical problem with Chinese firms, he did not have to worry about being paid, since this deal was backed by the Chinese government itself.

## Making the Business Deal Work

Because of the importance of the S.A.M.E. project and the opportunity to work with a Chinese customer, Travis Maples took on the responsibility of Project Manager, in addition to the responsibilities he had as VP of Operations.

Despite the sudden change in agents, Travis was pleased with the choice of the Freeson Company. In addition to sealing the deal with SAME, through Freeson CEC was able to find a Chinese manufacturer, Nanjing Changjiang Heat Treatment Installation Factory (NCHTIF) to supply all of the external conveyor system except for the robots. The robots were to be supplied by ABB Company and programmed by a company called Factory Automation Services in Atlanta, Georgia. Even the robots would have been made in China as well if CEC had been able to find a competent manufacturer. As part of China's development policy, it was a requirement that Chinese companies manufacture at least some parts of the foreign investment project. Even with the Nanjing company, CEC was going to have to supply engineering guidance because NCHTIF had experience with low-tech conveyor systems only.

The contract specified the terms and timing of payment from SAME to CEC. They were as follows:

- Down payment with the order: 20%
- After the design conference in Shenyang: 20%
- After pre-acceptance at the plant in the U.S., and according to the timetable set up in the letter of credit: 50%
- Final acceptance: 10%

In terms of the technology, CEC wanted to protect their "3 in 1" patented process—sand removal, heat treatment, and sand reclamation—that allowed CEC to sell their equipment for about a third of the price of their competitors. Travis knew that there was a real danger that some Chinese company would try to copy CEC's technology once it was up and running in China. In this case, though, he was more comfortable with the fact that SAME was a joint venture with Mitsubishi, and that Mitsubishi would require SAME to honor the patent. The process was patented in Japan as well as in the U.S. In addition, if another Chinese company copied the equipment, Travis felt CEC would be able to prevent export of any of the products made with the CEC technology, but that CEC would be powerless to do anything about the domestic market. Finally, while the machinery itself could be copied, the process could not be duplicated without a lot of help from CEC, which of course would not be available. Hence Travis was excited that this project could safely become CEC's China entry job, and that he was the project manager.

## The Design Conference at S.A.M.E. Plant—Shenyang, China

In mid-June, 1998, Volker, Travis, and Matt, the project engineer, met with SAME personnel at their plant in Shenyang, China. Charles Yang was there as well. According to Travis,

> "The purpose of the meeting was for CEC to obtain approval of the engineering for the project. This would allow us to proceed with the purchasing and manufacturing of the equipment. Gaining acceptance during this meeting was critical because it also meant that we were entitled to ask for the second payment—over $500,000. We were worried that lack of acceptance was going to have a big impact on our ability to deliver and get paid on time."

This was Matt's and Travis's first visit to China. The meetings were held in SAME's plant cafeteria. They ate lunch with the SAME employees in that cafeteria each day—an experience in itself. The first day during the afternoon meetings, two old women sat near them chopping fish into small pieces. They placed these pieces into a large pot, including heads, tails, and entrails. The next day, fish soup was served at lunch, which the team politely refused. Travis, especially, just could not handle that fish eye looking back at him. The team did try some of the other items and found that lunch was not as bad as they had feared.

The design conference turned into something quite different than the CEC representatives envisioned. The people they were meeting with from SAME were not the same ones that had ordered the equipment, and had very little knowledge of the product or its operating characteristics. The Foundry Director, Mrs. Xin, seemed to be in charge of these meetings. Mr. Zhao from the sales office attended, as did Mr. Zhang, the engineer in charge of the CEC project, and Mr. Qiu, the project manager for heat treatment. An older man, Mr. Huang, also appeared from time to time, whose titles on his business cards were Professor, General Engineer, and Technical Minister. The CEC team spent a lot of time explaining how the system operated and what SAME should expect in the way of performance. The language barrier was less of a problem than expected, mostly due to Charles Yang's handling of the translation.

Then things turned sour. As the meetings progressed, Mr. Qiu began to ask for changes, a couple of which were significant. He made it very apparent that SAME was not interested in paying any additional costs, yet expected the changes to be made.

These requests tested the team's negotiating skills not to "give away the farm." The team agreed to a few, minor, low cost concessions while trying to convey to Mr. Qiu that CEC would not make substantive changes without SAME issuing a change order to cover the additional costs.

> "After meeting three days, the CEC and SAME teams were successful in agreeing on all engineering aspects. Mr. Qiu said SAME would prepare a memorandum of understanding for all parties to sign. This document was to summarize the agreements reached during our meetings. The document was prepared first in Chinese and then translated by our agent, Charles Yang."

The translation was presented to Travis for his signature. Before signing, Travis read the document carefully. A short but very significant paragraph had been inserted that stated CEC would supply all the drawings, including fabrication details, along with the equipment. Travis immediately pointed out that this had never been discussed and that CEC would not do this under any circumstances. The contract specified that CEC would supply "... the Buyer with such drawings for erection work of the shipped Goods ..." and "... complete sets of Drawings and manuals for Operation and Maintenance (two copies in English) in accordance with the Schedule of Training assigned by two parties."

Mr. Qiu became very upset and asked Travis repeatedly why he refused to accept this part of the agreement. Travis answered that CEC did not supply this information to their American customers and were certainly not going to start supplying it in China. Mr. Qiu asked if they were going to have to buy all of their spare parts from CEC and Travis replied, absolutely, as far as proprietary parts were concerned. Mr. Qiu did not like the answer but realized that Travis' position was not going to change. Travis thought that the customer had been caught trying to pull a fast one and knew it. Mr. Qiu's indignation seemed to be a little forced and insincere. Perhaps they had not expected to be caught.

### The Pre-acceptance Meeting at CEC's Plant – Kennesaw, GA, USA

The contract required CEC to notify the customer 60 days prior to the intended shipping date and the customer had to respond with a Letter of Credit (LC) with a value of half of the total contract amount. This LC was the instrument that would guarantee payment upon proof of shipping. Although CEC had used LCs a great deal in their international sales, this was the first time that Travis had to know what to do. He was sorry that his MBA program had not taught him more about what seemed like immense complications and details involved in this part of the deal.

A SAME team planned to visit CEC's plant in Kennesaw in January 1999 to inspect and accept the equipment before shipping. Training was also to take place during this visit.

Notification took place early in November 1998 that shipping would take place on February 5, 1999. This meant that SAME had to supply the LC by December 22, 1998 to comply with the contract. Just before the deadline in December, the customer notified CEC, through their agent, that they were going to postpone their trip to the US until February. This meant CEC was going to have to delay shipping and any claim for payment by at least a month.

CEC was also asked to submit formal, written invitations to the SAME team to visit CEC in the US. The invitations were required in order for them to obtain visas. This turned into a major letter writing campaign to the American Consulates in Beijing and Shenyang. After several weeks of intense communications, the US consulate issued visas to two SAME personnel, one employee of the Nanjing company who was CEC's subcontractor, and CEC's agent. According to Travis:

> "Our contract required us to furnish transportation and lunch for the customer during their visit. According to our agent, the customer's representatives were allotted $50 US for motel and $20 US per day for food. CEC agreed to subsidize all costs incurred over this amount during this visit. This decision cost us about $6,000 for the two weeks the Chinese were here, including sightseeing. We were not sure if we did the right thing or if we were taken on this one, especially when the Chinese delegation added on a trip to Atlantic City."

The two SAME representatives were Mrs. Xin and Mr. Zhang—two of the people Travis, Matt and Volker had met in Shenyang. They were not the people that would be operating the CEC equipment after it was delivered and installed. Because of this, the training scheduled for SAME personnel during the pre-acceptance was scrapped. Why SAME made this decision was not clear, but CEC knew that this was ultimately going to cause problems during the actual start-up in China.

The CEC team spent the first week demonstrating the equipment and running each system. The

As of : Jan. 30, 1999

**Project No. 01-2672**
**Shenyang (S.A.M.E.)**
**Project Manager: Travis Maples**

| Item | Budget | Actual to Date | Committed Cost | Total Cost to Date | % Budget Complete | Estimate to Complete | Estimate at Completion | Over/(Under) | % Variance |
|---|---|---|---|---|---|---|---|---|---|
| Mech. Engineering | $ 48,210 | $ 51,008 | | $ 51,008 | 105.8% | | $ 51,008 | 2,798 | 5.8% |
| Electrical | $ 48,600 | $ 40,019 | | $ 40,019 | 82.3% | $ 7,200 | $ 47,219 | (1,381) | -2.8% |
| Shop | $ 59,130 | $ 111,590 | | $ 111,590 | 188.7% | | $ 111,590 | 52,460 | 88.7% |
| Installation Labor | | | | $ - | | | $ - | | |
| Project Mgt. | $ 45,000 | | | $ - | 0.0% | | $ - | (45,000) | -100.0% |
| Materials | $ 778,857 | $ 596,143 | $ 3,369 | $ 599,512 | 77.0% | $ 10,000 | $ 609,512 | (169,345) | -21.7% |
| Outside Mfg. | $ 190,000 | $ 207,632 | | $ 207,632 | 109.3% | | $ 207,632 | 17,632 | 9.3% |
| Installation Sub. | $ 74,000 | | | $ - | 0.0% | $ 74,000 | $ 74,000 | | |
| Other (Contingency) | $ 82,823 | | | $ - | 0.0% | $ 20,000 | $ 20,000 | (62,823) | -75.9% |
| Testing | | | | $ - | | | $ - | | |
| Shipping | | | | $ - | | | $ - | | |
| OH (Mfg.) | $ 119,577 | $ 197,063 | | $ 197,063 | 164.8% | $ 4,800 | $ 201,863 | 82,286 | 68.8% |
| Comm. & Patent Fees | $ 63,070 | $ 109,527 | | $ 109,527 | 173.7% | | $ 109,527 | 46,457 | 73.7% |
| WBC | $ 150,658 | | | $ - | 0.0% | $ 150,658 | $ 150,658 | | |
| **Total** | **$ 1,659,925** | **$ 1,312,982** | **$ 3,369** | **$ 1,316,351** | **79.3%** | **$ 266,658** | **$ 1,583,009** | **$ (76,916)** | **-4.6%** |

| | | | |
|---|---|---|---|
| Committed Cost | $ 1,316,351 | % Complete for Revenue Calculation | 83.2% |
| $ Invoiced to Customer | $ 901,000 | Percent Invoiced | 40.0% |
| $ Recv'd From Customer | $ 901,000 | Percent Cash Received | 40.0% |
| $ Rrcv'd from Customer this Month | | | |
| Amount More than 30 Days Over Due | | | |

| | |
|---|---|
| Total Contract Amount | $ 2,303,000 |
| Est. Contract Cost | $ 1,583,009 |
| Gross Margin | $ 719,991 |
| SG& A @ 18.7% | $ 296,023 |
| Net Profit | **$ 423,968** |
| Gross Margin as a % of Contract Price | **31.3%** |
| Profit as a % of a Contract Price | **18.4%** |

Exhibit 1

As of : Jan. 30, 1999

**Project No. 01-2672**
**Shenyang (S.A.M.E.)**
**Project Manager: Travis Maples**

| Item | Budget | Actual to Date | Committed Cost | Total Cost to Date | % Budget Complete | Estimate to Complete | Estimate at Completion | Over/(Under) | % Variance |
|---|---|---|---|---|---|---|---|---|---|
| Mech. Engineering | $ 48,210 | $ 51,008 | | $ 51,008 | 105.8% | | $ 51,008 | 2,798 | 5.8% |
| Electrical | $ 48,600 | $ 40,019 | | $ 40,019 | 82.3% | $ 7,200 | $ 47,219 | (1,381) | -2.8% |
| Shop | $ 59,130 | $ 111,590 | | $ 111,590 | 188.7% | | $ 111,590 | 52,460 | 88.7% |
| Installation Labor | | | | $ - | | | $ - | | |
| Project Mgt. | $ 45,000 | | | $ - | 0.0% | | $ - | (45,000) | -100.0% |
| Materials | $ 778,857 | $ 596,143 | $ 3,369 | $ 599,512 | 77.0% | $ 10,000 | $ 609,512 | (169,345) | -21.7% |
| Outside Mfg. | $ 190,000 | $ 207,632 | | $ 207,632 | 109.3% | | $ 207,632 | 17,632 | 9.3% |
| Installation Sub. | $ 74,000 | | | $ - | 0.0% | $ 74,000 | $ 74,000 | | |
| Other (Contingency) | $ 82,823 | | | $ - | 0.0% | $ 20,000 | $ 20,000 | (62,823) | -75.9% |
| Testing | | | | $ - | | | $ - | | |
| Shipping | | | | $ - | | | $ - | | |
| OH (Mfg.) | $ 119,577 | $ 197,063 | | $ 197,063 | 164.8% | $ 4,800 | $ 201,863 | 82,286 | 68.8% |
| Comm. & Patent Fees | $ 63,070 | $ 109,527 | | $ 109,527 | 173.7% | | $ 109,527 | 46,457 | 73.7% |
| WBC | $ 150,658 | | | $ - | 0.0% | $ 150,658 | $ 150,658 | | |
| **Total** | **$ 1,659,925** | **$ 1,312,982** | **$ 3,369** | **$ 1,316,351** | **79.3%** | **$ 266,658** | **$ 1,583,009** | **$ (76,916)** | **-4.6%** |

| | | | |
|---|---|---|---|
| Committed Cost | $ 1,316,351 | % Complete for Revenue Calculation | 83.2% |
| $ Invoiced to Customer | $ 901,000 | Percent Invoiced | 40.0% |
| $ Recv'd From Customer | $ 901,000 | Percent Cash Received | 40.0% |
| $ Rrcv'd from Customer this Month | | | |
| Amount More than 30 Days Over Due | | | |

| | |
|---|---|
| Total Contract Amount | $ 2,303,000 |
| Est. Contract Cost | $ 1,583,009 |
| Gross Margin | $ 719,991 |
| SG& A @ 18.7% | $ 296,023 |
| Net Profit | **$ 423,968** |
| | |
| Gross Margin as a % of Contract Price | **31.3%** |
| Profit as a % of a Contract Price | **18.4%** |

**Exhibit 2**

mechanical tests could be fully run but due to power limitations in CEC's shop, they were not able to heat the units since the Chinese used electric powered radiant coils as a heat source. In spite of this problem, the team worked through all the issues raised and managed to gain verbal approval for the two systems. Simultaneously Matt was working with Mr. Xia, the representative of the Chinese subcontractor from Nanjing, to finalize their design of the equipment they were to furnish. Matt was able to finalize this design while Travis handled the majority of the meetings with SAME.

After meeting in CEC's office for five days, the entire Chinese contingent left for New York and Washington for sightseeing. They returned four days later. This second part of the visit was to continue the discussions and to finalize the acceptance in accordance with the contract. In addition, they were waiting for the arrival of a third SAME representative who would have the authority to sign-off for SAME. During the next few days, the discussions were primarily about spare parts and delivery.

At this stage Travis had not received the Letter of Credit and he was becoming concerned. He continually asked the SAME representatives for confirmation of its issuance and was told it was on its way.

> "The Chinese team seemed to get a little aggravated with my questions about the LC. It was important to me, however, to keep pushing this issue because CEC could not ship until we had confirmation of the LC's receipt. Although they continued to say it was on its way, the LC did not arrive during their visit."

Two days before the end of their visit to CEC, the third person from SAME arrived, another Mr. Zhang. He was an older engineer that was apparently brought out of retirement to help SAME with this deal. Matt and Travis quickly noted that the other two SAME representatives were somewhat afraid of Mr. Zhang. Immediately he requested to see the equipment. After about two hours, they all met to discuss his findings. Much to Travis' dismay, Mr. Zhang began to request a number of changes.

At this time they presented Travis with a document, written in Chinese, that supposedly covered the pre-acceptance agreement. They were scheduled to leave immediately to visit the supplier of the robots for the project, which was located in South Atlanta. CEC had a Chinese engineer working for them at the time. Unbeknownst to the Chinese side, Travis left the document with Matt and the engineer to have it translated while they were gone.

During the visit to the robot company Travis told SAME, through CEC's agent, Charles Yang, that he thought they had agreed earlier that the equipment had been accepted and all requested changes had been made. Travis tried to keep his cool but became agitated and told them that it would be impossible to "satisfy every set of eyes in China." Travis felt strongly that CEC had met the contractual acceptance requirements and any additional changes should be made only if SAME was willing to issue change orders with additional funds to cover them.

## Travis' Decision

Time—and Travis' patience—was running out and a decision had to be made. The Chinese team was scheduled to leave early the next morning, and the protocol banquet had already been arranged for that evening. Half of the revenue from this deal depended on the Chinese side accepting the equipment at this meeting, and there were penalties up to 5% of the contract price written into the contract covering late deliveries. Travis felt pressure to make at least some of the changes, or he might lose the deal altogether. If successful, this sale would represent a significant amount of CEC's revenues for both 1998 and 1999. (See Exhibit 1 for the financials on the project as of January 1999.) But he couldn't get out of his mind the fact that CEC could sell the equipment elsewhere.

## Notes

1. We would like to thank Volker Knoblock and Matt Westendorf for their help in preparing this case.

2. Helen E. White and Gail Van Cleave, "Conference Report: The Automotive Industry in Asia," *Journal of Asian Business,* 12.2 (1996):73.

3. Ibid., p.79.

# Case 2.6

## KIWI SAMURAI:

### *SecureFit Industries in Japan*

DAVID C. THOMAS

Rain streaked the windows of his Christchurch office as Eion Williams, Chairman of The SecureFit Group, prepared for his 34th trip to Japan. It was September 29th and spring had yet to arrive in New Zealand, but Eion knew the early autumn weather in Osaka would be very pleasant. He was quite looking forward to his semi-annual trip now that all the preparations had been made. He had just finished reviewing the last six months of correspondence with Masanobu, Inc, SecureFit's major distributor in Japan, and the gift for its president Mr. Kiyomitsu was being crated for the trip. Eion was very pleased with the magnificent hand-blown glass orb that would be his gift to Kiyomitsu-san, this year's part of a ritual that had been going on for over fifteen years now. After so much time, it had been difficult to think of something new, which also reflected the magnitude of SecureFit's business relationship with Masanobu. Japan was the largest export destination for SecureFit's products and was by far the most profitable. The gifts for the three principal managers would be easier. He always picked up a few bottles of the 30 year old whisky that they seemed to prefer. By telling them that he had simply taken advantage of the airport duty-free shop he had always been able to prevent the traditional[1] return of a gift from each of them that he didn't really want and would only weigh down his luggage.

Eion Williams was a creature of habit and this trip would follow a pattern established many years earlier. He would stick to an established itinerary, stay in the same hotels, take the same airline flights, and even sit in the same seats on the aircraft as he had on previous trips. This, he felt, was one of the advantages of being Executive Chairman and being able to set your schedule a year in advance. There would be a significant difference on this trip, however. This time he was taking someone with him. That someone was Mark Blyth who, upon Eion Williams's retirement the following year, would assume responsibility for the firm's business in Japan. As Eion Williams prepared for this trip to Japan, his next to last as Executive Chairman of SecureFit, he reflected on the growth of SecureFit over the past 33 years.

Founded on November 24, 1961 as The SecureFit Fence Company, SecureFit Industries was built on an innovative retaining wall system, which was designed to withstand the unique New Zealand soil conditions. The wall system, invented by Colin Freeman and

AUTHOR'S NOTE: This case was prepared as a basis for classroom discussion rather than to illustrate the effective or ineffective handling of an administrative situation. The preparation of this case study was supported by a grant from the Carnegie Bosch Institute for Applied Studies in International Management. The names of individuals and companies in this case have been disguised. Used by permission of the author.

marketed by Eion Williams, became an instant success and many examples of the product are still to be found around New Zealand. In the early to mid 1960's, while retaining wall systems remained the principal product, Colin Freeman designed a number of other products many of which were produced by SecureFit. The name of the firm was changed to SecureFit Industries in 1964. In 1967 SecureFit introduced a retraction mechanism for automobile seat that employed a Colin Freeman designed sealed nylon bearing. The product locked the seatbelt position in response to increasing tension. This development, coupled with the introduction of automobile assembly in New Zealand, led to substantial growth in the company as sales of this unique product skyrocketed. Saturation of the domestic market led SecureFit to its first offshore venture, a license to manufacture the product in Australia to Aaron Hinton Pty Ltd. Bolstered by a loan from the Development Finance Corporation of New Zealand based on this export potential SecureFit was on solid ground. However, Eion Williams was convinced that SecureFit's future depended on developing the export potential for its product. By 1970 SecureFit had established a market for its unique products in England, Singapore, Malaysia, Thailand, and South America.

Eion Williams recalled those early trips overseas. While government export incentives had helped to offset much of the travel costs, it was still necessary to work at a tremendous pace to get the most out of the opportunity. Even for someone who was as fit as he had been in those days, it was arduous work. One of the early trips had involved stops in 27 countries in 10 weeks. The glamour of travel had worn off very quickly on that trip and by the time he had got to South Africa he had become quite irritable and impatient with potential customers. The lower back pain that often emerged after long periods of sitting was a constant reminder of another less than entirely pleasant overseas journey. An aircraft controller's strike at Heathrow had turned a trip from Christchurch to Stockholm into a 54 hour ordeal with no opportunity to rest his back. He had grabbed a heavy bag out of a taxi seriously injuring his back. And, he had to be in 13 different cities in over the next 14 days. On returning to Auckland he had the injury attended to. The operation to repair the crushed disc and subsequent recuperative period had been the only time he had missed work due to illness or injury in over thirty years.

By 1971 all the overseas travel had begun to pay off with 39,000 pairs of seat belt mechanisms shipped in 31 separate consignments. In 1972 this grew to 136,000 pairs. By the late seventies exports had then taken on an increased significance and accounted for about 20% of all sales.

By 1977, Eion Williams had visited 56 countries to evaluate markets and/or introduce SecureFit's products. SecureFit was exporting regularly to about 10 different countries at this time. While the company had been successful in many areas of the world, others such as South America, had presented difficulties because of uneven economic growth or political instability. A report from the British trade office had impressed Eion with the point that the 500 most successful exporters from Britain, while exporting to 160 countries, made 80% of their profits from only 20% of their markets. Thus began the search for a market that had political stability and economic growth and, in short, would be the best place to be in 10 years. Even in 1977 it became clear to Eion that this would be Japan.

A friend of Eion's, who at the time worked in the Auckland office of the giant Japanese firm Mitsui, provided SecureFit with its first exposure to the Japanese market. Eion had given him samples of products and brochures to be sent off to Japan with an eye toward establishing an agent relationship with Mitsui. About a month later Eion received a telex from Mitsui saying that they had completed their market survey, and would he come to Japan to learn the results. It was February 1978 and Eion had booked the first available flight to Tokyo. He remembered how impressive the big black, 60 storey Mitsui building had been, how it had dominated the Shinjuku district of Tokyo. He also remembered the smooth English-speaking Japanese junior executives with whom he met. In effect they said that most (90%) of Japanese automobile parts and accessories were manufactured locally and hence there were no opportunities for SecureFits product in Japan. Then the guy just said, "End of meeting." Eion was irritated at having been brought to Japan just to be told that and recalled that this had been his first and last meeting with fluent English speakers in Japan. He had gone straight around to the New Zealand embassy and borrowed an interpreter. Then, he spent the next several days going around Tokyo showing the product samples he had brought to the major automobile parts manufacturers. He had also taken a video with a Japanese narration that showed SecureFit's product being manufactured in New Zealand. This approach had been helpful in Latin America where it had been difficult to explain that SecureFit made only the retraction mechanism, not the entire seatbelt, and were therefore a supplier and not a potential competitor.

Dealing in the automobile component industry in Japan was very different from other Japanese industries, such as automobiles themselves or electronics, which were much more used to dealing with foreigners. The window manufacturers in Japan sell only to the domestic market and, therefore, had little prior experience with foreign firms. Eion's approach at each facility had been to ask (through his interpreter) who was the best component manufacturer, importer, agent or distributor in Japan. The name that kept popping up was Masanobu. So, he had contacted Masanobu. Fortunately, their managing director recognized some opportunities for the products and expressed interest in being SecureFit's agents in Japan. After several months of correspondence in which he had prepared a detailed marketing plan Masanobu agreed to be the exclusive distributor in Japan. The plan had included that Eion would make the Japanese market his personal responsibility, visit twice a year, meet their demands for quality and service, ship product within one month of receipt of orders, and airfreight at SecureFit's expense if they missed the first available ship.

It was on his second visit to Japan in October of 1978 that Eion Williams met Ichikawa Kiyomitsu, Managing Director of Masanobu, at their headquarters in Osaka. Kiyomitsu-san, now 75 years old, was an energetic chain smoker and hard drinker without particularly good English language skills. Eion had come to regard him as very intelligent, with a feel for western ways of doing things. He also seemed to have a keen awareness of what was transpiring around him. On that trip he had arranged for Eion to be taken around the country to meet Masanobu's major customers. One such customer, Kobe Automotive Products was ultimately the first Japanese company to use SecureFit's products. The general manager of Kobe at the time was a Mr. Tamagawa. Mr. Tamagawa, Eion recalled, was a great believer in testing and more testing. He took SecureFit's seat belt mechanism which was normally tested to operate a minimum of 360,000 times before failure, and subjected it to 1.8 million operations, the equivalent of 60 years of normal operation.[2] He found that a part failed in the last few operations unless a screw was added on the underside of a hollow aluminium rivet on the mechanism. He demanded that SecureFit incorporate this modification into the product, for which he was willing to pay an additional 20 yen per unit. Actually, it had proved to be more efficient for Masanobu to make the modification in Japan, which they did for five years until Eion was able to prove to Mr. Tamagawa that a new version of the product would last as long or longer without the modification.

By the time the first order had actually been placed from Japan, Eion Williams had made three visits to Japan and established a pattern that has lasted over 15 years. Part of that pattern concerned the Japanese obsession with quality. Every six months on the first Monday in October and April Eion would be picked up from his hotel and driven to Masanobu's headquarters. The first meeting would inevitably be in the large meeting room with 15 or 16 of Masanobu's managers from around the country in attendance. After the ritual exchange of greetings and calling cards, Mr. Kiyonaga, their quality manager, would come in with a box of faulty SecureFit product and tip it out on the table in front of Eion. It might have been only one fault in 10,000 but it looked terrible. Since Japanese automobile manufacturers guarantee the car and all of its components, faulty components created a big problem for them. While Eion explained what action had or was being taken on each fault the rest of the managers just seemed to glare at him. If a particular fault was ever subsequently repeated all hell would break loose and they would send rude telexes saying things like don't you train your people or don't they care? Although, these meetings put him in a difficult position as a supplier, particularly when he was seeking a price increase, they had also provided some lessons regarding quality control. In fact, it was from this experience that SecureFit had developed its fault report system, which subsequently became a cornerstone of its quality control programme.

The need to maintain quality always had to be balanced against the constant demands for new and innovative designs by the Japanese automobile industry. Large automotive component manufacturers in Japan produce biannual catalogues and are constantly looking for something that will differentiate them from their competitors. Eion felt that the Japanese manufacturers had come to depend on SecureFit for new products, but knew he would not sacrifice quality. He had said "no" more than once when asked to rush a product into production in order to meet the deadline of the forthcoming catalogue. Holding hundreds of patents worldwide as well as SecureFit's ability to continuously innovate gave Eion the power he needed to say no to the Japanese. This ability was something he valued very much.

All being said, Eion Williams was pleased with what he and SecureFit had accomplished in Japan. However, he knew that the relationships that had been built over years could not be left unattended. That's where Mark Blyth came in. In June of next year, when Eion Williams will have retired, Mark would take over responsibility for the Japanese market. The transition would begin with this trip on which Mark would take on the role of observer while Eion followed his normal routine. The following

Spring, Eion would be the observer as well as being the honoured at a number of functions because of his retirement. Eion intended for this transition to be seamless both at home in Christchurch and in Japan. Steven Campbell would take on most of his remaining duties, as in fact he already had. He had always said that nothing would please him more than after his retirement for someone to say "Where's Eion, I haven't seen his car in the parking lot lately?" Of course he will still probably go back to Japan once a year to play golf with Mr Kiyomitsu, or something like that—just what company presidents are supposed to do.

Mark Blyth was also preparing for the trip to Japan. It had been three and one half years since he had left Japan with Sachiko, his wife, to return to New Zealand. In that time, he had completed his MBA at Canterbury University and found what seemed an ideal situation for someone with his skills. SecureFit had needed someone with an affinity for the Japanese market and an understanding of manufacturing. His eleven years of experience in Japan, fluency in the language, and engineering background made the fit seem obvious. More than that, though, SecureFit seemed to be getting it right in a number of areas. They had won numerous export and quality awards, were an innovator in team-based management, plus the place seemed to have the kind of culture he had been looking for. Halfway through his MBA, Mark had drawn up a short list of 5 companies who did business in Japan and appeared to have the kind of strategic vision he thought was necessary to compete effectively there. After a three-week trial period at SecureFit he had become convinced that this was the kind of company he was looking for. Also, SecureFit's growth and the fact that the top management team was changing (as a result of Eion Williams's upcoming retirement) suggested that advancement opportunities might be good. An interview with Steven Campbell clinched it. Steven's vision of SecureFit in five to ten years was something that he had really bought in to; something that he had found lacking in the short-term perspectives of other New Zealand firms.

Now, after four months on the job at SecureFit, he was on his way to Japan to be introduced as the new Marketing Director who would be responsible for the Japanese market. He knew that the title of Marketing Director was partly a result of the need to assure Masanobu that they would be dealing with a very senior SecureFit executive. He also knew that this did not diminish the importance of his role. He had some concern that the Japanese might think that at age 37, he was too young to hold such a high position. Perhaps his prematurely grey hair would disguise his age. He felt that it was important that the Japanese be convinced that he would be authorized to make decisions. After all, they had been dealing with Eion, who was not only the Executive Chairman (the equivalent to the company president in Japan), he was a founder of the company with an encyclopaedic knowledge of the industry. The transition would be a tricky one, but one that he felt could be managed effectively. The importance of his performance on this trip could not be overemphasized. His career, and to some degree the future of SecureFit, depended on how well these initial meetings went.

Mark Blyth was confident in his ability to deal effectively with the Masanobu executives. His eleven years at Matsushita[3] not only gave him experience with the Japanese it gave him credibility. He knew through Naoko MacDonald, the Japanese translator employed by SecureFit in Christchurch, that the Japanese were impressed with his credentials. And, credentials always overly impress the Japanese. Mark also had some unique connections that he thought might be used to advantage at some stage. One of his wife's relatives, a cousin, was an executive with Nissan. Perhaps he could help fill what Mark perceived as an information gap between SecureFit and their end user, the Japanese automobile industry. Also, the silver symbol for *Ju* that he wore as a tie tack would not go unnoticed in the automotive components industry. *Ju* stands for Judo, and Mark Blyth had originally gone to Japan in 1982 because of his interest in Judo[4]. He was a 4th *dan,* a level that would garner respect among enthusiasts, and the automotive components industry was full of Judo enthusiasts. And if his Judo connections weren't a competitive advantage, perhaps his prowess at Shogi[5] would be. He had often found that playing Shogi with someone gave him some insight into their character. Certainly his level of Japanese language skill was an advantage that not many foreigners enjoyed. However, he reminded himself that he had to be careful in his use of Japanese on this trip. He almost wished that Eion had not told the Japanese that he was fluent in the language. In the past, he had found it useful to keep his level of language skill hidden until late in a negotiation. This was a tactic that he had learned from the Japanese who often understood English very well but didn't show it. He understood from Naoko that the Japanese were looking forward to being able to converse with someone from SecureFit in their own language. While he felt that his language skills would improve communication with Masanobu in the longer term, it might pose a problem on this trip. Since Eion Williams did not speak Japanese it was important that all the meetings in which Eion participated were conducted through the translator. Direct communication with Mark in Japanese would take Eion out of the loop and potentially be very confusing. Mark considered that he might revert to the rough Kobe dialect, which was characteristic of the Japanese language he first learned in western Japan. He had always feared slipping into this speech pattern when making formal presentations in Tokyo for Matsushita. However, now this ability to speak "less than perfect" Japanese when needed might be an advantage. He wondered how the executives at Masanobu would react to this tactic.

Mark was excited about the trip to Japan the next day and felt that he had prepared well. After having read the last three years of correspondence with Masanobu (and skimming five years worth) he felt he knew the relationship fairly well. He also knew that only one of the meetings would be in Osaka with Ichikawa Kiyomitsu and that Kiyomitsu-san would retire in about three years time. At that time, his son Torii would take over as president. Torii had a marketing background and was described by Eion as very un-Japanese. Torii had acted as Eion's translator for the past seven or eight years. At age 37, he had been promoted very rapidly through the ranks of Masanobu and was now Managing Director of the firm's Tokyo office. Mark understood that Torii's rapid rise had been against the wishes of the other directors and that something of a power struggle had occurred. However, with Torii's promotion to the Tokyo office, it now seemed clear that he would be the next president. Mark felt that he should use this trip as an opportunity to start building a relationship with Torii. Since he planned to stay in Japan a week longer than Eion, Mark thought he would take the opportunity to visit Torii at Masanobu's Tokyo office. This, he thought, would give the two men an opportunity to get to know each other without the restrictions imposed by the head office environment of Osaka. He might also use this time to explore other issues that interested him about SecureFit's relationship with Masanobu.

As Mark thought about what he wanted to accomplish on this trip to Japan he felt that establishing the relationship with Torii was paramount. He was no use to SecureFit if he couldn't make that relationship work. However, he also felt that he should spend a significant amount of time observing Eion Williams. After all, Eion had cracked one of the toughest markets in the world and managed to stay on top of it for seventeen years.

Mark found Eion Williams to be an intriguing man. He was especially impressed by Eion's apparent ability to control the flow of events in Japan. For example, he would send his agenda for the meetings at Masanobu on the day he left New Zealand for Japan. This, Mark thought, doesn't really give the Japanese much time to prepare. Also, from reading the transcripts of meetings he knew that Eion wouldn't allow smoking at any meeting in which he was in attendance. Mark thought this must have made many of the Japanese, who smoke like crazy, pretty nervous after a time. He also understood that Eion didn't really engage in the after hours drinking and socializing so prevalent in Japan. More importantly, Eion had often been able to say no to the Japanese on issues ranging from local manufacture of products to the timing of new product introduction. In Japan, being able to say no to a customer and make it stick was something that Mark had found to be very unusual. He had also heard, again through Naoko, that many of the Japanese were afraid to tell Eion exactly what they thought. Perhaps this was because of Eion's stature as Executive Chairman or maybe it was because Eion didn't speak Japanese. In any case, watching how the Japanese reacted to Eion should prove educational.

Also on Mark's agenda was to investigate a number of issues which he thought might suggest the need for change in the relationship with Masanobu in the years to come. These included some changes in market conditions including the breaking down of distribution barriers, increased consumerism, and a change toward safer cars. He felt that communications with Masanobu had not in the past been adequate to keep SecureFit abreast of changes in the Japanese market, which he knew could change very quickly. He wasn't sure if Masanobu just wasn't collecting the information or if it wasn't getting back to Christchurch. In any case, he felt that communications must be improved. Also, part of that improvement in the relationship must involve more visits to New Zealand by technical staff at Masanobu. For example, there was an engineer who accounted for about a third of the faxes that SecureFit got from Japan. Mark felt certain that a visit to Christchurch could sort out some of the issues he was raising. Probably, no one at Masanobu had suggested a visit because his superior had never visited. Again, he thought, that's the kind of thing his knowledge of Japan and the Japanese could help him sort out.

Mark Blyth was confident as he prepared to return to Japan in his new capacity as an Marketing Director of SecureFit. However, he also knew that there was a lot that he didn't know, couldn't know, after only four months with the firm. There are things that you just can't learn from reading the files, he thought. He also knew, through Naoko, that

Masanobu had some concerns about the relationship and he wondered what those might be. Find out the problems, he thought, that's all he needed to do. After all, he wasn't taking over on this trip.

Eion Williams, who had made a practice of delegating half of his responsibilities every five years, was confident in his plan for handing over his most important responsibility, the Japanese market. He felt that his success had been due, at least in part, to the fact that he was the Executive Chairman and could make commitments that would bind the company. A salesman wouldn't be able to do that. Mark Blyth would go to Japan with the title of Marketing Director on his cuff and he would be responsible for that market, just as all directors of SecureFit were responsible for markets.[6] Masanobu had been aware of Eion's retirement for years so the timing of the transition would not be a surprise. Also, Mark was extremely well qualified and he certainly knew Japan and the Japanese well. One of Eion's concerns was that perhaps Mark knew Japan too well. His 11 years of servitude, as Eion thought of it, in Japan certainly had to have had an effect. Eion had never really been enamoured with the Japanese, he just respected their business ability. They knew about power relationships, but so did he, and he knew when he could say no. He wondered if Mark Blyth would be able to say no.

## Notes

1. The giving of a gift in Japan places a burden on the other person (*on*) which is lifted when a comparable gift is returned.

2. SecureFit guarantees its products for 20 years.

3. Matsushita is a large manufacturing firm marketing products under the Panasonic and National brand names among others.

4. Mark Blyth had been captain of the New Zealand Judo team that travelled to Japan in 1982.

5. Shogi is a Japanese board game somewhat similar to chess.

6. For example, the accounts director was responsible for Malaysia and the technical director for Australia and Papua New Guinea.

**SecureFit Corporate Statement**

**Purpose**

To be the leading supplier of our products by determining customers' needs and developing products to meet those needs.

**What We Value**

We believe in the importance of:

- Delighting our customers
- Empowering our people
- Quality and innovation
- Keeping the promises we make
- Teamwork as a way to get things done
- Making work fun
- Being fair
- Celebrating our achievement
- Being willing to take risks

# Appendix

## Patent Protection in Japan

SecureFit Industries depends on innovation to remain competitive and spends about 10% of annual sales on research and development. To protect this innovation SecureFit owns over 300 patents worldwide. The price of this patent protection is not cheap, costing an estimated NZ$5000 per patent per country.

Two attempts at patent infringement have occurred in Japan. In the first case, one of the largest auto components companies in Japan and a large SecureFit customer, Yoshida, had approached SecureFit about developing locks for a new seatbelt mechanism. SecureFit had advised them that they would be pleased to produce the product, but that it would be six months before they could start the development program. Twelve months later SecureFit learned that the component had appeared on one of Yoshida's products which infringed SecureFit's patent. Through their patent attorneys, SecureFit advised Yoshida that they were infringing the patent and would have to cease. Toyonobu, a Tokyo manufacture who was making the product on tooling financed by Yoshida, immediately contacted SecureFit. Toyonobu attempted to negotiate a settlement of a 2 1/2% royalty to be paid to SecureFit. SecureFit's response was that if Toyonobu would transfer the tooling and technology to Masanobu (SecureFit's exclusive distributor in Japan) SecureFit would not sue them for damages or back royalties of 10% covering the infringing products they had produced. The matter was complicated by the fact that Yoshida, as part of the new product design, had incorporated and patented an improvement on the mechanism. After several months of negotiations Toyonobu agreed to move the tooling to Masanobu and transfer ownership of the new patent to SecureFit. In return, SecureFit (through Masanobu) would charge Yoshida a 5% royalty on the project whereas the price to all other customers would include a 10% royalty.

A second patent infringement involved an engineering company in Osaka, coincidentally also named Toyonobu but unrelated to the firm mentioned above. This Toyonobu had introduced an almost identical copy of SecureFit's largest selling product. It was made of stainless steel and differed on one small detail, unrelated to function, through which they had sought to circumvent SecureFit's patent.[1] SecureFit was not prepared to accept this particular situation and sought an injunction from the Osaka Patent Court. It took thirteen months but SecureFit finally won and Toyonobu was required to cease manufacture. This being Japan, there were no damages, court costs or royalties awarded. In fact, Toyonobu was allowed several months to continue production while they redesigned the product.

## SecureFit's Fault Report System

Any fault or complaint on any part or system is recorded on a bright yellow complaint form. The intent of the form is to provide information to prevent the error from occurring again. The form is applied rigorously and the directors and the CEO review all complaint forms on a monthly basis.

Note: As opposed to being able to patent a single novel feature of a design, as in most parts of the world, the Japanese patent office requires that each and every aspect of a design be detailed in the application. The effect of this is that it is relatively easy for a Japanese infringer to change just one of these details to circumvent the patent. Many business people would argue that it is extremely difficult to beat a Japanese company in a Japanese court on this type of patent infringement case.

# Case 2.7

# RUS WANE EQUIPMENT

## *Joint Venture in Russia*

STANISLAV V. SHEKSHNIA AND SHEILA M. PUFFER

"John, yesterday Lev presented me with a candidate for the human resource manager's position. Tomorrow he is going to ask the board to appoint Sasha Neresyan. What do you think?" Ronald Chapman, Wane Machines, Inc.'s Country Manager for Russia asked John Swift, Deputy General Manager of Rus Wane Equipment, as they discussed Wane's Russian joint venture on the eve of its third anniversary in November 1993.

The question came as quite a surprise to John who had virtually given up hope that the human resource manager position would be filled. But he would never have considered 30-year-old Sasha as a candidate for the job—not that he lacked desirable qualities as an employee. Sasha had joined Rus Wane in June 1992 as a customs clearance officer. He had earned a very good reputation in the company by skillfully negotiating with bureaucratic and often corrupt Russian government officials who could turn importing of crucial goods and components into a nightmare for the joint venture. Before joining Rus Wane, Sasha had retired from the Army with the rank of captain, having worked in the Middle East using his background as a military translator. His excellent communication skills and fluency in English had helped him build good relations with many local and all expatriate Rus Wane employees.

But being a good customs clearance officer, John thought, hardly makes one a qualified human resource professional. As Ron paused, John wondered aloud: "Will Sasha be respected by senior Rus Wane managers, even though he is at least twenty years younger than they are? And what does he know about HR practices?" John did not have the answers to these questions, but he knew that Sasha was a smart and hard-working young man. What really bothered John was the fact that Sasha had been brought to Rus Wane by the general manager, Lev Novikov, who had been a long-time patient and friend of Dr. Neresyan, Sasha's father. This hiring proposal was the latest episode contributing to the strained relations between the Russian general manager of the joint venture and his American deputy general manager.

### The U.S. Partner, Wane Machines, Inc.

During its 150 years of operation, Wane Machines, Inc. had grown from a one-person – one-invention

AUTHORS' NOTE: This case was written solely for the purpose of stimulating student discussion. All events and individuals are real, but names and industries have been disguised. The authors gratefully acknowledge the valuable suggestions of Editor John Seeger, three anonymous reviewers, and Northeastern colleague, Daniel J. McCarthy.

workshop in New York City into a multi-billion-dollar multinational corporation with manufacturing, sales and service operations in dozens of countries. Wane had always remained in one industry, engaging in the manufacture, installation and maintenance of large-scale heating and cooling equipment for office and apartment buildings. In the late 1890s, Wane began its international expansion by setting up operations in Europe. From the outset, its strategy had been to be recognized as a local company in every market it entered, and to establish long-term relationships with customers by providing a complete package of services, including product maintenance, repair, and upgrading. Following this strategy consistently for nearly a hundred years, Wane Machines became a global market leader with a network of more than 50 companies operating in 160 countries.

Wane Machines had four regional divisions: domestic (USA and Canada), Europe, Latin America, and Asia. In the 1980s domestic operations lost its sales leadership to the European division, as the market for new construction in the United States dropped precipitously during the severe economic recession. After a decade of spectacular growth, the European market also declined sharply in the early 1990s as the United Kingdom, and later France and Germany, entered an economic recession. To attempt future growth, Wane management began to explore the markets that had begun to open in Eastern Europe and the Soviet Union. In 1989 Ronald Chapman was appointed Wane's country manager for the Soviet Union. Ron, who had a Harvard MBA and 20 years' experience with Wane, was charged with studying the USSR market and setting up Wane's operations in Moscow and St. Petersburg. Before this assignment, he had managed Wane's joint venture in Taiwan after working in Japan and Hong Kong for 10 years. In his new function, Chapman reported to the area vice-president for Central and Eastern Europe who was located in Wane's European division in Brussels.

## Entering the USSR Market

The Soviet market was not total *terra incognita* for Wane, as it had been exporting its products to the USSR through its Austrian company since the early 1970s. During that period Wane sold its high quality heating and cooling equipment for installation in several Soviet government buildings as well as an American-built hotel. However, it could not penetrate the huge domestic market for several reasons. The ruble could not be converted to hard currency to pay for imported goods, few Soviet enterprises had access to hard currency, and until 1988 all purchases of imports were controlled by government foreign trade organizations with whom enterprises were required to negotiate for imported equipment and other supplies.

By the late 1980s the market potential in the USSR for Wane's products was the largest in the world, as 85 percent of the country's 290 million people lived in apartment complexes, most of which required upgrading of their large-scale heating and cooling systems. In addition, more housing was planned under President Gorbachev's "Housing 2000" program, announced in 1986 with the goal of providing every Soviet family with a separate apartment by the year 2000. This would be a massive undertaking, as some 25 percent of families lived in communal apartments in which they shared kitchen and bathroom facilities with other families. Because of these conditions, demand for large-scale heating and cooling systems was expected to double through the remainder of the century.

According to the Ministry of Building Equipment Manufacturing, in the late 1980s annual demand for large heating and cooling equipment was approximately 100,000 units, while Soviet enterprises manufactured a total of 60,000 units. Production planning, resource allocation, and customer selection were all controlled centrally by government bodies such as Gosplan, the state planning ministry, and Gossnab, the government supply organization. The domestic heating and cooling industry was fragmented with manufacturing plants reporting to the Ministry of Building Equipment Manufacturing, installation units attached to the State Construction Committee, and maintenance services operated by local civic authorities. The major cities of Moscow, St. Petersburg, and Kiev had their own manufacturing facilities and installation units.

For more than 20 years, Soviet factories manufactured the same, unimproved heating and cooling equipment for the domestic market, having little incentive or ability to upgrade them under the system of central planning. Artificially low prices were established by state authorities with little regard to actual costs or customer demand. For their part, customers, who were construction ministries and building management organizations attached to local governments, paid for goods not with their own money, but with funds allocated by the government. They were usually glad to receive the scarce equipment, even though it was of poor quality and low reliability.

## Formation of the Joint Venture

In 1989 the Soviet Ministry of Foreign Trade put Wane in touch with NLZ, a medium-sized factory located just outside Moscow that manufactured heating and cooling equipment similar to Wane's, but of lower quality. In February 1990, after what appeared to Wane's management as lengthy and sometimes frustrating negotiations, a joint venture called Rus Wane Equipment was formed, with the primary purpose of establishing a new plant to manufacture products virtually identical to Wane's European models. Registered as a Soviet-Belgian joint venture, the new company had initial capital funds of US$11.5 million. Wane contributed $8 million in hard currency and equipment for the new factory to be built with the Soviet partner. The latter contributed use of the facilities in the existing plant to manufacture components, as well as the site for the new factory. Whether NLZ or the government owned the land was unclear, however, because of ambiguous legislation on property. Wane Machines had a 57 percent share of the joint venture, and NLZ, 43 percent. At about the same time, Wane signed a second joint venture with a St. Petersburg partner to install and service Rus Wane's products in Western Russia.

Wane's strategy for Russia consisted of three major elements. First, they did not expect to make money for the first three years. Second, they planned to develop export potential for Eastern Europe. Third, Wane hoped that the Russian ruble would become a convertible currency in the near future.

The highest governing body of the Rus Wane joint venture was the board of directors. The chairman of the board was Wane Europe's area vice-president for Central and Eastern Europe. The other board members were the legal counsel of Wane Europe, Wane's country manager for the Soviet Union Ron Chapman, Rus Wane Equipment's general manager Lev Novikov, and an official from the Soviet ministry of building equipment manufacturing. The board of directors met quarterly to review developments since the previous meeting, review business plans and progress toward them, approve capital expenditures, and appoint direct reports. Organization charts depicting the Rus Wane Equipment joint venture and its relationship with Wane Machines are provided in Exhibits 1 and 2.

At the time of Wane's initial negotiations, joint ventures were the primary form of market entry into the Soviet Union. The Joint Venture Law of 1987 had opened the door for foreign investment in the USSR and accorded preferential taxation status and other privileges to foreign joint ventures. Initially, Soviet law restricted foreign ownership of joint ventures to a maximum of 49 percent, and the head of the operation was required to be a Soviet citizen. In 1988, these provisos were withdrawn by the Russian government, permitting greater foreign ownership and control.

Although Soviet law no longer required a Soviet citizen to hold the most senior position, Wane's policy throughout the world was to put local managers in charge, because they were believed to be the most knowledgeable and capable individuals to run local operations. Therefore, Lev Novikov, a 58-year-old mechanical engineer by training, was appointed general manager of Rus Wane Equipment. He also remained general manager of the Soviet partner, NLZ, a position he had held for 15 of the 25 years he had worked in the industry. His experience, enthusiasm, and strong leadership led Wane's management to view him as the driving force who could manage construction of the new manufacturing facility and see it through to completion under very difficult circumstances.

## Construction of the Plant

In October 1990, shortly after the joint venture agreement was signed, Wane's management took the bold step of beginning construction of a plant in the Moscow area to produce heating and cooling equipment for the Russian market. The multimillion-dollar investment was one of the first major commitments by a Western firm to manufacture products in Russia, since most companies were unwilling to take such a risk in Russia's highly unstable political and economic environment.

The state-of-the-art plant was built in full compliance with Wane's specifications, making it technologically comparable to Wane's European facilities. The plant was completed in June 1992, an extremely short period of time, especially in the Soviet Union where such building projects usually took years, and sometimes as long as a decade. Furthermore, the external environment at the time of construction was marked by the breakup of the Soviet Union, severely deteriorating economic conditions in Russia including monthly inflation exceeding 20 percent, disintegration of the centralized resource allocation system, and confusing and vacillating legislation on corporate taxation, business development, and the status of foreign operations. Inconsistent government policy on foreign direct investment, including taxation and ownership rights, along with erratic domestic policy concerning government subsidies, business law, and ownership of property, contributed to the external problems confronting international firms in Russia.

Rus Wane Equipment's plant was designed to manufacture Wane's European models of heating and cooling equipment, with minor modifications for the Russian market. Product characteristics, such as length of service and number of call-backs per unit, showed that the quality of Wane's products was more than four times that of Russian competitors', and required half the energy to operate. Wane maintained a pricing policy not to exceed twice the price of the grossly inferior Russian models. The first product was scheduled to be shipped from the new factory in June 1993, and full capacity of 5,000 units annually was projected for 1995.

In August 1993, only six weeks behind schedule, Rus Wane Equipment celebrated its first shipment with toasts of Möet champagne and Stolichnaya vodka. By September the factory was fully operational with an available production capacity of 85 units per month. Most of the joint venture's office employees and factory workers came from NLZ, the Russian partner. A select group, they were full of enthusiasm to work for the joint venture, and looked forward to excellent working conditions in the new plant as well as democratic and participative Western management methods.

## Sales and Service Operations

While the plant was under construction, Rus Wane also set up an organization to sell, install, and maintain Wane's imported and locally produced equipment. Field personnel, who numbered 150, were recruited from various Moscow installation and service agencies. This part of the business was quite successful, offering Western-style maintenance service to numerous foreign organizations and some Russian companies that could afford it.

## Early Obstacles

Construction of a state-of-the-art manufacturing facility and establishment of a sales and service network were achievements that few joint ventures had accomplished in Russia up to that time. However, reaching these goals by no means guaranteed Rus Wane's success. Among the obstacles confronting the firm once it became operational were an unexpected downturn in demand, difficulty in securing reliable suppliers, and an unpredictable legal and economic environment.

Despite the Soviet Union's vast market potential that had attracted Wane to build a manufacturing facility there, much of Rus Wane's production capacity sat idle in the initial months because of weak customer demand. As a result, only 17 units were manufactured in September, 12 in October, and 15 were planned for November. As Russia and the other countries of the former Soviet Union entered a severe economic crisis, new construction declined dramatically and demand for heating and cooling systems plummeted. No one had exact data, but Rus Wane's management estimated annual domestic sales in Russia to be 6,000 units, while the total combined capacity of domestic manufacturers was 30,000 to 40,000 units.

Under this tremendous supply pressure, aggravated by the extremely difficult financial position of most of their customers, price became a major factor in the purchase decision. Rus Wane's product, sold even at zero profit margin, was still nearly twice as expensive as domestic equipment because of small production runs and costs associated with the sophisticated design. Prospective Russian customers, primarily state- or municipally-owned construction and engineering enterprises, were caught in a squeeze. They suffered a cash shortage resulting from sharply reduced government subsidies of their operations, and hyperinflation had eroded their purchasing power. A limited number of price-tolerant and quality-sensitive customers, such as commercial banks, foreign hotels and joint ventures, appreciated the quality of Rus Wane's products, but even those often preferred to buy competitors' systems manufactured in Western Europe, considering their foreign origin to be more prestigious. High inflation of the ruble, along with its devaluation against foreign currencies, eliminated virtually all cost advantages of manufacturing in Russia, and did not allow Rus Wane to sell profitably to customers outside the country as it had planned.

Developing relationships with reliable domestic suppliers was an objective that proved challenging to implement. The company carefully sought out enterprises that had produced for the military sector because they had been held to higher quality standards and stricter delivery schedules than other enterprises under the former central planning system. Such enterprises also often had idle capacity and faced layoffs resulting from drastic cuts in government orders, and hence were eager to find customers. However, even these suppliers were not easily able to meet Rus Wane's standards, and they required a considerable amount of Rus Wane's time and energy for training and monitoring.

Like other companies operating in the Russian market, Rus Wane had to struggle with a constantly changing legal framework and unpredictable government policy. For example, in 1992 the Russian government froze the company's bank account for six months. The State bank had run out of cash and arbitrarily withheld payments owed to Russian and foreign enterprises. In another unfortunate financial incident, Rus Wane was forced to pay $1.5 million in taxes on their new factory building when the Russian government introduced a value-added tax (VAT), even though the building had been completed well before the introduction of the tax.

In spite of such problems, the company was growing and its management systems were being developed. With significant cash flows from its sales and service field operations compensating for the losses in manufacturing, Rus Wane was a profitable organization overall, with 320 employees and monthly revenues of $600,000.

### Staffing Key Managerial Positions

According to the joint venture agreement, Wane Machines was responsible for sending three experienced executives to serve as Rus Wane's deputy general manager, manufacturing manager, and financial manager for the first two to three years. Russian nationals would take over the positions at the end of this initial period. The major objectives of this policy were to provide "assistance in technology and management skills transfer, management systems and processes development, and local personnel coaching." Two other senior management positions, sales and service manager and human resources manager, were to be filled by local nationals from the beginning because they involved regular contact with Russian customers or workers at various levels, thus requiring a thorough knowledge of local culture and employment practices.

Other than the sales and service manager's position, which was filled by an experienced local manager, the remaining key managerial positions were not easily filled. Wane fell behind schedule in sending its expatriates to Russia, and Lev Novikov, the general manager, delayed hiring a local for the human resources position, preferring to administer that function himself.

John Swift, a 35-year-old American, was appointed as Rus Wane's deputy general manager in late 1991. For nearly ten months he commuted frequently from European headquarters in Brussels, and settled in Moscow in September 1992 after having problems finding suitable accommodations for his family. John had joined Wane in 1989 after graduating from business school. He then completed the corporate management development program and worked for two years in Western Europe as a field operations manager. Before 1991 John had never been to Russia nor, he said, had any intention of going there. He was, however, ambitious, and readily accepted the job offer, seeing it as a valuable career move. As deputy general manager, he reported to Lev Novikov, the joint venture's general manager, and was responsible for supervising technology transfer, sales, pricing, and personnel. He also served as the liaison between the joint venture and Wane's European headquarters, and reported to Ron Chapman, Wane's country manager for Russia.

Jean-Pierre Dumont, Rus Wane's manufacturing manager, had 15 years of engineering experience with Wane Machines in his native France, but the Russian appointment was his first management position. Like John Swift, he too found Russia to be a land of mystery, yet was equally eager to take the job. He explained: "It's very rare these days that an engineer gets a chance to work in a factory created from scratch. I am lucky to get this chance and I'm not going to miss it."

Convincing an experienced financial manager to relocate to Russia was not an easy task. After an intensive and lengthy search, Jeff Nichol, a 27-year-old Englishman who had been working at Wane for two years as a corporate auditor, was selected in October 1991. Because of Jeff's limited experience, Ron Chapman sent him for training in Brussels for six months before going to Russia. In the meantime, Lev appointed Katya Karaseva, NLZ's chief accountant, to head Rus Wane's finance department. Katya had worked in the industry for 24 years, 17 of them with Lev.

Wane's Russia country manager, Ron Chapman, worked out of Wane's European headquarters in Brussels, but flew to Russia at least once a month to visit Wane's St. Petersburg joint venture as well as Rus Wane Equipment in Moscow where he would review the joint venture's situation with the general manager, Lev Novikov and his deputy, John Swift.

### Tensions in the Finance Department

When Jeff Nichol arrived at Rus Wane in the spring of 1992, Lev suggested that he be a consultant for a while rather than immediately assuming the duties of financial manager, citing his young age, his need to adjust to the local culture, and his lack of Russian language abilities. Ron accepted the arrangement because he wanted Jeff to spend some of his time at the St. Petersburg joint venture. For a while, Jeff traveled between Moscow and St. Petersburg, spending most of his time learning the Russian language as well as Russian accounting systems, and developing financial procedures for both joint ventures.

Early in 1993, when a financial manager had been recruited for the St. Petersburg operation, Jeff decided it was the right time for him to become financial manager at Rus Wane. John Swift fully supported him. By that time Rus Wane had eight employees in the finance department: Jeff, Katya, and six accountants, most of whom came from NLZ. Unfortunately, this small group was unable to work smoothly together. As John explained to Ron: "We've got total confusion in the finance department: people don't know who's the boss, Katya does what she wants, and Jeff is running out of patience. His contract expires in March and I don't think he's looking forward to staying any longer. Ron, we can't allow this situation to continue—the company needs a financial manager."

To compound the problem, the accountants expressed their disappointment to John that Western management practices that they had hoped would give them greater participation in decision making had not been implemented. They also complained about not being rewarded on merit, and about the Westerners, whom they considered to be doing comparable work, receiving substantially higher compensation.

From the beginning, communication between Jeff and Katya had not been easy. For one thing, he did not speak Russian and she did not speak English. But that was not the only problem. Several times Jeff had organized training sessions for Rus Wane's finance personnel, yet each time Katya had found excuses not to participate. When, after a year at the joint venture, Jeff had become conversational in Russian, communication between him and Katya failed to improve in any meaningful way. Even though they worked virtually side by side, with Katya in a private office and Jeff in an adjacent common area, they communicated only through interoffice mail.

Jeff made a number of appeals to Lev to try to get his point across. He wrote several memos, with copies to the vice-president of finance for Wane Europe, in which he described Katya's mistakes, but the general manager never replied and continued to show his full support for Katya. In addition, the finance staff had been expanding, yet Jeff had never been involved in the selection process. When he raised the issue with Lev, the latter responded that hiring was his problem, not Jeff's.

## Discord Over the General Manager

In February 1993, John Swift sent a memo to Lev suggesting that he propose Jeff's appointment as acting financial manager to Rus Wane's board of directors for approval, as required by company policy. Lev did not respond. A month later John raised the issue again and received the categorical reply: "He cannot be a financial manager." Without challenging that conclusion, John forwarded his suggestion to Ron Chapman who had shown full understanding of John's viewpoint. The subject of the financial manager's appointment was put on the agenda for the next board meeting. However, the day before the meeting, the item was withdrawn from the agenda. Ron later explained to John that Lev had convinced him not to be in a hurry to appoint Jeff to the position.

Meanwhile, tensions in the finance department continued to escalate. The joint venture experienced some delays in consolidating its first business plan, as well as difficulties in cash management and inventory control. On several occasions Jeff openly expressed his low opinion of his Russian colleagues' professional qualifications. These problems deeply concerned the deputy general manager, but the country manager did not take the matter seriously. Neither did Ron seem to be concerned about other signs of poor morale. For example, the first Russian hired as a sales person, and who had been trained in the U.S. and Western Europe and was highly respected in the company, left to work for a Russian trading venture. In addition, turnover in the factory was 5 percent a month.

In a discussion the two had about the finance department, Ron assessed the situation quite differently from John: "I think you're dramatizing the situation, John. Rus Wane has an excellent cost accounting system, our corporate financial software has been successfully introduced, and the skills of the finance people have improved tremendously."

"Yes, but Jeff has done it all himself," John replied.

"That's because he doesn't know how to delegate. He needs to work at improving his management style. I am beginning to understand why Lev can't see him as a financial manager. Jeff doesn't know how to manage people and he is becoming paranoid about Katya. I'm afraid that if on Saturday night his girlfriend doesn't show up for a date, he'll find a way to blame it on Katya. By the way, John, Lev is looking for a financial manager from the outside. It could be a good solution."

John was very surprised to hear the proposal—Lev had mentioned nothing about it to him. "You know, Ron, it's always very difficult to communicate with Lev. First, he doesn't like to share any information with me and he prefers to make all the decisions himself. And second, he is simply never here. The last time I saw him was ten days ago."

Although Lev had officially become a full-time employee of Rus Wane Equipment in January 1993, he had never resigned from his position of general manager of NLZ, which was still manufacturing its old product next door to the joint venture's new plant. Some people at Rus Wane were concerned about the situation which they interpreted as their general manager also being their competitor's general manager. There had been rumors about the old plant being in a difficult financial situation, but no one had reliable information. Yet it was well known that NLZ had been going through the process of privatization, as mandated by the government, and Lev had been leading it. A major task would be to determine what percentage of shares would be owned by various managers and other employees.

John thought that there was a clear conflict of interest between Lev's role at the old factory and his position in the joint venture. He tried to raise the issue with Ron during one of his monthly visits: "Lev is preoccupied with his own interests, not Rus Wane's. When you are not here, he spends all his time at the old factory trying to turn it into his private property."

Ron angrily interrupted: "Let's drop the subject. This is not your responsibility, John."

## Hiring a Human Resource Manager

John suppressed his instinctive response, feeling his anger growing. On several previous occasions he had tried to raise the subject of Lev Novikov's management style with Ron, but the latter never wanted to discuss it. Now, totally frustrated with personnel management issues at the joint venture, John shifted to another sore point: "As you know, Ron, we still don't have a human resource manager here at Rus Wane. I believe Lev hasn't filled the position on purpose. He wants to continue to do things the old Soviet way—to run the company like a tsar."

Ron looked up sharply: "That's a pretty strong statement, John. You've got to have facts to prove it."

John was sure he had the facts. A human resource manager was supposed to have been hired as soon as the joint venture had been founded three years earlier, in order to organize the selection process for other positions. However, Lev had decided to manage this function himself. As a result, all of the joint venture's senior managers other than the expatriates, and most of the lower-level managers, had come from NLZ. John considered this move a dangerous mistake. What was worse, he believed, was that quite a few senior managers' relatives had also been hired. The most notable, Lev's son, had already built an astonishing career within 12 months, starting as an assistant, becoming purchasing manager, and then going to Western Europe for 18 months' practical training. John had strongly opposed the decision to send Novikov Junior abroad, arguing that there had been better candidates, and that Rus Wane's reputation among its employees for fairness and democracy would suffer. Ron had ignored these concerns, and John began to detect from employees' behaviors and attitudes, just as he had anticipated, silent but strong disapproval and disappointment.

Unhappy with Lev's hiring practices, John championed the introduction of selection and hiring procedures that had been developed for Russian operations by Wane's European headquarters (Exhibit 3). The procedures to implement Wane's standard corporate practices of preparing job requisitions, advertising vacant positions, evaluating candidates' resumes, and having HR and line managers conduct interviews, had been approved by Ron Chapman and were supposed to be mandatory at Rus Wane. However, the Russian managers ignored the procedures. For instance, a week before John's meeting with Ron, an angry Jean-Pierre Dumont told John that a new machine operator had been hired for the factory without his knowledge. It took John some time to find out that the 18-year-old new employee was the son of a local customs officer who often cleared shipments for Rus Wane. The young man had no manufacturing skills and was eligible for the army draft the following spring.

When John described the incident to Ron, he got a rather philosophical reply: "Well, you've got to remember the specifics of the country you are operating in. Russia has an Asian culture and European faces should not mislead you. American standards do not always work here. If hiring people you have known for a long time, and therefore trust, is a local custom, you can't change it overnight. And, you probably don't need to change it."

John didn't challenge his boss, but neither had he changed his mind about hiring practices. He strongly believed that hiring friends and relatives was equally bad whether one was in the USA, China or Russia. Now Ron was telling him that Lev was going to appoint his doctor's son as human resource manager. John had always regarded a human resource manager as one of the primary business officers responsible for enforcing high

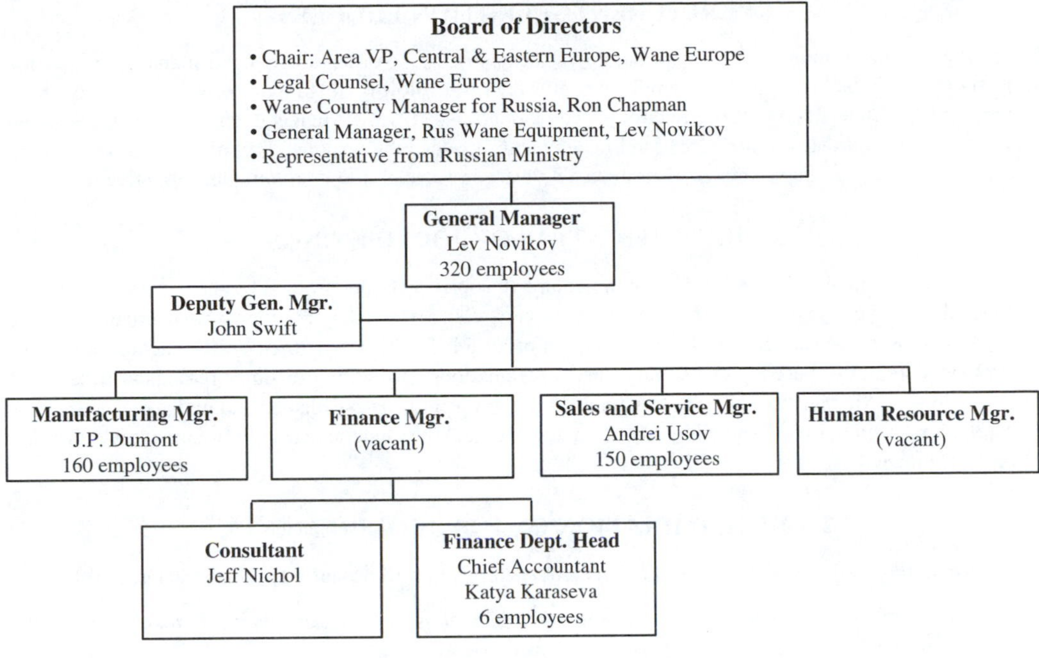


**Exhibit 1.** Rus Wane Equipment's Organization Chart

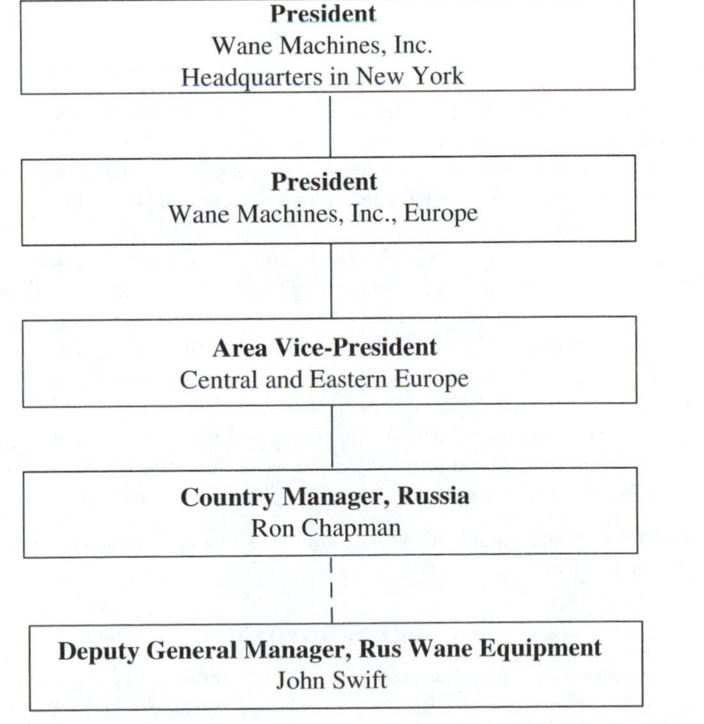


**Exhibit 2.** Wane Machines, Inc.'s Organization Chart (Abridged)

## RECRUITMENT/SELECTION PROCESS

The following Recruitment/Selection principles are established in order to help the management of the company in hiring the better qualified employees. It is the responsibility of Human Resources Department to manage and facilitate Recruitment/Selection in collaboration with Line Management but final decision on selecting/hiring candidates is made by Line Management. It is also the responsibility of the company's management to ensure that the principles mentioned above are in force and to maintain their effectiveness.

### 1. IDENTIFICATION OF JOB OPENINGS

The number of positions to be staffed in the company is primarily determined by the workforce forecast established every year as part of the business plan. Input is then provided by the Line Management along the year with necessary adjustments to the plan made in order for the HR Department to take action in recruiting and selecting. Any vacancy or opening due to resignation, termination or other reasons will be filled according to Line Management's request. A final list of job openings is established and updated as necessary.

A job requisition has to be signed by Line Management and the General Manager before every recruiting action (see attached form).

### 2. DETERMINATION OF JOB REQUIREMENTS

In close collaboration with the Line Management each position to be staffed is documented as follows:

- A list of professional and technical requirements as well as a list of personal traits required to do the job (strengths, orientation of the personality, background, etc.).
- A proper job description outlining the basic responsibilities of the position and the main tasks to fulfill the position requirements and to deliver the output.

These two documents will be established jointly and approved by Line Management.

### 3. ATTRACTING APPLICANTS

A list of possible Human Resources outsourcing is established here below. One or several sources listed may be used with consideration given to availability costs and likelihood of success.

- *Spontaneous Candidacies* are examined and each of them is answered to. (A Curriculum Vitae and a letter of motivation are necessary documents.)
- *Advertisements* for jobs may be inserted in local or national newspapers: they advertise not only the content of the job through a short description, but also the required profile of the candidate. Presenting the company is also recommended.
- *State Agencies*: Contracts for employees research can be used with existing recognized agencies. Requirements of the company are made clear through job requirements position description.
- *Education Institutions*: It is necessary for the company to develop and maintain regular and frequent relationships to local or national technical or nontechnical institutions considered as potential sources of candidates for the positions to fill. It is appropriate to present the company to the students/pupils schooled in these institutions. Job postings may be sent to these schools.
- *Private Agencies for Headhunting*: Restricted to managerial positions, headhunting companies may be used for research of candidates and screening interviews. This type of research has to be cost effective and conditions of the services rendered are clearly stated in a contract.

The use of one of these options results in a list of candidates including detailed information collected on forms filled obligatorily by them.

### 4. PRESCREENING

The Human Resources Department established a final list of candidates by eliminating applicants whose profile is not in line with requirements. At this stage the Human Resources Department informs the candidates who are not selected for interviews.

**Exhibit 3** Wane's Human Resources Policies for Rus Wane Equipment

## 5. SCREENING INTERVIEWS

The Human Resources Manager convenes listed candidates for interviews with the aim to assess:

- their knowledge of the company (product, service, culture when appropriate). More information may be given in order to clarify questions;
- their background (education, experience) is consistent with their application to the position as anticipated from the information previously collected. This answers the question, "Can the individual perform the job?"
- the motivation of the applicant to perform the job in the company and to develop within the specific culture of the company. This answers the question, "Will he/she do the job?"

## 6. LEVEL OF APPROVAL FOR CERTAIN RECRUITMENT

The General Manager will be involved in any recruitment for a position reporting directly to him. The final decision will be made by him.

The General Manager will also interview candidates for positions reporting to his direct report. His approval will be necessary before filling this position.

## 7. PRESELECTION

These interviews result in written evaluation of the candidate by the HR Manager (attached forms to be used). These forms are reviewed with the Line Manager involved in the recruitment process and a list of candidates to be interviewed is then established jointly.

## 8. INTERVIEWS WITH LINE MANAGEMENT

The preselected candidates are convened for interviews with the Line Manager supervising the position to be filled. The interview aims at determining again that professional aptitude based on experience and skills (technical/nontechnical) will allow the applicant to perform the work. Also the interviewer assesses the candidate's motivation to work for the company and to respond to the company's overall requirements (culture, etc.).

At the end of these interviews, evaluation forms are filled out by the interviewer.

## 9. EVALUATION OF CANDIDATES AND HIRING DECISION

A common evaluation of the candidates by the Line Manager and the Human Resources Manager is based on properly filled evaluation forms and subsequent ranking of the candidates.

## 10. HIRING DECISION

The Line Manager makes the final decision to hire one of the candidates interviewed based on assessment of their capabilities and aptitude to develop in the company.

At that stage, the candidates turned down are informed by letter from the HR Manager of the company's decision. The selected candidate is informed by the HR Manager.

## 11. OFFER TO THE CANDIDATE

A formal offer is prepared by the HR Manager in cooperation with the Line Manager. This offer (including contract and conditions of employment, etc.) is extended to the selected candidate. In the same time, administrative documents are handed over to the future employee for registration.

## 12. INTEGRATION IN THE COMPANY

The Human Resources Manager assists the Line Manager in facilitating the newcomer's integration into the company.

*(Continued)*

A welcome guide is given to the new employee upon his/her arrival in addition to all necessary documents and/or badges, punching cards, safety brochures, internal regulations, etc. The required training (safety) is coordinated by the HR Manager as well as any specific training necessary in the first days of the new employee's collaboration.

## 13. INTEGRATION'S FEEDBACK MEETING

Six weeks after starting date of employment, the Human Resources Manager invites the new employee for a feedback meeting aiming at determining how well the integration in his/her place of work is proceeding. Any obstacle to a real integration needs to be dealt with in the frame of the company's regulations.

The HR Manager gives feedback to the new employee's supervisor and follows up on any decisions made to ease the newcomer's integration in the company.

---

ethical standards in the company. Would Sasha be able to fulfill such an important responsibility? How much credibility would he have? And how independent would he be from his boss and likely mentor? These were some of the questions for which John did not have a ready answer.

### Prospects for the Future

This latest hiring decision only added to John Swift's growing frustration over the management of the joint venture. He had been appointed to provide expertise in Western management systems and to coach local personnel. Yet, his attempts were foiled at virtually every turn. He didn't know who was more to blame—Lev for sticking to his former Soviet practices, or Ron for letting Lev get away with such seemingly counterproductive behavior.

All of these issues contributed to John's worries about the future of Rus Wane Equipment. With the prospect of privatization turning NLZ into more of a competitor than a partner, and the advantages of joint ventures declining as a result of changing government legislation, John wondered whether Rus Wane had the right organizational structure and management systems in place to be a viable player in Russia's rapidly changing business environment. And not the least of his worries was whether there would be a place for him at Rus Wane that would allow him to be taken seriously.

# RUS WANE EQUIPMENT:

## *Joint Venture in Russia*

### Epilogue

John resisted Sasha's appointment as human resources manager, but to no avail. Sasha turned out to be very enthusiastic about his job, and was willing to learn and introduce new things. To John's surprise, Sasha was very independent in his actions and did not seem to be afraid to challenge Lev Novikov. He ensured that everyone in the company follow the hiring procedure developed by Wane, and worked quite well with John.

John was subsequently transferred to the U.S. without replacement. Jeff Nichol was appointed by the board of directors as Rus Wane's financial manager. However, his relations with Lev and Katya did not improve, and he asked for a transfer four months after assuming the position. Wane Machines sent a new financial manager, a 59-year-old Indian national whom Lev Novikov had interviewed and approved of.

Rus Wane Equipment was still struggling with low demand and poor collections, but no major top management changes were made. Ron Chapman remained country manager for Russia. The company converted from joint venture status to a joint stock company in 1994, since joint ventures no longer enjoyed special tax or other benefits from the Russian government. A joint stock company was similar to a conventional Western limited liability company.

NLZ was privatized into employee ownership, with the State owning no shares. Some employees later sold their stock to Lev for cash. How much stock Lev personally owned was unknown, but he was rumored to have more than 50 percent ownership of NLZ.

In early 1995, Lev left Rus Wane Equipment and returned to work exclusively for NLZ. No Rus Wane employees followed him. Ron Chapman moved to Moscow and became acting General Manager of Rus Wane, while retaining his job as Country Manager for Russia. Wane Machines planned to merge Rus Wane Equipment with Wane's newly created service joint venture with another Russian enterprise in Moscow.

The President of Wane Machines, Inc.'s 1994 Assessment of the Company's Investments in Russia:

"We invested early in Russia and moved as quickly as we could. Our company has invested $40 million already in several joint ventures, and discussions are continuing on possible additional ventures.

"Although our new Russian employees may lack expertise in sales, marketing, and accounting, their engineering skills are terrific. For example, they have already identified mistakes in some of our drawings. The transfer of Western technology into the ventures is going relatively smoothly for that reason.

"Of course, we would love to see better commercial banking facilities and improvements in communication and transportation. And we wouldn't object if networks of small supplier businesses were developed and import regulations simplified. Being realistic, however, we do not expect to make a quick profit on our investment.

"As the former Soviet republics struggle with the transformation to free-market economies, we will continue to be patient. We fully expect that our strategy in Russia will pay off, and we are confident in Russia's long-term future."

# PART III

## International Management Challenges

The articles and cases in this section are devoted to some of the significant challenges that managers in an international environment face. A key challenge facing these managers involves getting the most out of work groups and teams that are composed of members who are culturally different, and who may also be separated by time and geography. Managing multicultural work groups involves trying to find ways to maximize the positive effects of cultural diversity while at the same time minimizing the negative consequences. Another challenge facing the international manager is designing effective organizational structures. In an international environment this increasingly means forming some type of alliance with a foreign firm, and all the challenges that these ventures entail. Finally, one of the most difficult situations that international managers face is a temporary assignment in a foreign country.

# Reading 3.1

# VIRTUAL TEAMS

## *Technology and the Workplace of the Future*

ANTHONY M. TOWNSEND,
SAMUEL M. DEMARIE, AND ANTHONY R. HENDRICKSON

**Executive Overview**

Managers are challenged to develop strategically flexible organizations in response to increasingly competitive marketplaces. Fortunately, a new generation of information and telecommunications technology provides the foundation for resilient new organizational forms that would have not been feasible only a decade ago. One of the most exciting of these new forms, the virtual team, will enable organizations to become more flexible by providing the impressive productivity of team-based designs in environments where teamwork would have once been impossible.

Virtual teams, which are linked primarily through advanced computer and telecommunications technologies, provide a potent response to the challenges associated with today's downsized and lean organizations, and to the resulting geographical dispersion of essential employees. Virtual teams also address new workforce demographics, where the best employees may be located anywhere in the world, and where workers demand increasing technological sophistication and personal flexibility. With virtual teams, organizations can build teams with optimum membership while retaining the advantages of flat organizational structure. Additionally, firms benefit from virtual teams through access to previously unavailable expertise, enhanced cross-functional interaction, and the use of systems that improve the quality of the virtual team's work.

> You have no choice but to operate in a world shaped by globalization and the information revolution. There are two options: Adapt or die. . . . You need to plan the way a fire department plans. It cannot anticipate fires, so it has to shape a flexible organization that is capable of responding to unpredictable events.
>
> —Andrew S. Grove,
> Intel Corporation[1]

Just as the personal computer revolutionized the workplace throughout the 1980s and 1990s, recent developments in information and communication technology are on the verge of creating a new revolution in the coming decade. A group of technologies, including desktop video conferencing, collaborative software, and Internet/Intranet systems, converge to forge the foundation of a new workplace.

This new workplace will be unrestrained by geography, time, and organizational boundaries; it will be a virtual workplace, where productivity, flexibility, and collaboration will reach unprecedented new levels.

This exciting new potential comes at a time when increasing global competition and recent advancements in information technologies have forced organizations to reevaluate their structure and work processes. Many organizations have downsized and there are continuing pressures to implement increasingly flat (or horizontal) organizational structures. While these new organizational structures may achieve gains in efficiency, flat organizational structures, of necessity, disperse employees both geographically and organizationally, which makes it more difficult for those members to collaborate in an effective manner.

One popular response to this challenging new environment has been to outsource a number of organizational functions, replacing traditional structure with an interorganizational network or virtual organization. Virtual organizations have received substantial attention in both popular and academic literature.[2] While the interorganizational challenges presented by virtual organizations are important, this leaner new competitive landscape presents important intraorganizational challenges as well.

During the past several years, one of the most dominant intraorganizational initiatives has been the development of team-based work systems. Many organizations have recognized that team-based structures have the potential to create a more productive, creative, and individually fulfilling working environment. A majority of U.S. corporations use some form of team structures in their organizations, and many report that teams enhance their ability to meet organizational goals.[3] In general, teams have provided firms with significant gains in productivity, and as such, have become a fixture among contemporary organizations. But what happens to the team advantage when fundamental organizational structures begin to change? Can teams survive amidst radical transitions in the greater organization? Perhaps more importantly, can radically transformed organizations recapture the productive potential of team-based work?

Recapturing the benefits of team systems will require flat organizations to create teams whose members may no longer be located together, or may even include members from outside the organization. Fortunately, this period of radical organizational change has been accompanied by an equally radical change in telecommunications and computer technology. Thanks to these new technologies, teams can now be effectively reconstituted from formerly dispersed members. Thus, a key component of successful, twenty-first century organization will be the effective use of virtual teams.

Virtual teams are groups of geographically and/or organizationally dispersed coworkers that are assembled using a combination of telecommunications and information technologies to accomplish an organizational task. Virtual teams rarely, if ever, meet in a face-to-face setting. They may be set up as temporary structures, existing only to accomplish a specific task, or may be more permanent structures, used to address ongoing issues, such as strategic planning. Further, membership is often fluid, evolving according to changing task requirements.[4]

Virtual teams provide additional benefits in that they also can be used to address evolving interorganizational challenges that occur when organizations outsource some of their key processes to more specialized firms. By creating virtual teams, both within virtual organizations and within organizations undergoing other forms of transformation, firms can ultimately realize the competitive synergy of teamwork and exploit the revolution in telecommunications and information technology.

## Why Virtual Teams?

Although the modern organization faces a number of challenges in its competitive environment,[5] the imperative for moving from traditional face-to-face teams to virtual teams derives primarily from five specific factors:

1. The increasing prevalence of flat or horizontal organizational structures.
2. The emergence of environments that require interorganizational cooperation as well as competition.
3. Changes in workers' expectations of organizational participation.
4. A continued shift from production to service/knowledge work environments.
5. The increasing globalization of trade and corporate activity.

The emergence of the flat or horizontal organization is largely a response to intensifying competitive operating environments brought about by increased global competition and recent advancements in both information and transportation technologies.[6] Organizational flattening pushes decision authority to lower levels in the organization, reducing the need for several layers of management. With fewer layers of centralized, hierarchical management structure, organizations become increasingly characterized by structurally and geographically distributed human resources. While the organization may retain the collective talent it requires, there is a reduction in the opportunity for linkages between remaining employees (e.g., personnel and offices close enough to facilitate traditional interaction). This kind of environment occasions the need to reconstitute the benefits of the large, resource rich organization within the context of the new flattened organization.

A second trend is a shift from traditional competitive business environments toward strategic cooperation among a synergistic group of firms that may not only coexist, but also actually nurture each other.[7] In the past, firms vertically integrated to maintain more control of processes from the acquisition of raw materials to the manufacture of the final product. However, diversification and specialization have made direct management of far-flung processes unwieldy. Thus, firms have responded to this problem by eliminating their superfluous processes to concentrate on their core, value-added processes. Strategic partnering and/or outsourcing allows efficient span of control while maintaining larger economies of scale for the cooperative organizational group.

Although this segmentation enables more efficient management of each individual process, it often fails to provide an overarching structure by which these specialized organizations can compete within a large global market. These cooperative groups of organizations become increasingly interdependent, with the success of each individual organization enhancing the success of the cooperative organizational system.

A prominent example of this synergistic cooperation is the collaboration among a number of computer hardware and software developers. Unlike IBM in previous decades, firms such as Intel and Microsoft have avoided vertical integration and achieved unprecedented growth and dominance in the distributed computing environment. This success is largely due to their concentration on their respective core disciplines, thus avoiding the lack of focus inherent in vertically integrated organizations. While they have created and nurtured an environment in which both organizations flourish, the ultimate value of each is dramatically dependent upon the other. Without significant advances in chip technology, demand for personal computing software tools and distributed computing systems is limited. Conversely, advancements in computing software have led to an insatiable demand for faster, more powerful microprocessors.

Group success is dependent on effective communications and knowledge sharing among members. Microsoft's success in a variety of industries, including personal computers, corporate computing, telecommunications, and consumer electronics, is directly attributable to the firm's networking with software developers within these supplier organizations. By providing developmental versions of new software, Microsoft facilitates communication with its customers and acquires invaluable feedback prior to releasing final versions of its products. Product development is no longer an isolated task within the organization, but a collaborative effort in which product identity and loyalty is created via close customer involvement in the development process. Virtual teams provide an effective platform for these groups by using advanced technologies to facilitate their complex communication processes.

The third major trend in the business environment centers on changes in employee expectations of how they will participate in the workplace. Future employees, who have grown up in an environment of personal computers, cellular phones, and electronic classrooms, will be more likely to expect organizational flexibility. The new generation of workers will be technologically sophisticated, and will expect technological sophistication from their employing organization.[8] An example of how changing employee expectations are already affecting the workplace can be seen in the increasing number of employees who are opting for telework alternatives. Teleworkers operate from their homes or some other remote location, connected to a home office primarily through telephones, fax machines, computer modems, and electronic mail. Telework provides cost savings to employees by eliminating time-consuming commutes to central offices and offers employees more flexibility to coordinate their work and family responsibilities. Teleworkers currently make up the fastest growing segment of the workforce.[9]

Virtual teams provide a platform for organizations to actually exceed these new employee expectations. For example, telework is usually limited to relatively independent job categories that involve low levels of collaboration. A virtual team format can expand telework's potential range by allowing employees involved in highly collaborative teamwork to participate from remote locations.

A fourth factor encouraging the development of virtual teams is the continued shift from manufacturing and production jobs to service and knowledge work. Production processes, by their very nature, are often more structured and defined. Service activities often require cooperation of team members in dynamic work situations that evolve according to customer requirements. The hallmark of successful service firms has been their ability to flexibly respond to the customer's needs as quickly as possible. This requisite flexibility fuels the movement from highly structured organizational forms to more ad hoc forms. Virtual teams enable this organizational flexibility because they integrate the effectiveness of traditional teamwork with the power of advanced communication and information technologies, allowing them to accommodate increased dynamism in both team membership and task structure.

Finally, the increasing importance of global trade and corporate activity has radically altered the working environment of many organizations. Recent trade agreements, such as GATT and NAFTA, coupled with economic reforms in China and Eastern Europe, have created increased opportunities for international trade. Whereas in the past, multinational operations were solely the domain of the world's largest corporations, technological advances in both communications and logistics have enabled smaller firms to compete in the global marketplace. Regardless of firm size, multinational operations require high levels of cooperation and collaboration across broad geographical boundaries.[10] Turning these networks of collaborators into fully connected virtual teams has the potential to increase both the efficiency and quality of communications in this challenging environment.

## The Technology of Virtual Teams

Virtual teams are possible only because of recent advances in computer and telecommunications technology. Because these technologies define the operational environment of the virtual team, it is critical to examine how these technologies come together to form the infrastructure of virtual teamwork. Although all of the systems are somewhat interdependent, it is helpful to consider them as belonging to one of three broad categories of technology: desktop videoconferencing systems (DVCS); collaborative software systems; and Internet/Intranet systems. These three technologies provide an infrastructure across which the virtual team will interact and provide technological empowerment to the virtual teams' operation.[11]

### Desktop Videoconferencing Systems (DVCS)

DVCS are the core system around which the rest of virtual team technologies are built. Although virtual teams would be possible with simple e-mail systems and telephones, DVCS recreates the face-to-face interactions of conventional teams, making possible more complex levels of communication among team members. While the technology of videoconferencing is not new, traditional videoconferencing systems typically involved dedicated meeting rooms that were very costly to set up and maintain. These videoconference rooms were also cumbersome and inconvenient to use, requiring specially trained technicians to facilitate even the simplest of meetings. The most sophisticated DVCS currently cost less than $1,000 per station, can be added to most any new generation of personal computer, and can be used with no outside facilitation. This combination of affordability and operational simplicity make DVCS an affordable organizational communications solution.[12]

Although technologically sophisticated, the DVCS is a relatively simple system for users to operate. A small camera mounted atop a computer monitor provides the video feed to the system; voice transmissions operate through an earpiece/microphone combination or speakerphone. Connection to other team members is managed through software on the user's computer; to ensure user familiarity, the software uses an on-screen version of a traditional telephone to control the system. The final component of the system is a high-speed data connection, which may be accomplished through local area network connections, or specialized digital phone lines. DVCS create the potential for two primary types of group communication:

1. All team members are actively connected in a session. With current technology, groups of up to sixteen team members can simultaneously videoconference, meaning that each user can see and hear up to fifteen other team members on his or her computer monitor. Functioning in this mode, the entire team or subunits of the team can conference as needed.

2. A face-to-face group can interact with a non-present team member or outside resource. The same DVCS used for individual interaction also permits a conference table of team members to have a traditional teleconference with one or more outside parties. Because the DVCS allows for multiple conference connections, a local group can connect with up to fifteen different individuals or groups.[13]

In addition to providing video and audio connections, most DVCS provide users with the ability to share information and even applications while they are interconnected. For example, users can simultaneously work on documents, analyze data, or sketch out ideas on shared whiteboards. In many respects, the DVCS creates a work environment where users have more options available to help them collaborate and share data than would be possible working around a conference table or huddled around an office computer.

### Collaborative Software Systems

Collaborative software systems are the second component of the virtual team technical infrastructure. Effective collaboration requires team members to work both interactively and independently; collaborative software is designed to augment both types of group work activity and to empower teamwork processes.[14]

The simplest collaborative software application involves sharing traditional software products through the DVCS. As noted above, most DVCS allow users to share any application running on any one of their individual computers. Used in this manner, a variety of existing software applications become powerful collaborative tools, allowing multiple team members to create, revise, and/or review important information.

A second category of collaborative software systems is designed to empower real time group decision making and other creative activities. These systems, called group support systems (GSS), are specifically designed to create an enhanced environment for brainstorming, focus group work, and group decision making. These systems provide their users with a variety of support tools to poll participants and assemble statistical information relevant to the decision activity. Finally, these systems also allow users to "turn off" their individual identities during a brainstorming session and interact with relative anonymity, which can be very helpful in certain contexts.[15]

As with traditional teams, a substantial portion of the work of virtual team members may be conducted independently, and then passed along to the rest of the team at appropriate stages of the team's project. For this noninteractive aspect of the virtual team's work, there is also a developing body of software. This family of software provides specific support for collaborative accomplishment (e.g., project management, product design, document creation, and information analysis) when team members are working independently on team projects. The major focus of these collaborative software applications is to facilitate multiple authorship of documents and presentations, and joint development of databases, spreadsheets, and other information resources.

Collaborative software systems also may provide a comprehensive environment for group work. Lotus Notes, a dominant collaborative software product, is designed specifically for asynchronous teamwork (e.g., communication and data sharing where parties are working either at different times or independently) and combines scheduling, electronic messaging, and document and data sharing into one common product. By combining a number of collaborative applications and communications systems into an integrated framework, products like Lotus Notes facilitate both the production and communication necessary to effective teamwork. Although most of these types of software systems have been designed to facilitate teamwork in traditional work environments, they provide an equally powerful foundation for the collaborative empowerment of virtual teams.

### The Internet and Intranets

The enormous popularity of the Internet is a significant indicator that a friendly medium can overcome the technophobia of a vast number of people, and this lesson has not been lost on business organizations. Recognizing that the explosion of the Internet is a microcosmic glimpse of the potential for employee interest and use of this new interconnective technology, a number of firms have adapted state of the art Internet technologies into internal internets, or Intranets. The Federal Express Corporation provides a good example of this adaptive process. After finding that its Internet website was a cost-saving solution for customer service, the company decided to try out the technology on an internal basis. In 1995, the firm operated over sixty Intranet Websites among thirty thousand worldwide office employees.[16]

Intranets provide organizations the advantage of using Internet technology to disseminate organizational information and enhance interemployee communication, while still maintaining system security. With the Internet and Intranets, organizational users realize the benefits of the familiarity of the same connective interface, whether working with internal or external information. For the virtual team, the Internet and Intranets provide an important communicative and informational resource. They allow virtual teams to archive text, visual, audio, and numerical data in a user-friendly format. The Internet and Intranets also allow virtual teams to keep other organizational members and important outside constituents such as suppliers and customers up-to-date on the team's progress, and enable the team to monitor other ongoing organizational projects that might affect the task at hand.

The Internet and Intranets make a significant contribution to the collaborative environment because of the way that information is managed on both systems. They have proven to be a rich source of qualitative information, and new methods of information search and retrieval have been developed to effectively sort through their enormous volume of information. Systems such as Digital Equipment Corporation's AltaVista search engine provide a means to quickly and effectively locate information—first on the Internet, and now on Intranets and individual computers. Unlike traditional database software, which requires highly structured data, advanced search engines are able find text-based information from within a jumble of file types and formats. Most recently, these products have been enhanced to incorporate the very latest in user-friendly interfaces, further improving users' effectiveness by making an information search a more intuitive process. By enabling users to locate documents and text-based information from anywhere in their workgroup, these new data management tools provide a workable way to manage the distributed information resources of virtual teams.

Taken together, DVCS, collaborative software applications, and Internet/Intranet technologies form an informational infrastructure within which virtual teams can match or even surpass the effectiveness of face-to-face teams. Unfortunately, technology provides only a foundation for virtual teamwork; the real challenge to virtual team effectiveness is learning how to work with these new technologies. Although these new technical systems provide an incredibly rich communication context for virtual team members, they do not truly replicate the face-to-face environment. As such, virtual team members are challenged to recapture the effectiveness of face-to-face interactions using the virtual tools that are available to them.

## Virtual Team Building

Developing effective virtual teams goes well beyond the technical problem of linking them together. As workers increasingly interact in a virtual mode, it is imperative that they rebuild the interpersonal interaction necessary for organizational effectiveness. While the virtual team presents a number of challenges in this area, it also presents the potential to recreate the way work is done. Within the virtual connection lies an opportunity for efficiencies and team synergy unrealized in traditional work interaction. John Verity writes:

> That is the essence of virtualization: rather than simply recreating in digital form the physical thing we know as a letter, e-mail reinvents and vastly enhances letter-writing. Unbound by barriers of time and space and endowed with new powers, the electronic letter does something new altogether. The same sort of thing happens when business, the arts, or government are reborn in digital form.[17]

Recreating teams in virtual mode requires resolution of the challenges and opportunities inherent in virtual team technology, as well as the development of a new team sociology.

## New Challenges in Structure, Technology, and Function

As discussed earlier, changes in organizational structure and advances in informational technology define the environment in which the virtual team operates. While many of these challenges are present in traditional work settings, they become more pronounced in the virtual environment. Consider the following:

- More so than a traditional workgroup, the virtual team will probably have membership representing a number of different geographic locations within the organization, and may also include contingent workers from outside the organization.
- Virtual team members will be challenged to adapt to the telecommunication and informational technologies that link its members. Virtual team members will have to learn to use effectively new telecommunications systems in an environment where an important client or coworker is frequently never physically present.
- The virtual team's role transcends traditional fixed functional roles, requiring virtual team members to be prepared to adapt to a changing variety of assignments and tasks during the life of any particular team.

All of these factors affect the environment in which the individual members of virtual teams must learn to operate.

Virtual teams, because they have the potential to significantly decrease the amount of travel required of team members, can significantly increase the productive capacity of individual members. For this reason, virtual team members may be asked to participate in a higher number of separate team situations than was practical in traditional face-to-face teamwork. Thus, virtual team members may have multiple (and even competing) alliances outside their specific virtual team. This same challenge has been observed in traditional work settings, both in situations where contingent workers interact with permanent workers and when members of teams or workgroups are also members of other groups competing for their time and attention. Although problems associated with these factors are not new, outsourcing, organizational partnering, and the efficiencies afforded by advanced information technologies have increased the potential for conflict caused by multiple organizational roles.

Furthermore, the virtual team environment represents a pronounced structural difference from traditional workgroup participation because of their ability to transform quickly according to changing task requirements and responsibilities. Virtual team membership will be substantially more dynamic than traditional teams and virtual teams will be more likely to include members from locations that would not traditionally have worked together. This dynamism requires virtual team members to be particularly adaptable to working with a wide variety of potential coworkers.

Differences in the functional role of the virtual team within the broader organization also create a different environment for the virtual team and its members. Virtual teams provide the capability for more flexible organizational responses, which means that the role of the virtual team, as well as the roles attributed to its members, will be substantially more dynamic than in traditional settings. The Danish hearing aid manufacturer, Oticon, exemplifies this concept. After several years of attempting to turn the company around using traditional cost-cutting and strategic marketing techniques, the president decided to restructure the organization into what is essentially a giant virtual team. Conceptualizing the entire staff as one large 150-member team, the firm now draws the necessary skills for specific projects from a pool of workers whose diverse skills most appropriately fit the project and task requirements.[18]

Each employee's physical location is no longer a barrier to effective team structure. What remains critical is how individual skill sets meet project requirements driven by an ever-evolving business environment. Virtual teams like these are more capable of addressing an evolutionary mission because their technological infrastructure is designed to facilitate transformations in response to changing organizational requirements.

By far the greatest difference in the working environment of virtual team members is the process of virtual interaction. Although electronic mail and various document-sharing capabilities have been in use in traditional work settings for some time, these systems have generally been supported by face-to-face meetings and geographic proximity to other workgroup members. In the virtual work environment, traditional social mechanisms that facilitate communication and decision making are effectively lost and participants must find new ways to communicate and interact, enabling effective teamwork within the new technical context.

### Changes in Work and Interaction

The challenges detailed above have the potential to create a radically different work environment for the virtual team participant, both because of the change from face-to-face to some degree of virtual interaction, and because the virtual team is expected to operate in a different form of organization and assume new organizational roles. These changes in the work setting affect the way that team members conduct their work and how they communicate and express themselves:

- Virtual team members must learn new ways to express themselves and to understand others in an environment with a diminished sense of presence.
- Virtual team members will be required to have superior team participation skills. Because team membership will be somewhat fluid, effective teams will require members who can quickly assimilate into the team.
- Virtual team members will have to become proficient with a variety of computer-based technologies.
- In many organizations, virtual team membership will cross national boundaries, and a variety of cultural backgrounds will be represented on the team. This will complicate communications and work interactions, and will require additional team member development in the areas of communication and cultural diversity.

Research has indicated that when the trappings of traditional communicative patterns are absent, communication dynamics are substantially altered. For example, in workgroup systems where members' primary interactions are through some form of electronic mail, the absence of traditional communicative cues (i.e., facial expression, gesture, and vocal inflection) make subtleties in communication more difficult to convey.[19] Additionally, when participants are able to use a communication system anonymously, the group also begins to lose distinctions among members' social and expert status.[20] Thus, the loss of traditional cues creates an environment that is substantially different from face-to-face interaction, requiring participants to reconstruct a viable workgroup dynamic. Within this reconstructed environment, there is an opportunity for enhanced organizational democracy and participation in work and decision making. Although technology certainly presents an opportunity for such development, the team's sociology will ultimately be a function of technology, the larger organizational culture, and the team's task requirements.[21]

Within the larger organizational culture and the technical environment, the group dynamic of a virtual team depends on the socialization process of the individual team. Unlike many traditional teams, virtual teams will be expected to be able to repeatedly change membership without losing productivity; little time will be available for team members to learn how to work together. Thus, effective virtual team members will have to be particularly adept at fitting into a variety of team situations.

The traditional factors identified with high team performance come into play in the virtual environment as well. Effective communication skills, clarity of goals, and a performance orientation will continue to be critical attributes for virtual team members.[22] To fully exploit the advantages of the new environment, virtual team members will require basic teamwork training and development, and will also need training to enhance team workers' facility with the new information and communication technologies. Effective training in such virtual function skills as how to best use telecommunicative capability and collaborative systems, may ultimately result in teams that function as naturally in a technologically empowered, virtual environment as teams currently do around a conference table. Additionally, when team members represent a variety of national or cultural groups, there will also be the need to teach team members how each of their respective cultures may differ and how they can overcome these differences and use them to the team's advantage.

Advanced technologies may also be used to improve or streamline the socialization of new team members. For example, Intranets allow teams to archive a wide range of information. New team members potentially could access a complete electronic history of the team's work, including not only text-based and graphical information, but also video and audio recordings of important team meetings. The availability of this rich history may allow new members to be brought up to speed on team task, culture, and members' personalities much more quickly than in traditional face-to-face teams.

Recall too that technology presents the opportunity to enhance a team's effectiveness by empowering the teams' collaborative activity. Both research and industry experience indicate that collaborative systems can augment a group's decision quality and performance potential,[23] and will likely do so in the virtual environment as well.[24] Given a proper set of communicative protocols (e.g., telephones, DVCS, electronic mail, and Internet/Intranets), collaborative software systems will add enormous performance potential to the virtual teams' environment. While learning to use collaborative tools is no more difficult than learning many other software systems, the effective use of collaborative tools likely will reorient the attitude of users toward the process of work. Michael Schrage writes:

> Collaborative tools and environments will spark the same kinds of questions and concerns as other fundamental technologies, which will in turn determine the effectiveness of both individuals and enterprises. "Why won't he get out the good collaborative tools with me?" is a question not unlike "Why won't he talk with me on the phone?" . . . The technology becomes a frame of reference and a new infrastructure for the way people relate to one another.[25]

Thus, among virtual team members, collaborative tools not only enhance the productive capacity of the team; they also become a central medium of the team's work process.

## Capitalizing on Virtual Teams

It is important to stress that virtual teams are not an organizational panacea and that the degree to which organizations will benefit may differ. Developing the technology and employee skills necessary for effective virtual team implementation carries a cost in time and financial investment that must be offset by the competitive advantage virtual teams afford. Digital Equipment Corporation provides an excellent example of the productive potential of virtual teams, having used them to develop computer systems for years. These teams share databases, simulation and modeling systems, and advanced communication systems to support the collaborative design of new products. This organizational structure has enabled Digital to increase the productive capacity of its technical experts, and maintain its position as a leader in its field.[26]

Therefore, although virtual teams provide many exciting opportunities, organizations require clear understanding of the purpose and goals they have for virtual team implementation. The organizational challenge is first to effectively create the virtual team and, second, to overcome the inherent resistance that inevitably accompanies large scale innovation.

## Creating Virtual Teams

Once an organization determines that it has a need for virtual teams, the next challenge is to actually put them in place. At this juncture, the organization must define the teams' function and organizational role, develop the technical systems to support the teams, and assemble individual teams, as well as a cadre of potential team workers.

### *Managerial Direction and Control*

Just as in any team environment, managers will need to clearly establish expectations about the virtual team's performance and criteria for assessing the team's success. Because of the dispersion of team members, effective supervision and control of the virtual team may appear problematic. However, the virtual team's rich communicative environment, along with the system's capacity for archiving data and communications, actually empowers considerably more managerial monitoring than is possible in traditional environments. Managers could, for example, actually view archived recordings of team meetings to assess member contribution and team progress. Finally, the reporting and administrative relationship between the team and its external manager or managers must be clearly established. Again, because none of the team members will necessarily be located in the same place as external management, clear schedules must be established of when the team will provide reports, interim deliverables, and final product.

It is also critically important that managers clearly define the virtual team's role within the context of the organization's greater mission, including the limits of the team's scope and responsibility. This will help the team to focus its efforts on activities that support the strategic direction of the firm.

## Defining the Team's Organizational Role and Function

Virtual teams may be implemented as a response to one or a number of conditions detailed in the preceding sections. In turn, these underlying reasons for the introduction of virtual teams should determine the configuration of individual teams, dictate their mission, and ultimately determine the type of technical system required and the requisite skills and orientation of the team and its members. The following description of two types of team roles, while certainly not exhaustive, illustrates some of the range of the role and function of the virtual team.

Teams that are created to provide strategic responses to rapidly changing market conditions will operate in the most fluid of all virtual team environments. In addition to all of the challenges associated with virtual teamwork, these teams will be required to continuously evolve to meet changing tactical conditions. The configuration of these teams will be highly dynamic and dependent on current task and planning requirements. The role of these teams (and of the range of their potential participants) will be as highly adaptive response units, whose mission is to respond to market challenges and exploit market potentials. For example, Lithonia Lighting developed virtual marketing response teams from among independent sales agents, outside distributors, and their own electrical engineers. These virtual teams, which represent both product developers and end-user suppliers, provide the company with a unique capability to respond quickly to changes in the market and customer needs. Using these virtual teams, the company has dramatically increased both sales volume and customer satisfaction, while supply chain administrative costs have remained constant or decreased.[27]

Although flexibility is one of the potential virtues of the virtual team, virtual teams may also be created to operate in environments characterized by long-term membership and long task cycles. Virtual teams involved in complex development projects, for example, will capitalize on their ability to access a broader range of expertise and to more easily link to diverse functional resources. The role of these teams will be to manage and execute traditional organizational processes, but with the advantage of resources and expertise unavailable save for their virtual construction.

## Developing the Teams' Technical Systems

Once the role and mission of the teams have been clarified, the technical systems that will enable the teams' work will have to be designed and brought on line.

Teams whose task environment requires a high degree of informational integration and/or creative group participation are candidates for greater use of collaborative software applications, in addition to DVCS. This collaborative software will benefit teams whose members must produce group documents and presentations, interactively develop and analyze data, or engage in complex team-level planning and decision making. System design must also reflect an understanding that not all teams need all systems; system design must be task-oriented in order to avoid unnecessary technical overload of team members. The Xerox Corporation met this challenge when it connected two groups of scientists (one in Palo Alto, the other in Portland, Oregon) by arranging for constantly active phone, computer linking, and video conferencing between central areas in the two offices. The two sets of scientists, although 500 miles apart, could communicate with each other just as easily as if they were walking into the next room. No communication systems had to be operated; no complex protocols followed. Scientists simply walked up to the camera and started talking, or shared information back and forth through their computer links. Scientists working on the project report that the richness of the communication system significantly assists them in their work; because the system provides such high-quality communication, users regard their communications with long distance colleagues casually and indicate that their geographical separation no longer inhibits their collaboration.[28]

Teams whose task environment requires a high degree of personal interaction may simply require basic DVCS systems. However, depending on the frequency of use and the number of participants, these teams may need more advanced DVCS systems that use dedicated high-speed phone lines that allow information to flow more quickly between participants and allow for near broadcast quality video transmission. Although the more advanced systems add considerable cost to the DVCS, the increased costs may be justified where video interaction must be as absolutely seamless as is possible, such as in client presentations or sensitive negotiation sessions.

## Developing Teams and Team Members

In addition to developing the hardware and software infrastructure for virtual teams, it is equally critical to develop the teams themselves and to develop employees who can effectively participate in this new environment. This means that current potential team members must be trained and acclimated to the virtual team environment. Additionally, to fully exploit the virtual team's potential for optimized membership, organizations must extend their definition of human resources to include the broad range of consultants and contingent workers who may potentially participate on a team in only a virtual mode.

Training and developing virtual team members is in many ways no different from training and developing good team members in general; developing skills in communication, goal setting, planning, and task proficiency are all as important for the virtual team as for the traditional team. What is different about the virtual team is the amount of technical training that is required to empower the team member to function in the virtual environment. Learning to use all of the traditional team skills in an environment where most interactions take place through a telecommunications medium is a critical challenge. This is particularly true since technology continues to evolve and reinvent itself at an ever-increasing rate. Training to maintain technical proficiency will be an important component of any virtual team member's continuing education program.

Since virtual team members' interactions may take place across a relatively alien set of telecommunications systems, the first priority in virtual team preparation is to effectively teach team members how to fluently communicate with each other within the new media. Although team members can easily be taught to operate new technologies, they must be given an opportunity, through training and team development, to establish their own slang terminology and communications protocols. Over time, the team will develop a variety of methods to ensure that their communication is both efficient and accurate.

When team flexibility is highly stressed, team members will also require a very different attitude toward the team than would traditional team workers. Traditional teams provide members with feelings of cohort and social presence; in an extremely flexible virtual team environment, employees will have to learn to join teams and accept new members into teams without the benefit of time-related socialization. Thus, teams will benefit from learning to express explicit norms and role expectations to new members, who will in turn, be required to quickly acculturate according to the team's guidelines. It will be critical to the functionality of the virtual team that members are instilled with the same commitment to the virtual group activities as they would to any traditional team function.

In addition to training and developing team resources, human resources planners will have to identify potential team members from outside traditional organizational boundaries. As noted earlier in the paper, the virtual team provides the opportunity to build teams out of personnel who could not possibly work together under traditional circumstances. If the potential of virtual teams is fully realized, firms will have the opportunity to greatly expand access to expertise, overcoming constraints that might have been prohibitive in the past. Additionally, organizations will have to rethink how to compensate these individuals, whose contribution to a particular team may be less than full time.

Given the diversity of potential personnel available to the virtual team and the potential fluidity of team membership, organizations may want to consider the development of team development specialists. Team development specialists would function as resources to teams, assisting them with technical problems and facilitating their interaction when necessary. Providing this level of support would allow the virtual team to focus more on its objectives, rather than on the processes associated with teamwork in the virtual environment.

## Challenges and Obstacles

Like any organizational innovation, the introduction of virtual teams will encounter a number of challenges and obstacles. Virtual teams require organizational restructuring and the introduction of new work technologies. The potential for startup problems and deliberate resistance is substantially greater than for changes in structure or technology alone. In discussing virtual teams with professional managers, the following four areas of potential resistance were consistently identified.[29]

### Technophobia

Although an increasing percentage of the workforce is computer-literate (and even computer-oriented), a significant number of valuable employees are uncomfortable with computers and other telecommunications technologies. One of the greatest challenges in the introduction of virtual teams is the successful incorporation of valuable, technophobic personnel into the virtual team environment. Part of this problem will be obviated as both computer and telecommunications technologies become more user-friendly. The introduction of graphical operating systems (such as Microsoft Windows 95) opened up computing to a number of new users, and similar introductions of simplified operating systems, intuitive programs, and speech recognition capabilities should encourage even the most technologically recalcitrant to use sophisticated computer systems. In the meantime, organizations can more easily facilitate migration to the virtual team environment by providing training and technical support specifically geared to system novices.

### Trust and Cohesion Issues

In an environment where one's primary interaction with others takes place through an electronic medium, it is only natural to expect that participants will wonder whether the system is being used to monitor and evaluate them. The free flow of team members' communication, which once might have taken place away from the office, may now be inhibited by concerns about privacy and system security. To counter this problem, organizations must establish clear policy regarding communications privacy, and must then strictly adhere to that policy. Over time, participants will realize that the virtual team system is a safe medium across which to share ideas and concerns.

### Burnout and Stress

One of the benefits of the virtual team environment is its ability to efficiently connect people and enable greater levels of productivity. This may result in employees' being assigned to more teams, creating a more complex and potentially stressful work environment. Organizations must be careful not to overextend virtual team members and saddle them with levels of responsibility that they cannot reasonably satisfy. One important supervisory role will be to ensure that virtual team members have enough private time to complete their individual assignments and prepare for their team participation.

### Structural Resistance

The introduction of virtual teams will require significant amounts of organizational restructuring. Aside from the reasons detailed above, some resistance will occur because organizational members do not see this particular kind of change as desirable or necessary. To overcome their concerns, management must carefully design an implementation program that highlights the contribution that virtual teams will make and ties these contributions to important organizational values.[30]

## Looking to the Future

The world of the virtual team is far from static; continuing changes in technology and competitive environments will present new opportunities and imperatives for virtual teamwork. Nicholas Negroponte writes, "Computers are getting smaller and smaller. You can expect to have on your wrist tomorrow what you have on your desk today, what filled a room yesterday."[31] As telecommunication technologies continue to evolve, the virtual interface will provide more realistic presence, while simultaneously costing less and becoming easier to use.

Many of these same technological advances will create more virtual interaction in workers' private lives as well. This change will increase employee expectation of working in a virtual mode; as an increasing number of people socialize and shop in cyberspace, these same virtually-savvy people will be expecting a similar experience in their workplace. The economic imperative for virtual teams, combined with changing societal experience of the virtual, may well transform the virtual team from an innovative source of competitive advantage into a dominant organizational form.

## Notes

1. Grove, A. S. 1995. A high-tech CEO updates his views on managing and careers. *Fortune,* September 18: 229–230.
2. See Dess, G., Rasheed, A., McLaughlin, K. & Priem, R. 1995. The new corporate architecture. *Academy of Management Executive,* 9 (3): 7–20; Davidow, W. H. & Malone, M. S. 1992. *The virtual organization.* New York: Harper Collins; Byrne, J., Brandt, R. & Port, O. 1993. The virtual corporation. *Business Week,* February 8: 98–102.
3. Ranney, J. & Deck, M. 1995. Making teams work: Lessons from the leaders in new product development. *Planning Review,* 23(4): 6–13; Lawler, E. 1992. *Ultimate advantage.* San Francisco: Jossey-Bass.
4. Townsend, A. M., DeMarie, S. M. & Hendrickson, A. R. 1996. Are you ready for virtual teams? *HR Magazine,* 41 (9): 122–126; Pape, W. R. 1997. Group insurance: Virtual teams can quickly gather the knowledge of even far-flung staff. *Inc.* June 15: 29–30.
5. Bettis, R. & Hitt, M. The new competitive landscape. 1995. *Strategic Management Journal,* 16 (S1): 7–19; Moore, J. 1996. The death of competition: Leadership and strategy in the age of business ecosystems. New York: Harper Collins; Schrage, M. 1995. *No more teams! Mastering the dynamics of creative collaboration.* New York: Currency/Doubleday.
6. Bettis and M. Hitt, *op. cit.*
7. Moore, *op. cit.*
8. Schrage, *op. cit.*
9. Yap, C., & Tng, H. 1990. Factors associated with attitudes towards telecommuting. *Information and Management,* 19 (4): 227–235.
10. Hitt, M. A., Keats, B. W. & DeMarie, S. M. 1998. Navigating in the new competitive landscape: Building strategic flexibility and competitive advantage in the twenty-first century. *Academy of Management Executive,* forthcoming.
11. Osterlund, J. 1997. Competence management by informatics in R&D: The corporate level. *IEEE Transactions on Engineering Management,* 44 (2): 135–145.
12. Brookshaw, C. 1997. Virtual meeting solutions. *Infoworld,* 19 (22): 96–108.
13. Powell, D. 1996. Group communication. *Communications of the ACM,* 39 (4): 50–53.
14. Schrage, *op cit.*
15. Townsend, A., Whitman, M. & Hendrickson, A. 1995. Computer support system adds power to group processes. *HR Magazine,* 40 (9): 87–91.
16. Ibid.
17. Verity, J. 1994. The information revolution, *Business Week,* Special Bonus Issue: 12–18.
18. Lucas, H. 1996. *The T-form organization: Using technology to design organizations for the 21st century.* San Francisco: Jossey-Bass.
19. Kiesler, S. & Sproull, L. 1992. Group Decision Making and Communication Technology. *Organizational Behavior and Human Decision Processes,* 52 (1): 96–123; Siegel, J., Dubrovsky, V., Kiesler, S. & McGuire, T. 1986. Group processes in computermediated communication. *Organizational Behavior and Human Decision Processes,* 37 (1): 157–187.
20. Dubrovsky, V., Kiesler, S. & Sethna, B. 1991. The equalization phenomenon: Status effects in computer-mediated and face-to-face decision-making groups. *Human-Computer Interaction,* 6 (1): 119–146; Finholt, T. & Sproull, L. 1990. Electronic groups at work. *Organization Science,* 1: 41–64.
21. Mantovani, G. 1994. Is computer-mediated communication intrinsically apt to enhance democracy in organizations? *Human Relations,* 47 (1): 45–62.
22. Scott, K. D. & Townsend, A. M. 1994. Teams: Why some succeed and others fail. *HR Magazine,* 39 (8): 62–67.
23. Alavi, M. 1991. Group decision support systems: A key to business team productivity. *Journal of Information Systems Management,* 8 (3): 36–41; Jessup, L. M. & Kukalis, S. 1990. Better planning using group support systems. *Long Range Planning,* 23 (3): 100–105; McCartt, A. T. & Rohrbaugh, J.

1989. Evaluating group decision support system effectiveness: A performance study of decision conferencing. *Decision Support Systems,* 5 (2): 243–253.

24. Jessup, L. M., Connolly, T. & Galegher, J. 1990. The effects of anonymity on GDSS group process with an idea-generating task. *MIS Quarterly,* 14: 313–321; Jessup, L. M. & Tansik, D. A. 1991. Decision making in an automated environment: The effects of anonymity and proximity with a group decision support system. *Decision Sciences,* 22: 266–279.

25. Schrage, *op. cit.*

26. Grenier, R. & Metes, G. 1995. *Going virtual: Moving your organization into the twenty-first century.* Upper Saddle River, NJ: Prentice Hall.

27. Lucas, *op. cit.*

28. Schrage, *op. cit.*

29. For a more in-depth discussion of the challenges of implementing change, see *Academy of Management Executive,* 8 (4), 1994, special issue on restructuring, reengineering, and rightsizing.

30. Reger, R. K., Mullane, J. V., Gustafson, L. T., & DeMarie, S. M. 1994. Creating earthquakes to change organizational mindsets. *Academy of Management Executive,* 8 (4): 31–46.

31. Negroponte, N. 1995. *Being digital.* New York: Alfred A. Knopf.

# Reading 3.2

## MINDING YOUR METAPHORS

### *Applying the Concept of Teamwork Metaphors to the Management of Teams in Multicultural Contexts*

CRISTINA B. GIBSON AND
MARY E. ZELLMER-BRUHN

**The Challenge**

At Eastman Chemical, USA, team leaders are called "coaches," and their main role is to help teams set performance goals, assist teams in resolving personnel problems, and manage upsets and emergencies. At Wilson Corporation, USA, during the annual rewards and recognition dinner, gold, silver and bronze achievement medals are awarded to winning teams based on process improvements. At Sabre Inc., North America, team training is administered through the "Tour de Teams" program, in which teams progress along a route of programs, pass various milestones, and receive a "yellow jersey" if they are ahead of other teams.

In each of these examples, managers apply the concept of being on a sports teams to work teams, with the intent to use the mental images that sports teams invoke to motivate and guide team member behavior. To many U.S. workers for whom team sports are a common part of their personal, first-hand experience, and where professional sports are a dominant national pastime, this makes a lot of sense. However, would this same concept of teamwork resonate when Eastman Chemical operates a subsidiary in Southeast Asia? Or if Sabre Inc. expands operations to Europe? Recent research suggests the answer is "no." In fact, making the language of sports the dominant tool in Asia or Europe may be confusing, de-motivating, and counter-productive. In this article we explore why this might be the case. In doing so, we demonstrate that language is a powerful tool for multinational managers and explain how it can be used to manage teams across cultures more effectively.

The issue of how to best manage teams across subsidiaries in a multinational firm becomes all the more important given the increased role of teams in new product development, workplace innovation, and knowledge management, and the increasing degree to which these team functions are now located throughout the world, not just at U.S.-based headquarters.

Teams are a design mechanism that promotes effective collaboration, and increasingly this collaboration takes place across cultural contexts. Whether members of a team are all from one culture and must collaborate with other teams from other cultures, or whether the team itself is multicultural, collaborating across cultures is challenging. Nations,

SOURCE: Reprinted from *Journal of World Business, Vol. 31*, Gibson et al., "Minding Your Metaphors," pp. 102-116.

organizations, and functions each have their own cultures, and representatives of these identity groups see the world in unique ways, gather and process information differently, and often have contrasting expectations and priorities. This can be a source of competitive advantage or of dysfunctional conflict. Cultural differences often become obvious when work is conducted by teams. Teams allow for increased interaction, and help to structure interdependence between members to foster mutual accountability. During processes of communication and information exchange, members often become aware of each other's unique views and perceptions. Language in general, and metaphor in particular, plays a key role in these revelations.

## Metaphors for Teamwork

Metaphors are mechanisms by which we understand our experiences. We use metaphors whenever we think of one experience in terms of another. They help us to comprehend abstract concepts and perform abstract reasoning. Further, our behavior reflects our metaphorical understanding of experience. Consider for example, the following statements from workers in U.S. teams: "Among the sales people on our team, Jack is the star quarterback" and "Our team leader acts more like a coach than a referee." These statements reflect a metaphor that could be characterized as "Work team as sports team." Using this metaphor involves understanding one target domain of experience (work teams) in terms of a very different source domain of experience (sports teams). There are correspondences between aspects of a sports team (e.g., the coach, the players, the players' positions, the team's field position, the score, their ranking in the competition) and aspects of a work team (e.g., the leader, the team members, their roles, their progress, their objectives, their performance ranking in the organization). It is via such mappings that an individual in the U.S. is likely to project expectations they hold about sports teams onto the work team domain. For example, one team member from the U.S. used the sports team metaphor when he said:

> I think it's easy to have individual recognition within the team and still have a clear direction, but the team results are what's important. We have outstanding individuals on the team. And, very similar to a sports team, somebody needs to hit the home run; somebody needs to stop the ball. You know, somebody needs to catch'm and drag'm out. So I think it's a combination, but I think it's very difficult to play together as a team now. You know, we have bench players too. And we need bench players. We need the people that can get up and go fix the equipment every day.

This person's understanding of the sports metaphor will influence his expectations of leading, or participating in, a work team. In this way, metaphor goes beyond language and plays an important role in the way we think and reason and our expectations for practice and management. In fact, employees' understanding of what it means to work in a team can be identified by examining the metaphors they use when describing their team. Further, the use of the metaphors varies systematically across cultural settings.

We observed these differences while conducting research around the world between 1995 and 1998 with support from a National Science Foundation Grant. We traveled to match facilities of six pharmaceutical firms in four different geographic areas (Europe, Southeast Asia, Latin America and the U.S.), in total visiting over 20 different sites. For example, we visited subsidiaries of a major manufacturer of baby care and personal hygiene products in France, the Philippines, Puerto Rico, and the U.S. We repeated this process with each of the other firms. In each subsidiary, we conducted 1 hour interviews with team members, team leaders, and team customers. Elsewhere, we have reported the techniques we used to derive the metaphors and analyze their use. By way of summary, our first step was to develop a list of words that capture how people talked about teamwork in our interviews. Next, we asked five raters from each country involved in the study to sort them into groups they felt represented metaphors for teamwork. Through a process of discussion, negotiation, and elimination, the raters arrived at five piles, each of which represented a different metaphor: "family, sports, community, associates, and military." Finally, we used a content analysis computer program to pull excerpts from the text database containing each term representing a metaphor. This resulted in a subtext database consisting of approximately 400 pages. We read each excerpt to determine how each term had been used, and to code what the use of each metaphor implied. As a final step, we applied ethnostatistics, in which text data is transformed into word frequency counts. We analyzed this numeric data using advanced statistical techniques to understand the systematic variation in the use of the metaphors.

## Metaphors Convey Expectations for Team Scope, Roles and Objectives

A long history of previous research suggests that most people's mental images of a team include characteristics such as what a team does (activity scope), who is on the team (roles) and why the team exists (objectives). While these basic categories of characteristics may be shared across people from different cultures and settings, within each characteristic there is room for a wide variety of interpretation. For example, when some people think of a team, they picture a project team whose activity is limited in scope to the time during which members work on the project, whereas others may picture a team more like a family whose activity is broad and extends across a number of life domains. Likewise, some concepts of teamwork may include clearly differentiated roles, such as leaders and members, whereas others may be less structured. Finally, some people define teamwork by clear outcomes; others have argued that multiple, sometimes implicit benefits can be derived from teamwork. The teamwork literature tells us that nearly all mental images that people hold of teams contain these three elements. We used our extensive interview database to examine each of the five teamwork metaphors to determine the expectations each metaphor conveyed concerning scope, roles and objectives. Below, we explain these and offer sample quotations to illustrate the differences we found.

### The Sports Teamwork Metaphor

Interviewees suggested that sports teams tend to have a narrow scope, with activity limited to physical and social interaction. In other words, members of sports teams of the type most people have experienced first-hand typically only interact during practices and competitive events, and perhaps during an occasional social event. Sports teams typically have fairly clear roles, encompassing various positions on a playing field (e.g., catcher, pitcher, quarterback, center). Although there may be a coach, captain, or star player, there typically is fairly little hierarchy on sports teams. Finally, objectives are specific, with clear consequences (e.g., win or lose), and they are measurable, as represented by the myriad statistics maintained for a multitude of performance parameters. People who describe their work team with a sports metaphor are likely to hold these expectations for their work team. Use of the sports team metaphor is illustrated in the following quotation:

> Sports are what I'm thinking. There is a coach, and there are all these players, and among these players, there is somebody who is a very good one, a strong performer.

### The Military Teamwork Metaphor

Military teams also tend to have a fairly limited scope, with activity limited to professional, physical and educational activities. There are strong hierarchically arranged roles, such as commander, second in charge, and the "rank and file" soldiers. Rank is indisputable and clearly recognized. Finally, objectives in military teams are typically extremely clear and salient, with outcomes such as life and death, survival and defeat. There is an order about the activity in the team, in that it is fully directed at these clear objectives. Use of the military metaphor is exemplified in the following quote:

> Obviously, it's about how do I win the battle in this society. How do I survive, as opposed to, you know, what it is that I need to do to benefit everybody. [The team is] carefully measured on whether we meet objectives. Every year the company sets an annual objective and this is something that I'm going to do battle with soon.

### The Family Teamwork Metaphor

Families also have clear hierarchical roles, but the "leaders" in a family (e.g., father and mother) tend to be more nurturing and caring than in a military team. Other clear roles in families mentioned by our interviewees included referring to team members as "brothers" and "sisters." Activity in a family is the most broad in scope of all the metaphors. Family members often interact across nearly all domains in life including the domain of private life, psychological domain, physiological domains (food, shelter, clothing, safety, etc.), physical activity, socializing, entertainment, education, and in the case of a family owned business, professional activity. Finally, "objectives" in the formal sense are typically non-existent in a family. One might make the argument that a family exists to "feed and clothe" offspring, or that families struggle "to get along," but these are typically not explicit nor easily measurable goals. The family metaphor is used by the following interviewee:

> I think maybe you've heard it from the other people, the idea of *pakikisama* [a Filipino word meaning teamwork]. The *pakikisama* is a value of working. It's more than friendship, it's more family, mother, father, brother, sister. It's something in the team, everyone is caring for each other.

### The Community Teamwork Metaphor

Like families, communities are also broad in scope, often encompassing activity across a number of domains in life, including socializing, entertainment, education, and professional activity. However, unlike a family, roles in a community are typically very informal, ambiguous, and may be shared or dynamic. Communities have goals that are somewhat more concrete than those of a family (e.g., to provide support or a safe place to live), but these objectives are not as clear and do not serve to orient all activity, as in the case of sports teams or military teams. Communities are amorphous. Boundaries are often blurred, and members come and go. This metaphor is illustrated in the following quote:

> Being a hero to your neighbors. I think that's one way to talk about teams. And then it's more negative than positive. People in our culture, also tend to prefer to belong to an association. Like a neighborhood association. But you can also call it, "He's my *compadre,*" so he can't be wrong. So right or wrong, he's in my neighborhood.

### The Associates Teamwork Metaphor

A circle of associates is the last metaphor for teamwork we identified. Associates have the most limited activity, with interaction only occurring in the professional domain. There is some identification of roles, but there is likely to be little hierarchy, and roles may shift or be shared. Objectives in a circle of associates may be explicit, but tend to evolve and are less task oriented. Ties are based primarily on proximity and shared function. An example of this metaphor is provided by the following interviewee:

> Oh, I think the French culture is, I would say, very [indicates marching along with fingers], very directive. My team, my circle of associates, is more motivated by their own personal work performance, than by the collective discipline, surely.

Sample expectations that coincide with each of the metaphors that we discovered are summarized in Table 1.

Having identified the various components of the five primary metaphors we uncovered in our research, we next set out to discover where each was used. We developed specific predictions about why a given metaphor may be used more frequently in one context than in another, and then tested these predictions in our interview text database. We summarize those findings in the next section below.

## The Role of Culture: Where Each Metaphor Is Used Most and Why

Metaphors are categories in the minds of managers and workers. While these categories of meaning come from many sources, one very important source is national culture. National culture is a set of shared meanings that control behavior in that context. Cultures differ in specific ways. For example, cultures vary on power distance, or the degree to which members of a society accept and expect unequal distribution of power. Cultures low in power distance minimize inequalities and favor less autocratic, centralized leadership. Cultures high on power distance exhibit greater tolerance for inequalities and authoritarianism. Another important work-related value that differs across cultural settings is individualism. In individualistic cultures, there are weak ties among individuals and a strong "self" concept. In collectivistic societies, personal identity is deeply tied to the ingroup and there are strong connections among people.

Our interview research demonstrated that the very different cognitive frameworks existing in various cultures around the world resulted in different metaphors for teamwork and varied use of these metaphors. Specifically, our analyses indicated that particular elements of national culture—such as power distance and individualism—predicted use of specific metaphors. For example, individualistic interviewees used metaphors that were narrow in scope, such as the sports metaphor and the associates metaphor. Sports teams typically have clearly defined domains and limited scope of involvement. In contrast, the community metaphor is broader in scope and was less commonly used by individualistic interviewees. Power distance was related to the use of metaphors with clear objectives such as the military metaphor. We summarize how the characteristics of national culture are related to use of each of the teamwork metaphors in Table 2.

A second important force likely to shape teamwork metaphors is organizational culture, which is an identifiable set of beliefs and norms shared by members of an organization or subunit. Organizational culture is a source of shared understanding and shapes the behaviors of organizational members. Researchers have demonstrated that patterns of organizational orientations and practices can be used to explain differences in organizational cultures. Perhaps even more so, because language is an element of organizational culture, organizational culture is likely to play a role in the development of common teamwork metaphors in an organization.

**Table 1** Matching Practices to Metaphors

| *Teamwork Metaphor* | *Likely to Result in Expectations Such As . . .* | | |
|---|---|---|---|
| | *Roles* | *Scope* | *Objectives* |
| Sports | Explicit roles such as coach and players with positions, but a relatively flat hierarchy | Often limited to physical and social activity; sometimes also includes psychological domain | Clear and salient with outcomes such as win, lose, goals, scores, tallies, and statistics |
| Military | Hierarchical roles such as commander, second in charge, and soldiers, each with indisputable rank | Typically limited to professional, physical, and educational activities | Extremely clear and salient with outcomes such as survival, life, death, defeat, occupation, or conquer |
| Family | Hierarchical roles such as mother, father, brother and sister each with varying levels of paternalistic authority | Very broad scope with activity covering a number of domains in life (e.g., private, psychological, physiological, physical, social, entertainment, educational, professional) | Typically non-existent, ambiguous, or inherent (e.g., "to get along" to "feed and clothe") |
| Community | Informal, ambiguous, and shared roles | Broad scope with activity including numerous domains in life (e.g., psychological, social, entertainment, educational, professional) | Ambiguous and non-task oriented (e.g., to provide a safe environment or sense of support) |
| Associates | Little identification of roles | Typically limited to professional activity | Sometimes explicit, but evolving, and less task oriented (e.g., to share the work load, provide back-up, socialize) |

For example, a performance orientation in an organization captures the degree to which an organization emphasizes achievement, service, and efficiency. In our analysis, this dimension was related to the use of metaphors that included clear consequences of team activity, such as the sport and military metaphors. A second dimension of organizational culture, degree of control, captures the extent to which people take organizational membership seriously and with reverence, the degree to which members of an organization are expected to follow rules and procedures, the extent to which punctuality is emphasized, and the degree to which the organization is cost-conscious. In our analysis, these practices were related to the use of teamwork metaphors that contain clear role information and broad scope, such as the family metaphor. We summarize how organizational culture is related to the use of the teamwork metaphors in Table 3.

## Illustrative Examples

The metaphors, mappings, and corresponding expectations we have described thus far come alive when we consider their use in real, ongoing teams. In this section we draw on our rich intercultural interviews to describe two scenarios in which teamwork metaphors play a critical role in team effectiveness. In the first scenario, a single manager supervises two teams. These teams are both in the same organization, and they perform the same set of tasks, but they are located at different subsidiary locations, one in the U.S. and one in Asia. In the second scenario, we examine a virtual, multicultural,

**Table 2** Encouraging Metaphors Congruent with National Cultures

| *Teamwork Metaphor* | *Characteristics of National Cultures Where Metaphor Is Used Frequently (Understood and Welcomed in These Settings . . .)* | *Characteristics of National Cultures Where Metaphor Is Non-Congruent (Not as Well Received in These Settings . . .)* |
|---|---|---|
| Sports | Individualistic settings where teams are not expected to be broad in scope (e.g., the U.S.) | Collectivistic settings were membership is involuntary (e.g., Scandinavia) |
| Military | High power distance settings where objectives are mandated (e.g., Latin America) | Low power distance settings where objectives are ambiguous (e.g., U.S.) |
| Family | Collectivistic settings where teams are expected to be broad in scope (e.g., Latin America) | Individualistic settings where teams are not expected to be broad in scope (e.g., France) |
| Community | Collectivistic settings where teams are expected to be broad in scope (e.g., Southeast Asia) | Individualistic settings where teams are not expected to be broad in scope (e.g., the U.K.) |
| Associates | Individualistic settings where teams are not expected to be broad in scope (e.g., the U.K.) | Collectivistic settings where membership is involuntary (e.g., Latin America) |

self-managing team in which team members represent both different national cultures and different organizational cultures.

Scenario #1: Same Team Function Different Expectations

> What the team is, really, is the whole supply chain. I mean we start at marketing with the order or with the customer wherever we get the order from, and we end at manufacturing. We don't get into there, but anything else that has to do with the product, that is us. Customer service, product handling, transportation, demand planning functions, and inventory control.
>
> —By Fred, Director of Logistics, Photoco

As a first example, consider two logistic teams, each of which consists of six members, all responsible for logistics (i.e., receiving, warehousing and distribution) operations in a different region (e.g., one in Southeast Asia and the other in the U.S.). All the members of the two logistic teams are employed by "Photoco," a company that develops, manufactures, sells, distributes, and services imaging equipment and support products such as film. Photoco has been struggling for several years. The organization culture is fragmented as a result of divesting and downsizing. The focus has been on cost reduction and reinforcing the traditional, established excellence of a long-standing product line.

The manager in this scenario, Fred, supervises both the Asian and U.S. logistic teams. Although they have the same function and are from the same organization, the team in Asia has a very different set of cultural values than the team in the U.S. The Asian team emphasizes collectivism and high power distance, while the U.S. team emphasizes individualism and low power distance. As a result, the Asian team refers to itself as a community, using the community metaphor. For example, consider the following quote from Julia, a Filipino logistics coordinator:

> I think most Filipinos are very regionalistic. In the work place, most Filipinos would, would tend to clump together with co-town mates or *barrio* mates or province mates. They think of the team like that. That means it is a natural thing to just open up to anyone on the team. And that would be subtly felt in, let's say, in the process of training teams.

Coinciding with the use of this metaphor, the team members are comfortable with ambiguous informal roles, they are less task-oriented, and

**Table 3** Encouraging Metaphors Congruent with Organizational Cultures

| *Teamwork Metaphor* | *Characteristics of Organizational Cultures Where Metaphor Is Used Frequently (Welcomed in These Settings . . .)* | *Characteristics of Organizational Cultures Where Metaphor Is Non-Congruent (Not as Well Received in These Settings . . .)* |
|---|---|---|
| Sports | Organizations that place an emphasis on performance (and thus have clear objectives) (e.g., Photoco (Kodak) and Medco (GE)) | Organizations that place an emphasis on tight control (and thus have clear hierarchical roles) (e.g., Chemco (Pfizer)) |
| Military | Organizations that place an emphasis on tight control (and thus have clear roles) or on performance (and thus have clear objectives) (e.g., Pharmco (Merck)) | Organizations that emphasize loose control and empowerment (and thus emphasize shared roles) (e.g., Healthco (J&J)) |
| Family | Organizations that emphasize tight control (and thus have clear roles). (e.g., Chemco (Pfizer) and Pharmco (Merck)) | Organizations that emphasize performance (and thus have clear objectives) (e.g., Photoco (Kodak)) |
| Community | Organizations that emphasize loose control (and thus have shared roles) (e.g., Photoco (Kodak) and Medco (GE)) | Organizations that place an emphasis on tight control (and thus have clear hierarchical roles) or those that emphasize performance (and thus have clear objectives) (e.g., Pharmco (Merck)) |
| Associates | Organizations that emphasize loose control (and thus have shared roles) (e.g., Healthco (J&J)) | Organizations that place an emphasis on tight control (and thus have clear hierarchical roles) (e.g., Pharmco (Merck), Biomedco (SKB)) |

instead focus on social opportunities, educational activities, and support of one another across all domains of activity. In contrast, the U.S. team refers to itself as a circle of associates, using the associates metaphor. For example, consider the following quote from Sam, a U.S. logistics operations specialist:

> The responsibilities, which we ask each team member to hold, help us to function as if we were a franchise, or a circle of associates. Members are given as much autonomy and freedom and empowerment as we possibly can give, to make decisions at the local level.

In contrast to the community metaphor, this "mental picture" of a team carried with it very different expectations. Members were relatively autonomous. They interacted in a professional sense only, and did not socialize outside of the work place. Roles and responsibilities were very clear.

Because the Asian team and the U.S. team did not directly interact with one another, these different concepts of teaming, in and of themselves, are not that problematic. The turmoil occurred when their supervisor Fred attempted to manage the two teams in exactly the same manner. Fred was from the U.S., and therefore shared some of the common assumptions about teams that the U.S. logistics team held. The associates metaphor came naturally to him, as did the associated expectations for roles, scope and objectives. He applied those assumptions to manage the Asian team in "cookie cutter" fashion, and as a result, met great difficulties.

The Asian team members expected much more direction from Fred than he offered. The Asian team members were disappointed with his leadership style and felt as though he wasn't doing his job adequately. They expected Fred to interact socially with the team whenever he was in the country, and to be involved with the team members at a more personal level, engaging with them about activities that extended beyond the team task. When he did not do so, they perceived his behavior (or lack of it) as insensitive and uncaring, and therefore did not trust him. When he attempted to implement changes in teamwork processes, they were skeptical and resisted. In the final analysis, the team was deemed ineffective, and Fred was counseled for poor leadership. Had Fred been aware of the concept of teamwork metaphors, and listened to the language being used by team members across the two teams, he may have been able to use the concept as a diagnostic tool. This may have helped him to avoid the difficulties he faced, as we describe below, after a description of Scenario #2.

### Scenario #2: Multiple Multicultural Metaphors

> I'm very heavy on my belief in teams, the use of teams. And when I came here, I started coming up with teams that would be involved with certain activities. One of the most active ones would be the strategy team, composed of heads of all the regions.
>
> —By Mike, Director of Strategic Initiatives, Marketing Strategy Consortium, Pharmco

As a second example, consider the Marketing Strategy Consortium (Team MSC), that consists of 12 members, each of whom represents a different pharmaceutical company within a variety of countries in the U.S., Central America, and Latin America. The team is a "parallel" team, meaning that it pulls people from different organizations (or jobs) to perform functions that the regular organization structures are not well equipped to perform. Parallel teams typically have limited authority, and often make recommendations to people higher up in their respective organization. Parallel teams are often used for problem solving and improvement activities. The objective of Team MSC is to develop a consistent marketing strategy for the industry across products and nations, in order to strengthen the overall state of the industry in the region.

The countries that members of Team MSC are from have very different cultures. Specifically, they differ in terms of the national cultural values—individualism and power distance—that we mentioned earlier. Latin Americans and Central Americans tend to be low on individualism and high on power distance. People in the U.S. tend to be high on individualism and low on power distance. Further, although all of the members of Team MSC are employed by organizations that develop, manufacture, sell, and distribute pharmaceutical products, these organizations differ dramatically in their organizational cultures. For example, one of the companies, Pharmco, emphasizes tight control, and clear roles and hierarchy. A second company, Healthco, on the other hand, emphasizes results and objective-driven performance, as well as flexibility and extensive autonomy for subsidiaries.

As a result of their cultural differences (both national and organizational), the members of Team MSC use a variety of metaphors for teamwork in their everyday language as they interact with each other. For example, consider Margie, a Puerto Rican director of marketing representing Pharmco. The national cultural values representative of Puerto Rico are collectivistic, and the organizational culture of Pharmco emphasizes tight control. Likely as a result, Margie tends to talk about Team MSC as if it were a family. A quote that exemplifies this is:

> We are a Pharmco family. So, you can see day by day that we work "among." Among. And if I produce a lot that goes to the next step—that is advertising strategy—and they have problems on that stage, I have to be involved with them to make sure to correct that problem. I guess I am the mother, but there is also a father, and sisters and brothers. So, we always socialize and always work together, like a family.

In contrast, Jack, a regional marketing manager from the U.S., represents the Healthco corporation. People from the U.S. tend to be individualistic and Healthco emphasizes performance and clear objectives. As a result, Jack describes Team MSC as a sports team. A quote that exemplified this is:

> The other thing that happens, when you say to the team, "Okay, you're empowered," you can use the sports analogy, you'll find the second baseman running out to center field to try and catch the fly ball. "You say, no, no, no, no, wait!" However, if there is a line drive out to left field and it hits the ground and he picks it up and he throws on to first base—if you ever notice at a baseball game, every time that happens, the catcher runs out from behind home plate and he gets behind—those boundaryless things, I think, need to happen for a successful team.

These contrasting metaphors caused real challenges on the team, because they carried very different implicit expectations in terms of roles, scope and the structuring of objectives. Margie expected that the team would be run like a family, that members would be fully involved in each other's lives and would share in personal milestones, celebrations and concerns. She expected there to be a maternal or paternal leader. In contrast, Jack expected that the team would be more a like a sports team with a focus on winning and losing, players with "positions," and the "score." No matter which intervention was implemented, team members were constantly in conflict over how the team should be managed. They disagreed on basic work processes, and more fundamentally, on scope, roles and objectives of the team. Again, had the team members been aware of the metaphors they utilize, and the corresponding expectations the metaphors imply, they may have been better equipped to address the challenges of multicultural teaming.

## Using Metaphors in Management

As illustrated above, on a basic level, our findings suggest that the meaning of teamwork is culturally contingent. As a result, the implementation of universal team practices across subsidiaries in different countries will not work. Rather, managers can be more effective if they make the effort to identify which teamwork metaphors are likely understood and welcomed in each context. As illustrated above, in some contexts, the use of certain metaphors may be confusing, or at the extreme even insulting. Below, we describe three ways in which teamwork metaphors can be utilized in practice.

### Matching Practices to Metaphors

Our results have several key implications for international management practice. First, managers need to consider matching practices and actions with dominant metaphors (see again Table 1). In Scenario #1, Fred failed to do this, but could have if he had been more cognizant of the metaphors being used in each of the settings. For example, the associates metaphor conveys clear information about professionalism and scope. In a setting where the associates metaphor is dominant, it may be appropriate to develop and implement very specific task definitions, and to limit work to the task context, since this is a central element in members understanding of teamwork. Such objectives will meet members' expectations and enhance their ability to work together. Alternatively, the community metaphor does not convey as much information about goals and objectives, but instead emphasizes teams as small social support groups. If the community metaphor is dominant, then a focus on the professionalism of the team may backfire because team members do not envision this as representative of teamwork. In this way, managers can use metaphors as a way to identify team members' expectations about their roles and the role of team.

For example, demonstrating the impact of the military metaphor one respondent in the Puerto Rico team said:

> As the leader, I am supposed to be an active shooter in terms of assisting, you now, liaisoning with the people and making sure that [the company's] kinds of problems are run at sort of a management level. At the moment it is very [prevalent in the] rank and file, but not really with the staff. We have not really gone to the reduction of a lot of employees. So I'm helping to do that. Right now we're having to think in terms of manpower.

In this quote, the metaphor implies prescriptions for attitudes and team behavior. Specifically, the military metaphor resulted in the belief that the leader has a clear role as conduit to upper management. Activity was directed at upward reporting of problems associated with manpower. The quote implies that teams that utilize the military metaphor will likely be more effective when managed in a way that recognizes status relationships and incorporates these into the team structure. In the Puerto Rico setting, team members are likely to be more receptive to teams managed in a way consistent with the military metaphor.

### Establishing Metaphors Congruent with National and Organizational Cultures

There is a second way that metaphors can guide practice. Intercultural research has established that organizations are more effective when management practices in a work unit are congruent with national culture. Given that multinational organizations often operate across several cultures, these organizations face great challenges in managing teams. We argue that identifying and appropriately reinforcing particular metaphors that are congruent to and reinforce the values emphasized in a given culture is likely to have a positive impact on team effectiveness.

For example, the Philippines is a very collectivistic national context. As we suggest in Table 2, the community metaphor is consistent with collectivistic values, in that a community is broad in scope, and collective behavior encompasses many aspects of life in a collectivistic culture. Demonstrating the use of the community metaphor, one respondent in the Philippines said:

> That's called a *nipa* hut. Sometimes you do require that the hut be moved from one location to another. And in the old days, *nipa* huts would probably be located along the safe side of a river because there's water there, fish would be there. Some erosion could happen and you would need to relocate the hut to a safer ground. In the Philippines, you would gather your neighbors, call them, and you would put on handles and literally lift the house—in one, big haul, the house as one big piece, and move it to a new location. And that's called the *bayanihan* spirit. I think that would best describe in my culture, how teams can work.

Using the same metaphor, another Filipino respondent said:

> I think most Filipinos have where they're very regionalistic, I think. That most Filipinos would, would tend to clump together with, with co-town mates or barrio mates or province mates. That, I think itself, uh, it it's natural thing to just opening up to just anyone.

These excerpts demonstrate that the community metaphor shaped beliefs about who should be considered a part of a team and how central a role the team will serve in the respondents' work life. Again, drawing upon the rationale of cultural congruence, we would expect that where a cultural assessment reveals that collectivism is valued, managers who emphasize the community metaphor over other metaphor categories would meet with more team success. Further, as implied with the community metaphor, the team will be most effective when it is defined broadly, consisting of many individuals who have some connection to each other, even if these individuals are on the periphery of the central activity of the team.

In addition to helping managers consider the choice of metaphors *among* the categories we identified (e.g., community over military), we also suggest that these results can help managers tailor choices *within* metaphor categories. We must make it clear that our work does not suggest that managers in cultural contexts such as the Philippines would be wrong to use a sports metaphor (or other metaphor conveying similar information), but rather that even *within* metaphor categories there are likely to be some choices. For example, if a manager of a Philippine team decides to use a sports metaphor to explain her expectations to the team, she would be best served by referring to a sports team that more accurately portrays the typical expectations of the country culture. Soccer may be more readily understood as the subject of a sports metaphor in Latin America than U.S. football. Soccer has much less clear hierarchy and role definition than U.S. football, for example, so in addition to familiarity because it is a national pastime in many Latin American countries, the information about scope and roles is more closely aligned with the cultural values as well.

As a result of the issues we illustrated with the U.S. team and the Asian team and their metaphor use, a second alternative for Fred, the manager in Scenario #1, would be for him to attempt to better understand the cultural context in each country. For example, this understanding can be facilitated by measuring the cultural values mentioned in tables 2 and 3. This assessment is typically completed by attitudinal measures (e.g., a survey instrument), or by discussion and observation. With cultural values and orientations identified, the manager might then encourage metaphors (both by category and within category) in each context that are consistent with the dominant cultures, using these metaphors in his own language, during communication with the team.

### Sharing Metaphors and Building Mutual Understanding

Finally, as illustrated in Scenario #2, research on multicultural teams suggests that a serious challenge faced by these teams is a lack of shared understanding and meaning. Having team members define their understanding of teamwork prior to commencing work may help to bridge these gaps in understanding. In this way, managers can use conscious identification and sharing of metaphors within the team as a tool to promote understanding and proactively identify sources of potential conflict within multinational teams. In contrast, no effort was undertaken in Scenario #2 to share expectations for teamwork. This may have been a key explanation for the demise of the team.

International management scholar Martha Maznevski and her colleagues suggest a three-step process for sharing within multicultural teams that involves: (1) understanding differences in cultures, (2) bridging the differences, and (3) integration. To help in understanding cultural differences, we suggest that cross-cultural teams hold an initial session at their formation to discuss teamwork metaphors, and corresponding expectations about specific team behaviors which are felt to be critical to the team's success. Each member might be asked to describe their preferred approach, identifying where problems might arise across members. From this discussion, potential problem areas could be identified along with possible solutions. This method, of course, assumes that team members are able to articulate cultural norms which in reality may not necessarily be the case. Given this dilemma, it may be useful to have an third party intervene who could advise teams at the onset what they might expect in terms of cultural differences and how these might manifest themselves in dysfunctional ways.

The second step—bridging—requires finding commonalities among members. A specific process that enables this is *de-centering,* defined as the process of sending and receiving communication with the other person's perspective in mind. The fundamental idea of de-centering is empathy: feeling and understanding as another person does. This may require some initial training for the team in active listening and interpersonal behavioral skills. Also in conjunction with this step, the team might consider carefully the task, objectives and priorities that comprise their mandate. It may be that certain metaphors are more appropriate for certain missions. In this way, focusing on the team's mission may help them to de-center and arrive at a shared understanding of expectations for teamwork.

The final step—integration—requires blame-free explanations and problem solving. Research indicates that the single best predictor of effective group integration is team members' willingness to suspend blame for problems and to explain problems by trying to understand how members' different perspectives could have led the group as a whole to experience difficulties. This leads the team onward toward exploring alternatives and building a shared reality, developing trust and common rules, and building confidence in the team's ability to use different perceptions productively.

Another means of overcoming differences in groups is the development of a mutually agreed upon set of expectations, referred to by scholar Chris Earley and his colleagues as a "hybrid culture." A hybrid team culture refers to a set of rules, expectations, and member perceptions that individuals within a team develop, share, and create after mutual interactions. A shared group culture appears to be important for team functioning. Shared metaphors for teamwork are likely an important component of hybrid cultures, and leaders may play an role in creating and managing hybrid cultures, by identifying key issues and points of contention around which shared understanding should be developed. In particular, managers in multinational organizations can help create hybrid cultures by bridging the home office and overseas office cultures, which can mean facilitating the proper handling of seemingly incongruent values and priorities.

## Conclusions

The concept of teamwork metaphors advances the practice of multinational management. Due to the lack of empirical research regarding teams across cultures, leaders within multinational organizations have, up to this point, been forced to make educated guesses as to the most appropriate method of implementing teams across their various geographic facilities. Among other key insights, the concepts described here provide guidance regarding the meaning systems that must be managed in order to successfully implement teams interculturally. More specifically, these ideas shed light on the impact metaphors for teamwork, on the quality of the work experience, and the effectiveness of teams.

### Selected Bibliography

For a detailed account of the derivation and intercultural variation of teamwork metaphors see Cristina Gibson and Mary E. Zellmer-Bruhn's article entitled "Metaphors for Teamwork: An Intercultural Analysis of the Concept of Teamwork" in *Administrative Science Quarterly,* 2001, 46, 274–303. For a more comprehensive discussion of the theory underlying the management of multicultural teams, see P. Christopher Earley and Cristina Gibson's book entitled *Multinational Teams: A New Perspective* (Lawrence Erlbaum and Associates, 2002). For a general discussion about the use of self-managing work teams in a multinational context, see Bradley Kirkman, Cristina Gibson and Debra Shapiro's article entitled, "Exporting Teams: Enhancing the Implementation and Effectiveness of Work Teams in Global Affiliates," in *Organization Dynamics,* 2001, 30, 12–29; and Bradley Kirkman and Debra Shapiro's article "The Impact of Cultural Values on Employee Resistance to Teams: Toward a Model of Globalized Self-Managing Work Team Effectiveness," in *Academy of Management Review,* 1997, 22, 730–757. For an empirical test of the propositions found in the above article, see their article, "The Impact of Cultural Values on Job Satisfaction and Organizational Commitment in Self-Managing Work Teams: The Mediating Role of Employee Resistance," in *Academy of Management Journal,* 2001, 44, 557–569.

For more information on bridging cultural differences, see Martha Maznevski's book with Henry Lane and Joe Destefano entitled *International Management Behavior* (Blackwell Publishers, 1997) and her article entitled "Understanding our Differences: Performance in Decision-Making Groups with Diverse Members," in *Human Relations,* 1994, 47, 531–552; and P. Christopher Earley's article with Elaine Mosakowski entitled, "Creating Hybrid Team Cultures: An Empirical Test of Transnational Team Functioning," in *Academy of Management Journal,* 2000, 43, 26–50.

For additional reading on cultural value differences between countries in general, see Michael Gannon's book *Understanding Global Cultures: Metaphorical Journeys Through 17 Countries* (Sage, 1994); Geert Hofstede's book, *Culture's Consequences* (Sage, 1980); his article entitled, "Motivation, Leadership, and Organizations: Do American Theories Apply Abroad?" in *Organizational Dynamics* (Summer, 1980); and his article entitled, "Cultural Constraints in Management Theories," in *Academy of Management Executive* (February, 1993); Fons Trompenaar's book, *Riding the Waves of Culture* (Irwin, 1993); Miriam Erez and P. Christopher Earley's books entitled, *Culture, Self-identity and Work* (Oxford, 1993) and *The Transplanted Executive* (Oxford, 1997); and K. Newman and S. Nolan's article entitled, "Culture and Congruence: The Fit Between Management Practices and National Cultures," in *Journal of International Business Studies,* 1994, 27, 753–779.

For additional perspectives on the meaning and use of metaphor, see George Lakoff's chapter entitled, "The Contemporary Theory of Metaphor," in Andrew Ortony's (Ed.), *Metaphor and Thought* (Cambridge University Press, 1993, 202–252) and Cora Strauss and Nancy Quinn's book *A Cognitive Theory of Cultural Meaning* (Cambridge University Press, 1997).

# Reading 3.3

## END-GAMES IN INTERNATIONAL ALLIANCES

MANUEL G. SERAPIO, JR. AND WAYNE F. CASCIO

### Executive Overview

> *"The end-game is in many ways the most important phase of the game. It is here that the hard-won advantages of earlier play can be transformed into a win, draw, or worse."*
>
> —Tony Kosten, British International Chess Master

In recent years there has been an explosive growth in international alliances. As more of them mature, the issue of exit, the end-game scenario, will escalate in importance. As a general theme, we have observed that partners in international alliances do not often prepare for the eventual termination of their alliances, and some are caught off guard when their other partners are better prepared to deal with issues related to termination of the alliance. In this article we will explore three issues: why alliances end, how they end, and key issues to consider. Then, using the lessons that we learned from studying more than two dozen divorces in international alliances, we provide a list of dos and don'ts for prospective suitors.

Consider the following examples:

*Daewoo Motors (South Korea) and General Motors (U.S.)*

After a rocky relationship spanning eight years, Daewoo and GM ended their 50–50 joint venture in Inchon, South Korea, in 1992. The partnership began in 1984, when GM and Daewoo launched a joint venture to build the Pontiac LeMans in South Korea, using the design of GM's Opel unit in Germany. As the Inchon facility reached its production capacity of 270,000 cars per year, Daewoo planned to export half of its output to the United States, and to sell the other half in South Korea.[1]

Unfortunately, the Pontiac LeMans experienced disappointing sales in the U.S. market, peaking at fewer than 50,000 cars in 1988. Daewoo and GM each blamed the other for the lackluster performance of the LeMans in the U.S. Daewoo accused GM of failing to market the LeMans aggressively in the United States, while GM maintained that the initial poor quality of the LeMans and the on-again off-again availability of supplies soured dealers on the car.

After several years of attempting to survive this uneasy relationship, the two partners terminated their joint venture in 1992. The actual termination took several months as lawyers and executives from both sides worked out the details of the divorce. The major sticking point was the relative value of each partner's share in the facility. After several months of negotiation, Daewoo agreed to buy out GM's share of the joint venture.[2]

*Lesson:* Divorce is difficult, but partners to an alliance should be prepared for it, and also be prepared to tackle the sometimes difficult issues in exiting an alliance.

*Sover S.P.A. (Italy) and Suzhou Spectacles No. 1 Factory (China)*

In June 1991, Sover S.P.A., a small Italian spectacles maker, proposed to liquidate its 50%-owned sunglasses factory in Suzhou, China. The company alleged that its Chinese partner, Suzhou Spectacles No. 1 Factory, sold pirated copies of the joint venture's product in the domestic market. The Chinese partner denied any wrongdoing, and refused to approve the liquidation of the venture. Since dissolution required unanimous approval by the board of the joint venture, Sover found itself in the difficult position of not being able to get out of its partnership venture in China.

Sover sought help from Suzhou City's Foreign Economic Relations and Trade Commission, the agency that approves foreign investment in China. It got nowhere. The Commission referred a Sover representative to the Light Industrial Bureau, which did not help either. According to Carlo Molinari, the Sover representative, a Commission official urged him not to terminate the venture, saying, "When a son is sick, you should not hang him."[3]

*Lesson:* Quitting a venture in China is not easy, and the costs in legal fees, time, and effort, can be very high. Both the Chinese partner and the government are often unwilling partners in the termination of a partnership.

*Borden, Inc. (U.S.) and Meiji Milk (Japan)*

After nearly 20 years of partnership, Borden, Inc. and Meiji Milk terminated their alliance in 1991. The two firms jointly entered into a licensing agreement in 1971. Borden marketed its products throughout Japan by using Meiji Milk's vast distribution network. In exchange, Borden provided Meiji Milk with the technology to process cheese, margarine, and ice cream. Together, Borden and Meiji successfully created a premium market for ice cream. During the 1980s, Borden's "Lady Borden" brand dominated the upscale ice cream market in Japan, with over a 60% market share.

By the early 1990s, however, Lady Borden's market share in Japan started to decline. An ice cream boom and the liberalization of imports to Japan increased competition. Pillsbury's Haagen Dasz, Breyer's Grand Ice Cream, and other domestic and foreign competitors gradually eroded Lady Borden's market share.

Borden became increasingly dissatisfied with Meiji Milk, claiming that its executives did not respond aggressively to the competition. Borden threatened to end its collaborative relationship with Meiji Milk if the latter did not agree to expand the partnership and to yield greater control to Borden's executives over the marketing of Borden products in Japan.

Borden spent several months trying to get Meiji Milk to recraft their joint agreement. It was obvious from the start that Meiji Milk did not want to end the partnership, but it also did very little to respond to Borden's demands. Talks got nowhere. Finally, in June, 1991, Borden severed its ties to Meiji Milk and announced plans to sell Lady Borden on its own in Japan.

However, since Borden's standing license agreement with Meiji Milk had not expired, Meiji Milk insisted in carrying the Lady Borden brand in Japan until its license expired the following year.

Some observers were puzzled over the clumsy and tentative separation process between Borden and Meiji Milk. As Ken Honma, a manager in Taiyo Fishery, observed: "I can't understand it. It's just as though you keep dating your wife that you divorced."[4]

*Lesson:* Don't be afraid to terminate an alliance that is not working. Hanging on could just make matters worse.

## Why Do Alliances End?

Exhibit 1 provides additional examples of alliances that have terminated or are likely to terminate and the possible reasons for termination. In our study (see Appendix A), we found that alliances typically end for one or more of six reasons: (1) the alliance is not successful; (2) differences between partners (e.g., people incompatibilities, different management styles, disagreement over objectives); (3) breach of agreement; (4) the alliance no longer fits the goals/strategies of a partner; (5) a partner needs to exit the alliance because of financial difficulties or to take advantage of financial opportunities; and (6) the alliance has met its goals. Now let's consider examples of each of these.

*The Alliance Is Not Successful.* Vitro and Corning ended their equity ventures, Corning Vitro and Vitro Corning, in 1993 because the ventures had failed to help them integrate the sales and distribution of their products in the United States and Mexico. The joint ventures suffered from the different administrative practices of their two parent companies. "Managing from two countries was more complicated than we anticipated," said a Corning manager. "There were different management structures, styles, and accounting systems."[5] The companies agreed to sell their stakes to each other, and Corning agreed to pay Vitro $131 million, roughly the amount Vitro paid Corning when the joint venture was established. By terminating their partnership and maintaining separate ownership structures, both companies hoped to concentrate on their respective businesses and not be bogged down by the complexities of managing two different operations in rapidly-changing markets.

In the pharmaceutical industry, product problems, such as longer-than-expected product development or approval times, or outright failure to secure approval for testing and development, often lead to the termination of an alliance. One such case is the divorce between Norsk Hydro and Telios Pharmaceuticals in Europe. One year after launching their partnership in January 1992, Norsk Hydro returned its 55% stake in the joint venture to Telios because of greater-than-anticipated product development time and costs.[6]

*Differences Between Partners.* The breakup between AT&T and Olivetti, one of the most publicized divorces in the international alliance arena, demonstrates how differences between partners can impede the alliance's success. Robert Kravner, an AT&T senior executive, blamed most of the problems in the alliance on differences in culture and management style. He said: "I don't think we or Olivetti spent enough time understanding behavior patterns. We knew that culture was different but we never really penetrated. We would get angry and they would get upset."[7]

In a more recent case, Rubbermaid, Inc. sold its 40% stake in Curver Rubbermaid Group to the joint venture partner, Dutch Chemical Company DSM Group N.V. The alliance, launched in 1990 to manufacture and market plastic and rubber housewares in Europe, the Middle East, and North America, provided about $110 million in sales to Rubbermaid in 1993. However, reports indicated that Rubbermaid was disappointed with Curver's performance and management. According to Robert Moses, an analyst with McDonald and Co., "Curver was not run the way Rubbermaid wanted."[8] Rubbermaid and Curver's management differed on a number of management and strategic issues. For instance, Rubbermaid wanted to invest in product development and expansion in order to combat sluggish demand in Europe. In contrast, Curver's management is believed to have balked at new investments in the face of a European recession. In lieu of relying on European partners, Rubbermaid decided to expand its business on its own in Europe. The company recently established its European headquarters and a $10 million Little Tikes toy manufacturing facility in Luxembourg.

*Breach of Agreement.* The case of Sover S.P.A. (Italy) and Suzhou Spectacles No. 1 Factory, mentioned earlier, demonstrates how an alleged material breach of agreement could lead to the termination of an international alliance. Sover S.P.A. alleged that its Chinese partner sold pirated copies of the joint venture's product in the Peoples Republic of China. The company maintained that this constituted a violation of the terms of its partnership and called for the liquidation of the joint venture.[9]

In another case, the three-way research and development (R&D) alliance between Green Cross, Alpha Therapeutic, and Univax ended in arbitration. Alpha alleged that Univax failed to complete milestones and misrepresented status, costs, and its ability to perform the project. On the other hand, Univax alleged that Alpha failed to make payments to Univax as required by the alliance.[10]

*The Alliance No Longer Fits the Goals/Strategies of a Partner.* The decision by British Aerospace (BAe) to quit the car industry and bail out of its alliance with Honda in Europe is a recent example. In 1994, BAe sold its controlling interest in Rover, which it owned jointly with Honda, to BMW for £800 million (U.S. $1.2 billion). This move by BAe shocked Honda, as reflected in the following statement: "Rover, the last hope for a viable British-owned motor industry, has enjoyed a remarkable resurgence. For nearly 15 years, Honda was Rover's partner in recovery. But (in an unexpected turnaround), Rover turned abruptly to BMW. The last large British car maker becomes German, leaving Honda's European strategy in tatters."[11]

*A Partner Needs to Exit the Alliance Because of Financial Difficulties or to Take Advantage of Financial Opportunities.* Some observers contend that BAe's decision to sell Rover was partially motivated by financial considerations. Before the sale, BAe was said to have a daily average of £200 million (U.S. 300 million) debt on its balance sheet attributable to Rover, and another £700 million (U.S. $1.050 billion) tied up in working capital. Add

| Partners | Nature of Alliance | Outcome |
|---|---|---|
| Norsk Hydro (Norway) and Telios Pharmaceuticals (U.S.) | Joint venture in Europe to market Telios products | Terminated: Norsk Hydro returned its 55% stake in the venture to Telios because of greater-than-anticipated development time and cost of Telio-Derm in Europe. |
| Elders IXL Ltd. (Australia) and Guangxi Province (PRC) | Elders IXL Ltd. of Australia to grow pineapple in China | Terminated: Elders IXL Ltd. surrendered its 50% stake to its Chinese partner and wrote off its Australian $1 million investment, after suffering from 3 consecutive years of losses due to crippling frosts. |
| Greenwich Pharmaceutical (U.S.) and Syntex (France) | Co-development and co-promotion of Greenwich's drug for arthritis | Terminated: Syntex reevaluated research portfolio and restructured—laid off 500 employees and closed manufacturing plants. |
| Coors Brewing Company (U.S.) and Molson Breweries (Canada) | Molson to market Coors products in Canada | Contested: Coors sued and served Molson with an arbitration notice, after Molson agreed to form a separate partnership with Miller Brewing Company. |
| Ralston Purina Co. (U.S.) and Taiyo Fishery Co. (Japan) | Joint venture to market Ralston Purina's products in Japan | Terminated: Ralston Purina ended its 20-year partnership with Taiyo Fisheries in order to start its own pet food subsidiary in Japan. |
| Forest Laboratories (U.S.) and Rhone-Poulenc Rorer (France) | Development and testing of Forest's Micturin | Terminated: Failures to get FDA approval at the time of the dissolution of the partnership. |
| Price/Costco (U.S.) and Controladora Commercial Mexicana S.A. (Mexico) | Joint venture, Price Club de Mexico, to establish membership warehouses in Mexico | Price/Costco formally notified its Mexican partner of its intent to sell its 50% interest in Price Club de Mexico. |

**Exhibit 1** Divorces in International Alliances

SOURCE: Academy of Management Executive by Serapio, M. G., Jr., & Cascio, W. F. Copyright 1996 by Academy of Management. Reproduced with permission of Academy of Management via Copyright Clearance Center.

to that the £800 million ($1.2 billion) of the sale, and BAe is expected to save or receive interest on a total of £1.7 billion (U.S. $2.55 billion).[12]

Likewise, in 1991, Chrysler Corporation sold its 50 percent stake in Diamond Star Motors in Bloomington-Normal, Illinois, to joint venture partner Mitsubishi Motors for $100 million. In addition, Mitsubishi also assumed Chrysler's debt in the joint venture, allowing Chrysler to remove $105 million in negative book value from its balance sheet. Chrysler's sale of its stake at Diamond Star Motors and its prior sale of Mitsubishi stock in 1989 helped the cash-strapped company pay for refurbishments and marketing costs on its new LH models and Jeep Grand Cherokee.[13]

*The Alliance Has Met Its Goals.* Failure of an alliance or problems during its life are not the only reasons for exiting an alliance. Successful alliances often terminate after meeting the partners' goals. Project-oriented alliances, such as partnerships between international design and construction firms in building airports and other large

| Divorce Scenarios | | Examples |
|---|---|---|
| Planned | → | General Motors (U.S.) and Toyota (Japan) |
| vs. | | |
| Unplanned | → | AT&T (U.S.) and Olivetti (Italy) |
| Friendly | → | Vitro (Mexico) and Corning (U.S.) |
| vs. | | |
| Unfriendly | → | Coors Brewing Co. (U.S.) and Molson Breweries (Canada) |
| Both Agree | → | Ralston Purina (U.S.) and Taiyo Fishery (Japan) |
| vs. | | |
| One Partner Refuses to Agree | → | Sover S.P.A. (Italy) and Suzhou Spectacles No. 1 Factory (China) |
| **Outcomes** | | **Examples** |
| Termination by Acquisition | → | Daewoo Motors (South Korea) and General Motors (U.S.) |
| Termination by Dissolution | → | Meiji Milk (Japan) and Borden (U.S.) |
| Termination by Reorganization/ Restructuring of the Alliance | → | Matsushita Electric Industries Co. (Japan) and Solbourne Computer (U.S.) |

**Exhibit 2** How Do Alliances End?

projects, terminate after the project's successful completion.

The alliance between Sandoz and Sankyo, two major pharmaceutical multinationals from Europe and Japan, respectively, dissolved in 1990 after Sandoz had achieved its goal of establishing an independent business in Japan and Sankyo had gained access to Sandoz's major-selling brands. At the time that the alliance was dissolved, Sankyo was selling 22 Sandoz drugs in Japan and was generating 82 billion yen in revenues.[14]

## Divorce Scenarios

Exhibit 2 shows three possible divorce scenarios (planned/unplanned, friendly/unfriendly, both agree/ one partner refuses to agree), and three possible outcomes of the termination of an alliance.

*Planned/Unplanned.* The alliance between General Motors and Toyota Motors provides an interesting example of a planned divorce scenario. In 1984, the U.S. Federal Trade Commission authorized the formation of New United Motor Manufacturing, Inc. (NUMMI), a manufacturing collaboration between General Motors and Toyota Motors, with a provision that the joint venture will have a limited life of twelve years.[15] As a result of the twelve-year limit imposed by the U.S. Federal Trade Commission on NUMMI, both General Motors and Toyota Motors knew at the beginning of their joint venture that they would have to plan for their divorce.

Planned divorces, such as the case of NUMMI, are the exception rather than the rule. Divorces between companies in an international alliance are typically unanticipated. Most companies enter into an international alliance without really knowing how long their partnership will last. The dissolution of the collaborative partnerships between General Motors and Daewoo Motors, Meiji and Borden, and AT&T and Olivetti are examples of unplanned divorces.

*Friendly/Unfriendly.* Some international alliances terminate under friendly terms, while others do not. The divorce between Vitro and Corning, mentioned earlier, is an example of an alliance that ended on friendly terms. Both companies amicably agreed to terminate their equity ventures, and Corning paid Vitro its original investment in the joint venture. In addition, both companies agreed to continue their distributorship agreements.

Friendly separations are typically handled through negotiated settlements. In contrast, unfriendly divorces are often contested in courts or end up in arbitration proceedings. One such case is the ongoing dispute between Coors Brewing Company and its Canadian partner and licensee, Molson Breweries. Coors sued and served Molson with an aribitration notice after the latter agreed to form a partnership with Miller Brewing Company. According to Coors, Miller's purchase of a 20 percent stake in Molson contributed to a consolidation of the North American beer industry and endangered Coors' competitive position. Coors also maintained that the Miller-Molson alliance provided Miller, a key competitor of Coors in the United States, with highly confidential marketing strategies and brand performance information that Coors had given Molson under their licensing agreement.[16]

The financial condition of the international alliance at the time of the divorce often determines whether a separation is handled on friendly or unfriendly terms. According to William Mooz, an attorney in the law firm of Holland and Hart in Denver, "Partners are more willing to work with each other if the venture is making money. It is usually more difficult to negotiate the termination of an alliance in cases when the venture is losing money."[17]

*Both Agree/One Partner Refuses to Agree.* Having a partner that refuses to terminate an alliance presents one of the most complex divorce scenarios. To illustrate, a major U.S. computer company attempted to terminate its alliance with a Japanese partner three years ago. Although the alliance was doing well financially, the U.S. partner decided to exit the alliance because of a major shift in its strategic focus. The U.S. company's joint venture contract with the Japanese partner allowed it to exit, but the Japanese partner insisted on maintaining the alliance. The Program Director of Alliance Management of the U.S. company described her company's unsuccessful efforts to exit from the alliance as follows: "Our Japanese partner refused to accept our position. They could not understand how we could walk away from a successful venture. To our partner, ending our joint venture meant a loss of face—that they have failed. Our talks with them to end the joint venture have gone nowhere. They have managed to delay and prolong our discussions."

## Possible Outcomes of Termination

What are the possible outcomes of the termination of an international alliance? We found three common outcomes: termination by acquisition, termination by dissolution, and termination by redefinition of the alliance.

In a majority of the divorces that we studied, the alliance terminated with one of the partners acquiring the stake of the other partner. Termination by acquisition could also take the form of one partner selling its equity stake in the joint venture to another company (e.g., British Aerospace selling its equity stake in Rover to BMW), or both partners selling their shares to a third company.

Termination by acquisition is most common in international equity alliances. In contrast, most non-equity alliances, such as licensing agreements or marketing/ distributorship partnerships, terminate by dissolving their contractual arrangements (e.g., Meiji and Borden).

Another possible outcome of termination is the redefinition of the alliance agreement. In lieu of termination, partners to an international alliance may agree to redefine or restructure their original agreement. For example, Matsushita Electric Industries, Co. of Japan (MEI) and Solbourne Computer, Inc. of Colorado entered into an ambitious partnership in 1987 to compete with Sun Microsystems' SPARC computers. When the venture failed, MEI and Solbourne agreed in 1992 to recraft their initial agreement into a more limited partnership arrangement.[18]

## Key Issues to Consider

Before they formalize their working arrangements, prospective partners should consider some key legal and business issues. These issues vary depending on the type of alliance (equity vs. non-equity), the partners involved, the reasons for termination, and the divorce scenario. Let us begin by considering important legal issues. The standard issues included in the exit clauses of contract documents typically address four areas: (1) conditions of termination; (2) disposition of assets; (3) disposition of liabilities; and (4) dispute resolution mechanisms.

*Conditions of termination.* Partners to an international alliance must agree on the circumstances that would allow each partner to exit or call for the dissolution of an alliance. Events such as the following might trigger such a call: (1) material breach of agreement; (2) breach of law; (3) repeated (two or more) deadlocks among the members of the board of directors; (4) changes in the laws and regulations of the home or host country; (5) failure to meet a specific target; and (6) after a certain time period has lapsed. In addition, the partners must agree on voting rights and voting procedures for dissolving an alliance. For example, termination may require either a majority or unanimous approval by the board of directors.

*Disposition of assets.* How will the alliance liquidate its assets? How will the partners share in the assets of the alliance? Asset valuation or pricing is a major source of disagreement during a divorce. The partners should specify the methods to be used in valuing assets. For example, will one partner be given the opportunity to bid on the equity share of the other, will asset valuation be based on the actual amounts invested by the partners, the findings of an independent appraiser, or an offer from one of the partners or an external buyer?

*Disposition of liabilities.* How will the partners deal with the liabilities of the alliance? How will the alliance deal with contingent liabilities? For example, terminating a venture in host countries such as Italy, Spain, or Belgium, could be very expensive because of significant severance benefits that the governments of these countries require employers to pay terminated employees. To illustrate, terminating a 45-year-old manager with 20 years of service who is earning $50,000 (U.S.) per year costs about $130,000 (U.S.) in Italy, $125,000 in Spain, and $94,000 in Belgium, compared to an average of $19,000 in the United States.[19] Partners to an international alliance must be prepared to address these and other types of liabilities related to terminating an alliance.

*Dispute resolution.* How will the partners resolve their disputes? Will disputes be resolved judicially or through arbitration? Partners to an international alliance should be aware of the advantages and disadvantages of each alternative before selecting a particular mode of dispute resolution. If the partners agree to resolve disputes judicially, with certain exceptions, the partners are free to specify which country's laws will govern any dispute.[20]

In addition to these issues, partners to an alliance must address related legal issues that are material to the alliance. These may include distributorship arrangements, intellectual property arrangements (licensing agreements), rights over sales and territories, and obligations to customers.

*Distributorship arrangements.* Partners to an international distributorship alliance should specify the rights and obligations of the manufacturer and distributor in the event that the partnership is dissolved. Many countries provide distributors with protections against termination approaching those offered to terminated employees. Terminating a distributor in such countries can require substantial payments designed to compensate the distributor for expenses that it has incurred and for the goodwill that it has developed for the manufacturer.[21]

*Protection of proprietary information and property.* In alliances that involve an exchange of intellectual property (e.g., patents, know-how, trademarks, copyrights, tradenames) the partners have to weigh the impact of the termination of the alliance on proprietary information and property. Questions such as the following must be addressed: What intellectual property rights will belong to the exiting partner(s)? What will remain in the alliance? How will licenses be handled?

*Rights over sales territories and obligations to customers.* Upon termination of an alliance, it is important to specify who will have responsibility over various sales territories and who will support the customers of an alliance. Such longterm considerations should not be left unaddressed until the partnership is on the brink of dissolution. Rather, they should comprise integral parts of advanced planning.

All too often, unfortunately, partners to an international alliance leave these issues to their lawyers by default. This is a mistake! The provisions in these legal considerations should reflect the preferences of the partners. Attorneys experienced in international alliances often prod their clients to confront such issues. For example, William Mooz requires his clients to answer the following question: "Suppose the alliance does not work out. What do you want to do?"

## Business Issues to Consider

In addition to the legal considerations, the partners to an international alliance must be prepared to address important business issues related to termination.

These issues include: the decision to exit, people-related issues, and relations with the host government.

*The decision to exit.* Partners to an alliance should know at what point they are willing and prepared to exit. For example, a major U.S. computer company uses a scorecard to monitor the performance of its international alliances. If an alliance falls below expectations, the company will consider exiting the alliance.

*People-related issues.* In an earlier paper, Cascio and Serapio observed that people-related issues offer some of the most complex challenges in an international alliance.[22] This is particularly true when it comes to terminating an alliance. What happens to the employees of the alliance after it is dissolved? Are they terminated? Are they absorbed by one of the partners? For example, employees of one of the alliances of a U.S. computer firm expected the company to rehire all of the employees of the failed alliance because at the time the company followed a no-layoff policy.

In another case, the expatriate manager sent by a U.S. partner to manage its joint venture in Europe sued the U.S. parent company after the alliance was terminated, claiming that, under the host country's labor laws, he was entitled to the same significant severance benefits that the local employees of the European joint venture received.

*Relations with the host government.* The host government of a partner may be unwilling to permit the alliance to terminate. It could object to the termination in an overt way, such as not permitting a foreign partner to sell its interest in the alliance. There are also subtle ways to discourage a partner from leaving an alliance, such as blocking the repatriation of the foreign partner's investments in the alliance. Finally, it is important to consider carefully the long-term effects of terminating an alliance on the ability of the company to do business in the same host country in the future.

## Do's and Don'ts for General Managers

Based on our accumulated knowledge and understanding of how international alliances actually operate in practice, we offer nine recommendations to general managers. Following them will permit managers to leverage the end-game scenario for maximum advantage.

1. Know as much as possible about your partner before entering into an alliance. Investigate issues such as the following: your partner's track record, goals and objectives, and strengths and weaknesses. One good way of finding out is through "dating." You may want first to form a partnership on a limited scale before entering into a full-fledged alliance. Remember: your contract is only as good as the reputation and integrity of your partner.
2. Know as much as possible about the country in which you are going to do business. In particular, know the host country's relevant laws and regulations governing the termination of alliances. Take the time to study the host government's policies towards divestments by international direct investors.
3. Ask hard questions before entering into an alliance, questions such as: What are my key assumptions in entering the alliance? In the worst case scenario, what is most important to me? What am I prepared to lose?
4. Don't be afraid to walk away from the deal if it does not seem right. Be patient, and be prepared to look for other partners.
5. Termination is not just a legal issue. It is an important business issue. Don't leave this important responsibility to your lawyers by default.
6. The terminology and phraseology of the contract are very important. Where different languages are involved (e.g., in different countries), take the necessary steps to make certain that all parties have a common understanding of the agreement.
7. Don't expect to cover everything in the contract that governs the alliance. Build "intelligent flexibility" into the contract. For example, although it is impossible to derive a specific economic value for an asset in a future time period, both parties may agree on a method to be used in valuing the asset at the appropriate time.
8. Take the time to develop a personal relationship with your new partner that will permit unforseen issues to be resolved amicably.

   And last, but certainly not least,
9. Do think about the endgame before entering an alliance, and have an exit clause in your contract.

## Appendix A: About Our Study

Our discussion in this article relies heavily on the lessons that we learned from studying more than two dozen divorces in international alliances. The alliances in this study span several industries, including automotive, pharmaceuticals, computers, computer software, heavy equipment, alcoholic beverages, glass, telecommunications, and retailing. The majority of the alliances were collaborative ventures between U.S. and European firms, or U.S. and Asian companies. The partners in these alliances represented major multinational companies from the United States, Switzerland, France, the United Kingdom, Germany, the Netherlands, Italy, Canada, Australia, Japan, China, South Korea, and Mexico. More than two-thirds of the alliances were production joint ventures and marketing/distributorship arrangements; the other third were licensing ventures and R&D partnerships.

To collect data for this study, we conducted personal interviews of executives of eight partnerships that terminated, and monitored the divorces of several others. The personal interviews were conducted between 1991 and 1994 in the United States, Japan, and South Korea. The executives interviewed included senior managers of the alliance, the partner companies' in-house legal counsels, and key alliance managers in the parent companies.

To help us better understand the legal aspects of terminating an alliance, we also sought the assistance of attorneys in the law firms of Holland and Hart; and Holme, Roberts, and Owen, both located in Denver, Colorado. Both firms have significant and growing international practices. The lawyers that assisted us all have significant experience in negotiating international joint ventures and strategic alliances. One of the attorneys heads her firm's international practice. Another attorney oversees his firm's practice in Mexico and Latin America.

## Notes

1. J. Treece, "Why GM and Daewoo Wound up on the Road to Nowhere," *Business Week,* September 23, 1991, 5.
2. D. Darlin and J. White, "Failed Marriage: GM Venture in Korea Nears End. Betraying Firms' Fond Hopes," *Wall Street Journal,* January 16, 1992, A1.
3. J. Leung, "For China's Foreign Investors the Door Marked Exit Can Be a Tight Squeeze," *Wall Street Journal,* March 12, 1995, A5.
4. Y. Ono, "Borden's Breakup with Meiji Shows How a Japanese Partnership Can Curdle," *Wall Street Journal,* February 21, 1991, B1.
5. D. Fraser, "Vitro and Corning End Venture," *Financial Times,* December 16, 1993.
6. In *Vivo,* "Twixt Cup and Lip," May 1993, 45.
7. B. Wysocki, "Cross-Border Alliances Become Favorite Way to Crack New Markets," *Wall Street Journal,* March 26, 1990, Al/A6.
8. R. Narisetti, "Rubbermaid Brings to End Europe Venture," *Wall Street Journal,* June 1, 1994.
9. J. Leung, *op. cit.*
10. In Vivo, *op. cit.*
11. T. Jackson, "Rover Ownership Contentious to the End," *Financial Times,* February 1, 1994, 20.
12. T. Jackson, *Ibid.*
13. R. Johnson, "Chrysler Nets $205 Million by Halving Stake in Mitsubishi," *Automotive News,* June 29, 1992.
14. J. Bleeke and D. Ernst, *Collaborating to Compete* (New York, NY: John Wiley and Sons, 1993).
15. M. Duerr, "NUMMI at Midlife," in A. Negandhi and M.G. Serapio, Jr. (eds.), *Japanese Direct Investment in the United States: Trends, Developments, and Issues* (Greenwich, CT: JAI Press, 1992).
16. J. Lieb, "Coors Bellies up to Bar," *Denver Post,* March 31, 1994, lC/3C.
17. W. Mooz, *Personal Communication, December* 19, 1994.
18. P. Burrows, "How a Good Partnership Goes Bad," *Electronics Business,* March 30, 1992, 66–90.
19. *Fortune,* "Goodbyes Can Cost Plenty in Europe," April 16, 1992, 16.
20. Holland and Hart, *Outbound Joint Ventures: Business, Legal, and Tax Strategies* (Salt Lake City, UT: Holland and Hart/BYU Center for International Business Education and Research, 1994).
21. Holland and Hart, *Ibid.*
22. W.F. Cascio and M.G. Serapio, Jr., "Human Resource Systems in an International Alliance: The Undoing of a Done Deal?" *Organizational Dynamics,* Winter, 1991, 63–74.

# Reading 3.4

## SAME BED, DIFFERENT DREAMS

### *Working Relationships in Sino-American Joint Ventures*

JAMES P. WALSH, ERPING WANG, AND KATHERINE R. XIN

Mao Zedong died on September 9, 1976. Less than two and one half years later, the Chinese leadership at the Third Plenum of the Eleventh Central Committee announced that China would "open to the outside world" (Pearson, 1991). Notwithstanding years of isolation and a fear of problems that would accompany foreign direct investment (FDI) in China, foreign investment was now seen as a way of invigorating China's sluggish economy. The joint venture form of governance was seen as a particularly attractive way of absorbing foreign capital, advanced technology, management skills and access to export markets, while at the same time, enabling some state control over the attendant negative influences that could accompany such outside influence (Pearson, 1991; Child, 1994). China's potentially huge domestic market proved to be an irresistible lure for outside investors. Table 1 reveals that tens of thousands of FDI projects have been pledged in China since 1979. Notwithstanding the billions dollars of foreign investment in China over the years, we know less than we might imagine about how this money has been put to work within these collaborative enterprises.

The goal of this research is to begin to shed some light on how foreign and local managers view each other and work together in China. In particular, we will focus on the relations among the managers in Sino-American joint ventures. This focus on Sino-American joint ventures does not diminish others' investment interests in China (indeed, as revealed in the Appendix, if one rank-orders total used FDI in China from 1978 to 1996, the United States falls behind Hong Kong/Macao, but ahead of Japan, the United Kingdom, Germany, Canada and Australia as a source of such FDI) but rather, this focus reflects the limitations of our data and as such, our contemporary insight.[1]

Many studies of international joint ventures (IJVs) find their premise and rationale in an acknowledgment that such ventures are unstable and prone to failure (Killing, 1982; Morris & Hergert, 1987), especially IJVs in developing countries (Beamish, 1985). Of course, given the different motives behind the choice of a venture partner (Geringer, 1991) and their creation (Teargarden & Von Glinow, 1991), it is no surprise that the definition of joint venture success and failure itself is quite problematic (Anderson, 1990; Geringer & Hebert, 1991; GomesCasseres, 1987; Osland & Cavusgil, 1996; Yan & Gray, 1995). We know that management practice in China can be difficult and that

**Table 1** Foreign Direct Investment in the People's Republic of China

| *Year* | *Total FDI* | *FDI in Joint-Ventures* | *FDI in Cooperative Operations* | *FDI in Cooperative Developments* | *FDI in Foreign Enterprises* | *Used FDI* | *Used FDI in Joint-Ventures* | *Used FDI in Cooperative Operations* | *Used FDI in Cooperative Development* | *Used FDI in Foreign Enterprises* |
|---|---|---|---|---|---|---|---|---|---|---|
| 1979–1982 | 163.16 (922) | 4.50 (83) | 96.56 (793) | 50.35 (13) | 11.76 (33) | 41.29 | 3.54 | 18.80 | 17.56 | 1.42 |
| 1983 | 57.15 (470) | 6.20 (107) | 16.60 (330) | 33.03 (18) | 1.32 (15) | 20.99 | 2.44 | 7.49 | 9.63 | 1.42 |
| 1984 | 85.09 (856) | 34.25 (741) | 47.63 (1089) | 0.00 (0) | 3.21 (26) | 40.38 | 8.19 | 14.93 | 16.79 | 0.48 |
| 1985 | 174.95 (3073) | 59.87 (1412) | 103.11 (1611) | 10.62 (4) | 1.36 (46) | 48.99 | 17.11 | 17.25 | 14.19 | 0.38 |
| 1986 | 78.84 (1498) | 38.25 (892) | 37.78 (582) | 2.25 (6) | 0.56 (18) | 52.14 | 22.37 | 22.09 | 7.23 | 0.45 |
| 1987 | 96.17 (2233) | 50.56 (1395) | 33.27 (789) | 0.13 (3) | 12.21 (46) | 60.00 | 38.53 | 16.08 | 4.75 | 0.65 |
| 1988 | 115.88 (5945) | 68.56 (3909) | 35.53 (1621) | 1.29 (5) | 10.52 (410) | 69.87 | 43.21 | 17.04 | 4.66 | 4.94 |
| 1989 | 104.02 (5779) | 49.41 (3659) | 20.12 (1179) | 3.79 (10) | 30.72 (931) | 63.00 | 37.84 | 13.97 | 4.31 | 6.89 |
| 1990 | 119.98 (7273) | 49.18 (4091) | 22.81 (1317) | 3.53 (5) | 44.46 (1860) | 63.43 | 34.31 | 12.26 | 4.44 | 12.42 |
| 1991 | 211.62 (12978) | 107.49 (8395) | 37.78 (1778) | 1.63 (10) | 64.83 (2795) | 77.19 | 40.64 | 13.51 | 2.99 | 20.07 |
| 1992 | 975.10 (48764) | 488.66 (34354) | 222.37 (5711) | 0.72 (7) | 263.32 (8692) | 184.66 | 102.59 | 35.60 | 4.19 | 42.28 |
| 1993 | 1651.65 (83437) | 817.76 (54003) | 377.95 (10445) | 4.52 (14) | 451.40 (18975) | 407.81 | 227.48 | 77.64 | 6.28 | 96.43 |
| 1994 | 1006.98 (47549) | 488.62 (27890) | 247.24 (6634) | 2.87 (18) | 267.32 (13007) | 411.26 | 218.41 | 86.72 | 8.26 | 97.87 |
| 1995 | 968.45 (37011) | 421.63 (20455) | 189.11 (4787) | 0.60 (8) | 357.09 (11761) | 398.07 | 202.41 | 79.95 | 6.26 | 109.46 |
| 1996 | 732.76 (24556) | 318.76 (12628) | 142.97 (2849) | 2.93 (17) | 288.10 (9062) | 417.25 | 207.54 | 81.09 | 2.55 | 126.06 |
| Total | 6541.79 | 3003.70 | 1630.81 | 118.26 | 1808.18 | 2356.32 | 1206.59 | 514.40 | 114.09 | 521.21 |

*Notes:* Foreign Direct Investment refers to the total value of foreign capital invested through signed contract agreements that year.
Used FDI refers to the amount of foreign direct investment actually utilized that year.
All values for pledged projects (those in parentheses) are numbers of projects, whereas FDI is expressed US$100,000,000 dollars, adjusted by the Retail Price Index (1996 is the base year).

*Sources:* Various issues of the China Statistical Yearbook and the Almanac of China's Foreign Economic Relations and Trade, 1984–1998.

foreign companies do leave in frustration (Beamish, 1993; Yan, 1998; Yatsko, 1997). Indeed, Table 1 reveals that the number of joint ventures in China peaked at over 54,000 in 1993. They have been declining ever since. Three years later, their numbers were cut by more than 75 percent. In fact, we now see an investment shift away from joint ventures and toward wholly-owned foreign enterprises (The joy of being single, 1998; Vanhonacker, 1997). That said, our focus here is not to predict which foreign companies will stay or leave, realize their profit or market share expectations, achieve their learning objectives, efficiently adjust their numbers of expatriate managers, shift their equity commitments over time, or examine other plausible indicators of performance. Rather, we want to examine the day-to-day managerial life in these joint ventures. Regardless of each side's discrete objectives, we believe that the ability of the foreign and local managers to effectively work together is a necessary condition for success, however defined. In Pearson's (1991, p. 177) words, "Chinese managers and officials, and foreign managers, often expressed that success of their ventures depended on the relationship between the two sides, particularly trust (chengyi) and cooperation (peihe [or perhaps hezuo]). . . ." Our goal is to take a closer look at this attribution and examine the relationships among Chinese and American managers in Sino-American joint ventures.

Our observation that we know less than we think do about management in China may strike some as odd. Indeed, China has served recently as a frequent focus of inquiry, for both practice-oriented research and theory-driven investigations. Looking at the work grounded in organization and management experience in China, we know something about how multinational firms choose to enter China (Pan, 1996, 1997; Pan & Tse, 1996; Tse, Pan, & Au, 1997), how to conduct the JV negotiations (Eiteman, 1990), how the relationship between the parents affects the control of a joint venture (Yan & Gray, 1994), and how the boards of directors in these JVs function (Bjorkman, 1995) and even which joint ventures seem to be the most successful (Hu & Chen, 1996). We also know that managing human resource management systems across the two cultures is problematic (Von Glinow & Teargarden, 1988); more specifically, managing the reward systems can be particularly difficult (Chen, 1995). It is no surprise that the way an internationally diverse labor force is managed can affect JV employees' job satisfaction (Leung, Smith, Wang, & Sun, 1996). Finally, we are aware that Chinese negotiation styles differ from those in the West (Adler, Brahm, & Graham, 1992; Kirkbride, Tang, & Westwood, 1991; Shenkar & Ronen, 1987; Ting-Toomey, Gao, Trubisky, Yang, Kim, Lin, & Nishida, 1991; Tse, Francis, & Walls, 1994), that decision making, communication and personnel practices differ (Child & Markoczy, 1993), that notions of ideal management practices differ (Baird, Lyles, & Wharton, 1990) but may be evolving toward American ideals (Wang, 1986), and that conflict within and between American and Chinese managers is experienced differently (Doucet & Jehn, 1997) and that when resolved, this successful conflict resolution is linked to satisfaction with the venture itself (Lin & Germain, 1998). Case studies of joint venture successes and struggles are also available (Goldenberg, 1989; Mann, 1989).[2] Indeed, we now know enough to feel comfortable offering prescriptions for doing business in China (Davidson, 1987; Earley, 1994; Hendryx, 1986; Shenkar, 1990; Strutton & Pelton, 1997; Weiss & Bloom, 1990).[3]

All of that said, our understanding of organization and management in China is still preliminary. After reviewing nearly all of the research conducted on management in China, Child (1994, p. 279) concluded: "The process of managing Sino-foreign joint ventures, and indeed international strategic alliances in general, remains one of the least understood aspects of international management." What is missing? Three recent reviews of the JV literature provide a clue. Setting up their case study analysis of upward influence in an IJV, Lyles and Reger (1993, p. 383) argued that "no research has focused on JV management issues from the perspective of JVs." Olk and Earley (1995, p. 224) would likely agree. They asserted that "most theories that address international joint ventures focus almost exclusively on organizational and industrial characteristics and do not incorporate an explanation of individual difference" (p. 224). And most recently, Pearce (1997, p. 204) observed that "researchers have not yet begun to explore systematically the performance implications of management processes within the JV firm (emphasis in the original)." We believe that a focus on the daily managerial experiences of American and Chinese joint ventures, as revealed in their own words, will do much to bring us closer to an understanding of how to best manage Sino-foreign joint ventures. Given the financial and political investment in China's reform initiative, the stakes are very high. Our inductive study of Sino-American joint venture management is an attempt to attenuate the risks associated with these investments.

## Methods

### Overview

We created a Sino-American joint venture to study Sino-American joint ventures. Our research team is a particular manifestation of a longstanding partnership between the University of Michigan and the Chinese Academy of Sciences. The team comprises an American professor, a Chinese professor, and a bi-cultural professor who was born and raised in the People's Republic of China, educated in both the PRC and the US, and who now is jointly employed by an American and a Chinese university. With only a few exceptions, investigators from both research teams interviewed our respondents in their native languages.

We began by interviewing representatives from the US and Chinese governments and various local business experts to provide some contextual insight for our study. Next, we identified six Sino-American JVs that represented a wide variety of business interests in China and secured their commitments to have us interview their senior managers. Finally, after we analyzed these interview data, we identified four other Sino-American JVs and interviewed their senior managers. We asked these managers the same basic questions as we did with the first group of managers but then took another step and shared our preliminary conclusions with them, and asked for their reactions.

### Sample

Our background interviews with those familiar with US business interests were conducted with US embassy analysts, American Chamber of Commerce officers, and the head of a US-China trade association. Our understanding of China's business interests was informed by discussions with local journalists, union and labor officials, think tank representatives, and representatives from an entrepreneurial association and the Beijing city government. While we did not formally analyze these interviews, they were important to our understanding of the institutional business environment in China. Our ten JVs included firms representing a variety of business interests. They include a pharmaceutical, food service, financial services and a telecommunications company, as well as two industrial products firms, two high technology companies, and two consumer goods manufacturers. In all, we interviewed sixteen managers representing the American firms' interests and seventeen managers representing the Chinese interests in these ten JVs.

### Interview Protocols

We employed a semi-structured interview approach. After collecting descriptive information about the history of the JV, the management team and their own career histories, we asked each respondent a number of open-ended questions. In particular, we asked them to identify: (a) any problems they have had working with managers from the other country; (b) any particular successes that mark their working relationships; (c) any puzzles about working with each other; and (d) any pleasant surprises they encountered in their time together. And again, in the interviews with the second group of four companies, we asked our respondents to respond to the tentative conclusions we drew from our first round of interviews.

In all but four cases (where we relied upon our interview notes), the interviews were tape recorded, transcribed in their native language, and then translated into either English or Mandarin. Our bi-cultural professor resolved any translation ambiguities.

## Results

We approached the analysis of our data in a manner prescribed by Glaser and Strauss (1967) and Miles and Huberman (1984). We cycled through our interview notes over and over again until we discovered a set of mutually exclusive categories that we believe represent these data. We saw seven themes in these interviews. These themes capture the positive and negative impressions that the managers hold of each other in the areas of expertise and effectiveness, effort, management style, allegiance, time horizons, standards, and trust. We will share many of the words of these managers that give form to these themes. We will then reveal the puzzles and surprises that we heard. And finally, we will note some of the reflections that the managers in our second group of joint ventures offered about these seven themes.

We will discover that the results of this research are somewhat disconcerting. The views that the American and Chinese managers hold of each other are rather negative. Starkly put, the Americans view their Chinese partners as lazy (or hard working with dubious motives); self-interested and under-educated; unable to make a decision, assume responsibility, take a risk or delegate; unaware of what quality means to contemporary business practice; and narrowly focused on the short term. Not surprisingly, a sense of mistrust or distrust can hang over these relationships. The Chinese, on the other hand, seem to appreciate that their American collaborators bring valuable technological and managerial expertise to their country but recognize that they can be arrogant and condescending when they do so. And while they appreciate the Americans' managerial objectives, they wonder why the Americans need to be so strict, martial and unyielding in their approach. Like the Americans, they worry that the time horizons of their partners are too short, in this case worrying that their expatriate colleagues are inclined to focus on performance objectives that will be met only while they are living in China. Nevertheless, the Chinese managers appear to have some empathy for why the Americans act and feel the way they do. They acknowledge that it can be very difficult for foreigners to come to terms with life in China. With this overview as context, we will examine some of the specific comments that give form to this summary.

### Positives and Negatives

#### *Expertise and Effectiveness*

The comments about expertise, capability and managerial effectiveness were complementary. The Americans were not particularly impressed with their Chinese counterparts and the Chinese were not particularly impressed with their colleagues' views of them. The comments can be rather blunt. Here are the words of two U.S. managers on this topic.

> I haven't met, frankly, any Chinese manager in any company, in any joint venture in China that is capable of doing his job. In my experience, in two and one half years, there is no such animal.

> The Chinese keep saying that we need to do it the "Chinese way." There is no "Chinese way" in building or designing [our product]. You've got to learn; you've got to internalize; you've got to implement; and then you can improve or modify. Okay? Industry is science. It has nothing to do with Mao Zedong, the Qing Dynasty or Chinese history. This is science. One plus one equals two. You can argue about the history of the world all you want but one plus one has to equal two.

The Chinese managers noticed these kinds of perceptions. The following quotes are representative of the Chinese managers' opinions about these kinds of American attitudes.

> The Chinese have an old saying, "If the vinegar bottle is half full, it makes the most noise." This means that people who think they know Chinese culture, but they only understand a little bit of Chinese culture or they only know the surface of Chinese culture, tend to be those who make the most complaints about the Chinese people. Those are the people who are arrogant and hard to deal with.

> Some Americans, not all Americans, are full of air. They are very arrogant. They are the only ones who know how to do things.

These kinds of comments suggest that the effectiveness of a national policy on FDI and the accompanying hope of transferring Western management capability to China may be very dependent on the day-to-day life experiences in these collaborative enterprises. The following Chinese managers' comments about their American partners also affirm that daily managerial life can be quite difficult in China.

> The expats become dumb or lost after coming to China. Actually, the expats are very smart but after they joined the Chinese system, they almost cannot function or show their talents and expertise. Even if they have excellent experience, they cannot do anything. I guess there are two reasons for this. The first is personal. They cannot adapt to the Chinese operating system and are unable to find a clue to get the system to work. They always stay outside the system and rely on the Chinese to do the job for them. The second difficulty is language. I think language is a very big barrier.

> It is useless to mention the positive impact of expats on JVs. The Chinese have long had a concept that the expats are not so talented. The systems are different. They come here but they cannot adapt to it. They cannot display their full potential.

Interestingly, both sides seemed to be aware of their own limitations. An American general manager observed that the Americans who are willing to move to China for a few years might not be the most able managers within the firm.

> Realistically, the biggest problem is with the people who are willing to come here. People who are willing to be released [from normal duty] may not be the strongest, even in their own home country. So, a lot of these people came. I think they all try hard. But, their ability can be limited.

The Chinese managers' views of their own limitations ranged from a simple acknowledgment of their limitations, to a sense of foreboding about their potential to develop, to a more hopeful sense that with experience, their colleagues can be every bit as talented as any other world-class manager.

> The things we learned in college are not the same as what they learned; there are many things we cannot manage.

> The weakness we need to overcome is laziness and inertia. We need to learn the management skill and spirit from others. Habit is a very strong thing. The Chinese always think that their styles are good and that it is useless to learn from others.

> We try to localize. We try to use more local Chinese, but you know China has just been opened up for less than 15 years. Our new managers are very intelligent and very enthusiastic, but they just don't have international experience. They just don't have the international experience and exposure to make big strategic decisions. I'm Chinese. It's really a realistic concern.

*Effort*

The question of effort generally came up for the Americans. There were stark differences of opinion on this issue. The positive comments could not have been more positive, while the negative comments could not have been more negative.

> The labor force is all screwed up. On the one hand, people want to work in joint ventures. On the other hand, they have to work harder. And God forbid that anyone should put in eight hours of work.

> They are not committed to hard work. This applies to anyone from the "state owned enterprises generation." There is a big difference from ones that were raised in that generation and the modern generation. In the state owned enterprise, five hours a week of hard work may be reasonable. But five hours of hard work is not appropriate for our business.

Contrast these general managers' comments with two of their peers' views.

> I would say that the individuals are very eager to work. Very, very motivated. Much more attentive at times than some of the individuals in the U.S. . . . and that's been a real pleasure.

> I'm very proud of the people we have here. They really care about the company. Frankly, when I see how they work and the commitment they have, I worry sometimes for the United States. They are unbelievable.

*Management Style*

The Americans and Chinese had clear opinions about each other's management styles. The Americans were not particularly impressed with the practices they encountered. The Chinese seemed to appreciate what the Americans were trying to accomplish but they were not very comfortable with their approach. We will begin by reviewing what the Americans had to say about Chinese decision making and risk-taking behavior. Then, we will review what the Chinese managers said about working under an American management style.

*Chinese Decision Making*

The Americans' views of the Chinese approach to decision making and decision responsibility were very negative.

> Typically, managers who have gone through the Cultural Revolution are psychologically twisted. You have people who have done nothing their whole life but be told how to do every aspect of their life—when to eat, where to live, where they work, what they do. The decision making process in the Chinese managers' minds is non-existent. They wait for instructions. And I don't know how to correct that. Not in my lifetime anyway.

> The Chinese mentality is "Oh, I don't want to take a responsibility. You, you as boss—you take the responsibility."

> Nobody here wants to take responsibility. They say that "everybody takes care of this" but unless you have accountability, responsibility and feedback, you get what you bargain for . . . which, most of the time, is nothing.

*Chinese Risk Taking Behavior*

The issue of risk aversion came up a number of times in our interviews. The American managers were not impressed with the initiative they encountered in their new colleagues.

> The Chinese managers are reluctant to talk because they all think it's something that's gonna be used against them.

> The mentality is that the best and safest way to avoid making a mistake is to do nothing. This idea goes beyond the Communist Party; it goes back thousands of years. It is ingrained in the culture. That's why people don't want to take risks, have their names in print, or take assignments. It's safer. You won't get fired if you don't do anything but you will get fired if you make a mistake.

*American Management Styles*

The Chinese managers seemed to appreciate the broad administrative approach that the Americans employed.

> They are clearly managing people objectively . . . look at this fact objectively rather than look at the personal factor. The managers will assess employees purely and completely on their work performance, achievement and contribution. Interpersonal relations are relatively equal. In the mainland, interpersonal relations are the major conflict, which influences their work. This is quite unique. It creates a harmonious workplace.

> The foreign manager stresses efficiency. This is worth the study of Chinese managers. The enterprise does not support idle people; what it stresses is work efficiency. Chinese enterprises could learn from this. This has left deepest impression on my mind.

On the other hand, our Chinese respondents did react to the details of the American management approach. A number of people expressed misgivings about how the Americans implement their philosophies.

> They are exceptionally martial in their decision, believing that whatever they say goes; it cannot be altered and is simply right.

> To take some simple Western managerial forms and mechanistically and rigidly apply them to Chinese management will not work . . . especially a strict attitude toward the workers.

> Under the American method, your position is threatened; you can be dismissed or fired. After you have exhausted your efforts in a position, if they've discovered that you are not suitable, they won't employ you anymore. They manage the enterprise through this threat of dismissal, rather than by encouraging you to do more work.

These misgivings were not universally shared, however. One manager liked the transparency of this approach.

> I think the managerial methods of the American managers are fairly casual, not so strict as those of Japanese companies. In U.S. companies, as long as you take good care of matters, that will pretty much do it. There really isn't any feeling of oppression when you go into an American company.

*Allegiance*

The issue of allegiance came up in our interviews. For the Americans, it took the form of a question about the relationship between self-interest and a concern for the organization. Our American respondents were sometimes wary of their Chinese counterparts' motivations. Interestingly, the Chinese managers spoke of the importance of placing the needs of the organization above self-interest. We will hear from the Americans first.

> An employee maturity issue spans all JVs. Can they really look out for the company's interests ahead of their own? In most cases, no. They cannot. I've seen it time and time again here. I've challenged them with a lot of issues regarding employee benefits, trying to get their feedback, and every time they come back to me . . . it's something that's more favorable to them, personally. They can't take on really increasing responsibilities—in terms of company interest, general management, senior management—until they demonstrate a kind of employee maturity that I have never seen.

> They typically don't share information. Information is power to the Chinese. They worry much more about political relationship in the organization—not as much about the organizational goals and how to achieve them.

> They've got a term for it—jumping. They jump from job to job. There's no loyalty to the company. Money is everything.

> What I see is that people make decisions in their own interest. I'm not sure that an individual in

> the United States wouldn't do the exact same thing.

One Chinese manager spoke of the dual focus on the self and the firm, while another spoke about how the firm's practices mitigated self-interest. Finally, one Chinese manager alerted us to be wary of those who profess to serve the interests of those beyond the boundaries of the firm.

> The things that I manage to do will allow me to expand myself—one purpose is to provide service for society's enterprises and another is to expand myself.

> In serving as a manager of a company, the most important thing is to see if one can connect one's own fate with that of the enterprise. Whenever one does something, one gives highest priority to the interests of the company—this is of the utmost importance. I believe that once one arrives at a company, one should act with the interests of the company in mind and exhaust one's efforts on behalf of the company's development.

> The last means of "defense" for those managers who fail is to announce that they love their country. Once they find themselves unsuccessful, they will say how they have protected the benefits of their companies and country (the state-owned enterprises) and how they refused their partner's unreasonable requests.

*Time Horizons*

The problem of short time horizons came up in both sets of interviews. With one exception, the Americans and the Chinese thought the others were too limited in their thinking. The first three comments are from Americans.

> They don't plan ahead. They're not very good planners. They basically deal with crises as they come up.

> They've got a planned economy that would do very little planning. They don't plan. They are very short-term oriented. They don't know where they are going.

> These guys are originally farmers. They don't see beyond the next crop year. That's really a problem. And although they say they understand the long term, I don't think that they really do. They never live with the long term in mind. It's always, "What can I get from you this year?"

One Chinese manager expressed a concern about the limited time horizons of expatriate managers.

> Expatriates are on 3-year or 5-year term. So they usually do not think long-term, other than three or five years. They do not want to build up a foundation for five years later. They want to get their results, especially short-term results. There is a very big impact on the business. For us, we may stay here longer. When we do something or make some decisions, usually we have to care what the long-term impact is. You can get some short-term positive result but the long-term may be negative. For the expatriates, sometimes they do not care much about the long-term.

One American manager seemed to echo this same sentiment.

> One Strong part of a local person is that they have a longer-term strategy. They are looking forward to working here for perhaps the rest of their life. They have a family. They have houses. They've got mortgages. They've got things that everybody has. They've got to come here and work for the next forty years! They look at this job as a long-term commitment. If you hired a non-local person, that is not the case.

*Standards*

The question of quality and standards came up in our interviews. The Americans seemed to think that the Chinese standards were too low, while the Chinese were simply coming to terms with the Americans' concerns in this area.

> Quality, they have absolutely no idea what we're talking about. They don't see why it matters. In China, especially with our partner, chabuduo—which means 'almost'—is okay. And the word I always tell an employee that I hate the most, I don't want to hear, is chabuduo. They just don't, absolutely don't understand.

> In China, there tends to be what I call a quick any dirty attitude. Let's do the job, get it done, and get it done quick. As opposed to getting it done thoroughly, completely and with 100% quality. You can see it in the construction of the houses. On a macro scale, the house looks beautiful. But if you look at the quality of how the

door was hung or how they put caulking around the bathtubs, it's just full of imperfections. Nobody took the time to do these details. In lots of cases this introduces problems that you have to go back and fix. I think it is a problem here.

[My spouse and I] believe that if you stay in China too long as a manager, you begin to settle for mediocrity. You lose your sense of standards.

The Chinese managers seemed to appreciate the logic for a focus on total quality management but at least one manager seemed bemused by it.

Deming's entire program of Total Quality Management has been brought into our company, Periodic training in it is carried out. This, too, is a main reason why our company has been successful.

What was astonishing is how Americans in the food products industry have such a high level of concern over quality. I had no sense of this when I was working at a hotel and so, I had a deep impression upon coming here. For instance, if a sack of flour coming into port has bugs on the outside, [our boss] still has it sent back.

*Trust*

The issue of trust appears as a follow-up to the question of self-interest and as a topic of concern in its own right. Suspicion seems to hang over these relationships. Views of the Americans will follow a compendium of views we heard about the Chinese.

Because China was poor for so long . . . individual mid-level managers . . . we don't trust them to put the company's interests in front of their interests. Our observations indicate that the local managers, especially the young ones, tend to seek their personal gains first in any decisions made with the company.

You know, we all get undressed in front of the Chinese everyday. They see everything. The Chinese show nothing. And it's not only to the foreigners. They don't show anything to each other.

There's a lot of mistrust between the Chinese and the foreigners.

People in the United States are trained to have a "play fair" mentality. It is not the same here. It is not uncommon for someone to say, "Oh, we're negotiating with your competitor—perhaps we forgot to mention it."

I was very trusting in the beginning. I am very cautious now.

The Chinese managers seemed well aware of the possibility that their American counterparts did not trust them entirely.

The Chinese side places greater emphasis on the management of people, entrusting a person to do a job and then judging his work abilities on the basis of the results. The foreign side takes suspicion of everyone as their premise, and formulates procedures of internal control.

Basically, he [the general manager] trusts us. But all the more, he does not put his mind at ease. As for the majority of those on the Chinese side, they are earnest and sincere about their work. And so, his vigilance is unnecessary.

Look at our top management team, 85% or 80% of them—the people who really have a say in the business directions of [our JV] are all expatriates. They don't trust the Chinese. They will never put us in a position where we can make policy decisions. That's where I want to be. So no matter what the President is saying in all those meetings about promoting local Chinese, that's all a bunch of nonsense. Don't believe that. They will never put us in a position that we'll make strategic decisions. Period. Case closed.

One Chinese manager's comment may shed light on why trust can be so difficult to engender in this context.

[It is difficult] to understand the behavior of the local people. Sometimes no is not really no; sometimes yes is not really yes. Sometimes the Chinese say no but they don't know why the Chinese say no. So it takes two or three years for them to understand the hidden agenda or the language behind something. So it is very difficult for them to understand.

Puzzles and Surprises

Our own surprise was that we heard less about puzzles and surprises than we expected, especially among our Chinese respondents. That may be because admitting to such insights is akin to revealing some personal limitations. Nevertheless, we did hear some. In general, the American's puzzles speak to questions about particular workplace practices and impressions of the Chinese. One Chinese manager was puzzled by the American's management style. The surprises connect to attributions about each other. The surprises are more positive than not.

*Puzzles*

A number of day-to-day matters puzzled the Americans. For example, one person wondered why he never saw a secretary in a state-owned enterprise. Closer to the focus of this research, some aspects of their Chinese colleagues' behavior puzzled them as well.

> I'm not sure it's a puzzle. You just get used to it. But everything here is very dogmatic. As much as they say they break the rules and that relationships matter, they are very dogmatic in the way they do certain things. And that's very interesting. But it's not puzzling because that's the nature of the culture here.

> I think the greatest shock I've had since I got here is the awareness that the Oriental thought process is so different from ours. It is 180 degrees different. I still fail to understand how they get to a solution to a problem. And I may never understand how they get there. While we in the West tend to go automatically to the heart of a problem to identify it quickly, they're all around it. It's different. And I don't understand how they get to the same conclusion that I probably will. They first worry about a thousand reasons why you can't do it before they focus on the reasons that you can. This is 180 degrees different from my whole logic pattern in my life. They worry about the "can'ts" versus the "cans" first. And I find it very interesting. And that's a shock. I've never had that in working in 30 countries outside of Asia.

> I'm just not really sure what motivates our partner. In a joint venture, it's easier to see. I give 'em money, I give 'em benefits, I give 'em more responsibility, and there's the sense of belonging and things you can identify that are normal to us. People can prioritize what makes them tick at work. But the joint venture partner, I don't understand what motivates them to want to be part of this partnership. Because they don't get the money. What makes them tick? Why are they here every day going through this and wanting to be a part of all this?

> How do you get people to go beyond the minimum? Right now, we are trying to connect salary with performance. I don't know if it will work.

A Chinese manager's puzzle was grounded in an assumption about what constitutes punitive managerial behavior.

> A puzzle? It relates to how top level expatriate managers intervene in the work of lower level Chinese staff. For example, supervisors should report to the department managers, but the upper level managers sometimes intervene in the work of the supervisors directly. They would later say that they misunderstood the process. They didn't mean to punish someone.

*Surprises*

Next, let's consider the surprises. In a few cases, the Americans spoke of disappointments. One manager reported a growing sense of mistrust seeping into his relationships and another told a story of a broken promise. Another said simply, "the worst surprise is just the amount of time it takes to get something done here." Beyond that, the comments were all about pleasant surprises. One Chinese manager spoke about the Americans being more open that they expected. Another focused on our commonalities. We will begin with the Americans' words.

> I would say that the individuals are very eager to work.

> My [expatriate] manager was away recently and so I worked with a local individual. I am really surprised at what he came up with. It makes me wonder whether our managers are giving them a chance. Maybe we are not giving them enough credit. Or maybe we are not testing them enough, or not motivating them enough.

> My pleasant surprise is the sense of unity that Chinese employees have. There have been one or two exceptions—they don't accept people that are physically unattractive or have any kind of physical disability. I had an employee with a hearing impairment that they never accepted. But beyond that, anyone who is quote unquote normal in their view, they have a real sense of unity. To me it's unparalleled. I've just never experienced that in the U.S. We're

much more competitive and cutthroat and individual.

A Chinese manager reflected on the question and said that "I can't think of any particularly perplexing, unintelligible or difficult-to-understand issues." When pressed about why, he shared the following observation about our commonalities. Another manager invoked human nature as a source of common bonds.

> In basic terms, no matter what the cultural backgrounds of the Chinese and Western sides may be, no matter what their managerial methods are, there is still a most basic point of commonality. That is, the enterprise must develop and make a profit. The production capacity of the enterprise must be raised. In simple terms, the enterprise must be made to make a profit, to make money—this is the same no matter who is involved in the joint venture. With such common ground, many contradictions can be eliminated.

> I do not feel any surprise. They are also human beings. They have emotions and need friends. I do not see anything special.

### Reactions to These Observations

We were fortunate to be able to learn how some American and Chinese managers reacted to these comments. We are reminded of Karl Weick's now famous dictum, "I'll know what I think when I see what I say." We wanted to share our picture of these working relationships with a group of managers to discover if they would agree with these revealed sentiments when they were presented to them directly. Perhaps not surprisingly, we received a few strong reactions and many equivocal ones. One American general manager said that we were "one standard deviation too negative" here. He said that if we were to write a book on the pitfalls of going to China, these kinds of comments would be useful to keep in mind. On the other hand, he said that joint ventures like his own (which he described as "very high on the up side") "won't sell newspapers." He did not believe that observers of business ventures in China were very interested in hearing success stories. The strongest reaction of all came from an American manager who rescinded his offer to let us interview the Chinese managers in his joint venture after hearing these kinds of comments. Interestingly, when answering the questions himself, he sometimes spoke rather harshly of his experience with the Chinese business community (e.g., noting the lack of a Chinese work ethic and a sense of fair play, a history of broken promises, and their inability to support a decision once they endorsed it). Nevertheless, when he heard that some Chinese managers had negative things to say about Americans, he became quite upset. A comment about broken career promises particularly offended him. When he was told that some Chinese managers complained about Americans making false promises about their future, he sat up in his chair visibly offended and said, "I found that reversed. The reverse is true!" Our interview ended minutes later.

The comments about expertise were the only ones that went unchallenged. The Americans acknowledge that the Chinese can be well educated, but often not in ways that are practically useful in a joint venture. They also pointed out that, unfortunately, the Americans can be overbearing and arrogant. The Chinese managers recognized some of their own deficiencies but also noted that the comments about condescension were on target too. All of the other summary comments were simultaneously endorsed, challenged, and qualified.

The comments about Chinese decision making illustrated the kinds of responses we received. Speaking about the Chinese's seeming inability to make a decision, we heard from Americans that yes, "Americans think that the Chinese do not want to decide things and even if they do, they will not stick to it." Another said that yes, "they have different agendas; they sign up for a decision but won't support it." Yet, on the other hand, another American manager said, "I disagree with this almost entirely. I have no fear or hesitation whatsoever. I trust the judgment and decision making of my managers. They want more power that I can and am willing to give them. So it is not a question of trying to avoid responsibility. They want more; it is difficult to try to get the responsibility to give it to them." As for the Chinese, when speaking to the Americans' view of them, one endorsed them and said that "Yes, we are not as decisive on issues." Another qualified them and said that this is true but only for "the people in those very typical and old state-owned organizations, not the joint ventures, not the foreign-owned companies. For the young manager, I disagree with the statement." And still another Chinese manager offered a very different interpretation of these attributions. He noted that this kind of decision avoidance behavior can be traced to American management styles. He argued that "it depends on the company culture. If somebody makes a decision and it is wrong, is he punished? If so, a lot of people will be hesitant to make decisions. In a group decision, nobody is really responsible . . . otherwise they may be put in jail, fired, or get a very big punishment."

In all, this reflective exercise was useful in assessing the veracity of these insights. At one level, no one was surprised by any of these comments. Everyone could imagine that these comments were articulated by both American and Chinese managers in joint ventures. We appear to have tapped into some truths about these working relationships. That said, our second group of managers was quite free in offering their own interpretations and qualifications of these comments. This leaves us encouraged by the possibility that we might have discovered underlying qualities that define these working relationships, but also cautious about making too much of them. Therein lies both the attraction and the perhaps limitation of this kind of intensive interview-based investigation. We now know much more about how Chinese and American managers work together in Sino-American joint ventures but we also know much less than we might like. Subsequent research will be needed to investigate both how these perceptions are formed and how they may affect the operation of the joint ventures itself.

## Discussion

An old saying in China, "same bed, different dreams," may foreshadow the kinds of sentiments we discovered in this research. The two partners in the joint venture "bed" have very different dreams. These different dreams may fuel the kinds of negative perceptions that we found here. As we noted earlier, the Chinese typically want foreign capital (in the form of foreign investment and export revenue) and both technological and managerial expertise. The Americans want a foothold in what they see as an enormous emerging domestic market and, of course, profit. One Chinese manager spoke of the common dream for profit and how its joint pursuit could help resolve conflict and contradiction. Our results suggest, however, that their different goals (or "dreams") may contribute to problems between the two management groups. Combine a high stakes and a culturally challenging overseas assignment with basic Western attribution processes, add the Chinese partner's manifest desire for managerial expertise, and you have a recipe for Americans making condescending person attributions about their Chinese colleagues. The social psychology of this phenomenon is certainly not unique to the China setting. Rather, we believe that the circumstances in China will trigger these kinds of person perceptions. Moreover, the circumstances may make it particularly difficult to change these perceptions once they form. The commercial consequences of this phenomenon are unknown.

By all accounts, life for a Westerner in China can be unsettling. It can be full of frustration and exasperation, as well as mystery and magic (Holm, 1990). Managers enter this country in a very visible way. They embody their company's very high expectations for its future in China's emerging market. They also enter knowing that they have little margin for error or time to make their presence known. China's business environment is growing more competitive by the day and, of course, they know that their overseas assignment is time bound. What happens when they confront their inevitable business difficulties? Social psychology tells us that they will be quick to make person attributions for troublesome behaviors and circumstances (Gilbert & Malone, 1995). That is, they will be quick to blame the Chinese people for their business problems (whether this attribution is correct or not is another matter, our point is that other attribution options are unlikely to be considered). And just who are these "Chinese people"? Most likely, they are their partners and coworkers. China's manifest goal of inviting American and other foreign managers to come to China with their much needed state-of-the-art technological and managerial acumen only contributes to these attributions. This kind of formal policy aspiration exacerbates these growing negative person attributions. It buttresses the foreigner's sense that their Chinese collaborators are deficient in some important ways. Thus, a seductive vicious circle can emerge. The Americans nervously blame the Chinese managers for their shortcomings and then have this perception reinforced when they are told that they have been invited to China precisely to remediate their Chinese partners' business deficiencies. In time, the American's perceptions can harden into an unyielding worldview. The circle is broken when the Chinese managers have a (perhaps unexpected) chance to showcase their talents (recall the words of one general manager who spoke of his surprise when he discovered his colleague's initiative and stellar performance—"It makes me wonder whether our managers are giving them a chance. Maybe we are not giving them enough credit."

The Chinese managers' seeming patience with the Americans' attributions and attitudes may reflect a pragmatic orientation, whereby they must take the "bad" (the Americans' attitudes) with the "good" (American capital and expertise). However, recent work in social psychology suggests that East Asians are more likely to be attentive to situational factors than Westerners when making attributions

(Choi, Nisbett, & Norenzayan, 1998). The Chinese may be psychologically predisposed to examine the Americans' situational context and so, develop some empathy for the difficult setting they find themselves in. The Chinese managers may be less likely to make unabashed negative person attributions toward the Americans as a result.

The discussion is speculative at this point. Subsequent research is needed to examine these sorts of plausible inferences. One problem with this kind of interview-based inquiry is that we have no way of knowing if these perceptions are "one standard deviation too negative" or not. A large-scale investigation of intercultural person perceptions in a Sino-foreign business context would give us the answer to such a question. Our work tells us that an examination of expertise, effort, management style, allegiance, time horizons, standards and trust would be a good place to begin. The next step is to investigate such perceptions in a wide variety of business contexts in China. Of course, it will be critically important to link the investigation of managerial relationships to measures of the success or failure of the collaborative venture itself. We know that doing management research in international joint ventures is some of the most difficult work we attempt to do in our field (Parkhe, 1993). We also know that the return on billions of dollars of foreign investment, as well as the economic and political future of China itself, may hinge on the ability of managers from various countries to work well together in China. We cannot shy away from subsequent investigations of these relationships simply because the work is difficult. As we mentioned at the beginning of the paper, the stakes are simply too high.

## Doing Business in China: The Search for Common Ground in Unfamiliar Terrain

The question to consider now is just what our interview findings imply for business practice in China today. Do we have any basis here to offer prescriptive guidance? We believe that the answer is yes, but before we suggest what form this counsel might take, we need to consider the costs and benefits of acting on the results of our study. The costs would mount if we discover in subsequent research that the sentiments revealed here are unusually negative and only rarely held. If we assume a great many managers hold these kinds of beliefs when they do not, then we risk insulting, if not alienating, the managers who hold more positive views of their colleagues and business life in China. The benefits of acting now, of course, will be apparent if these kinds of beliefs turn out to be prevalent in China. We believe that the benefits of taking action to limit the pernicious effects of negative person perceptions will outweigh the possible costs of insulting those who already recognize that such beliefs can form in China. Addressing the problem once it exists is rather straightforward. Preventing its occurrence in the first place is another matter.

In 1982, Baruch Fischhoff discussed ways to help individuals with a variety of judgment biases. The approach to take depends upon whether the individual is seen as perfectible or incorrigible. If the person is seen as perfectible, then the prescribed approach is to warn the person of the problem, describe it in detail, and provide feedback about the person's particular manifestation of the problem. Training can then be offered to correct the problem. If the person is seen as incorrigible, then the alternatives are either to live with the biases and their consequences or to simply replace the individual who manifests the problem. That broad counsel seems appropriate here.

Our interview results can be used to warn managers that such perceptions exist. The results may even begin to offer a plausible description of the person perception problem itself. Readers can ask themselves whether or not they and their colleagues hold similar views. If the perceptions are present and false (and so, reflect a person perception bias), then the views need to be ameliorated. In this case, the next steps would be to document the nature of such views in the JV, provide everyone with feedback and evidence that shows their limitations or inaccuracy, and then devise a training program to correct them. On the other hand, if these perceptions are found to be accurate, then the training intervention must address the sources of these perceptions that lie beyond the psychology of the managers themselves. Training has always been seen as a key to effective JV management (Black & Mendenhall, 1990). Such training simply needs to take into account the possibility that these kinds of pernicious attitudes can develop quickly in China.

We believe that leaders can build effective managerial relationships by intervening in multiple ways. At the broadest level, the JV parents need to emphasize the shared strategic intent and so, build common interests and establish a foundation for trust. In this way, the parents will build the common ground that one Chinese manager argued can help "resolve contradictions." Within the JV itself, it is important to focus on reward systems. Tying incentives to the adoption of any new management initiative (for example, a quality program) is an obvious way to facilitate its implementation. Beyond that, providing

**Appendix** Sources of Foreign Direct Investment in the People's Republic of China

| | *Hong Kong and Macau* | | | *United States* | | | *Japan* | | | *United Kingdom* | | |
|---|---|---|---|---|---|---|---|---|---|---|---|---|
| *Year* | *Pledged FDI* | *Used FDI* | *Pledged Projects* | *Pledged FDI* | *Used FDI* | *Pledged Projects* | *Pledged FDI* | *Used FDI* | *Pledged Projects* | *Pledged FDI* | *Used FDI* | *Pledged Projects* |
| 1978–1982 | 130.19 | N/A | N/A | 13.53 | N/A | N/A | 30.45 | N/A | N/A | 0.60 | N/A | N/A |
| 1983 | 21.18 | N/A | 482 | 15.77 | N/A | 32 | 3.13 | N/A | 52 | 10.06 | N/A | 17 |
| 1984 | 69.81 | 24.01 | 1870 | 5.30 | 8.22 | 62 | 6.52 | 7.22 | 138 | 0.42 | 3.15 | 4 |
| 1985 | 121.92 | 28.19 | 2631 | 33.98 | 10.53 | 100 | 13.89 | 9.29 | 127 | 1.30 | 2.09 | 8 |
| 1986 | 40.31 | 31.49 | 1155 | 14.66 | 8.76 | 102 | 5.84 | 5.59 | 94 | 1.20 | 0.75 | 8 |
| 1987 | 51.19 | 41.44 | 1785 | 8.87 | 6.82 | 104 | 7.80 | 5.70 | 113 | 0.65 | 0.13 | 12 |
| 1988 | 78.38 | 45.83 | 4771 | 8.09 | 5.16 | 269 | 6.04 | 11.27 | 237 | 0.92 | 0.74 | 21 |
| 1989 | 60.25 | 38.60 | 4244 | 11.91 | 5.28 | 276 | 8.15 | 6.61 | 294 | 0.59 | 0.52 | 19 |
| 1990 | 71.72 | 34.80 | 5001 | 6.51 | 8.29 | 357 | 8.31 | 9.15 | 341 | 2.16 | 0.24 | 23 |
| 1991 | 132.72 | 43.97 | 8879 | 9.69 | 5.71 | 694 | 14.36 | 9.42 | 599 | 2.33 | 0.62 | 36 |
| 1992 | 696.73 | 129.33 | 31892 | 52.36 | 8.57 | 3265 | 36.45 | 11.91 | 1805 | 4.81 | 0.64 | 126 |
| 1993 | 1137.59 | 264.73 | 50868 | 100.98 | 30.58 | 6750 | 43.87 | 19.62 | 3488 | 29.47 | 3.28 | 348 |
| 1994 | 593.04 | 245.72 | 25527 | 73.20 | 30.34 | 4223 | 54.08 | 25.27 | 3018 | 33.47 | 8.39 | 390 |
| 1995 | 446.77 | 217.49 | 17713 | 79.26 | 32.71 | 3474 | 80.55 | 32.97 | 2946 | 37.95 | 9.70 | 457 |
| 1996 | 284.50 | 212.58 | 10682 | 69.16 | 34.43 | 2517 | 51.31 | 36.79 | 1742 | 25.42 | 13.01 | 326 |
| Total | 3936.33 | 1358.17 | | 503.26 | 195.40 | | 370.76 | 190.83 | | 151.35 | 43.25 | |

| | *Germany* | | | *Canada* | | | *Australia* | | | *Others* | | |
|---|---|---|---|---|---|---|---|---|---|---|---|---|
| *Year* | *Pledged FDI* | *Used FDI* | *Pledged Projects* | *Pledged FDI* | *Used FDI* | *Pledged Projects* | *Pledged FDI* | *Used FDI* | *Pledged Projects* | *Pledged FDI* | *Used FDI* | *Pledged Projects* |
| 1978–1982 | 1.27 | N/A | N/A | 0.04 | N/A | N/A | 0.25 | N/A | N/A | 86.11 | N/A | N/A |
| 1983 | 0.03 | N/A | 4 | 2.14 | N/A | 7 | 2.64 | N/A | 8 | 8.28 | N/A | 36 |
| 1984 | 3.37 | 0.26 | 18 | 0.00 | 0 | 1 | 0.13 | 0 | 10 | 6.74 | 2.70 | 63 |
| 1985 | 0.59 | 0.71 | 7 | 0.27 | 0.27 | 5 | 0.41 | 0.41 | 8 | 14.42 | 6.19 | 187 |
| 1986 | 1.20 | 0.53 | 6 | 2.45 | N/A | 13 | 0.89 | 1.67 | 8 | 12.30 | 3.37 | 112 |
| 1987 | 3.45 | 0.08 | 11 | 0.67 | 0.26 | 6 | 1.17 | 0.13 | 10 | 22.38 | 5.45 | 192 |

**Appendix** Continued

| | *Germany* | | | *Canada* | | | *Australia* | | | *Others* | | |
|---|---|---|---|---|---|---|---|---|---|---|---|---|
| *Year* | *Pledged FDI* | *Used FDI* | *Pledged Projects* | *Pledged FDI* | *Used FDI* | *Pledged Projects* | *Pledged FDI* | *Used FDI* | *Pledged Projects* | *Pledged FDI* | *Used FDI* | *Pledged Projects* |
| 1988 | 1.03 | 0.33 | 22 | 0.88 | 0.13 | 31 | 0.37 | 0.09 | 20 | 20.17 | 6.32 | 575 |
| 1989 | 2.77 | 1.50 | 19 | 0.78 | 0.32 | 25 | 1.56 | 0.82 | 27 | 18.00 | 9.38 | 875 |
| 1990 | 0.84 | 1.16 | 13 | 0.27 | 0.15 | 39 | 0.31 | 0.45 | 29 | 29.85 | 9.37 | 1470 |
| 1991 | 9.86 | 2.85 | 24 | 0.55 | 0.19 | 68 | 0.78 | 0.27 | 74 | 41.44 | 14.16 | 2604 |
| 1992 | 2.18 | 1.49 | 130 | 5.30 | 0.97 | 394 | 4.63 | 0.59 | 358 | 172.63 | 31.17 | 10794 |
| 1993 | 3.69 | 0.83 | 320 | 17.55 | 2.03 | 959 | 9.46 | 1.63 | 769 | 309.04 | 85.12 | 19935 |
| 1994 | 15.02 | 3.15 | 314 | 10.84 | 2.63 | 630 | 10.34 | 2.29 | 527 | 217.00 | 93.46 | 12920 |
| 1995 | 17.61 | 4.10 | 355 | 10.42 | 2.73 | 560 | 13.34 | 2.47 | 471 | 282.55 | 95.91 | 11035 |
| 1996 | 9.98 | 5.18 | 256 | 8.23 | 3.38 | 431 | 5.22 | 1.94 | 366 | 278.95 | 109.94 | 8236 |
| Total | 72.89 | 22.17 | | 60.38 | 13.05 | | 51.49 | 12.76 | | 1519.85 | 472.53 | |

*Notes:* Foreign Direct Investment refers to the total value of foreign capital invested through signed contract agreements that year.
Used FDI refers to the amount of foreign direct investment actually utilized that year.
All values for pledged projects (those in parentheses) are numbers of projects, whereas FDI is expressed in US$100,000,000 dollars, adjusted by the Retail Price Index (1996 is the base year).

*Sources:* Various issues of the Almanac of China's Foreign Economic Relations and Trade, 1984–1998.

incentives for more personal initiative and risk taking behaviors among the local managers might address some of the issues we discovered here. Coincidentally, these incentives may prompt the expatriate managers themselves to take the risk of giving their local colleagues more responsibility. In so doing, they would give themselves the opportunity to be as surprised by the talents of their local managers as our American manager was. Additionally, we sense that a fear of punishment may lie behind many of the Chinese managers' perceptions. A corporate culture that is built upon incentives that reward success (rather than punish failure) may be particularly effective in China.

Considering the management group itself, it may be that a particular mix of foreign and local managers may comprise a more effective management team than some other configurations. Staffing may be key. Until research results give us some precise guidance, each JV will need to experiment to find its appropriate staffing configuration. In addition to training focused explicitly on these person perception problems, teambuilding and cross-cultural communication training should help to bridge gaps between the Chinese and foreign managers. And finally, we cannot forget that we are dealing with human nature here. There may be no substitute for simple human contact. Social gatherings between local and foreign managers may be essential for joint venture success.

As plausible and effective as all of this prescriptive counsel may be, we find that we are continually drawn to the wisdom that one general manager shared with us in Beijing. When we told him about the mindset that many of his expatriate colleagues seemed to have about doing business in China, he offered the following advice.

> Recognize that the people who live in this system are as bright and creative as people anywhere else in the world are. When they do something that strikes you as odd, bite your tongue and do not be judgmental. Assume that there is a logical and compelling reason for their behavior. Your job is to keep your mouth shut, not be judgmental, and learn. Try to find out what their logic is and then work to optimize the situation.

This advice seems to be as relevant for the local managers as it is for the foreign managers. If everyone held such an appreciative attitude, managerial relationships in China might be much more harmonious (and we suspect, productive) than they are right now.

**Acknowledgements:** The authors wish to thank the many people who helped to build the relationships that enabled us to complete this project—JoAnn Brooks, Hongshen Che, Long Chen, Tom D'Aunno, Ken DeWoskin, Liluo Fang, Kent Foster, Xiaolan Fu, Pat Gurin, John Hulpke, Qicheng Jing, Wenquan Ling, Dawei Liu, Gary Olson, Judy Olson, Rick Price, Ted Snyder, Harold Stevenson, Hui Wang, Liancang Xu, Frank Yates and Kan Zhang. The authors also wish to thank Stewart Black, J. T. Li, Ken Lieberthal, Ellie Weldon, and Frank Yates for detailed feedback on an early draft of this article; Sarah Allen and Scott Cook for translation help; all the individuals in China that invited us into their lives and shared their time and insights with us so freely; and the University of Michigan Business School, the William Davidson Institute, the Center for International Business Education and the Department of Psychology, all at the University of Michigan, and the School of Business Administration at the Hong Kong University of Science and Technology for their support.

## Notes

1. We should also point out that this focus on joint ventures necessarily ignores other organizational aspects of China's reform experience. While it is beyond the scope of this paper to review all of this work, we can point the interested reader to recent research that investigates these broader questions. Rawksi (1994, 1995) provides a summary overview and assessment of the reform experience. Boisot and Child (1996), Nee (1992) and Walder (1995) discuss the kinds of innovative organizational arrangements that have emerged in China's new institutional setting. Naughton (1994) and Woo, Hai, Jin, and Fan (1994) provide a look at the performance of state enterprises in the reform period. And focusing more directly on management practices, Guthrie (1997) examines the diversification strategy of firms previously sheltered from market pressure, while Groves, Hong, McMillan, and Naughton (1994) show us how management practices have changed inside state enterprises.

2. Of course, this work in China is part of a longer tradition of work that examines broad questions of foreign entry mode (Agarwal & Ramaswami, 1992; Anderson & Gatignon, 1986; Hill, Hwang, & Kim, 1990; Kogut & Singh, 1988; Osborn & Baughn, 1990), comparative corporate governance (Roe, 1993), joint venture development (Gulati, 1998; Harrigan, 1985; Hennart, 1988; Kogut, 1988), and control (Mjoen & Tallman,

1997), and human resource management practices in international joint ventures (Shenkar & Zeira, 1987).

3. In addition to this work rooted in management practice considerations, China has served as a setting to examine perhaps more basic theoretical interests. The hypothesized difference between Eastern and Western psychology undergirds much of this work. The distinction between the independent and interdependent self (Markus & Kitayama, 1991) or individualism and collectivism (Triandis, McCuster, & Hui, 1990), for example, guides comparative investigations of basic attribution processes (Lee, Hallahan, & Herzog, 1996; Morris & Peng, 1994) and group dynamics (Earley, 1989, 1993).

## References


Adler, N. J., Brahm, R., & Graham, J. L. (1992). Strategy implementation: A comparison of face-to-face negotiations in the People's Republic of China and the United States. *Strategic Management Journal, 13:* 449–466.

Agarwal, S., & Ramaswami, S. N. (1992). Choice of foreign market entry mode: Impact of ownership, location, and internationalization factors. *Journal of International Business Studies, 23:* 1–27.

Anderson, E. (1990). Two firms, one frontier: On assessing joint venture performance. *Sloan Management Review, 31:* 19–30.

Anderson, E. & Gatignon, H. A. (1986). Modes of foreign entry: A transaction cost analysis and propositions, *Journal of International Business Studies, 17:* 1–25.

Baird, I. S., Lyles, M. A., & Wharton, R. (1990). Attitudinal differences between American and Chinese managers regarding joint venture management. *Management International Review, 30:* 53–68.

Beamish, P. W. (1985). The characteristics of joint ventures in developed and developing countries. *Columbia Journal of World Business, 20:* 13–19.

Beamish, P. A. (1993). The characteristics of joint ventures in the People's Republic of China. *Journal of International Marketing, 1:* 29–48.

Black, J. S., & Mendenhall, M. (1990). Cross-cultural training effectiveness: A review and a theoretical framework for future research. *Academy of Management Review, 15:* 113–136.

Boisot, M., & Child, J. (1996). From fiefs to clans and network capitalism: Explaining China's emerging economic order. *Administrative Science Quarterly, 41:* 600–628.

Bjorkman, I. (1995). The board of directors in Sino-western joint ventures. *Corporate Governance, 3:* 156–166.

Chen, C. C. (1995). New trends in rewards allocation preferences: A Sino-U.S. comparison. *Academy of Management Journal, 38:* 408–428.

Child, J. (1994). *Management in China during the Age of Reform.* Cambridge: Cambridge University Press.

Child, J. & Markoczy, L. (1993). Host-country managerial behavior and learning in Chinese and Hungarian joint ventures. *Journal of Management Studies, 30:* 611–631.

Choi, I., Nisbett, R. E., & Norenzayan, A. (1998). Cultural variation and causal attribution. Unpublished manuscript, Department of Psychology, University of Michigan.

Davidson, W. H. (1987). Creating and managing joint ventures in China. *California Management Review, 29:* 77–94.

Doucet, L., & Jehn, K. A. (1997). Analyzing harsh works in a sensitive setting: American expatriates in communist China. *Journal of Organizational Behavior, 18:* 559–582.

Earley, P. C. (1989). Social loafing and collectivism: A comparison of the United States and the People's Republic of China. *Administrative Science Quarterly, 34:* 565–581.

Earley, P. C. (1993). East meets West meets Mideast: Further explorations of collectivist and individualist work groups. *Academy of Management Journal, 36:* 319–348.

Earley, P. C. (1994). Self or group? Cultural effects of training on self-efficacy and performance. *Administrative Science Quarterly, 39:* 89–117.

Eiteman, D. K. (1990). American executives' perceptions of negotiating joint ventures with the People's Republic of China: Lessons learned. *Columbia Journal of World Business, 25:* 59–67.

Fischhoff, B. (1982). Debiasing, Pp. 422–444 in D. Kahneman, P. Slovic, & A. Tversky (Eds.), *Judgment under uncertainty: Heuristics and biases.* Cambridge: Cambridge University Press.

Geringer, J. M. & Hebert, L. (1991). Measuring performance of international joint ventures. *Journal of International Business Studies, 22:* 249–263.

Gilbert, D. T., & Malone, P. S. (1995). The correspondence bias. *Psychological Bulletin, 117:* 21–38.

Glaser, B. G., & Strauss, A. L. (1967). *The Discovery of Grounded Theory: Strategies for Qualitative Research.* New York: Aldine.

Goldenberg, S. (1989). *Hands across the ocean: Managing joint ventures with a spotlight on China and Japan.* Boston: Harvard Business School Press.

Gomes-Casseres, B. (1987). Joint venture instability: Is it a problem? *Columbia Journal of World Business, 22:* 97–102.

Groves, T., Hong, Y., McMillan, J., & Naughton, B. (1994). Autonomy and incentives in Chinese state enterprises. *The Quarterly Journal of Economics,* (February): 183–209.

Gulati, R. (1998). Alliances and networks. *Strategic Management Journal, 19:* 293–317.

Guthrie, D. (1997). Between markets and politics: Organizational responses to reform in China. *American Journal of Sociology, 102:* 1258–1304.

Harrigan, K. R. (1985). *Strategies for joint ventures.* Lexington, MA: Lexington Books.

Hendryx, S. R. (1986). The China trade: Making the deal work. *Harvard Business Review, 24:* 75–84.

Hennart, J. (1988). A transaction cost theory of equity joint ventures. *Strategic Management Journal, 9,* 361–374.

Hill, C. W. L., Hwang, P., & Kim, C. (1990). An eclectic theory of the choice of international entry mode. *Strategic Management Journal, 11:* 117–128.

Holm, B. (1990). *Coming home crazy.* Minneapolis, MN: Milkweed Editions.

Hu, M. Y., & Chen, H. (1996). An empirical analysis of factors explaining foreign joint venture performance in China. *Journal of Business Research, 35:* 165–173.

Killing, J. P. (1982). How to make a global joint venture work. *Harvard Business Review, 20:* 120–127.

Kirkbride, P. S., Tang, S. F. Y., & Westwood, R. I. (1991). Chinese conflict preferences and negotiating behavior: Cultural and psychological influences. *Organization Studies, 12:* 365–386.

Kogut, B. (1988). Joint ventures: Theoretical and empirical perspectives. *Strategic Management Journal, 9:* 319–332.

Kogut, B., & Singh, H. (1988). The effect of national culture on the choice of entry mode. *Journal of International Business Studies, 19:* 411–432.

Lee, F., Hallahan, M., & Herzog, T. (1996). Explaining real life events: How culture and domain shape attributions. *Personality and Social Psychology Bulletin, 22:* 732–741.

Leung, K., Smith, P. B., Wang, Z., & Sun, H. (1996). Job satisfaction in joint venture hotels in China: An organizational justice analysis. *Journal of International Business Studies, 27:* 947–962.

Lin, X., & Germain, R. (1998). Sustaining satisfactory joint venture relationships: The role of conflict resolution strategy. *Journal of International Business Studies, 29:* 179–196.

Lyles, M. A., & Reger, R. K. (1993). Managing for autonomy in joint ventures: A longitudinal study of upward influence. *Journal of Management Studies, 30:* 383–404.

Mann, J. (1989). *Beijing Jeep: The Short, Unhappy Romance of American Business in China.* New York: Simon and Schuster.

Markus, H. R., & Kitayama, S. (1991). Culture and the self: Implications for cognition, emotion, and motivation. *Psychological Review, 98:* 224–253.

Miles, M. B., & Huberman, A. M. (1984). *Qualitative Data Analysis: A Source Book of New Methods.* Beverly Hills, CA: Sage.

Mjoen, H., & Tallman, S. (1997). Control and performance in international joint ventures. *Organization Science, 8:* 257–274.

Morris, D., & Hergert, M. (1987). Trends in international cooperative agreements. *Columbia Journal of World Business, 22:* 15–21.

Morris, M. W., & Peng, K. (1994). Culture and cause: American and Chinese attributions for social and physical events. *Journal of Personality and Social Psychology, 67:* 949–971.

Naughton, B. (1994). What is distinctive about China's economic transition? State enterprise reform and overall system transformation. *Journal of Comparative Economics, 18:* 470–490.

Nee, V. (1992). Organizational dynamics of market transition: Hybrid forms, property rights, and mixed economy in China. *Administrative Science Quarterly, 37:* 1–27.

Olk, P., & Earley, P. C. (1995). Rediscovering the individual in the formation of international joint ventures. *Research in the Sociology of Organizations, 14:* 223–261.

Osborn, R. N., & Baughn, C. C. (1990). Forms of interorganizational governance for multinational alliances. *Academy of Management Journal, 33:* 503–519.

Osland, G. E., & Cavusgil, S. T. (1996). Performance issues in U.S.—China Joint Ventures. *California Management Review, 38:* 106–130.

Pan, Y. (1996). Influences on foreign equity ownership in joint ventures in China. *Journal of International Business Studies, 27:* 1–26.

Pan, Y. (1997). The formation of Japanese and U.S. equity joint ventures in China. *Strategic Management Journal, 18:* 247–254.

Pan, Y., & Tse, D. K. (1996). Cooperative strategies between foreign forms in an overseas country. *Journal of International Business Studies, 27:* 929–946.

Parkhe, A. (1993). 'Messy' research, methodological predispositions, and theory development in international joint ventures. *Academy of Management Review, 18:* 227–268.

Pearce, R. J. (1997). Toward understanding joint venture performance and survival: A bargaining and influence approach to transaction cost theory. *Academy of Management Review, 22:* 203–225.

Pearson, M. M. (1991). *Joint Ventures in the People's Republic of China.* Princeton, NJ: Princeton University Press.

Rawski, T. G. (1994). Chinese industrial reform: Accomplishments, prospects, and implications. *American Economic Review, 84:* 271–275.

Rawski, T. G. (1995). Implications of China's reform experience. *The China Quarterly, 35:* 1150–1173.

Roe, M. (1993). Some differences in corporate structure in Germany, Japan, and the United States. *The Yale Law Review, 102:* 1927–2003.

Shenkar, O. (1990). International joint venture problems in China: Risks and remedies. *Long Range Planning, 23,* 82–90.

Shenkar, O., & Ronen, S. (1987). The cultural context of negotiations: The implications of Chinese interpersonal norms. *The Journal of Applied Behavioral Science, 23:* 263–275.

Shenkar, O., & Zeira, Y. (1987). Human resources management in international joint ventures: Directions for research. *Academy of Management Review, 12:* 546–557.

Strutton, D., & Pelton, L. (1997). Scaling the great wall. The *yin* and *yang* of resolving business conflicts in China. *Business Horizons, 40:* 22–34.

Teargarden, M. B., & Von Glinow, M. A. (1991). Sino—foreign alliance types and related operating characteristics. Pp. 99–108 in O. Shenkar (Ed.), *Organization and Management in China 1979–1990.* Armonk, NY: M. E. Sharpe, Inc.

The joy of being single. (1998). *Business China,* (September 14): 1–3.

Ting-Toomey, S., Gao, G., Trubisky, P., Yang, Z., Kim, H. S., Lin, S-L., & Nishida, T. (1991). Culture, face maintenance, and styles of handling interpersonal conflict: A study of five cultures. *The International Journal of Conflict Management, 2:* 275–296.

Triandis, H. C., McCuster, C., & Hui, C. H. (1990). Multimethod probes of individualism and collectivism. *Journal of Personality and Social Psychology, 59:* 1006–1020.

Tse, D. K., Francis, J., & Walls, J. (1994). Cultural differences in conducting intra and inter-cultural negotiations: A Sino–Canadian comparison. *Journal of International Business Studies, 25:* 537–555.

Tse, D. K., Pan, Y., & Au, K. Y. (1997). How MNCs choose entry modes and form alliances: The China experience. *Journal of International Business Studies, 28:* 779–805.

Vanhonacker, W. (1997). Entering China: An unconventional approach. *Harvard Business Review, 75,* 130–140.

Von Glinow, M. A., & Teargarden, M. B. (1988). The transfer of human resource management technology in Sino–U.S. cooperative ventures: Problems and solutions. *Human Resource Management, 27:* 201–229.

Walder, A. G. (1995). Local governments as industrial firms: An organizational analysis of China's transitional economy. *American Journal of Sociology, 101:* 263–301.

Wang, R. L. (1986). Transferring American management know-how to the People's Republic of China. *SAM Advanced Management Journal,* (Summer): 4–8.

Weiss, J., & Bloom, S. (1990). Managing in China: Expatriate experiences and training recommendations. *Business Horizons, 33:* 23–39.

Woo, W. T., Hai, W., Jin, Y., & Fan, G. (1994). How successful has Chinese enterprise reform been? Pitfalls in opposite biases and focus. *Journal of Comparative Economics, 18:* 410–437.

Yan, A., & Gray, B. (1994). Bargaining power, management control, and performance in United States–China joint ventures: A comparative case study. *Academy of Management Journal, 34:* 1478–1517.

Yan, A., & Gray, B. (1995). Reconceptualizing the determinants and measurement of joint venture performance. *Advances in Global High-Technology Management, 5:* 87–113.

Yan, R. (1998). Short-term results: The litmus test for success in China. *Harvard Business Review, 76:* 61–75.

Yatsko, P. (1997). *Rethinking China. Far Eastern Economic Review,* (December 18): 52–57.

# Reading 3.5

# THE CONTEMPORARY INTERNATIONAL ASSIGNMENT

## *A Look at the Options*

GLENN M. McEVOY AND BARBARA PARKER

### Three Expatriates

Gerald Borenstein's selection for Bandag's Honk Kong office seemed a perfect fit for company needs. Not only had Borenstein authored a marketing plan for China, he had lived in another country before and had years of experience at Bandag—the leading U.S. maker of retread tires. Borenstein himself had good reasons to accept an overseas assignment: the job offered strategic opportunities and an increase in rank, Bandag's international revenues were growing, and the perquisites combined far exceeded those usual for the Muscatine, Iowa home office (e.g., a fully-paid 3-bedroom apartment, a full-time housekeeper, private school for the children, and a travel allowance). Soon after Borenstein arrived in Hong Kong in 1997, Asian sales began to slow and domestic competitive pressures increased. Borenstein found it difficult to cut costs fast enough to satisfy headquarters, and those who had selected Borenstein for the Hong Kong job had retired or been reassigned. Within only 18 months, the Hong Kong job evaporated, and Bandag was unable to find a new job for Borenstein. Borenstein and his wife packed their belongings and, with their two small children, returned to the U.S. to launch his career anew (Kaufman, 1999).

Stephanie Thompson's route to expatriation began in a different way. Born in a rural U.S. town, Stephanie was scarcely aware of an outside world until a dynamic university class revealed new options. After completing an international studies degree, Stephanie explored those options teaching English in Ecuador. Her relieved family welcomed her return at the end of a year, and was filled with pride as one success followed another: budding career, completion of a part-time M.B.A. program, a series of promotions. But Stephanie felt there was something missing in her life, and after some years decided to return to Latin America. It took time for her family to accept the decision, and even more time to liquidate her belongings. But in 1998 Stephanie returned to Ecuador with high hopes. Stephanie's personal network helped her secure a job she had first seen posted on the Internet—a job that draws on Spanish-language skills combined with her business acumen.

On the evening of the day he'd been offered an assignment in London, Robert Nathan returned home with a map. Unfolding it on the family table, he announced "we have some decisions to make." Nathan explained that the job represented an important promotion for him, but he asked the family to consider how taking the job could change their

SOURCE: Preverisly published in *Reading in International Human Resourse Management*, 2000 (pp. 470-486). Cincinnati, OH: South-Western College Publishing. Reprinted with permission.

lives. He described opportunities he'd experienced in an overseas posting before he had a family: to travel worldwide, make new friends, learn more about how other people live. Further, he outlined some of the costs: leaving old friends at home, adjusting to a new country, learning new habits. For his wife, it meant postponing her career for a few more years. For the children it would mean new schools and a different educational system. He described the job he'd been offered and laid out the possibilities he saw for his job and the family. The company expected to provide pre-departure training to help Nathan and his family adjust to their new life, but Nathan cautioned that some cross-cultural challenges cannot be anticipated. Acknowledging this, Nathan asked: should we take this international assignment?

Gerald Borenstein, Stephanie Thompson, and Robert Nathan all can be thought of as expatriates—people who decide to leave their home to live in another country. As theirs and other stories would illustrate, expatriates can follow one of many routes to an overseas assignment, including education, company selection, personal choice, and even chance. Additionally, while these experiences may seem unique, in fact almost all expatriate experiences differ according to variables that can be classified as personal, organizational, and contextual characteristics (such as where one works abroad). For example, Gerald Borenstein's expatriate experience might have turned out quite differently had his job been located somewhere other than Asia during the 1997 economic downturn. In combination, personal, organizational, and contextual characteristics motivate decisions to create or take overseas jobs. And, as the three experiences described above show, the expatriate experience contributes to career opportunities, affects self esteem, and contributes to relationships with family, friends, and colleagues. For some, a job abroad can be and often is more than a job; it is a life-changing experience that affects all dimensions of one's life.

## The U.S. Expatriate Experience

The expatriate experience has not always been viewed as one that ties together personal, organizational, and contextual factors. In the early 1950s when significant numbers of U.S. expatriates first began to work abroad, the overseas assignment usually was viewed only as it related to job characteristics. Accordingly, the majority of U.S. firms selected expatriate employees based on technical skills alone. For example, if overseas expansion strategies called for increased production abroad, the likely personnel choice would have been someone with outstanding experience and success in domestic production. For many firms, yet another reason motivated selection of expatriate home-country managers: with them in place, headquarters could exert more control over the foreign operation. Further, like Gerald Borenstein, the expatriate could expect to be better compensated abroad in salary or benefits. For example, perceived "hardship posts" were sometimes compensated at one-and-a-half to two times domestic salary. Additionally, most expatriate assignments from the U.S. were of relatively short duration—a few months to two years at most. Finally, unlike today, few women or minority group members were considered for overseas assignments, and it was considered very unusual for U.S. citizens to become "voluntary" expatriates like Stephanie Thompson.

By the late 1970s and into the 1980s these practices had begun to change, brought about largely by international competition that affected U.S. firms in two ways. First, cost reduction efforts led firms to send fewer expatriates abroad from headquarters. Second, among those who were sent abroad, the growing need for employees who were both technically successful and culturally adaptive could not easily be satisfied by U.S. employees. Many companies satisfied dual job/cultural needs by hiring host- or third-country nationals familiar with cultural attributes of the host country, but then discovered that this practice too was flawed. Principal among the problems were three: a) hiring host- and third-country managers with no company experience made it more difficult to transmit company values to employees abroad; b) competition for host- and third-country managers made it difficult to retain good ones; and c) managers at headquarters were gaining too little international experience even as international growth became more important to many firms. These and similar challenges led many U.S. firms to develop more managers from home and abroad who know their jobs well, are personally adaptive to life and work abroad, and are knowledgeable about other countries and cultures.

Like Gerald Borenstein, Stephanie Thompson, Robert Nathan and the many thousands of U.S. expatriates who work abroad each year, success depends not only on personal and organizational attributes but also on contextual variables beyond the control of the individual and the organization. This suggests that expatriate jobs both provide opportunities but also carry risks. Although some people control the decision to work abroad and have ample time to balance opportunities and risks (as Stephanie Thompson did), for others the offer of an overseas assignment arises almost overnight (as it did for Robert Nathan). Descriptions of these opportunities and risks on the following pages will help you assess your own interests in, and suitability for, seeking work in another country, and will prepare you to answer the question: should you take or seek an overseas assignment?

## Success and Failure in International Assignments

Reported failure rates in overseas assignments are high, particularly for U.S. expatriates and this can easily derail or delay a career trajectory. Someone is typically considered to have "failed" in an international assignment when he or she returns home before the anticipated end of the assignment. Using this definition, it has been suggested that between 15 and 70 percent of all expatriates "fail" by returning home early (Borstorff, Harris, Feild, & Giles, 1997). Problems in personal adjustment, family accommodation, and worries over career derailment can all contribute to an early return.

Given the high potential for failure, you must carefully consider the pros and cons of an international assignment before accepting or seeking it. On the upside, an international assignment represents an opportunity to expand your personal horizons, experience other cultures, and enhance your creativity and problem solving skills. It requires that you learn to live with—and capitalize on—diversity. Expatriates who overcome the innumerable obstacles of an international assignment are like athletes or Outward Bound participants who live with the self-confidence of one who has experienced success outside of one's comfort zone. An international assignment puts you in close contact with a different set of stakeholders, including customers and suppliers, and therefore provides you with first-hand knowledge of how to contribute to the success of the business. It can be a wonderful learning opportunity for your partner and children, and, with the right organization, can be an essential stepping stone to further career advancement. Finally, many international assignments carry with them an excellent package of perquisites, including enhanced salary; home leave arrangements, and educational and housing allowances. The higher cost of hiring expatriates usually motivates firms to send only one or a few people abroad, and those sent abroad can therefore develop generalist skills to supplement the specialist skills that may have led to the overseas assignment.

On the downside, an international assignment can be a source of career derailment. Some companies tend to forget about their expatriates—"out of sight is out of mind." There may or may not be a promotion waiting for you when you return. You may lose track of valuable mentors or insider information critical for career success as Gerald Borenstein did. Companies sometimes suggest that international postings are critical to career advancement, but the backgrounds of senior executives reflect the opposite. The position itself can be uncomfortable if the expatriate is viewed as the home country "spy" or the person charged with telling host country nationals how the work is done back home. You may learn skills or styles that actually hurt you in your career back home (e.g., learning to be accommodating and to value harmony in an Asian posting), you may find a specialist job less challenging following a generalist position abroad, or you may become so enamored with the host country culture that you "go native" and either do not want to return home or arouse loyalty concerns among sponsors back home. Your partner may have to give up his or her job to accompany you, and getting back on a career track for either of you may be difficult upon return. If you are going to a less developed economy where the technology in use is out of date, you may suffer in terms of keeping your technical skills on the cutting edge. A posting to a country where you must learn another language requires time and commitment. The financial perquisites, as good as they sound, may not cover the additional costs of living in some expensive international cities. Finally, family safety, health, living standards, and education may require compromises in some parts of the world. For example, the educational system in smaller, less developed economies may not be appropriate for college-bound teens and could mean sending students home to finish their high school education.

Of course, there is a lot more to "success" or "failure" in an international assignment than simply sticking out the posting until the designated return date. Expatriates may finish out their assignments and yet perform poorly in the assigned tasks, may behave in ways that alienate the host country nationals with whom they work, or may be so maladjusted to the international assignment that they quit the organization upon repatriation or harbor ill-will toward the notion of international assignments throughout the remainder of their careers.

One way of thinking about the issue of success or failure is to view it as a two-by-two matrix, as presented in Figure 1. The two general dimensions of success are adjustment and performance. Adjustment is more internally and personally

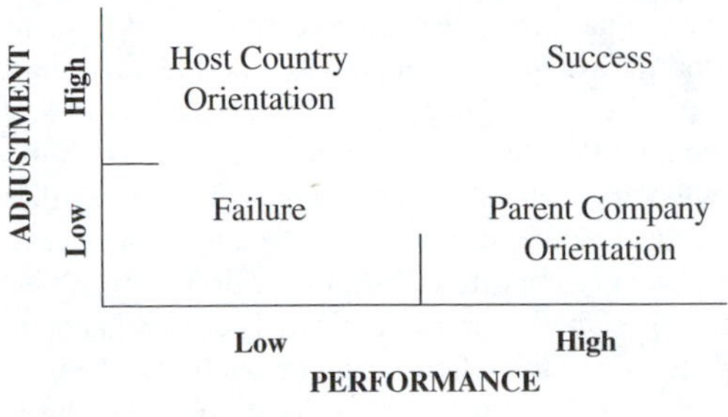


**Figure 1** Possible International Assignment Outcomes

focused, and refers to the general degree of psychological comfort the individual has with various aspects of a host country, including working in the country, interacting with the locals, and critical features of the host country such as education, food, climate, and medical facilities (Black & Gregersen, 1991). Performance is more externally and organizationally focused and, while it may include premature returns, it is more indicative of achievement relative to established organizational objectives (e.g., the development of host or third country nationals to assume greater responsibility) or subsidiary or joint venture performance indicators (e.g., market share, revenue, costs, cash flow, turnover). Viewed this way, performance incorporates the possibility that the expatriate may return early because the assignment was finished ahead of schedule, and thus is a success rather than a failure. Overall, this model incorporates the notions of both employee satisfaction and employee satisfactoriness with the assignment.

Using the model in Figure 1, success and failure relate to the combined effects of performance and adjustment. Intermediate levels of success may be achieved in either the Parent Company Orientation cell or the Host Country Orientation cell. Persons in the former may be expected to exhibit substantially more commitment to the parent firm than to the local operation, substantially more organizational commitment than career commitment, and a greater intent to return early but stay with the parent company upon return. Persons in the Host Country Orientation cell may be likely to exhibit opposite outcomes: higher commitment to the local operation and to their personal careers, less likelihood of returning early, but greater likelihood of quitting the parent company upon return (Takeuchi, 1997).

Of course, the optimum outcome in the model in Figure 1 is to be high in both performance and adjustment. Once you've decided that the potential rewards of an international assignment outweigh the potential risks for you, your next concern should be to identify what situations increase the likelihood of a fully successful international assignment in your case. This requires the examination of the three interrelated sets of factors we identified earlier: personal, organizational, and contextual (Parker & McEvoy, 1993).

## Personal and Professional Skills and Attitudes

The first questions to answer before accepting an international assignment revolve around the skills and temperament you have to be successful in another culture. First, what is your motivation for wanting to go abroad? Did you study or live abroad as a student? Do you take the opportunity to interact with foreigners in your home country when you have a chance? Do you just plain enjoy the opportunity to get to know people who are different than you?

Extensive interviews with returned American expatriates suggest that important prerequisites for a successful international experience are a willingness to go, a sense of adventure, and a desire for challenge and learning (Osland, 1995). Of course, if you've gotten this far in the process, you apparently have the willingness to go. This is important because expatriates forced to go abroad against their will are likely to be poorly adjusted. A sense of adventure is also critical. Do you feel more "alive" when experiencing something new and completely different? Successful expatriates sometimes feel something akin to a "mission" in their international work, idealism that they are doing good work not only for their company, but also for their country and the world. Lastly, the nature of most international assignments requires that expatriates confront challenges and be open to learning new ways of doing things. A narrow-minded, ethnocentric view of the world ("my way is the best") is a setup for failure.

Next, what is your temperament? Are you willing to accept a "cultural mentor," someone to show you the ropes and "break the code" (i.e., explain how things work) in a different country? Do you get frustrated and impatient when you can't figure things out on your own? Are you willing to ask for help without feeling that you have diminished your personal power base?

Other personal attributes that tend to predict success in an international assignment include a certain amount of extroversion or gregariousness, cultural empathy, perceptual accuracy, tolerance for ambiguity and stress, a sense of humor, and some ability to laugh at oneself (Parker & McEvoy, 1993). At the same time, the expatriate who is able to enjoy his or her own company may find it easier to weather feelings of isolation and loneliness that sometimes arise during an overseas assignment. Each of these characteristics is important in fostering both personal adjustment to a different culture and high performance in an environment much different from the one at home.

Viewed from the perspective of prerequisite skills, research has suggested three general categories of skills critical to successful adaptation to an international assignment: personal, people, and perceptual (Mendenhall & Oddou, 1985). Personal skills include such things as mental and emotional well-being, and stress reduction techniques such as effective delegation, time management, meditation, prayer, or physical exercise. People skills include capabilities in effective interaction with others, including communication, listening, conflict resolution, influence, and leadership. Depending on the country of assignment, they also include the willingness to attempt to learn another language and the confidence to try to use it despite the fact that it is not altogether familiar. Perceptual skills assist you in understanding why foreigners do things the way they do. They allow you to be conscious of social cues and behaviors. It is important to resist the tendency to jump to conclusions in an international setting because the cues and meanings are often quite different from the ones you learned at home.

There is also evidence that both maturity and predeparture knowledge of a country can assist the expatriate in successful acculturation (Parker & McEvoy, 1993). Of course, the two are interrelated, assuming that older expatriates have had the opportunity to travel more and gain more international experience, both directly and indirectly (reading, self-study, discussions with returned expatriates, etc.). The reason some organizations invest in training or orientation programs for expatriates is they believe that such preparation assists the expatriate to "hit the ground" running upon arrival in the host country. Training can vary from introductions to the history and geography of the country, to cultural orientations, language training, or sensitivity to cultural differences (Tung, 1982). But inasmuch as only about 5% of U.S. firms train employees for the overseas assignment, much of this training will have to be self-initiated. If you are unwilling to make this investment, you should seriously reconsider your decision to seek an international position.

One expatriate summed up his experience by saying: "For me the most important thing was to understand that I was in a continual adjustment phase. I would go through many periods of hating it and loving it, happiness and depression. It was realizing that my current emotions would only be temporary; understanding and grasping the fact that the first one-and-a-half to two years will not be easy is also very important. You won't fit, you won't be one of them, so just be yourself. The grass is not as green as you thought it would be but it is still a nice yard, just different. I am not sure if I have been 'successful' as an expat but I am still living abroad after nearly two years and have started calling my new country of residence 'home'" (Kidd, 1997).

## The Organization's Philosophy and Practices

The second category of factors that predicts success in an international assignment is organizational factors. What is the organization's general philosophy toward expatriation and repatriation? What specific policies and practices are in place to facilitate expatriate success? There is a good deal of research that suggests organizational practices can make or break an assignment, and this research is relatively unambiguous in suggesting what it takes to be successful.

### The Strategic Importance of International Assignments

The first question you should explore is the strategic importance of international assignments in general (and the specific assignment you are considering in particular) to your organization in building your career. Strategic importance in general can be assessed by the degree to which international experience is valued by the firm when making promotion decisions. Do senior executives have multicultural backgrounds and international exposure? If so, you can assume that this experience is valued. A few years ago, only 20 percent of U.S. CEOs had any real first hand international experience (Adler, 1991). And while that has improved in recent years, the level of senior executive international expertise is still a key indicator you should consider. Caution is advisable because executives who have not worked overseas will not really understand the difficulties and challenges involved, nor will they appreciate the personal growth and skill development that takes place in such an assignment.

Of course, some organizations have a commitment to international expansion but are in transition from domestic to global orientations. They may have few internationally seasoned managers presently on board, and it will take time to build such a corps. In cases like this, you might ask questions such as the following. Does there appear to be a logical career path for you upon repatriation that builds directly on the experiences you will have in the potential international assignment? Have recently returned expatriates obtained desirable positions with growth potential? Is there a long term strategic commitment to develop an internationally experienced corps of senior managers?

As an indicator of genuine upper management commitment to internationalization, ask about the support and communication system in place to facilitate expatriate success. The research is clear that such support and communication systems are vital to successful expatriation and repatriation (Black, Gregersen, & Mendenhall, 1992). One overseas subsidiary has a support system whereby the highest-ranking expatriate, as part of his or her job, is expected to help other expatriates adjust to the country of assignment. Duties include informal counseling and the sponsorship of monthly social gatherings to discuss successes and problems of expatriation. In addition, the spouse of this senior expatriate serves as a mentor for other spouses before they depart and after they arrive in the country of assignment (Mendenhall & Oddou, 1988).

Such efforts are exemplary. However, it is common for a single expatriate to be assigned to a particular overseas site. How do firms support their expatriates under such circumstances? The better ones provide regular telephone and email contact, including counseling with both work and family problems. Frequent trips back to headquarters for the expatriate (and home leave for spouse and family) are helpful. A committed firm also provides advice on how to gain the support needed in the local community. For example, the organization may provide information about nearby groups for those who are active in an organized religion, or service clubs such as Rotary or Lion's for those who participate in such organizations. In larger international cities, there are frequently organizations of expatriates from a single country, or related countries (e.g., Hash House Harriers), working for different international firms that share information on how to ease the transition into the local culture and can provide a local support network for an expatriate and his or her spouse.

If you intend to stay with the same firm over a long period of time, be leery of firms that practice the "out of sight, out of mind" philosophy of managing expatriates. This approach reflects the lack of a genuine strategic commitment to international work. In one company an expatriate complained that calls to headquarters were routinely ignored and that there were no organized social systems for either him or his spouse. Mentors were unavailable for advice and no counseling was provided either predeparture or within country. The total experience put extreme pressure on his marriage and he eventually sent his family home early and then remained overseas just a short time longer alone (Mendenhall & Oddou, 1988).

Don't leave home without knowing what kinds of support systems will be in place to help you succeed once you reach the country of assignment. These support systems should include not only the features mentioned above, but they should also provide you with a clear link to the job you will have upon repatriation. The stronger the support system, and the more it is directed not only to you but also to your spouse and family, the greater the likelihood of success.

The specifics of the assignment under consideration are also important. Is the assignment with a strategically critical subsidiary or highly visible international joint venture? For example, you may be offered a position as vice president for marketing in the Caribbean region. This position may be considerably less desirable than vice president for marketing in the rapidly expanding Far East region. Even within the same region, some business ventures will be rapidly expanding and therefore of more strategic significance than others. Ask to see past financial statements and future performance predictions for any business you are considering. It's much easier to be "successful" in some emerging markets than others.

## The Human Resource Management System for International Assignments

Other critical success factors for an international assignment pertain to the human resource (HR) management system the organization has to facilitate successful expatriation. How sophisticated is the expatriate selection system? How much lead time is typically provided for expatriates to decide on an assignment? How extensive is the predeparture training and orientation given for the expatriate and family, and what type of relocation assistance is provided? How clear are the job responsibilities and the amount of authority inherent in the position? How will performance be measured and rewarded overseas? What is the compensation and benefits package, and how is it tailored to the country of assignment? How tightly is the international assignment tied to career development and what arrangements in advance are made for eventual repatriation?

Expatriate selection systems are critical. How were you chosen? Did someone simply say, "Hey, do you want to go abroad?" Or was there an in-depth, competitive screening process used to identify not only the willing but also the qualified? The vast majority of organizations select their expatriates on the basis of technical or managerial expertise. Of course, this is only the foundation for success. Critical traits and skills such as those mentioned earlier (openness to others, perceptual skills, cultural empathy, comfort with ambiguity, self-deprecating sense of humor, and so forth) should also be criteria in a competent selection system. It is a vast simplification to believe that one's managerial and technical skills alone are adequate to ensure success in an international assignment. If this assumption exists in your organization, it is a sign that either upper management or HR—or both—has little first hand experience with the nature of international work.

Further, sophisticated selection systems take into account the needs and interests of the potential expatriate's spouse and family. Inability of a spouse and/or family to adapt to an international assignment is a frequent cause of premature returns (Black & Gregersen, 1991). As a result, the better organizations interview family members as part of the screening process and build their concerns into the overall placement and orientation systems. A critical challenge today is how to deal with dual-career families. Assistance in finding appropriate employment for a trailing spouse overseas and/or similar support upon repatriation is often critical to getting the best qualified expatriate to accept the assignment.

Training and orientation for expatriate assignments range from nonexistent to barely adequate. Few organizations believe they can spare much time for formal training either predeparture or post-arrival. Considerable experience with cross-cultural training exists in academic, religious, and diplomatic communities, but few firms avail themselves of this expertise. Churches have been sending missionaries abroad for years, as have schools been sending students, and the State Department diplomats. Many of these organizations have developed relatively sophisticated approaches to training "sojourners." For example, the Peace Corps started in the early 1960s with extensive predeparture training programs which included language and cross cultural training. With experience, they learned that a shorter predeparture training regimen, followed up with a more extensive in-country curriculum, was more effective (McEvoy & Aven, 1991).

When venturing to a country where the culture and language are quite different, it is useful to engage in a substantial amount of predeparture training, reinforced by occasional in-country refreshers. Techniques such as case analysis, role playing, culture confrontation, and behavior modeling are useful and can be effective. Returned expatriates can be used as trainers because they have the credibility that comes with personal experience. An extensive language and cross-cultural training program reflects a firm's commitment to you and your success in an international assignment. The odds are good that such a firm will also forecast worldwide HR needs well in advance and provide you with a career-enhancing position suitable to both your and their needs. On the other hand, if you are headed to Swaziland and are handed a brochure on your way to the plane as the only form of predeparture training, watch out. Other critical pieces of the HR support system are probably missing as well!

An important piece of the HR package is the performance measurement and appraisal system. Valid performance assessment is difficult enough in domestic operations. Thousands of miles away in a foreign country, you may rightly wonder how your boss will evaluate your performance in a fair and unbiased way. Given the inability to observe performance directly, your boss will be forced to assess the quality of performance using some combination of indirect and objective measures. What does the boss hear through the grapevine about your performance? How will he or she interpret your phone calls or e-mails asking for advice—as a weakness or as a willingness to keep the boss "in the loop"? Realistically, you can also expect that your boss will likely rely more on objective, organizational indicators of performance. What is the ROI for the business? The cash flow? Revenue growth? Costs? Quality improvement? Market share? These are indicators over which you do not have complete control. This realization reinforces the advice given earlier to pick your assignments carefully. It is easier to succeed in a favorable economic climate than a difficult one, and although stability is not perfectly predictable it can be estimated based on historical patterns. Finally, your performance appraisal is likely to rest more heavily on the success or failure of the business than on your individual behaviors and attitudes.

Another critical piece of the HR support system is the repatriation process. Studies have shown that attention to repatriation is lacking in many organizations, and, as a result, turnover among returned expatriates is very high, possibly as much as fifty-five percent within three years of repatriation (Black et al., 1992). This has been a serious concern for expatriates in recent years, and, possibly as a result, more firms are paying attention to this now. For example, Prudential Relocation International, a firm that assists organizations in overseas placements, reports that over fifty percent of companies with expatriates now guarantee those expats a position upon returning home (Coming home . . . , 1998). This is a significant improvement over past practice where returning expatriates frequently had to scramble and find their own jobs after returning. One American expatriate even lost his "identity" during repatriation. Apparently he did not exist on company records for the first three months after his return. He did not learn of the problem until he was denied two loans (car and home) because he was "unemployed" (Black et al., 1992).

Also complicating the return is the challenge of "reverse culture shock." Expatriates frequently report that the shock of re-entering their old home culture is every bit as severe—sometimes more so—as the shock they received on their outbound sojourn. Additionally, family members are likely to experience the same shock, but children may be less well able to describe their concerns. The problem here is likely one of expectations. When venturing abroad, you expect to be confronted with a different culture and lifestyle, and therefore you prepare for it mentally. However, most people are unprepared for the culture shock that comes when returning home. Only if you realize that you are now a different person because of your international experience do you appreciate that this is likely to be a problem. Therefore, if your organization has a program and a support system to help returning expatriates and their families readjust to living in their home country, you can assume this is a good sign that your firm understands the issues and wants to help. Firms offering family adjustment and readjustment programs find they ease entry and re-entry transition, and make others more willing to accept overseas assignments. For example, Motorola employees abroad are reimbursed for personal computers that improve telecommunications between family and their friends at home, and John Deere has developed youth programs to help teens make friends and fit in at school (Lublin, 1999).

Clearly, the advice given so far is contingent on the nature of the assignment as well as other contextual variables. Some expatriate assignments are of a long duration, two to four years, and attention to many of the suggestions above is warranted. However, contemporary organizations use a variety of types of international assignments depending on their goals and needs (Roberts, Kossek, & Ozeki, 1998). For example, firms sometimes use short-term "awareness-building" assignments that last only three months to a year. If you are considering such an assignment, issues such as repatriation and career advancement may be of much less concern. In other instances, you may be asked to join a "SWAT Team" for an even shorter time period, just long enough to complete a major assignment such as the installation of a computer information system. Under such circumstances, your family will probably not accompany you, so issues of spouse adjustment and children's education become moot. Lastly, given the advances in telecommunications, email, and video conferencing, you may be asked to join a global team without ever leaving home, a so-called "virtual team." Under these circumstances, even fewer of the concerns above are an issue.

The point is that the nature of the assignment and the organization determine what is important. There are other contextual variables as well to which you should attend. These are covered in the next section.

## The Context for the International Assignment

Contextual variables usually are influences outside the control of both the individual expatriate and the organization, and two types of contextual variables are particularly relevant to international assignment success: family/spouse adjustment and cultural novelty.

### Family and Spouse Adjustment

Many expatriates return early from an overseas posting due to adjustment issues for a spouse or children. This can play out in many ways. For example, following a spouse or partner overseas may mean giving up a rewarding job or career opportunities at home, with a resulting loss in self-esteem or income for the "trailing" spouse or partner. Companies can sometimes alleviate this risk by arranging for spousal employment abroad, but local laws and customs may be a barrier to this option. Engaging in satisfying cultural, volunteer, or family activities is another way partners can develop fulfilling lives during an overseas assignment, and these pursuits are often important when the expatriate works long hours or travels in the job. The general management role typical for many overseas assignments also may call for an active social life, and represent a perfect fit for partners who enjoy planning and implementing social events. Finally, partners often enjoy travel within and outside the assigned country. The opportunities described above show how a "trailing" spouse can find fulfillment abroad, but much depends on the individual and his or her personal characteristics. Just as the expatriate should complete a self-assessment on the personal and professional characteristics described earlier, so should the accompanying spouse and children. Doing so will help all members of the family rate their potential for success abroad.

Children create special challenges when contemplating life abroad. Young adults and teens may be reluctant to leave their friends at home, and it is important to consider how schools abroad will help them achieve educational goals. In settings where there are international schools, the costs of leaving a known educational system may be offset by cross-cultural learning that comes from making deep friendships with peers from many nations. Other family issues may arise. For example, differing laws and customs in some nations may conflict with family values. For example, many countries do not have a "drinking age." Others do not allow 16-year-olds to drive automobiles. For young adults, there may be dating issues that motivate an early return home. Younger children generally pose less of a challenge abroad than do teens, but there are issues to consider there as well. For example, an active social life for the expatriate family may mean leaving infants with full-time nannies who become central to the child's life. Because most expatriate postings are only for a few years, the child is almost certain to lose an important adult presence upon repatriation. Additionally, special needs for any child can be difficult to satisfy in some nations.

### Culture Novelty

Assumptions and habits reinforced in one's own country of origin often make it more difficult to adjust to countries where cultural habits and assumptions differ from—or even conflict with—one's own. Known variously as cultural "distance" or "toughness" (Mendenhall & Oddou, 1985), research generally shows that expatriate adjustment is more difficult with greater differences between the home and host culture. Among these differences are behavioral ones, such as punctuality, and more value-based ones, such as the role of family and friends in one's work life. A U.S. expatriate who believes that "time is money" may be disturbed by late arrivals at meetings in nations where time and work are less highly valued than in the U.S. For example, when a Brazilian says "work is not a rabbit, it will not run away," he or she is suggesting that work is less central in Brazil than in the U.S. Although it is possible for the expatriate to acquire cognitive knowledge of cultural differences like these, often it is only through failed interactions that the manager learns how these differences really work. For instance, the motivational systems so reasonable for U.S. individualism often fail in collectivist cultures where the opinion of friends or family is far more important than individual productivity. This can be frustrating for the American manager whose only experience is in motivating employees from individualistic cultures like the U.S.

Although the examples recorded above show how cultural distance can increase managerial difficulties and delay adjustment, cultural distance often is not a problem when the sojourner's net benefits are perceived to increase. For example, many expatriates to advanced economies—particularly those from developing economies—enjoy greater social mobility and the material goods offered in these consumer cultures. Similarly, expatriates from the U.S. may prefer differing host cultures, either because they offer a good fit with their own value systems or because they can live a better life abroad than in the U.S. Managerial assignments abroad can include interactions with high government officials, visiting dignitaries, and others one is unlikely to meet in the U.S. All this suggests that the degree to which a nation is "tough" for the expatriate depends in part on national conditions (e.g., health care systems, economic climate, product offerings), and in part on the expatriate and his or her aspirations and perceptions. Both point to the importance of advance preparation for any assignment abroad.

## Conclusion

If you've decided you want to go abroad, how do you prepare or position yourself to be selected and successful? First, review the section on Personal and Professional Skills and Attitudes to assess your current suitability for living and working abroad. If you have a life partner, ask your partner to engage in a similar assessment. Talk honestly with each other and reflect earnestly on your personal suitability for seeking an international assignment. If you can't predict how you'd feel in a new culture, find local opportunities to cross cultures. Depending on your community, you can find these opportunities by attending a Chinese New Year celebration, stopping in to tutor refugees at the Somalia Relief Center, or finding cultural events on your university campus.

Even visiting neighborhoods where you've never traveled is a way to assess your own comfort in new situations.

Also assess your current knowledge of geography, as well as cultural, social, and political events in other nations. Are there parts of the world about which you know very little? Other areas where your knowledge is deep? Answering these questions may lead you to focus your interests on a particular region of the world as Stephanie Thompson did, and perhaps acquire language fluency. If like Gerald Borenstein and Robert Nathan you need to be open to whatever posting your company offers, limited regional knowledge may call for a self-study program so that you become more of a generalist.

Weigh your current strengths and weaknesses for an expatriate assignment, set clear and measurable objectives for addressing them, and then follow through. Take a university class that moves you outside your comfort zone; attend an event that introduces you to a new culture; make friends with people who are not just like you. Crossing cultures—even within your own town—often is difficult to do, but if you begin today you are on your way to preparing for an international sojourn. Enjoy the adventure!

## References


Adler, N. J. 1991. *International dimensions of organizational behavior* (2nd ed.). Boston: PWS-Kent.

Black, J. S., & Gregersen, H. B. 1991. The other half of the picture: Antecedents of spouse cross-cultural adjustment. *Journal of International Business Studies, 22:* 461-477.

Black, J. S., Gregersen, H. B., & Mendenhall, M. E. 1992. *Global assignments: Successfully expatriating and repatriating international managers.* San Francisco: Jossey-Bass.

Borstorff, P. C., Harris, S. G., Feild, H. S., & Giles, W. F. 1997. Who'll go? A review of factors associated with employee willingness to work overseas. *Human Resource Planning, 20:* 29-40.

Coming home: Companies prepare warmer welcome for returning expatriates. 1998. *The Wall Street Journal,* October 27, p. A-1.

Kaufman, J. 1999. The castaways: An American expatriate finds Hong Kong post a fast boat to nowhere. *The Wall Street Journal,* January 21, pp. A1, A6.

Kidd, G. K. 1997. From "Expat Chat." {GOTOBUTTON BM 1 www.expatforum.com/msgboard/webx.cgi?13,} September 2.

Lublin, J. S. 1999. To smooth a transfer abroad, a new focus on kids. *The Wall Street Journal,* January 26, pp. B1, B14.

McEvoy, G. M., & Aven, F. F. 1991. *What multinational corporations should know about Peace Corps expatriate training.* Paper presented at the western regional meeting of the Academy of International Business, April 4, Pomona, CA.

Mendenhall, M., & Oddou, G. 1985. The dimensions of expatriate acculturation: A review. *Academy of Management Review, 10:* 39-47.

Mendenhall, M.E., & Oddou, G. 1988. The overseas assignment: A practical look. *Business Horizons,* September-October, 78-84.

Osland, J. S. 1995. *The adventure of working abroad: Hero tales from the global frontier.* San Francisco: Jossey-Bass.

Parker, B., & McEvoy, G. M. 1993. Initial examination of a model of intercultural adjustment. *International Journal of Intercultural Relations, 17:* 355-379.

Roberts, K., Kossek, E. E., & Ozeki, C. 1998. Managing the global workforce: Challenges and strategies. *Academy of Management Executive, 12*(4): 93-106.

Takeuchi, R. 1997. *Expatriate success and failure revisited: A taxonomy and consequences of international assignment outcomes.* Paper presented at the annual meeting of the Academy of Management, August 8-13, Boston, MA.

Tung, Rosalie. 1982. Selection and training procedures of U.S., European, and Japanese multinationals. *California Management Review, 25*(2), 57–71.

# Reading 3.6

# EXPATRIATE ASSIGNMENT VERSUS OVERSEAS EXPERIENCE

## *Contrasting Models of International Human Resource Development*

KERR INKSON, MICHAEL B. ARTHUR, JUDITH PRINGLE, AND SEAN BARRY

In this paper we posit two contrasting models whereby international experience is: (1) obtained, and (2) used to support the development of career, company, and national competencies both within and outside the country in which the experience takes place. The two models are *expatriate assignment* and *overseas experience.*

In Expatriate Assignment (EA), the initiative for the international experience comes primarily from a company which operates internationally. A position may become available in a subsidiary outside the country in which the company is based. The job requires both knowledge of the company's strategy, procedures, etc., and the ability to work and live successfully in a foreign environment. A suitable individual is assigned on a temporary basis, and subsequently returns to another position in the same company in the original country. Hopefully, the experience will result in career development for the individual, component completion of the job assignment, and organizational learning from the transfer of new skills and knowledge from the expatriate after return.

In Overseas Experience (OE), the initiative for the international experience comes from the individual. Typically, he or she will save money to bankroll the trip, resign from work, and set off overseas autonomously. Sometimes a job will be pre-arranged in a new company, but most often it will not be. The person will often shuttle between jobs, and between different areas or countries, and attempt to spend leisure and vacation time visiting new places. The obligation to pay one's way can involve accepting relatively unskilled temporary work with little apparent career value. After a period from a few months to several years duration, the person returns home, seeking to resume his or her career, or possibly start a new one.

Table 1 contrasts EA and OE. The initiation, goals, and funding of EA are, in large measure, company-mediated, though the individual may politic for an overseas posting, set personal objectives as well as pursuing company ones, and provide personal funding to enhance the experience. OE is, by definition, a personal odyssey, initiated

AUTHORS' NOTE: Recipient of the "Best International Paper" award at the Academy of Management Meeting, Boston, MA, August 1997. The authors wish to thank David Thomas for helpful comments on an earlier draft of this chapter.

SOURCE: Reprinted from *Journal of World Business, Vol. 34*, Inkson et al., "Expatriate Assignment Versus Overseas Experience," pp. 351-368. Copyright © 1999, with permission of Elsevier Science.

**Table 1** Contrasting Qualities of Expatriate Assignment

| | *E.A. (Expatriate Assignment)* | *O.E. (Overseas Experience)* |
|---|---|---|
| Initiation: | Company | Individual |
| Goals: | Company Projects (specific) | Individual development (diffuse) |
| Funding: | Company salary & expenses | Personal savings & casual earnings |
| Career Type: | Organizational career | Boundaryless career |
| Research Literature: | Large | Nil |

and resourced by the self. Typically, the initial goals are diffuse—"see the world," "try something different," "find myself," etc. EA is a microcosmic international representation of the "organizational career" in which the individual moves from role to role building company-relevant skills and ascending in status within one company; whereas OE is a microcosmic representation of the "boundaryless career" (Arthur & Rousseau, 1996) in which the individual moves between companies developing skills by reference to a wider labour market. There is a large literature on EA, whereas OE is largely unresearched.

The importance of EA and OE varies across countries, both in their overall importance and in their importance relative to each other. Our data are from New Zealand, where OE has traditionally been prominent, and where a relative paucity of multinational head offices makes EA more of a rarity. In contrast, the literature suggests EA is dominant in the US. However, the EA literature may make less and less sense in the boundaryless career era. In this era, boundaries between and within companies are dissolving (Inkson, 1997), and careers are becoming increasingly fluid, characterized more and more by temporary assignments and centered on building skills across companies rather than ascending hierarchies within companies. As careers change, and as the economy becomes increasingly global, OE may become a more prominent option worldwide. Popular US programs for working abroad—notably the Peace Corps (Starr, 1994)—or for studying abroad (Carlson, Burn, Useem, & Yachimonicz, 1990) may be precursors of a broader trend calling for increased attention.

In the context of boundaryless careers, both EA and OE form a primary basis for building competencies in individuals, in companies, and in nations. Careers operate as "repositories of knowledge" (Bird, 1996), enabling the transfer of skills between companies and between nations. EA, if thoughtfully planned, may provide short-term advantage to the originating company, enabling it to build knowledge abroad, "import" that knowledge, and integrate it as part of the company's broader knowledge resources. EA may also be used by the repatriate to enhance his or her career within or across companies. However OE offers greater flexibility to leverage the career development of the individuals involved, the competencies of specific companies, and the national human resources of the countries through which they move.

## Expatriate Assignment

There is a substantial, and growing, largely American literature on expatriate assignment of corporate executives. This literature is largely based on the results of surveys of expatriates, repatriates, and the companies that employ them. It focuses mainly on the human resource management (HRM) context of the company. Howard (1973) set the tone with a study of 81 returning expatriates; he noted a number of problems that needed addressing. Expatriates, it seemed, on their return from overseas lost authority, autonomy in decision making, and promotional opportunities. There tended to be no job waiting for returning expatriates and they were resented by colleagues.

These problems have been confirmed in a number of more recent studies. While expatriate assignment may be presented as a career opportunity (Oddou, 1991), and may facilitate short-term career progress, most returning expatriates report that the net effect is not positive (Oddou & Mendenhall, 1991). According to Napier and Peterson (1991), 40% of expatriates return early from their assignments. Scullion (1992) is among the writers finding that repatriation issues are not adequately addressed, and Oddou (1991) reports that nearly 50% of returnees had no position waiting for them on return. Birdseye and Hill (1995) and Engen (1995) report high rates of quitting the company by repatriates. Expatriate assignment, in short, seems to have a way of destabilizing the assignees. The costs may be high—$50,000 to $150,000 for a failed expatriate assignment (Stephens & Black, 1991), and over $250,000 for the loss, and replacement, of an employee leaving the company after return from assignment (Murray & Murray, 1986). The problem, of course, may be a largely American one—to be expected in a large country whose economy is still primarily domestic—since Japanese and European expatriates have a record of serving longer assignments than Americans, being looked after in an extended time frame with a clearer career perspective, and showing lower turnover rates (Tung, 1987).

Solutions to the "problem" of expatriate assignment are also apparent in the literature. These solutions reflect the traditional conceptualization of HRM as a centralized bureaucratic company activity. The management of expatriates must be based on a "strategic international human resource management system" backed by "policies and procedures" to enforce it (Oddou & Mendenhall, 1991). Such systems should include specific succession planning and "career pathing" for expatriates (Mendenhall, Dunbar, & Oddou, 1987). Candidates for expatriate assignment should be rigorously selected, for cross-cultural adaptability rather than for technical expertise, including the administration of psychological tests to them and their families, and properly trained in cross-cultural behavior (Mendenhall et al., 1987; Mendenhall & Oddou, 1988). Mentoring systems between repatriated staff and expatriates should be established (Mendenhall et al., 1987). "Company programs to assist reintegration" of repatriates should be introduced (Harvey, 1989; Harris, 1989). Oddou (1991) summarizes by saying that the key means of "managing your expatriate" are appropriate selection criteria, preparation of the expatriate, provision of overseas support, and career planning, particularly in respect of repatriation.

The research literature summarized above is striking in both its omissions and its assumptions. The problems with the approach put forward may be considered at three levels: the individual, the company, and larger collectivities such as the industry or the nation.

At the *individual* level, one is struck by the total, rather demeaning, powerlessness attributed to the expatriate/repatriate in the process. The causes of success or failure of AE are attributed solely to the company, and the remedies for failure are apparently in the company's hands alone. The expatriate or repatriate is apparently at the mercy of superior corporate forces of HRM, which may be seen as intensive, rational, and therefore benign, or alternatively loose, ad hoc and therefore malign. Yet most expatriates cite as their reasons for accepting international assignments not their desire to achieve project results, be good corporate citizens, or advance their company careers, but their personal development, sense of adventure, and wish to work in different cultures (Mendenhall & Oddou, 1988). The failure of writers on EA to focus on individual dynamics is compounded by their consideration of EA as a discrete short-term phenomenon, separate from the long-term life history and career dynamics of the person (Feldman, 1991).

In contrast, career theory sees career development as an outcome of complex forces, including individual self-direction as well as organizational career frameworks (Arthur, Hall, & Lawrence, 1989). There is much evidence that people "sculpt" their own careers rather than allowing themselves to become corporate sculptures (Bell & Staw, 1989). Individual career behaviors create organizational patterns and inadvertently build company expertise and shape company structures (Weick, 1996). The proactive role of the expatriate/repatriate in controlling her or his own life and in building company and cross-company expertise goes largely unacknowledged in the EA literature.

At the *company* level, to which the literature is most clearly oriented, the diagnosis of faulty HRM and the prescriptions for improved HRM are doubtless valuable to companies seeking ways to facilitate the job satisfaction, adjustment in the company, and long-term employment of expatriates. However, we would suggest that these issues of adjustment and commitment are peripheral. In the short-term, the question of what the company objectives for EA are, and the question of whether these objectives are achieved, should be the primary consideration. A related question is whether these objectives might be achieved in different ways, such as the employment of contracting of overseas locals rather than the assignment of expatriates. In the long-term, after repatriation, we should be interested in the specific competencies which the repatriate brings "home," the value of these competencies to the company, and the mechanisms for the reciprocal development of company and repatriate through ongoing exchange of knowledge and competence. But in much of the literature, expatriate assignment is accepted as a given, not something to meet company goals but something to be coped with. The key objective in handling EA appears to be to avoid the disruption and costs of employee distress, mobility, and turnover. Repatriate departure from the company is seen, in the context of the company, as little short of a tragedy, though of course it may also, paradoxically, represent triumph for the repatriate or for the employer to whom the repatriate moves or for the industry in general.

At the level of the *industry* or *nation,* EA represents a significant means of building inter-firm, industry, regional, and/or national expertise. The assumption, implicit in the literature, that the expatriate's acquired skills, including language and cross-cultural skills, are applicable only in the company in which the individual was when she or he acquired them, is clearly false. Through boundaryless careers, skills are transferred and developed more and more between rather than within companies, often through inter-firm networks and regional and industry groupings (Saxenian, 1996). EA is therefore not just an individual and company issue but an issue relevant to industrial and national development. In the knowledge society, expatriates and repatriates become exporters, importers, and local traders of expertise, the most precious resources of all. To view them merely as deviant company employees requiring additional socialization into productive corporate behavior is to trivialize the whole process of expatriation.

Additionally, we suspect that the focus in EA on corporate employees, often identified by researchers as being all "executives" and "managers" creates a major sampling bias in our understanding of the process of career development and skills acquisition through expatriate experience. The activities and knowledge-building of traveling entrepreneurs, small-company salespeople, plus the many people who travel overseas when young to "see the world" (to be discussed under OE) are ignored. In short, the expatriate experience covered in mainstream accounts of EA represents only a small and limited a sample of experience imported from overseas.

EA is further constrained by corporate sexism: it is estimated that fewer than 3% of expatriates are female (Brewster, 1991). The literature on women and EA suggests that women may be systematically excluded from these career options (Adler, 1994), possibly as part of a broader sex segregation of the labor market whereby, as globalization proceeds, men move into an international arena where key decisions are made, while women function in "second best" domestic positions (Calas & Smircich, 1993). There is also evidence that women prepare themselves better than men for EA and are more culturally sensitive than men (Dallalfar & Movahedi, 1996; Scullion, 1992). It may be that women are more suited than men to international assignment, even in countries apparently hostile to women, such as Iran (Dallalfar & Movahedi, 1996).

In framing EA as an issue of HRM in single companies, the EA researchers are of course merely echoing an increasingly questionable conceptualization of humans as resources, of resources as inert (or at least predictable) and therefore strategically plannable and manageable, and of employees as permanent and company-committed. In large companies which are genuinely able to maintain "lifetime employment" policies and expectations for large sections of their workforces, this may be reasonable. But in a world of increasing intercompany mobility (Stroh, Brett, & Reilly, 1994), ongoing restructuring and rationalization, inter-company collaboration, outsourcing and project work, boundaryless careers become normative and expatriation can no longer be considered as solely a company HRM issue.

Mendenhall's recent extension of his line of enquiry into EA bears out the above conclusion. EA may be seen as a complex and unpredictable adaptive system. Tiny events such as an expatriate's spouse's shopping experiences create multiple "butterfly effects" resulting in idiosyncratic outcomes. EA phenomena may therefore be better understood not as predictable effects of HRM policies but from a perspective of non-linear dynamics (Mendenhall & Macomber, 1997).

### Expatriates as Heroes

Osland (1995) titles her book on expatriation, "The Adventure of Working Abroad: Hero Tales from the Global Frontier." This book goes some way towards de-trivializing expatriate experience. Osland's data is not dry questionnaire box-ticking, but rather "tales told by expatriates." Expatriate experience is thus personalized, and takes on the rich texture of adventure stories in exotic locations. Osland uses Campbell's (1968) "myth of the hero's adventure" to show how the expatriate can be viewed as hero called to adventure, heeding the call, and crossing the threshold into the unknown, and into a place with the potential to enable transformation and spiritual rebirth. After a series of trials and ordeals the hero crosses back across the return threshold, now the master of two worlds instead of one. However, it often becomes apparent that the hero's transformation, and changes in the world left behind, may lead to fresh problems and challenges.

Osland's stories, collected from returned US expatriates, map well on to the adventure myth. The call is experienced as drama, and creates excitement, angst, and foreboding. The cultural differences between "home" and the assignment not only provide their own physical tests and obstacles, but also throw up paradoxes which provide the opportunity for cross-cultural learning. "Magical" assistance comes from local mentors, found through networking, who can interpret the culture and provide guidance through it. Transformation takes place as the hero lets go of previously unquestioned assumptions and frames of reference, accepts new roles, norms, customs, and schemas, and becomes "addicted to novelty and learning" (Osland, 1995, p. 152). Finally comes the return, from hero to company resource, from big fish in little pond to little fish in big pond, to others who aren't interested in stories, to companies who can't, or won't, use new skills, let alone new frames of reference: in short, to repatriation blues.

Osland's approach, it seems to us, represents a significant move toward better understanding of expatriate experience. The expatriate, rather than being seen as an HRM ping-pong ball, is recognized as the protagonist in an adventure of survival, learning, and accomplishment. The heroes' stories focus strongly on their social (nonwork) roles as travelers, consumers, spouses, parents, partakers of recreation and leisure, reminding us of the integrative nature of human development and the huge influences that lie (fortunately) outside company control. The stories also highlight and authenticate the physical differences and cross-cultural paradoxes which expatriates encounter.

From a boundaryless careers perspective, however, the presentation is still incomplete. The company is still there, albeit in the background, part of the narrative. The hero is called by the company, has air tickets paid and accommodation booked by the company, has mentors provided or recommended by the company, and finally returns through the company's threshold in the expectation that the company will provide a career path that makes use of the newly-acquired skills. Like the other HRM authors, Osland (1995, pp. 193–222) even provides a chapter on expatriate management, including familiar material on strategic career planning, selection criteria, pre-training, spouse and family programs, repatriation planning etc. This may create a company fit for heroes to live in, but does it create one in which ordinary people can become heroes? The hero Jason set off on his ship the Argos, to find the Golden Fleece beyond its protective dragon. Suppose Jason had received a proper induction course, dragon-slaying training, the assistance of cultural attaches in all ports of call, and a guaranteed promotion on return, would he have been more of a hero? One suspects not!

Again, Osland focuses on the hero's company as the only suitable repository of the "great boon' of personal transformation that the hero has gained. Why? What would be wrong with examining expatriates' experiences in their wider social roles and in the new companies to which they move or in the new careers which they make, careers which will forever be informed and energized by the skills, attitudes, and transformations of the expatriate experience? Why should the crossing of national boundaries be heroic but the crossing of corporate boundaries not worth a mention? Whatever the benefits of expatriates' experiences to themselves and to their companies, what about their benefits to their country (and for that matter to the countries into which they are expatriated)? We are forced to the conclusion that Osland's model needs further extension. To move toward such an alternative, let us now consider OE.

## Overseas Experience: "The Big OE"

In New Zealand or Australia, one does not say "overseas experience," one says, simply "OE," or affectionately, "the big OE," because everyone knows what it means. Every year thousands of young people head overseas for a prolonged period of travel, work, and tourism. Traditionally, because of historical and cultural ties and traditions, they have gone first to Britain, and used that as a base for seeing Europe. But increasing numbers are nowadays seeking to enter the U.S., Australia, Japan, and other countries. A few well-qualified candidates secure professional overseas jobs in advance, but most just set out planning to take what work they can get, with the presumption they will at least be able to pay for necessities and continue their travels.

Table 2 indicates some key characteristics of OE. Individuals do not usually embark on OE as an exercise in work-career development. Cultural experience and geographical exploration are also sought, and individuals may make short-term career sacrifices and accept employment in unskilled work in order to facilitate valued nonwork experience. Geographical mobility is high, and savings and vacations are used to leverage travel opportunities. The traveler is motivated by broad curiosity rather than specific goals, and the learning agenda is personally improvised. The person is largely self-supporting, though valuable social networks may also be created. Although he or she may give good service to employing companies, attachments formed to these companies are by their nature temporary and tend to be weak.

In conventional views of OE, jobs are regarded as temporary, and career development as coming from cultural experience rather than from work. The exercise is seen as recreational and social more than career-oriented. OE participants have a good

**Table 2** Characteristics of OE

| |
|---|
| 1. Cultural experience as important as work |
| 2. Geographical mobility |
| 3. Curiosity-driven |
| 4. Personal learning agendas |
| 5. Individual is self supporting |
| 6. Weak company attachments |

reputation as hard and willing workers, but their attachment to any employing company is weak. Most eventually return to their homeland, and when they do their overseas development enriches both the companies they subsequently work for and the national labor resource. Park, Pringle, and Tangri (1995) interviewed a sample of tertiary educated New Zealand women in midlife who had undertaken OE in their earlier lives. Most reflected on the importance of their broadening of perspectives and knowledge, their awareness and appreciation of cultural differences, and their building of confidence and independence. However, the greater specifics of the contributions OE makes to subsequent careers remain largely unexplored.

The case material below comes from a larger study of career development in New Zealand, which enables us to provide examples of both OE experiences and its consequences for the individuals involved. The cases come from in-depth interviews with 75 broadly representative, randomly chosen, workforce members, focusing on their career development in the decade 1985–95. The data from the larger study are currently being analyzed, and some preliminary results are available from the authors (Arthur, Inkson, & Pringle, 1996; Inkson, Arthur, & Pringle, in press). The data here are drawn from reported OE experiences over the period of study, along with background information about earlier experiences. It turned out that over 50% of younger respondents in our study had some form of OE in the decade in question.

In the reports below, we will respond in turn to each of the limitations of the EA literature identified earlier, concerning individual, company and industrial or national levels of analysis. As an extension of the last level we will also look at entrepreneurship and self-employment.

### Individual Initiative

A common feature of OE episodes is that they come at the initiative of the person, rather than that of a corporate employer. OE is typically pursued out of a personal motivation to explore and learn, rather than in response to an employer company's specification of a role to be performed. In turn, re-entry into the home country involves further "sculpting" (Bell & Staw, 1989) of the career, independent of any existing company obligations. Three cases from our data illustrate the long-term career consequences that OE can have.

1. *Susan:* graduated and worked as a food technologist before going abroad and finding the same kind of work "doing sauces and things" for a UK company. However, the work was becoming monotonous when she found "an opening in the marketing department and that's when I changed over as a marketing assistant and I loved it." Susan returned home to an economy in recession, but she persisted in finding and taking work with a marketing rather than food technologist emphasis. Her persistence paid off when she landed a job as a product manager in a global company where "you learn everything the proper way." She now regards herself as a professional with transferable skills, and would leave her company if the right opportunity were to be offered. Susan "found herself," at least in a career sense, through her OE, and through an unpredictable job transfer she gained after the OE experience began. Now Susan is bound neither by national frontiers nor by attachment to a company. Her loyalty is to herself, and to the profession she loves.

2. *Peter:* left high school and trained as a computer programmer. He went on OE early, at age 20, spending two years in Europe. "The stuff I did . . . before I left was far in advance of anything I did (in Europe), but I came back with overseas experience (on contract work for a telecommunications system) as 'walk on water' stuff. You sort of explain it to people but they don't believe it so you play along with it, take advantage of it." He leveraged his experience to gain a senior programming manager's position on his return. His rapid success continued through a series of executive positions at a major computer company, positions carefully selected to broaden Peter's understanding of the software programming marketplace. Then came a restructuring that left Peter as CEO at age 35 of a profitable independent software company. The company has grown from twelve to forty employees in its first four years of operation.

3. *Jeff:* went to Australia as a freshly-minted draftsman, but one "already losing interest rapidly" in the field of his qualifications. His further experience confirmed his discomfort with "the politics of

the big office," but while in Australia he put together the visualization skills of the draftsman, a family tradition of being interested in gardens, and his disappointment with regular employment and resolved to be a self-employed landscape designer. With financial support from his schoolteacher wife, Jeff returned home to begin a second apprenticeship. He purposefully sought employment with the very best landscape gardeners at minimal wages in return for the opportunity to learn his new craft. Jeff's emergent success is symbolized by a comfortable family home on ten acres of land (largely planted with long-term investment and landscaping crops) and the new Porsche he keeps and drives for a hobby.

### Company Experiences

While the EA literature focuses on return to employment in the same company and firm system, the OE experience typically involves inter-company rather than intra-company job transfers. The Susan and Peter cases already described illustrate how these kinds of transfer—and accompanying knowledge transfer—can happen. Some further examples are offered below.

1. *Isabel's story:* illustrates how employers can collaborate to provide the kind of experience under OE that is aspired to under EA. She is a research engineer at the cutting edge in the analysis of geothermal data, with a PhD as a direct by-product of the work she performed for her employer. An overseas company in correspondence with Isabel's boss was struggling to conclude the computer modeling necessary for successful completion of a high-profile project. The boss volunteered "I know someone who can do it," and arranged for Isabel to be transferred to do the work. Both the overseas and home employers stood to benefit, as Isabel returned home wiser for the experience she had gained. We must report, though, a somewhat disappointing follow-up that also relates to EA experience. Isabel subsequently became frustrated with her home employer's inability to offer fresh work in response to her increased competence.

2. *Henry:* is another computer programming specialist who benefited from two tours of overseas duty, one in the early 1980s and another in the early 1990s. His latest trip was in response to "an offer I couldn't refuse" from a former colleague. However, the principal learning was personal, as he struggled to help a project that was hopelessly behind schedule and for which he was at high risk of being made the scapegoat for failure. He reports, looking back, that he became confident "in the fact that I could take a project from nothing and push it right through and handle everything that came along." He returned home to spend time with his family while upgrading his computer skills for the next twelve months at a local college. When Henry returned to employment it was with the help of overseas connections. In Henry's words "the area I work in, around the world, is a small family." Put another way, Henry's network, rather than any single employer, provided the framework for successful repatriation to happen.

3. *Wendy:* had dropped out of university and was stuck in "incredibly boring" clerical work before deciding to go abroad. Once away, she became "really really focused" as she realized she had to compete with local candidates for job opportunities. She finally landed an "excellent job" as sales administrator for three entrepreneurs setting up a niche computer terminal and programming company. From there, she leveraged her emergent customer service experience to move to an overseas pharmaceutical company. At the conclusion of a difficult interpersonal relationship Susan returned home to find and successfully apply for a marketing assistant position advertised in the same pharmaceutical industry. She rejoices that "the reason why I got that other job (before returning home) . . . was to prepare me for this job." Yet "that other job" was not on the horizon when Susan first went abroad.

### Industry/Country Experiences

Several of the above cases suggest how industry experience gained overseas can be valuable to the host country, but not to any previous employer, on the expatriate's return. The cases also suggest the benefits of experience beyond the typically male, middle managers usually the subject of EA studies. Three further cases elaborate on these industry and country possibilities.

1. *Joan:* had been stuck in what she perceived to be a dead-end laboratory job when she decided to go overseas in her mid-twenties. Her initial intention was to stay away for just six months, but she ended up traveling widely for the next two and a half years, doing casual jobs to support herself along the way. When she returned she turned her travel experience into a virtue as she successfully earned a place on a competitive travel-agency-sponsored training school program, and built customer rapport based on her own travel experience. Joan is now a company

manager actively engaged in the rapid pace of change of the industry, and managing her own branch office as an "experimental office" where her company initiates multiple trial marketing projects. As part of her work, Joan now teaches at the training school that first caught her interest when she returned from abroad.

2. *Bruce:* a manual worker, went overseas to escape unemployment and a broken home after his attempts to encourage his union to modernize its collective bargaining practices backfired. He landed a job running a bar for a friend he had once met on vacation, then found himself carrying increased responsibility as the business went insolvent and he became duty manager for the appointed receivers. Upon returning home, he was able to claim new-found "people skills" and took employment as a car salesperson. After two successful years selling cars, he used the combination of his engineering background and emergent people and selling skills to gain a position as a customer representative for an engineering supplies company. Bruce appears successful and highly trusted by his boss, the owner of the company, and is developing new ideas that increasingly involve him in the company's competitive strategy.

3. *Damien:* is a chef who has had a range of positions over his fourteen years in the trade, with each job move designed to expose him to new techniques and situations. Experience as a catering manager before going to England helped him land a job running the catering side of an old English pub, with accommodation for himself and his wife thrown in. Damien's regular responsibilities covered 150 meals a day and events for up to 400 people. He later returned home, needing work, to find a job advertisement for a second-in-command at a major new restaurant just opening. Helped by the depth of this experience, Damien quickly progressed to joint and then sole head chef, and is closely associated with the continuing success that the new restaurant enjoys.

### Self-Employment Experiences

Our stories so far tell not only of people finding themselves, and their career direction, through OE, but also of an emergence of an enterprising spirit reminiscent of Osland's (1995) previously discussed heroes. Moreover, the heroic behavior often extends upon repatriation into self-employment, as it did in the cases of Peter and Jeff already noted. The three cases below elaborate on how the shift to self-employment can happen.

1. *Kirsty:* tumbled through a succession of reception, secretarial, and waitressing jobs, in the US, before eventually thriving as an assistant in a florist's shop. She came to value the creative aspects of working with flowers, the small, nonbureaucratic scale of operations and the opportunity to identify with and deliver high customer satisfaction. Says Kirsty, "I basically came back . . . thinking I was going to have a flower shop." However, an evaluation of the New Zealand market led her to a different conclusion, and she shifted her retailing experience to try to help her father's ailing flooring business. Although this eventually proved unsuccessful, Kirsty's passion for both self-employment and retailing survived, and she now runs her own tiling supply and installation company.

2. *Phillip:* had several years of experience as a town planner before moving to Australia and explicitly searching private sector employment opportunities. Through a "Yellow Pages" search of planning consultants, he landed a job where he learned "retail feasibility analysis work" as well as "how they ran their business (and) how I could do a better job myself." He later came home, "bought a suit, got a haircut, got some cards printed" and with the help of a consultant friend who passed some introductory jobs his way, set up on his own. He is successful as an independent consultant and plans to continue in self-employment. A particular motivation is that self-employment will allow him to work part-time, and from home, after his first child arrives, to accommodate his wife's full-time employment.

3. *Owen:* carried a science degree and early experience as a government fisheries researcher into a seemingly carefree travel adventure with his girlfriend, now his wife. They eventually arrived in London, England, where Owen's interest in aquaculture led him to apply for twenty jobs and subsequently receive five job offers. He took a job for a year as manager of a trout hatchery: "The main reason I stayed there was to get a reference which might enable me to get a loan (back home)." More apparently carefree travel brought him to Scotland, where he and his girlfriend were both employed scallop farming. He found the work satisfying, because in scallop farming "the environment was the controlling factor, not us, the humans." Upon returning home, he continued with his scientific work, but soon met and worked casually for an oyster farmer, which led in turn to taking out a lease on his own oyster farm. The farm, however, doesn't take all of his time, so Owen exercises his science background doing computer work for a local sawmill, as well as occasionally helping out his sheep-farming parents.

**Table 3** Common Themes in OE Stories

| |
|---|
| 1. Self-directed experimentation |
| 2. Self-designed apprenticeships |
| 3. Cast off negative past legacies |
| 4. Find occupational/industry identity |
| 5. Develop confidence and self-reliance |
| 6. Return with clearer career focus |
| 7. Increased interest in self-employment |

Table 3 lists some common themes of OE experience as recounted by our career actors. Our suggestion in this paper is that OE may represent a more important means of individual enrichment and collective human resource development than does EA. In an open market economy, the acquisition of overseas expertise may be better performed fortuitously by individual career builders pursuing personal objectives rather than strategically by expatriate company servants pursuing corporate goals. As well as specific "overseas" expertise, travelers learn self-confidence, flexibility, mobility, and cross-industry skills. These are hard to acquire in corporate settings but are core human attributes in an enterprise-driven economy. Of course, similar results may accrue to other forms of novelty-seeking behavior, such as moving to a new state, or from city to country or vice versa, or adding part-time self-employment to a full-time job. EA and OE are more important as prototypes of contrasted forms of career development than as key career mechanisms in their own right.

## Conclusion: OE, HRM, and National Competitiveness

Our suggestion in this paper is that OE may represent a more important means of knowledge acquisition, individual enrichment, and national human resource development than does EA. Our related suggestion is that the current management literature lends a false importance to EA as a means for getting international career experience. We also suggest that, in an open market economy, there are advantages to a system where the expatriate individual rather than an employing company makes decisions as to her or his career placement, development, and reintegration into the "home" environment. Thus, the acquisition of overseas expertise and its importation to the "home" environment is primarily performed fortuitously by individual career builders pursuing personal objectives rather than strategically by expatriate company servants pursuing corporate goals.

If we are right, there are important implications for HRM. The dissolution of secure corporate structures and the destabilization of hierarchical corporate careers is already leading to the reformulation of employment principles in many companies (Arthur, Claman, & DeFillippi, 1995). As companies become less reliant on "core" hierarchical career-builders and more reliant on contingent contractors and short-term employees, they must increasingly locate the expertise they need from outside, and pay for that expertise as and when they use it rather than by bartering promises of future advancement. Development opportunities for employees must recognize the likelihood that they are unlikely to remain permanently, or even long-term, with the company. The company must identify the explicit and implicit skills of its members and ensure that when she or he leaves relevant expertise has been shared and remains behind.

In this scenario, "corporate career-planning for expatriates is almost an oxymoron" (Mendenhall & Macomber, 1997). Expatriates, like other company members, become less "employees" to be "managed," and more "project partners" to be "related to" in a mutual exchange of benefits over a finite period. Probably this is more true of expatriates than of other members, because of their distance from "home." The focus in HRM must move from, "How do we plan, prepare, and protect our people so that EA doesn't cause them to leave?" to "What are the benefits we seek from this exchange and how do we ensure that we get these benefits?" In forming new relationships, companies must learn to identify and leverage the overseas experience already available inside and outside their workforces. In many cases the use of EA to manage an overseas situation probably represents the company's wish to continue control through the assignment of a "company servant" from the base country, rather than the employment of an unknown local. Perhaps some companies should experiment with more decentralized and federal structures and develop new ways of managing the interface between the base country and overseas operations.

The role of OE in economic development is worthy of consideration both by academics and by policy makers at the national level. The traditions of the nation's young people, streaming overseas at the early, "exuberant" phase of their careers (Arthur & Kram, 1989) can create a national reservoir of talent, which may be able to be used to good effect in an increasingly global and increasingly competitive economy. If this is correct, however, it is important that any policy relating to OE should be sensitive to the fact that its strength, in contrast to EA, is the freedom it gives to individuals to find their own learning from the opportunity. Any attempt at "national planning" of OE, prearrangement of projects, etc. would be to repeat at the national level the limitations which we believe already limit the potential of EA.

Frank Fluke, the hero of Keith Ovenden's novel, "O. E.," understands the phenomenon well by the end of the story:

> The thing that surprises me now is how things come together in the most surprising way. Whenever I've bothered to think about people in the past going off to get their OE. I saw it from the point of view of what made them do it, why they went, how they went. I saw it all from the perspective of motivations, never from the perspective of effects. You know, that people's actions have consequences in the world irrespective of that they intend . . . I've come to see that you perhaps can't ever know what motivates people, you can only ever know the effects, and then try to add them up into some sort of plausible story. (Ovenden, 1986, p. 244)

In this way people construct the lifescripts which they use to make ongoing career decisions. In this way the fragmentary explorations and experiments of the OE traveler assemble themselves into the powerful learnings which will later create and transform companies (Weick, 1996; Arthur et al., 1996). The problem with EA, considered as an investment in individual, company, and national development, is perhaps that it provides those who undertake it with too clear and too narrow a motivation to encourage truly creative development. If the cases cited by Osland (1995) are any guide, some of the most important learnings of the expatriate take place in less constrained settings. In OE it is the freedom from fixed purpose or formula, the implicit invitation to "broaden oneself," the release of the human spirit to determine its own learning, which give it its potential as a major source of learning for both those who undertake it, and for the companies which subsequently employ them.

## References


Adler, N. (1994). Competitive frontiers: Women managing across borders. In N. Adler & D. Izraeli (Eds.), *Competitive frontiers: Women managers in the global economy.* Cambridge: Blackwell.

Arthur, M. B., Claman, P. H., & DeFillippi, R. J. (1995). Intelligent enterprise, intelligent careers. *Academy of Management Executive, 9*(1): 7–20.

Arthur, M. B., Hall, D. T., & Lawrence, B. S. (Eds.) (1989). *Handbook of career theory.* UK: Cambridge University Press.

Arthur, M. B., Inkson, K., & Pringle, J. K. (1996). Enactment and boundaryless careers in deregulated economies and organizations. *British Academy of Management.* Birmingham, UK, September.

Arthur, M. B. & Kram, K. E. (1989). Reciprocity at work: the separate, yet inseparable possibilities for individual and organizational development. Pp. 292–312 in M. B. Arthur, D. T. Hall, & B. S. Lawrence (Eds.), *Handbook of career theory.* New York: Cambridge University Press.

Arthur, M. B. & Rousseau, D. M. (Eds.) (1996). *The boundaryless career: A new employment principle for a new organizational era.* New York: Oxford University Press.

Bell, N. E. & Staw, B. M. (1989). People as sculptors versus sculpture: the roles of personality and personal control in organizations. Pp. 232–251 in M. B. Arthur, D. T. Hall, & B. S. Lawrence (Eds.), *Handbook of career theory.* UK: Cambridge University Press.

Bird, A. (1996). Careers as repositories of knowledge: considerations for boundaryless careers. Pp. 150–168 in M. B. Arthur & D. M. Rousseau (Eds.), *The boundaryless career: A new employment principle for a new organizational era.* New York: Oxford University Press.

Birdseye, M. & Hill, J. (1995). Individual, organizational, and environmental influences on expatriate turnover tendencies: an empirical study. *Journal of International Business Studies, 22:* 787–813.

Brewster, C. (1991). *The management of expatriates.* London: Kogan Page.

Calas, M. & Smircich, L. (1993). The "feminine-in-management" meets "globalization." *Business Horizons, 33* (March-April): 71–81.

Campbell, E. (1968). *Hero with a thousand faces.* NJ: Princeton University Press.

Carlson, J. S., Burn, B., Useem, J., & Yachimonicz, D. (1990). *Study abroad: The experience of American undergraduates,* New York: Greenwood Press.

Dallalfar, A. & Movahedi, S. (1996). Women in multinational corporations: old myths, new constructions and some deconstruction. *Organization, 3*(4): 546–559.

Engen, J. (1995). Coming home. *Training, 32*(3): 37–40.

Feldman, D. C. (1991). Repatriate moves as career transitions. *Human Resource Management Review, 1:* 163–178.

Harris, J. (1989). Moving managers internationally: The care and feeding of expatriates. *Human Resource Planning, 12*(1): 49–53.

Harvey, M. (1989). Repatriation of corporate executives: an empirical study. *Journal of International Business, 20:* 121–144.

Howard, C. (1973). The expatriate manager and the role of the MNC. *Personnel Journal, 48*(1): 25–29.

Inkson, K. (1997). Organisational forms and the restructuring of careers, Pp. 165–185 in T. Clark (Ed.), *Advancement in organisational behaviour,* Aldershot, UK: Ashgate Publishing.

Inkson, K., Arthur, M. A., & Pringle, J. K. (in press). Restructuring and the careers of older workers. In M. Patrickson & L. Hartmann (Eds.), *Managing the aging workforce,* Sydney: Pearson Professional.

Mendenhall, M. E., Dunbar, E., & Oddue, G. (1987). Expatriate selection, training, and career-pathing: A review and critique. *Human Resource Management, 26:* 331–345.

Mendenhall, M. E. & Macomber, J. H. (1997). Rethinking the strategic management of expatriates from a nonlinear dynamics perspective. In Z. Aycan (Ed.), *Expatriate management: Theory and research,* Vol. 4. Greenwich, CT: JAI Press.

Mendenhall, M. E. & Oddou, G. (1988). The overseas assignment: a practical look. *Business Horizons, 31*(5): 78–84.

Murray, F. T. & Murray, A. H. (1986). Global managers for global businesses. *Sloan Management Review, 27:* 75–80.

Napier, N. & Peterson, R. (1991). Expatriate reentry: what expatriates have to say. *Human Resource Planning, 14*(1): 19–28.

Oddou, G. (1991). Managing your expatriates: what the successful firms do. *Human Resource Planning, 14*(4): 301–308.

Oddou, G. & Mendenhall, M. (1991). Succession planning for the 21st century: How well are we grooming our future business leaders? *Business Horizons, 34*(1): 26–34.

Osland, J. S. (1995). *The adventure of working abroad: Hero tales from the global frontier.* San Francisco: Jossey-Bass.

Ovenden, K. (1986). *O. E.* Auckland: Benton Ross.

Park, J., Pringle, J. K., & Tangri, S. (1995). *New Zealand Women's Life Paths Study.* Working paper, Departments of Anthropology and Management and Employment Relations. University of Auckland.

Saxenian, A. L. (1996). Beyond boundaries: open labor markets and learning in Silicon Valley. Pp. 23–39 in M. B. Arthur & D. M. Rousseau (Eds.), *The boundaryless career: A new employment principle for a new organizational era.* New York: Oxford University Press.

Scullion, H. (1992). Attracting management globetrotters. *Personnel Management, 24*(1): 28–32.

Starr, J. M. (1994). Peace corps service as a turning point. *International Journal on Aging and Human Development, 39*(2): 137–161.

Stephens, G. & Black, J. (1991). The impact of spouse's career orientation on managers during international transfers. *Journal of Management Studies, 28*(4): 417–428.

Stroh, L. K., Brett, J. M., & Reilly, A. H. (1994). A decade of change: managers' attachment to their organization and their job. *Human Resource Management, 33*(4): 531–548.

Tung., R. (1987). Expatriate assignments: enhancing success and minimising failure. *Academy of Management Executive, 11*(3): 241–244.

Weick, K. (1996). Enactment and boundaryless careers: organizing as we work. Pp. 40–57 in M. B. Arthur & D. M. Rousseau (Eds.), *The boundaryless career: A new employment principle for a new organizational era.* New York: Oxford University Press.

# Case 3.1

# TEAM SPIRIT AT SINO-AMERICAN SHANGHAI SQUIBB (SASS)

ANNE MARIE FRANCESCO

Zhou De Fu, the CEO of Shanghai-American Shanghai Squibb, sat quietly in his office sipping his tea. It was still early and the phones and visitors were not yet calling for his time. His years with the company had been good. SASS was a good company to work for, and each year the sales and number of employees were growing. People in China considered SASS to be a leading company in the pharmaceutical industry, and the way they managed their business was entirely modern.

However, Mr. Zhou was concerned about the new teams that had been functioning for almost a year now. They seemed to be achieving some positive results, but some of them had slowed down and were not doing as much as they had when they first started. On the other hand, some employees who belonged to teams thought they could do much more and wanted the company to expand the team concept even further.

### Sino-American Shanghai Squibb Pharmaceuticals Ltd.

Sino-American Shanghai Squibb Pharmaceuticals Ltd. (SASS) was a joint venture company located in Shanghai, People's Republic of China. SASS was established in 1982 by Bristol-Myers Squibb (BMS), an American company, and two Chinese organizations, the Shanghai Corporation of Pharmaceutical Economic and Technical International Cooperation and the China National Pharmaceutical Foreign Trade Corporation. BMS originally owned 50% but by late 1998 had increased their share to 60%.

SASS produced a wide range of pharmaceutical products including cardiovascular, antibiotic, analgesic, and vitamin lines. About 12 % of total sales were for export with the bulk of products being sold in China. Within China, SASS had a national sales network with distribution centers in 14 cities. SASS employed 923 people, including a sales force of 350.

SASS strove to be a world class organization in every respect. The three partners were all considered to be good companies, and in SASS their intention was to combine the strengths of all three. SASS executives worked continuously to update their management systems, and they had a strong customer orientation. Human resource management was also considered to be very important. HR policies and procedures were clearly spelled out and representative of internationally-recognized "best practice" approaches.

The technical competence of SASS was evident as the relevant authorities in the U.S., Canada, and New Zealand had certified their pharmaceuticals, and SASS was the first Sino-American joint venture

 This research was supported by a U.S. Department of Education International Research and Studies grant to Pace University with the author as principal investigator.

to export their products to the U.S. SASS also took a proactive response on social responsibility. In 1993, the company set up the SASS Medical Development Foundation to promote Chinese medical research. They also made donations of products for disaster relief and were known for supporting the Chinese Red Cross Society.

The company's mission, values, and vision were also clearly articulated. The SASS mission was "to extend and enhance human life by providing products of the highest quality," and the vision was "to be the leading ethical and OTC pharmaceutical company in China by the year 2000."[1]

## Core Values

As with other companies with well developed management systems, SASS had defined its core values:

High Productivity

Customer Focus

Operational Excellence

Teamwork Orientation

Accountability

Openness and Trust.

Company management took the core values seriously and was concerned with situations where practice was not consistent with the values.

In early 1998, Mr. Zhou realized that many operational problems were not being solved as effectively as possible and that some technical processes could be made more efficient. However, since each employee had a clear job description and accountability for accomplishing certain tasks, employees were reluctant to get involved if they felt that the problem was not part of their own or their department's job. Even worse, they would try to place the blame for the problem on another person or department. Clearly, this was not consistent with SASS's core values.

For example, product cycle time seemed to be longer than needed. From the time the company placed the order for raw material till the final product was supplied to the customer took 123 days—far too long from Mr. Zhou's perspective. Why was this happening? Well, it seemed to Mr. Zhou that each department was too concerned about itself and the work it had to do, rather than considering the whole process.

## Developing Team Spirit

In consultation with the management at BMS, Mr. Zhou decided that developing teams at SASS might be a way of handling this type of problem. A plan was developed, and an American training specialist from BMS, Mr. Nick Micale, was brought in to help them get started. Mr. Lang Yu He, the compliance supervisor from the Compliance and Audit Department, was asked to act as team coordinator.

The goals of the new team program were to

1. Increase productivity
2. Reduce costs
3. Enhance the company image

Since customer focus was an important value, SASS wanted to move towards an even better record of customer satisfaction.

At the beginning, ten teams were set up. Each team had a different focus, for example, cost savings, reducing product cycle time, product quality, customer complaints, and improving product quality analysis. Depending on the team's focus, appropriate members were chosen from different parts of the company, often from different levels. Some teams had mostly workers and supervisors, and others included more divisional level managers. Only certain employees were asked to join the teams, and they were usually the better performers. Work for the team was in addition to ongoing job responsibilities, and members were not given any extra compensation for being on a team. However, the company did recognize the team members' contributions by giving them small souvenirs, such as a watch, or inviting them to a special dinner.

Each team had a leader, usually someone who had responsibility in the area of focus and who could benefit from solving the problem under consideration, but the leadership within the team rotated approximately every two months in order to keep everyone motivated and give them the experience of the leadership role. Most teams were cross-functional in order to tackle problems that affected more than one department, but some included members from only one work area.

Times for team meetings varied from team to team but were usually once a week or once every two weeks for about half an hour or an hour. Between meetings, team members might also have to find information or carry out other tasks for the team.

Mr. Lang's job was to coordinate all aspects of the team functioning. He had to set up the teams and decide whom to include on each one. Since his job as compliance supervisor gave him a cross-company perspective, he could decide which departments should be involved in which team. Mr. Lang also monitored the frequency with which the teams held meetings and their progress. If he could, he tried to attend the team meetings himself. This gave him the chance to encourage discussion. From time to time, Mr. Lang also organized a big gathering of all the teams to discuss their progress with top management.

## Team Accomplishments

By December 1998, many teams had achieved substantial results. For example, the product cycle team reduction team was able to reduce the time from 123 days to only 38 days. This resulted in cost savings of over RMB100 million.[2]

The Bin team designed a standard bin (container) to transfer materials from one section to the next during the production process. Previously, no standard bin was used. The Bin team included members from Production, Engineering, Quality Assurance, and Technical Service. The members worked together to come up with a design for a bin and an associated procedure for using it. In late 1998, the team was doing trials of the new procedure, using one locally made bin and one imported bin. Initial results were positive, and the expectation was that the new procedure would become a standard practice very soon.

The Three Swordsmen team was a three person team with the objectives of improving productivity and reducing waste material. From May to December 1998, the Three Swordsmen had implemented three successful ideas:

1. A procedure that allowed wooden pallets delivered with imported materials to be reused for products that were being exported. This meant that the company saved money both by reducing the number of wooden pallets they needed to purchase and by avoiding waste disposal costs for the incoming pallets.

2. A new formula for calculating projected needs for packaging materials that was more accurate than the computer projections that had been used. Computer projected materials needs had routinely been higher than needed. The team figured out how to calculate the actual use from production so they could order less.

3. A method for reducing the number of status labels. Formerly, one label was put on each package, which meant that 12 labels were needed for each pallet. Now the entire pallet only needed one.

The first idea alone resulted in savings of RMB40,000 per year.

The Engineering team included five members of the Engineering Department, some from the electronic division and the rest from the mechanical division. Their objectives were to increase the quality and efficiency of work and to improve the equipment used on the production line. From March to December, they also had some notable results:

1. Responding to customer complaints about receiving empty or partially full medicine bottles, the team developed a new procedure to eliminate this problem. An automatic weighing machine was installed on the production line, and any items that were not the correct weight would be rejected. This had been successfully tested on one production line, and there were already plans to install the weighing device on lines throughout the factory.

2. Another customer complaint the team responded to was the problem of the aluminum seals on the tops of the bottles getting burned. The team designed a mechanism that would automatically take out any bottles that got stuck in the sealing machine so that the others could go through without getting burned.

Another successful team was the one working on reducing overtime hours worked. Including members from Planning, Engineering, and Production, the team was able to develop a plan which resulted in a 30% overall reduction in overtime.

## Team Rewards

Team members did not receive extra compensation for their work on the team. However, there were other rewards, besides the dinners and tokens of appreciation given by SASS. When team members were able to successfully implement an idea, they could apply for the President's Award given by the president of BMS. The team that reduced overtime was able to win one of the awards, and each member received RMB4,000.[3] A team that was able to source local packaging material also won an award.

Another benefit that members received from being on a team was they could include it in their performance reports. Each employee at SASS needed to prepare a yearly report on his or her performance, and team involvement was considered a positive contribution that could be noted.

Finally, team members could realize intangible benefits. Those working on teams talked about being able to expand their thinking, acquiring more knowledge, and improving relationships with other departments.

## A Changing Mindset

Many of the projects that the teams were working on were initiated in response to customer complaints. In the "old days" (before the teams were formed), the Sales Department handled all customer complaints. Now with the Customer Complaint Team, employees from different departments could try to understand what was bothering the customer. If there was a misunderstanding, that could be cleared up, but if there was a real problem, the team could try to figure out why it occurred, rather than merely offering the customer a replacement product. As Mr. Yuan Song Fan, a senior engineer and licensed pharmacist in the Warehouse and Distribution Department said, "There's no need to find out who made a mistake. We need to find out how to solve it."

When members of all the teams met with Zhou De Fu and the rest of the top management, this helped the top managers to understand what was going on in the teams and to appreciate the contributions of the members. Team members also felt that having higher level people at their meetings would help the teams to get their ideas implemented faster.

The teams were also seen as one way of making SASS a learning organization where the employees could learn both from people in other departments and those outside the organization. The changing cultural environment in SASS was encouraging increased positive feedback and emphasized self-development. There were frequent opportunities for training, and 40 percent of the yearly bonus was based on overall organizational performance. Employees who could develop themselves and make a contribution to the organization could benefit, but those who did not might find themselves out of a job.

Management at SASS was always trying to make people feel like they were part of a big family. One way of doing that was to make sure they knew what their employees were thinking. Two or three times per year, a survey was sent out to ask employees' opinions about benefits, the organizational culture, working conditions, and other aspects of work.

## What to Do?

Mr. Zhou realized that many teams had been very successful within a rather short period of time. Many people viewed the team approach as very important and necessary and believed that the good results achieved proved that to be true. Without a team, particularly a cross-functional one, many of the problems would be difficult for one person or one department to solve alone.

But, some other teams had not shown much result. When the team was not improving anything, the managers of the members involved often thought it was a waste of time.

Most team members saw membership as something beneficial, but a few just viewed it as extra work. There were also some cases of teams within a single department that didn't survive for very long because they were not as useful as the cross-functional teams.

As Mr. Zhou pondered what to do about the teams, his secretary came in to announce his first visitor.

## Notes

1. Sino-American Shanghai Squibb Pharmaceuticals Ltd., Company Brochure, 1997.
2. In December 1998, US$1 was equal to approximately RMB8.28.
3. The average salary in Shanghai in late 1998 was about RMB900 per month so this represented a substantial sum.

# Case 3.2

## JOHANNES VAN DEN BOSCH SENDS AN EMAIL

JOSEPH J. DISTEFANO

After having had several email exchanges with his Mexican counterpart over several weeks without getting the expected actions and results, Johannes van den Bosch was getting a tongue-lashing from his British MNC client, who was furious at the lack of progress. Van den Bosch, in the Rotterdam office of BigFiveFirm, and his colleague in the Mexico City office, Pablo Menendez, were both seasoned veterans, and van den Bosch couldn't understand the lack of responsiveness.

A week earlier, the client, Malcolm Smythe-Jones, had visited his office to express his mounting frustration. But this morning he had called with a stream of verbal abuse. His patience was exhausted.

Feeling angry himself, van den Bosch composed a strongly worded message to Menendez, and then decided to cool off. A half hour later, he edited it to "stick to the facts" while still communicating the appropriate level of urgency. As he clicked to send the message, he hoped that it would finally provoke some action to assuage his client with the reports he had been waiting for.

He reread the email, and as he saved it to the mounting record in Smythe-Jones's file, he thought, "I'm going to be happy when this project is over for another year!"

---

AUTHOR'S NOTE: The author prepared this mini-case as a basis for class discussion rather than to illustrate either effective or ineffective handling of a business situation. The mini-case reports events as they occurred. The email exchanges in both cases are reported verbatim, except for the names, which have been changed. Professor DiStefano acknowledges with thanks the cooperation of Johannes van den Bosch in providing this information and his generous permission to use the material for executive development.

*Message for Pablo Menendez*

| | |
|---|---|
| *Subject:* | *IAS 1998 Financial statements* |
| *Author:* | *Johannes van den Bosch (Rotterdam)* |
| *Date:* | *10/12/99 1:51 P.M.* |

*Dear Pablo,*

*This morning I had a conversation with Mr. Smythe-Jones (CFO) and Mr. Parker (Controller) re the finalization of certain 1998 financial statements. Mr. Smythe-Jones was not in a very good mood.*

*He told me that he was very unpleased by the fact that the 1998 IAS financial statements of the Mexican subsidiary still has not been finalized. At the moment he holds us responsible for this process. Although he recognizes that local management is responsible for such financial statements, he blames us for not being responsive on this matter and inform him about the process adequately. I believe he also recognizes that we have been instructed by Mr. Whyte (CEO) not to do any handholding, but that should not keep us from monitoring the process and inform him about the progress.*

*He asked me to provide him tomorrow with an update on the status of the IAS report and other reports pending.*

*Therefore I would like to get the following information from you today:*

- *What has to be done to finalize the Mexican subsidiary's IAS financials;*
- *Who has to do it (local management, B&FF Mexico, client headquarters, B&FF Rotterdam,*
- *A timetable when things have to be done in order to finalize within a couple of weeks or sooner;*
- *A brief overview why it takes so long to prepare and audit the IAS f/s*
- *Are there any other reports for 1998 pending (local gaap, tax), if so the above is also applicable for those reports.*

*As of today I would like to receive an update of the status every week. If any major problems arise during the finalization process I would like to be informed immediately. The next status update is due January 12, 2000.*

*Mr. Smythe-Jones also indicated that in the future all reports (US GAAP, local GAAP and IAS) should be normally finalized within 60 days after the balance sheet date. He will hold local auditors responsible for monitoring this process.*

*Best regards and best wishes for 2000.*

*Johannes*

# Johannes van den Bosch Receives a Reply

A little more than an hour later, with his own patience again wearing thin, Johannes van den Bosch watched with relief as Pablo Menendez's name popped into his Inbox messages. His smile quickly turned to disbelief, and then horror, as he read the response from Mexico City. Not only was the client's need still unmet, but now he had another problem! Stung by the apparent anger from Menendez, and totally puzzled as to the cause, he reread the email to make sure he had not misunderstood the message.

———Original Message——

| | |
|---|---|
| *From:* | *Menendez, Pablo (Mexico City)* |
| *Sent:* | *Wednesday December 10, 23:11* |
| *To:* | *van den Bosch, Johannes (Rotterdam)* |
| *Subject:* | *RE: IAS 1998 financial statements* |
| *Importance:* | *High* |

*Dear Johannes,*

*I am not surprised of the outcome of your meeting with Mr. Smythe-Jones (CFO). However, I cannot answer your request until I heard from local management. As it was agreed on the last meeting, we were precluded from doing any work without first getting approval from management at the headquarters and we were instructed by local management from not doing anything until they finalized what was required from us. It appears to me to be a Catch 22 game! I believe we (your Firm and ours) should not fall in the game of passing the ball to someone else before getting a clear understanding of what is going on. We have had several meetings with local management where the issue has been raised and were responded that other priorities were established by the headquarters (on my end I thought they tell you everything they have been instructed of locally, unfortunately it does not seem to be the case). In my opinion it looks very easy that you accept from management at the headquarters to hold us accountable from something we are not responsible of, and this does not mean I do not understand the pressure you are receiving from your end. However, we are not the enemy. I am not sending copy of this message to our client because I believe that internal issues have to be primarily dealt of internally without involving our clients in the internal politics. The last is what myself truly believe.*

*Could you tell me how can you accept a deadline from our Firm without first having involved local management? Don't you think they are the first to be involved local management? Don't you think they are the first to be involved on this? I may be wrong but if we are in an international Firm I think we should understand the other side and not just blame someone else of our client's problems.*

*I really do not want to be rude, but you do not let me any option.*

*Despite the differences we have had, it has been a pleasure working with you.*

*Best regards and seasons greeting.*

*Pablo Menendez*

Worried that he had somehow offended Menendez, van den Bosch printed off a copy of the email which he had sent the day before, and asked the two partners on either side of his office for their reaction to the message. The audit and tax specialists, one Dutch and the other Belgian, had nearly identical replies. "It seems to me that you got the point across clearly, Johannes," they said. "You laid out the facts and proposed actions to solve the problem. Why do you ask?" they queried. When he showed them the letter, they too were puzzled. "Smythe-Jones will no doubt be the next person to send me a message!" he thought. As a frown reflected his increasingly grim mood, van den Bosch wondered what he should do now.

# Case 3.3

# MASS MERGER

## *THE CASE OF AON SINGAPORE*

ANNE MARIE FRANCESCO

### Case Synopsis

This case describes the Aon Singapore merger process and reactions of the people working there. It is based on field research done by the author. The Aon Group, an American insurance services holding company ranked number two in size worldwide, included insurance brokerage, consulting, and consumer insurance companies. The case is presented from the point of view of Richard Tan, who had the major responsibility for bringing the merged organizations together. The history of the Singapore merger is given, followed by comments from a management researcher (the author) who interviewed a wide range of employees. The researcher felt that Aon needed to address issues such as communication, motivation, corporate culture, and teamwork. Although Richard is not surprised at the feedback from the researcher, he is left at the end of the case wondering what he should do next.

*Chicago, Oct. 21, 1996 (Reuter)—Insurance giant Aon Corp. said on Monday that it completed the acquisition of Bain Hogg Group, an insurance brokerage firm, from Inchcape PLC, creating the largest retail broker in both the United Kingdom and in the Far East.*

*Chicago, Jan. 15, 1997 (Bloomberg)—Aon. Corp. completed its purchase of Alexander & Alexander, a $1.23 billion transaction that will create one of the nation's largest insurance companies.*

*Chicago, IL—(Business Wire)—April 11, 1997—Aon Corporation and The St. Paul Companies announced today that they have entered into a definitive purchase agreement for the sale of the Minet Group to Aon.*

Richard Tan Bin Huat[1] was the head of Alexander Insurance Managers in Singapore, a small management services company. He was in charge of finance, accounting, information technology, human resources, and administration. He had been satisfied in his career so far, but when he heard the news that his company had been acquired, he wondered what the future would be like. As a senior manager of a company being acquired by such an international giant, he wondered whether he might have to start looking for a new job soon.

 This research was supported by a U.S. Department of Education International Research and Studies grant to Pace University with the author as principal investigator.

## Aon Corporation

Shortly after his company was acquired, Richard learned that Aon Corporation was headed by Mr. Patrick Ryan, an Irish-American, and that the name Aon meant *unity* in the Gaelic language. The insurance services holding company included insurance brokerage, consulting, and consumer insurance companies. The global organization offered services at 500 offices in over 100 countries and employed over 30,000 people. Richard also found that the company was listed on the stock exchanges of New York, London, and Chicago, and in 1996, Aon Group revenues were approximately US$5.5 billion.

In the last few years, Aon had been on a buying spree. In 1992, they acquired three of the world's largest insurance brokerage firms, Hudig-Langeveldt B.V., Frank B. Hall Cos. Inc., and Rollins Burdick Hunter Group Inc. Then, in October 1996, Aon acquired Bain Hogg Group P.L.C., Alexander & Alexander Services Inc.(A & A) in January 1997, and Minet Group in May 1997. These various firms were headquartered in the U. S. or Europe and had offices around the globe. As a result of the many acquisitions, Aon Group Inc. was the world's second largest insurance broker in 1997.

Aon established Singapore's first insurance brokerage in 1959. As the different Aon acquisitions took place on an international level, each of the firms in Singapore continued to operate independently under its original name. In early 1997, after the acquisition of A & A and while the Minet sale was still in progress, Aon decided that in Singapore all these companies should operate together under the Aon name.

## The Merger Committee

As a result of that decision, a group of key executives, including Richard, was selected to form the Merger Committee. Their task was to plan and implement all the activities needed to bring the companies together into Aon Singapore. Although the overall plan for the reorganization had already been decided by the top management in Chicago, the committee had to decide how to make it work in Singapore. Each of the merging companies had its own way of doing everything from how they hired staff to how they processed a claim. In addition, they all were located in different places and used different computer systems. The merger committee had to decide how the new organization would be structured, who would fill each position, where everyone would work, how the various systems and procedures would be integrated into one, and how client accounts would be handled during the transition and in the future. In each case, the committee had to decide whether to use a single existing approach, some combination of what was now being done, or find something totally new.

As each company merger was finalized, representatives from that company were invited to join the merger team. After much deliberation, the merger committee decided how the merging companies would fit the new Aon corporate structure.

Bain Hogg-Inchcape would be renamed Aon Risk Services Singapore Pte Ltd and would include Heath Hudig Langevelt, Alexander & Alexander Pte Ltd, and Minet Singapore. It would be responsible for retail broking. Inchcape Insurance Agencies were renamed Aon Insurance Agencies and subsumed under Aon Risk Services.

Nicholson Leslie was renamed as Aon Reinsurance Brokers Asia Pte Ltd. (Aon Re) and also included the Alexander Howden Group comprising Alexander Howden Reinsurance Brokers and Alexander Howden Far East. Aon Re would focus on handling reinsurance services.

Rollins Hudig Hall was renamed as Aon Benefits Insurance Brokers Singapore Pte Ltd and would specialize in employee benefits and human resources. Finally, Alexander & Alexander Asia Holding remained a separate regional entity.

Robin Yeo would become the managing director of Aon Risk Services, Bengt Johnson would head Aon Re, and Richard Tan Gim Hock would lead Aon Benefits. Staff functions including administration, human resource management, information technology, and finance and accounting would be grouped under the Finance Director. The managing directors of the three companies and the finance director would all report to the CEO for Aon Singapore, and the CEO of Aon Singapore would report to the CEO of Aon Asia who was based in Hong Kong. Exhibit 1 shows how the merged companies were reorganized.

The committee also decided that all of Aon Singapore would work at the same location, rather than making use of existing premises and facilities. After several months of hard work and many decisions, it was time to make the formal launch.

The Launch

On June 16, 1997, the official launch of Aon Singapore was held at the Mandarin Singapore Hotel with all Aon staff in attendance. There was a Happy Hour for people from the different companies to get acquainted, and members of management announced the merger timetable. Bernie Fung, CEO of Aon Asia, Chris Lawrence, an executive from the Hong Kong office, and Keith Pearson, CEO of Aon Singapore were all present. During the event, employees received a copy of the Aon mission statement and a short video about Aon was shown.

The employees from the different companies were pleased to be receiving more news about what would happen in the newly merged company, and of course, it was fun to be at the cocktail. However, most people tended to stay with their friends from their former companies so they didn't really have much chance to meet their new colleagues.

On June 17, there were two big events. In the morning, a press conference was held to brief the Singapore media on Aon Singapore. Bernie Fung, Chris Lawrence, and the managing directors of the three divisions, Robin Yeo, Bengt Johnson, and Richard Tan Gim Hock, made the formal announcement and answered questions from the media. After the press conference, Bernie and Chris held interviews with the *Wall Street Journal* and Reuters. Later the same day, Aon held a combined client and industry cocktail party for clients, insurers, and reinsurers. In addition to Bernie and Chris, all Aon management team members including account executives were present.

The merger was now official. This made Aon Singapore the largest broker in the Singapore market. About 180 employees worked for the three companies, and the combined annual brokerage revenue was over S$21 million.[2]

On July 1, Chris Lawrence was named the new CEO for Aon Singapore, and Richard Tan Bin Huat became finance director.

## Early Days

In addition to supervising all the staff functions, Richard Tan was expected to be the key player in making the merger into Aon Singapore work. Although the merger committee had already spent much time and effort to make many decisions, Richard expected that it would take some time before the new Aon Singapore actually functioned as a single integrated company.

## Staff Reactions

In November 1997, Dr. Anne Marie Francesco, a management researcher visited Aon Singapore to assess staff reactions to the merger. Interviews were held with a wide range of employees in all three divisions. The following is part of her report to management:

### *The Beginning*

*Most people described the beginning of the merger process as rather rocky. Often they learned about the merger through external sources: rumors, the newspapers, friends in the know. Many were shocked, surprised, or disappointed when they heard the news. People were generally unhappy with the amount of information given to them, and there was great uncertainty about whom they would be working with and for, or even if they would have a position in the newly created firm. Many people left and those that stayed knew that there were other job opportunities available if things did not work out as planned.*

### *The Good News*

*In spite of the difficult beginning, the overall feeling of people I spoke to was optimistic. Most of them felt that it was exciting to be working for a large, professional organization, and that they would have more opportunity to learn, to develop new areas of expertise, and to advance their careers in Aon. Although they cited many current problems that need to be solved, the overall reaction was that things would work out over time, and when that happened, Aon would be a good place to work. As one person stated so clearly, "It is a learning process for all of us."*

*The employees are working very hard: putting in long hours and in many cases needing to duplicate tasks (using both the old and developing systems) until the new systems are fully operational. People do see progress, but they also hope that more can be done to make things better.*

*The members of top management that I interviewed generally have an awareness of what is going on and how employees are reacting to it. For the most part, the problem areas that they identify are the same ones that other employees see as concerns. Many of these problems are people-related and thus need more time and patience to be solved. For the most part I agree with the overall approach that top management is taking, but I would like to make explicit what I think are the major areas that need attention and suggest how top management might respond.*

## *Employee Concerns*

### *Communication*

*The need for improved communication was emphasized over and over in the interviews. People want to understand Aon. Just giving them a copy of Aon's mission statement is not enough. There is a need for both the employees and the clients to know what Aon is now and what it is trying to become in the future. Employees need to see how they fit into the overall organization and current business plan. If they have a good understanding of what the company is, they can pass that information on to clients and make them feel more comfortable with the new organization.*

*Given the nature of the merger process, particularly when so many companies are involved, it is natural that many changes will need to be made. Employees can accept this. However, this becomes a problem when information does not flow freely.*

*Employees do not feel that they are receiving adequate amounts of information from top management. It is easy to say that it is the job of middle management to transmit information down the line, and to lay the blame there. However, it is the responsibility of top management to assure that all employees are getting the information that they need, and top management needs to take a more active role in making greater amounts of information available to all employees.*

### *Motivation*

*From all reports and my own personal observation, the staff is working very hard and often long hours as well. When I was in the office at 6 or 7 P.M., there were still many people working.*

*Many employees, however, reported that they felt they were not being adequately "appreciated" or rewarded for their efforts. One person suggested that "Management should give equal priority to 'treasuring staff' and getting business." Others mentioned that they were doing more work than in their previous positions but receiving the same compensation. Some suggested that management needs to give more recognition or incentives for good performance. Although the feeling expressed was that most people were working hard, there was also mention of some non-performers. These non-performers reportedly were not receiving any negative feedback and thus other staff felt that it was unfair to those who were doing their work.*

*Given the nature of the job market in Singapore, management must make an extra effort to maintain well qualified staff. Top management needs to develop appropriate human resource management systems to motivate the staff. In the meantime during the transition, all managers and supervisors must be sensitive to the needs of their employees and use other means to motivate them. These could include taking time to talk personally with each staff member, giving praise and recognition for good effort and performance, and providing small rewards such as occasionally buying dinner for groups of people working late.*

### *New Corporate Culture*

*One of the greatest challenges in a merger of this type is to cultivate a new corporate culture. Employees from the various companies that were merged had grown comfortable with their former working environments and want as much as possible to preserve them in Aon. In order to be successful though, Aon must get all its employees to understand and become part of its own corporate culture. Management must integrate the workings of the old companies and emerge as a unified Aon.*

*The first step in this process is communication. As mentioned earlier, employees need to know whom they are working for. As systems still are in the development stage, top management needs to inculcate what Aon's basic values are. Then as new systems and processes are developed, they should reflect these corporate values. In addition, various means of socializing employees into the new culture can be used. These include hiring new employees whose work experience and values are compatible with those of Aon, implementing an orientation program for new employees to familiarize them with Aon, introducing reward systems that reinforce corporate values, and developing other activities that promote the corporate culture on an ongoing basis.*

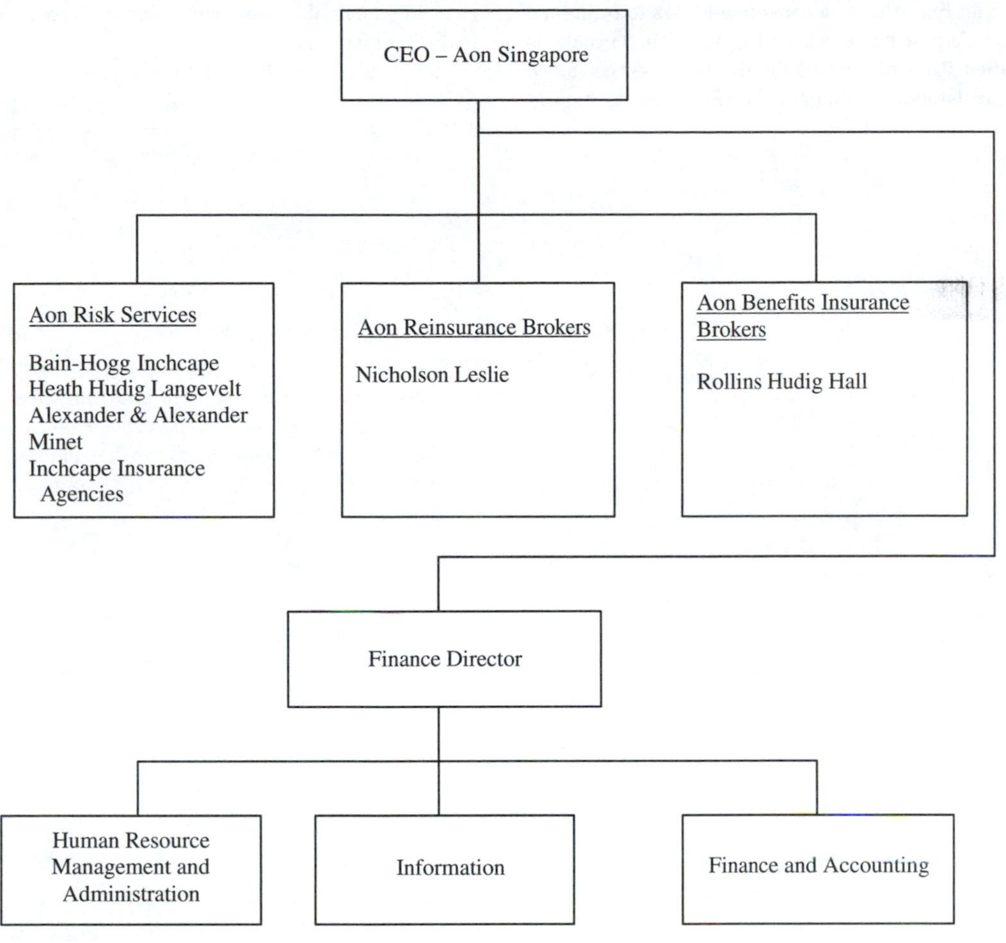


**Exhibit 1** Aon Singapore Organizational Chart

*Teamwork*

*In order for the newly integrated Aon to run smoothly, there must be coordination and cooperation. From many clients' perspectives, they now need to deal with two or more Aon representatives compared to the pre-merger days when one person handled all their needs. In order to make this as comfortable as possible both for the clients and the staff, Aon must promote coordination and cooperation across units.*

*Staff should be recognized for giving assistance to other divisions. Also, various coordinating mechanisms could be put into place such as having a department liaison for clients who have business with more than one Aon unit or creating cross-unit teams who work together to sell and service a package of products. Management needs to make explicit how individuals should work together as a team.*

## What Next?

When Richard received his copy of the report from Dr. Francesco, he was not really surprised with what she said. He agreed with many of her observations and recommendations. But, he now had to decide, "What next?"

## Notes

1. Chinese generally put their surname before their given names. In Singapore, many Chinese also

use an English given name in addition to or instead of a Chinese name. Richard Tan Bin Huat usually is called Richard and his family name is Tan. Since there is another Richard Tan in a key position at Aon Singapore, they use their Chinese given names to differentiate.

2. On July 17, 1997, US$1 was equal to S$1.46.

# Case 3.4

# THE ROLE OF THE AREA MANAGER

ASBJORN OSLAND

## Overview

Armando, the general manager of Playa Negra, a large production facility in Central America, wondered how to bring about the organizational change required at the middle management level in the TQM program they had undertaken. He wanted them to be less directive and more facilitative in their problem-solving role.

## Tropical Export Company

The Tropical Export Company's production facility was a very large bureaucratic organization with long-established work routines. The facility was dedicated to mass production. Decisions tended to be made at the top, by Armando and, in turn, his superiors at the US headquarters.

The Tropical Export Company was a family controlled North American based multinational corporation with very extensive production operations in Latin America that produced a labor intensive tropical export product for industrialized markets, mainly North America and Europe. The company was one of the four major players in the industry. There were a number of production divisions spread throughout Central and South America; Playa Negra was one such production division.

Playa Negra employed approximately 5,500 employees of whom around 550 were salaried; the rest were union members. Playa Negra exported an average of 20 million boxes of high quality product per year. Quality was vital to the customer and high export volume was the key to lowering costs through dilution of overhead costs.

The company had a century-long history in Latin America. It had contributed greatly to the development of some countries through the construction of railroads, ports, power generation plants, water systems, housing, schools, and hospitals. It had also educated and trained thousands of Latin Americans, sending many Latino managers' children to college in the United States. On the other hand, in the latter half of the twentieth century there were several well-documented cases of the company intervening in the internal affairs of governments, actually leading to the overthrow of one and bribery of a dictator in another. As recently as the mid 1990s there continued to be reports in the Wall Street Journal of strong pressure on one government to support the international trade policy the company was promoting. In the words of one general manager, "We're an arrogant company."

Though the total institution approach had changed from the neo-colonial period, the village-like, relatively closed environments in company towns such as Playa Negra created social situations that were more extreme than those found in other

SOURCE: Reprinted by permission of the author.

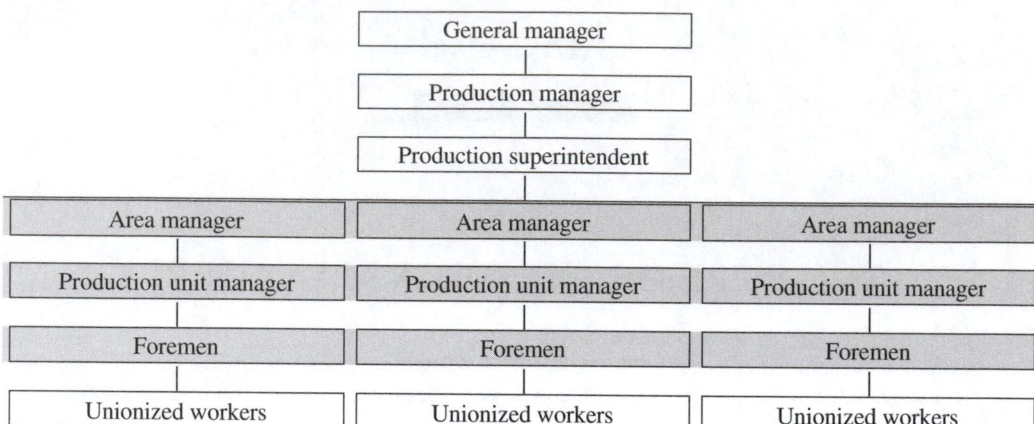


**Figure 1**

modern organizations; the distinction between one's work and social roles was blurred in such a company town.

Most of the supervisors did not have the academic background typically associated with their specialization. Instead they learned their jobs within the company. Metaphorically, one could say the production, transportation, exportation employees, and others directly involved in producing and shipping the product, comprised an "army of enlisted men." They were committed, loyal, and obedient members of a highly structured hierarchy and were generally not professionals. The non-professional managers and supervisors were usually insular in their perspective because their experience was almost entirely within the company and they did not have strong professional links outside the company.

Those who achieved the rank of department head gave ample consideration to what they perceived the desires of the general manager to be. According to one general manager, "Even if I ask a question, they are trying to guess what's on my mind."

According to an employee opinion survey done in Playa Negra in December 1991, Eric, the American human resources manager, had reconfirmed to Armando what he already knew: the group that felt most positively about working conditions was composed of male managers and supervisors over the age of 36. Membership in this in-group afforded these people status that was important within the community and influence that was critical to organizational effectiveness.

The heart of Playa Negra was the production function and one's position within it was a determining factor in the status one enjoyed in the community.

## Production Function

People within the company's production units worked under demanding conditions with a powerful union workforce. Each production unit consisted of approximately 250 full-time workers. The Playa Negra operation contained 18 such contiguous production units. The 18 production unit managers supervised the foremen and administrative staff who, in turn, were responsible for the supervision of the unionized workforce. Each of the three area managers supervised six production units. The production hierarchy is shown in Figure 1 with the shaded area the one under consideration here.

The production unit managers and the area managers had similar backgrounds—a high school degree and a few years of post-secondary education. There were fewer and fewer opportunities for promotion as the higher level positions in the production hierarchy were filled with men in their 30's or 40's. When the highly cyclical industry was booming, area and production unit managers from Playa Negra could look forward to well paid promotions to positions in other countries, as Playa Negra tended to be a training ground for the Tropical Export Company; there were not any universities that prepared production people for the industry. As with any ambitious subordinate, some of the production unit managers wondered why they were not in the slot of the area manager.

The foremen generally had only several years of secondary education or less. They were from the laboring class and were proud to have distinguished themselves by having moved up from union to salaried status and had no career aspirations other than eventual retirement.

## Adoption of TQM

Throughout the 80's and 90's a number of different measures had been taken by the company to improve quality, including the following:

1. naming a quality control coordinator for the region who provided consultation to troubled areas and diffused innovations to production operations;
2. quality bonuses to reward production, engineering, and shipping personnel for desirable quality outcomes in the market;
3. short term rotations of quality control and production personnel from the Tropics to the North American and European markets; and
4. improvements in processing, packaging and particularly shipping, in terms of speed and storage techniques.

Still, a more comprehensive approach to quality was sought. The director of organizational development and the vice president for engineering and quality at the US headquarters had both come to the company from a major food and beverage producer that had implemented a total quality program. They proposed this program to the CEO who supported it at the corporate level. Playa Negra was one of the first sites where TQM was implemented in late 1991, beginning with training. The objectives of the TQM training program were as follows:

1. become familiar with the basic elements of TQM and understand what it can do for the company;
2. understand the key roles in implementing the transformation to TQM and how to work within a TQM; and
3. learn the basic steps in beginning a TQM program.

The training seminars were motivational in design; the intent was to build enthusiasm for the process and get people speaking about TQM and shift from inspecting the final product to analyzing the processes used to produce, pack, and ship the product. The transition from traditional quality inspection of the final product to continuous improvement of TQM of work processes involved the following changes:

1. including the customers, mainly internal as these were production operations, in the analysis and revision of work processes;
2. focusing on the prevention of quality problems rather than inspection;
3. management of the process rather than management by results; managers were to work with subordinates in problem solving rather than simply revising results for variances from targets;
4. participative employees rather than subordinates waiting to be told what to do;
5. providing tools to teams of subordinates who would analyze problems using simple statistical tools such as Pareto charts, "fishbone" or cause-effect diagrams, control charts, histograms, and flow charts followed by presentations to managers committed to listening rather than deciding on intuition; and
6. continuous improvement of work processes ultimately reflected in higher quality scores and customer satisfaction in the market rather than relying on a commodity-low cost producer approach.

There was no connection established between the TQM program and compensation. Management viewed it as part of the participants' duties.

In addition to the introductory seminars, dozens of employees attended workshops conducted by external consultants. Topics covered included facilitation skills and leadership in participative workplaces and training in statistical process control.

Armando chose to train the entire salaried work force. The unionized workforce was not as yet included because he feared they would perceive it as a Machiavellian plot to overthrow their leadership, some of whom were Marxists.

He knew from past experience that his immediate subordinates, the department heads and supervisors, would likely be obstacles as they would see their power and autonomy threatened. Therefore, he did not expect them to change rapidly. He felt that those at the lower levels would prove very interested in TQM as it offered them a chance to have more impact through collaborative problem solving. On several occasions he was encouraged by consultants to press his direct reports to take more initiative in the quality council and to be more accepting of cross-functional teams. However, he refused to be strongly assertive, "I know I could beat them over the head and, like good soldiers, they'd do what I want. However, I could be transferred at any time and total quality would stop if they didn't assume ownership."

### Survey Results

Eric conducted a survey to investigate the impact of the TQM effort. As he explained to Armando, "You don't really see what's important in some organizations until you attempt to change them. Let's see what comes up in the survey (see attached tables 1 & 2)."

Armando listened to Eric discuss the results and concluded: "Looks like the TQM training and early participation in problem solving teams has had an impact." Eric continued with his explanation of the remaining table:

Eric summarized the results for Armando: "Though there were significant differences between the TQM and non-TQM groups (see Table 1), the most dramatic differences were between levels within the hierarchy of the production function (see Table 2): it differentiated the TQM participants from the non participants in the cases of both the foremen and the production unit managers but it also showed the impact of the work context. Foremen, in general, thought more highly of their supervisors, the production unit managers, than the production unit managers thought of their supervisors, the area managers. Thus, the training in TQM had an impact on attitudes and the work context did as well. In sum TQM seemed to complement the way work was done and, the way work was done within the production hierarchy seemed to complement TQM."

Eric had told Armando that it appeared to him that the area manager position seemed to be the focus of the tension within the organization as the company made its transition to TQM. To better understand this, Eric conducted interviews.

### Interviews in Playa Negra

Eric interviewed foremen, production unit managers, two area managers, the TQM coordinator and senior managers, including Armando. The interview results follow.

After attending one of the workshops, one area manager related his discomfort with feedback received from his subordinates during a workshop; he had been told he was autocratic but was frustrated because that was the style his superiors had shown him and he found it difficult to change.

One production unit manager stated: "He (the area manager) speaks with us periodically, on an average of once a day, to tell us or inform us of some details relating to production targets and criteria."

Statements from the production unit managers such as, "When there are production problems, I can almost always resolve them myself with my people," were common. However, the production unit managers also stated that they needed support from the area managers in terms of non-routine problems such as labor relations and problems with other departments.

Within the production unit itself, the production unit managers and the foremen discussed volume, cost, and quality related matters in their face-to-face collaborative encounters to solve the problems faced. In their discussions, they made extensive use of production statistics; the walls of almost all production offices seemed to be papered with charts and statistics. As is evident in the following quote, contact between the foremen and production unit managers was frequent:

> We speak to one another frequently: at six A.M. we speak to clarify what is to be done; . . . at 10 in the morning for the estimation regarding the boxes that one is to get in the day; at 12:00 noon to know what production is required, what problems there were in the morning . . .; at two in the afternoon we do another estimation to see if we're in agreement and the last time always at 3:30 or 4:00 in the afternoon to see if everything came out right and what is to be done the next day.

Bolivar, a production unit manager, spoke of the impact of TQM on the way they worked and innovation:

> Based on the experience that we had last year with a total quality group, we have the good fortune that . . . 80% of the administrative employees in the entire production unit worked in the TQM program (i.e., as members of quality action teams). . . . Based on this, we began meeting officially, in an organized manner, once a week each Monday. . . . From this come different ideas to put into practice . . . based on the consensus of the entire administrative group of the production unit. . . . We performed evaluations, checks. We kept certain statistical data to demonstrate that it was possible and it proved positive.

Another production unit manager but one not in TQM, Victor, responded in the following manner when asked about how innovations were put into practice:

> New practices, in general, are not developed without the consent of senior management and the company union. Supposing that an agreement has been reached between the two, the practices that they tell us are the practices we implement. They call us to a meeting and explain what is desired. Then we direct ourselves to our production units and call our personnel to a meeting and we tell them. . . . The foreman sometimes has already designated a person who is going to do this work. Then we all participate to see if what is said or desired is what is being done with the worker.

A foreman, though in an area uninvolved in TQM at the time of the interview, described his general perception of how the innovation process was changing the way people work together. He stated the following:

> . . . in the years I have worked in this unit, there have been good ideas developed right here by the personnel but all the ideas implemented came from outside. Lately some work has come out of the experimental unit. . . . A foreman had a few ideas that resulted positively. They took these to test them in another area. . . .
>
> One used to tell the overseer and the overseer had to ask the opinion . . . of the senior bosses. If he saw that they rejected it or didn't listen to him . . . everything died there. . . . This often used to happen years ago. Not like now, whatever idea that one has receives more attention. . . . Since total quality teaching came . . . more consideration has been given to the ideas that the foreman and worker have.

In the words of one foreman involved in TQM: ". . . the overseer (the former term for production unit manager) speaks with the manager and later goes to the field and tells us how the work is to be done. Then we have to follow-up. The ideas come from above."

Foremen generally used the term "overseer" when referring to the production unit managers whereas production unit managers did not. They were more apt to call themselves "administrators," the last title used in the evolution of this position rather than "manager," the current official title in Playa Negra.

One respondent explained that the titles reflect the evolution of the managerial style of the position. Decades ago, overseers used to wear pistols, ride mules, and require military-like discipline. The Spanish term for "overseer" is "mandador," which comes from the verb "mandar"—i.e., to give orders. Later the term administrator came into vogue as that was what the individual assigned to the production unit did—he carried out specific orders, attempted to follow a budget prepared by others in the production superintendent's office and so forth. The move in the early '90s, based on a desire to cut costs, was to make the production unit head a manager who controls his own costs on a daily basis, with the support of staff using personal computers. Yet, "overseer" was still in use in 1993 in the production areas and by some executives.

Eric asked the area manager who had successfully led the cross-functional team described below, if he saw himself as more of a coordinator or boss. The response was immediate and direct, "I'm the boss."

## Introduction of Cross-Functional Teams

The traditional importance given to "turf" made it difficult to introduce cross-functional teams in Playa Negra. Department heads and supervisors were regularly described by their mid-level subordinates in the production divisions as people to fear. Subordinates found it difficult to freely interact with peers from other departments when they were unsure about what their supervisor or department head desired. This demand from superiors for personal loyalty from their subordinates constrained cross-functional problem solving.

The TQM coordinator in Playa Negra related how they addressed this problem. Initially the cross-functional groups met with such resistance that Armando told him not to push interdepartmental problem solving quite so aggressively; instead Armando suggested limiting the problem solving teams to departments until the department heads became more accepting. Later, Armando instructed the TQM coordinator to adopt the following hybrid solution, as related by the TQM coordinator:

> An area manager, Anibal, was assigned a quality problem. He was then empowered to choose the members of his team, that included people from other departments. These people met and analyzed the specific problem. Significant improvements in

**Table 1** Significant Differences Between TQM Population ($n = 47$) and Non-TQM Sample ($n = 45$)

*Inclusion:* The TQM group felt that they were more apt to:

- meet with people from several levels and departments of the organization;
- receive information about the financial side of the organization and departmental objectives; know what information management used to make decisions and
- think that supervisors listen to suggestions.

*Upward influence:* The TQM group felt that:

- supervisors listen when one volunteers opinions on important matters;
- supervisors ask one's advice on important matters; and
- one is consulted when others want to change one's job.

*Activity feedback:* The TQM group also felt they received better feedback, in terms of:

- one receives feedback on when one does a good or bad job;
- people inside and outside one's department tell one how the quality of one's work affects them; and
- one can speak up and tell coworkers about the impact of the quality of their work.

*Attitude toward TQM:* Those involved in TQM had better attitudes toward TQM than the nonparticipants. They believe that:

- people seem enthusiastic about TQM and involvement in TQM groups;
- because of the TQM groups people will be more and more involved in the decision-making process;
- TQM groups should be given more responsibility and
- department heads support what the TQM groups are doing.

**Table 2** Significant Differences Between the Four Groups Within the Production Function

Significant differences existed between the following groups for the variables listed below. The first group (i.e., foremen in TQM) had the most favorable scores and the others follow in descending order:

| ***Number in group*** | ***Group*** |
|---|---|
| 5 | Foremen in TQM |
| 5 | Foremen not in TQM |
| 8 | Production unit managers in TQM |
| 5 | Production unit managers not in TQM |

The three variables were as follows:

*Facilitative leadership:* The TQM participants felt that:

- supervisors regularly let one know how one is doing;
- supervisors explain clearly what needs to be done; supervisors let one figure out the best way to do one's job and
- supervisors give guidance and help rather than orders.

The TQM participants also had better results in terms of *upward influence and activity feedback*, both described in Table 1.

quality outcomes resulted. The feedback from the market has been very positive.

The team leaders named people they felt were trustworthy and competent regarding the problem to be solved and with whom they enjoyed mutual respect. Though the team members came from various departments, they found common ground in their strong relationships with the team leader as well as their perceived competence.

## Final Questions

Armando wondered,

1. "What is it about the way the production unit managers and foremen work together that makes their relationship effective and mutually satisfying within the production units?
2. How has TQM had an impact on working relationships within the production hierarchy?
3. What appears to be the source of tension between the area managers and the production unit managers?
4. How should the role of the area manager change, if at all?
5. How could a general manager implement a change in the role of the area manager through the use of culturally effective controls?
6. Given the five or more years needed to make an organizational change stick, how likely is it that headquarters will consistently support TQM?"

# Case 3.5

# CATSKILL ROADS

J. B. RITCHIE AND ALAN HAWKINS

## Introduction

Autumn had come early to the Catskills this year, and a fresh coating of leaves covered the floor of the yellow woods. Kathryn Hill-Baker rolled down her van window and the fresh, cool, mountain air that poured in seemed to ease the tension that had mounted over the past two hours. Kathryn's husband, Brian, was driving slower now as he looked for the turn-off to the lodge where they planned to stay for the weekend. As they left the crowded highways of metropolitan New York City two hours ago, they talked intensely about the future. But discussion slowed as they approached the mountains, and now Kathryn was lost in her own thoughts.

A few weeks ago four senior partners from Kathryn's New York City law firm had announced their plans to leave the firm and form their own. One of those partners was Kathryn's mentor, and he asked Kathryn to come with them and to assume the lucrative litigation practice with the new firm. If she accepted the offer, it would mean a substantial increase in salary and a tremendous career boost. However, she was currently involved with an enjoyable and challenging project with her present firm's largest client, a multinational pharmaceutical company that was establishing a new operation in Argentina.

But what was an important career decision for Kathryn became a critical family problem two days ago when Jim Collins called Brian into his office. Collins is an executive vice president at Universal Bank. He wanted Brian to go to Mexico City to pull Universal Bank (UB) through the coming crisis. During the oil boom years, UB's Mexico City office was one of its most profitable units. No one anticipated the severity of the economic collapse in Mexico, which sent banks with big Mexican loan portfolios reeling. UB was among the hardest hit—over four-hundred million dollars in loans outstanding to Mexico. A few smaller loans had already come due and were renegotiated to avoid default. But the next eighteen months would be critical as many big loans would come due and would almost certainly need to be refinanced. With domestic profits already squeezed by deregulated competition, UB couldn't afford losses in Mexico. Top management wanted a savvy manager to go to Mexico City to take the reins and they were personally involved in the selection process. Brian Baker, with his familiarity with the Mexican loan operations, his technical competence, his international experience, and his fluent Spanish, was the obvious choice.

## Kathryn Hill-Baker

Kathryn, her husband Brian, and their two children currently live in an old but quaint house in a quiet

SOURCE: This case was previously published in *Readings and Cases in International Human Resource Management* edited by Mark Mendenhall and Gary Oddon, 2000, South-Western College Publishing. Reprinted with permission.

New Jersey suburb. She was born while her family was abroad. Her father was a commissioned officer in the U.S. Marines. She was the fifth of six children in her family, the second one born in Japan. However, she was the only girl, and the family lavished her with affection. The Hills were very religious. Every morning the family would gather and read a brief passage from the Bible before breakfast. And every Sunday the family attended church services on the base.

Kathryn's family lived on a military base near Tokyo until she was eight when her father was transferred to West Germany. They were only there two years. Her father retired from the military and took a management position with a large firm in Detroit that did a lot of contract work for the Defense Department. Through junior and senior high school, Kathryn excelled in both athletics and academics. She was a National Merit finalist and received a full-tuition scholarship to the University of Michigan where she was an English composition major. She also played on the junior varsity tennis team until her senior year. She graduated in the top five percent of the class.

Kathryn was initially attracted to Brian when they met during her senior year in an English literature class in which they studied Robert Frost poems. Over the summer, she gradually fell in love with a sensitive and warm man. He was different from her macho brothers and the guys she had usually dated in high school and college. Kathryn's family attended the wedding but her parents were upset that she was marrying outside her religious faith.

## Brian Baker

Brian was born in Panama City where his father was a diplomat for the U.S. government. When he was five his family moved to Mexico City where his father became the head of the U.S. Consulate there. His father was a decorated World War II fighter pilot and his mother had been an army nurse.

After the war, Brian's father finished up his degree in Public Administration and International Relations at American University, while his mother worked for a VA hospital in Virginia. His father graduated summa cum laude and was offered a diplomatic position in Panama City. Brian was born two weeks after their arrival there. Despite the demands of a young baby, his mother was actively involved in UN efforts to upgrade health care in Panama. Brian's earliest memories were tagging along with his mother as she inspected hospitals in the more rural areas of Panama.

The family moved to Mexico City when Brian's father was promoted to an important consulate position there. Brian attended a private Catholic school and most of his companions were children of wealthy Mexican industrialists and government officials. Over the years he learned to speak Spanish as fluently as he spoke English.

Summers were the source of Brian's richest memories. When summer vacation began, Brian and his mother would fly to Vermont where his maternal grandparents lived. They usually spent about a month there. Then they would fly to Michigan and meet Brian's dad and spend another month or two at a summer cabin in northern Michigan owned by Brian's paternal grandparents. The cabin was right on a lake and Brian probably spent three-fourths of his waking hours in or on the water, swimming, sailing, water skiing, and fishing. In the evenings they barbecued on the beach, ate and watched the sun sink into the lake, painting the sky with streaks of warm colors.

When Brian was 16, his father suffered a mild stroke and decided to ease up and take a "cushy, state-side desk job." They moved to New York where Brian finished his senior year of high school. He was accepted to the honors program at the University of Michigan and decided to go there and live with his grandparents. He studied political science and journalism, planning to eventually go to law school. After graduating he worked for a year at a local insurance company before beginning his graduate work. He was disappointed when he was not admitted to the University of Michigan Law School. But he enjoyed his work at the insurance company and decided to apply to the business school and was accepted.

The summer before he began in the MBA program at Michigan, he took a couple of evening classes to sharpen his math skills. Just for fun he also took an English literature class, something he never seemed to have time for as an undergraduate. There he met an attractive English major, Kathryn Hill, who was attending summer school in order to graduate by fall. They often studied together at night in the library and then went to an ice cream parlor where they talked until it closed. They were married in August.

## Work and Graduate School

After a honeymoon, Kathryn worked as a staff reporter for a Detroit newspaper and edited and typed student papers to earn extra income. Brian started the MBA Program at Michigan and although busy, they enjoyed their marriage and looked forward to starting their own family when Brian graduated. The only significant friction between them was a result of Kathryn's desire to attend Sunday services each week. Busy schedules didn't allow them much time together during the week, and they felt it was important to spend weekends together. Eventually, Kathryn decided to curtail her church attendance to every other week, and would spend the other weekends with Brian up at his grandparents' cabin.

Brian did well in school although he didn't "set the world on fire." His writing ability and hard work put him in the top third of his class. He received two good job offers, one with a small but respected brokerage firm, the second with a large multinational bank. Both offers would put the Bakers in New York City where Brian's parents lived. The brokerage firm offered more money, but the bank offered more exciting career opportunities. Brian hoped to go abroad in the future. Universal Bank had branch operations all over the world with many internationally assigned managers. Kathryn liked the idea of living in New York with its endless cultural opportunities. And there would be ample opportunities in the future to continue her career in journalism, if she wanted. They accepted UB's offer and moved to New York.

## Universal Bank

Universal Bank was an established, somewhat conservative bank with a large portion of their business overseas. In an average year, UB earned nearly sixty percent of their revenues abroad. The year Brian began working the bank had revenues of nearly four billion dollars. The International Banking Division was run almost like a separate subsidiary and was the glamour division of the bank. However, they seldom hired entry level managers, preferring to take promising managers with good track records from the various domestic divisions. UB had strong footholds in most of the big cities in Europe and England. In recent years, they had gained ground in an increasingly competitive Far East market, where U.S. multinationals brought their capital and built many manufacturing facilities to escape the high labor cost in the U.S. During the start-up phase of a foreign operation, UB catered mostly to U.S. and other English-speaking industrialists doing business in a particular country. As they got to know the countries better and how local businesses operated, they would do more business with national firms.

The deregulation of the banking industry had strained UB's conservative management. Past strategy had been to put a UB branch "within two miles of nearly every resident and business in New York." As a result, UB owned the largest share of the deposit market in New York. However, recently several of UB's competitors had gone to an automated teller machine strategy with its significantly lower transaction costs. In addition, UB's competitors were rapidly expanding their product lines and services to attract the upper scale customers who were willing to pay a little more for what they really wanted. UB's philosophy had been to move deliberately and carefully into new product lines and services so as not to "overburden the standard customer who just wants a dependable bank in a convenient location." This strategy seemed now to have hurt UB. Profit margins slipped the last two years and their fixed assets-to-sales ratio was now, by a wide margin, the highest among New York banks.

Not surprisingly, a new top management team was installed in the late 1970s. They were young, brash and aggressive and determined to turn UB's domestic operations into a market-driven organization. They were depending on UB's healthy international operations to provide them the cash flow to put the domestic bank back up on its feet and in the race again.

## New York

Brian began at UB as a loan officer in a branch handling mostly small corporate loans from steady customers with revolving accounts. Although the job did not really push his skills, he enjoyed the regular, close contact with his clients and took pride in the growth of their small businesses. He spent a lot of time out of the office with his clients trying to get a better feel for their unique needs and problems.

His track record after two years was good, and he was transferred to the central office downtown and asked to handle the accounts of some large multinational companies. But these big companies were just after the best prices and personal contact was lacking in the job. After a year he took a third position with a branch that did a good deal of loan business with Mexican and South American multinationals operating in New York City. Personal contact was more available in the job, and he enjoyed using his fluent Spanish again.

Kathryn had given birth to their first child shortly after they arrived in New York, and a second child followed only 18 months later. Homemaking was challenging to Kathryn. She had always been so active before, but now taking care of two small children kept her at home almost constantly. After the second child was born, Kathryn suffered a depression. She tried to hide it from Brian, hoping it would go away soon. But it only got worse and Brian started asking questions. Brian suggested some counseling but Kathryn did not like the idea. She tried to find part-time work as a journalist, but no one seemed interested. Instead, she applied to law school and was accepted at Columbia University. Although Brian was a little jealous, he encouraged Kathryn to go. They arranged for a babysitter in the afternoons and Kathryn studied at night and on weekends. Brian would get home about five o'clock and take care of the children and do the housework. Kathryn's mood improved, and Brian gained an appreciation for the rigors of domestic life.

However, leaving work at four o'clock every day did not help Brian's career. Although he got to work early and kept a fair client load, he was unable to drink with his colleagues after work, a regular activity in his unit. Brian's performance evaluations were still excellent but he did not have inclusion in the strong social network of the bank that was valuable for career progress. And because "he couldn't be counted on after four o'clock," he was seldom given the "plum accounts." But Kathryn was happier, and Brian sincerely liked his "daddy" role and the daily counterpoint it provided to the kinetic pace of work. In a few years the kids would be in school, and he could get back on track at work. The drawbacks were that money was tighter because of Kathryn's tuition, and quality time for Brian and Kathryn was limited.

Kathryn's grades her first year were good enough to get her on the law review. She graduated in the top ten percent of her class and accepted an offer to work for a medium-sized law firm that serviced many of the pharmaceutical companies in New York City. The children began school, so with Kathryn's extra income they purchased a small home in a suburb with an excellent school system. Kathryn worked 60-hour weeks and Brian took on some extra work and tried to get back into the social network now that he didn't need to be home at five o'clock every night. However, after about a year of both Kathryn and Brian working, Brian began to feel restless. He had been in the same unit almost five years and was risking career stagnation. He began to look at other positions. Although he was attracted to a possible international assignment, he didn't see quite how it could be managed with his current family situation.

It wasn't long after this, though, that a chance for an international assignment surfaced. UB was opening a branch in Buenos Aires, Argentina. Brian had done some loan work with several small Argentine firms operating in New York and had a pretty good feel for how they did business. With his fluent Spanish, he would be a good candidate to manage that new branch. When he casually mentioned the opening to Kathryn one night at dinner, she was concerned.

"How can we manage that? My work is going so well now, and with the house and all, it just doesn't seem to be the right time, Brian," she remarked.

"My chances are pretty slim, anyway," Brian replied. "They've been cutting back their international managers the last few years because they're just too expensive. It takes $100,000 just to move them, and may be $300,000 a year for salary, bonus, benefits, and perks. It can be twice that much in some places where the cost of decent housing is so high, or where there's high inflation. Competition for these positions is stiff. And with all the money involved now, an executive-vice president has to make the selection decision. I doubt that they would search low enough in the ranks of the company to find me."

But Brian underestimated his credentials. When Bob Jasper, the Executive Vice-president for UB-International pulled Brian's name out of the computerized personnel planning system in the bank, he was interested and asked Brian to come talk to him. Their thirty-minute chat turned into a two hour lunch as they discussed Brian's background, his work experience, and plans for the new Buenos Aires unit. The British banks dominated among foreign banks in Argentina. Research had shown that times might be right to challenge the "stodgy British banks down there." Brian was honest about his family situation but he could hardly conceal his excitement about the prospects of such an assignment. He would have almost complete autonomy to formulate and implement a strategy for breaking into the Argentina market, as well as responsibility for getting the branch up and running.

Two weeks later Brian was back in Jasper's office.

"You're the man, Brian. We want you down there as soon as you can tie things up here—no more than six weeks. This is the break you need. You'll be in the limelight. This assignment can turn you into top management material."

Brian was nervous when he recounted his conservation with Jasper to Kathryn. He restrained his enthusiasm but still tried to highlight the positive aspects of the assignment.

"This kind of thing is really good for kids," he argued. "It gives them a better perspective of the world. We'll find them a good private school, and the bank said that they'd help in finding you a job somewhere. The bank pays for high class housing and maids. They'll fly us back once a year for a month-long vacation, and they pay for a two-week R&R leave every year as well. Jasper said that he'll bring us back in three years. This is a once-in-a-lifetime shot, Kathryn. I know it comes at a bad time for you with your work and all, but when we get back, I promise you that we'll settle in and you can pursue your career full steam!"

Kathryn wanted time to think. They continued to talk about it, usually until two or three in the morning. Kathryn wondered what she would do. Despite Brian's assurances, she was uncertain about the prospects of employment down there. She couldn't speak the language and knew little about the culture. Kathryn's firm told her that she could have her job back at any time, which made things easier, but still, the uncertainty was almost overwhelming. One night she phoned her parents to talk about it. Relations between Kathryn and her parents had become strained over the past few years. Although her parents would not actually come right out and say it, she knew that they felt she had "abandoned" Brian and the children when she went to law school and began working. Still, she wanted their input. They both encouraged Kathryn to go.

"Believe me, Kate," her father's voice boomed over the phone, "these kinds of opportunities come along only once. If you don't jump now, Brian may never get another chance."

That night, Kathryn informed Brian that she was willing to go. They had only four weeks to get their affairs settled and Brian was so busy at work that Kathryn had to do most of it herself while trying to wrap things up at work. The bank offered to pay for a week-long language and culture training program for Brian and Kathryn, but they simply didn't have the time to go. They stored the furniture, left the selling of the house to a real estate agent, packed their bags and were gone.

## Argentina

For the first 18 months in Buenos Aires Brian put in 16-hour days and traveled frequently. But it was just what he wanted: autonomy, challenge, responsibility, and excitement. The first few months he concentrated on putting together a good staff. Rather than bring down some Americans though, he hired away from other banks some local professionals who knew how business was done in Argentina and who had extensive contacts. And rather than target the big foreign multinationals, and compete head-on with the established British banks' bread and butter, he went after some middle- to large-sized domestic firms. Whereas English was usually the international language in business, Brian conducted all his business in Spanish. This meant he could usually deal directly with the president of the company rather than the designated English-speaking finance officer. His strategy was successful. The branch was soon profitable and growing rapidly.

His only major disappointment was that, contrary to Bob Jasper's "limelight" predictions, no one back in New York seemed to take notice of his accomplishments. Anonymity could be tolerated, but headquarters was painfully slow responding to any special requests. Of course, if his reports were late, he would get a call from some "knucklehead in the accounting department who thought Buenos Aires was another socialist state in the Caribbean."

Kathryn had a more difficult time adjusting to the move. The family spent the first two months in a hotel unable to find suitable housing within the bank's allotted housing allowances. Brian finally got someone in International Compensation back at headquarters to raise the allowance enough so they could afford a decent place to live. The children were sick much of the time the first few weeks.

Eventually they found a nice home to rent in a suburb of the city in a price range the bank would accept. But Kathryn hardly left the house the first few months. A maid did all the shopping and most of the housework. With the children in a private British school most of the day, Kathryn had more free time than ever before in her life. Much of it was consumed by Dickens' novels, which were enjoyable, but the loneliness grew more intense. Brian was concerned and hired a private Spanish tutor to come every day and help Kathryn learn the language, which the bank paid for. He also kept his eyes open for some kind of work for her. But women professionals were not well accepted in Argentina. After about a year there, he was able to pull some strings with a man who worked at the U.S. Embassy who had known Brian's father many years ago, and got her a position working with immigration cases, visas, and some sticky international licensing problems. Although apprehensive of her ability to speak the language, she was happy to be working and using some of her legal skills again. She quickly made some new friends.

At that point, things began to go well for the Bakers. Even though Brian still wasn't around much, Kathryn and the children took advantage of long school holidays to travel to scenic spots along Argentina's vast and beautiful coastline. Kathryn made close friends with some American women at work, and often they would travel together. Five years passed and no one seemed anxious to return to the United States.

Unfortunately, Brian's father's health had been deteriorating while Brian was in Argentina. Nevertheless, his death of a sudden stroke came as a shock to Brian. The family returned to New York for the funeral. While there, Brian dropped in to Jim Collins' office who had replaced Bob Jasper as Executive Vice President of UB International upon Jasper's retirement.

"It's good to get to meet you, Brian," Collins said. "You've done an outstanding job down there. You've put UB on the map in South America. As a matter of fact, we're thinking about opening a couple more branches in Chile and Brazil. If we do, I want you to move up and be a regional director for South America. I'll make you a senior vice president. You can still live in Buenos Aires if you want. Give it some thought, Brian."

Brian was flattered to finally be getting some recognition. Regional Director would be another exciting position. More importantly, Brian thought it was a signal from top management that he was being groomed for bigger things to come. Collins was a regional director in Europe prior to his promotion to Executive Vice-President at UB-International.

In addition, his family seemed genuinely happy. The children were receiving a superior education to what they would have received in the States. They had friends, and could speak the language. But they would soon be entering their teenage years and Kathryn was concerned that they might miss a crucial socialization period if they stayed abroad too much longer. If Brian took the Regional Director position, it would likely entail another five years of hard work. And Brian was concerned about the effect his long hours of work had on his marriage and his relationship with his children. He was also concerned about his mother, who was alone for the first time in her life. As her only child, Brian felt a responsibility to be closer to her now and help her adjust to his father's absence. It seemed clear to Brian and Kathryn that it was time to return to the States. Brian contacted Jim Collins and informed him of his plans to return in a few months when school let out for the summer. Collins was disappointed but said he would try to find a slot for him somewhere by the time he got back. With a feeling of pride for what they had accomplished during the last five and a half years, and anticipation for the future, the Bakers packed their bags and returned home to New York.

## The Repatriation

Coming home wasn't easy. They left the warmth of Argentina and returned to the cold of winter in New York. There were no "Welcome Home" banners for Brian when he returned to work. In fact, he wondered if he was even in the right place. He hardly recognized anyone. Some major restructuring of the organization left Brian confused about strategic directions of the bank. The new (to Brian) top management team had replaced the old "knife-and-fork" banking culture with a lean, market-driven organization. But there were more serious problems. No clear position was available for Brian when he returned. Brian felt that he needed to get back into domestic operations if he was going to become top management material. But it soon became clear that no one was all that interested in taking him on board.

"These repatriates are out of touch with domestic operations now," was a frequently expressed opinion at the bank. "They walk around dazed for six months and when they finally come out of shock, they want to run the whole show. Overseas they had it all to themselves, but back here they forget we're a team."

Brian was assigned to work on a few projects at UB-International while he waited for some position to open up for him. He got involved with some of the sticky negotiations going on with refinancing some of the Mexican loans the bank had outstanding. But he felt more like a translator than a decision-maker. These projects hardly used the management skills he developed while abroad.

Meanwhile, the Baker children were having serious difficulties readjusting to American life. In terms of their education, they were well ahead of their peers in junior high. Socially though, they were perceived as odd, even stuffy, and had difficulty making friends. Brian felt responsible for the problems they were having and tried to compensate for it by taking the children to movies and spending a lot of time with them at night and on weekends. Although tired from work, Kathryn spent a good deal of time in the evenings talking with the children and helping them deal with their problems.

Kathryn was the only family member who seemed to be readjusting well. She went back to work full-time for the firm that she had worked for before they left for Argentina. They were delighted to have her back, and even paid for some legal update sessions at a nearby university. The firm had grown as some of their client companies had grown. One client company was now in the planning stages for a new manufacturing facility in Argentina. Kathryn become valuable in that process with her language ability, familiarity with local legal systems, and contacts. She traveled several times to Argentina on business and was very busy.

Brian was hoping that their return to the U.S. would give the family more time to spend with each other. He did spend more time with the children, but Kathryn's work didn't allow them to spend much time together as a couple. The five and a half years in Buenos Aires with Brian working 70-hour weeks had left their marriage strained. Their ability to communicate with each other, which played an important part of the happiness of their early years together, was rusty. But more importantly, they felt as if they were two separate persons traveling the same road, but in different directions, loosely coupled only by a son and a daughter. Brian and Kathryn were spending some time now with a marriage counselor, trying to repair some of the damage before it was too late.

After eight months of project work, Brian was still unable to find a suitable position at the bank. He was angry, frustrated, and wanted to quit. But the financial shock that accompanied their return to the States militated against that action right now. With the economy down, jobs were not easy to come by. Despite Kathryn's income, they were still struggling to meet their financial obligations. Real estate prices and interest rates had soared while they were gone and their new home required both incomes. Brian hung on, hoping that something would soon open up.

Then Brian ran across a friend he had gone to school with at Michigan. His friend mentioned an opening in the small New Jersey bank at which he had a revolving account. The vice-president of the bank was retiring next month. Although promotion opportunities were limited because the president was only a few years older than Brian and likely to remain in the number one slot for a long time, this kind of position would allow Brian to use his management skills again, and he would only have to work forty- to fifty-hour weeks. It was a stable position, and he could drive to work in ten minutes rather than commute two hours a day. He seriously considered applying for the position.

That's when Jim Collins called and asked Brian to go to Mexico City for eighteen months to handle the crucial negotiations coming up.

"You draw up the ticket," Collins told Brian, "and I'll sign it. Any guarantees you need, you name them, we'll do them. You've got my word that I'll bring you back in eighteen months as a senior vice-president anywhere you want to be. We're counting on you, Brian."

When Brian mentioned the offer to Kathryn, she was visibly shaken. Kathryn was still trying to decide whether she wanted to go with the new law firm or stay with the old one. And now this.

Brian called his mother and asked her to come stay with the kids for the weekend. Then he and Kathryn jumped in the van and headed for the Catskills to do some hard choosing.

# Case 3.6

# ANDREAS WEBER'S REWARD FOR SUCCESS IN AN EXPATRIATE ASSIGNMENT—A RETURN TO AN UNCERTAIN FUTURE

GÜNTER K. STAHL AND MARK E. MENDENHALL

Andreas Weber's mind would not stop racing. Normally, an intense run in the evening had the effect of dissipating his worries, but tonight this did not work. The further he jogged along his standard route along the Hudson River, the more he could not get out of his mind the letter he knew he must write tomorrow. "How had it all come to this?" he wondered. This thought triggered his mind back seven years, to the initial event that had set in motion the process that led to his current trouble.

Andreas remembered the occasion clearly; Herr Goerner, the Managing Director, had walked into his office at the Frankfurt headquarters of his bank, and asked him to participate in a companywide international leadership development program. Herr Goerner explained that the program involved an international assignment with the intention of fostering the professional development of young, aspiring managers. After their overseas assignments, the trainees would constitute a pool of internationally experienced young managers with the potential for senior management positions at corporate headquarters. Andreas accepted the offer on the spot, with pride. He had worked very hard since joining the bank and felt that his efforts had finally paid off.

The program started with a one-week seminar that took place at a leading business school in the United States. The CEO had flown in from Frankfurt for this event, demonstrating the commitment of top management to this program. In his speech to the participants, the CEO stressed that the major challenge and "number one" priority for the bank in the future was globalization. He made it clear that international experience was a key value in the organization and a prerequisite for promotion into the ranks of senior management. Andreas felt confident that he had made the right decision in accepting the offer and in pursuing an international career.

Shortly after the program started, an unexpected vacancy occurred in the New York branch of the bank and Andreas was asked if he was interested in the position. He remembered calling his wife, Lina, to discuss it. The offer looked very attractive from all angles, and they both quickly agreed that Andreas should accept the position. Two months later, he was transferred to New York.

Andreas remembered the day of his arrival as if it were yesterday. He arrived at JFK Airport early in the afternoon. Since his only contact point about the job assignment was corporate HR in Frankfurt, he assumed that they had made all the necessary arrangements with the New York office about his arrival. However, no one came to the airport to pick him up. He took a taxi and went directly to the New York branch of the bank. When he arrived at the bank, he was not sure where he should go. He had not been informed about who he should contact after his arrival. So, he went straight to the office of the head of the corporate finance department where he was supposed to work. When he entered the office and told the secretary that he was the new manager from Germany, she looked at her notebook, shook her head, and told him that they were not expecting anybody. Confused, Andreas rushed to the HR department and soon found that several misunderstandings had occurred. First, it was not the corporate finance department but the credit department that had requested his transfer. Second, contrary to what he was told in Frankfurt, there was only a nonmanagement position vacant. They were looking for a credit analyst, basically the same job that he had done in Germany.

Andreas shook his head in reaction to the memory: "There I stood, in what was supposed to be my new office, with three pieces of luggage on the desk, and wondering whether I should stay or take the next plane home!"

Why he decided to stay in New York, he could never quite figure out. In retrospect it was probably just a split second decision to make the best of the situation. The whirl of images of the next two months flashed across his memory: rushed days and nights trying to learn the ropes of a new office with new procedures, looking for a place to live, meeting new people, and exploring new places. Then a clear memory intervened the collage of memories of those first two months—Lina's arrival. Lina, his wife, and their three-year-old daughter, Anne-Marie, followed Andreas to New York two months after his arrival. They moved into a small house in the outskirts of New York. Lina knew New York pretty well, as she had lived there for a couple of months as an intern in a New York-based reinsurance company. She arrived excited to rediscover her favorite cafés, art galleries, and museums.

Except for occasional attacks of homesickness, Lina was satisfied with her new life. The week after they had moved into their new house, they received a dinner invitation from a young married couple who lived next door. To their surprise, their American neighbors quickly embraced the Webers. Since Lina was not able to get a working permit, she joined her new acquaintance in doing voluntary work at a local art museum. Anne-Marie spent every second afternoon at a local kindergarten, which gave Lina plenty of time to pursue her own interests. At the end of their first year in the United States, a second daughter, Elena, was born. By then, the Weber's had already made several more new friends, both Americans and other expatriates. When the Webers stepped off the plane at JFK after their first home leave to Germany, it felt more like they were coming home than returning to a temporary assignment.

Professionally, things had gone well during this time period. The New York branch of the bank had been right at the beginning of a boom-phase that lasted for several years. Throughout the boom, the bank's staff increased significantly. After eight months of working in the back office, Andreas was promoted to supervisor of a group of credit analysts. Then, one year after his first promotion, an unexpected vacancy occurred at the senior management level. The deputy head of the rapidly expanding corporate finance department—a German expatriate—had unexpectedly left for a job at one of their American competitors, and the bank had to fill his position with a manager who spoke fluent German, was familiar with the finance departments of a number of German and other European companies, and was instantly available. Andreas was asked if he was willing to extend his foreign service contract for another three years and accept the position as deputy head of the corporate finance department. After discussing it with Lina, Andreas accepted the offer.

In the fifth year of his assignment, Andreas made another step upward in his career. His boss retired, and Andreas was promoted to head of the corporate finance department. He was now one out of five managing directors in the branch. When Andreas signed his new contract, it was agreed that he would stay with the New York branch of the bank for another three years and would then return to the bank's German headquarters.

These were warm memories, memories that somewhat buffered the intensity of Andreas' emotions of frustration and anger. But as he continued running, the warmth of the past dissipated into the turmoil of the present. He felt tense again, and the beauty of the park's foliage, resplendent in full autumn color, did nothing to ease the burden he felt. His current troubles came to the forefront of his mind and would not leave.

"It all started with that promotion," he muttered to himself. As head of the corporate finance department, Andreas' professional as well as his private life had unexpectedly changed. He was now responsible for a huge area—his business activities no longer concentrated on North American subsidiaries of foreign-based companies, but on their headquarters in Europe and East Asia. In the first six months of his new job, Andreas had traveled almost

100,000 miles, mainly on business flights to Europe. Due to his extensive traveling, Lina began to complain. She felt alone, and started to be concerned about their children's education. Their eldest daughter, Anne-Marie was now nine years old and had spent most of her life outside of Germany. Lina was also concerned about her missing out on a German high school education. Anne-Marie's German language skills had gradually deteriorated over the last two years, and that troubled Lina as well. Their second daughter, Elena, was attending kindergarten, and except for the yearly home leave, she had no contact with other German children. Elena's German was quite poor. In fact, both Anne-Marie and Elena considered themselves Americans.

Lina also started to be more and more discontented with her life as a housewife. Obtaining a working permit in the United States remained impossible, and it was not easy for her to find new volunteer activities to quench her interests. To make things worse, Lina's father fell ill and died in that same year, before she could return to be by his side, leaving her mother alone. Andreas remembered the long conversations he had had with Lina during this period of time, many of which were by telephone from hotel rooms in far away places. When he was home, they spoke often in the quiet of their living room, and on long walks—Andreas lost count of the multitude of times they had talked as they walked through the same park he was now running through.

"It was an extremely difficult situation," Andreas remembered, "not so much for the children, but for Lina and I. . . . From a professional standpoint, my assignment to New York was the best thing that could ever happen to me: I worked in the financial center of the world; I loved my job, the freedom of being away from the corporate bureaucracy, the opportunities to travel; I became a member of the senior management team at a very young age—impossible if I stayed in Germany. . . . Personally, we were also very happy: our children felt at home in New York; we were quickly embraced by our neighbors and the expatriate community; we had many friends here. . . . The question we continually wrestled with was: 'Does it make sense to give all these up for a return to an uncertain future in Germany?' In principle, the answer would clearly have been: 'No.' But on a long-term basis, moving back to Germany appeared to be the best solution for our children and for Lina's mother. After all, we felt responsible for their future."

After several weeks of consideration and discussion, Lina and Andreas decided to move back to Germany. This was about a year ago. Immediately after the decision was made, Andreas contacted the bank's corporate headquarters and informed the human resource executive in charge of international assignments about his decision. Three weeks later, Andreas received a short letter from him, stating that there was currently no position available in Germany at his level. Part of the problem, Andreas was told, was due to the current economic downturn in Europe; but, since several new branches were due to be opened in the Eastern part of Germany over the course of the next year, he was told that chances were good that the company would be able to find him a suitable return assignment within the next six months. Since then, Andreas had had several meetings with managers at corporate headquarters, as well as with managers of domestic branches of the bank, but he still had not been offered any reentry position.

Lina gradually became discouraged. She had told her mother that they were coming home immediately after they made their decision to return to Germany, but 8 months had passed, and her mother kept asking when they were coming. Andreas' parents were persistent in their queries as well. Finally, last week, Andreas received a telephone call from the corporate HR department, in which he was informed that they had found what they called a "challenging" return assignment. They offered him the position of deputy head of a medium-sized branch of the bank in the Eastern part of Germany. Andreas was told that a letter explaining the details of the position offer had already been sent.

The memory of opening that letter and reading it, and the resultant emotions of anger, betrayal, disbelief, and frustration all came back to him. He stopped running, and sat down on a park bench alongside the jogging trail. "Not only will I earn little more than half the salary that I currently make in New York, I will not be able to use the skills and experiences that I gained during my overseas assignment; I will be out of touch with all the important decisions being made at headquarters; and on top of that, I will be posted to this God-forsaken place!" he thought, bitterly.

With all the frustrations and anger welling up in his chest, Andreas thought, cynically, "The bank's promotion policy—if there ever was any rational policy—is to punish those who are really committed to the organization. . . . They assign you to one of those programs for high-fliers and send you abroad, but there is no career planning whatsoever. . . . If there just happens to be a job vacant when you return, you are lucky. If not, they let you wait and wait and wait, until you finally accept the most ridiculous job offer. . . . Their slogan that internationally experienced managers are important to the organization and that international experience is a key value and a prerequisite for promotion into the ranks of senior management is garbage! If you look at the actual promotion practices in this organization, it becomes clear it's only lip service . . . and lies!"

He began to wonder if he should accept the offer. Perhaps they should just stay in New York and make their home here. But then, images of Lina, Lina's mother, Anne-Marie, Elena, and his parents, and all of their combined needs enveloped him.

Leaning back on the park bench, he blankly stared down the path that would lead out of the park and into the street, and then home.

# INDEX

# ABOUT THE EDITOR

**David C. Thomas** is Professor of International Management and Area Coordinator of International Business at Simon Fraser University, Canada. A naturalized New Zealander, Dr. Thomas was born and educated in the United States, and received his PhD from the University of South Carolina in Organizational Behavior and International Business.

His research on the interaction of individuals from different cultures in organizational settings has prompted him to conduct studies in more than a dozen different countries. He is the author of *Essentials of International Management: A Cross-Cultural Perspective,* Sage Publications. His research has also appeared in such journals as the *Journal of International Business Studies, Journal of Applied Psychology, Journal of Cross-Cultural Psychology, Journal of Business Research, Advances in International Comparative Management, Research in the Sociology of Organizations, Leadership Quarterly,* and *Organizational Dynamics.* He serves on the editorial boards of the *Journal of World Business, Advances in International Management,* the *International Journal of Cross-Cultural Management,* and the *International Journal of Organizational Analysis* and is a reviewer for numerous other journals including the *Academy of Management Journal,* the *Journal of International Business Studies, Organizational Research Methods,* and *International Business Review.*

Prior to returning to academia in 1988, Dr. Thomas was a Vice President with the bank holding company NationsBank (now Bank of America). His previous academic postings have included positions at the Pennsylvania State University and The University of Auckland, New Zealand, where he was also Director of the Master of International Business Program. He has held visiting positions at The Chinese University of Hong Kong, the University of Hawaii, and ESCEM, Tours, France. In addition to his teaching at both undergraduate and post-graduate level, Dr. Thomas has developed Executive Education programs in Australia, New Zealand, Canada, and the United States and has served as a consultant to a number of multinational firms.